P9-DFC-516

THE OXFORD DICTIONARY OF AMERICAN USAGE AND STYLE

BOOKS BY BRYAN A. GARNER

A Dictionary of Modern Legal Usage

The Elements of Legal Style

Guidelines for Drafting and Editing Court Rules

A Dictionary of Modern American Usage

Securities Disclosure in Plain English

The Winning Brief

The Oxford Dictionary of American Usage and Style

BOOKS EDITED BY BRYAN A. GARNER

Texas, Our Texas

Black's Law Dictionary (pocket edition)

A Handbook of Basic Law Terms

A Handbook of Business Law Terms

Black's Law Dictionary (seventh edition)

The Oxford Dictionary of American Usage and Style

BRYAN A. GARNER

Oxford New York
Athens Auckland Bangkok Bogotá Buenos Aires Calcutta
Cape Town Chennai Dar es Salaam Delhi Florence Hong Kong Istanbul
Karachi Kuala Lumpur Madrid Melbourne Mexico City Mumbai
Nairobi Paris São Paulo Singapore Taipei Tokyo Toronto Warsaw

and associated companies in
Berlin Ibadan

Published by Oxford University Press, Inc.
198 Madison Avenue, New York, New York 10016

Library of Congress Cataloging-in-Publication Data is available
ISBN 978-0-19-513508-4

Printed in the United States of America
on acid-free paper

For my father

CONTENTS

PREFACE

This book is an abridgment of my *Dictionary of Modern American Usage*, published in 1998. The idea behind abridging that book was to produce a handy paperback that discusses the most common problems of usage and style.

In reading through this book, you might get the idea that the language has gone to pot. In fact, though, the language never was in a pristine state: things are always changing, sometimes for the worse. The purpose of a usage guide is to promote the good and combat the bad. If you're a writer or editor, the stakes are rather high: your credibility is on the line. Good usage will enhance your credibility in readers' minds; bad usage can ruin it.

Although there are good, clarifying forces at work on the language, there are also bad, obscuring forces. And these bad forces tend to work most perniciously on people who are heedless of their language. It's hard to know such a thing, but this segment of society may well be on the rise.

This book could never reach those people.

But some people still want to use the language well. They want to write effectively; they want to speak effectively. They want their language to be graceful at times and powerful at times. They want to understand how to use words well, how to manipulate sentences, and how to move about in the language without seeming to flail. They want good grammar, but they want more: they want rhetoric in the traditional sense. That is, they want to use language deftly so that it's fit for their purposes.

This book is for them.

First Principles

Before going any further, I should explain my approach. That's an unusual thing for the author of a usage dictionary to do—unprecedented, as far as I know. But a guide to good writing is only as good as the principles on which it's based. And users should naturally be interested in those principles. So in the interests of full disclosure, here are the ten critical points that, after years of working on usage problems, I've settled on:

1. **Purpose.** The purpose of a usage dictionary is to help writers, editors, and speakers use the language effectively: to help them sound grammatical but relaxed, refined but natural, correct but unpedantic.
2. **Realism.** To guide users helpfully, recommendations on usage must be genuinely plausible. They must recognize the language as it currently stands, encourage reasonable approaches to editorial problems, and avoid refighting battles that were long ago lost.
3. **Linguistic Simplicity.** If the same idea can be expressed in a simple way or in a complex way, the simple way is better—and, paradoxically, it will typically lead readers to conclude that the writer is smarter.
4. **Readers' Reactions.** Generally, writing is good if readers find it easy to follow; writing is bad if readers find it hard to follow.
5. **Tightness.** Omitting needless words is important. As long as it's accurate, the briefest way of phrasing an idea is usually best because the brevity enhances speed, clarity, and impact.
6. **Word-Judging.** A word or phrase is somewhat undesirable if it has any one of the following characteristics, and is worse if it has two or more:

   (a) it sounds newfangled;
   (b) it defies logic;
   (c) it threatens to displace an established expression (but hasn't yet done so);
   (d) it originated in a misunderstanding of a word or its etymology;
   (e) it blurs a useful distinction.

7. **Differentiation.** If related words—especially those differing only in the suffix—begin to take on different senses, it's wise to encourage the latent distinctions when they're first emerging and then to follow them once they're established.
8. **Needless Variants.** Having two or more variant forms of a word is undesirable unless each one signals a distinct meaning.
9. **Conservatism.** If two constructions are current, and one of them has been widely condemned by authorities whose values are in line with those outlined in #6, the other construction is better.

10. **Actual Usage.** In the end, the actual usage of educated speakers and writers is the overarching criterion for correctness. But while actual usage can trump the other factors, it isn't the only consideration.

Reasonable though these points may seem to the professional writer or editor, they're likely to induce hissy fits among modern linguists, for whom #10 is the only valid concern (and then only after deleting the word *educated*). The problem for professional writers and editors is that they can't wait idly to see what direction the language takes. Writers and editors, in fact, influence that direction: they must make decisions.

And a good usage dictionary should help in those decisions. H.W. Fowler's groundbreaking *Dictionary of Modern English Usage* did that in 1926 and for generations after; Theodore M. Bernstein's book *The Careful Writer* did it in 1965; and Wilson Follett's *Modern American Usage* did it in 1966. That has traditionally been the job of the usage dictionary: to help writers and editors solve editorial predicaments. As Joseph Epstein, the longtime editor of *The American Scholar*, has observed, "The English language is one vast San Andreas fault, where things are slipping and sliding every moment."[1] English usage is so challenging that even experienced writers need guidance.

Quotations; Judgment Calls

This book contains nearly 2,000 quotations from published sources. Most are from newspapers, but many are from books and scholarly journals. These quotations came to my hand in various ways.

First, they came from my own reading. For many years, I've traveled a good deal, and whenever I go somewhere I make a point of reading and marking at least one local newspaper, usually more. When I return, I enter those sentences into my database.

Second, I have dozens of allies—members of the H.W. Fowler Society, an informal organization I founded—who send me clippings from newspapers. These Fowlerians, who are spread throughout the English-speaking world, have contributed enormously to the book with hundreds of examples.

Third, I've supplemented entries with examples gleaned from two online databases: NEXIS and WESTLAW. For two de-

[1]Joseph Epstein, "Mr. Fowler, He Live," *Weekly Standard*, 20 Jan. 1997, at 29.

cades, they have provided full-text searchability for millions of published documents—a luxury that earlier lexicographers never enjoyed. It's fair to say that the guidance given here is based on a greater corpus of current published writings than any usage guide ever before published. For contemporary usage, the files of our greatest dictionary makers pale in comparison with the full-text search capabilities now provided by NEXIS and WESTLAW. Thus, the prescriptive approach here is leavened by a thorough canvassing of actual usage in modern edited prose.

In this respect—the consideration of voluminous linguistic evidence to back up judgment calls—this book represents a radical departure from most other usage guides.

As you might already suspect, I don't shy away from making judgments. I can't imagine that most readers would want me to. Some linguists don't like it, of course, because judgment involves subjectivity. It isn't scientific. But rhetoric and usage, in the view of most professional writers, aren't scientific endeavors. You don't want dispassionate descriptions; you want sound guidance. And that requires judgment.

Yet this willingness to judge should be tempered by scholarship. The touchstone for writing well about usage, it seems to me, is a mixture of scholarship and criticism. Whether or not I've reached it, that has been my goal.

Along the way, friends and family have helped enormously. For their contributions to this abridgment—and to the big book on which this one is based—I thank these allies:

Frank Abate
Sheridan Baker
Beverly Ray Burlingame
Lance A. Cooper
Sir Brian Cubbon
Betty S. Flowers
Alexandra B. Garner
Caroline B. Garner
Gary T. Garner
Pan A. Garner
Linda Halvorson
Mark LaFlaur
Karen Larsen
Thomas B. Lemann
Karen Magnuson
David O. Moore
James L. Nelson
Jon Nichols
Elizabeth C. Powell
David W. Schultz
John R. Trimble
John W. Velz
Sir David Williams
Charles Alan Wright

—B.A.G.
August 1999

LIST OF ESSAY ENTRIES

This book contains essentially two types of entries: (1) word entries, which discuss a particular word or set of words; and (2) essay entries, which address larger questions of usage and style. For ease of reference, the essay entries—which appear throughout the book in small capitals—are listed below.

LIST OF ABBREVIATIONS

adj. = adjective
adv. = adverb
AHD = *The American Heritage Dictionary of the English Language* (3d ed. 1992)
Am. = American
AmE = American English
arch. = archaic
A.S. = Anglo-Saxon
Aus. = Australian
Br. = British
BrE = British English
c. = century
ca. = (*circa*) around
Can. = Canadian
cap. = capitalized
cf. = (*confer*) compare with
COD = *The Concise Oxford Dictionary of Current English* (8th ed. 1990)
colloq. = colloquial
conj. = conjunction
DAEU = Margaret Nicholson, *A Dictionary of American-English Usage* (1957)
DCAU = Bergen Evans & Cordelia Evans, *A Dictionary of Contemporary American Usage* (1957)
ed. = edition; editor
e.g. = (*exempli gratia*) for example
Eng. = English
esp. = especially
ex. = example
fig. = figuratively
fr. = from; derived from; found in
Fr. = French
G.B. = Great Britain (i.e., England, Scotland, and Wales)
Ger. = German
Gk. = Greek
id. = (*idem*) in the same work
i.e. = (*id est*) that is
Ital. = Italian
Jap. = Japanese
L. = Latin
l.c. = lowercase
lit. = literally
MAU = Wilson Follett, *Modern American Usage* (1966)
ME = Middle English
MEU1 = H.W. Fowler, *A Dictionary of Modern English Usage* (1926)
MEU2 = H.W. Fowler, *A Dictionary of Modern English Usage* (Ernest Gowers ed., 2d ed. 1965)
MEU3 = R.W. Burchfield, *The New Fowler's Modern English Usage* (1996)
n. = noun

no. = number
Norw. = Norwegian
OAD = *The Oxford American Dictionary* (1980)
obs. = obsolete
OE = Old English
OED = *The Oxford English Dictionary* (2d ed. 1989)
OED Supp. = *A Supplement to the Oxford English Dictionary* (4 vols., 1972–1986)
OF = Old French
OGEU = *The Oxford Guide to English Usage* (1983)
orig. = originally
p. = page
phr. = phrase
pl. = plural
pmbl. = preamble
pp. = pages
p.pl. = past participle
prep. = preposition
pron. = pronoun
pr.pl. = present participle
quot. = quotation
repr. = reprinted
rev. = revised by; revision
RH2 = *The Random House Dictionary of the English Language* (2d ed. 1987)
Russ. = Russian
Scot. = Scottish
sing. = singular
SOED = *The New Shorter Oxford English Dictionary* (1993)
Sp. = Spanish
specif. = specifically
U&A = Eric Partridge, *Usage & Abusage* (1942)
U.K. = United Kingdom (i.e., Great Britain and—since 1922—Northern Ireland)
U.S. = United States
usu. = usually
vb. = verb
v.i. = intransitive verb
v.t. = transitive verb
W2 = *Webster's New International Dictionary of the English Language* (2d ed. 1934)
W3 = *Webster's Third New International Dictionary of the English Language* (1961)
W10 = *Merriam-Webster's Collegiate Dictionary* (10th ed. 1993)
WDEU = *Merriam-Webster's Dictionary of English Usage* (1989)
WNWCD = *Webster's New World College Dictionary* (3d ed. 1995)

PRONUNCIATION GUIDE

ə *for all the vowel sounds in* amok, burger, London
a *as in* fact, vat
ah *as in* calm, father
ahr *as in* bar, start
air *as in* flare, lair
aw *as in* tall, law
ay *as in* page, same
b *as in* balk, job
ch *as in* chief, bench
d *as in* deck, red
e *as in* leg, ferry
ee *as in* flea, tidy
eer *as in* mere, tier
f *as in* fence, off
g *as in* go, mug
h *as in* harp, hold
hw *as in* which, while
i *as in* rib, akin
ɪ *as in* time, eye
j *as in* jump, magic
k *as in* keep, school
l *as in* lever, pill
m *as in* muck, drum
n *as in* note, clown
ng *as in* long, plank
o *as in* hot, wash
oh *as in* loan, home
oi *as in* join, ploy
oo *as in* rule, tomb
oor *as in* poor, lure
or *as in* board, court
ow *as in* plow, loud
p *as in* poem, drop
r *as in* rank, hear
s *as in* seek, pass
sh *as in* sharp, trash
t *as in* time, boot
th *as in* thin, math
th̲ *as in* there, bathe
uu *as in* took, pull
v *as in* vague, shiver
w *as in* witch, away
y *as in* year, union
z *as in* zone, please
zh *as in* measure, vision

A

a. A. Choice Between *a* and *an*. The indefinite article *a* is used before words beginning with a consonant sound, including /y/ and /w/ sounds. The other form, *an*, is used before words beginning with a vowel sound. Hence *a European country*, *a Ouija board*, *a uniform*, *an FBI agent*, *an MBA degree*, *an SEC filing*.

Writers on usage formerly disputed whether the correct article is *a* or *an* with *historian*, *historic*, and a few other words. The traditional rule is that if the *h-* is sounded, *a* is the proper form. Most people following that rule would say *a historian* and *a historic*—e.g.: "Democrat Bill Clinton appears within reach of capturing the White House in Tuesday's election, but Republicans hope that late momentum can enable President Bush to win *a historic* upset" (*Dallas Morning News*). Even H.W. Fowler, in the England of 1926, advocated *a* before *historic(al)* and *humble* (*MEU1*).

The theory behind using *an* in such a context, however, is that the *h-* is very weak when the accent is on the second rather than the first syllable (giving rise, by analogy, to *an habitual offender, an humanitarian, an hallucinatory image,* and *an harassed schoolteacher*). Thus no authority countenances *an history*, though a few older ones prefer *an historian* and *an historical*.

Today, however, *an hypothesis* and *an historical* are likely to strike readers and listeners as affectations. As Mark Twain once wrote, referring to *humble, heroic,* and *historical*: "Correct writers of the American language do not put *an* before those words" (*The Stolen White Elephant*, 1882). Anyone who sounds the *h-* in such words should avoid pretense and use *a*. See **herb & humble.**

B. In Distributive Senses. *A*, in the distributive sense <ten hours a day>, has traditionally been considered preferable to *per*, which originated in COMMERCIALESE and LEGALESE. But *per* has muscled its way into idiomatic English in phrases such as *60 miles per hour*, *one golf cart per couple*, and *five books per student*. Although *an* could be substituted for *per* in the first of those phrases, *a* wouldn't work well in the second or third.

When the construction requires a PHRASAL ADJECTIVE, *per* is the only idiomatic word—e.g.: "Our *per-unit* cost is less than $1,000."/ "The *$50-per-parent* fee seems unreasonably high."

abandon, n.; **abandonment.** The usual idiom is *wild abandon* or *reckless abandon* (= unrestrained impulsiveness), not *abandonment* (= the giving up of something). In the following sentences, *abandon* would better accord with modern usage: "One worrisome puzzlement: How can my countrymen celebrate in such wild *abandonment* [read *abandon*] on the carnage of so many helpless children and the thousands that are disease-ridden and dying every hour?" (*Ariz. Republic*)./ "Like a ventriloquist, the President put these words in the mouth of Dr. King: '. . . I did not fight for the right of black people to murder other black people with reckless *abandonment* [read *abandon*]' " (*Philadelphia Inquirer*).

ABBREVIATIONS. A. Acronyms and Initialisms. Five points merit our attention here. First, we should be aware of the difference between the two types of abbreviated names. An *acronym* is made from the first letters or parts of a compound term. It's usually read or spoken as a single word, not letter by letter (e.g., *radar* = radio detection and ranging). An *initialism* is also made from the first letters or parts of a compound term, but it's usually sounded letter by letter, not as one word (e.g., *r.p.m.* = revolutions per minute).

Second, the question often arises whether to place a period after each letter in an acronym or initialism. Searching for consistency on this point is futile. The trend nowadays is to omit the periods; including them is the more conservative and traditional approach. Yet surely if an acronym is spoken as a single word (e.g., *UNESCO*), periods are meaningless. If an initialism is made up of lowercase letters, periods are preferable: *rpm* looks odd as compared with *r.p.m.*, and *am* (as opposed to *a.m.*) looks like the verb. One method of determining whether to omit or include periods is to follow the form that the organization itself uses (e.g., *IRS*, *HUD*), although inconsistencies are common. (For an anomalous abbreviation, see **ID.**)

Third, the best practice is to give the reader some warning of an uncommon acronym by spelling out the words and enclosing the acronym in parentheses when the term is first used. A reference to *CARPE Rules* may confuse a reader who does not at first realize that three or four lines above this acronym, the writer has made reference to a Committee on Academic Rights, Privileges, and Ethics.

Fourth, in AmE the tendency is to uppercase all the characters (e.g., *GAAP*, *MADD*, *NASA*). But in BrE, the tendency is to uppercase only the first letter, as in *Ifor* in this example: "More recently, U.S. officials have acknowledged that a few U.S. troops will be needed early next year because the U.S.-led Implementation Force (Ifor) will not be able to pull all its armour out in time" (*Fin. Times*).

Finally, as illustrated under (C), the use in a single text of too many abbreviated forms leads to dense and frustrating prose.

B. Redundant Acronyms. Some acronyms often appear as part of a two-word phrase, in which the second word is also what one of the acronym's letters stands for. Thus, a bank customer withdraws cash from an *ATM machine*, using a *PIN number* as a password. A supermarket clerk searches a milk carton for its *UPC code*. High-school seniors study hard for the *SAT test*. Economists monitor the *CPI Index*. American and Russian diplomats sit down to negotiate at the *SALT talks*. And scientists try to unlock the mysteries of the deadly *HIV virus*.

The problem with these phrases, of course, is that they are technically redundant (*automated-teller machine machine*, *personal-identification number number*, *Universal Product Code code*, *Scholastic Aptitude Test test*, *Consumer Price Index Index*, *Strategic Arms Limitation Talks talks*, and *human-immunodeficiency virus virus*). And while the redundancies may be passable in speech—especially with unfamiliar acronyms—they should be avoided in edited writing.

For a different type of redundant acronym, see **RSVP.**

C. Initialese. One of the most irritating types of pedantry in modern writing is the overuse of abbreviations, especially abbreviated names. Originally, to be sure, abbreviations were intended to serve the convenience of the reader by shortening names so that cumbersome phrases would not have to be repeated in their entirety. The purported simplifications actually simplified. But many writers—especially technical writers—seem to have lost sight of this goal: they allow abbreviated terms to proliferate, and their prose quickly becomes a hybrid-English system of hieroglyphs requiring the reader to refer constantly to the original uses of terms to grasp the meaning. This kind of writing might be thought more scholarly than ordinary, straightforward prose. It isn't. Rather, it's tiresome and inconsiderate writing; it betrays the writer's thoughtlessness toward the reader and a puerile fascination with the insubstantial trappings of scholarship.

Three examples suffice to illustrate the malady:

- "As a comparison to these item-level indices, the factor-level indices IFS and C_ANR [*sic*] were both computed for the maximum likelihood factors. . . . Compression of the factor space tends to decrease both IFS and C_ANR, while excessive expansion is likely to also decrease the C_ANR, while the IFS might be expected to be reasonably stable. Thus, four rotation solutions were computed based upon Matthews & Stanton's (1994) extraction of 21 factors, the Velicer MAP test indicator of 26 (PCA) and 28 (image) factors, and Autoscree indicators of 17 and 21 factors for PCA and image respectively. From these solutions, it was hypothesized that a full 31 factor rotation might provide the optimal C_ANR parameters for the OPQ scales. Further, as a by-product of the use of MLFA, it is possible to compute a test" (*J. Occupational & Organizational Psychology*).

- "For the initial model, the significant variable TRANS is only significantly correlated with SUBNO. SUBCTY is correlated with NI, with SUBNO, and with FSALEPER. NI, however, is significantly correlated with: (1) DOMVIN; (2) METH1; and (3) METH3. In the reduced model, these intercorrelations with NI are not an area for concern" (*Int'l J. Accounting*).
- "SLIP, like VALP and ECC, is a defeasible constraint that is obeyed by all the types of head-nexus phrase considered thus far. It guarantees that (except in SLASH-binding contexts that we turn to in a moment) the SLASH value of a phrase is the SLASH value of its head-daughter" (*J. Linguistics*).

And so it goes throughout each article.

In naming something new, one's task is sometimes hopeless: the choice is clear between *ALI–ABA CLE Review* and *American Law Institute–American Bar Association Continuing Legal Education Review*, but one cannot choose either enthusiastically. Both sponsors must have their due (in part so that they can have their dues), and the acronyms might gradually become familiar to readers. But they aren't ideal because they give bad first impressions.

Remember that effective communication takes *two*—the writer and the reader. Arthur Quiller-Couch reminded writers never to forget the audience:

> [T]he obligation of courtesy rests first with the author, who invites the seance, and commonly charges for it. What follows, but that in speaking or writing we have an obligation to put ourselves into the hearer's or reader's place? It is *his* comfort, *his* convenience, we have to consult. To *express* ourselves is a very small part of the business: very small and unimportant as compared with *impressing* ourselves: the aim of the whole process being to persuade.
>
> *On the Art of Writing* 291–92 (2d ed. 1943).

Abbreviations are often conveniences for writers but inconveniences for readers. Whenever that is so, they should vanish.

abdomen is most commonly pronounced /**ab**-də-mən/, though some people continue to use the old-fashioned /ab-**doh**-mən/.

ability; capacity. The traditional distinction is that while *ability* is qualitative, *capacity* is quantitative. Hence, *ability* refers to a person's power of body or mind <a writer of great ability>; *capacity*, meaning literally "roomy, spacious," refers figuratively to a person's physical or mental power to receive <her memory has an extraordinary capacity for details>.

For the distinction between *capacity* and *capability*, see **capacity.**

abjure; adjure. A. Senses Distinguished. *Abjure* may mean either (1) "to renounce" <Germany abjured the use of force>, or (2) "to avoid" <her evaluation abjured excessive praise>. In bygone days, people were sometimes required to "abjure the realm," i.e., go abroad. *Adjure* means "to charge or entreat solemnly" <Bush adjured the Russians to join him in this noble goal>.

B. Cognate Forms. The noun forms are *abjuration* (or *abjurement*—now defunct) and *adjuration*. The adjectival forms end in *-tory*. The agent nouns are *abjurer* and *adjurer*.

-ABLE. A. Choice of *-able* or *-ible*. Many adjectives have competing forms ending in *-able* and *-ible*. Some of these have undergone DIFFERENTIATION in meaning; the less commonly used forms in some pairs are merely NEEDLESS VARIANTS of the predominant forms. The lists that follow contain the most troublesome words of this class.

Unlike *-ible*, *-able* is a living suffix that may be added to virtually any verb without an established suffix in either *-able* or *-ible*. Following are only some of the hundreds of adjectives preferably spelled *-able*:

actionable
addable
admittable
advisable
affectable
allegeable
analyzable
annexable
arrestable
ascendable
assertable
assessable
averageable
bailable
blamable
changeable
chargeable
circumscribable
commensurable
committable
condensable
conductable
connectable
contestable
contractable
conversable
convictable
correctable
definable
detectable
diagnosable
discussable
endorsable
enforceable
evadable
excisable
excludable
expandable
extendable
extractable
ignitable
immovable
improvable
includable
inferable
inventable
investable
lapsable
mixable
movable
noticeable
offendable
patentable
persuadable
preventable
processable
protectable
ratable
redressable
referable
retractable
revisable
rinsable
salable
suspendable
tractable
transferable
transmittable
willable

Although *-ible* is now dead as a combining form in English, the following words still retain that suffix:

accessible
adducible
admissible
audible
avertible
collapsible
collectible
combustible
compactible
compatible
comprehensible
compressible
concussible
contemptible
controvertible
convertible
corrodible
corruptible
credible
deducible
deductible
defeasible
defensible
descendible
destructible
diffusible
digestible
discernible
dismissible
divisible
edible
educible
eligible
erodible
exhaustible
expressible
fallible
feasible
flexible
forcible
fusible
gullible
horrible
impressible
incorrigible
indelible
intelligible
interfusible
invincible
irascible
irresistible
legible
negligible
omissible
oppressible
ostensible
perceptible
perfectible
permissible
plausible
possible
producible
reducible
remissible
reprehensible
repressible
resistible
responsible
reversible
revertible
risible
seducible
sensible
submersible (*or* submergible)
suggestible
suppressible
susceptible
terrible
transfusible
transmissible
uncollectible
vendible
visible

Some adjectives with the variant suffixes have different meanings. Thus *impassable* means "closed, incapable of being traversed"; its twin, *impassible*, means "unable to feel pain" or, less distinctively, "impassive, emotionless." *Passable* and *passible* have correspondingly positive meanings. (These pairs are formed from different Latin roots, L. *passus* "having suffered" and L. *passare* "to step.") Similarly, *impartible* means "not subject to partition" and *impartable* "capable of being imparted." *Conversable* means "oral," while *conversible* is a NEEDLESS VARIANT of *convertible*. *Forcible* means either "done by means of force" <forcible entry> or "characterized by force" <forcible behavior>; *forceable*, much less frequently encountered, would be the better term to describe a door that is "capable of being forced open." See **forcible.**

Other variant adjectives, though, are merely duplicative. Typical examples are *extendable, extendible,* and *extensible.* The first of these is now prevalent in AmE (though labeled obsolete in the *OED*). *Extensible* was, through the mid-20th century, the most common form, but today it trails *extendable* by a substantial margin, while *extendible* continues to appear infrequently. Writers and editors ought to settle on the most firmly established form—*extendable*, which is as well formed as the variants—and trouble their minds with weightier matters. See NEEDLESS VARIANTS, DIFFERENTIATION & MUTE E.

B. Attaching *-able* to Nouns. This passive suffix is usually attached to verbs, as in *avoidable*, *forgettable*, and *reproachable*. But sometimes it's attached to nouns, as in *marriageable*, *objectionable*, and *salable*. These do not mean "able to be marriaged," "able to be objectioned," and so on. Although *marryable* and *objectable* would have been the more logical forms, time, idiom, and usage have made these and several other forms both ineradicable and unobjectionable.

C. Attaching *-able* to Intransitive Verbs. A few words formerly upset purists: *dependable* (*depend-on-able*), *indispensable* (*in-dispense-with-able*), *laughable* (*laugh-at-able*), *reliable* (*rely-on-able*), and *unaccountable* (*un-account-for-able*). They're indispensable to the modern writer—not at all laughable.

D. Converting *-ate* Verbs into *-able* Adjectives. When *-able* is added to a transitive polysyllabic verb ending in the suffix *-ate*, that suffix is dropped. Hence, *accumulable, calculable, regulable*, etc. (See -ATABLE.) Exceptions, however, occur with two-syllable words, such as *rebatable* and *debatable*.

E. Dropping or Retaining the Medial *-e-*. This question arises in words such as *irreconcilable*, *microwavable*, *movable*, *resumable*, and *salable*. Although writers formerly put an *-e-* before *-able*, both AmE and BrE generally drop the medial *-e-*, except in words with a soft *-c-* (*traceable*) or a soft *-g-* (*chargeable*). See MUTE E.

abortive; aborted. *Abortive* may mean (1) "unsuccessful because cut short," or (2) "inchoate." With sense 1, it takes on the figurative sense of *aborted* (= cut short), as *an abortive attempt*, i.e., one cut short. (Note that *-ive*, an active suffix, here has a passive sense.) E.g.: "In the 50 years after the 1916 rising, an *abortive* anti-British rebellion, nationalists incorporated the tragedy into their vision of 'a heroic struggle against seven centuries of British oppression' " (*USA Today*). *Abortive* is archaic in reference to abortions of fetuses, except in the sense "causing an abortion."

about. A. And *approximately*. When possible, use *about* instead of *approximately*, a FORMAL WORD. But *about* shouldn't appear, as it sometimes does, with other terms of approximation such as *estimate* and *guess*, because it means "roughly" or "approximately." E.g.: "[T]heir *estimate* that there are *about* [delete *about*] 110,000 minke whales in the northeastern Atlantic has been accepted by the International Whaling Commission" (*L.A. Times*).

B. And *around*. When there is a choice between *about* and *around*—as in *beat around (or about) the bush*, *strewn around (or about) the garden*, or *all around (or about) the city*—the word *around* greatly predominates in AmE. In those phrases, *about* sounds schoolmarmish.

C. *About the head*. Theodore M. Bernstein called this phrase "police-blotter lingo" (*The Careful Writer*, 1965) when used in the sense "on" <the victim was pounded several times about the head>. The phrase might still be common in police blotters, but in published print sources it appears only occasionally—e.g.: "[A] Malaysian companion, 15, suffered a punctured eardrum from the interrogator's *blows about the head*" (*Minneapolis Star Trib.*).

D. *At about*. This phrase is sometimes criticized as a REDUNDANCY, the argument being that *about* can often do the work by itself. But in many contexts, especially those involving expressions of time, the phrase *at about* is common, idiomatic, and unimpeachable <we'll arrive at about 9:00 tonight>.

above. A. Meaning "more than" or "longer than." Restrict this usage to informal contexts. "*Above* [read *More than*] 600 people attended the reception."/ "Now, the RBI has allowed only the incentive of one percent for one-year deposits, 1.5 percent for two-year deposits and two percent for deposits *above two years* [read *of two years or more* or *of longer than two years*]" (*Econ. Times*). Cf. **over (A).**

B. For *above-mentioned.* *Above* is an acceptable ellipsis for *above-mentioned*, and it is much less inelegant <the above statements are his last recorded ones>.

It was long thought that *above* could not properly act as an adjective. But the word has been used in this way throughout the 20th century, even by the best writers. The *OED* records this use from 1873 and says that *above* "stands attributively," through ellipsis, for *above said*, *above written*, *above mentioned*, or some other phrase.

Some critics have suggested that *above* in this sense should refer only to something mentioned previously on the same page, but this restriction seems unduly narrow. Still, it's often better to make the reference exact by giving a page or paragraph number, rather than the vague reference made possible by *above*. Idiom will not, however, allow *above* to modify all nouns: *above vehicle* is unidiomatic for *vehicle mentioned above*. (If you must say *mentioned*, put *above* after that word.) Better yet would be *the vehicle*, if readers will know from the context which one you're talking about.

Less common than the adjectival *above* is the noun use <the above is entirely accurate>. Robert C. Pooley's assessment still stands: "Any writer may feel free at any time to use 'the *above* statement,' and with only slightly less assurance, 'the *above* will prove.' In either case, he has the authority of scholars and standard literature" (*Teaching English Usage*, 1946).

absolutely, in the sense "really" or "very much," is often a meaningless intensive. *You should be absolutely ashamed of yourself* is the sort of thing a parent might say when scolding a child, but in polished writing the word *absolutely* adds nothing of value to that sentence.

Abstractitis. "How vile a thing . . . is the abstract noun! It wraps a man's thoughts round like cotton wool" (Arthur Quiller-Couch, *On the Art of Writing*, 1943). *Abstractitis* is Ernest Gowers's term for writing that is so abstract and obtuse (hence abstruse) that the writer does not even know what he or she is trying to say (*MEU2*). Far be it from the reader, then, to give such writing a coherent meaning.

One sympathizes with a keen judge who wrestled with the Internal Revenue Code: "[T]he words . . . dance before my eyes in a meaningless procession: cross-reference to cross-reference, exception upon exception—couched in abstract terms that offer no handle to seize hold of—leave in my mind only a confused sense of some vitally important, but successfully concealed, purport, which it is my duty to extract, but which is within my power, if at all, only after the most inordinate expenditure of time" (Learned Hand, "Thomas Walter Swan," *Yale L.J.*, 1947).

Perhaps the best antidote to this malady—which in some degree afflicts most sophisticated writers—is an active empathy for one's readers. Rigorous thought about concrete meaning, together with careful revision, can eliminate abstractitis.

An example from political science suffices to illustrate the malady:

> Rosenau defines linkage as "any recurrent sequence of behavior that originates in one system and is reacted to in another." While there remains little doubt that such linkages exist, it has nevertheless been convenient for scholars of comparative and international politics to disregard or, to use the more contemporary term, to hold constant, factors in the other sphere. Thus, for the student of international politics, the nation functions in the international environment on the basis of the givens of that system, unrestrained by any domestic considerations.
>
> Jonathan Wilkenfeld, Introduction, *Conflict Behavior & Linkage Politics* 1 (1973).

This passage doesn't give any examples of the principles it discusses. It combines PASSIVE VOICE with JARGON. And it has many of the archetypal abstract words known as BURIED VERBS—that is, words ending with these suffixes: *-tion, -sion, -ment, -ity, -ence, -ance*. Writers are well advised to take these longish nouns and turn them back into verbs if possible—that is, write *adopting*, not *the adoption of*, and so on.

The Fowler brothers quote the following sentence—laden with buried verbs—in *The King's English* (1906): "One of the most important reforms mentioned in the rescript is the unification of the organization of judicial institutions and the guarantee for all the tribunals of the independence necessary for securing to all classes of the community equality before the law" (42 words). Arthur Quiller-Couch's revision eliminates the buried verbs: "One of the most important reforms is that of the courts, which need to be independent within a uniform structure. In this way only can people be assured that all are equal before the law" (35 words) (*On the Art of Writing*, 1943). But the following revision is even better: "One of the most important reforms is to unify the courts to guarantee their independence and thus the equality of all people before the law" (25 words).

By some accounts, abstractitis leads to far worse things. "If concepts are not clear," wrote Confucius, "words do not fit." But he did not stop there: "If words do not fit, the day's work cannot be accomplished, morals and art do not flourish. If morals and art do not flourish, punishments are not just. If punishments are not just, the people do not know where to put hand or foot" (*Analects* XIII, 3). When we descend into abstractitis, more than just our language is afflicted.

Fred Rodell, a Yale law professor, realist, and semanticist who frequently criticized lawyers' language, issued his own inimitable warning about abstractitis: "Dealing in words is a dangerous business, and it cannot be too often stressed that what The Law deals in is words. Dealing in long, vague, fuzzy-meaning words is even more dangerous business, and most of the words The Law deals in are long and vague and fuzzy. Making a habit of applying long, vague, fuzzy, general words to specific things and facts is perhaps the most dangerous of all, and The Law does that, too" (*Woe Unto You, Lawyers!*, 1980).

accede; exceed. *Accede*, v.i., = (1) "to agree or consent"; (2) "to come into office or a position of stature"; or (3) "to enter a treaty or accord." It takes the preposition *to*. *Exceed*, v.t., means (1) "to surpass," or (2) "to go beyond the proper limits." The first syllable of *accede* should be pronounced with a short /a/ to differentiate its sound from *exceed*.

Occasionally *exceed* is misused for *accede* (sense 1)—e.g.: "Eighty potential jurors filed into the Santa Clara County superior court chambers of Judge Charles Hastings after he, *exceeding* [read *acceding*] to the wishes of Davis' attorneys, instructed Joel and B.J. Klaas, the slain girl's grandparents, to remove the memorial buttons from their lapels" (*S.F. Examiner*).

ACCENT MARKS. See DIACRITICAL MARKS.

access; excess. *Access* (= a means of reaching or getting in) is sometimes confused with *excess* (= [1] an overabundance, superfluity; or [2] the amount by which one thing exceeds another)—e.g.: "At the time, the real estate concern was losing in *access* [read *excess*] of $1 million annually" (*Greater Baton Rouge Bus. Rep.*).

access, vb. **A. Generally.** As a verb, *access* has its origins in COMPUTERESE. Like a number of nouns turned into verbs (e.g., *contact*), it now seems increasingly well ensconced in the language. As Ernest Gowers said about *contact*, it is an ancient and valuable right of English-speaking peoples to turn their nouns into verbs when they are so minded (*MEU2*). *Gain access to* or some other such equivalent is admittedly ungainly alongside *access*.

But outside computing and electronic contexts, using *access* as a verb still jars sensitive ears. Avoid the verb if there's a ready substitute—e.g.: "The residents had bypassed utility meters and were *accessing* [read *getting*] free gas, water, electricity and cable television, deputies said" (*Riverside Press-Enterprise*)./ "There are now over 130 miles of converted trails in New York, all easily *accessed* [read *accessible*] by, what else, train" (*Village Voice*).

B. For *assess*. Sometimes *access* is misused for *assess* (= to evaluate)—e.g.: "They track hundreds of trends, looking for connections and *accessing* [read *assessing*] the implications of major socio-economic and political events" (*New Orleans Times-Picayune*).

accessory, n. **A. And *accessary*,** n. *Accessory* now predominates in AmE and BrE in meaning both "abettor" and "a thing of lesser importance." Though H.W. Fowler championed a distinction between *accessory* and *accessary* (the first applying primarily to things, the second to persons [*MEU1*]), *accessary* is now merely a needless variant and should be avoided.

B. Pronunciation. *Accessory* should be pronounced with the first *-c-* as a hard *-k-*: /ak-**ses**-ə-ree/. A common mispronunciation is /ə-**ses**-ə-ree/. Cf. **flaccid & succinct.**

accompanist /ə-**kəm**-pə-nist/ is the standard form, not *accompanyist* (falsely formed from *accompany*)—e.g.: "Paxton was in wonderful form, and *accompanyist* [read *accompanist*] Eric Weissberg added just enough instrumental firepower on guitar and dobro to lend the songs some spark" (*Albany Times Union*).

accounting. See **bookkeeping.**

accuse; charge. One is *accused of*, but *charged with*, a crime. Perhaps under the influence of *charged with*, the verb *accused* is sometimes unidiomatically paired with *with*—e.g.: "Ross and Vince Fera, Local 57's recording secretary and a member of its executive board, were *accused with* [read *accused of*] violating the union's code of ethics" (*Pitt. Post-Gaz.*).

achieve, v.t., implies successful effort at something more than merely surviving to a given age. Thus *achieving manhood* and *achieving womanhood* are ludicrous phrases, but they and others like them are fairly common EUPHEMISMS—e.g.: "Others remember the excitement of seeing the world and the satisfaction of *achieving adulthood* [read *reaching adulthood*] in such difficult times" (*Boston Globe*).

acquaintanceship, a NEEDLESS VARIANT of *acquaintance*, adds nothing to the language except another syllable, which we scarcely need. E.g.: "[I]t becomes plain to . . . partisans that the Clintons and their cronies only have a passing *acquaintanceship* [read *acquaintance*] with ethics" (*Wash. Times*). (On the placement of *only* in that sentence, see **only.**)

acquiescence. See **permission.**

ACRONYMS. See ABBREVIATIONS.

act; action. These words overlap a great deal, and it's difficult to delineate the distinctions. Generally, *act* is the more concrete word, *action* the more abstract. *Act* typically denotes the thing done, *action* the doing of it. *Act* is unitary, while *action* suggests a process—the many discrete events that make up a bit of behavior.

ACTIVE VOICE. See PASSIVE VOICE.

actual fact, in. This phrase is a REDUNDANCY: all facts are actual, just as they are all true. When one is uncertain of the truth of allegations, then there might be "alleged facts." *In actual fact* is a pomposity for *actually*. Cf. **true facts.**

ACUTE ACCENT. See DIACRITICAL MARKS.

A.D. See **B.C.**

ad, short for *advertisement*, is acceptable in informal contexts.

addendum (= an addition or supplement) forms the plural *addenda*. It's sloppy to use *addenda* as a singular—e.g.: "Jim Dykes sent an *addenda* [read *addendum*] to my She Crab Soup recipe" (*Knoxville News-Sentinel*). See PLURALS (B).

addicted; dependent. Regarding people's reactions to drugs, the distinction between these terms can be important. One who is *addicted* to a habit-forming drug has a compulsive physiological need for it. One who is *dependent* on a drug has a strong psychological reliance on it after having used it for some time. *Addiction*, then, is primarily physical, whereas *dependency* (also known as *habituation*) is primarily psychological.

adequate. A. And *sufficient*. Though originally both words were used in reference to quantity, *adequate* now tends toward the qualitative and *sufficient* toward the quantitative. Hence *adequate* means "suitable to the occasion or circumstances," and *sufficient* means "enough for a particular need or purpose." For more on *sufficient*, see **enough.**

B. *Adequate enough*. This phrase is redundant. Either word suffices alone—e.g.: "While Tyrol doesn't have a particularly large or sophisticated snowmaking system, it is *adequate enough* [read *adequate*] to cover 100 percent of the slopes" (*Madison Capital Times*)./ "There will be no excuses *adequate enough* if the Bears lose this one" (*Chicago Trib.*). (A possible revision: *No excuse will be adequate if the Bears lose this one.*) See ADJECTIVES (B).

adieu (= farewell) for *ado* (= fuss, trouble) is a surprisingly common error—e.g.: "So without further *adieu* [read *ado*], here's an early-week primer for this 60th annual event" (*Cincinnati Post*). Sometimes a pun is clearly intended—e.g.: "And then there's Whitewater, which has taken on a miserable life of its own. If it ever ends, it'll be much *adieu* about nothing" (*S.F. Chron.*). The opposite error—*ado* for *adieu*—is exceedingly rare.

ADJECTIVES. A. Definition. An adjective is a word that modifies a noun. The word is sometimes used sloppily as if it meant "noun"—e.g.: " 'Excellence' is *an adjective* [read *a noun*] that describes something which is of the highest quality" (*Barrister*). (In that sentence, *describes* should probably be *denotes*, and *which* should be *that.*)/ "Indeed, greatness is *an adjective* [read *a word*] befitting this Irish-bred 5-year-old son of 1990 Breeders' Cup Turf champion In The Wings" (*Las Vegas Rev.-J.*). Of course, *excellence* and *greatness* are nouns; their corresponding adjectives are *excellent* and *great*.

B. Uncomparable Adjectives. A number of adjectives describe absolute states or conditions and cannot take *most* or *more*, *less* or *least,* or intensives such as *very* or *quite* or *largely*. The ILLOGIC of such combinations is illustrated in this sentence: "It is possible that this idea too has outlived its usefulness and soon will be *largely discarded.*" The literal meaning of *discard* impinges on the metaphor here: it is hard to imagine a single idea being halfway discarded, though certainly it could be halfway discredited. Cutting *largely* clears the meaning.

The best-known uncomparable adjective is *unique* (= being one of a kind). Because something is either unique or not unique, there can be no degrees of uniqueness. Hence *more unique* and *very unique* are incorrect. Yet something may be *almost unique* or *not quite unique*—if, for example, there were two such things extant. (See **unique.**) Many other words belong to this class, such as *preferable*: "Stoll said the city also plans dozens of hearings with groups, showing different scenarios of how growth could be handled and getting feedback on what is *most preferable* [read *preferable*]" (*Sunday Oklahoman*).

Among the more common uncomparable adjectives are these:

absolute	inevitable	stationary
adequate	irrevocable	sufficient
chief	main	unanimous
complete	manifest	unavoidable
devoid	minor	unbroken
entire	only	uniform
false	paramount	unique
fatal	perpetual	universal
final	preferable	void
ideal	principal	whole
impossible		

For example, the phrase *more possible* should typically be *more feasible* or *more practicable*, since something is either possible or impossible. E.g.: "The VA medical centers, which have a long history of hospitalizing patients, have been stepping up outpatient services as they become more and more *possible* [read *compatible*] with emerging technology" (*Omaha World Herald*).

This general prohibition against using these words in comparative senses should be tempered with reason. It has exceptions. Good writers occasionally depart from the rule, but knowingly and purposefully. For example, Thomas Jefferson used the phrase *more perfect* in the Declaration of Independence, and the phrase then made its way into the preamble to the U.S. Constitution: "We the People of the United States, in Order to form a *more perfect* Union, establish Justice, insure domestic Tranquility, provide for the common defence, promote the general Welfare, and secure the Blessings of Liberty to ourselves and our Posterity, do ordain and establish this Constitution for the United States of America." One writer criticizes this phrase and suggests that it "should read 'to form a *more nearly perfect* Union' " (*Ky. L.J.*). Although the Constitution is not without stylistic blemishes, this probably isn't one of them, and the suggested edit seems pedantic.

A few adjectives, such as *harmless*, are wrongly thought of as uncomparable. But it's hopelessly donnish to insist that something is either *harmful* or *harmless* and that you can't write *more harmful*, *more harmless*, or *relatively harmless*. The same is true of many other words.

C. Adjectives as Nouns. English words can frequently change parts of speech. Thus nouns may act as adjectives (*swing set*, *baseball player*, *library books*) and adjectives as nouns (*collectibles*, *edibles*, *receivables*, *rentals*). *Indigent* was originally an adjective (15th c.), but it came to be used as a noun (16th c.). The same process occurred with *hypothetical*, *postmortem*, *principal* (= [1] principal investment, or [2] principal administrator), *ignitables*, *potential*, *explosives*, and *recitative*. Among recent examples are *finals* (= final examinations) and *classifieds* (= classified advertisements). Similarly, we refer to *the poor*, *the homeless*, *the rich*, *the religious*, and *the elite*.

Though recent semantic shifts are typically unsuitable for formal contexts, we should resist the benighted temptation to condemn all such shifts in parts of speech if they help fill gaps in the language. But as one commentator notes, some shifts have little to recommend them: "Can't we at least use correct English? That would distinguish Richmond from those places where the likes of 'multicultural collaboratives' are springing up. *Collaborative*, of course, is not a noun; it is an adjective. There can no more be a *collaborative* for youth than there can be an *exhaustive* for marathoners or a *repressive* for dictators or a *suggestive* for exotic dancers" (*Richmond Times-Dispatch*). Cf. NOUNS AS ADJECTIVES & NOUNS AS VERBS.

D. Adjectives as Verbs. Though noun-to-adjective, adjective-to-noun, and even noun-to-verb transformations are common in English, adjective-to-verb transformations have never been common. They usually have a jargonistic quality (as in the first example below) or a trendy quality (as in the second). Careful writers avoid them or, when quoting someone else, distance themselves with telltale quotation marks (as in the first example): "The

New York City Fire Commissioner directed that her cargo tanks be *'inerted'* through the introduction of carbon dioxide into the tanks" (*The Law of Admiralty*, 2d ed. 1975)./ "Clinton would be well-advised to *low-key* the task force before it announces anything embarrassing" (*Newsweek*). Cf. NOUNS AS VERBS.

E. Coordinate Adjectives. When two adjectives, both modifying the same noun, are related in sense, they should be separated by a comma (or else an *and*). Thus, we say *a big, sprawling house* and *a poignant, uplifting film*. But when the consecutive adjectives are unrelated, there shouldn't be a comma—hence *a big white house* and *a poignant foreign film*.

Some consecutive adjectives present close questions—e.g.: "The *brief, unsigned Supreme Court opinion* said that the lawyers for Ms. Benten had failed to show a substantial likelihood that the case would be won if it were argued before the United States Court of Appeals for the Second Circuit" (*N.Y. Times*). Is the fact that the opinion is brief related to the fact that it is unsigned? If so, the comma is proper; if not, the comma is improper. Because signed opinions tend to be longer than unsigned opinions, the comma is probably justified. But the long phrase-as-adjective, which is awkward, could be improved: *The brief opinion, unsigned by any justice, said that the lawyers* . . . .

For more on the punctuation of successive adjectives, see COMMA.

F. Proper Names as Adjectives. When a proper name is used attributively as an adjective, the writer should capitalize only that portion used in attribution <a University of Florida student> <a John Birch Society member>.

The practice of using as adjectives place names having two or more words is generally to be resisted. But it is increasingly common. Although *California home* and *Austin jury* are perfectly acceptable, *Sacramento, California home* and *Austin, Texas jury* are not. To make matters worse, some writers place a second comma after the state. Thus, using a city plus the state as an adjective disrupts the flow of the sentence—e.g.: "Farmland's president, Marc Goldman, sent out sleuths who traced the missing containers to an *Elizabeth, N.J., warehouse* he says is filled with discarded bottles of designer water" (*Wall St. J.*). Such constructions contribute to NOUN PLAGUE, lessen readability, and bother literate readers.

G. Phrasal or Compound Adjectives. See PHRASAL ADJECTIVES.

H. Modification of Adjectives Ending in *-ed*. See **very (B).**

I. Adjectives Ending in *-ly*. See ADVERBS (B).

J. Dates as Adjectives. See DATES (C).

K. Comparative and Superlative Adjectives. See COMPARATIVES AND SUPERLATIVES.

adjournment = (1) the act of suspending proceedings to another time or place; or (2) an adjourned meeting, i.e., a meeting "scheduled for a particular time (and place, if it is not otherwise established) by the assembly's 'adjourning to' or 'adjourning until' that time and place" (*Robert's Rules of Order*, 1990). As *Robert's* points out, because sense 2 is susceptible to confusion with sense 1, the phrase *adjourned meeting* is preferable to *adjournment* in sense 2. Reserve *adjournment* for its ordinary meaning: sense 1.

adjure. See **abjure.**

administrate is an objectionable back-formation from *administration*. Avoid it as a needless variant of *administer*—e.g.: "Inevitably, his unenlightened attempts to teach and *administrate* [read *administer*] were doomed to failure" (*Wis. State J.*).

admission. A. And *admittance*. The distinction between these terms is old and useful, but it is all too often ignored. *Admittance* is purely physical, as in signs that read "No admittance."

Admission is used in figurative and nonphysical senses <admission to the club's membership>.

Sometimes *admittance* is misused for *admission*, as when the subject is being accepted for enrollment in a school—e.g.: "To the extent that some private colleges may not require B averages to gain *admittance* [read *admission*], it could be tougher to win a state scholarship" (*Atlanta J. & Const.*).

B. And *confession*. In criminal law, a distinction has traditionally existed between these words: an *admission* is a concession that an allegation or factual assertion is true without any acknowledgment of guilt with respect to the criminal charges, whereas a *confession* involves an acknowledgment of guilt as well as of the truth of factual allegations.

advance; advancement. Generally, the first refers to progress, the second to promotion. Hence, someone might get an occupational *advancement*, but we speak of the *advance* of civilization. In senses suggesting the action of moving up or bringing forth, *advancement* is the proper word <National Association for the Advancement of Colored People>.

The phrases *advance notice*, *advance warning*, and the like are redundant.

ADVERBS. A. Placement of Adverbs. Many writers fall into awkward, unidiomatic sentences when they misguidedly avoid splitting up verb phrases. Although most authorities squarely say that the best place for the adverb is in the midst of the verb phrase, many writers nevertheless harbor a misplaced aversion, probably because they confuse a split verb phrase with the SPLIT INFINITIVE. H.W. Fowler explained long ago what writers still have problems understanding: "When an adverb is to be used with [a compound] verb, its normal place is between the auxiliary (or sometimes the first auxiliary if there are two or more) and the rest. Not only is there no objection to thus splitting a compound verb . . . , but any other position for the adverb requires special justification" (*MEU1*). Other authorities agree and have long done so, as the following sampling shows—e.g.:

- "[The adverb] frequently stands between the auxiliary and the verb, as 'He . . . *was attentively heard* by the whole audience' " (Robert Lowth, *A Short Introduction to English Grammar*, 1782).
- "Those [adverbs] . . . which belong to compound verbs, are commonly placed after the first auxiliary" (Goold Brown, *The Institutes of English Grammar*, 1852).
- "When the tense of a transitive verb is compound, the adverb follows the first auxiliary if the verb is in the active voice [e.g., *the boy has always obeyed his father*], and immediately precedes the principal verb if the verb is in the passive voice [e.g., *the house can be quickly built*]." Josephine Turck Baker, *Correct English: Complete Grammar and Drill Book*, 1938).
- "The truth is that more often than not the proper and natural place for an adverb is between the parts of a compound verb" (Theodore M. Bernstein, *The Careful Writer*, 1965).
- "With a compound verb—that is, one made with an auxiliary and a main verb—the adverb comes between auxiliary and main verb (*He will probably telephone before starting / I have often had that thought myself / The clock is consistently losing five minutes a day*)" (Wilson Follett, *MAU*).

But confusion on this point is all but ubiquitous. The result is an unidiomatic, unnatural style—e.g.: "Circuit judges *currently are elected* [read *are currently elected*] in countywide races" (*Milwaukee J.*)./ "The five police commissioners who have criticized Williams' management and who have reprimanded him for allegedly lying *all were appointed* [read *were all appointed*] by [Mayor Richard] Riordan" (*L.A. Times*). See SUPERSTITIONS (C).

B. Awkward Adverbs. Adjectives ending in *-ly* and *-le* often make cumbersome adverbs, e.g., *chillily*, *friend-*

lily, *ghastlily*, *holily*, *jollily*, *juvenilely*, *lovelily*, *sillily*, *statelily*, *supplely*, *surlily*, *uglily*, and so on. You needn't be timid in writing or pronouncing such adverbs when they're genuinely needed; but if they seem unnatural, you can easily rephrase the sentence, e.g., *in a silly manner*. Words such as *timely* and *stately*, however, act as both adjectives and adverbs.

If you do use unusual adverbs, use them sparingly. Some writers display an unfortunate fondness for them, as by using such forms as *corollarily*, *consideredly*, and the spurious *widespreadedly*. Cf. -EDLY.

C. Adjectives or Adverbs After Linking Verbs. English contains a number of linking verbs (or copulas) apart from *to be*—e.g., *appear*, *seem*, *become*, *look*, *smell*, *taste*. These verbs connect a descriptive word with the subject; hence the descriptive word following the linking verb describes the subject and not the verb. We say *He turned professional*, not *He turned professionally*.

Writers frequently fall into error when they use linking verbs. One must analyze the sentence rather than memorize a list of common linking verbs, much as this may help. Often an unexpected verb of this kind appears—e.g.: "No other rule sweeps so *broadly* [read *broad*]." The writer intends not to describe a manner of sweeping, but to say the rule is broad. Cf. **badly (A).**

D. Double Adverbs. Several adverbs not ending in *-ly*—especially *doubtless*, *fast*, *ill*, *much*, *seldom*, *thus*—have NONWORD counterparts ending in *-ly*. Using *doubtlessly*, *fastly*, etc. is poor style. The terms with the superfluous *-ly* reveal an ignorance of idiom.

adverse; averse. Both may take the preposition *to*, but *averse* also takes *from*. To be *averse to* something is to have feelings against it <averse to risk>. The phrase usually describes a person's attitude. To be *adverse to* something is to be turned in opposition against it <Thailand was adverse to Japan during most of World War II>. The phrase usually refers to things, not people.

The most common problem is the misuse of *adverse* for *averse*—e.g.: "Botha is known to be strongly *adverse* [read *averse*] to pressure—whether from the international community or from South Africa's black townships" (*Christian Science Monitor*).

advice; advise. *Advice* /ad-**VIS**/ (= counsel that one person gives another) is a noun. *Advise* /ad-**VIZ**/ (= to counsel; try to help by guiding) is a verb. The spellings are often confounded—e.g.: "All the programs take pains to inform you with large disclaimers that they are no substitute for real medical professionals (good *advise* [read *advice*]) and as such cannot be responsible if you use them improperly" (*Asbury Park Press*).

advise for *tell*, *say*, or *explain* is a pomposity to be avoided—e.g.: "The judge *advised* [read *told*] Smith that he would not have the benefit of a skilled attorney who could identify legal issues or problems with the state's evidence" (*Hartford Courant*).

aesthetic; esthetic. Although some dictionaries have long recorded *esthetic* as the primary form in AmE, the form *aesthetic* remains more common in AmE and BrE alike.

affect; effect. In ordinary usage, *affect* is always a verb; it means "to influence; to have an effect on." *Effect*, as suggested by its use in that definition, is primarily a noun meaning "result" or "consequence." To *affect* something is to have an *effect* on it. But as a verb, *effect* means "to bring about; produce."

Using *affect* (= to influence) for *effect* (= to bring about) is an old error that looks as if it will be increasingly difficult to stamp out. The mistake is especially common in the phrase *to effect change(s)*—e.g.: "Throughout the book her winning personality *affects* [read *effects*] changes in the drab and pitiful 'sad' people she encounters" (*Ark.*

Democrat-Gaz.)./ "[It is] a good example of environmentalists working with corporations to *affect* [read *effect*] change" (*N.Y. Times*).

H.W. Fowler treated only the verb forms of these words, apparently because they didn't seem susceptible to confusion as nouns. But today even the confusion of nouns is fairly common—e.g.: "Mr. Nir's briefing must have had some *affect* [read *effect*] on Mr. Bush" (*N.Y. Times*). Likewise, *effect* is sometimes misused for *affect*. See **effect (B).** Cf. **impact.**

afflict. See **inflict.**

affluence; affluent. These words are preferably accented on the first syllable (/**af**-loo-ən[t]s/, /**af**-loo-ənt/), not the second (/ə-**floo**-ən[t]s/, /ə-**floo**-ənt/). See PRONUNCIATION (B).

affront. See **effrontery (A).**

afterward; afterword. *Afterward*, an adverb, is a variant form of *afterwards* (= later). *Afterword* is a noun meaning "epilogue." Cf. **foreword.**

For more on *afterward(s)*, see DIRECTIONAL WORDS (A).

agenda is (1) the plural form of *agendum*, which means "something to be done" (another, less proper plural of *agendum* being *agendums*); and, more commonly, (2) a singular noun meaning "a list of things to be done" or "a program." The plural of *agenda* in this second sense is *agendas*. Decrying *agendas* as a double plural is pointless.

aggravate for *annoy* or *irritate*, though documented as existing since the 1600s, has never gained the approval of stylists and should be avoided in formal writing. Strictly speaking, *aggravate* means "to make worse; exacerbate" <writing a second apology might just aggravate the problem>.

Even Oliver Wendell Holmes, Jr., nodded once, using *aggravate* for *irritate* in one of his letters to Sir Frederick Pollock in 1895: "our two countries *aggravate* each other from time to time" (*Holmes-Pollock Letters*, 1941). The lapse is common in modern writing—e.g.: "It has *aggravated* [read *irritated*] me when I have seen billboards that contained misspelled words, punctuation errors and other things that are fundamental to the English language" (*Florida Today*).

The confusion also occurs between the noun forms—e.g.: "Rush Limbaugh, still the industry giant, has an extra tone of *aggravation* [read *irritation*] as he denounces the unyielding poll leads of 'the Schlickmeister' and 'noted hetero fun-seeker,' President Clinton" (*N.Y. Times*).

-AHOLIC; -AHOLISM. These newfangled "suffixes" derive from *alcoholic* and *alcoholism*, which were extended to *workaholic* and *workaholism*, and from there to other words indicating various addictions or obsessions. Each new term is automatically a morphological deformity. Most examples, though, are nonce words (e.g., *beefaholic*, *footballaholic*, *spendaholic*, *wordaholic*).

ain't. Is this word used orally in most parts of the country by cultivated speakers? That's what *W3* said in 1961, and it provoked a firestorm of protests from journalists and academics. *W3*'s assessment was quite a change from that of *W2* (1934), which had given it a tag: "*Dial. or Illit.*" The editor of *W3*, Philip Gove, explained the change by conceding that he had no large files of empirical evidence: "[K]nowledge of some kind of language behavior comes through contact with its observers and is not always documented because there seems to be no reason to collect additional evidence" (Herbert C. Morton, *The Story of Webster's Third*, 1994). If that's the method, then one can confidently say that *W3*'s treatment was flawed in its incompleteness.

Yes, *ain't* is used by cultivated speakers, but almost always for either of two reasons: (1) to be tongue-in-cheek; and (2) to flaunt their reverse snobbery. For most people, it remains a shibboleth of poor usage—a NONWORD. All in all, the

1934 tag has either remained accurate or been bolstered.

Airlinese. The JARGON of the airline business is notable in several ways. First, it has an odd vocabulary, in which *equipment* refers to the airplane you wish you were boarding ("I'm sorry, but the flight has been delayed because we don't have any *equipment*—it's been delayed in Pittsburgh"). Second, it relies heavily on DOUBLESPEAK, with a heavy dose of BURIED VERBS: *seat cushions may be used as flotation devices* means "if we crash in water, use your seat cushion to float"; *in the event of a loss in cabin pressure* means "if we lose cabin pressure so that no one can breathe"; *please use the trash dispenser for anything other than bathroom tissue* means "don't try to flush paper towels or anything other than bathroom tissue down the commode." Third, it is often stilted and redundant—e.g.: "It is a federal requirement to comply with all safety regulations." Fourth, it has borrowed many nautical terms, both directly (*aft, bulkhead, crew, fleet, galley, hold, stowage*) and by analogy (*airworthy, flight deck*). Finally, it contains many NEOLOGISMS, some formed by combining nouns (*load factor, ground personnel*), some by affixation (*inflight*, adj.), and some by changing parts of speech (e.g., *overnight*, vb., as in "We'll have to overnight you"). Among other recent coinages are these:

- *enplane, enplanement*: "Though it recorded more than 600,000 *enplanements* in the mid-'70s, the state is now struggling to board about 350,000 passengers a year" (*Charleston Gaz.*).
- *hub-and-spoke*: "The industry's *hub-and-spoke* system of operating, in which short flights feed customers into big airports, where they board longer flights, has also increased demand for regional jets" (*N.Y. Times*).
- *interline*: "Southwest does not *interline* with other carriers, in part because it is simply unwilling to spend the extra time and money on the ground, waiting to board passengers from connecting flights that are often delayed" (Kevin Freiberg & Jackie Freiberg, *Nuts! Southwest Airlines' Crazy Recipe for Business and Personal Success*, 1996).
- *load factor*: "Instead of raising fares when *load factors* (ratio of passenger capacity to tickets sold) are up, Southwest increases the number of flights and expands the market" (*id.*).
- *pushback*: "[The] ramp agent unhooks the *pushback* from the aircraft and the plane taxis toward the runway" (*id.*).

Although these neologisms serve a genuine purpose, airlinese otherwise typifies some of the worst qualities of modern AmE (e.g., "We'll be on the ground *momentarily*"—see **momentarily**). And it has a debilitating effect because so many people are so frequently exposed to it. Small wonder that some of them feel tempted to dash for an emergency exit.

alibi. A. As a Noun for *excuse*. Strictly speaking, the words are not synonymous, although the confusion of their meanings is understandable. *Alibi* is a specific legal term referring to the defense of having been at a place other than the scene of a crime. By slipshod extension it came to be used for any excuse or explanation for misconduct, usually one that shifts blame to someone else. This broader meaning has its defenders—e.g.: "Cynicism and the common man's distrust of the law have tinged *alibi* with a suggestion of improbability and even of dishonesty. Purists insist that it should be restricted to its legal meaning, and those who wish to be formally correct will so restrict it. In so doing, however, they will lose the connotation of cunning and dishonesty which distinguishes it from *excuse*" (Evans & Evans, *DCAU*). Their point is well taken, but *alibi* to denote a cunning excuse remains a casualism.

B. As an Adverb. In recent years *alibi* has been used as an adverb (meaning "elsewhere" <he proved himself alibi>), but this usage should be avoided. Although "elsewhere" is the original Latin meaning of *alibi* (originally a locative of L. *alius* "other"), in English it has long served only as a noun, and harking back to the classical sense is an affectation.

C. As a Verb. Nor should *alibi* be used as a verb, as it occasionally has been since the early 20th century. The examples below are doubly bad since the misbegotten verb (meaning *excuse*) is based on the misused noun: "Tyson *alibied* [read *said* or *tried to excuse himself by saying*] that he 'snapped' when he bit Holyfield—twice" (*Atlanta J. & Const.*)./ "I'd say there's a danger and plain lousy taste in distorting a current president's words to zip up a movie. 'It's fantasy, entertainment,' Zemeckis *alibied* [read *rationalized*]. 'It adds verisimilitude' " (*Milwaukee J. & Sentinel*).

all. A. *All (of)*. The more formal construction is to omit *of* and write, when possible, "*All* the attempts failed." E.g.: "With the end to fighting, the group was disbanded, and *all* its members were ordered to burn their identity papers and go into hiding" (*Austin American-Statesman*). Although *all of* is more common in AmE than in BrE, it should generally be avoided in formal writing. See **of (A)**.

In two circumstances, though, *all of* is the better choice. The first is when a pronoun follows <all of them>, unless the pronoun is possessive <all my belongings>. The second is when a possessive noun follows—e.g.: "Beyond *all of* Jones' ego-stroking maneuvers and incessant need for attention, this is what he is talking about" (*Cincinnati Enquirer*).

B. With Negatives. *Not all*—as opposed to *all . . . not*—is usually the correct sequence in negative constructions. E.g.: "When he screened Foster's office files two days after his death, Nussbaum decided that *all* of the papers were *not* relevant to the suicide inquiry" (*Chicago Trib.*). (Two possible revisions to remedy the ambiguity of the original: *Nussbaum decided that none of the papers were relevant.*/ *Nussbaum decided that some of the papers were not relevant.*)

C. And *any*. *All* follows a superlative adjective <the best of all>; *any* follows a comparative adjective <more than any other>. Constructions such as *more than . . . all* are illogical. See COMPARATIVES AND SUPERLATIVES.

ALLITERATION. A. Purposeful Examples. How language affects the ear should be a critical concern of every writer. Writers frequently harness sounds for any of several effects. When they repeat sounds in nearby words, the result is called *alliteration* (which has two subsets: *assonance* for vowels, *consonance* for consonants).

Sometimes alliteration reinforces sarcasm, as when Vice President Spiro Agnew referred to the *nattering nabobs of negativism* or when Fred Rodell, a Yale professor, referred to due process as *that lovely limpid legalism*. Rodell, in fact, relished sarcastic alliteration, once referring to "the *tweedledum-tweedledee twaddle* of much that passes for *learned legal* argument" (*Nine Men*, 1955).

At other times alliteration merely creates a memorable phrase—e.g.: "Music is unique among the fine arts in that it calls for a response not only *from* the *head* and the *heart* but also, *frequently*, *from* one or more of the *feet*" (Frank Muir, *An Irreverent and Thoroughly Incomplete Social History of Almost Everything*, 1976).

Sometimes alliteration is risky. If it leads you into SESQUIPEDALITY just for the sake of sound, it will probably annoy some readers—e.g.: "Lukacs has an *eagle eye* for the *etiology* of *error* and the seductions of false logic" (*L.A. Times*). If that writer hadn't been lured by alliteration, he almost certainly would have used *cause* rather than *etiology* there.

B. Accidental Examples. The unconscious repetition of sounds, especially excessive sibilance (too many /s/ sounds, as in the phrase *especially excessive sibilance*), can easily distract readers: "[W]hen used by accident it falls on the ear very disagreeably" (W. Somerset Maugham, "Lucidity, Simplicity, Euphony," in *The Summing Up*, 1938). E.g.: "[E]verybody with a stake in solving the problem will have to *bear their fair share* of the costs involved" (*Fin. Times*). (A possible revision: *Everybody with a stake in solving the problem will have to bear some of the costs.*)

The best way to avoid the infelicity of undue alliteration is to read one's prose aloud when editing. See SOUND OF PROSE.

all . . . not. See **all (B).**

all of. See **all (a).**

allow; permit. These words have an important connotative difference. *Allow* suggests merely the absence of opposition, or refraining from a proscription. *Permit*, in contrast, suggests affirmative sanction or approval.

all ready. See **already.**

all right. So spelled. The one-word spelling (*alright*) has never been accepted as standard in AmE.

all together. See **altogether.**

almond is pronounced /**ah**-mənd/—not /**ahl**-mənd/ or (worse) /**al**-mənd/. See PRONUNCIATION (B).

almost. Like *only*, the word *almost* should be placed immediately before the word it modifies. But it's sometimes misplaced—e.g.: "There is *almost a childlike simplicity* [read *an almost childlike simplicity*] in their straightforward depictions" (*Allentown Morning Call*). See **only.**

alongside, prep., = at the side of. Hence, one car is parked *alongside* another, logs are stacked *alongside* one another. It is unnecessary—and poor style—to write *alongside of*. Cf. **of (A).**

along with. Like *together with*, this connective phrase does not affect the grammatical number of the sentence. See SUBJECT–VERB AGREEMENT (E).

a lot (= many) is the standard spelling. *Alot* is a nonstandard form.

aloud; out loud. The latter is colloquial when used in place of the former in expressions such as *read out loud*. Because of this—and because *read aloud* is 12 times more common than *read out loud*—*read aloud* should be preferred in edited prose. E.g.: "McGuffey's fifth and sixth readers had an abundance of the kind of poetry that demands to be read *out loud* [read *aloud*], like 'The Raven' by Edgar Allan Poe" (*N.Y. Times*).

already; all ready. *Already* has to do with time <finished already>, *all ready* with preparation <we are all ready>.

alright. See **all right.**

also. See **too (a).**

also not is usually inferior to *nor*—e.g.: "*He was also not* [read *Nor was he*] told until later, he says, about the allegations of military doctor Maj. Barry Armstrong that one of the Somali men may have been killed execution-style" (*Windsor Star*). But when a contraction precedes the phrase and the tone is intentionally conversational, *also not* seems the more natural wording—e.g.: "It's *also not* hard to imagine that students, in the privacy of their dorm rooms, haven't cut the rug a time or two in secret" (*Fresno Bee*).

alter; altar. *Alter* (= to change) is a verb; *altar* (= the table or structure used for sacramental purposes) is a noun. But writers have sometimes confused the two—e.g.: "[C]ivil liberties have been sacrificed on the *alter* [read *altar*] of zero tolerance" (*USA Today*).

altercation. The traditional view is that this word refers to "a noisy brawl or dispute," not rising to the seriousness of physical violence. For authority limiting the term to the sense "wordy strife," see the *OED*, *W2*, *W3*, and Eric Partridge's *U&A*. But in AmE, the word now often denotes some type of scuffling or fighting, especially in police JARGON—e.g.: "A 29-year-old drugstore manager who was punched in the chest last month during an *altercation* has died of his injuries, Suffolk police reported yesterday" (*N.Y. Newsday*). Some will lament this development as SLIPSHOD EXTENSION, but the purely nonphysical sense is surely beyond recall. The real battle now is to limit *altercation* to light roughhousing. That is, it's wrong to say that someone is killed during an altercation. But police (and the reporters who interview them) tend to talk this way—e.g.: "Police said they received a call about 2 a.m. that Kamosky had been killed *during an altercation* [read *in a fight*] with a friend" (*Richmond Times-Dispatch*).

alternate; alternative. A. As Nouns. *Alternative* is needed far more often than *alternate*. An *alternative* is a choice or option—usually one of two choices, but not necessarily. Etymological purists have argued that the word (fr. L. *alter* "the other of two") should be confined to contexts involving but two choices. Ernest Gowers termed this contention a fetish (*MEU2*), and it has little or no support among other stylistic experts or in actual usage. E.g.: "The county has *three alternatives* on how to meet the region's needs before its treatment plants reach capacity in 2010" (*Seattle Times*).

Indeed, *alternative* carries with it two nuances absent from *choice*. First, *alternative* may suggest adequacy for some purpose <ample alternative channels>; and second, it may suggest compulsion to choose <the alternatives are liberty and death>.

Alternate = (1) something that proceeds by turns with another; or (2) one who substitutes for another.

B. As Adjectives. *Alternative* = providing a choice between two or more things; available in place of another. E.g.: "Herman would not oppose the light without offering an *alternative* solution, he said" (*Baltimore Sun*).

Alternate = (1) coming each after one of the other kind; every second one <the divorced parents had agreed on an alternate visitation schedule for their daughter>; or (2) substitute <although he didn't make the first team, he was named the first alternate player>.

Alternate is sometimes misused for *alternative*, an understandable mistake given how close sense 2 of *alternate* is—e.g.: "Patton responded to the Atlanta Preservation Center's proposal for an *alternate* [read *alternative*] site for the classroom building" (*Atlanta J. & Const.*).

although; though. As conjunctions, the words are virtually interchangeable. The only distinction is that *although* is more formal and dignified, *though* more usual in speech and familiar writing. In certain formal contexts, however, *though* reads better. *Though* serves also as an adverb <he stated as much, though>.

Tho and *altho* are old-fashioned truncated spellings that were at one time very common, but failed to become standard. They should be avoided.

altogether; all together. *Altogether* = completely; wholly <the charges were altogether unfounded>. *All together* = at one place or at the same time <the board members were all together at that meeting>.

alumni; alumnae. *Alumni* (/ə-**ləm**-nɪ/) refers either to male graduates or to males and females collectively; the singular form, which is masculine, is *alumnus*. *Alumnae* (/ə-**ləm**-nee/) refers to female graduates and not, traditionally, to mixed groups; the singular is *alumna*.

A more common mistake than confusing the gender of these words is confusing their number, as by using *alumni* or *alumnae* as a singular—e.g.: "He was an *alumni* [read *alumnus*] of Massachusetts Institute of Technology (MIT) and UCLA" (*News Trib.*). See PLURALS (B).

Alum is a clipped form that dodges the gender issue. This slangy casualism appears often in chatty discussions about high-school and college sports—e.g.: "[A] group of former Kentucky residents and Wildcat *alums*—mostly female—gather to cheer on their team" (*Portland Oregonian*).

Alum is a better and more frequent spelling than *alumn*—e.g.: "Four Lancaster-Lebanon League *alumns* [read *alums*] are members of the 24th-ranked Penn State team" (*Lancaster New Era*).

a.m.; AM; p.m.; PM. Whether you use small capitals or lowercase, keep your document consistent throughout. The lowercase letters are now more common, and with lowercase the periods are preferred. But many editors prefer the look of AM.

These abbreviations stand for the Latin phrases *ante meridiem* ("before noon") and *post meridiem* ("after noon"). But some writers, when using the full phrases, mistake *meridiem* for *meridian*—e.g.: "Twelve noon is neither *ante meridian* [read *ante meridiem*] (before midday) nor *post meridian* [read *post meridiem*] (after midday)" (*Guardian*).

ambience; ambiance. The first (pronounced /**am**-bee-ən[t]s/) is an anglicized form that entered the language in the late 19th century. It's preferable to the second (pronounced /**ahm**-bee-ahn[t]s/), a Frenchified affectation that, since its emergence in the mid-20th century, has become a VOGUE WORD.

ambulance /**am**-byoo-lən[t]s/ is often mispronounced /**am**-byoo-lan[t]s/.

AMERICANISMS AND BRITISHISMS. A. Generally. Although this book points out many differences between AmE and BrE, that is not its primary purpose. For guidance on distinctions not covered here, see Norman W. Schur, *British English A to Zed* (1987); Norman Moss, *British/American Language Dictionary* (1984); and Martin S. Allwood, *American and British* (1964). For differences in editorial style, compare *The Chicago Manual of Style* (14th ed. 1993) with Judith Butcher, *Copy-Editing: The Cambridge Handbook* (2d ed. 1981).

B. Americanisms Invading BrE. During the 20th century, the English language's center of gravity gradually shifted from England to the United States. As a result, the most influential linguistic innovations occur in AmE, as a further result of which BrE speakers frequently bemoan American encroachments. For example, in February 1995, Steve Ward of Bristol said in a letter published in *The Times*: "Sir, I am disappointed to see that even *The Times*'s leader columns are succumbing to the relentless invasion of American English. In your leader of January 28, on the National Lottery, you state that 'stores which sell tickets for the draw have lottery-only lines on a Saturday.' Do you mean: '*Shops* . . . have lottery-only *queues*'?"

C. Britishisms Invading AmE. To some extent, transatlantic linguistic influences are reciprocal. In the late 20th century, it became common in AmE to use the Britishism *take a decision* (as opposed to the usual AmE *make a decision*). And many Americans have begun using *amongst* and *whilst*. On the whole, though, BrE's influences on AmE are so slight that few take any notice.

D. Related Entries. For several other differences between the two major strains of English, see -ER (B), -OR & SPELLING (B).

amicable; amiable. The first came directly from Latin, the latter from French, but the two forms are at base the same word. Yet the two have undergone DIFFERENTIATION. *Amiable* applies to persons <an amiable chap>, *amicable* to relations between persons <an amicable resolution>.

amn't I? See **aren't I?**

amok; amuck. Usage authorities once held firmly to the idea that *amuck* is preferable to *amok*—solely on the mistaken notion that *amuck* is older in English and *amok* (though a better transliteration of the Malaysian word) was a late-coming "didacticism." In fact, both forms date from the 17th century. And, in any event, *amok* is ten times more common than *amuck* today—e.g.: "For decades, the Buildings Department, which processes 35,000 permits a year, has resembled a satirist's vision of bureaucracy run *amok*" (*N.Y. Times*). But some publications fight the trend—as evidenced by the title of Charles Krauthammer's essay "Elephants Run *Amuck*: After Killing Big Government, the G.O.P. Suddenly Risks Stampeding Itself to Death" (*Time*). *Amok* is now the standard term.

among. A. And *amongst*. Forms ending in *-st*, such as *whilst* and *amidst*, are generally archaisms in AmE. *Amongst* is no exception: in AmE it is pretentious at best. E.g.: "Imagine a city where the electricity and water companies are owned by the local authorities and, thanks to progressive planning and construction, prices are *amongst* [read *among*] the lowest in the country" (*Seattle Times*).

Amongst is more common and more tolerable in BrE, where it doesn't suggest affectation—e.g.: "With the deft wit of a real technician, Marber sets up the relationships *amongst* the employees" (*Guardian*).

B. With Mass Nouns. Generally, *among* is used with plural nouns and *amid* with mass nouns. Thus one is *among* people but *amid* a series of arguments. (See COUNT NOUNS AND MASS NOUNS.) In the following sentences, *among* is misused for other prepositions: "*Among* [read *With* or *In*] the president's contingent are Mr. Robert Mosbacher, commerce secretary, and around 20 top U.S. executives" (*Fin. Times*)./ "The shotgun came to New Plymouth *among* [read *in* or *with*] a shipment of arms from Gothenburg, Sweden, addressed to a Hawera firearm collector" (*N.Y. Daily News*).

C. And *between*. See **between (a).**

amoral. See **immoral.**

amount; number. The first is used with mass nouns, the second with count nouns. Thus we say "an increase in the *amount* of litigation" but "an increase in the *number* of lawsuits." But writers frequently bungle the distinction—e.g.: "The *amount* [read *number*] of ex-players who talked shows that the authors did their homework" (*Austin American-Statesman*). See COUNT NOUNS AND MASS NOUNS.

amount of, in the. See **check in the amount of.**

amuck. See **amok.**

amuse. See **bemuse.**

an. See **a (A).**

analysis; analyzation. The first, of course, is the standard word. *Analyzation*, a pseudo-learned variant of *analysis*, is a NONWORD—e.g.: "The module assists in the computerized design and performance *analyzation* [read *analysis*] of wooden pallets and skids" (*Buffalo News*).

and. A. Beginning Sentences with. It is rank superstition that this coordinating conjunction cannot properly begin a sentence:

- "That it is a solecism to begin a sentence with *and* is a faintly lingering superstition. The *OED* gives examples ranging from the 10th to the 19th c; the Bible is full of them" (Ernest Gowers, *MEU2*).
- "A prejudice lingers from the days of schoolmarmish rhetoric that a sentence should not begin with *and*. The sup-

posed rule is without foundation in grammar, logic, or art. *And* can join separate sentences and their meanings just as well as *but* can both join sentences and disjoin meanings" (Wilson Follett, *MAU*).

- "There is no reason why sentences should not begin with *and*" (Roy H. Copperud, *American Usage: The Consensus*, 1970).
- "Many years ago schoolteachers insisted that it was improper to begin a sentence with *and*, but this convention is now outmoded. Innumerable respected writers use *and* at the beginning of a sentence" (William Morris & Mary Morris, *Harper Dictionary of Contemporary Usage*, 1985).
- "There is a persistent belief that it is improper to begin a sentence with *And*, but this prohibition has been cheerfully ignored by standard authors from Anglo-Saxon times onwards" (R.W. Burchfield, *Points of View*, 1992).
- "*And* the idea that *and* must not begin a sentence, or even a paragraph, is an empty superstition. The same goes for *but*. Indeed either word can give unimprovably early warning of the sort of thing that is to follow" (Kingsley Amis, *The King's English*, 1997).

As Follett and Amis point out, the same superstition has plagued *but*. (See **but (A)**.) Though using *and* as a transitional artifice is quite acceptable, you should do so in moderation. See SUPERSTITIONS (D).

The very best writers find occasion to begin sentences with *and*—e.g.:

- "[T]he characteristics of one period have generally had their beginnings in the previous period, and it is impossible to say with perfect accuracy when one period begins and another ends. *And* just as it is impossible to fix the precise date at which one period of a language ends and another begins, so also it is not possible to do more than fix approximately the date at which any particular sound-change took place" (Joseph Wright & Elizabeth M. Wright, *An Elementary Historical New English Grammar*, 1969).
- "*And* one had better make use of whatever beauty, elegance, riches the translator's language possesses, and hope that something emotionally, intellectually, aesthetically equivalent will emerge" (John Simon, *The Sheep from the Goats*, 1989).
- "*And* there is, come to think of it, that unsounded *b*, to keep alive some small doubt" (Christopher Ricks, *Beckett's Dying Words*, 1993).

B. For *or*. Oddly, *and* is frequently misused for *or* where a singular noun, or one of two nouns, is called for—e.g.: "While third-party candidates have mounted serious challenges for senator *and* [read *or*] governor in almost two dozen states this year, building an effective third-party apparatus is rare" (*N.Y. Times*). (The phrase should be *senator or governor*; as written, the sentence says that in each of almost 24 states both senator and governor races were entered by third-party candidates—an idea belied by the context of the article.)

C. In Enumerations. Some writers have a tendency, especially in long enumerations, to omit *and* before the final element. To do so is often infelicitous: the reader is jarred by the abrupt period ending the sentence and may even wonder whether something has been omitted. One may occasionally omit *and* before the final element in an enumeration with a particular nuance in mind: without *and*, the implication is that the series is incomplete—rhetoricians call this construction "asyndeton"; with *and* the implication is that the series is complete. This shade in meaning is increasingly subtle in modern prose.

D. Serial Comma Before *and* in Enumerations. On the question of punctuating enumerations, the better practice is to place a comma before the *and* introducing the final element. See ENUMERATIONS (B) & COMMA.

and etc. See **etc. (B)**.

and/or. A legal and business expression dating from the mid-19th century, *and/or* has been vilified for most of its life—and rightly so. To avoid ambiguity, don't use it. Many writers—especially lawyers—would be surprised at how easy and workable this solution is. *Or* alone usually suffices.

anecdote; antidote. *Anecdote* (= a brief story, usu. true and intended to amuse) is sometimes confused with *antidote* (= something that counteracts poison), resulting in a MALAPROPISM—e.g.: "One dog was poisoned but we found the *anecdote* [read *antidote*]" (*Fresno Bee*). The opposite error rarely if ever occurs.

anemone /ə-**nem**-ə-nee/ (= [1] a flower of the buttercup family; or [2] a flowerlike sea polyp) is so spelled—not *anenome*. But the misspelling (like the mispronunciation /ə-**nen**-ə-mee/) is common—e.g.: "The meadow is bursting with thousands of *anenome* [read *anemone*] *vulgaris* (pasque flowers)" (*Wis. State J.*). The phrase *any money* can be a helpful mnemonic device. See METATHESIS.

anesthetist; anesthesiologist. Generally, *anesthetist* will serve for "one who administers an anesthetic." The term dates from the late 19th century. *Anesthesiologist*, of World War II vintage, refers specifically to a physician specializing in anesthesia and anesthetics.

annoy. See **aggravate.**

annulment. See **divorce (A).**

antagonist. See **protagonist.**

Antarctica is frequently misspelled *Antartica*—e.g.: "Kroc expanded the golden-arches empire to every continent on the globe (except *Antartica* [read *Antarctica*])" (*N.J. Record*). In fact, this misspelling occurs in about 3% of the modern journalistic sources containing the word.

ANTE-; ANTI-. The prefix *ante-* means "before," and *anti-* "against." Thus *antecedent* (= something that goes before) and *antipathy* (= feelings against, dislike). In a few words *ante-* has been changed to *anti-*, as in *anticipate* (= to consider or use *before* the due or natural time) and *antipasto* (= an Italian appetizer, usu. consisting of an assortment of cheeses, vegetables, meats, and olives).

In some compound words, the prefix *anti-* may cause ambiguities, as in *antinuclear protester*. Is that a protester against nuclear energy or a protester against antinuclear activities?

antebellum. One word.

ANTECEDENTS, AGREEMENT OF NOUNS WITH. See CONCORD.

ANTECEDENTS, REMOTE. See MISCUES (C) & REMOTE RELATIVES.

antedate; predate. Both words are so common that it would be presumptuous to label either a needless variant. One sees a tendency to use *antedate* in reference to documentary materials, and *predate* in reference to physical things and historical facts. The DIFFERENTIATION is worth encouraging.

For another sense of *predate*, see **predate.**

antenna. When the reference is to insects, *antennae* /an-**ten**-ee/ is the usual plural. But when the reference is to televisions and electronic transmitters, *antennas* is better. See PLURALS (B).

ANTI-. See ANTE-.

anticipate = (1) to take care of beforehand; to preclude by prior action; forestall <they anticipated the problem by filing for bankruptcy>; (2) to await eagerly <this much-anticipated film is a great disappointment>; or (3) to expect <we anticipate that 40 people will attend>. Senses 2 and 3 have long been considered the result of SLIPSHOD EXTENSION. Sense 3 no doubt resulted from the unfortunate tendency for people to choose longer words. Generally, avoid *anticipate* when it's merely equivalent to *expect*.

The poor usage is now seemingly ubiquitous—e.g.: "It is *anticipated* [read *expected* or *estimated*] that the 70-team, invitation-only tourney will realize about $15,000 for the clubs" (*Sarasota Herald-Trib.*). Indeed, sometimes this usage leads to near-ambiguities. In the following example, *anticipate* means "expect," but it suggests "forestall"—e.g.: "The foreboding of traffic snarls, towing and overall melee in connection with last night's Ohio State University football game may have prevented the problems officials had *anticipated*" (*Columbus Dispatch*). See **expect.**

ANTICIPATORY REFERENCE is the vice of referring to something that is yet to be mentioned. Thus, a sentence will be leading up to the all-important predicate but before reaching it will refer to what is contained in the predicate. The reader is temporarily mystified. E.g.: "Conflict of laws is the study of whether or not, *and if so, in what way,* the answer to a legal problem will be affected because the elements of the problem have contacts with more than one jurisdiction." (A possible revision: *Conflict of laws is the study of whether the answer to a legal problem will be affected because the elements of the problem have contacts with more than one jurisdiction—and, if so, how the answer will be affected.*)

Only rarely can anticipatory reference be used in a way that doesn't bother the reader—e.g.: "We think it's clear—*and nobody has disputed this point*—that Carla has the first choice in deciding whether to take the furniture." Innocuous examples tend to involve personal pronouns <as if she thought she could get away with it, the girl stood on the billfold to try to hide it>.

But vexatious examples are more common. They occur in a variety of forms. First, they're frequent with *do*-constructions—e.g.: "New Mexico, as *do* most states, invests a great deal of money in its highways." (Either put *as most states do* at the end of the sentence or change the *as do* to *like.*)/ "English professors, *as do* [read *like*] novelists and journalists, produce a body of writing that can be analyzed to discern their underlying philosophies." (See **like.**) Second, sometimes *have* appears too early in the sentence—e.g.: "The president, *as have* [read *like*] many others, has tried to understand the dynamics of this dispute between the company and its workers." Third, problems frequently crop up with pronoun references that anticipate the mention of the noun itself. In effect, the antecedent comes before the noun—e.g.: "Mr. Hytner is a director who knows how to keep the pot on the boil; whether you agree with *them* [read *his points*] or not, he makes *his points* [read *them*] with boldness and panache" (*Sunday Telegraph*). (Another possible revision: *whether you agree with him or not, he makes his points* . . . .)

The best antidote to this problem is becoming a stickler for orderly presentation and developing an abiding empathy for the reader.

antidote. See **anecdote.**

antipathy (= strong aversion; intense dislike) is sometimes misused for *antithesis* (= opposite; contrast)—e.g.: "Jiang can wear tri-cornered hats and tour Independence Hall, but his regime represents the *antipathy* [read *antithesis*] of America's democratic values" (*Wis. State J.*). *Antipathy* usually takes the preposition *toward* or *against* <they feel strong antipathy toward each other> <antipathy against the lame-duck mayor is palpable>. Also, it sometimes takes *to* or *for* <in the late 1990s, antipathy to tobacco manufacturers reached an all-time high> <society has always had an antipathy for child abuse>.

antipodes. This noun, meaning "the exact opposite or contrary things," is used almost exclusively in the plural form—sometimes even when the sense is singular <greed is the antipodes of charity>. The word is pronounced /an-**ti**-pə-deez/.

But the singular *antipode* (/**an**-ti-pohd/) is also quite frequent—e.g.: "Mike Tidwell last wrote for Travel about Washington's *antipode*, the spot on the exact opposite of the world" (*Wash. Post*)./ "But Malkovich's Abel Tiffauges, a simple-minded Paris auto mechanic turned POW, is the *antipode* of an ogre" (*N.Y. Newsday*). This singular form is to be encouraged when the meaning is singular because it promotes DIFFERENTIATION and makes intuitive sense.

The capitalized plural—*Antipodes*—refers to Australia, New Zealand, and nearby islands (being on the opposite side of the planet from Europe). E.g.: "He toured the role in the *Antipodes* a few years ago, but this is Soul's first shot at the West End" (*Independent*).

antithesis. For a misuse of this word, see **antipathy.**

anxious. This word most properly means "uneasy; disquieted; worrying." E.g.: "Creator and anchorman Brian Lamb, the prince of un-chic, tirelessly fields the remarks of obnoxious callers, preening journalists, and *anxious* authors" (*Nat'l Rev.*).

To use the word merely as a synonym for *eager* is to give in to SLIPSHOD EXTENSION—e.g.: "He knows that motorists are *anxious* [read *eager*] to save on suspension parts and will give generously" (*Christian Science Monitor*).

any. A. Uses and Meanings. As an adjective, *any* has essentially six uses. (1) The most common occurrence is in conditional, hypothetical, and interrogative sentences, where *any* means "a (no matter which)" or "some" <if you have any salt, I'd like to borrow some> <If any problem were to arise, what would it likely be?> <Is there any evidence of the crime?>. (2) In negative assertions, it creates an emphatic negative, meaning "not at all" or "not even one" <it was not in any way improper> <she did not know any member who was at the event>. (3) In affirmative sentences, it means "every" or "all" <any attempt to flout the law will be punished> <you are required to produce any documents relating to the issue>. (4) In a sentence implying that a selection or discretionary act will follow, it may mean "one or more (unspecified things or persons); whichever; whatever" <any student may seek a tutorial> <pick any books you like> <a good buy at any price>. (5) In a declarative sentence involving a qualitative judgment, it means "of whatever kind" <you'll have to take any action you consider appropriate>. In this sense, there is often the implication that the quality may be poor <any argument is better than no argument>. (6) In a declarative sentence involving a quantitative judgment, it means "unlimited in amount or extent; to whatever extent necessary" <this computer can process any quantity of numbers simultaneously>. In a related colloquial sense, it may mean "of great size or considerable extent" when following a negative <we won't be able to make any real headway this week>.

As an adverb, *any* is used before a comparative adjective or adverb in questions and in negative sentences <Is he any better?> <they can't walk any faster>.

B. Singular or Plural. *Any* may take either a singular or a plural verb. The singular use is fairly rare—e.g.: "He and Didi prop Sissy up in front of an Elvis mural to see if *any* of them *is* tall enough to ride the Rock 'n' Rollercoaster" (*Tennessean*). In such contexts *any* is elliptical for *any one*. See **anyone (A).**

C. Ambiguous Use. Avoid such ambiguities as, "She was the best of any senior in the class." (Read: *She was the best senior in the class.*)

anybody. See **anyone (B)** & PRONOUNS (C).

anybody else's. See **else's** & POSSESSIVES (I).

anymore. Unless it appears in a negative statement <the playground has no sand anymore>, this word is dialectal in the sense "nowadays"—e.g.: "*Anymore* [read *Nowadays* or *These days*], the price of housing is outrageous."

anyone. A. And *any one*. For the indefinite pronoun, the one-word spelling is required <anyone could do that>. Though the phrase was formerly written as two words, its unification is now complete. *Any one* = any single person or thing (of a number). E.g.: "When he died, none of us could remember *any one* thing he'd said" (*Sports Illustrated*).

B. And *anybody*. The two terms are interchangeable, so euphony governs the choice in any given context. In practice, *anyone* appears in print about three times as often as *anybody*. Cf. **everyone.**

C. *Anyone . . . they*. In all types of writing, sentences like this one are on the rise: "If *anyone* thought Diana would be chastened, *they* were wrong" (*Newsweek*). Americans who care about good writing tend to disapprove—and strongly. But the tide against them is great, primarily because the construction is so handy in speech. For more on this subject, see SEXISM (B) & PRONOUNS (C).

D. *Anyone . . . are*. Although *anyone . . . they* might arguably be acceptable, *anyone . . . are* isn't—e.g.: "Indeed, *anyone* who thought he or she could solve *their* immigration problems by getting hitched *are* in for a shock" (*N.Y. Times*). (A possible revision: *Indeed, those who thought they could solve their immigration problems by getting hitched are in for a shock.*)

E. *Anyone else's*. See **else's** & POSSESSIVES (I).

anyplace is much inferior to *anywhere*—e.g.: "The old [athletic director] hasn't gone *anyplace* [read *anywhere*], though" (*Chattanooga Free Press*). When the meaning is "any location," *any place* should always be two words <at any place>. E.g.: "Readers out there are looking for . . . *anyplace* [read *any place* or *a place*] that serves a good Italian beef sub, like the ones Cousins used to sell" (*Minneapolis Star Trib.*). Cf. **someplace & noplace.**

anything; any thing. *Anything* is the far more general word, meaning "whatever thing." *Any thing*, for practical purposes, is limited to plural constructions <Do you have any things to donate?> and to contrasts with *any person* <Is there any thing or person that might be of help?>.

anytime, adv., = at any time; whenever. E.g.: "*Anytime* a seller rents back from a buyer, an interim occupancy agreement should be completed" (*S.F. Examiner*). Some writers consider this term a casualism, but it is highly convenient and has—for whatever reason—gained more widespread acceptance than *anymore* (in positive contexts) and *anyplace*. Cf. **anymore & anyplace.**

anywhere; anywheres. The first is standard. The second is dialectal. Cf. **nowhere.**

APOSTROPHE [']. This punctuation mark does three things. First, it often indicates the possessive case <Charles Alan Wright's treatise> <Jane Ortiz's appointment>. See POSSESSIVES. Second, it frequently marks the omission of one or more elements and the contracting of the remaining elements into a word (or figure)—e.g.: *never* into *ne'er; will not* into *won't; 1997* into *'97*. See CONTRACTIONS. Third, it is sometimes used to mark the plural of an acronym, number, or letter—e.g.: *CPA's* (now more usually *CPAs*), *1990's* (now more usually *1990s*), and *p's and q's* (still with apostrophes because the letters are lowercase). See DATES (D) & NUMERALS (D).

Two contradictory trends—both bad—are at work with apostrophes.

First, careless writers want to form plurals with wayward apostrophes—e.g.: "The *bishop's* [read *bishops*] of the United Methodist Church have issued an urgent appeal for funds to assist the victims of flooding in the Midwest" (*United Methodist Rep.*). The same problem occurs in third-person-singular verbs: In the early 1990s, a sign at an Austin service station read, "Joe *say's*: It's time to winterize your car."

The second unfortunate trend is to drop necessary apostrophes. Especially in BrE, there is a tendency to write *the hotels many shops* or *Martins Pub*. But the disease is at work in AmE as well. The only possible cure is increased literacy.

apparatus has the plural forms *apparatus* (the Latin form) and *apparatuses* (the native English form). Because the word has been thoroughly naturalized, *apparatuses* is standard. See PLURALS (B).

Apparati is not a correct plural, even in Latin. It's an example of HYPERCORRECTION—e.g.: "[E]ven out of competition, exercycles, ab crunchers, and personal-trainers-as-therapists are the *apparati* [read *apparatuses*] of life in the 90's" (*N.Y. Times*).

appear. The phrase *it would appear* is invariably inferior to *it appears* or *it seems*—e.g.: "*It would appear* [read *It appears*] that more than a few of us are desperate for an easy dinner" (*Virginian-Pilot & Ledger Star*). See **would** & SUBJUNCTIVES.

On the sequence of tenses in phrases such as *appeared to enjoy* (as opposed to *appeared to have enjoyed*), see TENSES (B).

appendixes; appendices. Both are correct plural forms for *appendix*, but *appendixes* is preferable in nontechnical contexts—e.g.: "The authors of 'The Bell Curve' tell readers that they may limit their perusal to the summaries that precede each chapter, and that they may skip the main text. Still, 'The Bell Curve' is 845 pages long, and a reader who skips even the *appendixes* will miss many of the points the authors are at pains to make" (*N.Y. Times*). See PLURALS (B).

apple cider. Strictly speaking, this phrase is a REDUNDANCY because *cider* has traditionally referred to a drink made from apple juice. But for many decades now, beverage manufacturers have marketed other types of "ciders," from the juice of peaches, raspberries, and the like. So if *apple cider* is redundant, it is also sometimes necessary for clarity.

APPOSITIVES point out the same persons or things by different names, usually in the form of explanatory phrases that narrow an earlier, more general phrase. Thus, in the sentence "My brother Brad is a musician," *Brad* is the appositive of *brother*. Typically, in phrases less succinct than *my brother Brad* (in which *Brad* is restrictive), the appositive is set off by commas or parentheses: "The officers also arrested Jessica Countie, 23, and her sister, *Jill L. Countie*, 21, both of 4 Center Rd." (*Providence J.-Bull.*). (*Jill L. Countie* is an appositive of *her sister*.)/ " 'Gotta watch what I do,' joked the dark-haired 18-year-old, the youngest child of Councilwoman Domenique Thornton and her husband, *Richard Thornton*" (*Hartford Courant*). (*Richard Thornton* is an appositive of *her husband*.)

Generally, commas (or, less frequently, parentheses) must frame an appositive except when the appositive is restrictive. Thus a person might write *my brother Blair* to distinguish Blair from another brother (say, Brad). But if Blair were the only brother, the reference would be to *my brother, Blair*. One telltale signal that the appositive is restrictive is the definite article *the* preceding the noun—e.g.: *The grammarian Henry Sweet provided Shaw a model for Henry Higgins*. (But reverse the order and it comes out differently: *Henry Sweet, the grammarian, provided Shaw a model for Henry Higgins*.)

Emphatic appositives (also termed "intensive pronouns") are never set off by commas—e.g.: "*He himself* flunked the test."

Unfortunately, some writers carelessly omit the comma that should follow an appositive introduced with a comma—e.g.: "In the lawsuit, Douglas Hartman, an Illinois air traffic controller[,] says he was forced to walk through a Tailhook-style gantlet during a workshop designed by Eberhardt to combat sexual harassment" (*Detroit News*).

As a matter of CONCORD, an appositive should match its noun syntactically. For example, it's wrong to use a noun appositive after a possessive—e.g.: "Merton W. Starnes's (Starnes) claim arrived in this office after the deadline had passed." The better strategy would be to avoid the shorthand definition altogether; on a second reference, *Merton W. Starnes* becomes *Starnes*—and no reasonable person would be confused.

appraise; apprise. To *appraise* is to put a value on or set a price for (a thing). To *apprise* is to inform or notify (someone). But writers often use *appraise* when they mean *apprise*—e.g.: "[T]he elder Hugh called up the Charlotte Bank and *appraised* [read *apprised*] them of the situation" (*Memphis Commercial Appeal*).

Occasionally, the opposite mistake occurs—e.g.: "The maximum loan-to-value is the percentage of the *apprised* [read *appraised*] value of the house the lender will finance" (*Seattle Times*).

appreciate = (1) to fully understand; (2) to increase in value; or (3) to be grateful for. The last meaning originated through SLIPSHOD EXTENSION but is now established.

Sense 3 is often part of a wordy construction: "I would *appreciate it if you would send* [read *appreciate your sending*] me an application." Better yet: "Please send me an application."

apprise. See **appraise.**

approximately. See **about (A).**

apropos (of). Both variations are generally unnecessary, though they might prove serviceable in informal letters. *Apropos of* (suggested by the French phrase *à propos de*)—meaning "with respect to"—is well established in English. Yet the GALLICISM *apropos* may be used as a preposition to mean "concerning, apropos of" <apropos your plans, let me tell you about our schedule>. Hence *of* can be included or omitted, as the writer desires. E.g.: "Then, *apropos of* nothing, he proclaims: 'I'm 105 years old!' " (*Atlanta J. & Const.*)./ "*Apropos* singing along, the Angel City Chorale's appearance Sunday will have as a warmup act a musical duo" (*L.A. Times*). See **of.**

The word is sometimes misused for *appropriate*, adj., a mistake usually signaled by the use of *to*—e.g.: "Just three years ago, Sears, Roebuck and Co.'s finance department built a data warehouse [that] the retailer, *apropos to* its business, calls a data mall" (*Computerworld*). (A possible revision: *Just three years ago, Sears, Roebuck and Co.'s finance department built a data warehouse called (appropriately) a data mall.*)

arbitrator; arbiter. An *arbitrator* is a person chosen to settle differences between two parties. *Arbiter*, by contrast, is more general, meaning "anyone with power to decide disputes, such as a judge." The terms overlap considerably, and they cause confusion on both sides of the Atlantic. Yet when referring to legal arbitration, the term should be *arbitrator*.

And when legal disputes aren't at issue, the better term is *arbiter*. Thus, in the popular phrase *final* or *ultimate arbiter*, the word *arbitrator* is inferior—e.g.: "Foreign attention enhances Assad's image as the *ultimate arbitrator* [read *ultimate arbiter*] in the region" (*Montgomery Advertiser*).

ARCHAISMS. A. Generally. Many writers indulge in antiquated phrasings known primarily through the King James Version of the Bible or through Shakespeare. Avoid them, unless you're being jocular. Among the ones to be especially wary of are these:

alack	fain	perchance
anent	haply	shew (for *show*)
anon	howbeit	spake
begat	maugre	to wit
belike	methinks	verily
divers	nigh	withal
durst	peradventure	wot

One writer aptly says of a similar list: "These are easily avoided by anyone of the least literary sensibility" (Herbert Read, *English Prose Style*, 1952).

B. Mistakes Caused by Archaism. Archaism could be faulted in itself. But the more embarrassing problem is that the indulgers don't understand how the phrasings work. In early Modern English, the following singular forms frequently appeared:

Second Person	***Third Person***
thou goest	he (or she) goeth

Up to the 17th century, the *-eth* suffix was merely an alternate third-person singular inflection for an English verb. Used primarily in southern England, it had, by the end of that century, become obsolete. *She calls* and *he answers* took the place of *she calleth* and *he answereth*. Some writers, straining for an archaic literary touch, use this suffix with no regard to whether the subject is singular or plural. The use of *-eth* with a plural subject has become lamentably common—e.g.: "The Pittsburgh Penguins *giveth* and *taketh* away" (*Wash. Post*). Sometimes the second-person *-est* appears in the third person or even the first person—e.g.: "These silver linings provided balm to some, while the editorial writers and columnists—as always—worried aloud: Whither we *goest* into this nuclear night?" (*Louisville Courier-J.*).

Sometimes an error creeps in from the mangling of a SET PHRASE. A famous quotation from Shakespeare's *Hamlet*, for example, is that "the lady doth protest too much" (3.2.230). Translate this to the first person, and you have: "Perhaps *I doth* protest too much; it's just that the players' timing could have been better managed, methinks" (*Roanoke Times & World News*). But that's equivalent to saying *I does*.

A similar example appears in the phrase *the ice man cometh*, from Eugene O'Neill's play by that name. Refer instead to *men*—or to some other plural noun—and you make a hash of the phrase: "The tax men *cometh*" (*L.A. Times*)./ "Tickets are hot in Denver now that they know the ice men [i.e., hockey players] *cometh*" (*Boston Globe*).

Even when the writer gets the grammar right, it's not very heartening because the archaism makes the sentence ring false—e.g.: "But *doth* Nippon see through the wooden masks of a Noh drama—slow, plotless, and mistily symbolic?" (*Kansas City Star*). And even in jocular contexts, the jocularity is typically lame: "But the big question for old hardcore fans, of course, is *doth* the new disc rock? *Yeth*, it does" (*St. Louis Post-Dispatch*).

Finally, even when the effect is to be humorous, one shouldn't betray an utter ignorance of how a given form was once used. In the mid-1990s, British Airways ran a commercial in which an Englishman strikes up a mock-Shakespearean dialogue that ends, " 'Tis the way we make you feeleth." This construction is doubly bad because *feel*, in that sentence, is actually an infinitive. There is an elliptical construction: " 'Tis the way we make you [to] feel[eth]." How awful. Maybe an ad agency was to blame.

area, an abstract word, is sometimes used almost as a space-filler: *a problem in the area of domestic policy* should be *a problem in domestic policy*. E.g.: "Madeline Andrews, a third-grade teacher from the North School, in Londonderry, . . . has developed activities using computers for each theme and *subject matter area* [read *subject*]" (*Manchester Union Leader*). Cf. **field.**

aren't I?; amn't I? *Aren't I*, though illogical, is the standard contraction corresponding to *am I not*. *Amn't* is dialectal and substandard usage. See **ain't.**

armful. Pl. *armfuls*. See PLURALS (F).

around. See **about** (B).

arse; ass. *Arse* is the traditional spelling—in the anatomical sense, that is, not in the horse sense. But increasingly *ass* carries both meanings.

as. A. Causal Words: *as*; *because*; *since*; *for*. In the causal sense *as* should generally be avoided, because (not *as*!) it may be misunderstood as having its more usual meaning "while," especially when it is placed anywhere but at the beginning of the sentence. H.W. Fowler states: "To causal or explanatory *as*-clauses, if they are placed before the main sentence . . . there is no objection" (*MEU1*). This is most common in BrE—e.g.: "*As* she didn't get the original money, could she please have the larger sum?" (*Times* [London]).

As Fowler suggested, however, the reverse order is infelicitous unless the reader necessarily knows what is to be introduced by the *as*-clause. So don't use it in midsentence—e.g.: "Indeed, some jurors confirmed later that they wished they had been given the manslaughter option *as* [read *because*] they didn't believe the au pair intended to harm the baby" (*Seattle Post-Intelligencer*).

Given the syntactic restrictions on *as*, we are left with three general-purpose causal conjunctions. *Because* is the strongest and most logically oriented of these. *Since* is less demonstratively causal and frequently has temporal connotations. But using *since* without reference to time is not, despite the popular canard, incorrect. (See SUPERSTITIONS (G).) *For*, the most subjective of the three, is the least used. If *because* points out a direct cause-effect relationship, *for* signals a less direct relationship, adding independent explanation or substantiation. Moreover, *for* is a coordinating conjunction and not, like *because* and *since*, a subordinating conjunction; hence it can properly begin a sentence—that is, one consisting only of an independent clause <I want to go home now. For I am tired>.

B. And *like*. See **like.**

as . . . as. A. And *so* . . . *as*. In positive statements, the *as . . . as* construction is customary—e.g.: "The corn, which should be *as* tall *as* I am at this time of year, is barely half my height" (*Time*).

In the mid-20th century it was commonly held that *so . . . as* is preferable to *as . . . as* in negative statements—e.g.: "[T]he Republican governor said he might support future efforts to raise the ballot bar on non-major party candidates, but *not so* high *as* Senate Bill 200 tried to set" (*Allentown Morning Call*). But *as . . . as* generally serves equally well in such negative statements, and examples abound in good literature.

B. Repetition of Verb After. Often, when the second *as* in this construction is far removed from the first *as*—or when there's otherwise an opportunity for ambiguity—the verb is repeated for clarity. E.g.: "Owner Ray Haynie—tall, slim and baritone-voiced—is *as* likely to be cleaning tables *as is* any employee" (*Richmond Times-Dispatch*). (If we deleted the *is*, employees might bring sexual-harassment claims against Ray.) But if the second verb isn't truly needed, omit it—e.g.: "Montreal is *as* likely to survive *as is* [read *as*] common civility" (*N.J. Record*).

C. *As* [+ adj.] *a* [+ n.] *as*. In AmE, writers sometimes err by inserting *of* after the adjective. But good usage rejects this—e.g.: "From the sidelines, Nunez became nearly *as good of a cheerleader* [read *as good a cheerleader*] as he was a running back" (*Austin American-Statesman*).

D. *As . . . than*. *Than* is sometimes misused for the second *as*—e.g.: "[A] Roper Starch poll says that 24 percent of consumers—twice *as* many *than* [read *as*] in 1987—say they never go to malls" (*Sales & Marketing Mgmt.*). See SWAPPING HORSES.

ascension; ascent. Both mean "the act of ascending." *Ascent*, however, has these additional senses: (1) "the act of rising in station or rank, or in natural chronological succession" <the ascent of man>; (2) "a method of ascending" <an unorthodox ascent>; and (3) "the degree of slope or acclivity" <a steep ascent>.

ascribe = to attribute to a specified cause <Van Gogh's cycles of mental disturbances have been ascribed either to epilepsy or to manic depression>. The word is often bunglesomely used for *subscribe* in the sense "to think of favorably." Although the mistake was once thought to be found only among the semiliterate, today it appears in print with some frequency—e.g.: "Most of us, of whatever religious belief (and even of no religious belief), *ascribe* [read *subscribe*] to basic rules of decency" (*N.Y. Newsday*)./ "A philosophy I *ascribe* [read *subscribe*] to: Be honest. If you're honest, you can go further in life" (*Charleston Post & Courier*).

as far as. In its figurative uses, this phrase must be followed by some complement such as *that's concerned*, *that goes*, or *I know*—e.g.: "*As far as* they're concerned, January 1, 2000, will bring enough of a hangover" (*PC Mag.*). When the complement is omitted, idiom is severely violated. This seems to happen most often in reported speech—e.g.: " '*As far as* Ron Lynn [insert *is concerned*], I have no idea what the inner workings of [his] team are' " (*Ariz. Republic* [quoting a coach]). This error is becoming fairly widespread in spoken English.

Idiom aside, however, *as far as* usually signals verbosity. Thus, instead of *As far as the Navy is concerned,* it's possible to save nearly half the words by writing *As for the Navy,* . . . .

as follows; as follow. *As follows* is always the correct form, even for an enumeration of many things. The expression is elliptical for *as it follows*—not *as they follow*.

as if; as though. Attempts to distinguish between these idioms have proved futile. Euphony should govern the choice of phrase. Eric Partridge observed that *as if* is usually preceded by a comma and that *as though* rarely is (*U&A*).

One plausible distinction is that *as if* often suggests the more hypothetical proposition, cast in the subjunctive <as if he were a god>.

asked /askt/ is sometimes mispronounced /ast/. See PRONUNCIATION (B).

as of yet. See **as yet.**

as per is commonly understood to mean "in accordance with." But writing texts have long condemned the phrase—e.g.:

- "**As Per.** This hybrid is inexcusable. Instead of 'as per your request' say 'in accordance with your request,' or 'in compliance with your request' " (Maurice H. Weseen, *Crowell's Dictionary of English Grammar*, 1928).
- "**as per,** 'in accordance with,' is such horrible commercialese that even merchant princes are less than riotously happy when their secretaries wish it on them" (Eric Partridge, *U&A*).
- "When used to mean 'according to' (*per* your request, *per* your order), the expression [*per*] is business jargon at its worst and should be avoided. Equally annoying is the phrase *as per*" (Charles T. Brusaw et al., *The Business Writer's Handbook*, 1987).

Originating in business, *as per* is redundant for *per*. Yet even *per* is a LATINISM in place of which any one of several everyday equivalents will suffice (e.g., *as*, *according to*, or *in accordance with*)—e.g.: "*As per her request* [read *At her request* or *As she requested*], her family scattered her ashes Saturday at the summit of Mt. Washington in New Hampshire, said her husband, James Gardner" (*N.Y. Newsday*)./ "So *as per our predictions* [read *as we predicted*], we'll have to give Foss' date at South

Sound Stadium with River Ridge on Oct. 24 the nod as the key game" (*Tacoma News Trib.*).

as regards, a much-maligned phrase, is sometimes called a solecism. Actually, it's simply inferior to *regarding* or *concerning*, but it's perfectly idiomatic —e.g.: "Southeast Asia's troubles could magnify what has already been a difficult summer for many U.S. multinational companies, at least *as regards* their ability to meet earnings growth targets" (*L.A. Times*).

Though *as regards* is no more objectionable than *with regard to*, the whole lot of such phrases is suspect: "Train your suspicions to bristle up whenever you come upon *as regards, with regard to, in respect of, in connection with, according as to whether*, and the like. They are all dodges of JARGON, circumlocution for evading this or that simple statement" (Arthur Quiller-Couch, *On the Art of Writing*, 1943). See **regard (A).**

ass. See **arse.**

assassin; assassinator. The latter is a NEEDLESS VARIANT—e.g.: "The *assassinator* [read *assassin*] of [Richard McSorley's] character has been Rep. Robert Dornan, the California Republican whose unfactual and dirty attacks on Clinton and on McSorley in early October caught the attention of Bush" (*Wash. Post*).

assault; battery. In popular usage, these two are virtually synonymous. Most people use *assault* in referring to an incident that might begin with a threat and end with hitting and kicking. In fact, most people wouldn't say that someone had been *assaulted* if the incident didn't include physical contact. So in the popular mind, *assault* is essentially the same as *battery* (a rarer term).

But in law these terms have precise meanings. Essentially, an *assault* is the use or threat of force that causes the person to whom the force is directed to have a well-founded fear of physical injury or offensive touching. A *battery* is the use of force or violence on another (in the criminal sense), or any repugnant intentional contact with another (in the tortious sense).

Shooting a gun just to the side of someone, if that person reasonably feared physical injury, or shooting a blank gun directly at someone, would be an *assault*. Hitting someone with a bullet would make the act a *battery*, even if the shooter never knew about the hit. In the noncriminal (tort) sense, an uninvited kiss by a stranger is considered a *battery*.

assess. See **access (B).**

ASSONANCE. See ALLITERATION.

as such. In this phrase, *such* is a pronoun requiring an antecedent—e.g.: "And so goes the parade of excuses that allow athletes to do things that usually would be considered crimes and dealt with *as such*" (*Indianapolis Star*). (*Crimes* is the antecedent of *such*.)

But some writers misuse the phrase by including no identifiable antecedent—e.g.: "Suspects should be considered innocent until proved guilty and should be treated *as such* [read *as if they are innocent*]" (*Des Moines Register*).

Sometimes, too, the phrase causes an ambiguity when the referent isn't clear. When that is so, substituting *in principle* or some like phrase is recommended—e.g.: "There could, accordingly, be no grounded objection to the existence of images *as such*" (*New Republic*). (A possible revision: *There could, accordingly, be no objection in principle to the existence of images.*)

Also, some writers faddishly use *as such* as if it meant something like "therefore"—e.g.: "[T]hese efforts represent a fundamental change in the way responsibility is spread throughout the organization, what practices and behaviors are nurtured and rewarded, and how care will be provided in the future. *As such,* [delete phrase] the change will not occur immediately nor easily" (*Hosp. & Health Servs. Admin.*). This misuse is perhaps a SLIPSHOD EXTENSION from correct sentences such as the following, in which *icon* is the antecedent of *such*, but the sentence could be misread in such a way that *as such* would mean "therefore": "She will become an icon; *as such*, she will be a role model for years to come" (*Bloomington Pantagraph*).

Obviously, this phrase requires much care.

assuming. For *assuming* as an acceptable dangling modifier, see DANGLERS (E).

assurance. See **insurance (B).**

assure; ensure; insure. A person *assures* (makes promises to, convinces) other persons and *ensures* (makes certain) that things occur or that events take place. Any predicate beginning with *that* should be introduced by the verb *ensure*, if the verb is in the active voice. *Insure* should be restricted to financial contexts involving indemnification; it should refer to what insurance companies do. *Ensure* should be used in all other senses of making certain.

asterisk /**as**-tə-risk/ is frequently mispronounced /**as**-tə-rik/. See PRONUNCIATION (B).

as though. See **as if.**

as to whether. See **whether (B).**

as well. When used at the beginning of a sentence, this phrase has traditionally been considered poor usage. But in Canada it's standard as an equivalent of *Also,* . . . or *In addition,* . . . . Each of the following examples comes from a Canadian publication. In AmE they would be edited as shown in the brackets: "*As well,* [read *And*] people would have to work longer to qualify for UI [unemployment insurance]" (*Toronto Star*)./ "*As well* [read *Also*], people can place a sticker announcing their donor consent on their driver's license at the time of renewal or on their Care Card" (*Vancouver Sun*).

as well as or better than. Some writers illogically leave out *as* after *well*—e.g.: "Women would write in detail why they were working *as well or better than* [read *as well as or better than*] their male counterparts" (*Observer Sunday*). See CANNIBALISM & ILLOGIC (B).

as yet; as of yet. These are both invariably inferior to *yet* alone, *still*, *thus far*, or some other equivalent phrase—e.g.: "Seven years ago, a woman, *not as yet* [read *not yet*] identified, died in a stream in Monroe, Clarion County" (*Pitt. Post-Gaz.*).

-ATABLE does not generally appear other than in *-able* adjectives derived from two-syllable verbs (e.g., *create, vacate*), because in those short words the adjectives would become unrecognizable. H.W. Fowler notes some long exceptions to the general rule (*inculcatable, inculpatable, incubatable*), and states his standard: "The practice should be to use *-atable* where the shorter form is felt to be out of the question" (*MEU1* at 36). Other examples with which the shorter form is impracticable are *anticipatable, translatable*, and *infiltratable* (so that *infiltrable* not be thought to be derived from *infilter* [= to sift or filter in] rather than from *infiltrate*).

The following words, which occur with some frequency, are better than the *-atable* forms:

abbreviable	agitable	calculable
abdicable	alienable	communicable
abrogable	alleviable	compensable
accommodable	allocable	confiscable
accumulable	ameliorable	corroborable
activable	annihilable	cultivable
administrable	appreciable	delegable
adulterable	appropriable	delineable
affiliable	arbitrable	demonstrable
aggregable	articulable	detonable

differentiable
eradicable
evacuable
evaluable
expropriable
generable
indicable
inebriable
inextirpable
inextricable
infatuable
invalidable
investigable
isolable
litigable
manipulable
medicable
navigable
obligable
obviable
operable
originable
participable
penetrable
perpetrable
perpetuable
predicable
propagable
regulable
replicable
repudiable
segregable
separable
subjugable
vindicable
violable
vitiable

At least one pair distinguished by the two suffixes has undergone DIFFERENTIATION. *Estimable* = worthy of esteem; *estimatable* = capable of being estimated.

at about. See **about (D).**

athlete has two syllables (/**ath**-leet/), not three (/**ath**-ə-leet/). See PRONUNCIATION (B).

ATM machine. For this redundant acronym, see ABBREVIATIONS (B).

attached hereto. This phrase, symptomatic of COMMERCIALESE and LEGALESE, is redundant. Delete *hereto*.

at the present time. See **present time.**

at this time. This phrase often smacks of waffling OFFICIALESE, especially when the phrase comes at a SENTENCE END—e.g.: " 'We don't have any comments *at this time*,' said Disney spokesman Ken Green. . . . 'Our revenues and profits are record-setting *at this time*,' Mr. Green said" (*Dallas Morning News*). The more natural wording would be something like this: *We don't have any comments right now. Our revenues and profits are currently setting records.*

attribute (= to credit [something] as resulting from a specified cause; to ascribe) is sometimes confused with *contribute* (= to play a significant part in producing something)—e.g.: "The Buccaneers made 22 percent of their shots in the first half and had 17 turnovers at halftime. Most of that can be *contributed* [read *attributed*] to Kansas' defense" (*Kansas City Star*)./ "Most of the Broncos' troubles this year can be *contributed* [read *attributed*] to their defense" (*Lewiston Morning Trib.*).

au jus. This adjectival phrase—in French, "with the juice"—traditionally appears after the noun it modifies, in the sense "(of a meat) served with its natural juice" <steak au jus>. But it has gradually been corrupted into a noun form <served with au jus> and then an attributive adjective <au jus sauce>—e.g.: "We had to ask the waitress to take the plate back, and to return it with horseradish sauce instead of the *au jus*" (*Ft. Lauderdale Sun-Sentinel*). These uses are so well ensconced in culinary talk that there seems little hope of ousting them.

To make matters worse, the phrase is typically pronounced /oh-**zhoos**/ or even /**oh**-joos/ instead of the more nearly correct /oh-**zhoo**/.

auspices. *Under the auspices* means "with the sponsorship or support of"—e.g.: "Hugo Boss has developed an art library *under the auspices* of the Guggenheim" (*N.Y. Times*). But the phrase is frequently misconstrued as meaning "in accordance with" or "by means of"—e.g.: "Quickly, it was moved and seconded that a name change be ordered *under the auspices of* [read *in accordance with*] Robert's Rules" (*Minneapolis Star Trib.*).

author, v.t., is becoming standard, though careful writers still avoid it when they can. Generally it's a highfalutin substitute for *write*, *compose*, *publish*, or *create*—e.g.: "Dougherty now represents some of the country's top archery firms, serves as a consultant, and also stays very busy *authoring* [read *writing*] books and articles about bowhunting" (*Tulsa Trib. & Tulsa World*). But *coauthor* has been considered more acceptable as a verb, perhaps because *cowrite* seems deadpan. See NOUNS AS VERBS.

With reference to *the author* (= I), see FIRST PERSON.

autonomy (= self-rule) is sometimes misused for *authority*—e.g.: "But Dave Checketts, president of Madison Square Garden, insisted that the 50-year-old Riley wanted part ownership and complete *autonomy of* [read *authority over*] the team, and that his heart was no longer in the job when those requests were denied" (*N.Y. Times*). This sentence suggests that Coach Pat Riley wanted the team to be entirely self-governing, but the context shows that he wanted authority for himself.

avenge, vb.; **revenge,** vb. & n. To *avenge* is to visit fitting retribution upon. *Avenge* and *vengeance* have to do with justice and the legal process—e.g.: "He longs to see his friends' deaths *avenged*, to get a date with Beth Penrose, and to keep her from the amorous advances of the FBI liaison working on the case" (*Orange County Register*).

To *revenge* is to inflict suffering or harm upon another out of personal resentment. *Revenge* has to do with getting even—e.g.: "In 1996, with Leslie at the lead, the Americans *revenged* that defeat" (*Cincinnati Enquirer*). Actually, though, sportswriters use the two verbs almost interchangeably. If they're looking for hype, the word should be *revenge*.

Often, too, *revenge* is a reflexive verb—e.g.: "Solon, for example, opposed waiting until the dissatisfied class *revenged* itself with revolution and confiscation" (*Greensboro News & Record*).

Finally, *revenge* can (and usually does) function as a noun, while *avenge* cannot.

averse. See **adverse.**

avocation; vocation. Although these words are quite different, many writers misuse *avocation* for *vocation*. The first means "hobby," whereas the second means "calling or profession." Here is the common mistake, worsened by REDUNDANCY: "My one life—my *professional avocation* [read *vocation*]—is to help prevent animal suffering" (*St. Louis Post-Dispatch*).

await; wait. *Await* is always transitive (i.e., it takes a direct object), and *wait* is always intransitive. One *awaits* something, but one *waits for* something or *waits on* someone. For more than a century, critics have objected to *wait on* to mean *await* or *wait for*—e.g.: "They *waited on* [read *waited for*] the jury's verdict." But even if it's not the best phrasing, *wait on* certainly can't be labeled substandard. And, of course, *wait on* is quite correct in denoting what waiters do.

Await shouldn't be confused with *wait for*, as in the unidiomatic *await for*—e.g.: "As police were *awaiting for* [read *awaiting* or *waiting for*] the arrival of more officers, Ruiz, Tapia and Sanchez fled along with another suspect" (*Boston Herald*).

And if no object is supplied, *wait* is the proper term. That is, if the verb ends the clause, it shouldn't be *await*—e.g.: "I went to the Palm at the appointed hour. My shaman/friend *awaited* [read *waited*]" (*Wash. Times*).

awake(n). See **wake.**

aweigh, in the phrase *anchors aweigh* (= anchors clear of the ground so that a ship can move), is often confused with *away*—e.g.: "Anchors *away* [read *aweigh*]: Shakeups in the Navy's chain of command have touched Adm. Patricia Tracey, commandant at Great Lakes" (*Chicago Trib.*).

awesome, in the 1980s and 1990s, became a VOGUE WORD <That movie was totally awesome!>. For the time being, the word has been spoiled by overuse.

awful. This word has undergone several transformations. Originally, it meant "inspiring or filled with awe." Its meaning then degenerated to "horrible, terrible" <what an awful accident>. And *awfully*, meanwhile, became an equivalent of *very*, but with greater intensity <Joe was awfully sorry about the mix-up>. Nobody objects to these uses in speech, and few would in writing. But some begin to object when *awfully* intensifies adjectives with positive connotations <they're awfully good people> <Tiger played awfully well>. Although these uses have been called humorously illogical, they're actually quite close to the original sense.

Occasionally, of course, *awfully* can be ambiguous—e.g.: "He is *awfully* educated." But in sentences in which that ambiguity doesn't appear, the intensive *awfully* must be accepted as standard.

awhile; a while. After a preposition, it should be spelled as two words <he rested for a while>. Generally, however, you're best advised to use the term adverbially without the preposition and spell it as one word <he rested awhile>.

awoke(n). See **wake.**

axel; axle. The first is a figure-skating maneuver; the second is a rod or pin connecting two wheels. But *axle* sometimes wrongly displaces *axel*—e.g.: "An Olympic silver medal, a million-dollar professional skating gig and Saturday's marriage to her agent, Jerry Solomon, have put her a few leaps, bounds and triple *axles* [read *axels*] ahead of former rival Tonya Harding" (*Sacramento Bee*).

axes is the plural of both *axis* and *ax*.

aye (= yes) is the standard spelling of this word, most commonly used in the parliamentary procedure of voting. The word is pronounced /ɪ/. *Ay* is a variant form.

B

Back-Formations are words formed by removing suffixes from longer words that are mistakenly assumed to be derivatives, most commonly when a *-tion* noun is shortened to make a verb ending in *-te*—e.g., from *emotion* comes *emote*.

Such back-formations are objectionable when they stand merely as NEEDLESS VARIANTS of already existing verbs:

Back-Formed Verb	*Ordinary Verb*
administrate	administer
cohabitate	cohabit
delimitate	delimit
evolute	evolve
interpretate	interpret
orientate	orient
registrate	register
remediate	remedy
revolute	revolt
solicitate	solicit

Many back-formations never gain real legitimacy (e.g., *enthuse*, *elocute*), some are aborted early in their existence (e.g., *ebullit*, *frivol*), and still others are of questionable vigor (e.g., *aggress*, *attrit*, *effulge*, *evanesce*). *Burgle* (back-formed from *burglar*) continues to have a jocular effect (in AmE), as do *effuse*, *emote*, *laze*, and the learned word *metamorphose*. See **burglarize.**

Still, many examples have survived respectably, among them *diagnose*, *donate*, *orate*, *resurrect*, *sculpt*, and *spectate*. *Enthuse* may one day be among these respectable words, although it has not gained approval since it first appeared in the early 19th century. Many others have filled gaps in the language and won acceptance through sheer utility.

The best rule of thumb is to avoid newborn back-formations that appear newfangled, but not those that, being only faintly recognizable as back-formations, are genuinely useful. Only philologists today recognize (much less condemn) as back-formations *beg* (from *beggar*), *jell* (from *jelly*), *peddle* (from *peddler*), *rove* (from *rover*), and *type* (from *typewriter*).

backward(s). See DIRECTIONAL WORDS (A).

bacteria, the plural form of *bacterium*, should take a plural verb—e.g.: "Scientists reported today a sharp increase in antibiotic-resistant strains of the *bacteria* that *cause* pneumonia" (*N.Y. Times*). If the verb is singular, use the singular noun—e.g.: "Legionella pneumophila, the *bacteria* [read *bacterium*] that *causes* it, is fairly widespread, said Storch" (*St. Louis Post-Dispatch*).

bade. See **bid.**

badly. A. And *bad*. When a linking verb—such as *is*, *feels*, *seems*, or *tastes*—appears in the main clause, the predicate adjective *bad* is required, not the adverbial complement *badly*. E.g.: "And that . . . is indeed a serving that both tastes *badly* [read *bad*] and is a small portion" (*San Diego Union-Trib.*). See **feel (B).**

B. In the Sense "very greatly" or "very much." This use, as in *badly in need*, was formerly criticized. Today it is perfectly idiomatic in AmE—e.g.: "Democrats demanded concessions in a bill tightening immigration laws, another measure Republicans want *badly*" (*Chattanooga Times*).

bail; bale. You *bail* water out of a boat but *bale* hay. *Bailing* water means dipping it out with a bucket. *Baling* hay means putting it into a large bundle, usually compressed and wrapped.

baited breath. See **bated breath.**

baloney; bologna. For the word meaning "nonsense," *baloney* is the spelling. For the sausage, *bologna* (pronounced like *baloney*) is the spelling.

In what appears to be an amalgam of the two words, *baloney* is sometimes misspelled *boloney*.

bandit has two plural forms, *bandits* and *banditti*. The native-English form (*bandits*) is preferred. The Italian plural is usually tongue-in-cheek.

banister (= the handrail on a staircase) is the standard spelling. *Bannister* is a variant form.

bankrupt, n. Although in popular speech and writing it is common to refer to a *bankrupt*—a common usage since at least the early 16th century—modern bankruptcy statutes use the term *debtor* instead.

banquet; banquette. *Banquet* = an elaborate feast or ceremonial meal <a black-tie banquet>. *Banquette* = a bench or sofa <a red leather banquette>.

barbaric; barbarous. These words share the basic sense "primitive, uncivilized." *Barbaric*, which is four times more common, typically describes a lack of culture that ranges from trivialities to anything less than heinous destruction of human life <the rock band's reputation for barbaric excess>. Occasionally, though, *barbaric* actions are shocking—e.g.: "Dog fights are illegal in Cuba, where all gambling is banned and professional boxing is officially considered *barbaric*" (*Rocky Mountain News*).

The word *barbarous* is reserved for contexts involving savage cruelty—e.g.: "Calling the rape of an Okinawan schoolgirl a premeditated and *barbarous* act, prosecutors yesterday demanded 10-year prison terms with hard labor for three accused U.S. servicemen" (*Wash. Times*).

barbecue; barbeque; bar-b-cue; bar-b-que. The first form is the predominant and the preferred spelling.

barbiturate is pronounced either /bar-**bich**-ər-ət/ or /bar-bi-**t[y]oor**-ət/. The pronunciation /bar-**bich**-ə-wət/, though increasingly common, is best avoided. Of course, if you've taken one before trying to say the word, your listeners will probably make allowances.

bare, v.t. (= to uncover), is sometimes confused with *bear* (= [1] to carry; or [2] to endure)—e.g.: "During her latest, controversial show she advances to the front of the stage and *bears* [read *bares*] her breast" (*Fin. Times*).

For the opposite error, see **bear out.**

basis. A. In Wordy Constructions. The word *basis* often signals verbosity in adverbial constructions such as *on a daily basis* and *on a regular basis*. A simple adverb, such as *daily* or *regularly*, almost always serves better.

B. Plural Form. The plural of *basis*, as well as *base*, is *bases*. The pronunciations differ, however: for *basis*, the plural is pronounced /**bay**-seez/; for *base*, /**bays**-ez/.

bastard. See **dastard.**

bated breath is the phrase from Shakespeare's *Merchant of Venice*: "Or shall I bend low and in a bondman's key, with *bated breath* and whisp'ring humbleness, say this: . . ." (1.3.122–25). The idea is that breath is *abated*, or stopped. *Baited breath* is a bungle—e.g.: "During its 'Creature Feature' blowout, the aquarium wants kids and adults alike to celebrate the holiday with *baited breath* [read *bated breath*]" (*Chicago Sun-Times*).

bathos; pathos. These two words sometimes cause confusion. *Bathos* means "a sudden descent from the exalted to the trite, or from the sublime to the ridiculous." *Pathos* means "sympathetic pity," and is useful, e.g., in reference to juries and theater audiences.

battery. See **assault.**

bawl out (= to excoriate) is the phrase, not *ball out*. But because the mistake is possible, it sometimes occurs—e.g.: "You could also be *balled out* [read *bawled out*] on the spot for allowing any clerk's error of addition while standing at the cash till" (*Baltimore Sun*).

B.C.; A.D.; B.C.E.; C.E. The abbreviation B.C. (= before Christ) is usually so printed—in small capitals. By convention, B.C. follows the year <Julius Caesar died in 44 B.C.>. But A.D. (= *Anno Domini* "in the year of our Lord") properly precedes the year <Hadrian's wall was completed in A.D. 126>, unless the abbreviation is paired with a time frame expressed in words <the second century A.D.>.

Some scholars condemn B.C. and A.D. as undesirably sectarian. What about non-Christians? they ask. Why should they have to measure their calendar from the birth of Christ? A trend has therefore emerged to use B.C.E. (= before the common era) and C.E. (= common era)—the traditional Jewish designations—in place of the Christian labels. Whether this trend will catch on is still uncertain. There has already been much wrangling on the point, and there is sure to be more.

By the way, many people mistakenly believe that A.D. means "after death." By that erroneous measure, about 33 years of history (during Jesus' lifetime) would be lost.

be. See BE-VERBS.

bear. See **born.**

bear out (= to support or confirm as evidence) is sometimes wrongly made *bare out*—e.g.: "A luncheon date with his offensive line next week *bares* [read *bears*] that out" (*Sacramento Bee*).

beat > beat > beaten. The archaic past participle *beat* persists only in the phrase *I'm beat*, meaning "I'm exhausted," and (vestigially) in the word *deadbeat*. See IRREGULAR VERBS.

because. A. Punctuation with. Generally, the word *because* should not follow a comma. The reason is that when a dependent clause (the *because*-clause) follows the main independent clause of the sentence, a comma does not separate the two. E.g.: "When residents and some alumni campaigned in the 1970s to have the house listed on the National Register of Historic Places, other alumni strongly opposed the move *because* they felt it might lower the house's value if it ever had to be sold" (*San Diego Union-Trib.*). Yet a comma may be all but necessary when the sentence is long or complex.

B. Causing Ambiguity. Putting a purpose clause or phrase after a negative often causes ambiguities, attested by a priest's unintentionally humorous statement: "I wear no clothes to distinguish myself from the congregation."

C. Coupled with *reason*. See **reason is because.**

D. Beginning Sentences with. See SUPERSTITIONS (F).

E. Wordy Substitutes for. *Because* is often needlessly replaced by a verbose phrase such as *for the reason that*, *due to the fact that*, or *on grounds that*—e.g.: "That led one local analyst, who asked not to be named *due to the fact that* [read *because*] he had not yet seen the filing, to speculate that the company was burning through cash and needed more to fuel its growth" (*Puget Sound Bus. J.*).

F. As a Causal Word Generally. See **as (A).**

begging the question does not mean "evading the issue" or "inviting the obvious questions," as some mistakenly believe. The proper meaning of *begging the question* is "basing a conclusion on an assumption that is as much in need of proof or demonstration as the conclusion itself." One might beg the question by saying, for example, that life begins at conception, which is defined as the beginning of life.

begin. A. And *commence & start*. *Begin* is the usual word, preferable nine times out of ten. *Commence*, a FORMAL WORD, is sometimes unnecessarily stilted. The *OED* notes that "*begin* is preferred in ordinary use; *commence* has more formal associations with law and procedure, combat, divine service, and ceremon[y]." Often *commence* appears where *begin* would be better—e.g.: "Scungio was told that if she hoped to build a house before the town *commenced* [read *began*] work on the road . . . , she should propose what sort of gravel thoroughfare she could pay for" (*Providence J.-Bull.*). *Start* usually refers to physical movement <to start running>. Both *begin* and *start* may be followed by an infinitive, but *commence* may not.

B. Past Tense and Past Participle. *Begin*, of course, makes *began* in the past tense and *begun* in the past participle. But writers occasionally misuse *began* as a past participle—e.g.: "The woman testified she thought Mitchell was her sometimes-lover until they *had began* [read *began*] having sex" (*Chattanooga Times*). See IRREGULAR VERBS.

begrudge. See **resent (A).**

behalf. The phrases *in behalf of* and *on behalf of* signify different things. The former means "in the interest or for the benefit of" <he fought in behalf of a just man's reputation>; the latter, *on behalf of*, means "as the agent or representative of" <on behalf of the garden club, I would like to thank our luncheon speaker> <she appeared on behalf of her client>.

behest, a stronger word than *request*, means (1) "a command," or (2) "a strong urging." *Bequest* (= a gift by will) is sometimes misused for *behest*—e.g.: "Pataki claimed he vetoed a bill initiated at his *bequest* [read *behest*] because he did not want to force new negotiations" (*N.Y. Newsday*). This error verges on being a MALAPROPISM.

behoof (= benefit, sake) is the noun; *behoove* (AmE) or *behove* (BrE) is the corresponding verb meaning "to be necessary or proper" <it behooves you to bite your tongue in such circumstances>. Both noun and verb have an archaic flavor.

belabor; labor, v.t. Although *belabor* is not traditionally used figuratively in phrases such as *to belabor an argument*, modern dictionaries suggest that the usage is now standard. And *belabor* vastly predominates over *labor* in this sense, so it should be accepted as standard—e.g.: "But too many effects are *belabored*, rather than springing organically from the text" (*Seattle Times*).

belief. People frequently speak of a *genuine belief*, a *bona fide belief*, or an *honest belief*. In fact, all such phrases are REDUNDANCIES, since it is quite impossible to believe something ungenuinely, in bad faith, or dishonestly. This is so despite the possibility of being a wishy-washy, casual, or unprincipled believer.

beloved. This word can be spoken with two syllables /bi-**ləvd**/ or three /bi-**ləv**-id/. The two-syllable form is usually reserved for the past participle <the queen was beloved by her subjects>, a somewhat archaic usage. The three-syllable form is used for the adjective <my beloved wife> or the attributive noun <dearly beloved, we are gathered here . . . >.

bemean. See **demean.**

bemuse; amuse. Although *bemuse* is frequently taken to be a fancy variant of *amuse*, the meanings differ significantly. *Bemuse* = (1) to make confused or muddled; bewilder <the jury was bemused by all the technical evidence>; or (2) to plunge into thought; preoccupy <the math student was bemused with the concept of infinity>. *Amuse*, of course, means "to entertain" or "to cause laughter in" <the speaker amused the audience with various anecdotes>.

beneficent; benevolent; benefic; beneficial. The etymological difference between *beneficent* and *benevolent* is that between deeds and sentiments. *Beneficent* = doing good, charitable (*benefic* now being merely a NEEDLESS VARIANT). *Benevolent* = well-wishing, supportive, (emotionally) charitable. The DIFFERENTIATION should be cultivated; we should reserve *beneficent* for "doing good," and *benevolent* for "inclined or disposed to do good." *Beneficial* has the general meaning "favorable, producing benefits."

beneficiary is pronounced /ben-ə-**fish**-ə-ree/ or perhaps /ben-ə-**fish**-ee-er-ee/—not /ben-ə-**fish**-ə-rer-ee/.

benefit, vb., makes *benefited* and *benefiting* in AmE, *benefitted* and *benefitting* in BrE. See SPELLING (B).

benevolent. See **beneficent.**

bequeath = (1) to give (an estate or effect) to a person by will <she bequeathed the diadem to her daughter>; or (2) to give (a person) an estate or effect by will <she bequeathed her daughter the diadem>. Using the word as a fancy equivalent of *give* or *present* is an ignorant pretension—e.g.: "Apparently Mayor Annette Strauss plans to *bequeath* [read *present*] the gift personally to Her Majesty—something rarely done, according to protocol experts. Usually, a gift is *bequeathed* [read *presented*] to the queen's secretary, who then *bequeaths* [read *gives*] it to the queen" (*Dallas Times Herald*).

bequest. See **behest.**

bereave, v.t., yields as past-tense forms *bereft* and *bereaved*, and the same forms as past participles. *Bereaved* is used in reference to loss of relatives by death. *Bereft* is used in reference to loss of immaterial possessions or qualities. To be *bereft of* something is not merely to lack it but to have been dispossessed of it.

berth (= a spot or position) is sometimes misspelled *birth*, often with hilarious results—e.g.: "It was the earliest he's ever clinched a playoff *birth* [read *berth*]" (*Tacoma News Trib.*).

beside (= [1] alongside; or [2] in comparison with) is surprisingly often misused for *besides* (= [1] other than, except; or [2] in addition)—e.g.: "Hill is the only man *beside* [read *besides*] Trevino to win on the Senior Tour this year" (*N.Y. Times*).

bet > bet > bet. *Bet*, not *betted*, is the preferred (and the far more frequent) past tense and past participle. Still, the form *betted* occasionally appears. See IRREGULAR VERBS.

bête noire; bête noir. The spelling *bête noire*—the only one with any standing in the dictionaries—is about four times more common than *bête noir* (in which, by the way, the gender of the adjective does not agree with that of the noun). The French term literally means "black beast," but in English it is used figuratively to mean "a person or thing that is strongly disliked or that should be avoided" <Senator Edward M. Kennedy, the darling of the liberals, is the *bête noire* of conservatives>.

better. A. For *had better*. Dropping the *had* in expressions such as *You (had) better be going now* is acceptable only in speech or recorded dialogue. E.g.: "[I]f the Flyers are going to make an offer, they *better* [read *had better*] do it in a hurry" (*St. Petersburg Times*). Cf. **get (C).**

Sometimes *best* replaces *better*, as in *We had best be on our way*. This phrasing—*had best* rather than *had better*—is quite casual.

B. And *bettor*. See **bettor.**

better than any (other). Ordinarily, *better than any other* is more logical than *better than any*, because the thing being proclaimed best is also one of the things being considered—e.g.: "Lad Daniels, chairman of the 1990 tournament, said he thinks the PGA Tour has done a *better job than any other* sport of building relationships with communities" (*Fla. Times-Union*). Writers who omit the word *other* fall into logical lapses—e.g.: "If there's been a down moment or a traumatic flashback in Monica Seles' 1996, then she's a *better actor than any* [read *better actor than any other*] athlete I've ever met" (*Boston Herald*). Cf. ILLOGIC (B).

bettor is the standard spelling for "one who bets or wagers." *Better* has also been used in this sense but is liable to confusion with the comparative form of *good*.

between. A. And *among*. *Between* is commonly said to be better with two things, and *among* with more than two. Ernest Gowers calls this a "superstition," and quotes the *OED*: "In all senses *between* has been, from its earliest appearance, extended to more than two. . . . It is still the only word available to express the relation of a thing to many surrounding things severally and individually; *among* expresses a relation to them collectively and vaguely: we should not say *the space lying among the three points* or *a treaty among three Powers*" (*MEU2*). The rule as generally enunciated, then, is simplistic. Although it is an accurate guide for the verb *divide* (*between* with two objects, *among* with more than two), the only ironclad distinction is that stated by the *OED*. *Between* expresses one-to-one relations of many things, and *among* expresses collective and undefined relations.

B. *Between* and Numbers. This causes problems if the numbers at both ends of the spectrum are intended to be included. E.g.: "Saleh met with several other defendants in a Queens garage *between June 23 and June 24* [read (depending on the meaning) *from June 23 to June 24* or *around June 23 or June 24*] to discuss getting cars for the conspiracy" (*N.Y. Newsday*).

When you intend to refer to a range of possibilities from a low point to a high point, *from . . . to* or *between . . . and* is the correct form, not *between . . . to*. E.g.: "The large pressure difference between the low and a high over the southern Plains will generate winds *between* [read *from*] 18 to 36 m.p.h. in the wake of a sharp cold front" (*Chicago Trib.*).

C. *Between you and me*; *between you and I*. Because the pronouns following *between* are objects of the preposition, the correct phrase is *between you and me*. Yet the phrasing *between you and I* is appallingly common—"a grammatical error of unsurpassable grossness," as one commentator puts it. Little can be added to that judgment. See PRONOUNS (B) & HYPERCORRECTION (B).

BE-VERBS. A. Circumlocutions with *Be*-Verbs. Verb phrases containing *be*-verbs are often merely roundabout ways of saying something better said with a simple verb. Thus *be determinative of* for *determine* is verbose. But *be determinative* is all right without an object <this factor may be determinative in a given situation>.

The following circumlocutory uses of *be*-verbs are common in stuffy writing. The simple verb is usually better:

be abusive of (abuse)
be applicable to (apply to)
be benefited by (benefit from)
be derived from (derive from)
be desirous of (desire or want)
be determinative of (determine)
be in agreement (agree)
be in attendance (attend)
be indicative of (indicate)
be in error (err)
be in existence (exist)
be influential on (influence)
be in receipt of (have received)
be possessed of (possess)
be productive of (produce)
be promotive of (promote)
be violative of (violate)

Many such wordy constructions are more naturally phrased in the present-tense singular: *is able to (can), is authorized to (may), is binding upon (binds), is empowered to (may), is unable to (cannot).*

B. For *say*. This has become a common verbal tic among the younger generations—e.g.: "I am, 'What do you think?' And she is, 'I don't know.' And I am, 'Well, I think . . . .' " The tic seems to be determined more by emotional development than by age alone. That is a question for sociolinguists to determine. But you can confidently call it poor usage. Cf. **go** & **like (C)**.

beyond the pale. See **pale, beyond the.**

BI-; SEMI-. One can remember the proper prefix in a given context by noting that *bi-* means "two," and *semi-* "half." Hence *bimonthly* = every two months (not "twice a month") and *semimonthly* = every half-month, or twice a month. *Biweekly* and *semiweekly* work similarly.

Still, *bi-* has been used to mean "occurring twice in a (specified span of time)" so often (and legitimately, e.g., in *biennial*) that, for the sake of clarity, you might avoid the prefix altogether when possible. See the next entry.

biannual; biennial; semiannual. *Biannual* and *semiannual* both mean "occurring twice a year." *Biennial* means "occurring once every two years." The distinction becomes important, for example, when contractual language provides for "*biannual* increases" or "*biannual* meetings." The best advice is not to rely on words like *biannual* and *biennial* in any contractual provision. For absolute clarity, use *semiannual* or *once every two years*. See BI- & **biennial.**

bias, vb., makes *biased* and *biasing* in AmE, *biassed* and *biassing* in BrE. See SPELLING (B).

bicep; biceps. Although *biceps* is traditionally a singular noun, it is now usually considered a plural. In AmE, *bicep* is now the standard singular.

bid. A. Past Tense. *Bid* (= to offer a bid) forms *bid* in the past tense <Williams bid more than any other bidder>. In the expression *bid farewell* (= to wish someone well upon parting), the past tense is *bade*, rhyming with *glad* <thousands of fans bade farewell to Florence Griffith Joyner>. In the phrase *to bid fair* (= to seem likely), the better past-tense form is *bade fair*.

B. Past Participle. The past-participial form is usually *bidden* <just before the accident, a police officer had bidden the man good day>. But in the sense "to make a bid," the past participle is *bid* <the contenders each bid more than $400 for the signature>.

biennial = occurring every two years. If we climb the numerical ladder, we have *triennial* (3), *quadrennial* (4), *quinquennial* (5), *sexennial* (6), *septennial* (7), *octennial* (8), *novennial* (9), *decennial* (10), *vicennial* (20), *centennial* (100), *millennial* (1,000). See BI- & **biannual.**

BIG WORDS. See SESQUIPEDALITY.

billfold. See **wallet.**

billion. In the United States and France, *billion* means "one thousand millions" (= 1,000,000,000); but in Great Britain and Germany, it means "one million millions" (= 1,000,000,000,000). An American *trillion* equals the British *billion.* In BrE, however, the AmE meaning is gaining ground, especially in journalism, technical writing, and even government statements about finance. See NUMERALS.

bimonthly; semimonthly. See BI-.

birth, v.i., was used with some frequency in the Middle Ages as a verb. It fell into disuse, however, and only recently has been revived in AmE <the birthing of babies>. Some dictionaries label it dialectal. But given its usefulness and its long standing in the language, it should be accepted as standard.

bite > bit > bitten. Writers occasionally fall into dialectal usage by using *bit*, the past-tense form, as a past participle—e.g.: "That probably would have happened by now had Barnes not been *bit* [read *bitten*] by a spider in Florida in May 1995" (*Indianapolis Star*). See IRREGULAR VERBS.

biweekly; semiweekly. See BI-.

black, vb.; **blacken.** Both verbs mean "to make or become black," but *black* is confined to the narrow, physical sense of using black polish <Frank blacked his boots>, while *blacken* is used in all other physical senses <the sky blackened> as well as in figurative senses <the candidate's reputation was considerably blackened when he cheated on his taxes>.

But the most common figurative sense—in which *blacken* means something like "to vilify, defame"—is widely avoided because of its invidious association with race.

blame, v.t. In the best usage, one *blames* a person; one does not, properly, *blame* a thing *on* a person. E.g.: "I *blame* the fires *on* him." (Read: *I blame him for the fires.*)

blandish; brandish. *Blandish* = to cajole; to persuade by flattery or coaxing <the candidates were relentlessly blandished with promises of favors and political support>. *Brandish* = to wave or shake in a menacing or threatening way <one raider brandished a gun, the other a knife>.

Misusages occur most frequently with the corresponding nouns, especially *brandishment* for *blandishment*—e.g.: "Bargaining with the touts was almost as difficult as staying civil with them; but neither was as difficult as resisting their *brandishments* [read *blandishments*] toward our sweet little thing" (*Tacoma News Trib.*).

blatant; flagrant. Despite a fairly well-defined distinction, each word is misused for the other. What is *blatant* stands out glaringly or repugnantly; what is *flagrant* is deplorable and shocking, connoting outrage. A perjurer might tell *blatant* lies to the grand jury to cover up for his *flagrant* breach of trust. Egregious criminal acts are *flagrant* <flagrant arson>, not *blatant*—e.g.: "No self-respecting country can permit the *blatant* [read *flagrant*] murder of four of its citizens to go unpunished" (*Baltimore Sun*).

Likewise, *flagrant* is sometimes misused for *blatant*—e.g.: "But all the singing performances were strong—Mary Westbrook-Geha as a *flagrantly* [read *blatantly*] unrepentant penitent" (*Boston Globe*). For the MALAPROPISM of misusing *fragrant* for *flagrant*, see **flagrant.**

blindman's buff (= a game in which a blindfolded player tries to catch and identify any one of several other players) is the traditional term; it dates from about 1600. But *blindman's bluff*, a variant term, is now common.

blintze; blintz. American dictionaries are about equally divided between these two spellings. The term refers to a rolled pancake stuffed with cottage cheese and other fillings. The original Yiddish term is *blintze*, and that spelling predominates in AmE by a 5-to-1 margin.

bloc; block. Political groups or alignments are *blocs*. *Block* serves in all other senses.

blond; blonde. In French, the *-e* is a feminine tag, the spelling without the *-e* being the masculine. This distinction has generally carried over to BrE, so that *blonde* more often refers to women and *blond* more often refers to men. In AmE, though, *blond* is preferred in all senses—e.g.: "Currently there's an 'Absolut Dallas' ad that pictures a *blond woman's* tiara-adorned bouffant hairdo in the shape of a bottle" (*USA Today*). But sometimes *blonde* is ill-advisedly applied to a man—e.g.: "It looks like these beautiful people are going to ride off into Madison Avenue bliss. But wait. The *blonde man* is kissing someone else. And that someone else is another man" (*Pitt. Post-Gaz.*). In that sentence, *blonde* should probably have been *blond*—unless the writer was subtly trying to suggest effeminacy. Cf. **brunet(te).**

When the word describes an inanimate object, the *-e* is invariably dropped <blond wooden chairs> <a honey-blond microbrewed beer>.

bobby socks. So spelled—preferably not *bobby sox.*

bogey; bogy. *Bogey* = one over par on a golf hole. *Bogy* = an evil spirit. *Bogie* is a variant spelling of both terms.

bologna. See **baloney.**

bombastic is sometimes misconstrued to mean "strident" or "violent." Properly, *bombastic* (lit., "full of stuffing or padding") means "pompous, highfalutin, overblown." But the error is all too common, perhaps because *bombastic* suggests *bomb*—e.g.: "In sharp contrast to the *bombastic* [read *incendiary*?] nature of violence in Colombia, Rosenberg paints a chillingly urbane and sophisticated face on Argentina's Dirty War" (*S.F. Recorder*).

bona fide. A. And *good-faith*, adj. *Bona fide*, adj., is understood by educated speakers of English; as a legal term, it is unlikely to give way completely to *good-faith*, adj.

B. Adjective or Adverb. *Bona fide* was originally adverbial, meaning "in good faith" <the suit was brought bona fide>. Today it is more commonly used as an adjective <it was a bona fide suit>. The phrase is sometimes hyphenated when functioning as a PHRASAL ADJECTIVE.

C. Meaning "genuine, authentic." The adjective *bona fide* is best avoided in the sense "genuine" or "authentic," which was arrived at through SLIPSHOD EXTENSION—e.g.: "Ms. Rebhun argued successfully that Michael's alcoholism was a *bona fide* [read *genuine*] illness that prevented him from taking responsibility for filing his taxes" (*N.Y. Times*).

D. Misspelled *bonified*. During the late 20th century, the spurious form *bonified* emerged—e.g.: "Calvin Klein's unisex fragrance . . . is more like refreshing citrus water than a *bonified* [read *bona fide* or, better, *genuine*] perfume" (*Portland Oregonian*).

***bona fides*, n. A. And *good faith*.** Though the adjective *bona fide* has been fully anglicized, the noun phrase *bona fides* has lost much ground—especially in AmE—to *good faith*, which is generally preferable. Perhaps the comparative infrequency of *bona fides* results from its pronunciation (/boh-nə-**fī**-deez/), which sounds foreign and bombastic in comparison with *good faith*.

B. Number. If the variable meanings of *bona fides*, together with its air of affectation, weren't enough to make it a SKUNKED TERM, the dilemma it presents certainly is. Technically, of course, the noun phrase *bona fides* is singular: *this bona fides is*, not *these bona fides are*. Making it singular sounds pedantic; making it plural is likely to offend those who have a smattering of Latin. Avoid it altogether—e.g.: "His campaign turf extends from the Republican hard right, where Dole's conservative *bona fides are* [read *credentials are*] sometimes questioned" (*Baltimore Sun*). Unfortunately, only a few careful writers will consciously avoid this usage. Most writers would never think to use the phrase at all, but the semi-educated—eager to impress—are likely to perpetuate the error.

bon mot /bohn-**moh**/ (= a well-turned phrase, witticism) traditionally makes the plural in the French way—*bons mots*. But much more commonly, the plural actually used in AmE is *bon* *mots*—e.g.: "And people who imagine him eating canapes, sipping champagne and swapping *bon mots* with movie stars at Cannes and London have it all wrong, Jarvis said" (*Des Moines Register*). This anglicized plural ought to be accepted on the same footing as *memorandums* and *syllabuses*. See PLURALS (B).

bon vivant. Although the traditional plural is the French *bons vivants*, the phrase is often considered anglicized enough to use the English plural *bon vivants*. Indeed, the anglicized form is now standard—e.g.: "There were the *bon vivants* who remained anchored to their bar stools, hoisting just one more brew in honor of the Yankees" (*N.Y. Times*). See PLURALS (B).

bookkeeping; accounting. *Bookkeeping* is the uncritical recording of debts and credits or summarizing of financial information, usually about a business enterprise. *Accounting* differs from bookkeeping because it is not mechanical: it requires judgment about such issues as when a specified type of transaction should be recorded, how the amount of the transaction should be calculated, and how a balance sheet and income statement should be presented.

born; borne. Both are past participles of *bear*—*borne* for general purposes <she has borne a child> <the burden he has borne> and *born* only as an adjective or as a part of the fixed passive verb *to be born* <she was born in 1987>. *Bear in mind* yields *borne in mind*—e.g.: "That point should be *born* [read *borne*] in mind today as Colorado voters review a long list of important primary elections in races for the U.S. Senate" (*Denver Post*).

both. A. *Both . . . and.* These CORRELATIVE CONJUNCTIONS must frame matching sentence parts—e.g.:

- "He was trying *both* to establish himself in his new league *and* to justify the contract extension he was given through 2002" (*Chicago Sun-Times*). (The conjunctions frame two infinitives.)
- "Gunshot residue was observed on Mr. Foster's right hand, consistent *both* with the test firings of the gun *and* with the gun's cylinder gap" (*Wash. Times*). (The conjunctions frame two prepositional phrases beginning with *with*.)
- "Immunocompromise presents unique challenges *both* to the pet lover *and* to the veterinarian involved" (*Denver Post*). (The conjunctions frame two prepositional phrases beginning with *to*.)

See PARALLELISM.

B. *Both . . . as well as.* This construction is incorrect for *both . . . and*. E.g.: "But I think it should be obvious—*both* to the characters *as well as* [read *and*] to the reader" (*Raleigh News & Observer*).

C. *Both (of) the.* Though the idiom is falling into disuse, *both the* (or *both these*) has a fine pedigree and continues in formal English—e.g.: "The hazard, in *both these* respects, could only be avoided, if at all, by rendering that tribunal more numerous" (*Federalist Papers*). The alternative phrasing, *both of the* (or *both of these*), is somewhat more common in AmE.

D. *Both (of) the last; both (of) the last two.* These phrases are unidiomatic and unnecessarily wordy for *the last two*—e.g.: "One aspect of the game the Vikings need to work on is breaking the full-court press, which plagued them in *both of* [delete *both of*] the last two losses" (*Virginian-Pilot*).

boughten. See **buy** (A).

bountiful; bounteous. *Bounteous* is poetic or literary for *bountiful*, the preferable term in ordinary contexts.

BRACKETS ([ ]). Square brackets enclose comments, corrections, explanations, interpolations, notes, or translations that were not in the original text but have been added by subsequent authors, editors, or others. E.g.: "My right honorable friend [John Smith] is mistaken."/ "They [Whig members of Congress] couldn't thwart President Jackson's legislative agenda." Unfortunately, many journalists use parentheses for this purpose—a slipshod practice.

Also, brackets often show parentheses within parentheses <Smith and her commander (Robert Parnell, also a [helicopter] pilot) both survived the crash>. But in some fields, such as law, it's not only acceptable but customary to use parentheses within parentheses <(citing Leonard Baker, *John Marshall: A Life in Law* 14 (1974))>. The "kissing" parentheses at the end of that citation appear throughout this book in parenthetical cross-references to subparts; for example, toward the end of PLURALS (F), a cross-reference reads, "(see (B))."

Usually in scholarly writing, brackets are used for adjustments in quoted matter, such as making lowercase a letter that was uppercase in the source of the quotation <"It is not surprising, in Alison Lurie's view, that '[i]nnovations in language are always interesting metaphorically' "> or signifying the omission of a word's inflection <"Good writers . . . sometimes prove[ ] to be among the toughest of editors themselves">. Some writers and editors, though, tacitly change the capitalization to keep their text free of brackets.

brandish. See **blandish.**

brand-new, adj. So spelled—not *bran-new.* Sometimes the phrase is written *bran'-new,* to show that the *-d* is usually dropped when the word is pronounced. Although sounding the *-d* in speech is more than a little pretentious, the contracted written form is unnecessary.

breach (= [1] n., an opening or gap; or [2] vb., to break open) can be a troublesome word. In general usage, it is confused with two other words, *breech,* n. (= [1] buttocks; or [2] the lower or back part of something, as a gun), and *broach,* v.t. (= [1] to make a hole in to let out liquid; or [2] to bring up for discussion). The confusion of *breach* with *breech* occurs most often when writers mistakenly use the latter where *breach* belongs—e.g.: "To fill the *breech* [read *breach*], factor in how much income your investments might spin off" (*Tampa Trib.*).

Also, *breech birth* (= the delivery of a baby buttocks-first or feet-first) is sometimes wrongly made *breach birth*—e.g.: "Called Danzante carvings, the panels show a woman writhing during a *breach* [read *breech*] birth, an Olmec warrior with a twisted arm, as well as other characters" (*Milwaukee J. Sentinel*).

The lapse with *broach* occurs when someone mistakenly writes of *breaching* a topic or subject—e.g.: "When Faldo *breached* [read *broached*] that subject to his wife of nine years, Gill wasn't exactly overjoyed" (*USA Today*).

breach, more honored in the. Strictly speaking, this phrase refers to an unjust rule that is better broken than obeyed. Thus, in *Hamlet,* where the phrase originated, Shakespeare has Hamlet say that the Danes' riotous drinking "is a custom/ More honor'd in the breach than in the observance" (1.4.15–16). But writers frequently misapply the phrase to a just rule that, in practice, is often broken—e.g.: "[I]t is an American custom (perhaps *more honored in the breach* [read *more often breached than observed*]) as well as a Chinese one to show respect for one's elders" (*Chicago Trib.*).

breakdown = (1) failure <the breakdown of the bus didn't delay them long>; or (2) subdivision <the breakdown on the financial statement showed which subsidiaries owed the most in taxes>. Sense 1 is much older (ca. 1832) and has long been established. Sense 2 was once considered OFFICIALESE, especially after it first appeared in the mid-20th century, but today is generally viewed as natural and useful.

break-in, n. So hyphenated.

breath; breathe. The first is the noun, the second the verb. But *breath* is often mistaken for *breathe*—e.g.: "It was as if the questioner could not fathom the fact that the carrier of two X chromosomes would be able to *breath* [read *breathe*] the same rarefied air as men" (*N.Y. Times*).

breathable. So spelled—not *breatheable*. See MUTE E.

breech. See **breach.**

BREVE. See DIACRITICAL MARKS.

bridal; bridle. These two are sometimes the victims of WORD-SWAPPING. *Bridal*, adj., = of, for, or relating to a bride or wedding. *Bridle*, n., = part of a horse's harness. But instances do occur in which writers misuse *bridal* for *bridle*—e.g.: "A horse *bridal* [read *bridle*] hangs around her neck like a necklace or dog leash" (*Phoenix Gaz.*). The opposite error also occurs—e.g.: "It is also supposed to be symbolic of the canopy once held over the *bridle* [read *bridal*] couple to protect them from the 'evil eye' " (*Durham Herald-Sun*).

brilliance; brilliancy. *Brilliance* is preferred in describing a quality or state. *Brilliancy*, not quite a NEEDLESS VARIANT, means "something brilliant" <the brilliancies in Edmund Wilson's writings>.

bring. A. Inflected Forms: *bring* > *brought* > *brought*. The form *brung*, a dialectal word, is not in good use except in variations of the jocular phrase *dance with the one that brung ya*. For example, one politician told a crowd, " 'The voters of the 25th District are the ones who *brung* me, and they are the ones I want to dance with' " (*Columbus Dispatch* [quoting a politician]). See IRREGULAR VERBS.

B. And *take*. *Bring* suggests motion toward the writer or reader <please bring me a soda>. *Take* suggests motion in the opposite direction <just after you put the soda down, he took it from me>.

The distinction might seem to be too elementary for elaboration here, but misuses do occur—e.g.: "If the gentleman wishes to *bring* [read *take*] you somewhere, he should say to the hosts, 'I have been seeing a great deal of someone whom I would like you to meet,' and then give them your name so that they can issue you a proper invitation" (*Chicago Trib.*).

Britain. See **Great Britain.**

Britisher. See **Briton.**

Britishism; Briticism. Although *Briticism* came first (in the mid-19th century) and is more often used by linguists, the term *Britishism* is more than twice as common in journalism. H.W. Fowler preferred *Britishism* on scholarly grounds (*MEU1*), but it has been mostly the nonscholarly writers who have followed his preference. Most American desktop dictionaries misguidedly list *Briticism* first.

BRITISHISMS. See AMERICANISMS AND BRITISHISMS.

Briton; Britisher. The word *Briton*—the word that Britons themselves recognize—is nearly 100 times more common than *Britisher*, an Americanism. For that reason, and because Britons often consider *Britisher* a vague insult, *Briton* should be preferred—e.g.: "It would not be a good idea to ask the famously crabby *Britisher* [read *Briton*] if this rush of Stateside success makes the prospect of working in Hollywood, with a decent-sized budget, attractive" (*Ft. Lauderdale Sun-Sentinel*).

broach. See **breach.**

broadcast; forecast; telecast; cablecast; radiocast. As verbs, these are the correct forms for the past tense as well as the present. Adding *-ed*, though fairly common, is incorrect. See **cast.**

brokerage; brokage. *Brokerage* = (1) the business or office of a broker <real-estate brokerage is a profession requiring knowledge and experience>; or (2) a broker's fee <brokerage differs from an underwriting commission>.

The archaic *brokage* (or, alternatively, *brocage*) means "the corrupt jobbing of offices; the bribe unlawfully paid for any office" (*OED*). It's also a NEEDLESS VARIANT of *brokerage*.

bronco; bronc; broncho. The standard form is *bronco* (= a wild, unbroken horse). *Bronc* is a colloquial clipping. *Broncho* is a variant spelling used for some sports teams; for example, the University of Central Oklahoma calls its players the *Bronchos*, and a few high-school teams use the same spelling. But the spelling *bronco* vastly predominates.

Pl. *broncos*. See PLURALS (C).

brother-in-law. Pl. *brothers-in-law*. See PLURALS (F).

brunet(te). Unlike its counterpart *blond(e)*, this word is seldom applied to males, even though the form *brunet* is the masculine in French. Some have suggested that *brunet* appears most often as a noun, while *brunette* is reserved for the adjective. But in fact *brunette* commonly serves both functions. Cf. **blond.** See SEXISM (D).

brung. See **bring (A).**

brusque; brusk. The first spelling is preferred. In AmE, the term is pronounced /brəsk/; in BrE, it's /broosk/.

bucketful. Pl. *bucketfuls*—not *bucketsful*. See PLURALS (F).

budget, vb., forms *budgeted* and *budgeting* in AmE, *budgetted* and *budgetting* in BrE. See SPELLING (B).

buffet. When speaking of the serve-yourself meal, say either /bə-**fay**/ or /boo-**fay**/. When speaking of the pummeling blow, say /**bəf**-it/. But in BrE, the pronunciation /**bəf**-it/ is common for both senses.

bulk, n., sometimes causes writers to doubt which form of a verb to use, singular or plural—e.g.: "Although nearly a third of blacks have moved into the middle class, the *bulk* of blacks *fall* [*falls*?] into a troubled underclass, as Andrew Hacker's *Two Nations* so cogently proves" (*Nation*). Most writers—who might find support in the principle of SYNESIS—would write *fall* in that sentence. And they have the better position: when the phrase *bulk of the* is followed by a plural COUNT NOUN, the verb should be plural. The form is attested from the early 19th century in historical dictionaries. Hence *the bulk of the criticisms are* is better than *the bulk of the criticisms is*.

bulk large is an acceptable variant of *loom large*, but both phrases have become CLICHÉS.

BULLET DOT [•]. This punctuation mark draws the eye immediately to one of several enumerated items. When you don't mean to imply that one thing in a list is any more important than another—that is, when you're not signaling a rank order—and when there is little likelihood that the list will need to be cited, you might use bullet dots. They enhance readability by emphasizing salient points. Examples appear throughout this book (see, for example, the three bullets under **both (A).**

There is a notable difference, however, between how the bullets appear in this book and how they ought to appear in most documents. Although here the bullets fall at the left margin, they should generally be indented a little farther than a paragraph indent. They are not indented here because the double-column format doesn't allow it.

Here are seven more tips on using bullets well: (1) end your introduction with a colon, which serves as an anchor; (2) keep the items grammatically parallel (see PARALLELISM); (3) if you begin each item with a lowercase letter, put a semicolon at the end of each item and use *and* after the next-to-last item—put a period after the last item; (4) if you begin each item with a capital—by convention, "fragments" are acceptable units here—end each with a period; (5) use hanging indents, which are extremely important in giving each bullet its full weight (see DOCUMENT DESIGN (H)); (6) ensure that the bullets are well proportioned both in their size and in their distance from the text they introduce, preferably with no more than one blank character-space between the bullet and the first word; and (7) resist the temptation to play with hollow characters, smiley faces, funky check marks, and the like: unless you're trying for an offbeat appearance, use real bullet dots.

buncombe; bunkum. This term—meaning "political talk that is empty or insincere"—derives from Buncombe County, North Carolina, because the U.S. congressman from the district embracing that county early in the 19th century felt compelled, despite other pressing business, to "make a speech for Buncombe" during a session of Congress. *Buncombe* has remained the standard spelling and is preferable because it recalls the interesting origin of the word.

Even so, the shortened slang term is *bunk* (= nonsense) <that's all bunk!>. A clipped form of *bunkum*, it dates from the early 20th century. Henry Ford immortalized the word when he said, "History is more or less bunk."

bureau. The better plural form is *bureaus*; the Frenchified plural, *bureaux*, should be avoided as pretentious. See PLURALS (B).

burgeon literally means "to put forth buds; sprout." Although some usage experts have considered the word objectionable in the sense "to flourish, grow," no good reason exists to avoid it in this figurative sense; but the word preferably refers to growth at early stages, not to full-blown expansion.

burglarize; burgle. *Burglarize* is an American coinage from the late 19th century meaning "to rob burglariously" (*OED*). It is still largely confined to AmE. *Burgle*, a BACK-FORMATION of comparable vintage, has the same meaning. Although *burgle* is usually facetious or jocular in AmE, it's standard and colorless in BrE. In AmE, *burglarize* appears about 30 times more often than *burgle*—e.g.: "A man who dressed in women's clothing and pretended he was injured so he could enter and *burglarize* homes has pleaded guilty in Hennepin County District Court" (*Minneapolis Star Trib.*).

BURIED VERBS. Jargonmongers call them "nominalizations," i.e., verbs that have been changed into nouns. Without the JARGON, one might say that a verb has been buried in a longer noun—usually a noun ending in one of the following suffixes: *-tion*, *-sion*, *-ment*, *-ence*, *-ance*, *-ity*. It is hardly an exaggeration—no, one hardly exaggerates—to say that whenever the verb will work in context, the better choice is to use it instead of a buried verb. Thus:

The Verb Buried	*The Verb Uncovered*
arbitration	arbitrate
compulsion	compel
computerization	computerize
conformity, -ance	conform
contravention	contravene
dependence	depend
enablement	enable
enforcement	enforce
hospitalization	hospitalize
incorporation	incorporate
knowledge	know
maximization	maximize
mediation	mediate
minimization	minimize
obligation	obligate, oblige
opposition	oppose
penalization	penalize
perpetration	perpetrate
perpetuation	perpetuate
reduction	reduce
utilization	utilize, use
violation	violate

Naturally, you will sometimes need to refer to competition or litigation or regulation as a procedure, and when that is so you must say *competition* or *litigation* or *regulation*. But if a first draft says *the insurance industry's attempts at regulation of doctors*, you might well consider changing the second draft to *the insurance industry's attempts to regulate doctors*.

Why uncover buried verbs? Three reasons are detectable to the naked eye: first, you generally eliminate prepositions in the process; second, you often eliminate BE-VERBS by replacing them with so-called "action" verbs; and third, you humanize the text by saying who does what (an idea often obscured by buried verbs).

A fourth reason is not detectable to the naked eye: in fact, it is the sum of the three reasons already mentioned. By uncovering buried verbs, you make your writing less abstract—readers can more easily visualize what you're talking about. (Compare: "After the transformation of nominalizations, the text has fewer abstractions; readers' visualization of the discussion finds enhancement.") See ABSTRACTITIS.

Though long neglected in books about writing, buried verbs ought to be a sworn enemy of every serious writer. In technical writing, they often constitute an even more serious problem than PASSIVE VOICE.

burn > burned > burned. As a verb, *burnt* is a chiefly BrE form, usually the past participle but sometimes the past tense. In AmE, *burnt* is almost exclusively an adjective <burnt orange> <burnt rubber>.

burst > burst > burst. As a past-tense or past-participial form, *bursted* is a mistake—e.g.: "Among emergencies that agencies and managers name are such things as a *bursted* [read *burst*] water pipe" (*Chicago Trib.*). See IRREGULAR VERBS.

bus, n. & v.t. The plural form of the noun (meaning "a large vehicle that holds many passengers") is *buses*. The verb (meaning "to transport by bus") is inflected *bus > bused > bused*; the present participle is *busing*. When the *-s-* is doubled, the sense is different: *bussed* means "kissed," and *bussing* means "kissing." Cf. **gases.** See SPELLING (B).

The verb *bus*, as a BACK-FORMATION from *busboy*, has the additional meanings "to work as a busboy or busgirl" and "to clear dishes from (a table)." Here, too, the better inflected forms are *bused* and *busing* <he helped pay his way through college by busing tables>.

but. A. Beginning Sentences with. It is a gross canard that beginning a sentence with *but* is stylistically slipshod. In fact, doing so is highly desirable in any number of contexts, and many stylebooks that discuss the question quite correctly say that *but* is better than *however* at the beginning of a sentence. See SUPERSTITIONS (D). Good writers often begin sentences with *but* and have always done so.

Some years ago, a researcher found that 8.75% of the sentences in the work of first-rate writers—including H.L. Mencken, Lionel Trilling, and Edmund Wilson—began with coordinating conjunctions (i.e., *And* and *But*). Francis Christensen, "Notes Toward a New Rhetoric," 25 *College English* 9 (1963). In *The New York Times* (front page during the 1990s) and *U.S. News & World Report* (in 1997), the figure is about the same. To the professional rhetorician, these figures aren't at all surprising.

B. More Than One in a Sentence. Putting this subordinating conjunction twice in one sentence invariably makes the sentence unwieldy and less easy to read. E.g.: "*But* this opening misleads because the focus dissipates as the play progresses and the scattershot climax drips with sentiment *but* is ultimately unsatisfying" (*Pitt. Post-Gaz.*). (A possible revision: *But this opening misleads because the focus dissipates as the play progresses. Although the scattershot climax drips with sentiment, it's ultimately unsatisfying.*)

C. For *and*. This lapse is surprisingly common. The misuse of *but* for *and* often betrays the writer's idiosyncratic prejudice. That is, if you write that someone is *attractive but smart*, you're suggesting that this combination of characteristics is atypical. E.g.: "Billy's father, Dr. Istvan Jonas, . . . is a man of sterling rectitude, *poor but honest* [read *poor and honest*], determined to pass his upcoming naturalization exams" (*Chicago Trib.*). (Is the writer really suggesting that poor people are typically dishonest?)

D. Preposition or Conjunction. The use of *but* in a negative sense after a pronoun has long caused confusion: is it *No one but she* or *No one but her*? When *but* is a preposition (meaning "except"), the objective *her* (or *him*) follows. But when *but* is a conjunction, the nominative *she* (or *he*) is proper.

The correct form depends on the structure of the sentence. If the verb precedes the *but*-phrase, the objective case should be used—e.g.: "None of the defendants were convicted *but him*." But if the *but*-phrase precedes the verb, the nominative case is proper: "None of the defendants *but he* were convicted." That sentence is considered equivalent to "None of the defendants were convicted, *but he was convicted*." (Although that rewording doesn't seem to make literal sense—given that he was one of the defendants—it serves to show the grammar of the sentence excepting him from the absolute word *none*.) *But* thus acts as a conjunction when it precedes the verb in a sentence, as in this one from Thomas Jefferson: "[N]obody *but we* of the craft *can understand* the diction, and find out what [the statute] means." Here the subject of *can understand* is *nobody*, and the *but* heads the understood clause: *nobody can understand, but we can understand*.

buy. A. Inflected Forms: *buy* > *bought* > *bought*. The form *boughten* (= store-bought as opposed to homemade) is an archaic past-participial adjective formed on the analogy of words such as *broken, driven,* and *frozen*. It still occurs in dialectal speech in the North and Northeast (in the sense "store-bought"), but not elsewhere. E.g.: "In those days any *boughten* [read *store-bought*] cookie we would see in Maine was made by the Loose-Wiles Biscuit Company, which had a huge brick factory near the railroad tracks in Boston's North End" (*Christian Science Monitor*). See IRREGULAR VERBS.

B. And *purchase*. As a verb, *buy* is the ordinary word, *purchase* the more formal word. Generally, *buy* is the better stylistic choice. As one commentator says, "Only a very pompous person indeed would say he was going to *purchase* an ice-cream cone or a bar of candy" (Robert Hendrickson, *Business Talk*, 1984).

Purchase may also act as a noun; *buy* is informal and colloquial as a noun <a good buy>.

bylaw; byelaw. Both the spelling and the sense differ on the two sides of the Atlantic. In AmE, *bylaws* are most commonly a corporation's administrative provisions that are either attached to the articles of incorporation or kept privately. In BrE, *byelaws* are regulations made by a local authority or corporation, such as a town or a railway.

The spelling without the *-e-* is preferred in AmE. Though etymologically inferior, *byelaw* (sometimes hyphenated) is common in BrE.

by the by (= incidentally) is the standard spelling. *By the bye* (archaic) and *bye the bye* are variant forms.

by virtue of. See **virtue of.**

byword (= [1] a proverb or saying; or [2] a person representing a specific quality) is best spelled as one word and not hyphenated.

C

-C-; -CK-. When adding a suffix to a word ending in *-c*, how do you keep the hard sound (/k/) from becoming soft (/s/)? With native suffixes (*-ed*, *-er*, *-ing*, *-y*), you do it by inserting a *-k-*. Thus *mimic* becomes *mimicked*, *traffic* becomes *trafficker*, *frolic* becomes *frolicking*, and *panic* becomes *panicky*.

But classical suffixes (*-ian*, *-ism*, *-ist*, *-ity*, *-ize*) don't take the *-k-* and thus become soft: *politician, cynicism, publicist*, *mendacity*, and *criticize*.

cablecast. See **broadcast.**

cacao. See **cocoa.**

cache; cachet. *Cache* /kash/ = (1) a hiding place or storage place; (2) something hidden or stored in such a place; or (3) a type of computer memory. (In COMPUTERESE, the term is sometimes mispronounced /kaysh/.) *Cachet* /ka-**shay**/ = (1) prestige, status, distinction; (2) an official seal, esp. one denoting approval; (3) a commemorative postal design; or (4) a wafer-like capsule used to dispense bad-tasting medicine.

Cache is sometimes mistakenly used in place of *cachet*—e.g.: "Through all its vicissitudes, the company has retained its reputation for impeccable quality and the *cache* [read *cachet*] of being the instrument of choice for every great pianist from Rachmaninoff to Awadagin Pratt" (*Baltimore Sun*).

cactus. Pl. *cactuses* or *cacti*. *Cactuses* is more common in ordinary usage, but *cacti* predominates in botanical contexts. See PLURALS (B).

caddie; caddy. *Caddie* = one who carries a golf bag, esp. for hire. *Caddy* = a box or other container. Occasionally *caddy* is mistakenly rendered *caddie*—e.g.: "In addition to such touches as a bookshelf with travel books and a globe, and a wheeled tea *caddie* [read *caddy*], there must have been upward of 100 pieces of silver plate" (*Virginian-Pilot*).

cadre (/**kad**-ree/ or /**kah**-dray/), meaning "a tightly knit group," usually takes a plural verb despite being grammatically singular. E.g.: "He intimidates many who work for him, yet a *cadre* of loyal executives has [read *have*?] followed him from company to company" (*Fortune*). This sentence presents a close call because, in using the singular verb, the writer might have wanted to emphasize the oneness of the group. For more on this grammatical issue, see SYNESIS.

caesarean section. See **cesarean section.**

calculated = (1) deliberately taken or made <a calculated risk>; or (2) likely <the weather is calculated to slow play in the Masters today>. Sense 2 represents a debasement in meaning that damages the utility of the word even in sense 1.

caldron. See **cauldron.**

caliber; caliper. *Caliber* = (1) the diameter of a cylinder, esp. the bore of a gun <a .44-caliber pistol>; or (2) degree of worth or competence; quality <the Wharton School of Business turns out CEOs of the highest caliber>. (The BrE spelling is *calibre*. See -ER (B).) *Caliper* = (1) (usu. pl.) a tool used for measuring thickness or diameter; (2) thickness, as of paper or cardboard; or (3) a part of a disc-brake system.

calk. See **caulk.**

callous; callus. The former is the adjective ("hardened, unfeeling"), the latter the noun ("hardened skin"). Unfortunately, during the early 1990s Dr. Scholl's—the company specializing in foot products—mistakenly advertised *callous removers* instead of *callus removers*, encouraging further confusion.

calvary; cavalry. Despite having wholly unrelated meanings, these words are often confused. *Calvary* = (1) (cap.) the place near Jerusalem where Jesus was crucified; (2) (sometimes cap.) a depiction or representation of Jesus' crucifixion; or (3) (l.c.) an experience of intense suffering; an ordeal. *Cavalry* = (1) a military unit mounted on horseback; or (2) a motorized military unit.

The reason for the confusion, of course, is the similarity in sound and spelling—both words contain the same seven letters. When spoken, the sounds in the word *cavalry* (/**ka**-vəl-ree/) are sometimes transposed (a process known as METATHESIS), resulting in a mispronunciation of the word as /**kal**-və-ree/. And because it is misspoken, it is also misused in print—e.g.: "After the second mile into the race, the Franklin Park environ resembled a *calvary* [read *cavalry*] charge with 40 runners near the front" (*Boston Herald*).

camaraderie is routinely misspelled *camraderie*, *comraderie*, and even *comradery* because of the mistaken association with *comrade*—e.g.:

- "Ah, yes, the *camraderie* [read *camaraderie*]" (*Boston Globe*).
- "But the *comraderie* [read *camaraderie*] hasn't spread to the assembly line" (*USA Today*).
- "In a show of *comradery* [read *camaraderie*], McNealy cut his own salary . . . in 1993 after Sun's stock had dropped dramatically" (*S.F. Chron.*).

Although the words *camaraderie* and *comrade* are related etymologically—both derive from the French *camarade*—the English spellings are well enough established that *camraderie* can indeed be labeled an error. Of course, careful speakers probably won't misspell *camaraderie*—it has five syllables: /kah-mə-**rah**-də-ree/.

can. A. And *may*. The distinction between these words has been much discussed. Generally, *can* expresses physical or mental ability <he can lift 500 pounds>; *may* expresses permission or authorization <the guests may now enter>, and sometimes possibility <the trial may end on Friday>. Although only an insufferable precisian would insist on observing the distinction in speech or informal writing (especially in questions such as "Can I wait until August?"), it's often advisable to distinguish between these words.

But three caveats are necessary. First, educated people typically say *can't I* as opposed to the stilted forms *mayn't I* and *may I not*. The same is true of other pronouns <why can't she go?> <can't you wait until Saturday?>. Second, *you can't* and *you cannot* are much more common denials of permission than *you may not* <no, you can't play with any more than 14 clubs in your bag>. Third, because *may* is a more polite way of asking for permission, a fussy insistence on using it can give the writing a prissy tone.

B. And *could*. These words express essentially the same idea, but there is a slight difference. In the phrase *We can supply you with 5 tons of caliche*, the meaning is simply that we are able to. But in the phrase *We could supply you with 5 tons of caliche if you'll send us a $5,000 deposit*, the *could* is right because of the condition tacked onto the end; that is, there is some stronger sense of doubt with *could*. See SUBJUNCTIVES.

And in interrogatives, *could* indicates willingness: *Could you meet me at 7:00 p.m.?* This asks not just whether you're able, but also whether you're willing.

In still another circumstance—in the subordinate clause of a complex sentence—the choice between *can* and *could* depends on the sequence of tenses. If the verb in the main clause expresses a past event, *could* appears in the subordinate clause <she asked me to go so that I could meet my great-aunt>. But if the verb in the main clause expresses a present or future event, *can* appears in the main clause <she is asking me to go so that I can meet my great-aunt> <she will ask me to go so that I can meet my great-aunt>. See TENSES (B).

candelabrum (= a branched candlestick with several candles, or a branched lamp with several lights) forms the plural *candelabra*, which is actually the more usual form of the word. Three problems commonly arise. First, some writers use *candelabra* as a singular—e.g.: "The holiday centered on lighting the eight-branch *candelabra* [read *candelabrum*] called the menorah" (*Capital Times*). Second, as a result of the false singular just mentioned, writers are then tempted to use the double plural *candelabras*—e.g.: "The dignity is leavened by some whimsical touches, such as chandeliers and *candelabras* [read *candelabra*] entwined with iron flowers and a giant piggy bank behind the small bar" (*Chicago Sun-Times*). Third, and least seriously, some writers stick to the native-English plural even though the foreign plural has been thoroughly established—e.g.: "But this Hanukkah season, which runs through Dec. 13, Mickey is appearing on menorahs—seven-branch *candelabrums* [read *candelabra*]—and dreidels—spinning toy tops" (*Chicago Sun-Times*). See PLURALS (B).

CANNIBALISM. This is H.W. Fowler's term for constructions in which certain words "devour their own kind" (*MEU1*). Words that commonly fall prey are *as*, *to*, and *that*. E.g.: "But the playwright's the thing, and he comes across *as* fascinating, mercurial and doomed *as* any of his fictional creations" (*USA Today*). The phrase *comes across as* has swallowed the first *as* in the phrase *as fascinating, mercurial and doomed as*. (A possible revision: *But the playwright's the thing, and he comes across as being as fascinating, mercurial, and doomed as any of his fictional creations.*)

There are two similar blunders. The first results from omitting *as* after *regard*, *treat*, *accept*, *acknowledge*, and other verbs that are unidiomatic without it (such as the PHRASAL VERB *come across*). E.g.: "We *regard* him *as* holy as a saint." Although the strictly correct phrasing would be *regard him as as holy as a saint*, the better course is to use another word: "We *consider* him as holy as a saint." Or: "We *believe* he is as holy as a saint." The second blunder occurs with incomplete comparisons—e.g.: *as bad or worse than*, *as much or more than*. The phrases should be *as bad as or worse than* and *as much as or more than*. E.g.: "They compromised at 8 feet, but in many spots the competition among walkers, dog walkers and runners has worn paths *as wide or wider than* [read *as wide as or wider than*] planners sought" (*Minneapolis Star Trib.*). See ILLOGIC (B).

Problems of this kind are most readily spotted by reading aloud. The ear tends to hear them even if the eye doesn't see them. See SOUND OF PROSE.

cannon. See **canon.**

cannot should not appear as two words, except in the rare instances when the *not* is part of another construction (such as *not only . . . but also*)—e.g.: "[H]is is among very few voices that *can not only* get away with numbers like 'You Are So Beautiful to Me' and a reggae/salsa remake of 'Summer in the City,' but actually make them moving" (*Toronto Sun*). *Cannot* is preferable to *can't* in formal writing. See CONTRACTIONS.

cannot help but; cannot help —ing; cannot but. In formal contexts, the last two phrases have traditionally been preferred—e.g.: "Engaged in these activities, the critic *cannot but* formulate value judgments" (John Simon, *The Sheep from the Goats*, 1989)./ "When I put this on the list, I *can't help feeling* a little puffed up"

(*S.F. Examiner*). Still, because *cannot help being* and (especially) *cannot but be* are increasingly rare in AmE and BrE alike, they strike many readers as stilted.

Cannot help but is becoming an accepted idiom that should no longer be stigmatized on either side of the Atlantic—e.g.: "Experts say Thomas' court performance *cannot help but* be affected by the traumatic Senate confirmation hearings" (*Philadelphia Inquirer*).

Occasionally writers twist the phrase not just unidiomatically, but illogically—e.g.: "I *cannot help from refraining myself* to comment on Ms. Gabor's flagrant disrespect of the law" (*L.A. Times*). If the writer couldn't help refraining, then the letter wouldn't have been written! On the misuse of *refrain* as a reflexive verb, see **refrain.**

canon; cannon. *Canon* = (1) a corpus of writings <the Western canon>; (2) an accepted notion or principle <canons of ethics>; (3) a rule of ecclesiastical law (either of the Roman Catholic canon law or of the Anglican Church); or (4) a cathedral dignitary.

Cannon = (1) a big gun; or (2) the ear of a bell, by which the bell hangs. *Cannon* incorrectly displaces *canon* surprisingly often—e.g.: "The state Criminal Justice Commission said yesterday in Wallingford that there was no evidence that Litchfield County State's Attorney Frank Maco violated the *cannon* [read *canon*] of ethics for lawyers by his remarks" (*N.Y. Newsday*).

can't hardly. There is some debate about this expression, only half of which need be taken seriously. Traditionalists call it a double negative—*not* and *hardly* both being negatives—and condemn the phrase on that ground. Descriptive linguists counter that *hardly* is not really a negative at all and say that *can't hardly* is perfectly acceptable.

But regardless of whether it's a double negative, *can't hardly* is not standard English. And the phrase can always be replaced by a more logical and more direct phrase in one of two ways. If a strong negative is intended, use *can't* (or *cannot*). If a soft negative is intended, use *can hardly* (or, more typically, *could hardly*).

can't help but. See **cannot help but.**

can't seem. Although this phrase is technically illogical (e.g., "I can't seem to find my coat" is more logically rendered "I seem to not be able to find my coat"), it is also undoubtedly idiomatic. Linguists use the term "raising" to describe the process of moving a negative from a subordinate clause to a main clause. Thus, "I think I will not go" becomes "I don't think I will go." The phrase *can't seem* is one of the more popular instances of raising.

Regardless of its label, this process is quite common, especially in speech. But it also occurs in writing—e.g.: "Shaq's mother *can't seem* to remember to give him the pill each morning, so Clifton got a doctor's permission to do it himself" (*Palm Beach Post*)./ "But all the lawsuits in the world *can't seem* to slow down tobacco profits" (*N.Y. Newsday*).

canvas; canvass. *Canvas*, almost always a noun, is the heavy cloth. In its rare verbal sense, it means "to cover with such a cloth." *Canvass*, v.t., = (1) to examine (as votes) in detail; (2) to discuss or debate; (3) to solicit orders or political support; or (4) to take stock of opinions, esp. those of individuals. The term is fairly common in all four senses. As a noun, the word *canvass* means "the act of canvassing."

capacity; capability. These words overlap, but each has its nuances. *Capacity* = the power or ability to receive, hold, or contain <the jar was filled to capacity>. Figuratively, it refers to mental faculties in the sense "the power to take in knowledge" <mental capacity>. In law, it is frequently used in the sense "legal competency or qualification" <capacity to enter into a con-

tract>. *Capability* = (1) power or ability in general, whether physical or mental <he has the capability of playing first-rate golf>; or (2) the quality of being able to use or be used in a specified way <nuclear capabilities>. See **ability.**

capital, n.; **capitol.** The former is a city, the seat of government; the latter is a building in which the state or national legislature meets (fr. L. *capitoleum,* the Roman temple of Jupiter). Until October 1698, when the Virginia governor specified that *Capitol* would be the name of the planned statehouse in a village then known as Middle Plantation, the word *capitol* had been used only as the name of the great Roman temple at Rome.

Capital, whether as noun or as adjective, is called on far more frequently than *capitol.*

CAPITALIZATION. Conventions of capitalization abound; several of the more important ones are here discussed. They vary, to be sure, since practices in capitalizing are governed as much by personal taste as by a set of rules. The following sections prescribe the usual conventions of capitalization.

A. All Capitals. Avoid them. They impair readability because the eye cannot easily distinguish among characters that are all of a uniform size. Try reading these passages, arranged by increasing readability:

> EXCEPT AS MAY BE OTHERWISE SPECIFICALLY PROVIDED IN THIS AGREEMENT, ALL NOTICES SHALL BE IN WRITING AND SHALL BE DEEMED TO BE DELIVERED WHEN DEPOSITED IN THE UNITED STATES MAIL, POSTAGE PREPAID, REGISTERED OR CERTIFIED MAIL, RETURN RECEIPT REQUESTED, ADDRESSED TO THE PARTIES AT THE RESPECTIVE ADDRESSES SET FORTH ON EXHIBIT B OR AT SUCH OTHER ADDRESSES AS EITHER PARTY MAY SPECIFY BY WRITTEN NOTICE.

vs.

> Except as May Be Otherwise Specifically Provided in This Agreement, All Notices Shall Be in Writing and Shall Be Deemed to Be Delivered When Deposited in the United States Mail, Postage Prepaid, Registered or Certified Mail, Return Receipt Requested, Addressed to the Parties at the Respective Addresses Set Forth on Exhibit B or at Such Other Addresses as Either Party May Specify by Written Notice.

vs.

> Except as may be otherwise specifically provided in this Agreement, all notices shall be in writing and shall be deemed to be delivered when deposited in the United States mail, postage prepaid, registered or certified mail, return receipt requested, addressed to the parties at the respective addresses set forth on Exhibit B or at such other addresses as either party may specify by written notice.

Oddly, capitalizing to draw attention makes a passage typographically impenetrable. Using all caps is bad enough; underlining them is even worse. If you feel impelled to use all caps, make sure that they do not run for more than one line.

Large and small caps, as in the titles of essay entries in this book, are preferable to all caps because they are easier on the eye. See DOCUMENT DESIGN.

B. Initial Capitals. When capitalizing only the initial letters of words—as in headings or titles—follow these conventions:

1. Capitalize the first letter of every important word, such as a noun, pronoun, verb, adjective, and adverb, no matter how short—even such words as *pi, it,* and *be* <"On Hearing an Irish Poem Read in the Linenhall Library," by Medbh McGuckian>.
2. Put articles (*the, a, an*) as well as conjunctions (*and, or*) and prepositions having four or fewer letters (*of, by, with*) in lowercase. Capitalize those having five or more letters <"I'm Through with Love"> <"Only Because It's You">.
3. Capitalize the initial letter of the first and last word, no matter what part of speech. Also, capitalize the first letter of any word following a colon or dash. But if a heading is followed by a period

with run-in text after it, a final preposition having four or fewer letters isn't capitalized—for an example, see the heading at **yet (A)**.

4. Capitalize nouns, adjectives, particles, and prefixes in hyphenated compounds <"The Nineteenth-Century Outlook"> <"The Anti-Idealist">. But don't capitalize after the hyphen in hyphenated single words such as *Re-enlistment* or *Fifty-fourth Street*.

capitol. See **capital.**

caramel (= [1] burnt sugar used to color or sweeten food; or [2] a smooth, chewy, caramel-flavored candy) is the standard spelling. The word is pronounced /**kar**-ə-məl/ (best), /**kar**-ə-mel/ (second best), or /**kahr**-məl/ (worst). *Carmel* is a misspelling that results from the third pronunciation—e.g.: "Another offering is the Cow Pie, which is made of chocolate, pecans and *carmel* [read *caramel*]" (*Memphis Commercial Appeal*). Another influence leading to this error might be a place name: Carmel, California (which is pronounced /kahr-**mel**/).

carat; karat; caret. These homophones have distinct meanings. *Carat* = a unit of weight for gemstones, equal to 200 milligrams <a 2-carat diamond>. *Karat* = a unit of fineness for gold <a 24-karat gold bracelet>. *Caret* = a typographic mark (‸) used to indicate an insertion <a heavily edited page filled with cross-outs and carets>.

Not surprisingly, the first two words are the most frequently confused—so much so that dictionaries list *carat* as a variant spelling of *karat* (in addition to defining *carat*'s ordinary sense). But the DIFFERENTIATION ought to be encouraged.

cardinal numbers; ordinal numbers. Cardinal numbers measure quantity or magnitude (*one*, *two*, *three*, etc.); ordinal numbers measure position (*first*, *second*, *third*, etc.). See NUMERALS (F).

careen; career, vb. *Careen* = (1) v.i., to tip or tilt <the sailboat careened and then sank>; or (2) v.t., to cause to tip or tilt <they careened the ship on the beach to scrape the barnacles and caulk the seams>. *Career* = to move wildly at high speed <the car was careering out of control>.

Since the early 20th century, AmE has tried to make *careen* do the job of *career*, as by saying that a car *careened* down the street. On September 7, 1992, in a campaign speech in Wisconsin, President George Bush said that "product liability has *careened* out of control."/ "Imagine yourself as Ridge Racer, *careening* in a rocket-powered car through an ever-changing, three-dimensional landscape" (*Newsweek*).

Despite the increasing currency of *careen* in this sense, however, careful writers reserve *career* for this use—e.g.: "Monday night, while he [Silvio Berlusconi] reaffirmed his promise to deliver a 'new Italian miracle,' supporters *careered* through the streets of Rome blasting their car horns and crying 'Silvio! Silvio!' " (*Time*)./ "A hot rod *careered* out of control during a drag race and flew into the grandstand Sunday" (*Chicago Trib.*).

Misuse of *careen* may have been influenced by the word *carom* (= to rebound after colliding)—e.g.: "Among those comforted were seven students, ages 10 to 15, who were riding their bicycles Sunday with Dale Tutkowski when two cars collided and one car *caromed* into the teacher" (*Milwaukee Sentinel*).

caret. See **carat.**

Caribbean is sometimes misspelled *Caribean*. The pronunciation /kar-i-**bee**-ən/ is preferred because of its derivation from *Carib* /**kar**-ib/, the name of the native inhabitants of the islands that Christopher Columbus landed on and explored from 1493 (the Lesser Antilles) and of the northern coast of South America. The pronunciation /kə-**rib**-ee-ən/ is common, however, especially in BrE.

carmel. See **caramel.**

carom. See **careen.**

case. Arthur Quiller-Couch condemned this word as "Jargon's dearest child" (*On the Art of Writing*, 1916). H.W. Fowler elaborated on the idea: "There is perhaps no single word so freely resorted to as a trouble-saver, and consequently responsible for so much flabby writing" (*MEU1*).

The offending phrases include *in case* (better made *if*), *in cases in which* (usually verbose for *if*, *when*, or *whenever*), *in the case of* (usually best deleted or reduced to *in*), and *in every case* (better made *always*, if possible). The word *case* especially leads to flabbiness when used in a passage with different meanings—e.g.: "The popular image of a divorce *case* has long been that of a private detective skulking through the bushes outside a window with a telephoto lens, seeking a candid snapshot of the wife *in flagrante delicto* with a lover. Such is not exactly the *case*" (Joseph C. Goulden, *The Million Dollar Lawyers*, 1978).

cast > cast > cast. Generally speaking, the form *casted* is incorrect as a past-tense or past-participial form—e.g.: "For a week, the three men swapped fish tales, told ghost stories, baited hooks, *casted* [read *cast*] both fishing and song lines" (*Virginian-Pilot*). The one exception occurs when *cast* means "to supply with a lineup of actors"—e.g.: "Hollywood honcho Frederick Golchan, the executive producer of the Richard Gere-Sharon Stone flick 'Intersection,' was in town the other day scouting locations for 'Kimberly.' Golchan's latest not-yet-*casted* project is about a woman coxswain who joins a men's rowing team" (*Boston Herald*).

catalog(ue). Though librarians have come to use *catalog* with regularity, *catalogue* is still the better form. *Cataloging* makes about as much sense as *plaging*. "If the professionals decline to restore the *-u-* to the inflected forms," wrote Wilson Follett, "let them simply double the *-g-*" (*MAU*).

catchup. See **ketchup.**

categorically = without qualification. E.g.: "Sells, a half-Serb, *categorically* condemns the behavior of the Serbian political, military and literary elite" (*New Republic*).

For a MALAPROPISM involving this word, see **uncategorically.**

cater-cornered; catty-cornered; kitty-cornered. These terms all mean "located at a diagonal." The original phrase, in Middle English, was *catre-cornered* (lit., "four-cornered")—*catre* deriving from the Latin *quattuor*. Today *cater-cornered* and *catty-cornered* are about equally common—e.g.: "Arkansas' only 'cyber cafe' sits in a low-tech-looking bungalow a block from the courthouse square and *catty-cornered* to the local university campus" (*Ark. Democrat-Gaz.*)./ "Mr. Lebewohl was honored on Thursday when the small park in front of St. Mark's Church-in-the-Bowery—*cater-cornered* from his deli, at Second Avenue and 10th Street—was renamed Abe Lebewohl Park" (*N.Y. Times*). The form *kitty-cornered* is less than half as common as either of the other forms.

In regional dialects, the *-ed* is dropped <the gas station is kitty-corner from the music building>.

catsup. See **ketchup.**

cauldron; caldron. The first is the preferred spelling in AmE and BrE alike. *Cauldron* outnumbers *caldron* by a 4-to-1 margin in AmE print sources.

caulk; calk. *Caulk* = (1) vb., to fill (cracks or seams) in order to make airtight or watertight; or (2) n., the paste-like material used for this purpose (also known as *caulking*). *Calk* = (1) n., a piece fitted to a shoe (esp. a horseshoe) to prevent slipping; (2) vb., to fit with calks; or (3) vb., to injure with a calk.

Both words are pronounced /kawk/ or /kok/.

Though *calk* is sometimes used for *caulk*, the words have undergone DIFFERENTIATION, so that the spellings are best confined to the respective definitions above.

cause célèbre (/kawz-sə-**leb**/ or /kohz-sə-**leb**/) does not mean "a famous cause or ideal," as it is sometimes used—e.g.: "To some fervent left-wingers, if you're not with them and their *cause célèbre* [read *cause*], you're against them" (*Palm Beach Post*).

Instead, the primary meaning is "a trial or decision in which the subject matter or the characters are unusual or sensational" (*Black's Law Dictionary* [pocket ed. 1996]). The term has been legitimately extended from the strict legal sense to mean "a famous or notorious person, thing, or event"—e.g.: "As the first clear-cut case of a genetic difference in taste, this phenomenon became a sort of scientific *cause célèbre* in the 1930's and 1940's" (*N.Y. Times*).

cavalry. See **calvary.**

-CE; -CY. Choosing between these two endings can be tricky. Many nouns, of course, have comfortably settled into one form (*avoidance*, *coincidence*, *forbearance*, *intelligence*) or the other (*agency*, *constancy*, *decency*, *vacancy*). But some words can have both endings—and when they do, they often bear quite different meanings: *dependence*, *dependency*; *emergence*, *emergency*; *excellence*, *excellency*. See DIFFERENTIATION.

Unfortunately, no general principles can accurately be deduced from the available specimens. The best advice is to stay alert to possible distinctions between spellings and to consult a good dictionary.

C.E. See **B.C.**

cease, a FORMAL WORD, can often be replaced by *stop* or *end*—e.g.: "The noises *ceased* [read *ended*] after three or four nights, and we have not seen any raccoons for a week or so" (*Boston Globe*)./ "About the time Compaq nuked its Mobile Companion, Microsoft *ceased* [read *stopped*] work on WinPad, an operating system designed for hand-held computers" (*Houston Chron.*).

CEDILLA. See DIACRITICAL MARKS.

censor; censure. A. As Verbs. To *censor* is to scrutinize and revise, to suppress or edit selectively. E.g.: "The news is severely *censored* by the Pentagon and the Arab information agency" (*St. Petersburg Times*). To *censure* is to criticize severely, to castigate. E.g.: "Acting on Steele's advice, majority members threatened to impeach Keefer, which they could not legally do, but settled for *censuring* her for betraying board confidences and lawyer-client communications" (*Pitt. Post-Gaz.*).

Occasionally *censor* is misused for *censure*—e.g.: "Burns was severely *censored* [read *censured*] for remarks made after their match at Falkirk" (*Daily Mirror*).

B. As Nouns. *Censor*, n., = one who inspects publications, films, and the like before they are released to ensure that they contain nothing heretical, libelous, or offensive to the government. Although it would be nice to pronounce this use of the term obsolete, censors remain prominent in some countries. E.g.: "A movie made to finesse Chinese *censors* can easily slip through the grasp of Western audiences" (*Village Voice*).

Censure, n., = (1) a judgment of condemnation; or (2) a serious reprimand. Sense 1: "There have long been calls to deny new livers to alcoholics as a form of moral *censure*" (*Sacramento Bee*). Sense 2: "Mack and O'Dell voted against *censure*, which Tobolski said applies to the one incident and can be repeated if legislators do not like Mack's comments" (*Buffalo News*).

censorious (= severely critical), oddly enough, is the adjective corresponding to the verb *censure*—not *censor*.

censure. See **censor.**

center around. Something can *center on* (avoid *upon*) or *revolve around* something else, but it cannot *center around*, as the center is technically a single point. The error is common—e.g.: "They said the debate now *centers around* [read *centers on* or *revolves around*] what price Sandoval should pay for her mistake" (*Denver Post*).

CENTURY DESCRIPTIONS. Some of us, apparently, forget from time to time that *19th century* describes the 1800s, that *18th century* describes the 1700s, and so on. Take, for example, R.B. Collins's article titled "Can an Indian Tribe Recover Land Illegally Taken in the Seventeenth Century?" (1985), which discusses land acquired by New York from the Oneida Indians in 1795. The title should refer to the *18th century*, not the *17th*.

What particular years make up the course of a century has also caused confusion. Strictly speaking, since the first century ran from A.D. 1 to 100, every century begins with a year ending in the digits 01. The last year of a century ends in 00. But the popular mind has moved everything back a year, in the belief that 2000 marks the beginning of the 21st century. This confusion is unfortunate but seemingly ineradicable.

One other point merits our attention. As compound adjectives, the phrases denoting centuries are hyphenated; but they are not hyphenated as nouns. Hence, "The 12th-century records were discovered in the 19th century." See ADJECTIVES (C).

cerebral. In AmE this word is pronounced /sə-**ree**-brəl/ in all contexts except one—the phrase *cerebral palsy*, which is most often pronounced /**ser**-ə-brəl-**pahl**-zee/. This exception derives from an old pronunciation of *cerebral*: in the early 1900s, the preference was for the first syllable to be accented.

ceremonial; ceremonious. The DIFFERENTIATION between these words lies more in application than in meaning; both suggest a punctilio in following the customs and trappings of ceremony. *Ceremonial* is the general word relating to all manner of ceremonies, but is used only in reference to things—e.g.: "Don Larsen, who pitched the only perfect game in World Series history, threw out the *ceremonial* first pitch" (*Allentown Morning Call*).

Ceremonious, a slightly disparaging word, suggests an overdone formality; it is used in reference both to persons and to things—e.g.: "Walking the plank would have been too *ceremonious* for the real pirates, who much preferred slicing their victims up in redblooded swordplay" (*Cleveland Plain Dealer*).

certainty; certitude. *Certainty* = (1) an undoubted fact; or (2) absolute conviction. Sense 2 is very close to that reserved for *certitude*, which means "the quality of feeling certain or convinced." E.g.: "The decision that thrust the world into the nuclear age and cast doubt on the moral *certitude* of the United States still has the power to incite bitter and contentious debate" (*USA Today*).

Justice Oliver Wendell Holmes stated, rather memorably, "*Certitude* is not the test of *certainty*. We have been cock-sure of many things that were not so" ("Natural Law," in *Collected Legal Papers*, 1920). Other writers sometimes echo this aphorism—e.g.: "He was the sort of thinker for whom (to borrow a phrase of Oliver Wendell Holmes) *certitude* was the only proof that *certainty* required" (*New Republic*).

cesarean section; caesarean section. The first is the standard spelling for the term denoting the surgical procedure for delivering a baby—with a lowercase *c*-. Otherwise, *Caesarean* (= of or relating to Caesar) is the standard spelling; *Caesarian*, *Cesarean*, and *Cesarian* are variant forms.

chair; chairman; chairwoman; chairperson. Sensitivity to SEXISM impels many writers to use *chair* rather than *chairman*, on the theory that doing so avoids gender bias. E.g.: "Jeanie Austin [is the] former national *co-chair* of the RNC" (*Wash. Post*). Certainly *chair* is better than *chairperson*, an ugly and trendy word.

Many readers and writers continue to believe, however, that there is nothing incongruous in having a female *chairman*, since *-man* has historically been sexually colorless. Thus, in 1967, *chairman* was paired with *he or she*: "The Lord Chancellor, following up his proposals about the retiring age for justices, has announced that no one may be elected *chairman* after he or she has reached the age of 70, though existing *chairmen* may continue" (R.M. Jackson, *The Machinery of Justice in England*, 1967).

In journalistic sources in the 1990s, *chairman* outnumbered *chairperson* by a 100-to-1 margin. Even so, the nonsexist forms are gaining ground and may well prevail within the next couple of decades. If we're to have a substitute wording, we ought to ensure that *chair* (which goes back to the mid-17th c.) and not *chairperson* becomes the standard term—e.g.: "Mrs. Berman was instrumental in founding the Rhode Island State Nurses Association, District One, and served as *chairperson* [read *chair*] for the Tucks Scholarship Fund" (*Providence J.-Bull.*).

One caveat: if we adopt a term such as *chair*, it must be used in reference to males and females alike. In recent years, there has been a lamentable tendency to have female *chairs* and male *chairmen*. That is no better than having *chairwomen* and *chairmen*. After all, in most circumstances in which people lead committees, the sex of the leader is irrelevant.

chaise longue /shayz-**long**/ (= a couchlike chair) forms the anglicized plural *chaise longues*—no longer *chaises longues*. See PLURALS (B).

Some people commit the embarrassing error of saying or writing *chaise lounge*—e.g.: "[R]esin manufacturers are now trying to shatter their low-rent stereotype with ambitious new designs like folding deck chairs and *chaise lounges* [read *chaise longues*] in designer colors like hunter green" (*Nat'l Home Center News*). The problem is that *lounge*, when put after *chaise*, looks distinctly low-rent. See METATHESIS.

challenged. On the use of this adjective to mean "disabled" or "handicapped" <physically challenged>, see EUPHEMISMS.

chaperon (= a person, esp. an elder, who accompanies others, esp. youngsters, to ensure good conduct) is the standard spelling. *Chaperone* is a variant form apparently misspelled as a result of the (correct) long *-o-* in the final syllable. That is, because the word is pronounced /**shap**-ə-rohn/ or /shap-ə-**rohn**/, some writers have mistakenly added the final vowel—e.g.: "When the Mall of America in Bloomington, Minn., . . . announced a curfew and *chaperone* [read *chaperon*] policy for adolescents in September, teenagers seemed well on their way to becoming pariahs" (*USA Today*).

character; reputation. Very simply, the semantic distinction is that *character* is what one is, whereas *reputation* is what one is thought by others to be.

charge. See **accuse.**

charted. For the mistake of writing *unchartered territory* instead of *uncharted territory*, see **uncharted.**

chasm is pronounced /**kaz**-əm/.

chasten; chastise. These words are close in meaning, but distinct. *Chasten* = to discipline, punish, subdue. *Chastise* = (1) to punish, thrash; or (2) to castigate, criticize.

Chastise is so spelled; *chastize*, an incorrect spelling, is not uncommon. See -IZE.

check in the amount of. Instead of this wordy phrasing <enclosed is a check in the amount of $75>, say *check for $75* or *$75 check.*

childlike; childish. *Childlike* connotes simplicity, innocence, and truthfulness <childlike faith>. *Childish* connotes puerility, peevishness, and silliness <childish sulking>.

Sometimes *childish* (the negative term) wrongly displaces *childlike* (the positive term)—e.g.: "The text rang out with honesty and simplicity, whether voicing Anne's *childish* [read *childlike*] innocence or her tragic sense of weariness" (*Rocky Mountain News*).

chimpanzee may be pronounced /chim-pan-**zee**/, /**chim**-pən-zee/, or /chim-**pan**-zee/. The first of those pronunciations now predominates.

choate. See **inchoate.**

chord; cord. *Cord* (= [1] string, rope; [2] a measure of wood equaling 128 cubic feet; [3] an electrical cable; or [4] a ribbed fabric) is the usual spelling. *Chord* is reserved for musical and geometrical senses. When the reference is to the voice-producing organs—in which the anatomical part resembles a string or rope—the spelling *cord* is correct. But writers occasionally err—e.g.: "Miss Anderson still likes to exercise her vocal *chords* [read *cords*] on Irish folk songs" (*Omaha World Herald*). And sometimes *cord* displaces *chord* in metaphorical references to music—e.g.: "The sound of the dulcimer reaches lightly to the soul. It strikes a resonant and responsive *cord* [read *chord*] in most people" (*Pitt. Post-Gaz.*).

choreograph, like *orchestrate*, has become a CLICHÉ when used figuratively. In the most jejune modern language, careers are *choreographed* and events are *orchestrated*. See VOGUE WORDS.

Christian name. See **surname.**

chronic (= persistent; frequently recurring) is sometimes loosely used for *habitual* or *inveterate*—e.g.: "High school football coaches are *chronic* [read *habitual*] exaggerators" (*Lewiston Morning Trib.*).

chronicle, n. & vb., is frequently misspelled *chronical*—e.g.: "Ruth Pasquine will talk about these works that *chronical* [read *chronicle*] Sigler's experience with the disease" (*Ark. Democrat-Gaz.*).

In its one near-legitimate use, *chronical* is a NEEDLESS VARIANT of the adjective *chronic*.

CHRONOLOGY. Many writing problems—though described in various other ways—result primarily from disruptions in chronological order. In narrative presentations, of course, chronology is the essential organizer. The brain can more easily process the information when it's presented in that order. So generally, the writer should try to work out the sequence of events and allow sentences and paragraphs to let the story unfold.

Even at the sentence level, disruptions can occur. The following example comes from a handbook for band directors: "Improved intonation often results when students take up their instruments after singing their parts aloud once the director realizes that there are intonation problems." This is in reverse chronological order. But the sentence can easily be recast: *A director who detects intonation problems should try having the students put their instruments down and sing their parts aloud. Then, when they play again, their intonation will often be improved.*

Another elementary example: "Eight people died after being taken to a hospital, and 26 were killed instantaneously, the radio said" (*Las Vegas Rev.-J.*). (A possible revision: *The radio report said that 26 were killed instantaneously and that 8 others died after being taken to the hospital.*)

But consider the more subtle problem presented by a legal issue phrased (as lawyers generally do it) in one sentence:

> Is an employee who makes a contract claim on the basis that her demotion and reduction in salary violate her alleged employment contract, and who makes a timely demand under the Attorney's Fees in Wage Actions Act, disqualified from pursuing attorney's fees under this statute without the court's addressing the merits of her claim?

Now let's date the items mentioned in that statement:

> Is an employee [hired Oct. 1997] who makes a contract claim [in Sept. 1998] on the basis that her demotion and reduction in salary [in June 1998] violate her alleged employment contract [dated Sept. 1997], and who makes a timely demand [in Aug. 1998] under the Attorney's Fees in Wage Actions Act, disqualified from pursuing attorney's fees under this statute without the court's addressing [in May 1999] the merits of her claim?

The dates (which no one would ever actually want in the sentence) show that the sentence is hopelessly out of order. But if we improve the story line by highlighting the chronology, we instantly make the issue more understandable:

> Lora Blanchard was hired by Kendall Co. as a senior analyst in October 1997. She worked in that position for eight months, but in June 1998 Kendall demoted her to the position of researcher. Two months later, she sued for breach of her employment contract, including attorney's fees. Is she entitled to those fees under the Attorney's Fees in Wage Actions Act?

Of course, part of the improved story line comes from the enhanced concreteness that results from naming the parties. But the main improvement is finding the story line.

Remember: chronology is the basis of all narrative.

chute. See **shoot.**

chutzpah /**huut**-spə/ is a curious word, having both positive and negative connotations in AmE. On the one hand, some consider it unfavorable:

> Alan Dershowitz, the white knight of religious correctness, should have been a tad more judicious in his choice of a title for his book *Chutzpah*. Leo Rosten's book *Hooray for Yiddish!* defines *chutzpah* as "ultrabrazenness, shamelessness, hard-to-believe effrontery, presumption or gall"—traits that many Jews and Gentiles would hardly classify as desirable.
>
> Chloë Ross, *New York* (Mag.) (1991).

On the other hand—and perhaps this says something about American culture—many consider *chutzpah* something desirable. *W10* defines it first as "supreme self-confidence" but then unnerves us with "nerve, gall." The word sits uneasily on the fence that divides praise and scorn.

Variant spellings include *chutzpa*, *hutzpah*, and *hutzpa*.

cider. See **apple cider.**

cinematographic; cinemagraphic. *Cinematographic*, the traditionally correct form, is at least ten times more common than *cinemagraphic*, the etymologically inferior form. The latter arose through the linguistic process known as "syncope"—the loss of an unstressed syllable in the middle of a word. Though increasingly common even among filmmakers, *cinemagraphic* is not yet recorded in general dictionaries and ought to be avoided—e.g.: "[B]ut 'Dragonheart' is a beautiful piece of *cinemagraphic* [read *cinematographic*] work" (*Wash. Times*).

Cinematographic is pronounced /sin-ə-mat-ə-**graf**-ik/.

CIRCUMFLEX. See DIACRITICAL MARKS.

circumstances. A. *In* or *under the circumstances.* Some writers prefer *in the circumstances* to *under the circumstances*. The latter is unobjectionable, however, and is much more common. E.g.: "*Under the circumstances*, we think that the board made the right decision." H.W. Fowler wrote that the insistence on *in the circumstances* as the only right form is "puerile" (*MEU1*).

B. *Surrounding circumstances.* This phrase, which is slightly more common in BrE than in AmE, is stigmatized as a REDUNDANCY for etymological reasons. The *OED* confirms this, noting that *circumstance* derives from the Latin *circumstantia* "standing around, surrounding condition." In AmE, it appears most commonly in legal contexts (but not exclusively there)—e.g.: "The emotional and physical shock of giving birth, as well as other *surrounding circumstances* [read *circumstances*], led doctors to believe that Kraft was not responsible for stabbing her child" (*Des Moines Register*).

citizen. A. And *resident*. With U.S. citizens, the terms *citizen* and *resident* are generally viewed as being interchangeable in reference to state residency or citizenship. But the words are not interchangeable when other political entities (e.g., cities) are the frame of reference, for *citizen* implies political allegiance and a corresponding protection by the state, whereas *resident* denotes merely that one lives in a certain place. It is possible to be a U.S. *citizen* while being neither a *citizen* nor a *resident* of any particular state. (That is, American citizens can reside abroad.)

B. And *subject*. *Subject* (= a person subject to political rule; any member of a state except the sovereign [*COD*]) is not merely the BrE equivalent of the AmE *citizen*. A *citizen* is a person from a country in which sovereignty is believed or supposed to belong to the collective body of the people, whereas a *subject* is one who owes allegiance to a sovereign monarch.

citizenry; citizens. Both are acceptable plurals of *citizen*, but *citizens* is the more general. Two aspects of *citizenry* distinguish it: first, it is a COLLECTIVE NOUN (although it frequently takes a plural verb), emphasizing the mass or body of citizens; and second, it is, as *W2* notes, frequently used by way of contrast to soldiery, officialdom, or the intelligentsia. Here it is opposed to one part of officialdom (some might say *intelligentsia*): "The written Constitution lies at the core of American 'civil religion'; not only judges but also the *citizenry* at large habitually invoke the Constitution."

-CK-. See -C-.

clamor; clamber. *Clamor* (= to make noise; raise an uproar) is sometimes misused for *clamber* (= to climb with effort or difficulty)—e.g.: "When we returned to the house, we opened the large windows, let the ocean breeze roll in, and *clamored* [read *clambered*] up the oak staircases to bed" (*Wall St. J.*).

classic; classical. *Classical* refers to anything relating to "the classics" (whether in Greek or Latin literature, English literature, or music); *classic* may also serve in this sense, although not in phrases such as *classical education* and *classical allusion*. *Classic*, an easily overworked word, has the additional sense "outstandingly authoritative or important."

clean, v.t.; **cleanse.** *Clean* is literal, *cleanse* figurative. Hence *cleanse* is often used in religious or moral contexts—e.g.: "Subsequently, a traditional Navajo medicine man and a Hopi spiritual leader conducted a *cleansing* ceremony that returned the spirit of the student's mother to its resting place and allowed students to come back to school" (*L.A. Times*).

cleanly. This word can be either an adverb or an adjective. Most commonly, it functions as an adverb meaning "in a clean manner"—e.g.: "Even when it hits off-center (as it does this month) instead of *cleanly*, the moon manages a total eclipse" (*Discover*). In this sense, the word is pronounced /**kleen**-lee/.

But sometimes *cleanly* functions as an adjective—and is pronounced /**klen**-lee/—in a sense corresponding to the noun *cleanliness*. It means either (1) "(of a person) habitually clean"; or (2) "(of a place) habitually kept clean." In sense 2, a simple *clean* is surely preferable. In the first example that follows, sense 1 applies. In the second, sense 2 applies: " 'Owing to the leaning and handling of dirty persons, tobacco-spitting, the deposit of broken fruit and waste of all sorts of eatables, and other filthy practices voluntary or otherwise, the summer houses, seats, balustrades, balconies of the bridges are frequently forbidding to *cleanly* persons, who are thus deprived of what they deem their rights upon the Park' " (*N.Y. Times* [quoting Frederick Law Olmsted])./ " 'Our whole approach to quality assurance is not cracking the whip but to point out why things like dusting the pictures, a *cleanly* [read *clean*] room, are important,' [Ray] Sawyer said" (*Hotel & Motel Mgmt.*). Note that both examples occur in reported speech. This usage is more common in speech than in writing.

cleanse. See **clean.**

clearly. Exaggerators like this word, along with its cousins (*obviously, undeniably, undoubtedly,* and the like). Often a statement prefaced with one of these words is exceedingly dubious. As a result—though some readers don't consciously realize it—*clearly* and its ilk are WEASEL WORDS. Just how much *clearly* can weaken a statement is evident in the following example, in which the author uses the word to buttress a claim about his own state of mind: "*Clearly,* I am not to be convinced that this is a small matter" (Stephen White, *The Written Word,* 1984). See OVERSTATEMENT.

cleave, v.t., = (1) to divide or separate, split; or (2) to adhere to firmly. In other words, it has opposite meanings. In sense 1, *cleave* yields the past tense *cleft* (or, less good, *clove*) and the past participle *cleft* (or, again less good, *cleaved*). The past-participial adjective is *cloven*. Hence, "He cleft the Devil's cloven hoof with a cleaver."

In sense 2, the verb is inflected *cleave > cleaved > cleaved.* The *COD* sanctions, for BrE usage, *cleave > clove > cloven* for all senses, though *cleft* is used adjectivally in SET PHRASES such as *cleft palate* and *cleft stick*. Luckily, the term is literary, so that generally only literary scholars must trouble themselves with these inflections. See IRREGULAR VERBS.

clench. See **clinch.**

CLICHÉS. Writing pundits frequently warn against clichés:

- "The purpose with which these phrases are introduced is for the most part that of giving a fillip to a passage that might be humdrum without them; they do serve this purpose with some readers—the less discerning—though with the other kind they more effectually disserve it" (H.W. Fowler, *MEU1*).
- "[M]odern writing at its worst does not consist in picking out words for the sake of their meaning and inventing images in order to make the meaning clearer. It consists in gumming together long strips of words [that] have already been set in order by someone else, and making the results presentable by sheer humbug" (George Orwell, "Politics and the English Language," in *Modern Essays on Writing and Style,* 1964).
- "Don't use [clichés] unwittingly. But they can be effective. There are two kinds: (1) the rhetorical—*tried and true, the not too distant future, sadder but wiser, in the style to which she had become accustomed*; (2) the proverbial—*apple of his eye, skin of your teeth, sharp as a tack, quick as a flash, twinkling of an eye.* The rhetorical ones are clinched by sound alone; the proverbial are metaphors caught in the popular fancy. Proverbial clichés can lighten a dull passage. You may even revitalize them because they are frequently dead metaphors . . . . Avoid the rhetorical clichés unless you turn them to your advantage: *tried and untrue, gladder and*

wiser, a future not too distant" (Sheridan Baker, *The Practical Stylist*, 1998).

As Baker suggests, you'll sometimes need clichés. That is, they're occasionally just the ticket, but only when no other phrase fits the bill. Despite that standard, you'll find more clichés in modern writing than you could shake a stick at. Among typical ones are these:

blissful ignorance
but that's another story
comparing apples and oranges
conspicuous by its absence
crystal clear
far be it from me
fast and loose
his own worst enemy
innocent bystander
moment of truth
more in sorrow than in anger
more sinned against than sinning
my better half
nip in the bud
pulled no punches
sea change
six of one, half a dozen of the other
throw the baby out with the bathwater
viable alternative

In deciding whether to use a cliché, consider the following approaches.

First, you might occasionally pun with the final word of a cliché to arrive at a new kind of memorable truth: a drink might be *conspicuous by its absinthe*; a dirt-talking disc jockey might be *his own worst enema*; a farmer might tend to his *better calf*; bankruptcy is sometimes *a fate worse than debt*. But if you're going to play with a cliché, it should usually be with a pun: don't simply change one word to arrive at the same meaning. That is, don't write *more in sorrow than in outrage* or *comparing apples and pomegranates*.

Second, if a cliché suggests itself you might go ahead and use it if (1) you work to replace it but can't find a good substitute, and (2) it doesn't strike your ear as being stale.

climactic; climatic. The word *climactic* is now established as the adjective corresponding to *climax*—e.g.: "In the *climactic* trial, Roxie beats the rap, only to be abandoned by reporters rushing on to the next case" (*Time*). *Climatic* is the adjective corresponding to *climate*—e.g.: "Long-term weather forecasts, which have been feeding the corn price frenzy, are seen by some as ominous because they include certain *climatic* events associated with droughts in the recent past" (*Wash. Post*).

Occasionally, though, *climatic* becomes a MALAPROPISM for *climactic*—e.g.: "In a *climatic* [read *climactic*] finish to more than four hours of questioning, prosecutor Chris Darden asked Lopez if she had told her friend Sylvia Guerra that she was going to be paid $5,000 for her testimony" (*S.F. Chron.*).

climb. A. Declension: *climb* > *climbed* > *climbed*. The past-tense *clomb* and the past-participial *clumb* are dialectal. They sometimes occur in reported speech, especially *clumb*—e.g.: "In 'The Busher Pulls a Mays,' Keefe writes to 'Friend Al' that 'the way we been going you would think we *clumb* in to 1st' " (*Chicago Trib.*).

B. *Climb down*. Although some purists have branded this phrasing illogical, in fact it is perfectly idiomatic—and certainly more natural-sounding than *descend*. E.g.: "When he [Esteban Toledo] was 8, he used to hide in the trees on the golf course in Mexicali. He would *climb down*, fish golf balls out of a pond with his toes, then clean the balls and sell them back to the golfers at the country club" (*L.A. Times*).

clinch; clench. Similar in meaning, these words are used differently. *Clench* is applied to physical matters, and *clinch* is used figuratively. Hence one *clenches* one's jaw or fist but *clinches* an argument or debate. E.g.: "Despite a script that makes him little more than a control freak with *clenched* jaws, Russell's O'Neil has a moment or two" (*Palm Beach Post*)./ "But one claim

. . . would really *clinch* the argument" (*Wash. Post*).

The exceptions to this distinction occur in boxing, carpentry, and metalworking: clutching one's opponent in boxing is *clinching*, and fastening something with a screw or a rivet is likewise *clinching*. Apart from these specialized meanings, *clinch* should be reserved for nonphysical contexts. Here it is used ill-advisedly: "After their speeches, Mr. Bentsen and Mr. Clinton *clinched* [read *clenched*] hands together with Gov. Ann Richards on the stage of the party's state convention as 'Deep in the Heart of Texas' played over the loudspeakers" (*Dallas Morning News*).

clique (= a small group of people who, for certain purposes, keep to themselves and treat others as outsiders) is pronounced either /klik/ or /kleek/. The corresponding adjective is *cliquish* /**klik**-ish/ (= snobbishly confining one's interests to a small in-group)—e.g.: "Jews and homosexuals appear in the hater's mind as small, *cliquish* and very powerful groups, antipathetic to majority values" (*N.Y. Times*). *Cliquey* (sometimes also spelled *cliquy*) is a NEEDLESS VARIANT.

clomb. See **climb (A).**

clothes is pronounced /klohz/. To pronounce the *-th-* is to engage in HYPERCORRECTION.

clove; cloven. See **cleave.**

clumb. See **climb (A).**

CO-. A. Hyphenation with. Generally, this prefix—which means "together with" or "joint"—does not take a hyphen (e.g., *coauthor, cosponsor*). The hyphen should appear only when the unhyphenated form might lead the reader to mistake the syllables (e.g., *co-occurrence, co-organizer*) or when the writer thinks that a word is a new form (e.g., *co-golfer, co-secretary*). See HYPHEN.

B. Attaching to Noun Phrase. This creates an awkward construction but is sometimes almost inevitable, as in *copersonal trainer*. Some writers and editors would make this *co-personal trainer*, which is hardly an improvement. The solution is simply to avoid the choice altogether, as by writing *fellow personal trainer*.

cocoa; cacao. *Cocoa* is a brown, chocolate powder or a drink made from this powder. *Cacao* is the tree or the seeds that are the source of cocoa powder. *Cocoa butter* and *cacao bean* are the standard terms—not *cacao butter* and *cocoa bean*.

coercion, though originally applicable only to physical force, is now commonly used to describe moral and economic pressures. E.g.: "[People are debating] whether 'economically disadvantaged' volunteers can fairly weigh the health risks of tests, or whether the lure of being paid $85 a day, plus room and meals, amounts to economic *coercion*" (*Indianapolis Star*). Such uses are a natural extension of the original sense ("the control by force of a voluntary agent or action").

cohabit, the verb for *cohabitation*, is analogous to *inhabit*—e.g.: "To cohabit is to dwell together," says one treatise, "so that matrimonial cohabitation is the living together of a man and woman ostensibly as husband and wife" (Joel P. Bishop, *Marriage, Divorce, and Separation*, 1891).

Cohabitate is a misbegotten BACK-FORMATION—e.g.: "There's little evidence that tax rates are pushing people to *cohabitate* [read *cohabit*] rather than marry (most *cohabitating* [read *cohabiting*] relationships end within two years)" (*Wash. Post*).

coleslaw; coldslaw. The latter is a common mistake—e.g.: "[A] mound of French fries and a big bowl of creamy *coldslaw* [read *coleslaw*] arrived" (*N.Y. Times*). In fact, the error derives from folk etymology, the mistaken notion being that the term refers to the temperature at which the dish is ordinarily served. The true etymology is that *coleslaw* comes from the Dutch *koolsla* [*kool* "cabbage" + *sla* "salad"]. See ETYMOLOGY (D).

coliseum; colosseum; Colosseum. For the amphitheater of Vespasian in Rome, *Colosseum* is the proper name. For any other large building or assembly hall, the word is *coliseum* (AmE) or *colosseum* (BrE).

collaborate. For the confusion of this word with *corroborate*, see **corroborate (C).**

collate (= [1] to compare critically; [2] to assemble in order; or [3] to verify the order of) is best pronounced /**kol**-ayt/ or /kə-**layt**/, not /**koh**-layt/.

COLLECTIVE NOUNS. A collective noun names an aggregate of individuals or things with a singular form. For example, *ensemble*, *group*, and *team* refer to several people, but each word is singular.

The main consideration in skillfully handling them is consistency in the use of a singular or plural verb. If, in the beginning of an essay, the phrasing is *the faculty was*, then every reference to *faculty* as a noun should be singular throughout the whole. On the other hand, a writer who wishes to emphasize the individual persons more than the body of persons may decide to write *the faculty were*, though *members of the faculty were* is preferable because it's more accurate.

But switching back and forth between a singular and a plural verb is lamentably common: "Mark Pattison's *Memoirs* is not strictly speaking an autobiography .... His *Memoirs* do not so much tell the story of his life .... Mark's father, as the *Memoirs* make plain, dominated his son's early years .... The *Memoirs* describes clearly" (V.H.H. Green, Introduction, Mark Pattison, *Memoirs of an Oxford Don*, 1988).

Apart from the desire for consistency, there is little "right" and "wrong" on this subject: collective nouns take sometimes singular and sometimes plural verbs. The trend in AmE is to regard the collective noun as expressing a unit; hence, the singular is the usual form. When the individuals in the collection or group receive the emphasis, the plural verb is acceptable <that deconstructionist school were not wholly in error>. But generally in AmE collective nouns take singular verbs, as in *the jury finds*, *the panel is*, *the committee believes*, *the board has decided*, etc.

Just the opposite habit generally obtains in BrE, where collective nouns tend to take plural verbs. The British tend to write, e.g., "The *board have* considered the views of the shareholders." BrE has gone so far in some contexts that many Americans would suspect a typographical error: "Oxford were the winners of the 136th University Boat Race, but many will say that Cambridge were the heroes" (*Sunday Times* [London]). See CONCORD (A).

But in modern AmE, singular verbs are often preferred with collective nouns. The question arises frequently with nouns such as *couple*, *faculty*, *majority*, and *press*—e.g.: "The French press *have* [read, in AmE, *has*] said he is too expansion-minded" (*Daily Telegraph*). These are largely questions of local idiom, not correct or incorrect grammar. See COUNT NOUNS AND MASS NOUNS.

Colombian, adj.; **Columbian.** *Colombian* = of or relating to the South American country of Colombia. *Columbian* = of or relating to America or to Christopher Columbus.

The adjective *pre-Columbian* (= of or relating to America before Columbus's arrival) should be so written—not *precolumbian*.

COLON [:]. This punctuation mark, which promises the completion of something just begun, has four uses.

First, it may link two separate clauses or phrases by indicating a step forward from the first to the second: the step may be from an introduction to a main theme, from a cause to an effect, from a general statement to a particular instance, or from a premise to a conclusion. E.g.:

- "Boeing left some chips on the table: It agreed to give up the exclusive-supplier agreements it had negotiated with American Airlines, Delta Air Lines, and Continental Airlines" (*BusinessWeek*).
- "Economists point to day care's problems as a classic case of 'market failure': Large numbers of parents need the service so they can work, but they are not willing to pay the fees that would be necessary for the well-trained, highly motivated workers they would like their children to have" (*U.S. News & World Rep.*).
- "My assignment: Identify and contact the CIOs for 100 companies that were selected on the basis of their productive and innovative use of information technology" (*CIO*).
- "Nor did the evidence submitted resolve the real question: whether Jackson is in fact Cosby's daughter" (*Newsweek*).

As in the examples just quoted, what follows the colon may be either a full sentence or just a phrase. When it's a sentence, authorities are divided on whether the first word should be capitalized. The first three bulleted examples above follow the prevalent journalistic practice: the first word is capitalized. But the other view—urging for a lowercase word following the colon—is probably sounder: the lowercase (as in this very sentence) more closely ties the two clauses together. Although the uppercase convention is a signpost to the reader that a complete sentence is ahead, that signpost generally isn't needed.

Second, the colon can introduce a list of items, often after expressions such as *the following* and *as follows*—e.g.: "The meetings are as follows: Central, Dec. 11 at the Municipal Auditorium, 5:30 p.m.–7:30 p.m.; South, Dec. 15 at the Mexican Cultural Institute, 5:30 p.m.–7:30 p.m." (*San Antonio Bus. J.*).

Third, the colon formally introduces a wholly self-contained quotation, whether short or long. If the quotation is in block form, the colon is mandatory, but if it's run in with the text, a comma is also permissible. E.g.: "By 1776 it seemed clear to numerous inhabitants of the western areas of the Connecticut River valley that the fight against tyranny had assumed a two-fold character: 'We are contending against the same enemy within, that is also without' " (*Creation of the American Republic*).

Finally, the colon often appears after the salutation in formal correspondence —e.g.: "Dear Ms. Johnsonius: . . . ."

colosseum. See **coliseum.**

columnist. In pronouncing this word, be sure to sound the *-n-*: /**ko**-ləm-nist/.

combat is pronounced /**kom**-bat/ as a noun, /kəm-**bat**/ as a verb. Although some authorities accept the inflected forms *combating* and *combated*, those spellings suggest the pronunciations /kəm-**bay**-ting/ and /kəm-**bay**-təd/. *Combatting* and *combatted* are more in keeping with general principles of AmE word formation. See SPELLING (B).

comedic. See **comic.**

come off it. This colloquial idiom is as old as Chaucer. For some reason, a few writers who use it feel inclined to make it *come off of it*, which is unidiomatic—e.g.: "There are some presenters who, without ever knowing it, prompt their audiences to think, 'Oh, *come off of it* [read *come off it*]' " (Ron Hoff, *"I Can See You Naked,"* 1992)./ "If you detect distance, or resistance, she is probably thinking, 'Oh, *come off of it* [read *come off it*]' " (same). See **off of.**

comic; comical; comedic. These words are confusingly similar. *Comic* and *comical* both mean "funny" or "humorous." *Comic* is generally used, however, for what is intentionally funny, and *comical* for what is unintentionally funny. Hence the latter term may mean "laughable" in a derisive sense—e.g.: "Kaelin, a struggling actor who was a shaggy-haired, *comical* figure at Simpson's criminal trial, appeared with his hair cut and neatly combed, wearing a white shirt, green tie and dark green sport coat" (*Austin American-Statesman*).

Comedic = of or pertaining to the form or nature of a dramatic comedy—i.e., a play that ends as the audience would wish (as the opposite of *tragic*). E.g.: "Director Paula Welter compares the W. Randolph Gavin play to the *comedic* style of television's 'Mad About You' " (*Sarasota Herald-Trib.*).

Sometimes *comedic* is misused for *comical*—e.g.: "Their first attempts to navigate the creek were *comedic* [read *comical*]—an aquatic, slapstick skit of unintended rammings and beachings" (*S.F. Chron.*).

COMMA [,]. This punctuation mark, the least emphatic of them all, is the one used in the greatest variety of circumstances. Two styles result in different treatments. The "close" style of punctuation results in fairly heavy uses of commas; the "open" style results in fairly light uses of commas. From the 19th to the 20th century, the movement was very much toward the open style. The byword was, "When in doubt, leave it out." Indeed, some writers and editors went too far in omitting commas that would aid clarity. What follows is an explanation tending slightly toward the open style, but with a steady view toward enhancing clarity.

Essentially, the comma has nine uses.

First, the comma separates items (including the last from the next-to-last) in a list of more than two—e.g.: "The Joneses, the Smiths, and the Nelsons." Whether to include the serial comma has sparked many arguments. But it's easily answered in favor of inclusion because omitting the final comma may cause ambiguities, whereas including it never will—e.g.: "A and B, C and D, E and F[,] and G and H." When the members are compound, calling for *and* within themselves, clarity demands the final comma. (See ENUMERATIONS (B).) Although journalists typically omit the serial comma as a space-saving device, virtually all nonjournalist writing authorities recommend keeping it—e.g.:

> When you write a series of nouns with *and* or *or* before the last one, insert a comma before the *and* or *or*. "The location study covered labor, tax, freight, and communications costs, all in terms of 1972 prices." While this rule is not observed by all publishers, it is valid and helpful. Professional magazines follow it frequently, and such authorities as David Lambuth support it. The reason is that the comma before the *and* helps the reader to see instantly that the last two adjectives are not joined. In the example cited, suppose the last comma in the series is omitted; *freight and communications costs* could then be read as one category, though it is not meant to be.
>
> David W. Ewing, *Writing for Results in Business, Government, and the Professions* 358 (1974).

Second, the comma separates coordinated main clauses—e.g.: "Cars will turn here[,] and coaches will go straight." There are two exceptions: first, when the main clauses are closely linked <Do as I tell you [no comma] and you won't regret it>; and second, when the subject of the second independent clause, being the same as in the first, is not repeated <Policies that help prevent crime are often better for the public [no comma] and are closer to the ideal of effective public administration>. (Another way of referring to the construction in that sentence is that it contains a "compound predicate.") Omitting the comma before the *and* in a compound sentence often causes an ambiguity or MISCUE: "I would love to see her and the baby and I will be here all day." (Insert a comma after *baby*; otherwise, it might sound as if the baby and the writer will be there all day.)/ "No one claimed responsibility for the attack nor for once were Chechen guerrillas seen as the prime suspects" (*Fin. Times*). (Insert a comma after *attack*; otherwise, it looks as if *for once* is parallel to *for the attack*.)

Third, the comma separates an introductory phrase or subordinate clause from the main clause so as to prevent misunderstanding. If there are three or more words in the introductory phrase, then the comma is generally needed—e.g.: "In the valley below[,] the villages looked very small." But the comma is also helpful with some shorter introductory phrases—e.g.: "In 1982[,] 1918 seemed like the distant past."

Fourth, the comma marks the beginning and end of a parenthetical word or phrase, an appositive, or a nonrestrictive clause—e.g.: "I am sure[,] however[,] that it will not happen."/ "Fred[,] who is bald[,] complained of the cold." Some writers mistakenly omit the second comma—e.g.: "After graduating from Rosemary Hall, an exclusive Greenwich girls' school in 1965, Ms. Close began touring with Up With People, the squeaky-clean pop group" (*N.Y. Times*). (Insert a comma after *school.*) Still others omit both commas, often creating a MISCUE: "Such a customer must at a minimum need help locating the maintenance department." (Insert a comma after *must* and after *minimum;* otherwise, one might read *at a minimum need* as a single phrase.)

Fifth, the comma separates adjectives that each qualify a noun in the same way <a cautious[,] reserved person>. If you could use *and* between the adjectives, you'll need a comma—e.g.: "Is there to be one standard for the *old, repulsive* laws that preferred whites over blacks, and a *different, more forgiving* standard for new laws that give blacks special benefits in the name of historical redress?" (*N.Y. Times*). But when adjectives qualify the noun in different ways, or when one adjective qualifies a noun phrase containing another adjective, no comma is used—e.g.: "a distinguished [no comma] foreign journalist"; "a bright [no comma] red tie." Writers often include the comma when it isn't necessary—e.g.: "The centerpiece of the Senate GOP package, which could be presented to the Senate Finance Committee for a vote as early as next week, is a *permanent, $500-per-child* [read *permanent $500-per-child*] tax credit for families. . . . Effective in 1996, families would be granted a *new, $500* [read *new $500*] tax credit for each child" (*L.A. Times*). See ADJECTIVES (E).

Sixth, the comma distinguishes indirect from direct speech—e.g.: "They answered[,] 'Here we are.' "/ " 'He did get excited,' Geoffrey said."

Seventh, the comma separates a participial phrase, a verbless phrase, or a vocative—e.g.: "Having had breakfast[,] I went for a walk."/ "The sermon *over* [or *being over*], the congregation filed out."/ "Fellow priests[,] the clergy must unite in reforming the system of electing bishops." Note, however, that no comma is needed within an absolute construction—e.g.: "The sermon [no comma] being over, we all left." Nor is a comma needed with restrictive expressions such as "my friend Professor Wright" or "my son John" (assuming that the writer has at least one other son—see APPOSITIVES).

Eighth, in informal letters the comma marks the end of the salutation <Dear Mr. Crosthwaite[,]> <Dear Rebecca[,]> and the complimentary close <Very truly yours[,]> <Yours sincerely[,]>. In formal letters, the salutation is separated from the body by a colon <Dear Sir[:]> <Dear Madam[:]>.

Finally, the comma separates parts of an address <#8 Country Club Dr., Amherst, Massachusetts> or a date <March 2, 1998>. Note that no comma is needed between the month and year in dates written "December 1984" or "18 December 1984"; a comma is required only when the date is written "December 18, 1984." See DATES.

Writers cause needless confusion or distraction for their readers when they insert commas erroneously. This typically occurs in one of four ways.

(1) Some writers insert a comma before the verb—something that was once standard. But the practice has been out of fashion since the early 20th century, and today it's considered incorrect—e.g.: "Whether or not the

shoes were bought at our store, [omit the comma] is not something we have yet been able to ascertain."/ "Only if this were true, [omit the comma] could it be said that John F. Kennedy was a great president." Even those who understand this principle are sometimes tempted to place a comma after a compound subject. That temptation should be avoided—e.g.: "Teachers who do not have a Ph.D., a D.M.A., or an M.A., [omit the comma] do not qualify for the pay raise."

(2) Commas frequently set off an adverb that doesn't need setting off. The result is a misplaced emphasis—e.g.: "We, *therefore,* [read *therefore* without the embracing commas] conclude that the mummy could not be authentic." Note that if the emphasis in that sentence is to fall on *We*—as clearly separated from some other group and its thinking—the commas should stand; but if the emphasis is to fall on *therefore* as a simple consequence of reasoning from the evidence, then the commas should be omitted.

(3) In compound sentences, an unnecessary comma is sometimes inserted before a second independent clause when the subject is the same as in the first clause. (As some grammarians put it, a comma shouldn't appear before the second part of a "compound predicate.") As explained above in the second rationale for using this mark, no comma appears before the conjunction when the second clause has an understood subject—e.g.: "They did their spring cleaning, and then had a picnic." (Delete the comma.)

(4) Some writers mistakenly use a comma as if it were a stronger mark—a semicolon or a period. The result is a comma splice—e.g.: "He said he didn't want to look, he wanted to remember her as she was in life." (Replace the comma with a semicolon.) See RUN-ON SENTENCES.

COMMA SPLICES. See RUN-ON SENTENCES.

commence. See **begin (a).**

commendable; commendatory. The former means "praiseworthy, laudable," and the latter means "expressing commendation, laudatory." Like other differentiated pairs ending in *-able* and *-atory*, these words are sometimes confused—e.g.: "[R]esponses of American business to disaster have included some *commendatory* [read *commendable*] actions" (*Miami Herald*).

comment; commentate. The longer form is a BACK-FORMATION from *commentator*, but an established one dating from the late 18th century. If *commentate* were only a NEEDLESS VARIANT of *comment*, its existence would be unjustified. But it enjoys the DIFFERENTIATION of meaning "to give a commentary on" or "to expound persuasively or interpretatively." Meanwhile, *comment* implies brevity. Hence scholarly commentators typically *commentate* rather than *comment* when expounding their disciplines. The word is, of course, grandiose when used of television journalists who cover sporting events, though it is too late to object to their being called *commentators.*

COMMERCIALESE. This is the peculiar JARGON of business, typified by words and phrases such as these (from correspondence):

acknowledging yours of
beg to advise
enclosed herewith
enclosed please find
further to yours of [date]
inst.
in the amount of
of even date
pending receipt of
please be advised that
please return same
pleasure of a reply
prox.
pursuant to your request
regarding the matter
regret to inform
thanking you in advance
the undersigned
this acknowledges your letter
ult.

we are pleased to note
your favor has come to hand
yours of even date

Books on business writing have long admonished writers to avoid these mind-numbing wads of verbiage—e.g.: "All stereotyped words [that] are not used in talking should be avoided in letter writing. There is an idea that a certain peculiar commercial jargon is appropriate in business letters. The fact is, nothing injures business more than this system of words found only in business letters. The test of a word or phrase or method of expression should be, 'Is it what I would say to my customer if I were talking to him instead of writing to him?' " (Sherwin Cody, *How to Do Business by Letter*, 1908).

For more on the subject, see the following books:

- L.E. Frailey, *Handbook for Business Letters* (2d ed. 1965).
- Maryann V. Piotrowski, *Effective Business Writing* (1989).
- Gary Blake & Robert W. Bly, *The Elements of Business Writing* (1991).
- Charles T. Brusaw et al., *The Business Writer's Handbook* (4th ed. 1993).

common. See **mutual.**

commonwealth. See **territory.**

COMPARATIVES AND SUPERLATIVES. A. Choice Between Comparative and Superlative. When two items are being compared, a comparative adjective is needed <the greater of the two>; when more than two are being compared, the superlative is needed <the greatest of the three>. The blunder of using the superlative adjective when only two items are being compared is not uncommon—e.g.:

- "The *tallest* [read *taller*] of the two pyramids is nearly 500 feet" (*Orlando Bus. J.*).
- "He has raced in *worst* [read *worse*] conditions, of course, and often won" (*Austin American-Statesman*).
- "With the first half of the game over, the *most* [read *more*] important half is yet to be played—this time on the voter's turf" (*Rocky Mountain News*).
- "The *youngest* [read *younger*] of Jean's two children from a previous marriage, a 16-year-old boy, lived with the couple until about a year ago" (*Virginian-Pilot*).

One exception occurs when we put our *best foot* forward, when (of course) we have only two.

B. Which to Use—Suffixes or *more* and *most*? Apart from anomalies like *good* > *better* > *best,* comparatives and superlatives are formed either by adding the suffixes *-er* and *-est* (e.g., *broader, broadest*) or by using the additional words *more* and *most* (e.g., *more critical, most critical*). Several words have a choice of forms (e.g., *commoner, -est* or *more, most common*; *tranquil(l)er, -est* or *more, most tranquil*; *stupider, -est* or *more, most stupid*; *naiver, -est* or *more, most naive*). The terminational forms are usually older, and some of them are becoming obsolete; the choice in any given context depends largely on euphony.

Still, if a word ordinarily takes either the *-er* or the *-est* suffix—and that formation sounds more natural—it's poor style to use the two-word form with *more* or *most*. E.g.: "Few things in this world short of yard work are *more dull* [read *duller*] than watching animated characters play basketball" (*Richmond Times Dispatch*)./ "The answers we sought proved *more simple* [read *simpler*] than we imagined" (*Hartford Courant*).

C. The Double Comparative. Among literate speakers and writers, the double comparative is fairly uncommon. But it does occasionally appear in print—e.g.: "Does it mean that change will be a bit *more slower* [read *slower*], a bit more careful, a bit more reasoned than totally revamping the health care system? Yes" (*Am. Medical News*).

D. Absolute Adjectives. See ADJECTIVES (B).

compare with; compare to. The usual phrase is *compare with*, which means "to place side by side, noting differences and similarities between" <let us compare his goals with his actual accomplishments>. *Compare to* = to observe or point only to likenesses between <the psychologist compared this action to Hinckley's assassination attempt>. Cf. **contrast (A).**

Compare and contrast is an English teacher's tautology, for in comparing two things (one thing *with* another) one notes both similarities and differences.

COMPARISONS, FALSE. See ILLOGIC (B).

compel; impel. *Compel* is the stronger word, connoting force or coercion, with little or no volition on the part of the one compelled. *Impel* connotes persuasive urging, with a degree of volition on the part of the one impelled.

compendious means "abridged, succinct," not "voluminous," as writers often mistakenly believe—e.g.: "In an archive at Harvard he found a *compendious* [read *bulky*?], multivolume, handwritten journal entitled 'Amos Webber Thermometer Record and Diary' " (*Wash. Post*).

compendium forms either of two plurals: *compendiums* or *compendia*. The native-grown plural is slightly preferable—e.g.: "One of the chief shortcomings of *compendiums* like this is finding what you want quickly" (*Seattle Times*). See PLURALS (B).

For the sense of the word, see **compendious.**

competence; competency. Though H.W. Fowler considered *competency* a NEEDLESS VARIANT, these terms have come to exhibit some DIFFERENTIATION, which should be further encouraged. *Competence* usually bears the general sense "a basic or minimal ability to do something." E.g.: "Inman got his reputation in the first place. Was it based on the ability of Washington insiders to judge the character and *competence* of public officials?" (*Chicago Sun-Times*).

Today *competency* is unnecessary in all but its legal sense: "the ability to understand problems and make decisions; the ability to stand trial." A severely mentally retarded person, an incompetent, is said to have legal *incompetency*. The usual phrase is *competency to stand trial*.

complacent; complaisant. The first means "self-satisfied; smug" <Mailer has become complacent about his place in the literary world>. The second means "obliging; tending to go along with others" <when dealing with the White House, the press isn't complaisant at all—it's sometimes downright hostile>.

complement. See **compliment & supplement.**

complementary. See **complimentary.**

complete. See ADJECTIVES (B).

completely, an intensive adverb, is often superfluous, as in the phrase *completely superfluous* (made doubly superfluous by further REDUNDANCY in the sentence that follows): "There's a *completely superfluous* [read *superfluous*] lemon-basil sauce on and around the fish *that's really not necessary* [delete phrase], but sopping it up with bread is nice" (*Nashville Banner*).

Indeed, the word *completely* creates redundancies when coupled with myriad adjectives—e.g.:

- "For 12 long minutes the board was *completely silent* [read *silent*], seemingly stunned by this news" (*Fortune*).
- "Naturally, the software industry wants to see this change happen, because no software is ever *completely perfect* [read *perfect*]" (*InfoWorld*).
- "No gallery of pictures can ever show the true breadth of Christmas because it is celebrated in a *completely unique* [read *unique*] and original manner within the heart of each person who treasures it" (*Life*).

See ADJECTIVES (B).

compliment; complement. Both as verbs and as nouns, these words are often confounded. *Compliment* = (1) vb., to praise <she complimented the book lavishly>; or (2) n., a laudatory remark <her generous compliments emboldened the young author>. *Complement* = (1) vb., to supplement appropriately or adequately <special Thai desserts complemented the curries nicely>; or (2) n., an adequate supplement <the flowering plants are a splendid complement to the trees offered at the nursery>.

The phrase *full complement* is sometimes misrendered *full compliment*—e.g.: "[T]he West Brookfield Police Department now has a full *compliment* [read *complement*] of six full-time police officers" (*Worcester Telegram & Gaz.*).

complimentary; complementary. This pair of adjectives is even more susceptible to confusion than the corresponding nouns. When a mistake occurs, *complementary* usually displaces *complimentary*—e.g.: "The reports were broadly encouraging. *Complementary* [read *Complimentary*] remarks were made about the extraordinary concentration by countries seeking to bring their infrastructure up to scratch" (*Fin. Times*).

compose. See **comprise (A).**

comprise. A. And *compose*. Correct use of these words is simple, but increasingly rare. The parts *compose* the whole; the whole *comprises* the parts. The whole is *composed* of the parts; the parts are *comprised* in the whole. *Comprise*, the more troublesome word in this pair, means "to contain; to consist of"—e.g.: "Summit Hall Farm *comprises* several hundred acres on the exterior portion of the original settlement of the Gaither family" (*Wash. Times*).

B. Erroneous Use of *is comprised of*. The phrase *is comprised of* is always wrong and should be replaced by some other, more accurate phrase—e.g.: "The Rhode Island Wind Ensemble *is comprised of* [read *has*] 50 professional and amateur musicians, ranging in age from 15 to 82" (*Providence J.-Bull.*).

C. *Comprise* for *are comprised in* or *constitute*. If the whole comprises the parts, the reverse can't be true—e.g.: "Of the 50 stocks that *comprise* [read *make up*] the index, 40 had gains, 8 had losses and 2 were unchanged" (*Fla. Today*).

D. *Comprise* for *are*. This is an odd error based on a misunderstanding of the meaning of *comprise*. E.g.: "They *comprise* [read *are*] three of the top four names in the batting order of the 30 most influential sports people in B.C. for 1997" (*Vancouver Sun*).

E. *Compromise* for *comprise*. See DOUBLE BOBBLES.

comptroller (= a government official in charge of finance, audits, and the like) is really the same word as *controller* (the spelling used for the equivalent person in private business). The word is pronounced /kən-**troh**-lər/—the same as *controller*. Sounding the *-p-* was traditionally viewed as semiliterate. (See PRONUNCIATION (B).) *Comptroller* is more common in AmE than in BrE, where it is archaic.

The strange spelling of *comptroller* originated in the zeal of 15th-century Latinists who sought to respell medieval French loanwords on the "purer" Latin model. Thus *account* became *accompt*, and *count* became *compt*. *Comptroller* is one of the few survivals among such respellings, and it is also one of the bungles perpetrated by those ardent Latinists: the *con-* in *controller* was mistakenly associated with the word *count*, when in fact it is merely the Latin prefix. Thus the respelling (which was never supposed to affect the pronunciation) should never have been. But we are several centuries too late in correcting it, the result being that many people have difficulty pronouncing the word.

COMPUTERESE, the JARGON of computer wizards, is making inroads into standard English. Thus *access* and *for-*

mat and *sequence* have become verbs, *input* has enjoyed widespread use as both noun and verb, and *online* and *user-friendly* have begun to be used as models for NEOLOGISMS (e.g., *on-stream* used of an oil well, *reader-friendly* used of well-written documents). No one can rightly object, of course, to computerese in computing contexts, where it is undeniably useful. But many computer terms have acquired figurative senses, thereby invading the general language. Careful users of language are wary of adopting any of these trendy locutions. Although some of the terms may remain and become standard, many others will keep their jargonistic stigma. Still others will thrive for a time and then fall into disuse. Such are the vagaries of the English vocabulary.

comrade; camarade. The latter, an archaic GALLICISM, is a NEEDLESS VARIANT. See **camaraderie.**

comstockery (often cap.) refers to prudish censorship, or attempted censorship, of supposed immorality in art or literature. In 1873, Congress passed the so-called "Comstock Law," a federal statute to control obscenity, pushed through by one Anthony Comstock (1844–1915), who was a leader of the New York Society for the Suppression of Vice. George Bernard Shaw invented the word *comstockery*, pejorative from the first, when he wrote in *The New York Times* in 1905: "*Comstockery* is the world's standing joke at the expense of the United States."

concept; conception. Both may mean "an abstract idea." *Conception* also means "the act of forming abstract ideas." H.W. Fowler wrote that *conception* is the ordinary term, *concept* the philosophical term (*MEU1*). Often the latter is just a high-flown equivalent of *design, program, thought,* or *idea*—e.g.: "That is good news for [Senator] Kerry, who was dragged kicking and screaming to the *concept of* [read *idea of*] a long series of debates that began in April" (*Boston Globe*).

conceptualize is often a bloated word that can be replaced by *conceive, think, visualize,* or *understand*—e.g.: "You can also ask to see a couple of units—actually standing inside the door of a 10- by 10-foot (100 square feet) space helps immensely, allowing you to *conceptualize* [read *visualize*] your belongings in place" (*Ariz. Republic / Phoenix Gaz.*).

concerto. The preferable plural is *concertos*, not the pretentious *concerti*. See PLURALS (B).

concierge /kon-see-**erzh**/ is frequently mispronounced /kon-see-**er**/ by those affecting a French pronunciation. In French, though, the *-g-* is pronounced /zh/ because the vowel *-e* follows it. Thus, the word is not like many other French words—*lait* and *rendezvous*, for example—in which the final consonant is silent.

Still, an informal survey at hotels throughout major American cities suggests that about half of all hotel employees use the incorrect pronunciation. See PRONUNCIATION (B) & HYPERCORRECTION (K).

concision; conciseness. Drawing a fine distinction, H.W. Fowler wrote: "*Concision* means the process of cutting down, and *conciseness* the cut-down state" (*MEU1* at 295). In fact, though, the two are generally used as synonyms for the cut-down state. As between these two words, surprisingly, *concision* occurs about 30% more often than *conciseness*—and, take note, in a sense that Fowler implicitly disapproved. This frequency might reflect the influence of *precision*, by analogy.

What ruling, then? If any DIFFERENTIATION is now possible, the word *conciseness*—like other *-ness* words—emphasizes a quality, whereas *concision* emphasizes a static condition. This is a fine distinction indeed, and one that not all writers will be able to apply. In that event, let euphony govern. But it would be a mistake (and a bootless one) to brand either word a NEEDLESS VARIANT.

CONCORD = grammatical agreement of one word with another to which it relates. Concord embraces number, person, case, and gender. It applies most often to (1) a subject and its verb; (2) a noun and its pronoun; (3) a subject and its complement; (4) a noun and its appositive; (5) a relative and its antecedent; and (6) an adjective and its noun. Errors in concord for (1), (2), and (3) are examined at (A), (B), and (C) below; for (4), see APPOSITIVES; for (5), see (D) below and REMOTE RELATIVES; for (6), see (E) below.

A. Subject–Verb Disagreement. Errors in SUBJECT–VERB AGREEMENT are, unfortunately, legion in AmE—e.g.:

- "Every one of us *have* [read *has*] a role to play" (President Bill Clinton, State of the Union Address, 23 Jan. 1996).
- In reference to Haiti: "The flow of desperate refugees to our shores *have* [read *has*] subsided" (President Bill Clinton, State of the Union Address, 23 Jan. 1996).
- "The price of sports tickets *are* [read *is*] rising" (*Seattle Times*).

Are these merely symptoms of the decay of 20th-century English? Consider: "[T]he adequate narration may take up a term less brief, especially if explanation or comment here and there *seem* [read *seems*] requisite to the better understanding of such incidents" (Herman Melville, *Billy Budd*, 1891).

Quoting Melville is not to excuse lapses of this kind: every generation can be more vigilant about its subjects and verbs. But we shouldn't consider these problems to have been unthinkable two or three generations ago.

The British—oddly to American eyes and ears—consider sports teams plural—e.g.: "On the field, England *were* going through their ritual reincarnation . . . . England *are* beset by similar urges" (*Observer*)./ "When the rain arrived yesterday, Australia *were* 201 runs ahead" (*Sunday Times* [London]). Kingsley Amis defends this construction: "Anybody with a tittle of wit knows that country-plus-plural refers to a sporting event or something similar. This is precisely what the verb is doing in the plural. It shows that a number of individuals, a team, is referred to, not one thing, a country" (*The King's English*, 1997). But Americans are no more accustomed to saying *England are* than they are to writing *anybody with a tittle of wit*. It's pure BrE, and *England are* surely isn't BrE at its best.

B. Noun–Pronoun Disagreement. Depending on how you look at it, this is either one of the most frequent blunders in modern writing or a godsend that allows us to avoid sexism. Where noun–pronoun disagreement can be avoided, avoid it. Where it can't be avoided, resort to it cautiously because some readers (especially speakers of AmE) may doubt your literacy—e.g.: "You can only teach a person something if that person can comprehend and use what is being taught *to them* [delete *to them*]" (J.M. Balkin, *Yale J. Law & Humanities*, 1990).

In BrE—to a surprising degree, and even when the purpose cannot be to avoid sexist usage—this type of disagreement in number is common. E.g.:

- "Anyone can set *themselves* up as an acupuncturist" (*Observer Sunday*).
- "A starting point could be to give more support to the company secretary. *They are*, or should be, privy to the confidential deliberations and secrets of the board and the company" (*Fin. Times*).
- "Under new rules to be announced tomorrow, it will be illegal for *anyone* to donate an organ to *their wife*" (*Sunday Times* [London]).

As this seeming sloppiness mounts—and bids fair to invade edited AmE—the complaints mount as well. For example: "Columnist James Brady . . . noted on page 38 that Richard F. Shepard was grammatically incorrect when he wrote, 'Nobody remembers a journalist for *their* writing.' Perhaps it was

Mr. Shepard who wrote the headline for the AT&T ad that appeared on Page 37 of the same issue: 'This florist wilted because of *their* 800 service' " (*Advertising Age*).

Why is this usage becoming so common? It is the most likely solution to the single biggest problem in sexist language—the generic masculine pronoun. Advertisements now say, "Every student can have *their* own computer," so as to avoid saying *his own computer*—a phrasing that would probably alienate many consumers. *The Macmillan Dictionary of Business and Management* (1988) defines *cognitive dissonance* as "a concept in psychology [that] describes the condition in which *a person's* attitudes conflict with *their* behavior." In his 1991 State of the Union address, President George Bush said: "If *anyone* tells you that America's best days are behind her, then *they're* looking the wrong way." And one of the best-edited American papers allows this: "If the newspaper can't fire him for an ethical breach surely *they* [read *it*?] can fire him for being stupid" (*Wall St. J.*).

For related discussions, see **each (A),** PRONOUNS (C) & SEXISM (B).

C. Subject–Complement Disagreement: Mismatched Number in Cause and Effect. Another common mistake, in AmE and BrE alike, is to attribute one result to two separate subjects, when logically a separate result necessarily occurred with each subject—e.g.: "In school, seats are not assigned, yet students tend to sit in the same seats or nearly the same each time, and sometimes feel vaguely resentful if *someone else gets* [read *others get*] there first and *takes 'their' seat* [read *take 'their' seats*]" (Robin T. Lakoff, *Talking Power: The Politics of Language in Our Lives*, 1990). (This might be broken into two sentences, the second of which would read: *They sometimes feel vaguely resentful if "their" regular seats are taken by others.*)/ "Designated hitter Jason Layne, already sporting a black eye, was hit by *a pitch* [read *pitches*] twice" (*Austin American-Statesman*). (The grammar here misleadingly suggests that the batter was hit twice by the same pitch.)

A related problem occurs in the following sentence, in which *both* is followed by a singular complement (*candidate*): "Today, both camps were enthusiastic about how *their candidate* fared" (*N.Y. Times*). The error could have been corrected by saying *each camp was . . . its candidate* or *both camps were . . . their candidates*.

D. Relative Pronoun–Antecedent Disagreement. This problem doesn't often arise, but a relative pronoun is supposed to agree with its antecedent in both number and person. Thus, it's correct to say *It is I who am here*, not *It is I who is here*. Because *I* is first-person singular, *who* must also be first-person singular, and the verb—it naturally follows—must be *am*. Strictly speaking, the following forms are correct:

- *me who know*;
- *I who have made*;
- *one who has*;
- *they who have*; and
- *I who am*.

E.g.: "I have said ugly things about gay people, and I've laughed at gay jokes. I, *who am* female and black, and *who know* firsthand the sting of contempt" (*Louisville Courier-J.*)./ "In fact, it is *they who have* been let down" (*L.A. Times*).

E. Adjective–Noun Disagreement. Some agreement problems arise between an adjective and the noun or nouns it modifies—e.g.: "In an outpouring of grief such as is seldom seen, the 'beloved community' of Martin Luther King's dream, Tony Brown's 'Team America' came to say good-bye to Barbara [Jordan]. People of *all races*, social *class* [read *classes*], national *origin* [read *origins*] and sexual *orientation* [*orientations*] joined in mourning her death" (*Daily Texan*). But that sentence might read better if *all* were replaced by the "singular" adjective *every* and if each of the nouns were made singular: *People of every race, social class,* *national origin, and sexual orientation . . . .*

concussion; contusion. *Concussion* = (1) violent shaking; (2) shock caused by a sudden impact; or (3) injury to the head caused by a heavy blow. *Contusion* = a bruise; an injury resulting from a blow that does not break the skin.

condemn; contemn. To *condemn*, in its main sense, is to render judgment against (a person or thing) <the court condemned the accused to life in prison>. The word has passed from legal into general usage mostly in the figurative sense "to disapprove forcefully; to declare reprehensible" <tribe members condemned the way Irving County reburied ancient artifacts>. *Contemn* = to hold in contempt; to disregard; esp., to treat (as laws or court orders) with contemptuous disregard. The *OED* notes that it is "chiefly a literary word" <rooted in the Shakespearean tradition, Richard Burton contemned trendy ploys to update the classics>.

condole, v.i.; **console,** v.t. To *condole* is to express sympathy; one *condoles with* another *on* a loss. E.g.: "Our king could devote himself to *condoling* with flood victims and boosting American products abroad" (*U.S. News & World Rep.*). To *console* is to comfort (another), especially in grief or depression. E.g.: "Clinton—who *consoled* victims' families earlier in the day—ordered that more baggage be screened or hand-searched and that aircraft making international flights be fully inspected" (*Detroit News*).

Occasionally, *condole* is misused for *console*—e.g.: "And as always, countrymen everywhere can continue *condoling* [read *consoling*] the forlorn Cubs, from sea to shining sea" (*Atlanta J. & Const.*).

conferencing. The *OED* records *conference* as a (rare) verb from 1846. The *SOED* and *W3* omit it. Though increasingly common in AmE, *conferencing* is often a bloated NEEDLESS VARIANT of *conferring*. The word has also become rather widespread in the forms *teleconferencing* and *videoconferencing*, favorite activities in American business. The word is likely to survive in those forms.

confess. A. *Confess to* for *confess*. Traditionally, confessors *confess* crimes, guilt, charges, weaknesses, faults, and the like. Less traditionally—though at least since the 18th century—confessors have *confessed to* these things. Euphony should govern the phrasing. Sometimes *confess to* sounds better than *confess* alone—e.g.: "I *confess to* never having attended a tractor pull" (*N.Y. Times*).

B. *Confess innocence* for *profess innocence*. This misusage is nothing short of a MALAPROPISM—e.g.: "Exactly six months ago, Daniel Strader stood before 2,000 members of his father's congregation and *confessed* [read *professed*] his innocence" (*Lakeland Ledger*).

confession. See **admission (B).**

confidant; confidante; confident, n. The forms *confidant* and *confidante* have an interesting history. Until 1700 or so, the English word was *confident* (= a trusty friend or adherent), the correct French forms being *confident* and *confidente*. But early in the 18th century, English writers began substituting an *-a-* for the *-e-* in the final syllable, perhaps because of the French nasal pronunciation of *-ent* and *-ente*.

Today the forms *confidant* and *confidante* predominate in both AmE and BrE, though *confidante* is falling into disuse because of what is increasingly thought to be a needless distinction between males and females. Despite the poor etymology, one can be confident in using *confidant* for both sexes, as it is predominantly used in American writing—e.g.: "In softer profile, [Hillary] Clinton comes across as a well-organized working mother and her husband's closest *confidant*" (*Cleveland Plain Dealer*).

In any event, it's wrong to make *confidante* refer to a male—e.g.: "He was the *confidante* [read *confidant*] of five U.S. presidents, from Woodrow Wilson to Franklin Roosevelt" (*Tampa Trib.*)./ "The leadership he applied to the process, the attention to contrary stratagems, was evident even earlier to another *confidante* [read *confidant*] who found himself suddenly consulted by Mr. Powell about the political art of a strategic retreat" (*N.Y. Times*).

conform takes the preposition *to* or *with*. H.W. Fowler objected to *conform with*, but most authorities find it quite acceptable. E.g.: "Libya said the investigations *conformed with* international law and did not violate its sovereignty" (*N.Y. Times*).

congenial; genial. A subtle difference exists and should be promoted. *Congenial* = (1) having similar tastes; compatible; kindred <a congenial married couple>; or (2) to one's liking; suitable; pleasant <a congenial workplace>. *Genial* = affable; friendly; cordial <her usual genial disposition>. Thus, *genial* applies to individuals, while *congenial* is generally reserved for persons collectively or for environments.

The DIFFERENTIATION is less pronounced with the noun forms, the word *congeniality* often doing the work for both adjectives—hence "Miss Congeniality" (not "Miss Geniality"). But *geniality* remains current, and there is no reason why beauty-pageant usage should control what careful writers do. *Congeniality*, then, might usefully be reserved for groups of people and environments, *geniality* for individual persons.

congeries (= a collection; aggregation) is a singular noun—e.g.: "Multiculturalism, by contrast, casts the world as a *congeries* of particularisms; and it regards the idea of an all-embracing humanity with suspicion" (*New Republic*). The form *congerie* (sometimes spelled *congery*) is a false singular noun recorded by the *OED* and *W3*, formed on the mistaken assumption that *congeries* (Fr. "a collection, aggregation") is the plural of such a noun. E.g.: "[T]he greatest effect of the closing will be what happens to the land under the century-old *congerie* [read *congeries*] of industrial buildings" (*N.Y. Times*).

In fact, although the singular *congeries* is most frequent, it can also be a plural—e.g.: "I learned [economic theory] all as *congeries* of interrelated propositions" (H.W. Arndt, *A Course Through Life: Memoirs of an Australian Economist*, 1985).

The word is pronounced /**kon**-jə-reez/, /kən-**jir**-eez/, or /kon-jə-**reez**/ in AmE; and /kən-**jeer**-eez/ or /kən-**jeer**-ee-eez/ in BrE.

Congress does not require an article, except in references to a specific session <the 104th Congress>. Although some congressional insiders use the phrase, *the Congress* is a quirk to be avoided in polished prose. The possessive form is preferably *Congress's*—e.g.: "Ms. Rosen said it is *Congress's* responsibility because it gave regulators the framework for RESPA" (*Nat'l Mortgage News*). See POSSESSIVES (A).

Congressperson is unnecessary for *representative*, *congressional representative*, *member of Congress*, *Congressman*, or *Congresswoman*. E.g.: "Be sure to check out the upcoming vote on the amendment just to see if your *congressperson* [read *representative*] has the guts to vote against something enormously popular and incredibly dumb" (*Idaho Statesman*). See SEXISM (C).

CONJUNCTIONS, CORRELATIVE. See CORRELATIVE CONJUNCTIONS.

connive = (1) to avoid noticing something that one should oppose or condemn; or (2) to conspire or cooperate secretly. Sense 1 is the original and the better one—e.g.: "Edward Heath railroaded Britain's entry into Europe through Parliament, courtesy of revolting Labour Europhile MPs who cheerfully *connived* at the deception Heath was perpetrating upon British voters" (*Observer*).

Because sense 2 is the product of SLIPSHOD EXTENSION, it can usually be improved on—e.g.: "A shipment of Norton McNaughton shirts and jackets still bore their original tags and enough unscrupulous shoppers *connived* [read *managed*] to get 'refunds' at department stores that some of Pittsburgh's better department stores called to complain" (*Pitt. Bus. Times & J.*).

connote. See **denote (A).**

consequently. See **subsequently (B).**

consider, when used alone, most often means "to think of as being" <she considered him rude>. The phrasing *consider as* is usually redundant. It has only one legitimate use, when meaning "to treat as for certain purposes" <this Dylan song, when considered as poetry, is a masterpiece>. It's usually desirable to drop *as* from *consider as*—e.g.: "The drug Depo Provera inhibits the sex drive and has been *considered as* [read *considered*] a kind of 'chemical castration' for chronic offenders" (*St. Louis Post-Dispatch*).

considerable, used adverbially, is dialectal—e.g.: "[G]uys such as Gwynn admitt[ed] that Montreal's defeat at Atlanta on the scoreboard was of *considerable* [read *considerably*] more interest than the Chargers' score updates against the Raiders" (*L.A. Times*).

considering. For this word as an acceptable dangling modifier, see DANGLERS (E).

consist in; consist of. American writers too often ignore the distinction. *Consist of* is used in reference to materials; it precedes the physical elements that compose a tangible thing. The well-worn example is that cement *consists of* sand, gravel, and mortar. *Consist in* (= has as its essence) precedes abstract elements or qualities, or intangible things. Thus, a good moral character *consists in* integrity, decency, fairness, and compassion.

console. See **condole.**

consul; counsel; council. *Consul* = a governmental representative living in a foreign country to oversee commercial matters. *Counsel* = a legal adviser or group of legal advisers. (See **counsel.**) *Council* = a body of representatives.

consult, as an intransitive verb, takes the preposition *with* (another person), or *on* or *about* (a matter). The verb may also be used transitively <to consult the document itself>.

consummate has one pronunciation as adjective /kən-**səm**-it/ and another as verb /**kon**-sə-mayt/. To pronounce the word /**kon**-sə-mət/ as an adjective is acceptable, but that pronunciation has long been considered an inferior one.

contact, v.t. Though vehemently objected to in the 1950s, *contact* is now firmly ensconced as a verb. Brevity recommends it over *get in touch with* or *communicate with*; it should not be considered stylistically infelicitous even in formal contexts. E.g.: "One former Palatine village official *contacted* during the investigation called the BGA report a 'sleazy witch hunt' " (*Chicago Sun-Times*)./ "The Goodmans *contacted* Searle and presented him with a detailed record of their claim to the painting" (*Time*).

If, however, the writer means either *call* or *write*, the specific verb is preferable.

contagious; infectious. These words are misused even by educated writers and speakers. A *contagious* disease is communicable by direct contact with those suffering from it. An *infectious* disease spreads by contact with the germs, as in the air or in water. Some *contagious* diseases are not *infectious,* and vice versa.

contemn. See **condemn.**

contemplative is preferably accented on the second syllable: /kən-**tem**-plə-tiv/. But /**kon**-tem-play-tiv/ is acceptable.

contend. See **contest (A).**

content, n. **A. And *contents.*** When referring to written matter or oral presentation, *content* refers to the ideas or thoughts contained (in words) as opposed to the method of presentation. Wilson Follett disapproved the modern tendency to use *content* as well as *contents* for "what is contained" (*MAU*), but the usage is old and is now common. And the DIFFERENTIATION it represents—as explained below—is genuinely helpful.

Whereas *content* invariably refers to nonmaterial things, *contents* refers most commonly to material ingredients—e.g.: "Birthdays, holidays and special occasions, Forman is usually greeted with that flat skinny box that makes no secret of its *contents*" (*New Orleans Times-Picayune*). But sometimes it refers to nonmaterial ingredients, especially when the suggestion is that many items are being considered—e.g.: "Kirkland police improperly kept secret the *contents* of a crime report on Northeast District Judge Rosemary Bordlemay and were ordered by a court to release the document" (*Seattle Times*).

B. And *contentment.* In the sense "the fact or condition of being fully satisfied (i.e., contented)," the word *contentment* is now standard. *Content* is reserved for a single idiom: *to (one's) heart's content.* But as an adjective it is frequent—e.g.: "She was *content* with her arrangement."

contest, v.t. **A. And *contend.*** In the sense "to fight (for)," *contest* is almost always transitive <to contest an election>, and *contend* is intransitive <to contend against an opponent>. *Contend* may be transitive when it means "to maintain, assert" and is followed by *that* <the striking workers contend that the pension fund is inadequate>.

B. Pronunciation. The noun is pronounced /**kon**-test/; the verb is pronounced /kən-**test**/.

context of, in the; in a . . . context. These phrases are often used superfluously. "During the seventh century B.C., Egypt was repeatedly though always briefly occupied by Assyrian armies and *later infiltrated by Greek and other Aegean elements in a military and subsequently a commercial context* [read *later infiltrated militarily and then commercially by Greek and other Aegean elements*]."

contextual is so spelled. But the mistaken form *contextural* has arisen from the false analogy of *texture/textural*—e.g.: "Amazingly, American television, including San Francisco's KQED, has passed on this strong, *contextural* [read *contextual*] documentary, made for British TV by independent filmmaker Micha X. Peled" (*S.F. Examiner*). For a similar mistake, see **contractual.**

contiguous means not merely "close to" or "near," but "abutting; sharing a boundary" <contiguous parking spaces>. It is commonly misused in the phrase *the 48 contiguous states,* which is illogical: only a few states can be *contiguous* to one another. (And *neighboring* is surely better than *contiguous*—it's more down-to-earth.) Technically speaking, the proper way to put the idea would be *the 48 conterminous states* or *the continental United States.*

Contiguous to for *next to* is sometimes a pomposity. *Contiguous* should always be construed with *to*—not *with.*

continual; continuous. *Continual* = frequently recurring; intermittent. E.g.: "And [the police are] removing [the homeless]—by police rides to the edge of town, by *continual* issuing of citations for camping, by mass towing of vehicles and by routine discarding of people's belongings" (*USA Today*). *Continuous* = occurring without interruption; unceasing. E.g.: "Crow Canyon archaeologists want to study the 12th- and 13th-century village to determine exactly when it was inhabited and whether it was occupied *continuously* or intermittently" (*Santa Fe New Mexican*). A good mnemonic device is to think of the *-ous* ending as being short for "one uninterrupted sequence."

The two words are frequently confused, usually with *continuous* horning in where *continual* belongs—e.g.: "*Continuous* [read *Continual*] interruptions are frustrating because *it often means* [read *they often mean*] you have to warm up all over again or don't get a complete workout" (*Montgomery Advertiser*)./ "The antidepressant Prozac has been in the news *almost continuously* [read *continually*] since it was introduced in Belgium in 1986" (*Tampa Trib.*).

continue on is a minor but bothersome prolixity—e.g.: "As he *continued on and on* [read *went on and on* or *continued*], uninterrupted by me, he proceeded to answer his own objections" (*Indianapolis Bus. J.*).

continuous. See **continual.**

CONTRACTIONS. A. Generally. Many writers, especially those who write in formal situations, feel uncomfortable with contractions. And perhaps contractions don't generally belong in scholarly journals.

But why shouldn't writers use them in most other types of writing? Some excellent writers use contractions to good effect, even in books—e.g.:

- "The ideal book reviewer['s] . . . own literary quality should be obvious in his prose. If he is an academic, he *shouldn't* allow this to show through" (Joseph Epstein, "Reviewing and Being Reviewed," in *Plausible Prejudices: Essays on American Writing*, 1985).
- "*It's* no longer the sheepish effusions that score for Byron, but his goatish satires and letters" (John Simon, *The Sheep from the Goats: Selected Literary Essays*, 1989).
- "Deep-seated conflict in the North was another story—it *wasn't* supposed to exist" (Nicholas Lemann, *The Promised Land*, 1991).
- "Victims *don't* occupy a higher moral plane. *They've* just suffered more" (Jonathan Rosen, "The Trivialization of Tragedy," in *Dumbing Down: Essays on the Strip Mining of American Culture*, 1996).

The common fear is that using contractions can make the writing seem breezy. For most of us, though, that risk is nil. What you gain should be a relaxed sincerity—not breeziness. Among the wisest words on the subject are these:

- "Don't start using . . . contractions . . . at every single opportunity from here on. It's not as simple as that. Contractions have to be used with care. Sometimes they fit, sometimes they don't. It depends on whether you would use the contraction in speaking *that particular sentence* (e.g. in this sentence I would say *you would* and not *you'd*). It also depends on whether the contraction would help or hinder the rhythm that would suit your sentence for proper emphasis. So don't try to be consistent about this; it doesn't work. You have to go by feel, not by rule" (Rudolf Flesch, *The Art of Readable Writing*, 1949).
- "Such common contractions as *it's, that's, they're,* and *she'll* are correct in almost all written communications in business and the professions. Whether or not you choose to use them is a matter of personal preference" (David W. Ewing, *Writing for Results in Business, Government, and the Professions*, 1974).
- "Use occasional contractions. They'll keep you from taking yourself too seriously, tell your reader that you're not a prude, and help you achieve a more nat-

ural, conversational rhythm in your style" (John R. Trimble, *Writing with Style*, 1975).

B. Ill-Advised Forms. While you can use contractions such as *can't, don't,* and *you'll* to good advantage, you may stumble if you contract recklessly. A few contractions that occur in speech don't translate well into writing because they're not instantly readable—the mind's tongue trips over them, however briefly. Examples of ones generally to avoid include *it'd, would've, should've,* and *who're*.

The form *who're* is particularly ugly: "How is it that many people *who're* [read *who are*] convinced that Oliver Stone's *JFK* was a documentary about a right-wing plot to get Jack Kennedy are satisfied that Vincent Foster's peculiar death in Fort Marcy Park was an open-and-shut case of suicide?" (*Ariz. Republic*).

C. Mispronounced Contractions. See PRONUNCIATION (B).

contractual is sometimes erroneously written (or pronounced) *contractural*, with an intrusive *-r-*. E.g.: "KCTS refused to release the budget figures, citing *contractural* [read *contractual*] obligations" (*Seattle Times*). For a similar mistake, see **contextual.**

contrast. A. Prepositions with. One *contrasts* something *with*—not *to*—something else. But it's permissible to write either *in contrast to* or *in contrast with*.

B. *Compare and contrast.* This is an English teacher's REDUNDANCY. See **compare.**

C. Pronunciation. As a noun, *contrast* is accented on the first syllable: /**kon**-trast/. As a verb, it's accented on the second syllable: /kən-**trast**/.

contribute. For the MALAPROPISM in which this word is confused with *attribute*, vb., see **attribute.**

controller. See **comptroller.**

controversial is preferably pronounced /kon-trə-**vər**-shəl/, not the affected /kon-trə-**vər**-see-əl/.

contusion. See **concussion.**

convict, v.t. A person is *convicted of* a crime, *for* the act of committing a crime, or *on* a particular count. But a person is not *convicted in* a crime: "A Palestinian suspected in the bombing of Pan Am Flight 103 was *convicted* today along with three co-defendants *in* [read *for*] a series of attacks in northern Europe four years ago" (*N.Y. Times*).

convince. See **persuade.**

co-op. The shortened form of *cooperative* (= an organization owned by and run for the benefit of those who use its services), *co-op* is hyphenated even though the longer form isn't. Without the hyphen, it looks like a pen for chickens.

COORDINATE ADJECTIVES. See ADJECTIVES (E).

copartner need not exist alongside *partner*. The joint relationship (i.e., that the existence of one partner implies the existence of one or more other partners) is clear to all native speakers of English. Because *copartner* adds nothing to the language, it should be avoided as a NEEDLESS VARIANT. E.g.: "In her firm, which she shares with Amy Newman, Rakinic feels it's a plus having a woman as a *copartner* [read *partner*]" (*Legal Intelligencer*).

COPULAS, ADVERBS OR ADJECTIVES AFTER. See ADVERBS (C).

copy, v.t., in the sense "to send a copy to" <he copied me with the letter>, is a voguish casualism to be avoided in formal contexts—e.g.: "It is therefore legitimate to *copy* [read *send a copy to*] the recipient's boss" (Mark H. McCormack, *What They Don't Teach You at Harvard Business School*, 1984).

copyright, n. & vb., is so spelled. *Copywrite* is a not infrequent mistake for the verb—e.g.: "You said you didn't know the author's name. Well, she's Portia Nelson, and her piece was *copywritten* [read *copyrighted*] in 1985" (*Chicago Sun-Times*)./ "Most of the really vicious stuff said, sung and written these days is the work of professional scumbags, syndicated, *copywrited* [read *copyrighted*], mass-marketed and protected by free-speech guarantees" (*Denver Post*).

Still another mistake is *copywright*—e.g.: "Barsky is a partner in Sonnenschein Nath & Rosenthal, where he practices and specializes in intellectual property, trademark and *copywright* [read *copyright*] matters" (*St. Louis Post-Dispatch*). For a similar error, see **playwrighting.**

cord. See **chord.**

corps. The singular *corps* is pronounced /kor/. The plural form—also spelled *corps*—is pronounced /korz/.

correctitude; correctness. *Correctitude* is a PORTMANTEAU WORD—a blend of *correct* and *rectitude.* It refers to what is proper in conduct or behavior, and it has moralistic overtones. E.g.: "It is to Henry VIII that Prince Charles owes the monarchy's anomalous position as supreme head of the Church, Defender of the Faith, by which was meant, at the time, the Catholic faith, in all its Catholic *correctitudes*" (*Evening Standard*).

Correctness serves as the noun corresponding to *correct*, adj., in all other senses. E.g.: "But the U.S. believes there is an inherent *correctness* and conviction in its positions with which the rest of the world invariably should agree" (*Christian Science Monitor*).

CORRELATIVE CONJUNCTIONS, or conjunctions used in pairs, should frame structurally identical sentence parts, sometimes called "matching parts." Simple nouns never cause problems: *both lions and wolves.* When we use constructions with noun phrases and even clauses, however, PARALLELISM may become a problem. Following are examples with some of the more common correlative conjunctions.

A. *Either . . . or.* "But here's where the obscenity surfaces: Whenever a black is hired to run anything in professional sports, the inference is always there that he was hired *either* because of affirmative action *or* because of a fluke" (*Atlanta J. & Const.*). See **either (B).**

B. *Neither . . . nor.* " 'Retire? That's for older fellas,' the former four-term Ohio governor said with a conviction that was *neither* false *nor* boastful" (*Columbus Dispatch*). See **neither . . . nor.**

C. *Both . . . and.* "As with the 1983 news coverage, it is through this sort of presentation that horror video watching becomes *both symptomatic* [read *a symptom*] of sickness *and* the precursor of despicable forms of behavior" (*Guardian*). See **both (A).**

D. Other Correlatives. Some of the other common correlatives in English are:

- *although . . . nevertheless*;
- *although . . . yet*;
- *as . . . as*;
- *if . . . then*;
- *just as . . . so*;
- *not only . . . but also*;
- *notwithstanding . . . yet*;
- *since . . . therefore*;
- *when . . . then*;
- *where . . . there*; and
- *whether . . . or.*

corroborate. A. Senses and Uses. *Corroborate* = (1) to support (a statement, argument, etc.) with evidence that is consistent; to confirm; or (2) to confirm formally (a law, etc.). Sense 1 is more common—e.g.: "Miss McLaughlin has recently declined to comment on the Toys project, but others have *corroborated* her account that the funds were intended for weapons" (*N.Y. Times*).

In either sense, this verb is transitive

<the last witness corroborated the testimony of other witnesses>. Thus, *corroborate with* is inferior to *corroborate*. But in the PASSIVE VOICE, the phrasing *corroborated by* is usual—e.g.: "The novelists Gaskell and Disraeli and Hardy were not so naive, and their realism is *corroborated by* this book" (*Economist*).

B. Pronunciation. In October 1991, during Justice Clarence Thomas's confirmation hearings, Senator Joseph Biden and other members of the Senate Judiciary Committee consistently mispronounced this word as if it were *cooberate*—in other words, *cooperate* with a *-b-* instead of a *-p-*. The correct pronunciation is /kə-**rob**-ə-rayt/.

C. And *collaborate*. The word *corroborate* is occasionally used where *collaborate* (= to work jointly with [another] in producing) belongs—e.g.: "The family *corroborated* [read *collaborated*] on a project to replicate a 1705 microscope" (*Ariz. Republic/Phoenix Gaz.*).

The opposite error (*collaborate* for *corroborate*) is also all too frequent—e.g.: "A testing specialist *collaborated* [read *corroborated*] personal testimony that blacks normally score lower on written examinations than whites" (*Tennessean*).

D. Corresponding Adjective. *Corroborate* makes *corroborable*, not *corroboratable*. See -ATABLE.

could. See **can (B).**

couldn't care less is the correct and logical phrasing, not *could care less*—e.g.: "The American people *could care less* [read *couldn't care less*] who's White House Chief of Staff" (George Will, on *This Week with David Brinkley*, 1994). If you could care some, that means you must care. In other words, if you could care less, you're saying that you do care. Invariably, though, writers and speakers who use the phrase mean that they don't care at all.

Although some apologists argue that *could care less* is meant to be sarcastic and not to be taken literally, a more plausible explanation is that the *-n't* of *couldn't* has been rubbed out in sloppy speech and sloppy writing. See ILLOGIC (A).

could of. See **of (D).**

council. See **consul.**

counsel (= a legal adviser or group of legal advisers) may be either singular or plural. Although in law it's usually plural, examples of the singular are common enough—e.g.: "*Counsel* arguing a case is permitted to assert that a precedent has had unhappy consequences" (Michael Zander, *The Law-Making Process*, 1985).

More typically, *counsel* is used as a plural—e.g.: "Dickstein, Shapiro & Morin, one of Washington's largest law firms, said yesterday that it has hired 13 partners and three *counsel* and made offers to more than 20 associate attorneys from Anderson Kill Olick & Oshinsky" (*Wash. Post*).

Counsels is sometimes mistakenly used as a plural of *counsel*—especially when nonlawyers are writing about the law. Part of this tendency comes from the popularization of the phrases *independent counsel* and *general counsel*. At the federal level, there are occasionally calls for *an independent counsel* to be appointed. And if two are needed, the tendency is to say *two independent counsels*. That makes the third example below understandable—even acceptable—but it doesn't excuse the first two:

- "[T]his might seem a strange approach for *counsels* [read *counsel*] responsible for representing not just Valeo and Henshaw but the interests of their employers, the U.S. House and Senate, as well" (Barbara H. Craig, *Chadha: The Story of an Epic Constitutional Struggle*, 1988).
- "[F]our lawyers were named Nov. 25 to serve as legal *counsels* [read *counsel*] for the transition" (*Nat'l L.J.*).

• "Independent *counsels* were created under a 1978 law that Congress allowed to expire in 1992" (*USA Today*).

COUNT NOUNS AND MASS NOUNS. Count nouns are those that denote enumerable things, and that are capable of forming plurals (e.g., *cranes, parties, minivans, oxen*); mass (noncount) nouns are often abstract nouns—they cannot be enumerated (e.g., *insurance, courage, mud*). Many nouns can be both count <he gave several talks> and mass <talk is cheap>, depending on the sense. These are few, however, in comparison to the nouns that are exclusively either count or mass. Use of these two types of nouns may implicate problems with number, especially when the use of count nouns strays into a use of mass nouns or vice versa. See PLURALS (I).

coup de grâce /koo-de-**grahs**/ means a "blow of grace," a compassionate act that puts a mortally wounded person or animal out of misery. The phrase is sometimes mispronounced /koo-de-**grah**/, as if the last word were spelled *gras* (as in *pâté de foie gras*). But worse than that, the phrase is occasionally written *coup de gras*—e.g.: "Keith pulled up and hit a wide-open Chris Federico for the *coup de gras* [read *coup de grâce*] and a 19–7 lead with 6:50 remaining in the game" (*Denver Post*). Even the sense is sometimes mangled. To make *coup de grâce* cruel, bloody, and painful is to torture the phrase—e.g.: "I saw a fox being torn to pieces by a pack of hounds. It was the final act, *the coup de gras* [delete erroneous phrase] in what we call a country sport" (*Evening Standard*).

couple, n. See COLLECTIVE NOUNS.

coupled with, like *together with* and *accompanied by*, results in a singular and not a plural verb when the first of the two nouns is singular. See SUBJECT–VERB AGREEMENT (E).

couple (of) dozen, hundred, etc. Omitting the *of* is slipshod in such a construction as this: "Is a used toilet seat worth $1 million? Or even a *couple* [read *couple of*] hundred thousand dollars?" (*N.Y. Times*). (Cf. **type of.**) In other words, using *couple* not as a noun but as an adjective is poor usage: instead of *a couple days ago*, say *a couple of days ago*.

For just the opposite tendency—the intrusive *of*—see **of (B).**

coupon should be pronounced /**koo**-pon/, not /**kyoo**-pon/. The mispronunciation betrays an ignorance of French and of the finer points of English. Imagine *coup d'etat* pronounced with /kyoo/ as the first syllable. See PRONUNCIATION (B).

court-martial. A. Generally. *Court-martial* (= an ad hoc military court convened to try and to punish those who violate military law) is hyphenated both as noun and as verb. The *OED* lists the verb as colloquial, an observation now antiquated. As to spelling, in AmE the final *-l* is not doubled in *court-martialed* and *court-martialing*, although in BrE it is. (See SPELLING (B).)

The plural of the noun is *courts-martial*. See PLURALS (F).

B. And *court marshal.* One meaning of *marshal* is "a judicial officer who provides court security, executes process, and performs other tasks for the court" (*Black's Law Dictionary* [pocket ed. 1996]). It's therefore not surprising that *court marshal* has become a frequent phrase—e.g.: "He became *court marshal* in 1989 and would start each court session by calling, 'Oyez, oyez'" (*Charleston Gaz.*).

Not surprisingly, therefore, the phrase *court-martial* is now often mistakenly written *court marshal*—e.g.: "[A] lieutenant gave him a summary *court marshal* [read *court-martial*], fined him $25 and booted him out of headquarters" (*Anchorage Daily News*).

couth, a BACK-FORMATION from *uncouth,* has never been accepted by authorities as a proper word.

covert was traditionally pronounced like *covered,* except with a *-t* at the end: /**kəv**-ərt/. Still, /**koh**-vərt/, nearly rhyming with *overt* (but for the stress), is the more common pronunciation in AmE nowadays.

coyote is, strictly speaking, pronounced /kɪ-**yoh**-tee/. But in the western United States, the pronunciation /**kɪ**-oht/ is often heard.

crane, v.t., = (1) to lift as if by a machine made for the purpose; or (2) to stretch (one's neck) for the purpose of seeing better. The word is sometimes wrongly written *crain,* which isn't a word—e.g.: "Restrained by yellow ropes and signs that read, 'Please Look, Don't Touch,' spectators *crained* [read *craned*] necks to get a few glimpses of the car's spotless interior" (*N.Y. Newsday*). This blunder obscures the metaphor in the phrase *to crane one's neck,* as the long-necked bird does when reaching out.

crape. See **crepe.**

crappie (= a freshwater sunfish found in the central and eastern United States) is the standard spelling. *Croppie* is a variant form, which is closer to a phonetic spelling. Both words are pronounced /**kro**-pee/.

crawfish; crayfish. Although *crayfish* has traditionally been considered standard AmE—and *crawfish* a dialectal variant—things have changed. With the rise in popularity of Cajun cuisine in the 1980s came a general awareness of such dishes as *crawfish étouffée.* And today, most people who buy the freshwater product for cooking call it *crawfish.* But in other contexts—for example, among zoologists—*crayfish* remains standard. *Crawdad,* another dialectal variant, is still current in parts of the South.

credible; creditable; credulous. *Credible* = believable <a credible story>. *Creditable* = worthy of credit; laudable <creditable goals>. *Credulous* = gullible; tending to believe <the credulous fools were taken in by the ruse>.

credulity (= gullibility) should not be confused with *credibility* (= believability), as it is in the phrase *it strains credulity*—e.g.: "And in all honesty, the story veers into an over-the-top territory that strains *credulity* [read *credibility*]" (*USA Today*).

crepe; crape. A *crepe* (/krep/ or /krayp/) is either a thin, French-style pancake or a type of thin crinkled fabric. In the pancake sense, *crêpe* often appears thus, with the circumflex. (See DIACRITICAL MARKS.) A *crape* (/krayp/) is a band made of that fabric and worn around the arm as a sign of mourning. *Crape myrtle,* not *crepe,* is the correct spelling of the tree (actually a shrub) *Lagerstroemia indica.*

crisis forms the plural *crises,* not *crisises*—e.g.: "Earlier this year, the Organization of African Unity (OAU) discussed setting up a rapid intervention force for such *crisises* [read *crises*] but shelved the idea" (*Christian Science Monitor*).

criterion. A. And the Plural Form *criteria.* *Criteria* is the plural, *criterion* the (originally Greek) singular. A Ph.D. in linguistics once defended *criteria* as a singular because "not everyone knows that the singular is *criterium*"! (See (C).) The plural *criterions* was tried for a time but failed to become standard. (Infrequently, though not infrequently enough, one even sees *criterias.*) Here are the correct forms: "The commission . . . has published its *criteria* for eligibility. Its central, repeated *criterion* for participation in the debates: 'the realistic chance of being elected' " (*Cincinnati Enquirer*)./ "Melissa Knierim wants an opera house in the Poconos, and if determination and hard work are the *criteria* for getting one, order your tickets now" (*Allentown Morning Call*).

But writers often want to make *criteria* a singular—e.g.: "Grade your business from 'A' to 'F' on each *criteria* [read *criterion*] (but with a numeric value where A=4.0 and C=2.0, etc.)" (*Ariz. Bus. Gaz.*). Cf. **media & phenomenon.** See PLURALS (B).

B. *Criterion* Misused as a Plural. Oddly, perhaps because *criteria* is so often wrongly thought to be a singular, the correct singular and plural forms have—in some writers' minds—done something of a role reversal. Thus, *criterion* is sometimes incorrectly used as a plural form—e.g.: "A state law adopted in 1959 outlines many *criterion* [read *criteria*] for consolidation, but no communities have ever met all the *criterion* [read *criteria*]" (*Wis. State J.*).

C. And *criterium*. Since about 1970, *criterium* has denoted "a bicycle race of a specified number of laps on a closed course over public roads closed to normal traffic" (*W10*). The word was borrowed from the French, in which *critérium* means "competition." E.g.: "Jonathan [Page], 17, won the 72-mile road race and placed fourth and fifth, respectively, in the *criterium* and the time trials in the 17- and 18-year-old division at the national junior cycling championships" (*Sports Illustrated*). The plural of *criterium* in the sense just given is *criteriums*, not *criteria*.

Occasionally, writers confuse *criterium* with *criterion*—e.g.: "My sole *criterium* [read *criterion*] was this: Did he make a difference?" (*Charleston Gaz.*).

critique, n. & v.t. Until recently, this word was almost always a noun. But in the mid-20th century, the verb became quite common as a neutral equivalent to the word *criticize*, which had by then acquired negative connotations. In fact, though, the verb *critique* dates from the mid-18th century.

crow, v.i. A cock *crows*. But if you want to describe what a cock has already done, do you say *crowed* or *crew*? The modern preference is for *crowed*—e.g.: "Above the din of car horns, a cock *crowed*" (*Boston Globe*). Occasionally, *crew* pops up in allusion to the King James Version—e.g.: "And immediately the cock *crew*." Matthew 26:74. Or sometimes the writer needs a rhyme, as in the following title: "When the Cock *Crew*, the Neighbors Started to Sue" (*Smithsonian*).

crummy; crumby. When the meaning is "worthless" or "inferior," the spelling is *crummy*. When the meaning is "consisting of or giving off crumbs," the spelling is *crumby*. But some writers err by using *crumby* when they mean *crummy*—e.g.: "You . . . are on the highway unsuccessfully trying to get them off with the *crumby* [read *crummy*] wrench that came with your car" (*N.Y. Newsday*).

cuckoo (= silly, crazy) is sometimes misspelled *coocoo*—e.g.: "I assumed Mr. Nelson's prolonged isolation had brought on that endemic Maine malady known sometimes as *cabin-coocoo* [read *cabin-cuckoo*] and sometimes as woods-nutty" (*Christian Science Monitor*).

cue; queue. A. As Nouns. Though pronounced the same, these words have different meanings. *Cue* = a signal to begin; a hint; or (2) a stick used in billiards, pool, or shuffleboard. *Queue* = (1) a line of persons or things waiting their turn; or (2) a hanging braid of hair.

Not surprisingly, the two are sometimes confused—e.g.: "Like most birds, teal don't start their migration based on air temperatures, but take their *queue* [read *cue*] to head south from the shortening hours of daylight" (*New Orleans Times-Picayune*).

B. *Cue up*; *queue up*. To *cue up* a videotape, an audiotape, or a compact disc is to have it ready for playing at a particular point. E.g.: "You can bet your remote control clicker that every network has already *cued up* video of the glowering Dole, eyes flitting, hanging that warmonger tag on an astonished Mondale" (*Boston Globe*).

To *queue up* is to line up. E.g.: "On my way to a week's cruise in the Galapagos on the Albatros, a luxurious 80-foot dive boat, I *queued up* in the airport in Quito, Ecuador" (*S.F. Examiner*).

cuisine is pronounced /kwi-**zeen**/ or /kwee-**zeen**/, not /kyoo-**zeen**/.

cultivable; cultivatable. The first predominates in AmE usage, being nearly four times more common than *cultivatable*, which has become a NEEDLESS VARIANT—e.g.: "Kenneth Hobbie, president and CEO of the U.S. Feed Grains Council in Washington, said that by 2050, Asia will have nine times more people than the Western Hemisphere per *cultivatable* [read *cultivable*] acre" (*Omaha World Herald*). See -ATABLE.

cultured; cultivated. Correctly, the former is used of the person, the latter of the mind. A *cultured* person has refined tastes; a *cultivated* mind is well trained and highly developed.

cummerbund (= a wide waistband worn with tuxedos and other formal dress) is the standard spelling. *Kummerbund* is a variant form. *Cummerbun* and *cumberbun* are simply errors—e.g.: "Long, elegant dresses, bow ties, *cummerbuns* [read *cummerbunds*] and corsages" (*Reading Times & Eagle*).

cumquat. See **kumquat.**

curriculum. Pl. *curricula* or *curriculums*. The Latin plural is slightly more common, but the English version may be gaining ground. E.g.: "To accommodate the semester conversion, some *curriculums* will be revised" (*Greensboro News & Record*)./ "Schools stressing rote memorization, rigid *curriculums*, and obedience to authority have produced disciplined and politically docile workers" (*BusinessWeek*). See PLURALS (B).

curtail means "to cut back," not "to stop completely." Therefore, the phrases *completely curtailed*, *totally curtailed*, and similar others are misuses—e.g.: "Their halcyon days of wine and roses, if not *totally curtailed* [read, perhaps, *totally over*], certainly would be cramped beyond recognition" (*St. Petersburg Times*). But *curtail* is the right word when there is only a scaling back—e.g.: "Banking and government offices will be closed or services *curtailed* in the following countries and their dependencies this week because of national and religious holidays" (*L.A. Times*).

CURTAILED WORDS. See BACK-FORMATIONS.

cut-and-dried, the age-old PHRASAL ADJECTIVE, is sometimes wrongly written *cut-and-dry*—e.g.: "The gift dilemma is further complicated currently by companies' increased activity in international markets, where the ethical questions tend to be much less *cut-and-dry* [read *cut-and-dried*]" (*Electronic Buyers' News*).

-CY. See -CE.

cyclops. Pl. *cyclopses* /**sɪ**-klop-səz/ or *cyclopes* /**sɪ**-klə-peez/. The classically formed plural, *cyclopes*, still predominates in modern usage. But *cyclopses* is becoming common—e.g.: "We are bombarded with vainglorious descriptions and fantastic illustrations of dragons, giants, *cyclopses*, griffins (lashed to a flying machine), the anthropophagi and men whose heads grow beneath their shoulders" (*Fin. Times*). It's wrong, by the way, to try to make *cyclops* itself into a plural—e.g.: "I remember . . . several *cyclops* [read *cyclopses* or *cyclopes*] and a fire-breathing dragon" (*Toronto Star*).

czar; tsar. The spelling *czar* is overwhelmingly predominant. *Tsar*, though closer to the Russian form, is archaic.

D

-'D. See -ED.

dachshund is pronounced /**dahk**-sənd/ or /**daks**-huunt/. It's occasionally mispronounced /**dash**-ənd/, and it's occasionally misspelled *daschund* or *dachsund*.

damp, v.t.; **dampen.** Both may mean "to make damp, moisten," but each word carries at least one additional sense. *Damp* = (1) to stifle or extinguish <damp the furnace>; or (2) to deaden the vibration of (a piano string). *Dampen* = to check, diminish, or depress <the news of Mr. Ratliff's illness dampened our spirits>. The words sometimes overlap in these additional senses, but they are best kept distinct.

dandruff is sometimes misspelled *dandriff*.

DANGLERS. A. Generally. So-called "danglers" are ordinarily unattached participles—either present participles (ending in *-ing*) or past participles (ending usually in *-ed*)—that do not relate syntactically to the nouns they are supposed to modify. That is, when the antecedent of a participle doesn't appear where it logically should, the participle is said to "dangle"—e.g.: "*Watching* from the ground below, the birds flew ever higher until they disappeared." In effect, the participle tries to sever its relationship with its noun or pronoun and thus to become functionally a preposition. Gerunds may also dangle precariously—e.g.: "By *watching* closely, the birds became visible." (See (D).) Usually, recasting the sentence will remedy the ambiguity, ILLOGIC, or incoherence: "Watching from the ground below, we saw the birds fly higher until they disappeared."/ "By watching closely, we were able to see the birds."

Most danglers are ungrammatical. In the normal word order, a participial phrase beginning a sentence ("Walking down the street,") should be followed directly by the noun acting as subject in the main clause ("I saw the house"). When that word order is changed, as by changing the verb in the main clause to the PASSIVE VOICE, the sentence becomes illogical or misleading: "Walking down the street, the house was seen." It was not the house that was walking, but the speaker.

Some danglers, though, are acceptable because of long-standing usage. Examples are easy to come by: "*Considering* the current atmosphere in the legislature, the bill probably won't pass." But avoiding the dangler would often improve the style: "With the current atmosphere in the legislature, the bill probably won't pass." Several other examples are discussed below in (E).

B. Present-Participial Danglers. In the sentences that follow, mispositioned words have caused grammatical blunders. The classic example occurs when the wrong noun begins the main clause, that is, a noun other than the one expected by the reader after digesting the introductory participial phrase. E.g.: "The newspaper said that *before being treated* for their injuries, *General Mladic* forced them to visit the wards of wounded at the Pale hospital, telling them, 'here's what you have done' and 'you have also killed children' " (*N.Y. Times*). That wording has General Mladic being treated for others' injuries. Thus, danglers are a type of bad thinking. See ILLOGIC (C).

Another manifestation of this error is to begin the main clause with an expletive (e.g., *it* or *there*) after an introductory participial phrase:

- "*Applying* those principles to the present situation, *it* is clear that the company must reimburse its employee." (A possible revision: *If we apply these principles to the present situation, it becomes clear that* . . . . Or better: *Given those principles, the company must* . . . .)

- "*Turning* to England, *it* ought to be noted first that that country, though late in doing so, participated fully in the medieval development sketched above" (Grant Gilmore & Charles L. Black, Jr., *The Law of Admiralty*, 1975). (A possible revision: *Although England was late in doing so, it participated fully in the medieval development sketched above.*)
- "*After reviewing* the aforementioned strategies, *it* becomes clear that there is no conclusive evidence regarding their success" (*SAM Advanced Mgmt. J.*). (A possible revision: *Even a detailed review of those strategies provides no conclusive evidence about how successful they are.*)

As in that last example, danglers occurring after an introductory word are just as bad but are harder for the untrained eye to spot—e.g.: "I have always found John Redwood thoughtful, intelligent and rather convivial. I sincerely hope that we can remain friends after the dust has settled. He has conducted a skilled campaign. Yet, *being* a thoughtful man, I suspect that in his heart of hearts he wishes some of his supporters . . . would just disappear" (*Independent*). (The writer here seems to attest to his own thoughtfulness. A possible revision: *Yet because he is a thoughtful man, I suspect that in his heart of hearts* . . . .)

C. Past-Participial Danglers. These are especially common when the main clause begins with a possessive—e.g.: "*Born* on March 12, 1944, in Dalton, Georgia, Larry Lee Simms's qualifications" (Barbara H. Craig, *Chadha: The Story of an Epic Constitutional Struggle*, 1988). (Simms's qualifications were not born on March 12—*he* was. A possible revision: *Born on March 12, 1944, in Dalton, Georgia, Larry Lee Simms had qualifications that* . . . .)

D. Dangling Gerunds. These are close allies to dangling participles, but here the participle acts as a noun rather than as an adjective when it is the object of a preposition: "*By instead examining* the multigenerational ethnic group, *it* becomes clear that the Irish had fully adjusted to American society by the time of the First World War" (*Canadian Hist. Rev.*). (A possible revision: *By instead examining the multigenerational ethnic group, we see that the Irish* . . . .)/ "*Without belaboring* the point, *the central premise* of this article is that the average pharmacist, preparing myriad prescriptions each day, does not have the time to provide CPS" (*Drug Topics*). (A possible revision: *In brief, the central premise of this article* . . . .)

E. Acceptable Danglers, or Disguised Conjunctions. Any number of present participles have been used as conjunctions or prepositions for so long that they have lost the participial duty of modifying specific nouns. In effect, the clauses they introduce are adverbial, standing apart from and commenting on the content of the sentence. Among the commonest of these are *according, assuming, barring, concerning, considering, judging, owing, regarding, respecting, speaking, taking* (usu. *account of, into account*). Thus:

- "Horticulturally *speaking*, the best way to prune the tree is probably to remove some of the lowest branches by cutting them off at the trunk" (*Seattle Times*).
- "*Assuming* everyone shows up who's supposed to (not a given in this sport of last-minute scratches), this could be the finest assemblage of talent for a Long Island road race in a decade" (*N.Y. Newsday*).
- "*Considering* how hated Belichick was in Cleveland, it's incredible that another owner would want him as a head coach" (*Houston Chron.*).

F. Ending Sentences with Danglers. Traditionally, grammarians frowned on *all* danglers, but during the 20th century they generally loosened the strictures for a participial construction at the end of a sentence. Early-20th-century grammarians might have disapproved of the following sentences, but such sentences have long been considered acceptable: "Sarah stepped to the door, looking for her friend."/ "Tom's arm hung useless, broken by the blow." Usually, as in the first example, the end-of-the-sentence dangler is introduced by a so-called "coordinating participle": *looking* is equivalent to *and looked*. Similarly:

- "Vexed by these frequent demands upon her time, she finally called upon her friend, *imploring* him to come to her aid." (*Imploring = and implored.*)
- "The New Orleans–bound steamer rammed and sank the freighter ten miles from its destination, *sending* her to the bottom in 10 minutes." (*Sending = and sent.*)
- "She died before her brother, *leaving* a husband and two children." (*Leaving = and left.*)

A few editors would consider each of those participles misattached, but in fact they are acceptable as coordinating participles. As for the few who object, what would they do with the following sentence: "The boy ran out of the house *crying*"?

DASHES. There are two kinds of dashes, which printers are able to distinguish by their length: the em-dash and the en-dash.

A. Em-Dash [—]. This dash, which is as wide as the capital *M*, is used to mark an interruption in the structure of a sentence. In typewriting, it is commonly represented by two hyphens, often with a space at each end of the pair (--). A pair of em-dashes can be used to enclose a parenthetical remark or to mark the ending and the resumption of a statement by an interlocutor. E.g.: "The last time I saw him I asked him if he still believed—as he once had written—'that we are at this moment participating in one of the very greatest leaps of the human spirit to a knowledge not only of outside human nature but also of our own deep inward mystery' " (Bill Moyers, Introduction to Joseph Campbell, *The Power of Myth*, 1988).

The em-dash can also be used to replace the colon—e.g.: "On July 22, the company was awarded the largest privatization contract ever for a prison—a 2,048-bed minimum-security facility in Taft, Calif." (*BusinessWeek*)./ "She returned to singing in 1996—after a stroke and complications from diabetes forced her to have both legs amputated" (*Newsweek*).

The em-dash is perhaps the most underused punctuation mark in American writing. Whatever the type of writing, dashes can often clarify a sentence that is clogged up with commas—or even one that's otherwise lusterless. Imagine the following sentences if commas replaced the well-chosen em-dashes:

- "It is noteworthy that the most successful revolutions—that of England in 1688 and that of America in 1776—were carried out by men who were deeply imbued with a respect for law" (Bertrand Russell, "Individual and Social Ethics," 1949).
- "Unfortunately, moral beauty in art—like physical beauty in a person—is extremely perishable" (Susan Sontag, *Against Interpretation*, 1966).
- "When David Nemer sat down with his 12-year-old daughter one night recently to watch a television sitcom—a treat for finishing her homework early—he was shocked by the behavior he saw in his living room" (*L.A. Times*).

Sometimes, perhaps as a result of the ill-founded prejudice against dashes, writers try to make commas function in their place. Often this doesn't work. In fact, the commas can result in a comma splice (one of two types of RUN-ON SENTENCE)—e.g.: "Don't worry about making it pretty, they will do that, just make sure the mathematics is right" (*Newsweek*).

When using dashes, be sure to place the dashes logically so that the PARALLELISM of the sentence remains intact. Sometimes writers put them in odd places—e.g.: "Criminologist Marvin Wolfgang compiled arrest records for every male born—and raised in Philadelphia—in 1945 and 1958" (*Newsweek*). (A possible revision: *Marvin*

Wolfgang, a criminologist, compiled arrest records for every male who was both born in Philadelphia in either of two years—1945 and 1958—and raised there. [On the reason for changing the position of *criminologist* in that sentence, see TITULAR TOMFOOLERY.])

B. En-Dash [–]. The *en-dash,* which is half as wide as an *em-dash,* is distinct (in print) from the *hyphen* and is used to join pairs or groups of words wherever movement or tension, rather than cooperation or unity, is felt. It is often equivalent to *to* or *versus.* In typewriting, it is commonly represented by one hyphen, occasionally with a space at either end (-). E.g.: "The 1914[–]1918 war"; "current[–]voltage characteristic"; "the Dallas[–]Toronto[–]Quebec route"; "the Fischer[–]Spassky match"; "the Marxist[–]Trotskyite split." The en-dash is also used for joint authors—e.g.: "the Prosser[–]Keeton text." But it's not used for one person with a double-barreled name: "the Lloyd-Jones hypothesis" (that's a hyphen, not an en-dash).

In circumstances involving a disjunction, the en-dash is usually preferable to the virgule—e.g.: "If we manage to get that far, the absurdity of attempting to preserve the 19th-century possessive–genitive dichotomy [not *possessive/genitive dichotomy*] will have become apparent."

dastard. *Dastard* (= coward) is commonly muddled because of its sound-association with its harsher rhyme, *bastard.* Although H.W. Fowler insisted that *dastard* should be reserved for one who avoids all personal risk (*MEU1*), modern writers tend to use it as a printable EUPHEMISM for the more widely objectionable epithet—e.g.: "Along with heroes, villains have changed, too. My guys' enemy was always a scheming *dastard* so obsessed with the bottom line that in a modern adventure film he would be the hero" (*Denver Post*).

British writers, on the other hand, have remained truer to the word's original sense—e.g.: "Last week I moved house from London to Brighton but like a genuine spineless *dastard* I flatly denied its implications on personal relationships to the last" (*Times* [London]).

data (/**day**-də/ or /**da**-də/) is a SKUNKED TERM: whether you write *data are* or *data is,* you're likely to make some readers raise their eyebrows. Technically a plural, *data* has, since the 1940s, been increasingly thought of as a mass noun taking a singular verb. But in more or less formal contexts it is preferably treated as a plural—e.g.: "While recent U.S. Census *data* show that the average working woman's pay has declined in the '90s, highly educated, high-paid women keep gaining ground" (*Money*).

Many writers use it as a singular, however, risking their credibility with some readers (concededly a shrinking minority)—e.g.: "But now NRG, hit by charges that its *data isn't* reliable, has some competition" (*Newsweek*)./ "[B]rowsing the World Wide Web these days is less like surfing than like crawling: *data drips* like molasses onto your computer screen, sometimes taking several minutes to create a single page of text" (*Time*). The one context in which the singular use of *data* might be allowed is in computing and allied disciplines. See COMPUTERESE.

In one particular context, though, *data* is rarely treated as a singular: when it begins a clause and is not preceded by the definite article. E.g.: "*Data* over the last two years *suggest* that the rate at which gay men get AIDS has finally begun to flatten out" (*N.Y. Times*).

Datum, the "true" singular, is still sometimes used when a single piece of information is referred to: "Confident that my brain—assuming it had any blood left in it—would react hysterically to any syllables remotely sounding like 'eject,' I took comfort in this *datum*" (*Forbes*). Still, in nonscientific contexts, *datum* is likely to sound pretentious.

As a historian of the English language once put it, "A student with one year of Latin [knows] that *data* and *phenomena* are plural" (Albert C. Baugh, "The Gift of Style," *Pa. B. Ass'n*, 1962). And that's what makes the term skunked: few people use it as a plural, yet many know that it technically is a plural. Whatever you do, if you use *data* in a context in which its number becomes known, you'll bother some of your readers. Perhaps 50 years from now—maybe sooner, maybe later—the term will no longer be skunked: everybody will accept it as a collective. But not yet. See PLURALS (B).

DATES. A. Order. One may unimpeachably write either *May 26, 1994* or *26 May 1994*. The latter—the primarily BrE method—is often better in prose, for it takes no commas. It appears in dates throughout this book.

Of the usual AmE method—*May 26, 1994*—the first editor of the *OED* said: "This is not logical: 19 May 1862 is. *Begin* at day, *ascend* to month, *ascend* to year; not *begin* at month, *descend* to day, then *ascend* to year" (James A.H. Murray, as quoted in *Hart's Rules for Compositors and Readers at the OUP*, 1983).

B. Month and Year. *February 1985* is better than *February of 1985*. There is no need for a comma between the month and the year.

C. As Adjectives. Modern writers have taken to making adjectives out of dates, just as they do out of place names. E.g.: "His July 1998 book contract resulted in a record advance." The more traditional rendering of the sentence would be: "In his book contract of July 1998, he received a record advance." Although occasionally using dates adjectivally is a space-saver, the device should not be overworked: it gives prose a breezy look.

And the practice is particularly clumsy when the day as well as the month is given—e.g.: "The court reconsidered its July 12, 1994 privilege order." Stylists who use this phrasing typically omit the comma after the year—and justifiably so: in the midst of an adjective phrase (i.e., the date), it impedes the flow of the writing too much. Still, that second comma sometimes surfaces—e.g.: "Harvey is accused of murder, robbery and burglary in the *June 16, 1985,* [read *June 16, 1985*] slaying of Irene Schnaps, 37, who suffered 15 blows to the head with a hatchet in her Hunters Glen apartment" (*Newark Star-Ledger*).

D. *1990s* vs. *1990's*. When referring to decades, most professional writers today omit the apostrophe: hence, *1990s* instead of *1990's*. See APOSTROPHE. On whether a decade is singular or plural, see SUBJECT–VERB AGREEMENT (K).

datum. See **data.**

daylight saving(s) time. Although the singular form *daylight saving time* is the original one, dating from the early 20th century—and is preferred by some usage critics—the plural form is now extremely common in AmE. E.g.: "When *daylight savings time* kicks in, a guard will be posted from 5 to 10 p.m." (*New Orleans Times-Picayune*).

The rise of *daylight savings time* appears to have resulted from the avoidance of a MISCUE: when *saving* is used, readers might puzzle momentarily over whether *saving* is a gerund (the saving of daylight) or a participle (the time for saving). Also, of course, we commonly speak of how to "save time" (of saving time), and this compounds the possible confusion. Using *savings* as the adjective—as in *savings account* or *savings bond*—makes perfect sense. More than that, it ought to be accepted as the better form.

Regardless of whether you use the plural or the singular, you can prevent most miscues by hyphenating the PHRASAL ADJECTIVE: *daylight-savings time* or *daylight-saving time*.

de. This particle commonly appears in French names. Two points merit attention. First, *de* should always remain part of the name. Referring to Charles de Gaulle as *Gaulle* or Alexis de Tocqueville as *Tocqueville* is sloppy.

Second, *de* is capitalized only when the name begins a sentence. Thus: "Sooner or later, as *de Tocqueville* remarked" (Alexander M. Bickel, *Politics and the Warren Court*, 1965)./ "*De Tocqueville* early remarked that" (same).

debacle is pronounced /di-**bahk**-əl/ or (less good) /di-**bak**-əl/—not /**deb**-i-kəl/.

debut, v.i., should be avoided as a VOGUE WORD. Even though the *OED* records examples as far back as 1830, the forms *debuted* and *debuting* have an ugly and newfangled look about them. And they're easily mispronounced.

decimate. Originally this word meant "to kill one in every ten," but this etymological sense, because it's so uncommon, has been abandoned except in historical contexts. Now *decimate* generally means "to cause great loss of life; to destroy a large part of." Even allowing that extension in meaning, the word is commonly misused in two ways.

First, the word is sometimes mistakenly applied to a complete obliteration or defeat—e.g.: "Incidentally, this particular cyclamen is one of the species that had been nearly *totally decimated* [read *obliterated*] in its native Mediterranean lands by mindless digging for commercial gain" (*N.Y. Times*)./ "When he did reach Preston Flats the town looked not only uninhabited but deserted, as if plague had swept through and *decimated it* [read *destroyed it* or, perhaps, *killed everybody*]" (Cormac McCarthy, *Outer Dark*, 1968).

Second, the word is misused when it is used lightly of any defeat or setback, however trivial or temporary, especially when applied to inanimate things—e.g.: "The Steelers may be *decimated* [read *hampered* or *plagued*] by injuries, but they possess great depth on defense" (*Boston Herald*)./ "House Republicans have eagerly attacked and, as of last year, effectively *decimated* [read *wiped out*] family-planning funds" (*Cleveland Plain Dealer*).

And sometimes the metaphor is simply inappropriate—e.g.: "He said he had watched lung cancer *decimate* [read *emaciate* or *destroy*?] his sister's body" (*Fresno Bee*).

In fact, though, the word might justifiably be considered a SKUNKED TERM. Whether you stick to the original one-in-ten meaning or use the extended sense, the word is infected with ambiguity. And some of your readers will probably be puzzled or bothered.

declaim; disclaim. To *declaim* is to speak formally in public (hence the adjective *declamatory*). To *disclaim* is to disavow, deny, or renounce (as a manufacturer sometimes does in its warranties).

deduction; induction. *Deduction* is reasoning from a general principle to a specific conclusion. *Induction* is reasoning from many specific observations to a general principle.

defamation; libel; slander. These three terms are distinguished in law. *Defamation* = an attack upon the reputation of another. It encompasses both *libel* (in permanent form, especially writing) and *slander* (in transitory form, especially spoken words).

defective; defectible. See **deficient.**

defense. A. Spelling. *Defense* is AmE; *defence* is BrE (or very antiquated AmE). Modern American writers who use the British spelling are likely to seem affected.

B. Pronunciation. The standard pronunciation has long been with the accent on the second syllable: /di-**fen[t]s**/. But primarily as a result of sports talk, the accent has shifted to the first syllable: /**dee**-fen[t]s/. If you want to sound like a general or a lawyer, use the first of these pronunciations; if you want to sound like a sports announcer or a cheerleader, use the second. Cf. **offense.**

deficient; defective; defectible. The primary difference to be noted is between *deficient* (= insufficient; lacking in quantity) and *defective* (= faulty; imperfect; subnormal). *Defectible*, the least common of the three, means "likely to fail or become defective."

definite. A. And *definitive*. These words are increasingly confused. *Definite* = fixed, exact, explicit. *Definitive* = authoritative; conclusive; exhaustive; providing a final solution.

The most frequent error is misuse of *definitive* for *definite*—e.g.: "He has some very *definitive* [read *definite*] views on golf-course architecture, and it's hard not to like what he says" (*Ft. Lauderdale Sun-Sentinel*).

B. As Misspelled. The word is sometimes misspelled *definate*. See SPELLING (A).

defunct, in a ghastly blunder, is sometimes written *defunk*—e.g.: "Several segments of the *defunk* [read *defunct*] 'Hotel' were filmed at the Fairmont" (*San Diego Union-Trib.*).

DEICTIC TERMS. See POINTING WORDS.

delegate. See **relegate.**

delusion. See **hallucination & illusion.**

demagoguery; demagogy. *Demagoguery* (= the practices of a political agitator who appeals to mob instincts) is more than twice as common as *demagogy*, which (in the absence of any useful DIFFERENTIATION) ought to be labeled a NEEDLESS VARIANT. E.g.: "Such *demagogy* [read *demagoguery*] aside, there are good grounds to object to this particular venture" (*Baltimore Sun*).

demean; bemean. Formerly, authorities on usage disapproved of *demean* in the sense "to lower, degrade," holding that instead it really means "to conduct (oneself)." For example, an early usage critic wrote that "*demean* signifies 'to behave' and does not mean *debase* or *degrade*" (Frank H. Vizetelly, *A Desk-Book of Errors in English*, 1909). The meaning "to behave," now somewhat archaic, is used infrequently in legal contexts—e.g.: "The oath of office now generally administered in all the states requires the lawyer to uphold the law; to *demean* himself, as an officer of the court, uprightly; to be faithful to his trust." In this sense, of course, the verb corresponds to the noun *demeanor*.

Yet the other sense, which has been with us since at least 1601, is now widespread—e.g.: "School district officials fired Maria de la Rosa last year after Latino students complained that the Philippines native *demeaned* and verbally abused them with ethnic slurs" (*L.A. Times*)./ "By the time he left Boston, Dawson was through as a player, and he *demeaned* himself by playing two more seasons for the Marlins as an extra outfielder and pinch-hitter" (*Providence J.-Bull.*).

Meanwhile, the word with which *demean* was confused in arriving at its popular meaning—*bemean* (= to debase)—has become virtually obsolete.

democracy. This term, meaning literally "government by the people," is often employed loosely, often tendentiously, often vaguely, and sometimes disingenuously (as when the post–World War II Soviet Union was referred to as a "democracy"). Originally a Greek term, *democracy* was understood by the Greeks in a very different sense from the current understanding: Greek democracy was an institution limited to male clan members who were citizens; a huge population of slaves and other subordinated classes were disenfranchised. The same, of course, might be said of the United States before the abolition of slavery and before women gained the right to vote. Notions of democracy change with changing notions of who "the people" are. Throughout history, the term has come gradually to be more and more inclusive.

Democrat. A. And *democrat*. The capital *D* distinguishes the sense "a member of the Democratic Party" from the broader sense, which is denoted by a lowercase *d*.

B. *Democrat(ic),* adj. During much of the late 20th century, Republicans were fairly successful in denigrating the word *Democrat,* which often appeared in such phrases as *tax-and-spend Democrats* and *big-spending Democrats.* Interestingly, though, the adjective *Democratic* didn't undergo this depreciation in meaning. In the 1980s and 1990s, therefore, some Republicans preferred to refer to the *Democrat Convention* as opposed to the *Democratic Convention.* The former suggests something like a drunken party, whereas the latter suggests dignified proceedings. In politics, of course, this type of semantic jockeying is a practice without end.

denote. A. And *connote.* *Denote* = to signify the literal meaning <in the Constitution, "President" denotes the highest officer of the executive branch of government>. *Connote* = to imply in addition to the literal meaning <the term "President" connotes an aura of power, grave responsibilities in world politics, and domestic popularity>.

B. Misused. Sometimes *denote* is misused for *denominate* (= to assign a name)—e.g.: "Teenagers whose parents are home at what the researchers *denoted* [read *denominated* or *called*] 'key times'—in the morning, after school, at dinner and at bedtime—are less likely to smoke, to drink or to use marijuana" (*Wash. Times*).

denounce; renounce. *Denounce* = (1) to condemn openly or publicly; (2) to accuse formally; or (3) to announce formally the termination of (a treaty or pact). *Renounce* = (1) to give up or relinquish, esp. by formal announcement; or (2) to reject or disown. Both senses of this word are common. Some writers use *denounce* when they mean *renounce*—e.g.: "Supreme Court Justice David Souter administered the oath to people who *denounced* [read *renounced*] their Russian, Guyanan and even Bosnian citizenships, among others, to become Americans" (*Quincy Patriot Ledger*).

deny (= to declare untrue; repudiate; refuse to recognize or acknowledge) is sometimes misused for *refuse* or *decline.* These words are synonymous in certain constructions, such as *He was denied* (or *refused*) *this.* But in modern usage *refuse* properly precedes an infinitive, whereas with *deny* this construction is an ARCHAISM—e.g.: "Zimmerman moved that Harmon dismiss herself. She *denied* [read *declined*] to do so stating, among other things, that the motion should have been filed much earlier" (*Houston Chron.*).

depart. This FORMAL WORD rarely does better than *leave.*

dependency. See **territory.**

dependent. See **addicted.**

deplane. This word, like *enplane* and *reinplane,* is characteristic of AIRLINESE, a relatively new brand of JARGON. Careful writers and speakers stick to time-honored expressions like *get off, get on,* and *get on again.*

deprecate; depreciate. The first of these has increasingly encroached on the figurative senses of the second, which has retreated into financial contexts. *Deprecate* = to disapprove regretfully. E.g.: "The Kocian ensemble plays that early work with respect and energy, showing that however Hindemith may have *deprecated* it, it is a monumental, expressive piece" (*Albany Times Union*). The phrase *self-deprecating* is, literally speaking, a virtual impossibility, except perhaps for those suffering from extreme neuroses.

Depreciate, transitively, means "to belittle, disparage"; and intransitively, "to fall in value" (used in reference to assets or investments). Thus *self-depreciating,* with *depreciate* in its transitive sense, has historically been viewed as the correct phrase—e.g.: "Sadly, Grizzard did not have the *self-depreciating* humor of a Jeff Foxworthy, the self-proclaimed redneck comedian" (*St. Louis Post-Dispatch*).

Unfortunately, though, the form *self-deprecating*—despite its mistaken origins—is now 50 times more common than *self-depreciating*. Thus, speakers of AmE routinely use *self-deprecating*. However grudgingly, we must accord to it the status of standard English—e.g.: "He's smart, articulate, funny, alternately *self-deprecating* and proud of his success" (*L.A. Times*)./ "Milken doesn't drive himself much anymore, but he has a *self-deprecating* explanation for why that's the case: He says he used to do so many things while driving that he kept having collisions" (*Fortune*).

depute, v.t.; **deputize.** To *depute* is to delegate <these responsibilities she deputed to her agent>. To *deputize* is to make (another) one's deputy or to act as deputy <the sheriff then deputized four men who had offered to help in the search>.

derisive; derisory. *Derisive* = scoffing; expressing derision <derisive comments>. *Derisory* = worthy of derision or of being scoffed at <a derisory first offer>. Although *derisive* and *derisory* at one time overlapped and were frequently synonymous, the DIFFERENTIATION is now complete, and using the two interchangeably is erroneous.

descendible. Traditionally so spelled—not *descendable*. (See -ABLE (A).) But this creates something of an anomaly because *ascendable* has long been preferred over *ascendible*. Such are the vagaries of language.

descent /di-**sent**/ is often mispronounced /**dee**-sent/. See PRONUNCIATION (B).

desirable; desirous. *Desirable* is used in reference to things (or persons, in the sexual sense) that are desired. *Desirous* is used in reference to the desirer's emotions. What is *desirable* is attractive and worth seeking; a *desirous* person is impelled by desire.

Occasionally, *desirous* is misused for *desirable*—e.g.: "John Ortego said telephone marketing and sales jobs created in Erie County at Ingram Micro and Softbank Services Group fit the description of *desirous* [read *desirable*] service-sector positions" (*Buffalo News*).

But even when *desirous* is correct, it usually appears in the wordy phrase *(be) desirous of*, which can be shortened to *desire* or *want*—e.g.: "The coaches *are desirous of building* [read *want to build*] a winning tradition in each of their sports" (*Dallas Morning News*).

destination. This word commonly appears in two supposed REDUNDANCIES—*final destination* and *ultimate destination*. But neither phrase is necessarily redundant. If a shipment has a series of stops or transfers—i.e., a series of "immediate destinations"—it may have a *final* or *ultimate destination*. You may be on your way to Bangkok, with a stopover in Tokyo. If on that flight to Tokyo someone asks about your destination, it would not be inappropriate to characterize Tokyo as the *immediate destination* (i.e., the destination of that particular flight) and Bangkok as the *ultimate destination* (the destination of the entire trip).

Yet the phrase *final destination* or *ultimate destination* should not be used (as it commonly is) in contexts in which such specificity is not called for. Cf. **final outcome.**

determine whether; determine if. Although *determine if* has historically been used almost as often as *determine whether*—even by reputable writers—today the *whether* form is considered better because *if* erroneously suggests a conditional statement as opposed to a neutral hypothetical. E.g.: "Without a clear, consistent method of evaluating the performances of the chief attorney and county administrator, it's difficult, if not impossible, for the commissioners and the public to *determine if* [read *determine whether*] these two top employees are meeting their goals and objectives" (*Sarasota Herald-Trib.*). For a similar problem with *doubt if* for *doubt whether*, see **doubt (A).**

Detroit /di-**troyt**/ is frequently mispronounced /**dee**-troyt/. See PRONUNCIATION (B).

deviant; deviate. A. As Adjectives. *Deviant* is normal. The first edition of the *OED* (1933) labeled both of these adjectives "obsolete" and "rare." The *OED Supp.* (1972) deleted the tag on *deviant* and cited many examples in the sense "deviating from normal social standards or behavior." The word is common—e.g.: "He wasn't a young rebel, *deviant*, troubled or neurotic, didn't die early and wasn't weirdly erotic" (*Chicago Trib.*).

Although *deviant* is the predominant adjective, it has had to compete—unfortunately—with *deviate*. The latter, a NEEDLESS VARIANT of *deviant*, is common in AmE—e.g.: "Nora Mae Roberts is charged with one count of first-degree violation of a minor, involving alleged intercourse or *deviate* [read *deviant*] sex with a 17-year-old boy" (*Ark. Democrat-Gaz.*).

B. As Nouns. Both *deviate* and *deviant* are used as (generally pejorative) nouns meaning "a person who, or thing which, deviates, esp. from normal social standards or behavior; specif., a sexual pervert" (*OED*). Although the two forms are about equally common, *deviant* should be preferred since the use derives from the adjective function. (See ADJECTIVES (C).) All in all, *deviate* is best reserved for its verb function.

DIACRITICAL MARKS, also known as "diacritics," are orthographical characters that indicate a special phonetic quality for a given character. They occur mostly in foreign languages. But in English a fair number of imported terms have diacritical marks. Sometimes they survive indefinitely, but often they fall into disuse as a term is fully naturalized. Nobody today, for example, writes *hôtel*. Although that spelling can be found in some 19th-century publications, it was falling out of fashion even during that period. To the extent that modern readers encounter diacritical marks, the main ones are as follows:

- **acute accent (´).** This mark generally indicates a stressed syllable or rising inflection. It sometimes appears in imported words to show that a final syllable is not silent, especially in words imported from French (as in *flambé* or *résumé*). It also appears over vowels in Spanish either to mark the syllable that has the highest degree of stress or to distinguish words otherwise identical in form but of different meaning.
- **breve (˘).** This mark, used most commonly in pronunciations, indicates that a vowel is short or unstressed. That is, in some pronunciation guides, /bĕt/ signifies the same thing as /bet/ does in this book.
- **cedilla (¸).** This mark appears under the French and Portuguese *c* when the letter is to be pronounced as an *s* rather than as a *k* (as in *façade*). Generally the cedilla is quickly dropped in English-language contexts—so today *facade* usually doesn't have one. See **facade.**
- **circumflex (ˆ).** This mark was used over vowels in ancient Greek to indicate a rising–falling tone. Today it appears most commonly over French vowels after which an *-s-* was once elided (as in *côte* [our *coast*] or *fête* [our *feast*]).
- **diaeresis [umlaut] (¨).** The diaeresis sometimes appears in English over the second of two adjacent vowels to indicate that the vowel is treated as a second syllable (as in *Chloë* or, archaically, *coöperate*). It appears in several Indo-European languages but is generally associated with German (in which it is termed an *umlaut*).
- **grave accent (`).** In ancient Greek, this mark signaled a lower inflection, in contrast to the higher inflection called for by the acute accent. In English, the grave is rarer than the acute accent, but it does appear on occasion to indicate a falling inflection or that a final syllable is to be pronounced separately (as in *blessèd* or *learnèd*). The grave accent is

used in French over the vowels *a*, *e*, and *u*.

- **macron (¯).** This mark, used most commonly in pronunciations, indicates that a vowel is long. That is, in some pronunciation guides, /bōt/ signifies the same thing as /boht/ does in this book.
- **tilde (˜).** This mark appears over the Spanish *n* to indicate the palatalized sound apparent in *señor*.

diagnosis; prognosis. There is an important distinction between these words. A *diagnosis* is an analysis of one's present bodily condition with reference to disease or disorder. A *prognosis* is the projected future course of a present disease, disorder, or disadvantageous situation. E.g.: "Mr. Yeltsin did not specify his *diagnosis* or the type of procedure he will undergo, making it difficult to comment about his *prognosis*, the American doctors said" (*N.Y. Times*).

diaeresis. See DIACRITICAL MARKS.

dice. In formal usage, the numbered cube used in games of chance is called a *die*, and two or more are *dice*. But the word *dice* is often used sloppily as a singular—e.g.: "You win the fight by rolling one *dice* [read *die*] two times" (*Wis. State J.*).

Julius Caesar's *the die is cast* (i.e., one of the pair of dice is thrown) is sometimes mistakenly thought to mean that a machinist's cutting or stamping device has been cast in the foundry.

different. A. *Different from; different than.* *Different than* is often considered inferior to *different from*. The problem is that *than* should follow a comparative adjective (e.g., *larger than*, *sooner than*, etc.), and *different* is not comparative—though, to be sure, it is a word of contrast. *Than* implies a comparison, i.e., a matter of degree; but differences are ordinarily qualitative, not quantitative, and the adjective *different* is not strictly comparative. Thus, writers should generally prefer *different from*—e.g.: "He performed to everything from jazz to the bossa nova to Brahms and Scarlatti, establishing a style very *different from* that of Bill (Bojangles) Robinson, Fred Astaire and the Nicholas Brothers" (*Dayton Daily News*).

Still, it is indisputable that *different than* is sometimes idiomatic, and even useful, since *different from* often cannot be substituted for it—e.g.: "This designer's fashions are typically quite *different* for men *than* for women."

Also, *different than* may sometimes usefully begin clauses if attempting to use *different from* would be so awkward as to require another construction—e.g.: "Life for Swann, who held out to sign a two-year, $7 million contract in August, is a lot *different than* it was for him in Lynn" (*Boston Herald*).

But whenever *from* nicely fills the slot, use it instead of *than*—e.g.: "One could argue that . . . Russia is no *different than* [read *different from*] other nations" (*Wash. Q.*).

But with the adverb *differently*, the word *than* often follows—a usage common since the 17th century. This usage is especially common in speech, but it also appears in print—e.g.: "In the future, however, HARP will be handling things *differently than* it did in the Quick case" (*Fresno Bee*). When there is no independent clause immediately following *differently*, though, *from* works well and is preferable—e.g.: "We found that businesspeople who have been dressing casually for five years react to salespeople's dress *different than* [read *differently from*] those who recently have gone casual" (*Houston Chron.*).

B. *Three different,* etc. When following a number, *different* is sometimes a superfluity <Bennett backed Forbes as a candidate for five different reasons>. Sometimes, however, the word *different* adds a desirable emphasis <scientists examined the problem using three different methods>. The word is emphatic in the same way as *distinct*. In fact, if you wouldn't feel comfortable replacing *different* with *distinct*, you shouldn't be using *different*.

DIFFERENTIATION is the linguistic process by which words of common etymology gradually diverge in meaning, each taking on a distinct sense. An appreciation of this linguistic value is essential to the true stylist. Meanwhile, that appreciation can lead to a continual disenchantment with the forces that seem to be exerted on language.

Richard Grant White, a 19th-century usage critic, extolled the virtue of differentiation while condemning the vice of SLIPSHOD EXTENSION. He used heavy prose typical of the time: "The desynonymizing tendency of language enriches it by producing words adapted to the expression of various delicate shades of meaning. But the promiscuous use of two words each of which has a meaning peculiar to itself, by confounding distinctions impoverishes language, and deprives it at once of range and of power" (*Words and Their Uses, Past and Present*, 1872).

differently abled. See EUPHEMISMS.

dilemma = a choice between two unpleasant or difficult alternatives. This word should not be used by SLIPSHOD EXTENSION for *plight* or *predicament*. Originally a Greek word meaning "a double assumption," the word often appears in the colorful CLICHÉ *horns of a dilemma*—e.g.: "[N]ews media moguls find themselves on the *horns of a dilemma*. They all feel they must have a presence on the Internet, but none has yet figured out how to make money there" (*Buffalo News*).

diminutive, meaning "small," is pronounced /di-**min**-yə-tiv/—not /di-**min**-ə-tiv/.

diphtheria is properly pronounced /dif-**thir**-ee-ə/, not /dip-**thir**-ee-ə/. See PRONUNCIATION (D).

diphthong is properly pronounced /**dif**-thong/, not /**dip**-thong/. See PRONUNCIATION (D).

DIRECTIONAL WORDS. **A. The Suffix *-ward(s)*.** In AmE, the preferred practice is to use the *-ward* form of directional words, as in *toward*, *forward*, and *westward*. Words ending in *-ward* may be either adjectives or adverbs, whereas words ending in *-wards*, common in BrE, may be adverbs only. These are typical preferred AmE forms:

cityward
coastward
downward
outward
rearward
seaward
shoreward
sideward
skyward
sunward
toward
upward

Two exceptions in AmE are the adverbs *afterwards* and *backwards*, which are almost universally used in preference to *afterward* and *backward*. It's anomalous that most people say *forward* but *backwards*.

B. Capitalization. The words *north*, *south*, *east*, and *west* should not be capitalized when used to express directions <we went north>. They are properly capitalized when used as nouns denoting regions of the world or of a country <Far East> <the South>.

But when a directional word appears as an adjective before a geographic proper name, it is lowercase <eastern United States> <southern Italy>. If, however, the adjective is part of the proper name, it should be capitalized <North Dakota> <East Anglia>.

C. Verbose Constructions. Use of such words as *easterly* in phrases like *in an easterly direction* is prolix. In fact, the simple word for the direction (*east*) usually suffices in place of the word ending in either *-erly* or *-wardly*. E.g.: "In Portsmouth, when you're going north on U.S. 17 on High Street, you're traveling *in a westwardly direction* [read *west*]" (*Virginian-Pilot*).

The one useful distinctive sense that forms such as *southwardly* and *southerly* convey is that the movement is more or less in the direction indicated—but not in a straight line. E.g.: "Many of the bees escaped from his lab and have moved steadily *northward* ever since" (*Fresno Bee*).

D. An Infrequent Error: *northernly* for *northerly*, etc. Occasionally writers err by making the directional words ending in *-erly* into words ending in *-ernly*—e.g.: "The districts of Downstate Democratic Reps. Richard Durbin of Springfield and Lane Evans of Rock Island would move clockwise in *westernly* [read *westerly*] and *northernly* [read *northerly*] directions under the GOP proposal" (*Chicago Trib.*)./ "[T]he models showed that the cloud of nerve gas initially traveled in a *southernly* [read *southerly*] direction from the blast site" (*N.Y. Times*). Though the *-ernly* words are recorded in the *OED*, they're noted as being rare and obsolete.

directly; direct, adv. *Directly* = (1) in a straight line; without interruption <we flew directly from Dallas to Frankfurt>; (2) immediately <they left directly after the decision>; (3) with no intervening agent <she was directly responsible>; (4) totally <directly opposite>; (5) soon <they'll be going directly>; or (6) as soon as <directly we saw him, we cheered to express our appreciation>. In sense 1, *direct* is interchangeable as an adverb <we flew direct from Dallas to Frankfurt>. Sense 5 is typical of southern AmE. Sense 6 is exclusively BrE.

directorial, not *directoral*, is the adjective corresponding to *director*—e.g.: "Mr. Wuhl makes his *directoral* [read *directorial*] debut in the film, which opens on Friday" (*N.Y. Times*).

DIRECT QUESTIONS. See QUESTIONS, DIRECT AND INDIRECT.

dis, v.t.; **diss.** *Dis*—preferably so spelled—is a clipped form of *disrespect* (or, less likely, *dismiss* or *disparage*). This slang term came into existence in the early 1980s and into vogue in the early 1990s—e.g.: "In the 'other body,' where four GOP members are running for president, Gingrich would like senators to ponder the theoretical possibility of a President Newt before they *dis* the bills he sends them" (*Newsweek*). The inflected forms are *dissed* and *dissing*.

disassemble. See **dissemble.**

disassociate. See **dissociate.**

disastrous is so spelled—not *disasterous*, a fairly common misspelling.

disbelief; unbelief; nonbelief; misbelief. *Disbelief* = (1) shocked incredulity; or (2) the mental rejection of something after considering its plausibility. In sense 2, *disbelief* results from active, conscious decision. *Unbelief* denotes the state of doubt, of not having made up one's mind. Thus, while an atheist's state of mind is *disbelief* (sense 2), an agnostic's state of mind is *unbelief*. *Nonbelief* is a NEEDLESS VARIANT of *unbelief*. A *misbelief* is an erroneous or false belief.

disburse; disperse. *Disburse*, from the Latin *bursa* "purse," is used chiefly in reference to distribution of money <the directors disbursed dividends to the stockholders>. *Disperse* is used in reference to distribution of all other things, such as crowds or diseases. But *disburse* sometimes appears erroneously in place of *disperse*—e.g.: "Sure enough, the car drew a crowd. When they *disbursed* [read *dispersed*], it took me a good 15 minutes to figure out how to remove [the top]" (*Albany Times Union*).

The corresponding nouns are *disbursement* and *dispersal*. It's incorrect to use *dispersement* (no such word is in the dictionaries) when *dispersal* is intended—e.g.: "What concerns Fresno

State coach Jerry Tarkanian is the Bulldogs' potential to be off-balance defensively, at least in the *dispersement* [read *dispersal*] of players on the floor" (*Fresno Bee*). Nor, finally, is it right to use the fictitious *dispersement* when *disbursement* is the intended word—e.g.: "[C]ompletion of the plan was slowed by disagreements among day-care providers over money *dispersement* [read *disbursement*]" (*Boston Globe*).

disc. See **disk (A).**

disc jockey is the standard spelling. *Disk jockey* is a variant form.

disclaim. See **declaim.**

discomfit. A. And *discomfiture.* *Discomfit* (= to frustrate, disconcert) is best used only as a verb. The preferred noun is *discomfiture.* Ill-trained writers use phrases such as *much to his discomfit,* in which either *discomfort* or *discomfiture* is intended.

B. And *discomfort.* *Discomfort* is preferably a noun, not a verb. Writers sometimes use it when they seem really to mean *discomfit*—e.g.: "Not only has it embraced what amounts to a social crusade—something that some journalists find *discomforting* [read *discomfiting*]—but it has set a goal it almost certainly will not meet" (*Newsweek*)./ "Sometimes his access was *discomforting* [read *discomfiting*] to the men at the top" (*Atlantic Monthly*).

C. The Form *discomforture.* *Discomforture* is incorrect for either *discomfort* or *discomfiture*—e.g.: "[T]he stubbornness of the owners in repeating their rhetoric in the past made it even harder to believe that they aren't on their way to re-experiencing their *discomfortures in* [read *discomfort of* or *discomfitures of*] the past" (*N.Y. Newsday*).

discrete; discreet. Although the two words ultimately have the same Latin origin, the spelling *discreet* came into English through French. Today the two spellings are treated as different words. *Discrete* means "separate, distinct"; *discreet* means "cautious, judicious." *Discreet* is most commonly used in reference to behavior, especially speaking or writing. The usual error is to misuse *discreet* for *discrete*—e.g.: "He is clearly not at home with strategic views, but prefers handling *discreet* [read *discrete*] issues rather than sweeping ideas" (*N.Y. Times*). Sometimes, though, the opposite blunder appears—e.g.: "The selections are tasteful with visceral mayhem, profanity, and sex almost nonexistent, or *discretely* [read *discreetly*] handled" (*Christian Science Monitor*).

disenfranchise; disfranchise. Though *disfranchise* has long been favored, *disenfranchise* is now more than 20 times as common. It's the standard term meaning "to deprive of the right to exercise a franchise or privilege, esp. to vote." E.g.: "Part of this holding back was the result of white men, the persons in power, being unwilling or unable to reach out and bring in persons who traditionally had been *disenfranchised*" (*San Diego Union-Trib.*).

disinformation; misinformation. These words are not synonyms. *Disinformation* = deliberately false information <Soviet disinformation>. *Misinformation* = incorrect information <widespread misinformation about HIV and how it is transmitted>. Sometimes the more pejorative word (*disinformation*) is misused for the less pejorative—e.g.: "Not surprisingly, the low level of scrutiny she was thought to deserve accounts for a significant amount of *disinformation* [read *misinformation*] in reference works" (*Profession*). That sentence appears in an article charging oversights, not deliberate lies.

disinterest; uninterest. *Disinterest* = (1) impartiality or freedom from bias or from chance of financial benefit <the judge showed disinterest in the way that every judge should>; or (2) lack of concern or attention <the team suffered from the disinterest of their tra-

ditional supporters>. Leading writers and editors almost unanimously reject sense 2, in which *uninterest* (recorded fr. 1952) is the better term because it is unambiguous—e.g.: "He may empathize with modern American theater, but his *uninterest* in American opera is resounding" (*N.Y. Times*).

But *disinterest* still predominates in this sense—e.g.: "Nancy Aldera, a Precinct 39 poll worker who had little to do in last Tuesday's school board election because only 24 people voted, said she doesn't know why there is so much *disinterest* in voting" (*Des Moines Register*). Reserving *uninterest* for this use would be tidier, but because *uninterest* remains comparatively rare, the DIFFERENTIATION seems unlikely on a broad scale.

disinterested; uninterested. Given the overlapping nouns, writers have found it difficult to keep the past-participial adjectives entirely separate, and many have given up the fight to preserve the distinction between them.

But the distinction is still best recognized and followed because *disinterested* captures a nuance that no other word quite does. A *disinterested* observer is not merely "impartial," but has nothing to gain from taking a stand on the issue in question. The following quotation deals with a journalist's disinterest: "In the film, Wexler's directorial debut, a cameraman portrayed by Robert Forster must wrestle with being a *disinterested* observer or becoming emotionally involved with what he sees through his lens" (*L.A. Times*).

Yet *disinterested* is frequently used (or, in the traditionalist's eyes, misused) for *uninterested*—e.g.: "On a day when seeded players fell by the wayside like overripe tomatoes, Agassi looked sickly and almost *disinterested* [read *uninterested*]" (*Toronto Sun*).

disk. A. And *disc*. *Disk* is the more usual spelling in all but four specific meanings. *Disc* is the spelling used for these senses: (1) "a phonograph record"; (2) "an optical disk (as a compact disc or videodisc)"; (3) "a tool making up part of a plow"; and (4) "a component of a brake system." Otherwise, *disk* is the preferred spelling for general reference to thin circular objects, intervertebral disks, celestial bodies, and computer disks.

B. And *diskette*. Both *diskette* and *disk* may refer to the computer-data storage medium. (The synonym *floppy disk* is declining in use—probably because the disks are no longer floppy.) *Disk* is commoner and shorter, but neither form can be fairly criticized.

disk jockey. See **disc jockey.**

disorganized; unorganized. The first means "in confusion or disarray; broken up." The second means "not having been organized," but not in a pejorative sense.

disorient; disorientate. The longer form is a NEEDLESS VARIANT of the shorter—e.g.: "There, upset and *disorientated* [read *disoriented*], Berkelbaugh drew the attention of a security guard" (*Pitt. Post-Gaz.*). See **orient.**

disperse. See **disburse.**

disquiet; disquieten. The standard verb is *disquiet* (= to bother or disturb). The form *disquieten*—a Britishism not recorded in *W10*—is a NEEDLESS VARIANT. E.g.: "[W]hat will Europe consist of, and who will decide about the future shape and destiny of that suddenly and dramatically *disquietened* [read *disquieted*] continent?" (*Independent*).

diss, v.t. See **dis.**

dissatisfied; unsatisfied. Some DIFFERENTIATION exists between these words. To be *unsatisfied* is to be less than completely satisfied, whereas to be *dissatisfied* is to be positively bothered by the lack of satisfaction. Thus, a person whose accounts are in arrears has debts that are *unsatisfied*—and creditors who are *dissatisfied*.

dissemble; disassemble. *Dissemble* = to present a false appearance; to conceal the truth. E.g.: "[T]he boy answered [my questions] simply, directly and honestly, unlike most adults, who *dissemble*, ramble or tell you everything but the answer to the question" (*Plain Dealer*). *Disassemble* = to take apart. E.g.: "The Edgewood trainees . . . [learn] along the way how to assemble, *disassemble* and repair [the computers]" (*Baltimore Sun*).

Unfortunately, some writers use *dissemble* when they mean *disassemble*—e.g.: "Rushakoff said that he had to spend a lot of money learning how to use the right tools and the right procedures to *dissemble* [read *disassemble*] computers" (*Am. Metal Market*).

dissociate; disassociate. *Dissociate* is the preferred term; *disassociate* is a NEEDLESS VARIANT. *Dissociate* takes the preposition *from*. E.g.: "To *dissociate* himself *from* such impairments, Dole released the medical summary of his exam last month" (*Cleveland Plain Dealer*).

dissolution of marriage. See **divorce (B).**

distinct; distinctive; distinguished. The first means "well defined, discernibly separate" <distinct speech>, and the second means "serving to distinguish, set off by appearance" <a distinctive red bow tie>. *Distinct* speech is well enunciated, whereas *distinctive* speech is idiosyncratically accented, different from that of surrounding speakers. *Distinctive* is sometimes misused for *distinguished* (= notable; famous).

distrustful; mistrustful. The difference here is subtle because both terms mean "having or showing doubt; lacking confidence." But *distrustful* implies suspicion or wariness based on an informed judgment, whereas *mistrustful* suggests uncertainty or uneasiness. Thus, one might be *distrustful* of a used-car dealer's puffing, yet *mistrustful* of a stranger's advice. Note that both adjectives take the preposition *of*.

dive > dived > dived. Although *dove* is fairly common in AmE, *dived* is the predominant form—and the preferable one.

divorce. A. And *annulment*. A *divorce* recognizes the existence of a valid marriage, whereas an *annulment* treats the marriage as if it had never existed. Even so, in most jurisdictions the "nonexistence" of the marriage is not considered absolute: any children produced by such a void or voidable marriage are considered legitimate.

B. And *dissolution of marriage*. In the 1970s, the word *divorce* was struck from many statutes and replaced by the EUPHEMISM *dissolution of marriage*.

divorcée; divorcé. The usual word—*divorcée*—properly refers only to a woman. The masculine form is *divorcé*, which has been AmE usage since the late 19th century. But some writers have tried to create male divorcées—e.g.: "Parents were lulled into security by Martin's plausible manner and his implied message that, as an ex-police officer, he was a man to be trusted. Gregarious *divorcée* [read *divorcé*] Martin was a familiar figure in Manchester in his open-top sports cars" (*Glasgow Herald*). (On the use of *gregarious divorcée* as a "title" in that sentence, see TITULAR TOMFOOLERY.)

djinni. See **genie.**

DOCUMENT DESIGN. Traditionally, writers have been relatively unconcerned with the look of their documents. This lack of concern didn't have such horrible consequences in the days of typewriters, when the primary design choices were the width of the margins and the amount of underlining and capitals.

But with the advent of word processing, document design has become much more important as writers are presented with all kinds of new printing options. Failing to use these options knowledgeably puts the writer at a disadvantage because—through books and other professionally printed materials—most readers have become accustomed to well-designed documents. In short, it has become essential to know something about typography and design.

In this space, of course, it's impossible to offer even the simplest primer on the subject. But a few points deserve mention:

A. Readable Typeface. For text, a readable typeface probably means a serifed typeface, such as the one used throughout this book, as opposed to a sans-serif (/san-**ser**-if/) typeface made up of only straight lines. A serif is a short stroke that projects from the ends of the main strokes that make up a character.

This is a serifed typeface: Times Roman.
This is a sans-serif typeface: Univers.

Although sans-serif typefaces often work well in headings and the like, they can be difficult to read in text. Among the better serifed typefaces are Bookman, Caslon, Garamond, Palatino, and Times Roman. The one typeface to avoid at all costs still predominates in American business: Courier. It's an eyesore.

B. White Space. Ample white space makes a page more inviting. The primary ways to create white space on the page are to use generous margins (for example, margins greater than one inch for letters and other business documents), to supply headings and subheadings, and to enumerate items in separate paragraphs, subparagraphs, or bulleted lists.

C. Headings and Subheadings. Artfully employed, headings and subheadings make a document much easier to follow. Not only do they serve as navigational aids for readers; they also help writers organize thoughts more logically than they might otherwise.

D. Avoiding All Caps. See CAPITALIZATION (A).

E. Avoiding Underlines. Generally, italicizing is preferable to underlining, which was traditionally nothing more than a (poor) substitute for italics. The effect of underlining is to take up white space between lines and therefore to make the lines harder to read.

F. Listing. Enumerate items by breaking down lists into paragraphs and subparagraphs. Using a tabulated list allows the writer not only to display the points better, but also to improve the sentence structure. Make sure that the list falls at the end of the sentence—not at the beginning or in the middle. See ENUMERATIONS.

G. Bullets. On this extremely useful device, see BULLET DOT.

H. Hanging Indents. In most texts, when you indent an item to be listed—whether it's a bulleted item or an entire paragraph—don't begin the second line of the item at the left margin. Instead, begin it just below the first one, with the enumerating signal hanging to the left. Examples appear throughout this book in bulleted lists.

I. Ragged Right Margin. Many readability specialists insist that unjustified right margins are more readable than justified ones. In letters, contracts, and the like, an unjustified right margin is often desirable.

J. Citations in Footnotes. Citations tend to clutter the text; you can easily minimize this cluttering by moving citations to footnotes (and avoiding footnotes for other purposes). See FOOTNOTES.

K. Characters per Line. Ideally, a line of type should accommodate 45 to 70 characters, but the "fine print" that characterizes so many legal documents often spans 150 characters to the line. In text of that kind, the reader's eye tends to get lost in mid-line or in moving from the end of one line to the beginning of the next. One way to improve a document with a large block of text—and, typically, small margins on each side—is to use a double-column format. That design can be extremely helpful, for example, in consumer contracts such as residential leases.

L. Select Bibliography. For more on this subject, see Philip Brady, *Using Type Right* (1988); Robert Bringhurst,

The Elements of Typographic Style (1992); and *Words into Type* (3d ed. 1974).

dogged. As a past-tense or past-participial verb, *dogged* is pronounced /dogd/ <they were dogged by problems>. But as an adjective, the word is pronounced /**dog**-id/ <golfers are the dogged victims of an inexorable fate>.

done (= finished), when used as an adjective, is sometimes criticized, but the word has been so used since the 19th century <call me when you're done>. Many stylists prefer *through* <call me when you're through>.

donut. See **doughnut.**

DOUBLE ADVERBS. See ADVERBS (D).

DOUBLE BOBBLES. A double bobble occurs when somebody reaches for a word—in fact, the *wrong* word—and then mistakes another word for the wrong word. It's a word twice removed from its correct use. Two ready examples are *Hobbesian choice* (when misused for a difficult choice) and *compromise* (when misused for *comprise*).

A *Hobson's choice* is really a take-it-or-leave-it choice. (See **Hobson's choice (A).**) By SLIPSHOD EXTENSION, though, the phrase came to refer to any difficult choice. And to compound the problem, some writers reach for the extended sense and miss entirely: they confuse Thomas Hobson, a relatively obscure man, with his famous contemporary Thomas Hobbes (1588–1679). The resulting MALAPROPISM is amazingly common—e.g.: "The Court said that clients had more than a '*Hobbesian choice*' of choosing between adding an attorney to an action and exposing privileged information, or forfeiting the right to sue" (*N.J.L.J.*). See **Hobson's choice (C).**

A similar error occurs when *compromise* is confused with *comprise*, which itself is often misused for *compose* or *constitute*. In the strictest usage, the parts compose the whole; the whole comprises the parts; the whole is composed of the parts; the parts are comprised in the whole. Thus, the phrase *is comprised of* is always wrong and should be replaced by *is composed of*, *is made up of*, or *comprises*. See **comprise.**

Sometimes, however, the writer wanting the incorrect *comprise* seizes upon a doubly incorrect word, *compromise*—e.g.: "Women *compromise* [read *make up*] 60 percent of the 400,000 California adults estimated to have been seriously mentally ill in 1989" (*Sacramento Bee*).

These misuses are so spectacularly wrong that they merit their own special name: hence "double bobbles."

DOUBLE COMPARISONS. See COMPARATIVES AND SUPERLATIVES (C).

double entendre; double entente. The English phrase—sometimes thought to be pseudo-French, but actually 17th-century French—is *double entendre*. The modern French form, *double entente*, is an affectation—e.g.: "Martin Booth writes the scripts, funny in a conventional way, with rather more *double entente* [read *double entendres*] than I expected" (*Fin. Times*).

Double entendre originally referred to any ambiguity (usually a pun) giving rise to more than one meaning, but now connotes that one of those meanings is indecent or risqué—e.g.: "The company has an owl logo, but it 'acknowledges that its name is considered a slang term for a portion of the female anatomy,' according to company literature, and the six businessmen who founded Hooters were aware of the *double entendre* when they chose the name" (*Asbury Park Press*).

DOUBLE GENITIVES. See POSSESSIVES (D).

DOUBLE MODALS. In grammar, a *modal* (short for *modal auxiliary*) is a verb such as *can, could, may, might, must, ought, shall, should, will,* or *would*. A modal is used with another verb to express grammatical mood—that is, to indicate the speaker's attitude toward the factuality or likelihood of what is being said: (1) the indicative expresses objective fact <Sam plays the piano>; (2) the imperative expresses a command or request <play it again, Sam>; and (3) the subjunctive expresses something hypothetical or contrary to fact <if Sam were up to it, he would play>. See SUBJUNCTIVES.

A double modal, as the name implies, is a combination of two modals in such nonstandard expressions as *might can*, *might could*, *might ought*, *might should*, and *should ought*. These phrases are not uncommon in regional American speech—especially in the South—but they rarely appear in print. E.g.: "Although I have only spent one day on the water at Lay Lake, and interviewed perhaps 20 percent of the field, I still believe I *might can* [read *might*] get pretty close" (*Ark. Democrat-Gaz.*).

The problem with most double modals, of course, is that only one of the verbs is needed. In the most common double modal, *might could*, the word *might* can usually be dropped without a change in meaning. Thus, unless you're recording dialect or creating fictional dialogue—or mimicking regional speech for comic effect—don't use double modals.

DOUBLE NEGATIVES. See NEGATIVES (B).

DOUBLE PASSIVES. See PASSIVE VOICE (B).

DOUBLESPEAK, the language of disinformation, is a subset of EUPHEMISM. In the words of a leading text on the subject:

> Doublespeak is language that pretends to communicate but really doesn't. It is language that makes the bad seem good, the negative appear positive, the unpleasant appear attractive or at least tolerable. Doublespeak is language that avoids or shifts responsibility, language that is at variance with its real or purported meaning. It is language that conceals or prevents thought; rather than extending thought, doublespeak limits it.
>
> William Lutz, *Doublespeak* 1 (1989).

In the language of doublespeak, poor people are *fiscal underachievers*; hobos or "street people" are *non-goal-oriented members of society*; prostitutes are *sexual service providers*; graffiti sprayers are *wall artists*; and students whose grades are borderline passing are *emerging students*.

Apart from a few words and phrases that have become very common—for example, *exceptional* used in reference to children with severe learning disabilities or subnormal intelligence—doublespeak is not the subject of this book. For good treatments, see Lutz's work cited above and several earlier works: Mario Pei, *Words in Sheep's Clothing* (1969); Mario Pei, *Double-Speak in America* (1973); Mario Pei, *Weasel Words: The Art of Saying What You Don't Mean* (1978); William Lambdin, *Doublespeak Dictionary* (1979); and Hugh Rawson, *A Dictionary of Euphemisms & Other Doubletalk* (1981).

DOUBLE SUBJECTS. Linguists term it "pronominal apposition"—the use of a dependent pronoun in a sentence such as *My brother he's the president*. Of course, the *he* is unnecessary there, and its use marks the speaker as uneducated—as belonging to one of the lower strata of society.

Interestingly, though, the difference between this substandard usage and standard usage is—though quite perceptible—somewhat slight. William Labov explains the kinship between the double subject in standard and in nonstandard speech:

> [I]t is not always realized that the "nonstandard" aspect is merely a slight difference in intonation. A standard speaker frequently says the same thing, with a slight break after the subject: *My oldest sister—she works at the bank, and she finds it very profitable*. There are many ways in which a greater awareness of the standard colloquial forms would help

teachers interpret nonstandard forms. Not only do standard speakers use pronominal apposition with the break noted above, but in casual speech they can also bring object noun phrases to the front, "foregrounding" them. For example, one can say

> My oldest sister—she worked at the Citizens Bank in Passaic last year.
>
> The Citizens Bank, in Passaic—my oldest sister worked there last year.
>
> Passaic—my oldest sister worked at the Citizens Bank there last year.

Note that if the foregrounded noun phrase represents a locative—the "place where"—then its position is held by *there*, just as the persons are represented by pronouns. If we are dealing with a time element, it can be foregrounded without replacement in any dialect: *Last year, my oldest sister worked at the Citizens Bank in Passaic.*

William Labov, "The Study of Nonstandard English," in *Language: Introductory Readings* 543, 547–48 (Virginia P. Clark et al. eds., 4th ed. 1985).

Labov's final examples—with the "foregrounding"—are quite informal, even if they are standard. Some journalists habitually use that type of sentence.

There is, of course, the more formal, oratorical type of double subject, as in *We the people of the United States* . . . .

doubt. A. *Doubt that, doubt whether & doubt if.* The phrasing *doubt that* is used primarily in negative sentences, statements of skepticism, and questions—e.g.: "Consider Ronald Reagan: he was widely considered an amiable, affable fellow—but no one *doubted that* he could be aggressive if he needed to be" (*Forbes*).

Doubt whether is used primarily in affirmative statements (again, though, of skepticism)—e.g.: "But even if the rules can survive legal challenge, they *doubted whether* David Kessler, the Food and Drug Administration's chief, can reach his goal of cutting youth smoking in half within seven years" (*Tampa Trib.*).

Doubt if is less sound because it suggests a conditional statement. The phrase *doubt that* will usually replace *doubt if*—e.g.: "Dr. Hughes *doubted if* [read *doubted that*] it would be used to screen all women as the test was not 100 per cent accurate" (*Scotsman*). This usage appears most commonly in BrE. Cf. **I'm not sure that & determine whether.**

B. Followed by a Negative. *Doubt* can be confusing when followed by a negative—e.g.: "I *doubt* whether the company *will not* take the further step when necessary." This sentence merely states that the writer thinks the company *will* take the further step.

doubt if. See **doubt (A).**

doubtlessly is incorrect for *doubtless* (a mild expression of certainty), *no doubt* (a stronger expression of certainty), or *undoubtedly* (the strongest of these three expressions of certainty). The word *doubtless* is itself an adverb <the Framers doubtless feared the executive's assertion of an independent military authority unchecked by the people>. The form *doubtlessly* is therefore unnecessary—e.g.: "Lebed, who has made no secret of his longing to be Russia's defense minister, *doubtlessly will* [read *will doubtless*] take great personal satisfaction from being courted by Yeltsin" (*Chicago Trib.*). (On the position of the adverb within the verb phrase, see ADVERBS (A).) Cf. **clearly.** For other adverbs with a superfluous *-ly*, see ADVERBS (D).

doubt that; doubt whether. See **doubt (A).**

doughnut; donut. The first spelling, which is more common, is preferred because it retains the name of the main ingredient (though on this rationale it might be aptly renamed *sugarnut* or *oilnut*). *Donut*—or, worse, *do-nut*—should be reserved for eatery names and advertising.

dour, in the best speech, rhymes with *lure*. But many people say it as if it rhymed with *sour*.

douse; dowse. These words are best kept separate. To *douse* (/dows/) is to soak with liquid, as by immersing or drenching <she immediately doused the flame with water>. To *dowse* (/dowz/) is to try to find something underground by "divining" for it, as with a divining rod that is supposed to help in locating water, oil, or buried treasure <with nothing more than a twig, they went dowsing for gold>.

Both words are sometimes misused. *Douse* sometimes displaces *dowse* from its rightful place—e.g.: "She walks over to a tree that stands at the edge of one circle of stones, picks up a stick that lies nearby, holds it out toward the circle like a *dousing* [read *dowsing*] rod" (*Tampa Trib.*). But the opposite error, *dowse* for *douse*, is even more common—e.g.: "As fire spread to the building, Piper made his way out and back to his house where his wife, Lynn, *dowsed* [read *doused*] his clothes with water in the shower, Clement said" (*Manchester Union Leader*).

dove. See **dive.**

downplay (= to de-emphasize), dating from the 1950s, is a VOGUE WORD today. If a casualism is desired, the PHRASAL VERB *play down* generally suffices—e.g.: "Theiss also *downplayed* [read *played down*] the importance of police groups altogether, saying many of them are 'vintage labor unions' that typically back Democrats" (*L.A. Times*). Both expressions are colloquial.

dowse. See **douse.**

dozen makes two plural forms: *dozens* and *dozen*. The first is used when the number is inexact or unspecified <dozens of geese>, the second when the count is precise <three dozen doughnuts>.

draft; draught. *Draft* is standard AmE in all meanings of the word. In BrE, *draught* is the usual spelling in all but the following three senses: (1) "a bank's payment order"; (2) "the compulsory enlistment of persons into military service"; and (3) "an initial or preliminary version." American writers who use *draught* are likely to seem pretentious or pedantic.

drag > dragged > dragged. The past-tense and past-participial form *drug* is a dialectal form common in the southern United States—e.g.: "Mazur said his father lipped the fish and *drug* it well back up on the bank so it couldn't get away" (*Austin American-Statesman*). The linguistic authorities have had some negative things to say. *W2* (1934), the last of the great prescriptive dictionaries, called *drug* "dialectal" and "illiterate." More recent dictionaries, such as *RH2*, call it, more chastely, "nonstandard." Surprisingly, the monumental *OED* is silent on the question.

The question, to a traditional grammarian, is whether *drag* is a regular or an irregular verb. (See IRREGULAR VERBS.) No existing grammars list *drag* among the irregular verbs. As a matter of distribution, perhaps the best summing-up is that of E. Bagby Atwood, the Texas linguist, in 1953: "*Dragged* . . . predominates among cultured informants everywhere, but it predominates among the other types only in N.Y., n. Pa., e. Va., S.C., and Ga. Elsewhere in these [noncultured] types it is more or less narrowly limited by the competing form *drug*" (*Survey of Verb Forms*, 1953). Whether President Bill Clinton would rank as a "cultured informant" might be a disputable point, but when he was debating Bob Dole on 16 Oct. 1996, he said: " 'Then we took comments as we always do. And there were tens of thousands of comments about how we ought to do it. That's what *drug* [read *dragged*] it out' " (*N.Y. Times*).

draperies; drapes. Usage critics and etiquette mavens have long preferred *draperies* over *drapes*, which has been stamped as a lowbrow usage. The term *curtains* is perhaps the best choice.

draught. See **draft.**

draw on. See PHRASAL VERBS.

drink > drank > drunk. Although *drank* is sometimes heard as a past participle <they had drank the wine>—and *drunk* as a past-tense verb <they drunk the wine>—both usages are substandard. See IRREGULAR VERBS.

drought; drouth. The latter is archaic in BrE, but still frequently appears in AmE texts. Still, *drought* is the preferred form in both linguistic communities. Misusing *drought* for *flood* is perhaps just an odd mental glitch—e.g.: "Spring is a time of heightened concern about *drought* [read *flood*]. In a typical year, melting snowpacks can conspire with increased rainfall to send rivers over their banks. Sometimes in northern areas, ice jams exacerbate the floods on swollen rivers. This year, spring flooding is less likely than normal" (*N.Y. Times*).

drown. A. *Drowned* and *drownded*. The past-tense form is *drowned*, not *drownded*—the latter being dialectal. E.g.: "True, [the flooding] helped duck and geese populations, but it also *drownded* [read *drowned*] millions of other living creatures who weren't favored targets" (*Buffalo News*).

B. *Drowned*; *was drowned*. In the best usage, if somebody *drowned* it was an accident, but if somebody *was drowned* foul play was involved.

drug, vb. See **drag.**

drunk, adj.; **drunken.** Traditionally, *drunk* has been an adjective appearing in the predicate <they were drunk>, whereas *drunken* has preceded the noun <a drunken sailor>. Today, the words mostly bear distinct senses. *Drunk* = intoxicated, inebriated. *Drunken* = given to drink; morbidly alcoholic.

Thus, *drunken* usually denotes a habitual state—e.g.: "Molly Ringwald stars as a waitress with a *drunken* buffoon of a father and a churchgoing mother she calls 'Ma' " (*Time*). This nuance is slightly counterintuitive, given that *a drunk* refers to one who is habitually drunk. Although *drunken* sometimes means merely "exhibiting intoxication," the better term for this meaning is *drunk*—e.g.: "[A] confidential computer disk containing the names of 4,000 AIDS patients was mailed anonymously to a newspaper after a *drunken* [read *drunk*] public health worker showed it to friends and dropped it outside a bar" (*Memphis Commercial Appeal*).

Drunken also frequently describes not a person or group of people, but their *brawl, orgy,* or *party*, through HYPALLAGE—e.g.: "[S]he agreed not to speak ill of Astra, which has been embroiled in a scandal since tawdry tales of *drunken* company parties and fraternity-party behavior were made public earlier this year" (*Boston Herald*).

drunken. See **drunk.**

dual (= double; twofold) is sometimes misspelled *duel*—e.g.: "The refinements . . . include a modified cam and carburetor, higher compression ratio, larger valves and *duel* [read *dual*] exhausts to trumpet the sound and strength" (*N.Y. Times*). Of course, *duel* originally meant "a formal combat between two persons, fought with weapons, under an accepted code of procedure, and in the presence of witnesses." Today, however, the word has come to mean "any contest between two opponents."

dubious = (1) causing uncertainty <his credentials were dubious>; or (2) doubting <we are dubious about whether we'll be able to attend>. Although sense 2 has occasionally been criticized, it is now in good use.

duct tape is so spelled, from its originally intended use around heating ducts. But the mistaken phrase *duck tape* has become quite common—e.g.:

"Their tactic is then to put the metal back in place with *duck tape* [read *duct tape*], and disguise the cut with paint" (*Christian Science Monitor*)./ "They brought insect repellent, wore head nets and, following the sage advice of yours truly, sealed their cuffs, leg bottoms and waist with *duck tape* [read *duct tape*]" (*Albany Times Union*). In the early 1990s, one company—Manco, Inc.—developed the brand name *Duck Tape* for its duct tape; the trademark, if the product is successful, will only aggravate the confusion.

duel. See **dual.**

due to. The traditional view is that *due to* should be restricted to adjectival uses in the sense "attributable to," usually following the verb *to be* (sometimes understood in context). But the stylist may wish to avoid even correct uses of the phrase, which one writer calls a "graceless phrase, even when used correctly," adding: "Avoid it altogether" (Lucile V. Payne, *The Lively Art of Writing*, 1965).

Despite the traditional view that the adjectival use is best (*due* being equivalent to *attributable*), the phrase is commonly used as a preposition or conjunctive adverb for *because of, owing to, caused by*, or *on grounds of*—e.g.: "*Due to* [read *Because of*] a mistake in Lincoln-Mercury's press material, which we didn't notice until we read Nissan's press material, the maximum cargo room listed for the Villager in our 1992 review was incorrect" (*N.Y. Newsday*)./ "Viewers were supposed to care about characters they knew little about and, *due to* [read *owing to*] expense and logistics, the adventures were limited to gimmicks and dialogue on the sub's bridge" (*Palm Beach Post*). See **owing to.**

Sometimes the examples are somewhat comical. For example, we all know what babies are due to. But what are big boys due to?—e.g.: "[O]nly the likes of Trigger and C'Lock can expect to compete with the big boys *due to* superior graphical interfaces and good quality, unique content" (*New Media Age*). Big boys who are due to what? the reader might momentarily wonder. New media age indeed!

In the following examples, the phrase is used in the traditionally preferred way. But as Payne notes, the sentences might be improved by eliminating it—e.g.: "The widening of the gap was *due* largely *to* the increase in black-female-headed families" (*Virginian-Pilot*). (A possible revision: *The widening gap has resulted largely from the increase in the number of families headed by black females.*)/ "The market's enthusiasm was *due to* [read *traceable to*] the belief—fuelled by Mr. Clarke's statements at the time—that he was moving ahead of events" (*Fin. Times*). (Another possible revision: *The market's enthusiasm swelled from the belief—fueled by Mr. Clarke's statements—that he was moving ahead of events . . . .*)

duffel, the preferred spelling for the bag, is an eponymous term deriving from the city Duffel, in Belgium. But because the *-el* spelling departs from analogous terms spelled *-le*—such as *muffle, shuffle, scuffle*, and also those such as *baffle, hassle, tussle*—the word is frequently misspelled *duffle*. (Mussels, the crustaceans, are exceptional.)

The less good spelling, which is about 25% as common as *duffel* in modern print sources, occurs even in well-edited newspapers—e.g.: "Across the street from Gypsy Me is Cedar Key Canvas, with a large seaman's *duffle* [read *duffel*] bag for $57" (*Ft. Lauderdale Sun-Sentinel*).

dumb = (1) unable to speak; or (2) stupid. Although sense 1, the traditional usage, has long been considered preferable <deaf and dumb>, sense 2 has predominated in such a way as to make the term a disparaging one. Today, *mute* is the generally preferred term for one who cannot speak. The origin of using *dumb* to mean "stupid" is probably that stupid people are often dumb because they don't understand the conversation.

duodenum is pronounced either /doo-oh-**dee**-nəm/ or /də-**wod**-ə-nəm/.

dwarf. Pl. *dwarfs.* The form *dwarves,* a nonstandard variant, occasionally appears—e.g.: "[T]he sculptors of Benin long have made their finest objects—their regal heads and life-size *dwarves* [read *dwarfs*], their animals and birds and ceremonial swords—out of molten brass" (*Wash. Post*). When he released his famous movie in 1938, Walt Disney got it right: *Snow White and the Seven Dwarfs.* See PLURALS (G).

dying; dyeing. *Dying* corresponds to the verb *die* (= to expire), *dyeing* to the verb *dye* (= to color with a dye).

Dyeing is often mistakenly written *dying*—e.g.: "From Fountain Valley, the water could be distributed by the Orange County Water District to golf courses, a *carpet-dying* [read *carpet-dyeing*] firm and other reclaimed-water users" (*Orange County Register*).

dysfunctional (= functioning abnormally) is occasionally misspelled *disfunctional*—e.g.: "[S]ome of the conservative leaders who were demanding less government jumped all over the Illinois Department of Children and Family Services for not preventing the murder and abuse of babies born into *disfunctional* [read *dysfunctional*] families" (*Chicago Trib.*).

DYSPHEMISM = (1) the substitution of a disagreeable word or phrase for a neutral or even positive one; or (2) a word or phrase so substituted. Dysphemism is the opposite of EUPHEMISM. Examples usually fall into the realm of slang—e.g.:

Ordinary Term	**Dysphemism**
accountant	bean-counter
athlete	(dumb) jock
cadaver, corpse	stiff
Christian fundamentalist	Bible-thumper, Bible-beater
civil servant	paper-shuffler
conservative	fascist
doctor	pill-pusher
environmentalist	tree-hugger
fashion model	clothes-peg
intellectual	egghead, nerd
lawyer	mouthpiece, shyster, pettifogger
liberal	bleeding heart, granola head
Marine	jarhead
mechanic	grease monkey
newscaster	talking head
police officer	fuzz, pig
psychiatrist	shrink
rural resident	bumpkin, hick, yokel
surgeon	sawbones
urbanite	city slicker

Many dysphemisms, of course, are hardly printable, as when the word *man* or *woman* is reduced in reference to the low word for a sexual organ. Most racist terms likewise illustrate this phenomenon.

Although they frequently appear in dialogue, dysphemisms rarely find a place in well-edited prose that is not intended to be jocular.

E

each. A. Number. The word *each* raises two problems of number. First, does it take a singular or plural verb, regardless of the construction? And second, must a pronoun referring to it be singular, or is *they* acceptable?

As for the first question, *each* traditionally takes a singular verb, and the best practice is to write *each . . . is* regardless of whether a plural noun intervenes (*each of the members is*)—e.g.: "Sapienza knows that *each* of the players *are* [read *is*] very gifted" (*Pitt. Post-Gaz.*).

The exception occurs when *each* acts in apposition to a plural subject but does not constitute the subject itself. When that is so, the verb should be plural—e.g.: "JR's four Tokyo commuter lines *each* has its own color" (Peter McGill, *The American Express Pocket Guide to Tokyo*, 1988). (Two possible revisions: [1] *JR's four Tokyo commuter lines each have their own color.* [2] *Each of JR's four Tokyo commuter lines has its own color.*)/ "The athletes each *are* seeking more than $50,000 in compensation and Carver and Miller are seeking reinstatement and damages in excess of $1 million" (*Tampa Trib.*). See APPOSITIVES.

As for the second question, pronouns having *each* as an antecedent are traditionally—and most formally—in the singular. E.g.: "Each of them got into *their* [read *his* or *her*, depending on context] car and drove off." But the word *they* has come to take on a singular sense in constructions of this type, as the generic masculine pronoun continues to decline in use. (See SEXISM (B).) The better practice, though, is to change the reference to a plural: "*Both of them* got into *their* cars." Or: "*All of them* got into *their* cars."

B. *Each . . . apiece.* This construction is a REDUNDANCY—e.g.: "Ben Tanner and Kirk Gammill *each* added a goal *apiece* [delete *apiece*]" (*Idaho Statesman*).

each and every. Unless you need a special emphasis, avoid this trite phrase.

each other. A. Possessive Form. The possessive form of this phrase is *each other's*. The noun that follows is often plural <each other's cars>, but the more logical construction is singular <each other's car> <they praised each other's presentation>.

B. And *one another.* *Each other* is most traditionally used in reference to two persons or entities <John and Bob helped each other>; *one another* is best confined to contexts involving more than two <all of them loved one another>. E.g.: "Horrible noise on the one hand; money on the other. How do you relate them to *one another* [read *each other*]?" (Richard A. Lanham, *Revising Prose*, 1979)./ "There is no getting around how important the two are to *each other* on the field" (*Sun-Sentinel*).

early on (= at an early stage) is not the odious locution that some people think. Slightly informal, it is perfectly idiomatic in both AmE and BrE. E.g.: "A chemistry professor who later turned to computer science as a profession, he learned *early on* to love the pleasures of long, solitary treks" (*People*). For *later on*, see **later (B).**

earth. In most contexts, *earth* is both preceded by *the* and lowercased. Although one writer has claimed that *earth* without *the* means "soil" <the excavation left a large pile of earth>, that isn't quite accurate. In fact, when the word is used as a proper noun (and therefore capitalized), the article is also usually omitted <Jupiter is larger than Earth>.

easier is an adjective often misused as an adverb, in contexts where *more easily* is called for—e.g.: "Although most people are still taking the postal route to employment, finding professional work is now being accomplished *much quicker and easier* [read *much more quickly and easily*] thanks to personal computers, modems and the Internet" (*Chicago Trib.*).

easily. See **easy.**

Easter Sunday. Though technically redundant, this phrase is unobjectionable. In fact, the REDUNDANCY is understandable: in many contexts, *Easter* refers to the holiday period beginning late Friday and ending Sunday—e.g.: "We're going to New York for the Easter vacation." That example can be shortened, with no change in meaning, to "We're going to New York for Easter." Thus, *Easter Sunday* is more specific than *Easter* as popularly used.

eastwardly. See DIRECTIONAL WORDS (C).

easy; easily. The word *easy*, an adjective, is understood as an adverb in two SET PHRASES: *go easy* (*on me*, etc.) and *take it easy*. But because the verb *go* and the PHRASAL VERB *take it* can also be understood as linking verbs, the word *easy* can then appear quite appropriately as an adjective. In all other contexts, of course, *easily* is the adverb.

eatable. See **edible.**

eat your cake and have it too. See **you can't eat your cake and have it too.**

ebullient /i-**buul**-yənt/ is frequently mispronounced /**eb**-yə-lənt/. See PRONUNCIATION (B).

economic. A. And *economical*. *Economical* means "thrifty" or, in the current JARGON, "cost-effective." *Economic* should be used for every other meaning possible for the words, almost always in reference to the study of economics. Hence we have *economic studies* and *economic interest* but *economical shopping*. See -IC.

B. And *financial*. *Economic* is increasingly often misused for *financial*. When the reference is to pecuniary affairs of a household or business, the word should be *financial*, not *economic* (which refers to larger-scale finances). There is an irony in the usage, since *economic* comes from a Greek word meaning "of the household." E.g.: "The firm financed a string of big-budget movies that perpetually left it on the brink of *economic* [read *financial*] ruin but managed to come up with a big hit often enough to stay afloat" (*Wash. Post*). But the phrase *economic ruin* is acceptable when the reference is to a geographic area (such as a town) or a country—e.g.: "The news these days is filled with dire predictions about the *economic ruin* awaiting our increasingly long-lived nation" (*Charleston Daily Mail*).

economics may be either singular <economics is a difficult science> or plural <his economics weren't very palatable to most voters>. Today it is more often singular. Cf. **politics.**

ecstasy. So spelled—not *ecstacy*.

ecstatic /ek-**sta**-dik/ is frequently mispronounced /e-**sta**-dik/. See PRONUNCIATION (B).

-ED; -'D. Although R.W. Burchfield says that the BrE preference is for past-participial adjectives such as *cupola'd arch*, *mustachio'd*, *shanghai'd sailor*, and *subpoena'd witness* (*MEU3*), the strong preference in AmE is for *cupolaed arch*, *mustachioed*, *shanghaied sailor*, and *subpoenaed witness*—and even *stockinged feet*. The past tense *OK'd* is an exception.

edible; eatable. These adjectives are broadly synonymous, but they can be differentiated. What is *edible* is capable of being eaten without danger, or fit for consumption <edible plants>. E.g.:

"With any type of *edible* wild mushrooms, it is very important that you always cook them thoroughly" (*Seattle Times*).

What is *eatable* is at least minimally enjoyable or palatable <the food at that restaurant isn't even eatable>. E.g.: "Along the way, they've maintained a live-and-let-live attitude with the gawkers who show up to watch as they paw through the garbage and recycle the *eatable* morsels" (*S.F. Chron.*).

Eatable is often used as an attributive noun, usually in the plural—e.g.: "We can assume that such concentrations of rich *eatables* made them natural synonyms, as time went on, for something politically desirable" (*Virginian-Pilot*).

-EDLY. With words ending in *-edly*, the classic adverbial formula *in a . . . manner* does not work; thus *allegedly* does not mean "in an alleged manner," *purportedly* does not mean "in a purported manner," and *admittedly* does not mean "in an admitted manner." Rather, the unorthodox formula for these words is *it is . . . -ed that*; i.e., *allegedly* means "it is alleged that," and so on. Instead of bewailing the unorthodoxy of these words ending in *-edly*, we should welcome the conciseness they promote and continue to use the several forms that have made their way into common usage. We have many of them, such as *admittedly, allegedly, assertedly, concededly, confessedly, reportedly,* and *supposedly*.

Even so, any new or unusual form ending in *-edly* ought to be avoided if a ready substitute exists—e.g.: " 'I'm as awkward an interviewee as you're likely to get,' he says, laughing *embarrassedly* [read *with embarrassment*]" (*Sunday Telegraph*).

educable. A. And *educible.* *Educable* = capable of being educated. *Educible* = capable of being elicited (or educed).

B. And *educatable.* Although the shorter form is correct, the longer sometimes crops up—e.g.: "Sooner or later, we have to go back to the realization that the only education the *educatable* [read *educable*] can ever get that will keep them from going to prison has to come from their parents" (*Phoenix Gaz.*). See -ATABLE.

-EE. A. General Principles. This suffix (from the French past-participial *-é*) originally denoted "one who is acted upon"; the sense is inherently passive. It's an especially active suffix; that is, people are continually creating NEOLOGISMS with it. Some of these look fairly ridiculous (e.g., *civilizee*), but some readily become quite familiar (e.g., *honoree*, dating from the early 1950s). Although there are exceptions (e.g., *biographee*), words ending in *-ee* are almost always made from verbs in the PASSIVE VOICE—e.g.:

arrestee	= one who is arrested
detainee	= one who is detained
expellee	= one who is expelled
indictee	= one who is indicted
invitee	= one who is invited
permittee	= one who is permitted
returnee	= one who is returned
selectee	= one who is selected
separatee	= one who is separated
smugglee	= one who is smuggled
telephonee	= one who is telephoned

The suffix has also a dative sense, in which it acts as the passive agent noun for the indirect object. This is the sense in which the suffix is most commonly used in peculiarly legal terminology:

advancee	= one to whom money is advanced
consignee	= one to whom something is consigned
disclosee	= one to whom something is disclosed
grantee	= one to whom property is granted
lessee	= one to whom property is leased
patentee	= one to whom a patent has been issued
trustee	= one to whom something is entrusted
vendee	= one to whom something is sold

At least one word ending in *-ee* has both a normal passive sense and a dative sense. *Appointee* = (1) one who is appointed; or (2) one to whom an estate is appointed. Sense 2, of course, is primarily legal.

The suffix *-ee*, then, is correlative to *-or*, the active agent-noun suffix: some words in *-ee* are formed as passive analogues to *-or* agent nouns, and not from any verb stem: *indemnitee* (= one who is indemnified; analogue to *indemnitor*); *preceptee* (= student; analogue to *preceptor*).

These are the traditional uses of the suffix. There is a tendency today, however, to make *-ee* a general agent-noun suffix without regard to its passive sense or the limitations within which it may take on passive senses. Hence the suffix has been extended to PHRASAL VERBS, even though only the first word in the phrase appears in the *-ee* word. Thus *discriminatee* (= one who is discriminated against) and *tippee* (= one who is tipped off). Then other prepositional phrases have gradually come into the wide embrace of *-ee*: *abortee* (= a woman upon whom an abortion is performed); *confiscatee* (= one from whom goods have been confiscated); *optionee* (= one against whose interests another has an option).

Some *-ee* words contain implicit possessives: *amputee* (= one whose limb has been removed); *breachee* (= one whose contract is breached); *condemnee* (= one whose property has been condemned). In still other words, *-ee* does not even have its primary passive sense:

arrivee	= one who arrives
asylee	= one who seeks asylum
attendee	= one who attends
benefitee	= one who benefits (or, possibly, "is benefited")
escapee	= one who escapes
signee	= one who signs
standee	= one who stands

Finally, the suffix is sometimes used to coin jocular words such as *cheatee* (= one who is cheated).

The upshot of this discussion is that *-ee* is subject to abuse and that writers must be careful about the forms they use. For active senses we have *-er*, *-or*, and *-ist* at our service; we should be wary of adopting any new active forms ending in *-ee* and do our best to see that *attendee*, *escapee*, *signee*, *standee*, and similar forms come to an eternal rest. Otherwise, we risk wasting any sense to be found in this suffix. For example, "the unskilled workers used to 'dilute' skilled workers in time of war should have been called *diluters* instead of *dilutees*; the skilled were the dilutees" (*MEU2* at 146).

B. Word Formation. The principles applying to words ending in -ATABLE apply also to agent nouns ending in *-ee*. Thus we have *inauguree*, not *inauguratee*; *subrogee*, not *subrogatee* (though the latter is infrequently used mistakenly for the former).

C. Stylistic Use of. Stylists know that *-ee* agent nouns are often inferior to more descriptive terms. They sometimes objectify the persons they describe, although the writer may intend no callousness—e.g.: "On October 19, 1966, a jury convicted Enriquez of capital murder of Kay Foss, the *abductee* [read *woman abducted*], and imposed the death penalty."

effect, v.t. **A. Generally.** This verb—meaning "to bring about, make happen" or "to occur, take place"—is increasingly rare in English generally. Besides sounding pretentious, it often spawns wordiness. The verb tends to occur alongside BURIED VERBS such as *improvement*—e.g.: "For some schools in the state, the present system of oversight has not *effected improvement* [read *improved things* or *improved anything*]" (*Greensboro News & Record*). (Another possible revision: *The present system of supervision has not improved many of the schools in this state.*)

B. And *affect*. *Effect* (= to bring about) is often misused for *affect* (= to influence, have an effect on). The blunder is widespread—e.g.:

- "Opponents say it would *effect* [read *affect*] only a small number of people—in

New York an estimated 300 criminals a year—and would have little effect on the causes of crime" (*N.Y. Times*).
- "Despite the injuries, Gauthreaux did not miss any time from work and Baylor admitted it did not *effect* [read *affect*] her work" (*Amarillo Daily News*).
- "It is clear that the business community is *effected* [read *affected*] by the ethical climate in which it operates" (*Providence Bus. News*).

It could be that the widespread misuse of *impact* is partly an attempt to sidestep the issue of how to spell *affect*. See **affect & impact.**

C. And *effectuate*. Most dictionaries define these words identically, but their DIFFERENTIATION should be encouraged. Although both mean "to accomplish, bring about, or cause to happen," stylists have generally considered *effect* the preferable word, *effectuate* a NEEDLESS VARIANT.

No longer need this be so. The growing distinction—common especially in law—is that *effect* means "to cause to happen, to bring about" <effect a coup>, while *effectuate* means "to give effect to, to bring into effect" <effectuating the purpose of the statute>.

effective. See **effectual.**

effectively = (1) in an effective manner; well <to speak effectively>; (2) in effect, actually <she has effectively become his mother-surrogate>; or (3) completely; almost completely <that resource is now effectively gone>. All three senses are common.

Effectually (= completely achieving the desired result) often wrongly displaces *effectively* in senses 2 and 3—e.g.: "And introduction of government assistance dictated secularization of the programs, he said, *effectually* [read *effectively*] cutting out the very heart that made it successful" (*Ft. Lauderdale Sun-Sentinel*). See **effectual.**

effectual; effective; efficacious; efficient. All these words mean generally "having effect," but they have distinctive applications. *Effective* = (1) having a high degree of effect (used of a thing done or of the doer) <the court's power to fashion an effective equitable remedy>; or (2) coming into effect <effective June 3, 1994>. *Efficacious* = certain to have the desired effect (used of things) <efficacious drugs>. *Efficient* = competent to perform a task; capable of bringing about a desired effect (used of agents or their actions or instruments) <an efficient organization>. *Efficient* increasingly has economic connotations.

Effectual, perhaps the most troublesome of these words, means "achieving the complete effect aimed at"—e.g.: "George Washington [remarked] in his first annual message to Congress in 1790 that to be prepared for war is one of the most *effectual* ways of preserving peace" (*Wash. Times*). Why the most troublesome? Because *effectual* is often stretched to describe a person instead of a person's action or some other thing—e.g.: "Jenkins . . . became a not wholly *effectual* [read *effective*] President of the Commission" (*Sunday Telegraph*). This stretch is all the more understandable because the negative form—*ineffectual*—usually describes a person <an ineffectual loafer>. But the history of *effectual* has not been parallel: most often, it doesn't refer to persons.

On the use of *effectually* for *effectively*, see **effectively.**

effectually. See **effectively.**

effectuate. See **effect** (C).

effeminate. See **female.**

effete, now a SKUNKED TERM, has traditionally meant "worn out, barren, exhausted"—e.g.: "In contrast, many of the new album's icily elegant, minor-chord-driven tunes sound uninspired, *effete*, even cynical—older indeed, but not necessarily in ways that one associates with creative growth" (*L.A. Times*). But today—thanks in large measure to Vice President Spiro Agnew, who used the phrase *effete corps of impudent snobs*—writers have made it the victim of SLIPSHOD EXTENSION, often making it mean "sophisticated and snobbish." This might have resulted from the similar sound of *elite*—e.g.: "The substantive problem is that the size of government has absolutely nothing to do with the scheming of *effete* snobs" (*Pitt. Post-Gaz.*). Still others use it as a genteelism denoting weakness or effeminacy—e.g.: "The point of all this sound and fury was to turn the stereotype of the *effete*, tuxedo-clad dandy tapper upside-down" (*Orange County Register*). As with other skunked terms, the thing to do is simply to avoid using it.

efficacious. See **effectual.**

efficacy; efficiency. *Efficacy* = the capacity for producing a desired effect; effectiveness <the drugs had greater efficacy when administered at bedtime>. *Efficiency* = the ability to accomplish something with minimum time or effort <the managers worked on improving their efficiency>. Thus, *efficacy* exists when you can do something at all, while *efficiency* exists when you can do something quickly and well.

efficient. See **effectual.**

effrontery. A. For *affront*. *Effrontery* (= shameless insolence), when misused for *affront* (= an open insult), is a MALAPROPISM. E.g.: "This is the ultimate *effrontery* [read *affront*] to the people who support the team—the fans" (*St. Louis Post-Dispatch*).

B. Misspelled *affrontery*. This error is becoming quite common—e.g.: "His fiery Spanish nature refused to allow him to accept such *affrontery* [read *effrontery*]" (*Atlanta J. & Const.*)./"And the provincial employees' *affrontery* [read *effrontery*] shrinks to nothing compared to that of Daryl Bean" (*Toronto Sun*). The correct form *effrontery* derives from the French *effronté* (lit., "shameless"). The erroneous form *affrontery* has no pedigree because it isn't a real word: the *OED* calls it an obsolete mistake for *effrontery*, and the permissive *W3* doesn't even record it. In fact, of course, the error results from confusion with *affront*, which derives from the French *affronter* (lit., "to confront" or "to strike on the head").

-EFY. See -FY.

e.g., the abbreviation for *exempli gratia* (= for example), introduces representative examples. In AmE, it is preferably followed by a comma (or, depending on the construction, a colon) and unitalicized. In BrE, curiously enough, the periods are sometimes omitted—e.g.: "The problem with seeking a legislative cure for the ethical disease is that most of the perceived outrages are either already illegal (*eg*, Pentagon officials taking bribes) or beyond the reach of the law (politicians' sexual adventures)" (*Economist*).

Using the abbreviation *etc.* after an enumeration following *e.g.* is superfluous because one expects nothing more than a representative sample of possibilities. But *etc.* might be required after *i.e.* (L. *id est* "that is") to show the incompleteness of the list.

Be sure to indicate clearly what the signal refers to: "Out-of-pocket losses include medical expenses, lost earnings, and the cost of any labor required to do things that the plaintiff can no longer do himself (*e.g.*, a housekeeper)." But "things the plaintiff can no longer do himself" are not exemplified by *a housekeeper*. (Or does the writer mean *be a housekeeper*?) In any event, wherever readers encounter an *e.g.* they rightly expect a sampling of appropriate items—not an ambiguous or all-inclusive listing. In the given example, it might be, *e.g., keep house, drive a car, tend the garden*. See **i.e.**

either. A. Number of Elements. Most properly, *either . . . or* can frame only two alternatives, and no more: "Now Mr. Arafat has failed for a year to keep the promise without which he never would have seen *either* the White House, its lawn, Mr. Clinton *or* Mr. Rabin [omit *either*]" (*Wall St. J.*).

It is understandable that writers would want to be able to say *any of the following* in fewer than seven syllables—and those who like *either* for this purpose may succeed in the long run. But the better practice, for the time being, is to rely on the disjunctive *or* for a list of many—not *either . . . or*.

B. Faulty Parallelism with *either . . . or*. This is a common problem: "New Hampshire Right to Life sends its newsletter to about 10,000 abortion opponents that Mrs. Hagan said *either contributed money or time* [read *contributed either money or time*] to the cause" (*N.Y. Times*). For more on *either . . . or*, see CORRELATIVE CONJUNCTIONS (A).

C. Singular or Plural. As the subject of a clause, *either* takes a singular verb—e.g.: "The law [is] . . . supposed to be 'family friendly,' but we suggest you keep the kids away from Mom or Dad next April when *either* of them *are* [read *is*] bouncing off the walls with the complex instructions for filing claims" (*Wall St. J.*).

Nouns framed by *either . . . or* take a singular verb when the second noun is singular, but a plural verb when the second noun is plural—e.g.: "[W]hat happens when grown children continue to pull on mom's apron strings or play on her 'mom guilt' for longer than *either they or she needs*?" (*St. Petersburg Times*)./ "[H]e gives every sign of not stopping until *either he or they are* thoroughly defeated" (*Rocky Mountain News*).

D. Meaning "each of two" or "both." *Either* in this sense <houses on either side of the street> is less common than *each* (or *both*). But it is perfectly idiomatic—e.g.: "The framed lists—there is one on *either* side of the chapel—are rolls of all the Dominican sisters from the Springfield Roman Catholic diocese" (*State J.-Register*).

For more on *either . . . or*, see CORRELATIVE CONJUNCTIONS & PARALLELISM.

eke out, a PHRASAL VERB, has traditionally meant "to supplement, add to, or make (a thing) go further or last longer." Today, this usage is rare, but it still sometimes appears—e.g.: "John Andre, their martyred co-conspirator, received a memorial in the Poets Corner of Westminster Abbey—something of an irony since he *eked out* his income by writing doggerel and was unpopular with his fellow officers who patronized him as an opportunist" (*Memphis Commercial Appeal*).

Today, though, the phrase is most commonly used in the sense "to succeed in obtaining or sustaining (a thing) with great difficulty"—e.g.: "In Tokyo, stocks *eked out* small gains by the end of Friday's session after a three-day winning streak" (*S.F. Examiner*). Although this usage began by SLIPSHOD EXTENSION, it is now firmly entrenched as standard.

Unfortunately, by still further extension, sportswriters have come to use *eke* without its Siamese twin *out*, as if it meant something like *squeak*—e.g.: "Actually, you surely noticed that Northwestern *eked* [read *squeaked*?] back into the Top 25 to take the last rung on the strength of whipping the mighty Ohio U. Bobcats" (*Orlando Sentinel*).

elder; eldest. These are variants of *older* and *oldest*, with restricted uses. You might refer to an *elder* brother or sister or to the *eldest* son or daughter, or to an *elder statesman* or *elder in the church* (or *church elder*). But if *older* or *oldest* works in context, it's probably the better choice.

elderly. This adjective is a EUPHEMISM for *aged* or *old*. Deciding at what age to call someone *elderly* must be left to your own good judgment.

-elect is uniformly hyphenated as a combining form—hence *president-elect*, *chair-elect*, etc.

electoral (= of or relating to electors) is so spelled. But *electorial* is a common misspelling—e.g.: "Their analyses of Liberal bills on *electorial* [read *electoral*] redistribution, settling Pearson airport contracts, and Yukon Indian settlements were thorough" (*Toronto Sun*). The word is preferably pronounced /i-**lek**-t[ə]-rəl/, not /ee-lek-**tor**-əl/.

electric; electrical; electronic. *Electric* = (1) of, relating to, or operated by electricity <electric train> <electric chair>; or (2) thrilling; emotionally charged <a musician's electric performance>. *Electrical* overlaps with sense 1 of *electric*—that is, it commonly means "concerned with electricity" <electrical engineering> <electrical outlet>. The choice between the two seems to be governed largely by euphony: although *electric* is more usual, *electrical* occurs in a few SET PHRASES beginning with vowels.

Electronic = (1) of or relating to electrons; or (2) of or relating to the branch of physics known as electronics, or to systems or devices developed through this science. Sense 2 is far more common—e.g.: "Toyota treats a blueprint for a change on an engineer's desk (or its *electronic* equivalent) the way it would an unfinished component" (*Fortune*).

ELEGANT VARIATION. See INELEGANT VARIATION.

elegy; eulogy. An *elegy* is a mournful song or poem, whereas a *eulogy* is a funeral oration or, by extension, a laudatory speech. Writers occasionally misuse *elegy* for *eulogy*—e.g.: "Speaking in precise, well-crafted paragraphs, Poland's most popular political figure delivered an extemporaneous *elegy* [read *eulogy*] to the movement that had spawned him" (*New Republic*).

elemental; elementary. *Elemental* is the more specific term, meaning (1) "of or relating to the elements of something; essential" <an elemental component of the machine>; or (2) "of or relating to a force of nature, or something like it" <elemental rage>.

elf. Pl. *elves*. See PLURALS (G).

elfin; elfish; elvish. The distinction is slight. *Elfin* = (1) of, relating to, or resembling an elf; or (2) having the magical qualities of an elf. *Elfish* = having the mischievous, prankish qualities of an elf. *Elvish* is a NEEDLESS VARIANT.

elicit. See **illicit & solicit (A).**

ELLIPSIS DOTS [. . .]. Ellipsis points—also called "period-dots"—come in threes. Each one is typographically identical to the period, but together they perform a special function: they signal that the writer has omitted something, usually from quoted matter. Consider the following sentence: "Shakespeare's speech—as exhibited in his works, at least—seems to have represented rather well the cultivated usage of Elizabethan England, particularly in the area around London; and what is more, it was sensitive to social levels" (Carroll E. Reed, *Dialects of American English*, 1967). If you quoted that sentence but omitted some words from the middle and at the end, it would look like this: "Shakespeare's speech . . . seems to have represented rather well the cultivated usage of Elizabethan England, particularly in the area around London . . . ." The final period-dot in that quotation, which is spaced evenly with the other three, is simply the period for the sentence; it's not technically part of the ellipsis.

else but; else than. Instead of either of these ungainly phrases, use a simple *but* or the more idiomatic *other than*—e.g.: "[T]his has nothing to do with some supposed slacker mentality that strikes 20-somethings deaf and dumb to anything *else but* [read *but* or *other than*] the boob tube" (*Hartford Courant*).

else's. Possessive constructions such as *anyone else's* and *everyone else's* are preferred to the obsolete constructions *anyone's else* and *everyone's else*. Although *whose else* is technically correct, modern usage prefers *who else's* by analogy to the forms made with *anyone* and *everyone*. See POSSESSIVES (I). .

else than. See **else but.**

elvish. See **elfin.**

EM-; IM-. See EN-.

e-mail; E-mail; email. The first is the prevalent form. The letter *e*—short for *electronic*—is sometimes capitalized, but the trend is to make it lowercase. The unhyphenated *email* is unsightly, but it might prevail in the end.

The word is also coming to be used as a verb <please e-mail me with the answer>.

embarrass. See SPELLING (A).

embassy; legation. Often assumed to be synonymous in diplomatic contexts, these words should be distinguished. An *embassy* is under an ambassador, and a *legation* is under a minister, envoy, *chargé d'affaires*, or other diplomatic agent.

embezzle; misappropriate; steal. *Embezzle* (= to fraudulently convert personal property that one has been entrusted with) is now always used in reference to fiduciaries. *Misappropriate* means "to take for oneself wrongfully" and may or may not be used of a fiduciary. *Steal*, like *misappropriate*, is a broader term than *embezzle*; it has the same meaning as *misappropriate*, but much stronger negative connotations.

EM-DASHES. See DASHES (A).

emigrate. See **immigrate.**

eminent. See **imminent.**

eminently (= notably, conspicuously) is frequently used, in mild hyperbole, to mean "very" <eminently qualified>. For some common misuses, see **imminent.**

Emmy (= the statuette given as a television award) forms the plural *Emmys*—not *Emmies*. See PLURALS (D).

empathetic; empathic. *Empathetic* (= of, relating to, displaying, or eliciting empathy) is the usual form, even though most American dictionaries put the main listing under *empathic*. In modern usage, *empathetic* is nearly five times more common—e.g.: "Five years ago, Harvard psychologist Carol Gilligan published 'Meeting at the Crossroads,' a luminously *empathetic* study of adolescents at an all-girls private school in Cleveland" (*L.A. Times*). *Empathic* should be classed as a NEEDLESS VARIANT.

empathy; sympathy. *Empathy* is the ability to imagine oneself in another person's position and to experience all the sensations connected with it. *Sympathy* is compassion for or commiseration with another.

employ is a FORMAL WORD for *use*—and is inferior whenever *use* might suffice.

employe(e). Although *employé*, the French form, might logically be thought to be better as a generic term, *employée* (which in French denotes the feminine gender) is so widespread—minus the accent mark—that it is not likely to be uprooted. Although *The Wall Street Journal* and a few other publications remain staunch adherents to *employe*, the form *employee* is standard.

EN-; IN-. No consistent rule exists for determining which form of the prefix to use before a given word. But it's fair to say that the French form *en-* is more a living prefix than *in-*. That is, *en-* has won most of the battles in which it contended against *in-*.

The following lists show the preferred form at left and the variant on the right. Of course, when the root word begins with a *-b-*, *-m-*, or *-p-*, the prefix typically becomes *em-* or *im-*.

Preferred Form	*Variant Form*
embalm	imbalm
embark	imbark
embed	imbed
embitter	imbitter
emblaze	imblaze
embody	imbody
embolden	imbolden
embosom	imbosom
embower	imbower
embrown	imbrown
empanel	impanel
empower	impower
encage	incage
encapsulate	incapsulate
encase	incase
enclasp	inclasp
enclose	inclose
enclosure	inclosure
encrust	incrust
encumber	incumber
encumbrance	incumbrance
endow	indow
endowment	indowment
endue	indue
enfold	infold
engraft	ingraft
engulf	ingulf
enlace	inlace
enmesh	inmesh
ensheathe	insheathe
enshrine	inshrine
ensnare	insnare
ensoul	insoul
ensphere	insphere
enthrall	inthrall
enthrone	inthrone
entitle	intitle
entomb	intomb
entreat	intreat
entrench	intrench
entrust	intrust
entwine	intwine
entwist	intwist
enwind	inwind
enwrap	inwrap
enwreathe	inwreathe
imbrue	embrue
impale	empale
impoverish	empoverish
inflame	enflame
ingrain	engrain
inquire	enquire
inquiry	enquiry
inure	enure

Especially troublesome to writers are word pairs with varying prefixes according to inflection: *enjoin* but *injunction*.

For a discussion of *in-* as both privative and intensive, see NEGATIVES (A).

enamored takes the preposition *of*, not *with*—e.g.: "There are also the areas we are becoming *enamored with* [read *enamored of*]: for example, health insurance, security companies" (*Crain's Detroit Bus.*).

enclosed please find; please find enclosed; enclosed herewith; enclosed herein. These phrases—common in commercial and legal correspondence—are archaic deadwood for *here are*, *enclosed is*, *I've enclosed*, *I am enclosing*, or the like. Interestingly, business-writing texts have consistently condemned the phrases since the late 19th century:

- "[*Please find enclosed*:] A more ridiculous use of words, it seems to me, there could not be" (Richard Grant White, *Every-Day English*, 1880).
- "*Inclosed herewith please find. Inclosed* and *herewith* mean the same thing. How foolish to tell your reader twice exactly where the check is, and then to suggest that he look around to see if he can find it anywhere. Say, 'We are inclosing our check for $2550' " (Wallace E. Bartholomew & Floyd Hurlbut, *The Business Man's English*, 1924). (In that sentence, *inclose* should be *enclose*.)
- "*Please Find Enclosed.* This worn-out formula is not in good use in letters, either business or personal" (Maurice H. Weseen, *Crowell's Dictionary of English Grammar*, 1928).
- "Business words and expression borrowed from an earlier generation can make your writing sound artificial and pedantic. Every letter will read like a form letter, and you will sound bored or, even worse, boring. Thinking up substi-

tute phrases is easy if you put your mind to it. Consider some of these revisions: ... *Enclosed please find* [becomes] *I am enclosing*" (Maryann V. Piotrowski, *Effective Business Writing*, 1989).

EN-DASHES. See DASHES (B).

endeavor, vb., is a FORMAL WORD for *attempt* or *try*—either of which is preferable in everyday contexts. But *endeavor* suggests more of a challenge and more of a sustained effort—e.g.: "If you are trying to prove that your ancestor arrived in Texas before the closing days of the Republic in the 1840s or if you are *endeavoring* to learn how, when and where your foreign-born Texas ancestors were naturalized, the voter registration lists will reveal these facts" (*Dallas Morning News*).

The same is true of *endeavor*, n., which means "an undertaking; earnest attempt." E.g.: "From that standpoint, [the march] has the makings of a worthy *endeavor*—one designed to promote pride in Latinos, a diverse group of ethnicities, as well as push political awareness" (*Riverside Press-Enterprise*).

endemic. See **epidemic.**

end(ing), n. *End*, not *ending*, corresponds to *beginning*. E.g.: "The turnover of the Sinai is a beginning, not an *ending* [read *end*]." Obviously, the writer was trying for parallel *-ings*. See PARALLELISM.

ENDNOTES. See FOOTNOTES (B).

endorse; indorse. The usual spelling is *endorse*, and that is the only acceptable spelling when the word is used figuratively to mean "to express approval of publicly; to support." E.g.: "The IRS, of course, doesn't sanction or *endorse* specific investments" (*Money*).

In legal discussions relating to checks and other negotiable instruments, *indorse* predominates in AmE. But popularly, *endorse* is the more frequent spelling in all contexts—and most checks have "Endorse here" printed on the back. *Endorse on the back* is a REDUNDANCY because the root *dors-* means "back."

end product is usually a REDUNDANCY for *product*.

end result is a REDUNDANCY for *result*. William Safire calls it "redundant, tautological and unnecessarily repetitive, not to mention prolix and wordy" (*N.Y. Times*). The only exception occurs when the writer needs to refer to *intermediate results* as well as *end results*. Cf. **final outcome.**

England. See **Great Britain.**

enormity; enormousness. The historical DIFFERENTIATION between these words should not be muddled. *Enormousness* = hugeness, vastness. *Enormity* = outrageousness, ghastliness, hideousness. For example, Alan Dershowitz once said that Noam Chomsky "trivializes the *enormity* of the Chinese massacre [at Tiananmen Square on 4 June 1989]" (*L.A. Times*). But President Bush was less fastidious when referring to a different event: on July 10, 1989, he was buoyed and cheered by what he called "the enormity of this moment," which he said presented a historic challenge to reform the Polish economy.

The following examples typify the careful writer's usage—e.g.: "The last question invites comparison of the mere misfortunes of the defendant with the *enormity* of the killing" (*Baltimore Sun*)./ " 'A limited encounter with the Devil,' his clansmen now try to explain, even as they realize the *enormity* of his sin" (*N.Y. Times*).

But *enormity* is all too often misused—e.g.: "A biographical sketch prepared by the university shows the *enormity* [read *magnitude*] of his energy and output" (*Charleston Daily Mail*)./ "Nothing in this story can make the Milky Way's incredible presence understandable. Yet one thing is certain. Its *enormity* [read *enormousness* or *enormous size*] places things in perspective" (*N.J. Record*).

Sometimes the term is ambiguous. Is the writer of the following sentence partisan? And if so, is the writer a Republican or a Democrat? "Pick a superlative, any superlative. Chances are it doesn't come close to portraying the *enormity* of the Republican victory Tuesday" (*Amarillo Globe-Times*).

enough, adj.; **sufficient.** Although *enough* modifies either count nouns <enough books> or mass nouns <enough stamina>, *sufficient* should modify only mass nouns <sufficient oxygen>. (See COUNT NOUNS AND MASS NOUNS.) There are of course exceptions to the general rule: *sufficient* (or more often *insufficient*) *funds* is a common phrase. But the following examples misuse *sufficient* for *enough*: "[P]resident Rosemary Brester reports she's encountering substantial problems finding *sufficient* [read *enough*] people to meet her expanding order book" (*Puget Sound Bus. J.*)./ "And even where there are *sufficient* [read *enough*] doctors, people are gradually realising that not every consultation needs a fully-qualified GP" (*Daily Record*). For more on *sufficient*, see **adequate (A).**

enough, adv.; **sufficiently.** The same rule of thumb that applies to the adjectives applies to the adverbs as well—though because of the strictures of grammar, errors with this pair are less likely to occur.

enplane. See AIRLINESE.

enquiry. See **inquiry (B).**

ensure; insure. See **assure.**

enthuse, vb., is a widely criticized BACK-FORMATION avoided by writers and speakers who care about their language. The verb can be either transitive or intransitive—e.g.:

- Transitive: "He *enthused* [read *stated enthusiastically* or, perhaps, *gushed*] that she was remarkable shortly after meeting her."
- Transitive: "They appeared on television; they *enthused* [read *inspired*] student volunteers with their ideas" (*Economist*).
- Intransitive: "Avon Editor in Chief Bob Mecoy *enthuses* [read *raves* or *rhapsodizes*] about the graphic-novel form" (*Newsweek*).

Although the adjective *enthused* is virtually always inferior to *enthusiastic*, it is increasingly common—e.g.: "Stabenow seemed *enthused* [preferably *enthusiastic*] about the possibilities last week" (*Newsweek*)./ "With reviews like that, Detroit is so *enthused* [preferably *enthusiastic*] about its prospects that it is positioning the new class of compacts as the centerpiece of an old-fashioned, '50s- and '60s-style all-out autumn advertising blitz" (*Time*).

entire is accented on the second syllable: /en-**tɪr**/, not /**en**-tɪr/. On this word as an uncomparable adjective, see ADJECTIVES (B).

entitle; title, v.t. The word *entitle* has two meanings: (1) "to provide with a right or title to something" <entitled to a discount>; and (2) "to give a title to" <a book entitled *Woe Unto You, Lawyers!*>. Sense 1 is more common. And sense 2, in the best usage, is confined to the past-participial adjective (as in the illustration with the book title).

As a transitive verb, *title* is preferred over *entitle*. Hence *What are you going to title your article?*, not *What are you going to entitle your article?*

ENUMERATIONS. A. *First(ly), second(ly), third(ly); one, two, three.* The best method of enumerating items is the straightforward *first*, *second*, and *third*. The forms *firstly*, *secondly*, and *thirdly* have an unnecessary syllable, and *one*, *two*, and *three* seem especially informal. E.g.: "This leaves but two possible effects of the service mark's continued use: *One* [read *First*], no one will know what CONAN means. *Two* [read *Second*], those who are familiar with the plaintiff's property will continue to associate CONAN with THE BARBARIAN." See **firstly.**

B. Comma Before the Last Element. The question whether to use the serial comma—or, as it's sometimes called, the "Harvard" comma or "Oxford" comma—is more vehemently argued than any other punctuation issue. Fashions in public-school textbooks and journalists' manuals come and go, but only one method is ironclad in avoiding unnecessary ambiguities: inserting a comma before the final element. Thus *a, b, and c* rather than *a, b and c*. The problems arise with elements containing two or more items, as *a and b, c and d, e and f, and g and h*. The last two elements are muddled if the comma is omitted. See COMMA.

C. Within a Single Sentence. To keep the sentence short, enumerate items with parenthetical numbers: *(1), (2), (3),* etc. Of course, if the sentence becomes overlong anyway, you're better off dividing it up into separate ones.

D. *And* Before the Last Element. See **and (C).**

E. Bullets. See BULLET DOT.

envelop is the verb ("to wrap or cover"), *envelope* the noun ("wrapper, covering"). The verb is pronounced /en-**vel**-əp/; the noun is pronounced either /**en**-və-lohp/ or /**on**-və-lohp/.

enviable; envious. That which is *enviable* arouses envy or is at least worthy of it. A person who is *envious* suffers from envy. *Envious* usually takes the preposition *of* <envious of her sister's success>, but historically has also taken *against* or *at*. See **jealousy.**

Some writers confuse the two words—e.g.: "Mr. Strauss's financial disclosure statement . . . details what is already widely known: the 72-year-old lawyer is a power broker of abundant wealth and *envious* [read *enviable*] political and corporate connections" (*N.Y. Times*).

envy. See **jealousy & enviable.**

epidemic; endemic. A disease is an *epidemic* when it breaks out and rages in a community, only to subside afterwards. A disease is an *endemic* when it constantly exists within a certain population or region.

The words are sometimes used as adjectives. *Epidemic* = extremely prevalent; widespread. *Endemic* = native to a particular region or group.

epigram; epigraph. Because these similar-sounding terms are similar in meaning, they are therefore often subject to WORD-SWAPPING. *Epigram* = (1) a short, witty poem; or (2) a concise, pointed, and usu. clever saying. *Epigraph* = (1) an inscription, esp. on a building or statue; or (2) a thematic quotation at the beginning of a book, chapter, etc. Thus, although an *epigram* can constitute an *epigraph*, the reverse does not hold true.

epitaph (= a gravestone inscription) is sometimes misused for *epithet* (= [1] a derogatory name; or [2] in grammar, a "dummy" subject such as *it* or *there* in the phrase *it is* or *there are*). Today the blooper is irksomely common—e.g.: " 'Protectionist' *epitaphs* [read *epithets*] are hurled at any American union that decries how its members are losing jobs as U.S. companies search for cheap labor" (*Buffalo News*)./ "Santiago, of the 3400 block of Lituanica, beat the mailman with a pool cue and shouted racial *epitaphs* [read *epithets*], Burnett said" (*Chicago Sun-Times*).

epithet; expletive. *Epithet* = (1) an especially apt adjective, whether the quality described is favorable or unfavorable; or (2) an abusive term, slur. Sense 2 is slowly driving out sense 1, a trend to be fought against.

Expletive = (1) an interjectory word or expression (esp. a profane or scatological one); (2) in grammar, a word that fills the syntactic position of another (most commonly *it* or *there*), as in

It is difficult to describe how . . . or *There are five . . . .*

epitome /i-**pit**-ə-mee *or* ee-**pit**-ə-mee/ = a summary, abstract, or ideal representation. E.g.: "In short, he is the *epitome* of all that many liberals find evil in the boardrooms of America" (*Boston Herald*).

The word doesn't mean "pinnacle" or "climax"—e.g.: "ESPN reached the *epitome* [read *pinnacle* or *zenith*] of boredom during its marathon coverage of the NFL draft" (*S.F. Chron.*).

equable; equitable. *Equable* = even; tranquil; level. *Equitable*, deriving from *equity*, has associations of justice and fairness, or that which can be sustained in a court of equity. To nonlawyers it generally means "fair," whereas to lawyers it may mean "fair," but just as often means "in equity" <equitable jurisdiction> <equitable remedies>.

equally as. This phrase is almost always unnecessary—e.g.: "Senior Darnell Morgan (5-9, 171) leads the way with 466 yards. Chapman plays defense *equally as* [read *equally*] well" (*L.A. Times*). Not every use, though, is incorrect: if the words *equally as* simply appear together, but are really parts of other constructions, all is well <I love you equally as a nephew and as a friend>.

equitable. See **equable.**

equivalent. A. Prepositions with. As an adjective, *equivalent* preferably takes the preposition *to*, not *with*—e.g.: "The $20 million is more than any other NFL coach will receive and approximately *equivalent with* [read *equivalent to*] the $3 million a year that Pat Riley and John Calipari earn in the NBA" (*Baltimore Sun*). As a noun, it almost always takes the preposition *of* <this Australian wine is an equivalent of a good, robust Burgundy>.

B. A Malapropism: *equivocal with*. Misusing *equivocal* for *equivalent* is a surprising MALAPROPISM, committed here by the chair of a college biology department: "Though physical sexual identity is not *equivocal with* [read *equivalent to*] sexual orientation, the point I am trying to make is that not all things are as black and white as some homophobes might like them to be" (*Ariz. Republic*).

-ER. A. And *-or*. These agent-noun suffixes can be especially vexatious. The historical tendency has been to make the Latinate *-or* the correlative of *-ee*, hence *indemnitee / indemnitor*, *obligee / obligor*, *transferee / transferor*, *offeree / offeror*, *donee / donor*. See -EE.

Attempts to confine *-er* to words of Anglo-Saxon origin and *-or* to those of Latin origin are fruitless because so many exceptions exist on both sides of the aisle. Nevertheless, Latinate words usually take *-or*, though there are many exceptions—a few of which appear below in the *-er* column:

-er	*-or*
adapter	abductor
conjurer	collector
corrupter	distributor
digester	impostor
dispenser	infiltrator
endorser	investor
eraser	manipulator
idolater	persecutor
promoter	purveyor
requester	surveyor

B. And *-re*. Words borrowed from French generally arrived in English with the *-re* spelling. Most such words have gradually made the transition to *-er*. A few words may be spelled only *-re*, such as *acre*, *chancre*, *massacre*, and *mediocre*, because of the preceding *-c-*. Still others—the great majority—have variant spellings, the *-er* ending usually being more common in AmE and the *-re* ending in BrE. The following words have variants subject to this distinction: *accouter, -re*; *caliber, -re*; *center, -re*; *goiter, -re*; *liter, -re*; *louver, -re*; *luster, -re*; *maneuver, manoeuvre*; *meager, -re*; *meter, -re*; *miter, -re*; *niter, -re*; *reconnoiter, -re*; *scepter, -re*; *sepulcher, -re*; *somber, -re*; *specter, -re*; *theater, -re*.

Occasionally, heated debates break out over how to spell such words. In the late 1970s and early 1980s, the Government Printing Office was accused of upsetting the balance of trade by recommending *liter* over *litre*. The pro-*litre* forces argued that other nations would be more likely to import American goods if those goods bore the *litre* spelling. But when the GPO conducted a worldwide survey, it found that more people spell it *liter* than *litre*. And so *liter* it remained in official American publications.

Some American companies have started using the *-re* spellings to distinguish themselves and perhaps to bring some cachet to their projects. Many major cities, for example, have downtown buildings called *Such-and-Such Centre*. Next door might be the *Such-and-Such Theatre*. People who go into such centers and theaters should be on their best behavior—no, make that *behaviour*.

C. And *-est*. See COMPARATIVES AND SUPERLATIVES.

err should properly rhyme with *purr*. It is incorrect, strictly speaking, to say it as *air*—a mispronunciation that mimics the first syllable in the word *error*.

errata. Like *addenda* and *corrigenda*, the plural form *errata* (= errors; corrections to be made) should be used only when listing more than one item. E.g.: "It is important to clarify some of its abundant *errata*" (*Chattanooga Times*). (See PLURALS (B).) If there is only one mistake, the singular *erratum* is called for <it was the most embarrassing possible erratum>. The English plural *erratums* is not used.

erroneous is sometimes erroneously spelled *erronious*.

escalate is pronounced /**es**-kə-layt/, not /**es**-kyə-layt/.

escapee (= one who escapes) should more logically be *escaper* or *escapist*. (See -EE.) The *OED* suggests that *escapee* is waning in use and that *escapist* is emerging as standard BrE. American writers seem to prefer *escaper*, which might be better for two reasons. First, *escapist* suggests Houdini, i.e., one who makes a living putting on "escapes" from difficult predicaments (also known as an *escapologist*). Second, *escapist* has irrelevant figurative uses, as in *escapist fiction* (i.e., as the adjective corresponding to *escapism*).

One writer defines *escapee* as "one who has been caught after escaping, or while preparing to escape" (Paul Tempest, *Lag's Lexicon*, 1950). Perhaps that is how a *lag* (= a convict sentenced to penal servitude) understands the term. But most writers and speakers would find nothing wrong with saying, "The *escapees* were never caught"—they would merely find something wrong with their not being caught.

especial; special. Traditionally, *especial* (= distinctive, significant, peculiar) is the opposite of *ordinary*. E.g.: "The public press is entitled to peculiar indulgence and has *especial* rights and privileges." *Special* (= specific, particular) is the opposite of *general* <this community has special concerns>, though increasingly *special* is driving out *especial*.

Especial is so rarely used in AmE today—even in learned journals—that some might term it obsolescent. But it does occasionally appear, most often when modifying a noun made from an adjective; that is, a writer who might otherwise refer to something that is *especially powerful* would refer to its *especial power*—e.g.: "I found myself wishing the NSO had packed a showstopper—an American work of *especial* power and virtuosity" (*Wash. Post*). The phrase *special power* might have connoted something like a superhuman or otherworldly power—surely not the intended sense.

espresso (= a specially prepared coffee through which steam is forced under high pressure) is so spelled—not *ex-*

presso. But writers frequently get this wrong—e.g.: "Paul Leighton, co-owner of the Coffee Corner Ltd., a Eugene-based coffee shop chain, said he expects a cup of coffee to cost $1 at most local coffee bars and *expresso* [read *espresso*] stands by summer's end" (*Eugene Register-Guard*).

Esq., in AmE, typically signifies that the person whose name it follows is a lawyer. The mild honorific is used nowadays with the names of men and women alike; it is incorrect, however, to use it with any other title, such as *Mr.* or *Ms.* In BrE, of course, *esquire* is used of any man thought to have the status of a gentleman.

-ESQUE. This suffix—meaning "like, resembling"—almost always creates a solid word, as in *romanesque, Rubenesque, statuesque*. E.g.: "One could almost see the *Clintonesque* curling and biting of the lip for dramatic effect" (*Omaha World-Herald*). Of course, given the suffix's meaning, it's wrong to add *-like* to the end of such a word—e.g.: "A man painted in white stands on a pedestal striking various *statuesque-like* [read *statue-like* or *statuesque*] poses" (*Orlando Bus. J.*).

-ESS. See SEXISM (D).

-EST. For antique verb forms such as *goest* and *sayest*, see ARCHAISMS (B). For superlative adjectives such as *strongest* and *finest*, see COMPARATIVES AND SUPERLATIVES.

estate agent. See **realtor.**

esthetic. See **aesthetic.**

et al. is the abbreviated form of the Latin phrase *et alii* (= and others). It is used only in reference to persons, whereas *etc.* is used in reference to things. American writers commonly punctuate it *et al*, *et. al.*, or *et. al*—all of which are wrong.

It does not fit comfortably alongside possessives: "Clifford T. Honicker's chilling account of Louis Slotin's, S. Allan Kline's *et al.* encounter with the Nuclear Age is as horrific as it is emblematic" (*N.Y. Times*). (Read: *Clifford T. Honicker's chilling account of Louis Slotin's, S. Allan Kline's, and others' encounter* . . . .).

For the misuse of *etc.* for *et al.*, see **etc. (C).**

etc. A. Generally. More than 400 years ago, John Florio wrote: "The heaviest thing that is, is one *Etcetera*." It is heaviest because it implies a number too extensive to mention. Following are some of the most sensible words ever written on *etc.*:

> Every writer should be on his guard against the excessive use of *etc.* Instead of finishing a thought completely, it is easy to end with an *etc.*, throwing the burden of finishing the thought upon the reader. If the thought is adequately expressed, *etc.* is not needed. If the thought is not adequately expressed, *etc.* will not take the place of that which has not been said. The use of *etc.* tends to become a slovenly habit, the corrective for which is to refrain from using *etc.* except in the driest and most documentary kind of writing.
> George P. Krapp, *A Comprehensive Guide to Good English* 229 (1927).

Whenever possible, try to be specific about what you mean rather than resorting to *etc.* Still, it would be foolish to lay down an absolute proscription against *etc.*, because often one simply *cannot* practicably list all that should be listed in a given context. Hence, rather than convey to the reader that a list is seemingly complete when it is not, the writer might justifiably use *etc.* (always the abbreviation).

B. *And etc.* This is an ignorant REDUNDANCY, *et* being the Latin *and*.

C. For *et al.* The term *etc.* should be reserved for things, not for people; *et al.* serves when people are being mentioned. But liberal ideologues might think the following usage quite appropriate: "The presidential heavyweight hopefuls—Dole, Sen. Phil Gramm, ex-Tennessee Gov. Lamar Alexander, *etc.* [read *et al.*]—were present and accounted for at the GOP Midwest leadership conference in Green Bay over the weekend" (*Chicago Trib.*). See **et al.**

D. Misspelled and Mispronounced. The abbreviation is surprisingly often misspelled *ect.*, perhaps because the *-t-* in the first syllable of *etc.* is often mispronounced as an *-x-* (as if it were *ex cetera*). See PRONUNCIATION (B).

E. Punctuating. Punctuate around this phrase just as if the words *and others* were substituted in its place. For example, don't put a comma after *etc.* if it's the tail end of a subject: *Carrots, potatoes, broccoli, etc. have the advantage of being vegetables.* The *Chicago Manual of Style* sits on the fence with this point, recommending the extra-comma approach but allowing the no-comma approach. But because it's more logical—and consistent with other phrases in a series—the more fastidious approach is to omit the comma.

F. Using with *e.g.* or *i.e.* See **e.g. & i.e.**

-ETH. See ARCHAISMS (B).

ethicist; ethician. *Ethician* is more than two centuries older (dating from the early 17th century) and is therefore given precedence in most dictionaries. But *ethicist* overwhelmingly predominates in modern usage—being about 400 times more common—so *ethician* is now a NEEDLESS VARIANT. E.g.: "George Annas, a Boston University medical *ethicist*, opposes the legislation and predicted it will never pass in Massachusetts" (*Quincy Patriot Ledger*).

-ETTE. See SEXISM (D).

ETYMOLOGY. A. English Etymology Generally. Etymology is the study of word derivations. Understanding etymology often leads to a greater appreciation of linguistic nuances. For example, knowing the history of words such as the following can open up vistas:

- *abominable*, L. *ab-* "off, away from" + *ominari* "to prophesy, forebode"—hence "being an evil omen."
- *exorbitant*, L. *ex-* "out of, away from" + *orbita* "wheel track"—hence "off track" or "out of line."
- *inoculate*, L. *in-* "into" + *oculus* "eye (i.e., 'bud,' as in eye of a potato)"—hence to graft a bud from one plant to another, where it will continue to grow. The sense of implanting germs to produce immunity from a disease dates from the early 18th century.
- *symposium*, Gk. *syn-* "together" + *posis* "a drink." The term was extended from "a drinking party" to "a convivial meeting for intellectual stimulation," and then was extended further to "a collection of articles published together on a given topic."

Learning the classical roots and prefixes of English words—as by studying Donald M. Ayers's *English Words from Latin and Greek Elements* (2d ed. 1986)—will certainly repay the effort.

But while the study can help considerably, making a fetish of it can lead to many linguistic fallacies. For many words, modern usage is pretty well divorced from etymology. For example, in distinguishing *assiduous* from *sedulous*, it doesn't particularly help to say that *assiduous* is "sitting to" a thing and that *sedulous* is merely "sitting." It would be more helpful to note that although the words are close synonyms, *assiduous* is much more common (by a 20-to-1 margin). And although the etymology of *assiduous* suggests greater intensity, the rarity of *sedulous* betokens a special intensity.

Another fallacy arises when pedants object irrationally to ill-formed words. Some, for example, insist that *homophobe*, in Greek, would refer to a self-hater. But in English, of course, *homo* is simply a slang shortening of *homosexual*, and *homophobe*—though at variance with classical word formation—is perfectly understandable to any reasonable speaker of AmE. The etymological "error" is no error at all.

So learn all you can about etymology, but temper that knowledge with other types of linguistic facts. Then you'll be in a position to choose words prudently.

And you'll be better equipped to answer questions such as these: Must *alternatives* be limited to two? Must a *decimation* involve the destruction of only 10% of a group of things? Which spelling is right: *idiosyncrasy* or *idiosyncracy*? For views on those questions, see the appropriate entries.

B. Native vs. Classical Elements. The English language has undoubtedly benefited from its diverse sources. This diversity springs mostly from the English Renaissance, when writers decided to supplement what they considered a meager vocabulary by importing words.

They borrowed freely from foreign languages—mostly Latin, French, and Greek—when adding to the English word-stock. Thus William Caxton, who introduced printing into England in 1477, is credited in the *OED* with the first use of *abjure*, *admiration*, *apparition*, *calumnious*, *capacity*, *desperate*, *factor*, *ingenious*, *inhuman*, *nuptial*, *seduce*, and *sumptuous*, among many others. It might be hard for modern readers to imagine a time when those words seemed foreign or absurd. But many of Caxton's other borrowings haven't fared so well: for example, *excidion* (= a rooting out), *exercite* (= army), *magistration* (= a command). Another early word-borrower, Thomas Elyot, wrote in the early 16th century. Like Caxton, Elyot had his word-coining successes (*animate*, *attraction*, *education*, *excrement*, *exterior*, *frugality*, *irritate*, *persist*) as well as his failures (*allective*, *applicate*, *assentatour*). In that respect, these writers are typical of the age.

Some coinages from that period seem not to have arisen from any felt need but from a particular writer's penchant for the far-fetched. Thus, our historical dictionaries are brimming with strange and ridiculous formations, such as *celeripedian* (= a swift footman). Many such terms, which appeared only once or twice in the recorded history of the language, were coined by fervent neologists who had little or no sense of linguistic necessity. See NEOLOGISMS.

The result of all this word-coining, though, is that English now has many sets of words formed from analogous etymological elements. Many of these words, having coexisted in English for many centuries, retain the same basic meanings:

Greek	Latin/French	Anglo-Saxon
enchiridion	manual	handbook
hypogeal	subterranean	underground
prolegomenon	prologue	foreword
prophesy	predict	foretell
sarcophagous	carnivorous	meat-eating

But others have undergone DIFFERENTIATION to varying degrees:

Greek	Latin/French	Anglo-Saxon
——	postpartum	afterbirth
prodrome	precursor	forerunner
prognosis	prescience	foreknowledge
sympathy	compassion	fellow feeling
thesis	position	placement

Those listings show that the Greek derivatives tend to be the most arcane, the Latin a little less so, and the Anglo-Saxon not at all. But this tendency has many exceptions. The Anglo-Saxon *gainsay* is certainly less common today than the Latin *contradict*. And the Greek is much more common than the Latin in the following pairs: *anonymous* (Gk.) and *innominate* (L.); *hypodermic* (Gk.) and *subcutaneous* (L.); *anthology* (Gk.) and *florilegium* (L.).

All in all, though, the generalization about Greek derivatives—when they have synonyms from Latin or Anglo-Saxon—holds true. Many Greek terms lie at the periphery of the English language—e.g.:

analphabetic (= illiterate [L.], unlettered [A.S.])
anamnesis (= reminiscence [L.])
chirography (= handwriting [A.S.])
exlex (= outlaw [A.S.])
peritomy (= circumcision [L.])

They therefore serve writers inclined toward SESQUIPEDALITY, but they seem laughable to those inclined toward PLAIN LANGUAGE.

Regardless of your bent, it's useful to enhance your awareness of Greek and

Latin word roots. You'll gain a greater sensitivity to the English language and its origins and nuances.

C. Etymological Awareness. Through wide reading and a conscious sensitivity to words and their origins, good writers become aware of etymological associations that may escape others. Ignorance of etymologies can easily lead writers astray, as when a journalist gave the label *holocaust* (Gk. "burnt whole") to a flood. Following are sentences in which writers wandered into etymological bogs:

- "The right to exclude or to expel aliens in war or in peace is an inherent and *inalienable* right of every independent nation." (The root *alien-* causes problems when we say that a country has an *inalienable* right to exclude *aliens.*)
- "What we are concerned with here is the automobile and its *peripatetic* [= able to walk up and down, not just *itinerant*] character."
- "This is a result which, if at all possible *consonant* [lit., "sounding together"] with *sound* judicial policy, should be avoided."

In the first and third specimens, an incongruous repetition of the root sense occurs; in the second, the writer has insensitively abstracted and broadened a word still ineluctably tied to its root sense. Cf. SOUND OF PROSE & VERBAL AWARENESS.

D. Folk Etymology. Popular notions of etymology are often quite colorful—and quite wrong. Indeed, word origins are a common subject of conversation in English-speaking countries. But such discussions ought to be well grounded because linguistic resources are widely available to serve as guides.

That wasn't always so, and folk etymology has left its mark on the language. Take a few common examples. *Pea* is a false singular of *pease*, which was mistakenly taken as a plural. Likewise, *a newt* is a historical error for *an ewt, an adder* for *a nadder*, and *an apron* for *a napron*. *Titmouse* now makes the plural *titmice* even though the word has no real connection with *mouse* or *mice*. *Primrose* and *rosemary* were earlier *primerole* and *romarin*, neither of which has anything to do with roses, but they were respelled precisely on that mistaken assumption.

Historical examples may be interesting, but modern examples are still reparable. To cite but one example, many quite educated people believe that *posh* means "port outward, starboard home," and that the word refers to the most desirable positions in an ocean liner. In fact, though, professional etymologists haven't ascertained that etymology—indeed, they've pretty much rejected it. Thus, under *posh*, most dictionaries say "origin unknown." Although the popular notion would make it a colorful term, the facts unfortunately get in the way of a good story.

A typical example of folk etymology occurs in the following sentence, in which the writer apparently wants the base word *mean* to bear its ordinary English sense in the word *demean*: "By ridiculing the idea of vampires ('Vampires haunt Russian psyche,' 14 November), you *demean* yourself (literally, deprive yourself—and us—of meaning) and hold out a less-than-supporting hand to the northern Russians whose plight you depict" (*Independent*). In fact, though, *demean* doesn't mean "to deprive of meaning"; rather, its sense is "to lower in quality or position."

For other examples of folk etymology treated in this book, see **coleslaw, helpmate, hiccup & Welsh rabbit.** For a good study on the subject, see Hugh Rawson, *Devious Derivations*, 1994.

EUPHEMISMS are supposedly soft or unobjectionable terms used in place of harsh or objectionable ones. The purpose is to soften; the means is usually indirection. To discerning readers, of course, some euphemisms may seem unnecessarily mealy-mouthed.

We euphemize if we say not that someone is drunk, but *inebriated* or *in-*

toxicated; not that someone is a *drug addict*, but (much more vaguely) that the person is *impaired*; not that someone has *died*, but *passed away*; not that someone is *mentally retarded*, but *exceptional* or *special*; not that someone is *disabled*, but *differently abled* or even *challenged*; not that someone is *malingering*, but that the person is *suffering from a factitious disorder*.

In some contexts, to be sure, you might prefer a euphemism. If plain talk is going to provoke unnecessary controversy—if talk about *illegitimate children* or *sodomy* will divert attention from your point by offending people—then use an established euphemism.

Indeed, the phrase *illegitimate children* exemplifies the need sometimes to throw over old forms of expression. One legal publisher's system of indexing legal topics went from *Bastards* in the 1960s to *Illegitimate Children* in the 1970s to *Children Out-of-Wedlock* in the 1980s. Some writers use *nonmarital children* to convey the idea. The point, of course, is that we shouldn't scar innocent children with ugly epithets.

Other euphemisms, however, are roundabout and clumsy. Some writers use *rodent operative* or *extermination engineer* in place of *rat-catcher*. We see *pregnancy termination* rather than *abortion*; *sexually ambidextrous* rather than *bisexual*; *armed reconnaissance* rather than *bombing*; *permanent layoff* rather than *firing*. For every unpleasant or socially awkward subject, some euphemisms are usually available.

Sometimes, though, euphemisms appear for words that might otherwise seem innocuous. In the workplace, for example, the terms *employee* and *worker* are sometimes thought to have unpleasant associations with the division between management and labor. So, in the 1990s, some companies promoted the terms *partner*, *teammate*, *crew member*, and the like to avoid what might be perceived as putting people down. As organizations become "flattened," traditional titles (such as *senior executive vice president*) and even generic terms (such as *manager*) fall by the wayside. Likewise, the lower spheres are upgraded as *secretaries* become *assistants* or even *administrative assistants*.

Still other euphemisms denote things that have historically caused serious discomfort. In law, *unnatural offense* (or *crime*) *against nature* is not uncommon in place of *sodomy*.

Euphemisms are often subtle. Thus *incident* appears in place of *accident* in a U.S. statute limiting total liability to $200 million for a single "nuclear incident," presumably because *incident* sounds vaguer and less alarming. Today *revenue enhancement* (= tax increase) and *investment* (= increased government spending) are commonly used by American politicians reluctant to call things by their more understandable names.

All in all, one can hardly disagree with the assessment that euphemisms are irrational and quaintly uncandid: "[T]hey are only intelligible when both parties are in on the secret, and their silly innocence masks a guilty complicity, which is why they almost invariably wear a knowing, naughty-postcard smirk. At the close of the taboo-breaking century, they ought to have become comically redundant" (*TLS*). Even so, they thrive as much today as ever. Cf. DYSPHEMISM.

In the end, too, they leave a linguistic garbage-heap in their wake. For once a euphemism becomes standard, it loses its euphemistic quality: "This is the usual destiny of euphemisms; in order to avoid the real name of what is thought indecent or improper people use some innocent word. But when that becomes habitual in this sense it becomes just as objectionable as the word it has ousted and now is rejected in its turn" (Otto Jespersen, *Growth and Structure of the English Language*, 1952). Thus, the vocabulary regarding unpleasant things remains in constant flux.

The only solution would be for people to be less squeamish in their use of language. And that's not likely to happen—

not in AmE, at any rate—without a cultural upheaval.

EUPHONY. See SOUND OF PROSE.

euthanasia. A. And *mercy killing.* These synonyms are widespread, the former perhaps being more connotatively neutral.

B. And *physician-assisted suicide.* In *euthanasia*, the doctor may take an active role in the death, as by administering a fatal dose of a drug. In *physician-assisted suicide* (sometimes shortened to *assisted suicide*), the doctor supplies the means of death but allows the patient to take the decisive step.

euthanize; euthanatize. These terms, meaning "to subject to euthanasia," are used most commonly in reference to pets. If we must have such a word, the longer version might seem the better candidate because it is properly formed, strictly speaking, and is older, dating in the *OED* from 1873. But in modern writing, *euthanize* greatly predominates and has become standard—e.g.: "Because the dog's vaccinations were not current, it was *euthanized*" (*Worcester Telegram & Gaz.*). See -IZE.

evacuable. So formed—not *evacuatable*. See -ATABLE.

evangelical; evangelistic. Today the older term *evangelical* (fr. ca. 1531) is so closely tied with fundamentalist, proselytizing Christians that it should not be applied more generally. *Evangelistic* (fr. ca. 1845), though also redolent with Christian associations, may be used more broadly to mean "militantly zealous."

even, adv., gives rise to syntactic problems similar to those arising from *only*. It should be placed directly before the word it modifies. Note, for example, the difference in meaning between *this summer is even hotter and wetter* and *this summer is hotter and even wetter*. See **only.**

event. The AmE phrase is usually *in the event that* [+ clause]—an equivalent of *if* <in the event that they fail>. The British generally write *in the event of* [+ noun phrase] (usually a BURIED VERB)—as Americans often do <in the event of failure>. Either phrase is typically inferior to *if*.

eventuality is a needless pomposity for several everyday words, each of which is more specific: *event*, *possibility*, *outcome*, *contingency*, or *result*. E.g.: "This is the way the world ends—with humans evolving into billions of electronic navel-gazers? Without navels, even? Ironically, the film cumulatively argues against such *an eventuality* [read *an outcome* or *a possibility*]" (*San Diego Union-Trib.*).

ever. For phrases in which *ever* is superfluous, see **rarely ever & seldom ever.**

ever so often. See **every so often.**

every. A. Singular or Plural? Today it is standard BrE to write, "Almost *everybody* now seems to be a 'victim' of something—of society or *their* own weaknesses" (*Sunday Times* [London])./ "[T]he compilation of the *OED* made it possible for *everyone* to have before *them* the historical shape and configuration of the language" (R.W. Burchfield, *Unlocking the English Language*, 1989). Here's a statement of the BrE view: "Jane Austen wrote 'every body' as two words and considered the phrase as singular; we now write one word, 'everybody,' and consider it as plural, equivalent to 'all people.' Hence the entry in the *Dictionary* under 'agreement' gives 'Everybody knows this, don't they?' as an example of notional concord, obviously rightly: we would not accept 'Everybody knows this, doesn't he or she?' " (*TLS*).

But most Americans continue to think of this usage as slipshod, *every-*

body requiring a singular; after all, they reason, nobody would say *everybody think* instead of *everybody thinks*. An early usage critic remarked insightfully (while disapproving): "[T]he use of this word is made difficult by the lack of a singular pronoun of dual sex . . . . Nevertheless, this is no warrant for the conjunction of *every* and *them*" (Richard Grant White, *Every-Day English*, 1884). A goodly number of Americans now take the same stand, thereby making a happy solution elusive. See SEXISM (B) & PRONOUNS (C).

B. Meaning "all." With an abstract noun—as opposed to a count noun—the word *all* is more apt than *every*. E.g.: "Now both the law enforcement community and, apparently, the judiciary, are going to the opposite extreme by giving the Freemen *every leniency they can* [read *all the leniency they can*]" (*Albany Times Union*).

C. *Each and every*. See **each and every.**

everybody. See **everyone (B)** & PRONOUNS (C).

everybody . . . they. See **every (A),** CONCORD (B), PRONOUNS (C) & SEXISM (B).

everybody else's. See **else's** & POSSESSIVES (I).

every day, adv.; **everyday,** adj. One tries to accomplish something *every day*; but an *everyday* feat would hardly be worth accomplishing.

everyone. A. And *every one*. This sentence should make the distinction evident: "*Every one* of the employees attended the company picnic, and *everyone* had a good time." If you're unsure about whether the single word *everyone* is right, mentally substitute the synonymous *everybody* to see whether the sentence still makes sense; if it does, *everyone* is the correct form.

B. And *everybody*. Because the terms are interchangeable, euphony governs the choice in any given context. In practice, *everyone* appears in print about twice as often as *everybody*. Cf. **anyone (B).**

On the question whether these words are singular or plural, see **every (A),** CONCORD (B), PRONOUNS (C) & SEXISM (B).

everyone else's. See **else's** & POSSESSIVES (I).

everyone . . . they. See **every (A),** CONCORD (B), PRONOUNS (C) & SEXISM (B).

everyplace should be avoided as a vulgarism; *everywhere* is the proper word.

every so often; ever so often. The first means "occasionally" <we go to Lockhart for barbecue every so often>. The second—a slightly quaint phrasing—means "with great frequency" <you're extremely thoughtful to call me ever so often>.

evidently. The pronunciation /**ev**-i-dənt-lee/ is preferred over /ev-i-**dent**-lee/—the latter evidently occurring only in AmE.

evoke; invoke. The difference between these words is fairly subtle—and thus sometimes lost on even the most careful of writers. *Evoke* = (1) to call to mind or produce (memories, emotions, etc.) <the photographs evoked feelings of disgust>; or (2) to elicit or draw forth <the commencement address evoked laughter and applause>. *Invoke* = (1) to call on (a higher power) for blessing, guidance, or support <Homer invoked the Muse in each of his epics>; (2) to cite as an authority <the newspaper's reply invoked the First Amendment>; (3) to solicit; entreat <the rebels invoked the aid of the U.S. military>; (4) to summon by incantation; conjure <the wizard invoked a host of evil spirits>; or (5) to put into effect; implement <after the bombing, the governor invoked tighter security measures>.

The most common mistake in using these words is substituting *evoke* for sense 1 or 2 of *invoke*. This error occurs especially in the phrase *evoke the name of*—e.g.: "Then Heard *evoked* [read *invoked*] the name of God in his next untruth wherein he accused the Zulu demonstrators of attempting to 'storm the ANC headquarters' " (*L.A. Times*).

EX-, when meaning "former," should always be hyphenated: "A bitter *exemployee* [read *ex-employee*] can do great harm . . . . [W]hen people feel they have been fired 'fairly' . . . they will be reluctant to bad-mouth their *excompany* [read *ex-company*]" (Mark H. McCormack, *What They Don't Teach You at Harvard Business School*, 1984).

A problem arises when using the prefix with a noun phrase. Is an *ex-brain surgeon* a former brain surgeon, one formerly having a brain, or a specialist in head-autopsies? Although a nitpicker might argue for either of the last two, most reasonable readers will understand that *ex-* applies to the entire phrase, not just to the attributive. Otherwise, where would the prefix go in the following example: "Others say that *ex-corporate middle managers* are prone to reproducing the world they knew" (*Memphis Commercial Appeal*).

For an illogical use of this prefix, see **ex-felon.**

ex, n., is colloquial in the sense "a former spouse or lover." The plural of *ex* is *exes*, and the possessive is *ex's*—but be aware that many readers will find these forms odd-looking.

exact same. This expression is a lazy truncation of *exactly the same*. Although *the exact same* is acceptable in informal speech, it's not an expression for polished prose—e.g.: "There is not one briefcase, however. There are several; they're *the exact same* [read *exactly the same*] shade of pale aqua, and they all get swapped by characters skulking in and out of various dressing cubicles" (*N.Y. Times*).

And because *exactly the same* is a phrase of pinpoint precision, to qualify the idea by saying *almost the exact same* is doubly bad—e.g.: "Yes, No. 4 Alabama (10–0) and No. 6 Auburn (9–0–1) play *almost the exact same* [read *almost the same* or *the same*] brand of football" (*Wash. Post*).

For a similar example involving *exact*, see **just exactly.**

exalt; exult. To *exult* is to rejoice exceedingly. To *exalt* is to raise in rank, to place in a high position, or to extol.

Exalt is rather frequently misspelled *exhalt* or *exhault*—e.g.: "God would . . . make him an instrument to *exhalt* [read *exalt*] His mightiness and reach out to others" (*Austin American-Statesman*). Such errors seem to result from confusion with words such as *exhale* and *exhaust*. In the latter word, the *-h-* isn't pronounced, and the vowel in the second syllable is generally sounded just as it is in *exalt*.

exceed. See **accede.**

except, prep. & conj. **A. As Preposition and Conjunction.** When *except* begins a noun phrase rather than a clause (i.e., a phrase with a finite verb), it is a simple preposition not followed by the relative pronoun *that* <all persons except farmers owning more than 500 acres> <no one must leave the room except with permission>. But when, as a conjunction, *except* introduces a clause, it should be followed by *that* <all vice presidents are to receive a 10% bonus in compensation, except that no bonus on previous bonuses is allowed>.

If a pronoun follows a prepositional *except*, the pronoun should be in the objective case, not the nominative—e.g.: "Everyone has been accounted for except *he* [read *him*]." See PRONOUNS (A), (B).

B. *Excepting.* This word should not be used as a substitute for *except for* or *aside from*, except in the phrase *not excepting*—e.g.: "*Excepting* [read *Except for*] Thomas Worthington, handily beaten by Watterson on Saturday, Ohio Division teams went 5–0 in their openers" (*Columbus Dispatch*). It's true that *excepting* is one word, not two, and that it might be considered an acceptable dangling modifier (or "disguised conjunction"). (See DANGLERS (E).) But many knowledgeable readers will disapprove it as a dangler. And in any event it's less natural-sounding than the edited versions—which add one more word but no extra syllables.

exceptional. A. And *exceptionable.* *Exceptional* = out of the ordinary; uncommon; rare; superior. *Exceptionable* = open to exception; objectionable. E.g.: "It is the same ideological insularity that found nothing terribly *exceptionable*—until the firestorm—with the racial spoils system advocated by Lani Guinier" (*Cincinnati Enquirer*).

Exceptionable, of course, is the much rarer term. And about 20% of the time it's misused for *exceptional*—e.g.: "Indian food holds up remarkably well on a buffet table and Khyber Pass's table is *exceptionable* [read *exceptional*]—especially at the bargain price of $8.95 during the week (it is $9.95 on weekends and $5.95 for lunch)" (*Chicago Trib.*).

B. Meaning "physically or mentally handicapped." The problem with using the word as a EUPHEMISM in this way is that it can result in ambiguity: *exceptional* can mean either "having above-average intelligence" (i.e., gifted) or "having below-average intelligence" (i.e., retarded). In passages such as the following, *exceptional* is symptomatic of DOUBLESPEAK: "The Resource Directory also lists state and federal agencies that can assist parents with *exceptional* children" (*Dallas Morning News*).

exception proves the rule, the. This phrase is the popular rendering of what was originally a legal maxim, "The exception proves (or confirms) the rule in the cases not excepted" (*exceptio probat regulam in casibus non exceptis*). Originally *exception* in this maxim meant "the action of excepting"—not, as is commonly supposed, "that which is excepted"—so that the true sense of the maxim was that by specifying the cases excepted, one strengthens the hold of the rule over all cases not excepted.

At least two spurious explanations of *the exception proves the rule* exist. One is that because a rule does not hold in all instances (i.e., has exceptions), the rule must be valid. This misunderstanding of the phrase commonly manifests itself in the discourse of those who wish to argue that every rule must have exceptions. A more sophisticated, but equally false, explanation of the phrase is that *prove* here retains its Elizabethan sense (derived from the Latin) "to test," so that the sense of the phrase is that an exception to a rule "tests" the validity of the rule. This erroneous explanation appears, of all places, in Tom Burnam, *A Dictionary of Misinformation* (1975).

By the way, the *MEU1* entry on this phrase is perhaps the only one in which the great H.W. Fowler is all but incomprehensible.

excess. See **access.**

excess verbiage. See **verbiage.**

EXCLAMATION POINT [!]. This punctuation mark is used after an exclamatory word, phrase, or sentence. It usually counts as the concluding full stop—e.g.: "I can almost hear the producer saying, 'Cut! Too much talk!' " (Phillip Lopate, "The Last Taboo," in *Dumbing Down: Essays on the Strip Mining of American Culture*, 1996). If used within square brackets, in or after a quotation, it expresses the quoter's amusement, dissent, or surprise.

excuse, n. See **alibi (A).**

excuse me; pardon me. Traditionally, *excuse me* was used for minor offenses such as bumping into someone; *pardon me* was reserved for more serious situations requiring a more explicit apology. Today, the terms are interchangeable, *excuse me* being slightly less formal. *Sorry* is even less so.

When the word *me* receives the stress, either *pardon me* or *excuse me* is used as a mild challenge of someone else.

exempli gratia. See **e.g.**

ex-felon is an illogical expression—except, perhaps, in reference to a pardoned offender—because a convicted offender does not lose the status of felon merely by serving out a criminal sentence. Once a felon, always a felon. But *ex-convict* is quite all right, *convict* now being viewed as a close synonym of *prisoner*.

exodus means "a mass departure or emigration." Thus, the common phrase *mass exodus* is a REDUNDANCY, perhaps a venial one—e.g.: "On the streets, buses lined the curb, waiting for the *mass exodus* [read *exodus*] of fans after the game" (*Columbus Dispatch*). As a corollary to that point, one person's leaving does not make an *exodus*—e.g.: "Jones' *exodus* [read *exit*] has sparked a discussion among university staffers and the deaf community over what went wrong with the training program" (*L.A. Times*).

exorbitant (lit., "having departed or deviated from one's track [*orbit*] or rut") is sometimes mistakenly spelled *exhorbitant*—perhaps because it is confused with *exhort*. E.g.: "The developers and tenants, however, insist the costs are far from *exhorbitant* [read *exorbitant*]" (*Boston Globe*).

expect is informal or colloquial for *think* or *suppose*, as here: "I *expect* that it will take three weeks," instead of, "I think it will take three weeks." Most properly, *expect* means "to look forward to and rely on." See **anticipate.**

expend is a FORMAL WORD that often seems less appropriate than *spend*—e.g.: "Cosmic bowling is not the first time Brunswick has *expended* [read *spent*] time and energy giving bowling a face lift" (*Chicago Trib.*).

expensive. Because the word means "high-priced," the phrase *expensive prices* is a REDUNDANCY—e.g.: "We settled for a reserve chardonnay at the *too expensive price* [read *unduly high price*] of $6.50 a glass" (*Virginian-Pilot*).

expletive. See **epithet.**

EXPLETIVES. In general usage, *expletives* are understood to be curse words or exclamations. This sense was fortified in AmE during the Watergate hearings in the early 1970s, when coarse language was replaced with *expletive deleted* in transcripts of the White House tapes. In grammar, however, an *expletive* is a word having no special meaning but standing (usually at the beginning of a clause) for a delayed subject. The two most common expletives are *it* and *there* at the beginnings of clauses or sentences. See **it & there is.**

express; expressed. See **implied.**

exquisite. A. Pronunciation. The word is better pronounced with the first syllable accented /**eks**-kwiz-it/; in AmE, however, stressing the second /ek-**skwiz**-it/ is acceptable.

B. Use. Although there is historical justification for using *exquisite* (= acute) in reference to pain, modern readers are likely to find this use macabre at best, for they generally understand the word as meaning "keenly discriminating" <exquisite taste> or "especially beautiful" <an exquisite vase>. For many readers, the obsolescent sense is merely a MISCUE—e.g.: "Steve R., a sign painter, suffered such *exquisite* [read *excruciating*] pain in his ankle that he could barely walk" (*Buffalo News*).

extant is preferably pronounced /**eks**-tənt/, not /ek-**stant**/—but the latter pronunciation is at least acceptable in AmE.

extraordinary is preferably pronounced with five syllables (/ek-**stror**-

di-ner-ee/), not six (/ek-strə-**or**-di-ner-ee/). See PRONUNCIATION (B).

extreme unction. See **last rites.**

exuberant (= [1] extremely joyful; or [2] flamboyant) is so spelled. But *exhuberant* is a fairly common misspelling—e.g.: "Unlike Washington Park's garden on the Downing Street side, famed for its large flower beds and *exhuberant* [read *exuberant*] colors, this garden is meant to be a place of tranquility and serenity" (*Denver Post*).

exult. See **exalt.**

eyes peeled. The phrase is so spelled, though some erroneously make it *pealed*—e.g.: "The mug can be lifted to the mouth, a necessity during the Super Bowl, when all eyes are *pealed* [read *peeled* or, better yet, *fixed*] on the television and not watching where soup may be dripping" (*Wash. Post*).

F

facade is pronounced /fə-**sahd**/. Today the cedilla beneath the *-c-* (*façade*) is usually dropped. See DIACRITICAL MARKS.

facility. This word is surplusage in phrases such as *jail facility* and *museum facility*—e.g.: "Airports that aren't well-served by airline clubs or that don't have major *hotel facilities* [read *hotels*] nearby will put in conference rooms of their own, he predicted" (*L.A. Times*). And sometimes the word is a EUPHEMISM for *building*—e.g.: "[T]he Fort Lauderdale development firm that bought the rest of the mall complex 16 months ago—including the main mall *facility* [read *building*], a nearby strip shopping center and the former Sam's Wholesale Club building—is studying redevelopment plans" (*Fla. Times-Union*). On the variation between *facility* and *building* in that sentence, see INELEGANT VARIATION.

Not only is *facility* often unnecessary; it has also become virtually meaningless. The word is so abstract that it refers to just about anything, from a laboratory to a stadium to a toilet.

facsimile transmission. See **fax.**

factional; factious; fractious. These words are confusingly similar. *Factional* = of or relating to a faction or factions. E.g.: "*Factional* fighting has dragged the people of Somalia's capital back to the darkest days of the civil war in 1992" (*Guardian*). *Factious* = given to faction; acting for partisan purposes. E.g.: "Louisiana Democrats are *factious* as well. Their division is largely along racial lines" (*New Orleans Times-Picayune*). *Fractious* = refractory, unruly, fretful, peevish. E.g.: "[P]erhaps . . . [Jewish and Christian] cultures and traditions are not really that far apart. After all, we all get frayed and *fractious* at Christmas" (*Independent*).

fact of the matter, the. This FLOTSAM PHRASE occasionally serves well in speech—to fill up space while the speaker thinks of what to say next—but generally has no justification in writing. Cf. **fact that.**

factor, n., properly means "an agent or cause that contributes to a particular result." It should not be used, by SLIPSHOD EXTENSION, in the sense "a thing to be considered; an event or occurrence."

fact that, the. It is imprudent to say, as some have, that this phrase should never be used. At times it cannot reasonably be avoided <they ignored the fact that all the elections had been against them>. One writer has suggested that *because* will usually suffice for *the fact that*. Yet rarely, if ever, is *because* a good substitute for that phrase (as opposed to the longer phrase *because of the fact that*)—e.g.: "*The fact that* singer-songwriters like Sarah McLachlan and Jewel have managed to break through the homogenized slop that record companies are distributing does not mean that music or women have been liberated" (*Time*).

When *the fact that* can easily be avoided, it should be—e.g.: "Aniston, who still admits a yen for Big Macs and mayo-on-white-bread sandwiches, objects to *the fact that* [read *how*] 'Hollywood puts pressure on women to be thin' " (*People*). But sometimes it's all but inescapable—e.g.: "He has learned to laugh again at little ironies, such as *the fact that* he, unlike several of his rescuers, did not get poison ivy that day" (*Wash. Post*).

fair. A. And *fare*. Properly an adjective or noun, *fair* is sometimes misused for the verb *fare* (= [1] to experience good or bad fortune or treatment; or [2] to happen or turn out)—e.g.: "Luckily for Lush, the album has *faired* [read *fared*] well" (*Wash. Times*).

B. *Bid fair.* For the past tense of this PHRASAL VERB, see **bid (A).**

falderol. See **folderol.**

false, in a phrase such as *false statement*, is potentially ambiguous, since the word may mean either "erroneous, incorrect" or "purposely deceptive."

On *false* as an uncomparable adjective, see ADJECTIVES (B).

FALSE COMPARISON. See ILLOGIC (B).

falsehood; falseness; falsity. *Falsehood* = (1) an untrue statement; a lie <many falsehoods were uttered during the campaign>; or (2) the act or practice of lying <truth and falsehood became difficult to distinguish>. *Falseness* = (1) the quality of being untrue <the speech carried an air of falseness>; or (2) tendency to lie; deceitfulness <falseness of character>. *Falsity* is synonymous with sense 1 of either word (although more commonly with *falseness*), but it appears too frequently to be labeled a NEEDLESS VARIANT.

fare. A. As a Noun. Because this word, in one of its senses, means "food," the phrase *food fare* is a silly REDUNDANCY—e.g.: "It takes little effort to incorporate pears into your holiday and winter *food fare* [read *food* or *fare* or *cooking*]" (*Atlanta J. & Const.*).

B. As a Verb. See fair (A).

far-flung; far-fetched. These adjectives are, literally speaking, etymological opposites—*far-flung* meaning "flung (i.e., cast) a far distance" and *far-fetched* meaning "fetched (i.e., retrieved) from afar." Of course, both words are now used almost exclusively in their figurative senses. *Far-flung* means "widespread" or "remote"; *far-fetched* means "improbable" or "strained."

Some dictionaries make *far-fetched* a single word, without the hyphen. Although that may signal the future of this word, it isn't now the predominant form.

farther; further. Both are comparative degrees of *far*, but they have undergone DIFFERENTIATION. In the best usage, *farther* refers to physical distances, *further* to figurative distances—e.g.: "Some [people] walk no *farther* than the synagogue on the Sabbath" (*Milwaukee J. Sentinel*)./ "But the sheriff's department did not investigate *further* after YMCA officials were unwilling to pursue the matter, Vance County Sheriff R. Thomas Breedlove said Tuesday" (*Durham Herald-Sun*). The superlatives—*farthest* and *furthest*—follow the same patterns.

fastly, an obsolete form, now exists only as a NONWORD, since *fast* serves as both adverb and adjective. Even so, writers occasionally perpetrate sentences with phrases such as *the fastly held rule* and *fastly becoming so*. In the first, *firmly*, and in the second, *fast*, would serve better. Journalists have gone quite far with this unnecessary adverb—e.g.: "Kraska has mixed emotions about the onslaught of bagel chains—*fastly expanding* [read *fast-expanding*] Bruegger's and newcomers Einstein Bros." (*Pitt. Post-Gaz.*). That sentence involves a PHRASAL ADJECTIVE (*fast-expanding*), but there is no more need for the *-ly* adverb in those phrases than anywhere else. For other adverbs with a superfluous *-ly*, see ADVERBS (D).

fatal; fateful. Though both are tied etymologically to the noun *fate*, they have undergone DIFFERENTIATION. *Fatal* means "of or relating to death," while *fateful* means "producing grave consequences." The most common mistake is to use *fatal* for *fateful*, but sometimes one would be presumptuous to suggest any change, so close is the call: "Like Henry Kissinger and other modern scholars, Mr. Gelb considers the *fatal* turning point not Munich in 1938, but the failure by France and Britain to oppose German reoccupation of the Rhineland in 1936" (*Wall St. J.*).

On *fatal* as an uncomparable adjective, see ADJECTIVES (B).

faux pas [Fr. "false step"] is both the singular and the plural spelling. But the singular is pronounced /foh-**pah**/ or (less good) /**foh**-pah/, and the plural is pronounced /foh-**pahz**/ or (less good) /**foh**-pahz/.

fax, n. & vb. This term is now all but universal, in the face of which *facsimile transmission* is an instant ARCHAISM—and a trifle pompous at that. *Fax*, which is now perfectly appropriate even in formal contexts, first appeared in the mid-1970s—e.g.: "In the past two years, *fax* installations have more than doubled from fewer than 50,000 to more than 100,000 units" (*BusinessWeek*). Pl. *faxes*.

faze; phase. *Faze* = to disconcert; daunt. *Phase*, vb., = to carry out (a plan, program, etc.) in stages. *Phase* for *faze* is an increasingly common blunder—e.g.: "Others said they had weathered so many rumors that nothing *phased* [read *fazed*] them anymore" (*Boston Globe*).

The mistake often appears as *unphased* (for *unfazed*)—e.g.: "But some analysts are *unphased* [read *unfazed*], given the company's growth prospects" (*USA Today*).

The opposite error (*faze* for *phase*) also occurs, but somewhat more rarely—e.g.: "All that while shooting guard Art Mlotkowski, shadowed all over the court by Northport senior Rob Sanicola, was *fazed* [read *phased*] out of the offense" (*N.Y. Newsday*).

fearful; fearsome. In a perfect world, there would be strict DIFFERENTIATION here: *fearful* would be confined to the sense "full of fear, afraid"; *fearsome* would be reserved for "causing fear, horrible." Alas, the world isn't quite so perfect, and there is considerable overlap.

feasible = (1) capable of being accomplished; (2) capable of being used or handled to good effect; or (3) reasonable, likely. Sense 3 is a classic example of SLIPSHOD EXTENSION. The extended sense is ambiguous. When saying that a cure for cancer is *feasible*, do you mean that a cure can definitely be found (if we work hard enough to find it), or do you mean that a cure might one day be found (but not necessarily)? To avoid this problem, it's best to reserve *feasible* for senses 1 and 2. When sense 3 is the intended meaning, *possible* or *probable* is the better choice. Cf. **viable.**

feature. The classic book popularly known as "Strunk & White" cautioned against using this word, citing the following example: "A *feature* of the entertainment especially worthy of mention was the singing of Miss A" (William Strunk, Jr. & E.B. White, *The Elements of Style*, 1979). The authors sagely advise: "Better use the same number of words to tell what Miss A. sang and how she sang it."

feel. A. For *think*. *Feel* is a weak and informal substitute for *think*, *believe*, *maintain*, or *submit*. E.g.: "We *feel* [read *believe*] that the plan should be summarized in considerable detail." When the idea is phrased on an emotional rather than a cognitive level, the resulting sentence seems to minimize the thoughts being reported—e.g.: "She *feels* [read *thinks* or *believes*] that crime prevention must start with helping small children find their way out of poverty and neglect, and that society's resources should go toward better education and housing, not more jails" (*Newsweek*).

B. *Feel bad; feel badly*. When someone is sick or unhappy, that person feels *bad*—not *badly*. Most professional writers know this, but a few get it wrong—e.g.: "Manager Dusty Baker's attention was divided. He felt *badly* [read *bad*] for Dunston and was depressed over a ninth-inning rally gone sour" (*Sacramento Bee*). Not to excuse these errors, but they may result from the misplaced fear that *feel bad* somehow suggests wickedness or personal evil.

But the same error crops up even with adjectives other than *bad*. Here it's *miserable*: "Every couple of years, the American Bar Association's monthly magazine publishes an article detailing how *miserably* [read *miserable*] many lawyers feel" (*Asbury Park Press*). See ADVERBS (C). Cf. **badly (A).**

C. *Feel like.* To avoid using *like* as a conjunction, writers usually need to change this phrase to *feel as if*. E.g.: "But on a combined income of $60,000, McDonald and his wife Cindy, who have five children, *feel like* [read *feel as if*] they're just scraping by" (*Newsweek*). See **like (A).**

feign; feint. These words, though deriving from the same French verb (*feindre* "to touch or shape"), have undergone DIFFERENTIATION in English. To *feign* is either to make up or fabricate <she feigned an excuse> or to make a false show of <he feigned illness>. To *feint* is to deliver a pretended blow or attack designed to confuse an opponent momentarily. *Feint* is also, in its older (but still current) sense, used as a noun meaning either a sham or a pretended blow or attack (i.e., the act of *feinting*).

female, adj.; **feminine; womanly; womanlike; womanish; effeminate.** These adjectives all share the sense "of or relating to women." *Female* is a neutral term usually used to indicate the sex of a person (or an animal or plant), in contrast with *male* <a female cadet> <my female coworkers>. *Feminine* typically refers to what are traditionally considered a woman's favorable qualities <feminine grace>. *Womanly* often carries these positive connotations as well <womanly intuition>, but it's also used to distinguish an adult female from a girl <her womanly figure>. *Womanlike* (the rarest of these words) is synonymous with *womanly*, though perhaps a bit more neutral <womanlike features>. Finally, *womanish* and *effeminate* are now almost always used in a derogatory way in referring to men who supposedly lack manly qualities <his womanish laugh> <his effeminate gestures>.

In this era of political correctness, the use of any of these terms can be offensive in certain contexts. Cf. **male.** See SEXISM.

FEMININE ENDINGS. See SEXISM (D).

FEMININE PRONOUNS USED GENERICALLY. See SEXISM (B).

festive; festal. *Festive* = (1) of or relating to a feast or festival; or (2) joyful, merry <a festive mood>. *Festal*, a rarer word, shares only sense 1 of *festive* and is probably the better word in that sense.

fetch. Because *fetch* means "to go get and bring back," the phrase *go fetch* is something of a REDUNDANCY—e.g.: "Next, the hijacker released a third man to *go fetch* [read *fetch*] the two escapees" (*L.A. Times*).

fever. See **temperature (B).**

fewer; less. *Fewer* emphasizes number, and *less* emphasizes degree or quantity. *Fewer number* and *fewest number* are illogical tautologies, since *fewer* means "of smaller number." E.g.: "The *fewest number* [read *smallest number*] of people use the library between 4:30 and 7:00 p.m." (Or, better, read: *The fewest people use the library between 4:30 and 7:00 p.m.*) See **less (A).**

few in number is a common REDUNDANCY—e.g.: "They were once prized for their tasty bacon, but when new breeds came along that were cheaper to raise and produced more bacon, the Tamworths declined and they are now *few in number* [read *scarce* or *uncommon*]" (*Chicago Trib.*).

fiancé; fiancée. A *fiancé* is male, a *fiancée* female. The better pronunciation is /fee-ahn-**say**/ (approximating the French). The middlebrow AmE pronunciation is /fee-**ahn**-say/. In AmE—unlike BrE—the accents are usually retained.

Fiancé is sometimes misused for *fiancée*—e.g.: "Howard has been dumped by the *fiancé* [read *fiancée*] he adored" (*Time*).

fictitious; fictive; fictional. These forms overlap to a great degree, but they have undergone some useful DIFFERENTIATION. *Fictional* = of, relating to, or having the characteristics of fiction. E.g.: "It's not hard to understand the retro appeal of a *fictional* hero such as Dirk Pitt" (*Orange County Register*).

Fictitious = (1) false, counterfeit; or (2) imaginary. Sense 1: "His 1993 Nissan Sentra had a *fictitious* license plate, said Phillip Roland, a spokesman for the Las Vegas Metropolitan Police" (*Tampa Trib.*). Sense 2: "First in the series of *fictitious* murders—Allen says there will be 666 in all, a suitably demonic number—is a photo captioned 'Slaughtered' [depicting] a woman in a blue dress plunging a large knife into a man heavily splattered in fake gore" (*Louisville Courier-J.*).

Fictive = having the capacity of imaginative creation <fictive talent>. Apart from this narrow sense, *fictive* is a NEEDLESS VARIANT of both *fictional* and *fictitious*—e.g.: "But when an earthly reality hovers too near a *fictive* [read *fictional*] one, it sends a shadow onto the landscape that can dominate, even supersede the imagination" (*Boston Globe*).

fiddle. It's often thought that *fiddles* are the instruments of country-and-western musicians, *violins* those of orchestral musicians. In fact, though, many great violinists refer to their *fiddles*, perhaps as a type of DYSPHEMISM.

field. The phrase *the field of* is vague and often unnecessary—e.g.: "Lindsey . . . accrued a 3.91 grade point average while studying *in the field of* [delete *in the field of*] communications" (*Knoxville News-Sentinel*). Cf. **area.**

fifth is pronounced /fifth/. Whether the version without the medial *-f-* (/fith/) is a mispronunciation, a hasty pronunciation, or a casual pronunciation is debatable. But one thing is certain: it's not as good. See PRONUNCIATION (B).

Fifth Amendment. The idiom is *take the Fifth*, not *plead the Fifth*—e.g.: "He was advised to keep silent and *plead* [read *take*] the Fifth Amendment" (*Minneapolis Star Trib.*).

filet mignon. The plural of this phrase is *filet mignons* (or, more stuffily, *filets mignons*). (See PLURALS (B).) But when the second word is dropped, the plural is *filets*. While AmE uses the spelling *filet* /fi-**lay**/, BrE spells it *fillet* /**fil**-ət/.

final analysis, in the. See **in the final analysis.**

final destination. See **destination.**

finalize = (1) v.t., to complete; bring to an end; put in final form; or (2) v.i., to conclude. Originally an Australianism, *finalize* has flourished as a VOGUE WORD in the late 20th century, a favorite of jargonmongers. For that reason alone, many writers avoid it. But the word's advantage is that it has the compactness of a single word, as opposed to its equivalents: *make final, put into final form,* and *bring to an end.* Today few people object to it, and it is all but ubiquitous—e.g.:

- "The show was taped for future broadcast, but theater officials have yet to *finalize* an air date and network contract" (*Wash. Post*).
- "Charles and Diana will *finalize* their divorce this spring" (*Toronto Sun*).
- "HUD also contends that the county failed to *finalize* a contract for an administrator to oversee task-force operations" (*Pitt. Post-Gaz.*).

Still, *complete* is a better choice when it will suffice, as in the last example quoted above. See -IZE.

final outcome; final result. These are common REDUNDANCIES, both *outcome* and *result* being generally understood as final. It may be, however, that because modern technology—whether in instant replays on television or in computer calculations—allows us to view all sorts of preliminary results, some further qualification is considered desirable. But that's merely an excuse, not a justification. And besides, writers often use the wordy phrases even when they don't mean them—e.g.: "A manual recount of absentee ballots indicated Saturday that Sheriff Bob Vogel's margin of victory was even greater than the *final results* [read *results*] on election night" (*Orlando Sentinel*). Cf. **destination.**

FINAL PREPOSITION. See PREPOSITIONS (B).

final result. See **final outcome.**

finance is pronounced either /fə-**nan[t]s**/ or /**fɪ**-nan[t]s/. The first is traditionally the better pronunciation.

financial. See **economic (B).**

fine-toothed comb; fine-tooth comb. The latter spelling is more than twice as common as the former. But because *fine-toothed comb* better reflects the literal meaning—a comb with teeth set close together, rather than a comb with fine (very thin) teeth—that spelling ought to be preferred, even in figurative senses <she went over the contract with a fine-toothed comb>.

finicky is the preferred spelling—not *finnicky*. *Finical* is a pedantic variant that is seldom used. Anyone who uses it is likely to be thought of as being, well, finical.

fire; terminate; lay off. *Fire* has the sense of dismissing an employee for cause, such as for inadequate performance or moral turpitude. The word implies abruptness and forcibleness and is therefore viewed as being derogatory. A common EUPHEMISM is *terminate*. *Lay off* means "to dismiss (an employee), often temporarily, because of slow business."

first and foremost is a CLICHÉ that should not be used merely for *first*. But the *OED* describes it as a "strengthened" phrase—i.e., an especially emphatic one—and dates it from the 16th century.

firstly, secondly, thirdly, etc. are today considered inferior to *first*, *second*, *third*, etc. Many stylists prefer *first* over *firstly* even when the remaining signposts are *secondly* and *thirdly*. See ENUMERATIONS (A).

FIRST PERSON. Immature writers use *I* and *me* at every turn. It's therefore a customary rite of passage for every grade-school student to write an essay without ever using first person. As a writing exercise, this is useful.

Yet it arguably does much harm as well. Many students come to believe that in writing, there's something inherently wrong with first person. So even later in life, they go to great lengths to avoid it, as by using phrases such as *the present writer*, *the author*, and so on. It leads them to PASSIVE VOICE and to BURIED VERBS. If you're the actor, the belief runs, omit the actor. It all leads to ABSTRACTITIS.

But graceless circumlocutions serve no real stylistic purpose and are inferior to the straightforward pronouns *I* and *me*. Late in his career as a writer, Jerome Frank confessed that he had long shunned the first-person pronoun, preferring *the writer* to *I* on the assumption that the indirect phrasing signified modesty. With age he became wiser and concluded: "To say *I* removes a false impression of a Jovian aloofness" (*Courts on Trial*, 1950).

Of one common set of self-obscuring devices—*it is suggested that*, *it is proposed that*, and *it is submitted that*—Fred Rodell observed, "[W]hether the writers really suppose that such constructions clothe them in anonymity so that people cannot guess who is suggesting and who is proposing, I do not know" ("Goodbye to Law Reviews—Revisited," *Va. L. Rev.*, 1962). We do know, however, that these phrases often make sentences read as if they had been "translated from the German by someone with a rather meager knowledge of English" (*id.*).

None of this should suggest that every personal opinion should include the word *I*. Most opinions are transparently just that, and they therefore need no direct mention of the writer—e.g.: "Though Einstein is routinely lionized as a great scientific mind, Newton was the most original thinker that science has ever produced." No moderately sophisticated reader would assume that this statement is anything more than an opinion. And it is much more convincingly stated without inserting the phrase *in my opinion*. See **myself** & SUPERSTITIONS (I).

fission. The standard AmE pronunciation today is either /**fi**-zhən/ or /**fish**-ən/. The first now predominates (probably to parallel the sound of the correlative term *fusion* /**fyoo**-zhən/) even though the second corresponds to analogous words such as *mission*.

fit > **fitted** > **fitted** (traditionally); *fit* > *fit* > *fit* (more modernly in AmE). Just since the mid-20th century, AmE has witnessed a shift in the past tense and past participle from *fitted* to *fit*. Traditionally, *fit* would have been considered incorrect, but it began appearing in journalism and even scholarly writing as early as the 1950s.

This casualism now appears even in what is generally considered well-edited journalism—e.g.: "This 'modified Münchausen syndrome,' in FBI terminology, occurs in someone who wants to be a hero so badly that he creates emergencies so he can rescue people. Jewell, a police wannabe, *fit* this profile and also had the characteristics of people who use pipe bombs—white single men in their 30s or 40s with a martial bent" (*Time*)./"He [Steven Morrissey] never quite *fit* as a proper rock star" (*N.Y. Times*). And it appears in fine scholarly writing—e.g.: "English land tenure, and the English way of life among landed gentry, *fit* this social order more than was true in the North" (Lawrence M. Friedman, *A History of American Law*, 1985).

The traditionally correct past tense still surfaces—especially in BrE—but in AmE it is becoming rarer (and stuffier) year by year: "A most interesting item in my coin collection is a disk that *fitted* the pressure-spray nozzle on our apple-orchard pump some 50 years ago" (*Christian Science Monitor*). Although *fitted* may one day be extinct as a verb form, it will undoubtedly persist as an adjective <fitted sheets>.

flaccid is pronounced /**flak**-sid/, not /**fla**-sid/. All the traditional pronunciation guides have said so—and they're right. Cf. **succinct.** (See PRONUNCIATION (B).) As a result of the mispronunciation, the misspelling *flacid* (on the analogy of *placid*) has arisen—e.g.: "Naomi, Toshiyuki and I unrolled the long, *flacid* [read *flaccid*] canopy while Richard positioned a huge electric fan at the mouth" (*Boston Herald*).

flack. See **flak.**

flagrant (= glaring) is occasionally confused with *fragrant* (= nice-smelling)—e.g.: "U.S. Secretary of State Madeleine Albright and United Nations Ambassador Bill Richardson huff and puff in one breath that Iraq's Saddam Hussein will not get away with *fragrantly* [read *flagrantly*] violating the United Nations" (*Augusta Chron.*). See MALAPROPISMS.

For more on the use of *flagrant*, see **blatant.**

flair. See **flare.**

flak; flack. *Flak* (orig. referring to antiaircraft guns) = unwanted criticism. *Flack* = a press agent. The most common problem with these words is that *flack* is misused for *flak*—e.g.:

"*Variety*'s Todd McCarthy says he received a good deal of *flack* [read *flak*] for his negative review" (*Village Voice*).

Occasionally, too, *flak* edges out *flack* from its rightful place—e.g.: "To reporters, they are derisively known as '*flaks*' [read *flacks*], whose main duties consist of peddling press releases" (Bryan Burrough & John Helyar, *Barbarians at the Gate*, 1990).

During the 1960s, the noun *flack* was made into a verb. A person who *flacks* provides publicity. But once again, *flak* has appeared in this context—not commonly, but often enough to warrant caution. E.g.: "Monday, I was all over Chicago *flakking* [read *flacking*] my new book *On the Line* (Harcourt Brace, $21.95), about last year's elections" (*USA Today*).

flammable; inflammable. The first is now accepted as standard in AmE and BrE alike. Though examples of its use date back to 1813, in recent years it has become widespread as a substitute for *inflammable*, in which some persons mistook the prefix *in-* to be negative rather than intensive. Traditionally, the forms were *inflammable* and *noninflammable*; today they are *flammable* and *nonflammable*. Purists have lost the fight to retain the older forms. See NEGATIVES (A).

flare; flair. *Flare* = a sudden outburst of flame; an unsteady light. *Flair* = (1) outstanding skill or ability in some field; or (2) originality, stylishness. By far the most common confusion occurs when *flare* displaces *flair*—e.g.: "Ms. Telesco has a real *flare* [read *flair*] for writing in very succinct, plain terms" (*Fresno Bee*).

flaunt; flout. Confusion about these terms is distressingly common. *Flout* means "to contravene or disregard; to treat with contempt." *Flaunt* means "to show off or parade (something) in an ostentatious manner," but is often incorrectly used for *flout*, perhaps because it is misunderstood as a telescoped version of *flout* and *taunt*—e.g.: "In Washington, the White House issued a statement that deplored the Nigerian Government's '*flaunting* [read *flouting*] of even the most basic international norms and universal standards of human rights' " (*N.Y. Times*).

Of course, *flaunt* is more often used correctly—e.g.: "He donates millions to religious and charitable groups, yet *flaunts* his own wealth" (*Fortune*).

Flout, meanwhile, never seems to cause a problem—e.g.: "A record rider turnout, fueled by the mayor's earlier pledge to end the escort and crack down on cyclists *flouting* traffic laws, poured into the streets on an improvised route" (*S.F. Examiner*).

flautist. See **flutist.**

flesh out; flush out. To *flesh out* is to put flesh on bare bones—that is, to move beyond the merest rudiments and to elaborate; to add some nuance and detail. To *flush out* (probably a hunting metaphor) is to bring something into the open light for examination. *Flush out* is sometimes misused for *flesh out*—e.g.: "Both sides say their case was hampered by the disappearance of Anait Zakarian, whom they said they needed to help *flush out* [read *flesh out*] some of the details" (*L.A. Times*).

flier; flyer. *Flier* is the standard form in AmE, *flyer* being a NEEDLESS VARIANT. But in BrE, *flyer* is standard.

flippant; flip, adj. *Flippant* = (1) inappropriately nonserious or disrespectful; pert; or (2) glib, talkative. Sense 2—the older one—has become archaic. *Flip*, a clipped form, is a casualism that is gaining ground on the more traditional word.

floes (= sheets of ice [fr. Norw. *flo* "flat layer"]) should not be confused with *flows*—e.g.: "But the shots from Galileo detailed Tuesday at a briefing at NASA's Jet Propulsion Laboratory in Pasadena, Calif., show surface features that resemble ice *flows* [read *floes*] in the polar seas on Earth, geysers, and crustal ridges where new material may be welling up from beneath the satellite's surface" (*Christian Science Monitor*).

flotation; floatation. *Flotation*, the standard spelling, first appeared in the mid-19th century. According to *The Oxford Dictionary of English Etymology*, "[t]he sp. with *flot-* has been adopted to make the word conform to [*flotilla* and *flotsam*], and *rotation*" (p. 364). A more recent work gives a different ETYMOLOGY: "The current spelling appeared . . . probably by influence of French *flottaison*, which was used in technical terms translated into English, such as *ligne de flottaison* line of flotation" (*The Barnhart Dictionary of Etymology*, 1988).

FLOTSAM PHRASES just take up space without adding to the meaning of a sentence. Thus there is usually no reason, where it is clear whose opinion is being expressed, to write *In my opinion* or *It seems to me that.* Other examples are *in terms of, on a . . . basis, my sense is that, in the first instance, the fact of the matter*, and *the fact that.* (Admittedly, some of these phrases may be useful in speech.) We have enough written words without these mere space-fillers. See **basis (A) & fact that.**

flounder; founder. Both verbs signal failure, but the literal senses, and therefore the images conveyed metaphorically, differ. To *flounder* is to struggle and plunge as if in mud. To *founder* is (of a person or animal) to go lame; (of a ship) to fill with water and sink; (of a building) to fall down or give way; (of a horseback rider) to fall to the ground; (of livestock) to become sick from overeating.

flout. See **flaunt.**

flowed; flown. Surprisingly, these words are often confused. *Flowed* is the past tense and past participle of *flow*. *Flown* is the past participle of *fly*. See **fly & overflow.**

fluid; liquid; gas. Nonscientists often confuse these terms. A *fluid* is any substance that is capable of flowing and that changes shape under pressure; in other words, a fluid is not a solid. Fluids include both liquids and gases. A *liquid* is a fluid that has a fixed volume (such as water or oil). A *gas* is a fluid that can expand indefinitely (such as oxygen or steam). Although these words should be kept distinct in scientific contexts, *fluid* is sometimes used as a loose synonym of *liquid* in nontechnical writing <bodily fluids>.

flush out. See **flesh out.**

flutist; flautist. *Flutist*, the much older word (dating from the early 17th century), is generally preferred by professional flute players in the United States. The old joke within the profession is that only second-rate flutists call themselves *flautists*. But that form predominates in BrE.

fly > flew > flown. Despite those inflections, in baseball it is standard to say that a player who has hit a *fly ball* (i.e., one hit high into the air) has *flied*—e.g.: "After getting a good rip on a 2-and-1 fastball but fouling it off the catcher's chest protector, Fielder *flied* out to the rightfield warning track" (*N.Y. Newsday*). Cf. **flowed.** See IRREGULAR VERBS.

flyer. See **flier.**

fob off. See **foist (B).**

focus. A. As a Noun. Pl. *focuses* or *foci* (/**foh**-SI/). The plural *foci*—typical in medical and other technical texts—may strike readers as pretentious in ordinary prose. E.g.: "Job retention and job creation were the central *foci* [read *focuses*] of BEST's efforts" (*Charleston Post & Courier*). See PLURALS (B).

B. As a Verb. *Focus* makes *focused* and *focusing* in AmE, *focussed* and *focussing* in BrE. See SPELLING (B).

foist. A. Preposition with: *off* vs. *on*. Traditionally speaking, *foist* takes the preposition *on*—e.g.: "That network has *foisted* innumerable Virtual Celebrities *on* us" (*Chicago Sun-Times*). When the phrase is as unidiomatic as *foist with*, a different verb is in order: "An employer *is foisted with* [read *bears the*] responsibility to a third party if his employee commits a tort in the course of his employment" (Stanley Berwin, *The Economist Pocket Lawyer*, 1986).

Foist off on is awkward and prolix. The *OED* quotes Charlotte Brontë as having written *foist off on* but calls the phrase "rare." It is fairly rare today. It ought to be rarer—e.g.: "[W]e always seem ready to *foist off on* [read *foist on*] young people those things that we don't wish to do ourselves" (*Denver Post*).

B. And *fob off*. *Foist* shares one sense with *fob off*: "to offer or pass (something) to someone falsely or fraudulently" <lemons foisted on unsuspecting car buyers>. But it should not also take the second sense of *fob off*: "to trick (someone) with something inferior." H.W. Fowler summed up the distinction well: "The public can be *fobbed off* with something, or the something can be *fobbed off* on the public; but *foist* has only the second construction" (*MEU1*). In fact, though, the first construction is pretty much confined to BrE—e.g.: "[C]ustomers are sometimes *fobbed off* with a car [that] does not entirely meet their expectations" (*Fin. Times*).

folderol; falderol. In journalism and other print sources, *folderol*—the preferred spelling—outnumbers *falderol* by a margin of more than 50 to 1. The word means either "nonsense" or "a useless trifle."

FOLK ETYMOLOGY. See ETYMOLOGY (D).

following (= after), when used to begin a sentence or clause, often results in a misplaced modifier and a MISCUE—e.g.: "*Following* [read *After*] lunch, the students came back to the high school and the art students took over" (*St. Louis Post-Dispatch*). The problem, of course, is that some readers might envision a line of hungry students trailing a caterer's truck.

But even when *following* doesn't begin the sentence, if it means "after" it can almost always be simplified—e.g.: "Javier Colon of Mission Hill and Ramon Peres of Roxbury, both 22, escaped after a 'routine trip' to the barber shop building on the grounds *following* [read *after*] breakfast" (*Boston Globe*).

foment, vb., = to incite or rouse <the rebels fomented a revolution>. Although the word was once used as a noun—the *OED* records sparse uses from 1540 to 1892—the corresponding noun has long been *fomentation* (= incitement, instigation). But some writers want to revive *foment* as a noun—e.g.: "In the social *foment* [read *fomentation*] of the 1960s and 1970s, Donahue was a pioneer in discussing both personal and political issues with a largely female audience" (*L.A. Times*). Perhaps this poor usage arises from confusion with *ferment* (= agitation). Indeed, *ferment* might be the better edit in the sentence just cited. It certainly seems the better choice here: "There hardly could be better circumstances to nurture political *foment* [read *ferment*]" (*Chattanooga Times*).

Although *fomentation* doesn't appear frequently, it remains much more common in printed sources than the noun uses of *foment*—e.g.: "For decades, extremists on both sides spoiled any hope of Arab acceptance of the Jewish state of Israel with their *fomentation* of hatred and bloodshed" (*USA Today*). So *foment*, as a noun, ought to be considered a NEEDLESS VARIANT.

FOOTNOTES. A. The Good and the Bad. Footnotes are the mark of a scholar. Overabundant, overflowing footnotes are the mark of an insecure scholar—often one who gets lost in the byways of analysis and who wants to show off. Underinclusive footnotes mark the scholar who (1) wants to write for a popular audience and fears that footnotes will be a turnoff; (2) doesn't really know the literature in his or her field very well; or (3) doesn't care to give credit where credit is due.

The difficult thing for any scholarly writer is to achieve a balance. Much depends on the subject matter, the intended audience, and the content of the writing. On the one hand, footnotes are "reminders that scholarship is an intrinsically communal enterprise—building on, revising or replacing the work of predecessors. History as we know it would not exist without source notes. Neither would philosophy, which even at its most original involves a dialogue with thinkers alive and dead" (*Newsweek*). On the other hand, footnotes can be "the horrid squeakings [that] arise when an author puts a brand new pair of shoes on his brain child. . . . [L]et all beware of too copious annotation, one of the deadly sins of literature" (Fairfax Downey, "Literary Chiropody," in *The Modern Writer's Art*, 1936).

A good rule of thumb is that footnotes are an excellent place for citations. But textual footnotes—those that contain talk—ought to be kept to a minimum.

B. Versus Endnotes. Whereas footnotes appear at the foot of the page, endnotes appear at the end of an article, chapter, or book. (Endnotes are often mistakenly called footnotes.) In general, footnotes are easier on the reader than endnotes, which require flipping through pages to locate references. But scholarly journals and books increasingly require endnotes to simplify printing and unclutter pages.

FOR-; FORE-. As you'll observe in many of the following entries, these prefixes cause a great deal of confusion. You can usually arrive at the correct prefix for any given word by remembering that *for-* means either "completely" or "against," and that *fore-* means "before."

for is one of several causal words in the English language, the most prominent others being the subordinating conjunctions *because*, *since*, and *as*. (See **as (A).**) And because *for* is roughly equivalent to those words, some grammarians have mislabeled it a subordinating conjunction. But unlike those words, *for* has always been proper at the beginning of an independent clause—e.g.: "[O]ur job is to study our fellow animals caught in the cages and learn from them. *For* they are us" (*Fla. Today*). The better grammatical view is this: "Because . . . *for* can stand at the beginning of an independent statement or even of a paragraph, it can be classed as a coordinating conjunction" (R.W. Pence & D.W. Emery, *A Grammar of Present-Day English*, 1963).

fora. See **forum.**

for all intents and purposes; to all intents and purposes. Both forms are used, *for* being more common in AmE and *to* in BrE—e.g.: "It is only when life has, *for all intents and purposes*, already abandoned the patient that Dr. Kevorkian steps in" (*Chicago Trib.*)./ "Vermeer's mainly domestic scenes . . . are also, *to all intents and purposes*, priceless" (*Daily Telegraph*). Either form, though, often qualifies as a FLOTSAM PHRASE.

Because some people mishear the phrase, the MALAPROPISM *for all intensive purposes* has arisen—e.g.: "*For all intensive purposes* [read *For all intents and purposes*], all six teams came away from Des Little Stadium with some glimmer of hope" (*St. Petersburg Times*).

for a period of. See **period of.**

forbad(e). See **forbid.**

forbear, v.t.; **forebear,** n. Though unrelated, these words are confused in every conceivable way. *Forbear*—the verb meaning "to refrain from objecting to; to tolerate"—is inflected *forbear* > *forbore* > *forborne*. But because the inflected forms appear only infrequently, writers sometimes fall into error—e.g.: "A borrower who lives in the home five years after doing the work may have the loan *forebeared* [read *forborne*]" (*Allentown Morning Call*). (See IRREGULAR VERBS.) *Forebear*—always a noun—means "ancestor" (usually used in the plural). *Forebearer* is an incorrect form of this noun.

Forbear is occasionally misused for *forebear*—e.g.: "[T]he founding fathers of cyberspace . . . , like their *forbears* [read *forebears*], were almost exclusively white, male, middle-aged and privileged" (*N.Y. Times*).

The opposite error, though less common, also occurs—e.g.: "The governor scrupulously *forebore* [read *forbore*] to notice Mark Green in 1986 and could barely conceal his hostility to Robert Abrams in 1992" (*N.Y. Newsday*).

forbearance. So spelled—not *forebearance*, which is a NONWORD. But some writers blunder—e.g.: "But the 1903 National League pennant went to the Pittsburgh Pirates, whose owner, Barney Dreyfuss, greatly appreciated the American League's *forebearance* [read *forbearance*] in not putting a team in his city" (*N.Y. Times*).

forbid > forbade > forbidden. In formal contexts, *forbid* traditionally takes the preposition *to* or, less formally, *from*. H.W. Fowler stated that *forbid from doing* is unidiomatic (*MEU1*), but it is increasingly common. In fact, it is probably more common today than *forbid to do*, but both forms appear frequently—e.g.: "In exchange, the Government prohibits newspaper vending machines, *forbids* small stores *from selling* papers and gives the union sole right to use the public sidewalks to sell newspapers" (*N.Y. Times*).

The past tense is *forbade* (rhyming with *glad*)—e.g.: "[Locke] sharply distinguished the respective spheres of Church and State and *forbade* each from meddling in the other" (Clifford Orwin, "Civility," in *Am. Scholar*, 1991). *Forbid* is sometimes wrongly used as a past-tense form—e.g.: "Susan has dropped the restraining order that once *forbid* [read *forbade*] him [from making] any contact with her" (*Palm Beach Post*).

Some writers—no doubt those who pronounce *forbade* correctly—use the variant spelling *forbad*. Avoid it—e.g.: "[T]he 1967 Age Discrimination in Employment Act . . . *forbad* [read *forbade*] bias based on age" (*Boston Globe*). See IRREGULAR VERBS.

forbore; forborne. See **forbear.**

forcible; forceable; forceful. Oddly, we have the spellings *enforceable* but *forcible*. The usual and preferred form, *forcible* means "effected by force against resistance"—e.g.: "Driving the 4% dip in violent crime through June were drops in homicide, 2%; *forcible* rape, 6%" (*USA Today*).

Forceable, though it might appear a NEEDLESS VARIANT, carries a passive sense: "capable of being forced" <she tried to coerce him, but he simply wasn't forceable>.

Because *forcible* properly refers only to physical force, it shouldn't be used where *forceful* is needed, the latter carrying figurative as well as literal meanings—e.g.: "A Washington Post–ABC News survey of U.S. voters taken Wednesday night confirmed the doubts *forcibly* [read *forcefully*] expressed by a dozen Illinois voters in a two-hour group interview in this Chicago suburb Monday" (*Houston Chron.*).

FORE-. See FOR-.

forebear. See **forbear.**

forebearance. See **forbearance.**

forebode (= to predict [usu. something bad]; foretell) is sometimes misspelled *forbode*—e.g.: "If the personalities of the principals on both sides of the table don't mesh, it *forbodes* [read *forebodes*] what well could be a bad marriage between the firms" (*Cincinnati Enquirer*). See FOR-.

forecast. See **broadcast.**

forego; forgo. Although a few apologists argue that these words are interchangeable, they have separate histories. And their meanings are so different that it's worth preserving the distinction. *Forego*, as suggested by the prefix, means "to go before." *Forgo* means "to do without; pass up voluntarily; waive; renounce."

Using *forego* where *forgo* is intended is a persistent problem. Examples of the poor usage are legion—e.g.: "Seed is excited that three members of the New Bedford basketball team have decided to *forego* [read *forgo*] a three-month spring break and pick up a bat and a glove" (*Boston Herald*)./ "That realization not only helped Lavelle's brother but convinced her to *forego* [read *forgo*] a career as a social worker or psychologist and instead become a teacher" (*L.A. Times*).

The opposite mistake—misusing *forgo* for *forego*—is much less common. E.g.: "The *forgoing* [read *foregoing*] arguments largely concern comparison of higher taxa" (*Science*).

Forwent and *forewent* are the past-tense forms. While *forewent* is hopelessly archaic <they forewent us to the theater>, *forwent* is occasionally useful—e.g.: " 'I'm not going to say never to anything,' said Moulton Patterson, who *forwent* a bid for reelection" (*L.A. Times*).

Forgone and *foregone* are the past-participial forms. *Foregone* is correct in the phrase *foregone conclusion* because the idea is that the conclusion "went before" the question: everybody knew the answer before the question was posed. But the past participle of *forgo* is *forgone*, without the *-e-*: "I would have given a lot for a few columns about what the Flynn years cost Boston in the way of *foregone* [read *forgone*] opportunities" (*Boston Globe*).

forehead traditionally rhymes with *horrid*, as in the nursery rhyme: "There was a little girl, who had a little curl/ Right in the middle of her forehead;/ When she was good, she was very, very good,/ But when she was bad she was horrid." But in AmE, the word is commonly (and acceptably) pronounced /**for**-hed/.

foreman. A. Generally. In the sense "a person in charge of a group of workers" <the foreman on the docks>, *foreman* dates from the 16th century. But there is pressure afoot to find gender-neutral alternatives, and the words *supervisor*, *chief*, and *leader* seem to be the most likely candidates. See SEXISM.

B. In Legal Sense. Of the three choices—*foreman*, *foreperson*, and *presiding juror*—the best is the last. E.g.: " 'We are working diligently,' the *presiding juror* concluded in the message" (*Houston Chron.*). The word *foreperson*, though one word, is less satisfactory because it uses the *-person* suffix. (See SEXISM (C).) Yet that form is, for the time being, ensconced in federal procedural rules and may be difficult to oust.

It's mildly surprising to see *foreman* and *foreperson* being used together for purposes of INELEGANT VARIATION—e.g.: "And since the *foreperson* is the single most influential person on a jury, lawyers will do anything to keep good *foreman* material off" (Robin T. Lakoff, *Talking Power: The Politics of Language in Our Lives*, 1990).

forename. See **surname.**

forewent. See **forego.**

foreword (= a preface) is often misspelled like its homophone, *forward*—e.g.: "[Tom] Kite . . . wrote the *forward* [read *foreword*] to this book" (*American Way*). See FOR-.

for free. See **free.**

forgo. See **forego.**

FORMAL WORDS are those occupying an elevated level of diction. The English language has several levels of diction, and it even has synonyms existing on the different levels. Thus *residence* is formal, *house* is the ordinary word, and *digs* (or *pad* or *crib*) is slang. Likewise, *proceed* is formal, *go* is ordinary, and *head on over* is slang.

In written AmE, the unfortunate tendency has long been to reach for the formal word that is widely known. Thus, writers steer away from SESQUIPEDALITY but choose pomposities that everyone recognizes. That's what leads people to write (or occasionally say) *be of assistance* instead of *help*, *attire* instead of *clothes*, *inebriated* instead of *drunk*. Early in the 19th century, the novelist James Fenimore Cooper worried that "[t]he love of turgid expressions is gaining ground, and ought to be corrected" ("On Language," in *The American Democrat*, 1838). For stylists, that worry is perpetual, as each generation becomes enamored of its own brands of linguistic inflation: DOUBLESPEAK, OFFICIALESE, and the like.

The problem with formal words is that they are symptomatic of those stylistic disturbances. One way or another, they lead to stuffiness—the great fault in modern writing: "For most people . . . in most situations, in the writing of everyday serious expository prose, it is the Stuffy voice that gets in the way. The reason it gets in the way, I submit, is that the writer is scared. If this is an age of anxiety, one way we react to our anxiety is to withdraw into omniscient and multisyllabic detachment where nobody can get us" (Walker Gibson, *Tough, Sweet & Stuffy*, 1966).

In the left-hand column below are some of the chief symptoms—not in every context, of course, but whenever the terms in the right-hand column would suffice:

Formal Word	*Ordinary Word*
accommodation(s)	room
accompany	go with
annex, vb.	attach
appear	look, seem
append	attach
approximately	about
arrive	come
attain	reach
attired	dressed
cast, vb.	throw
cease	stop
commence	begin, start
complete	finish
conceal	hide
continue	keep on
deem	consider, treat as
demise	death
depart	go
desist	stop
detain	hold
discover	find
donate	give
effectuate	carry out
emoluments	pay
employ (an instrument)	use
endeavor	try
evince	show
expedite	hasten
expend	spend
expiration, expiry	end
extend	give
forthwith	immediately, now, soon, promptly
henceforth	from now on
imbibe	drink
inaugurate	begin
indicate	show
individual	person
initiate	begin
inquire	ask
institute	begin, start
interrogate	question
intimate, vb.	suggest
luncheon	lunch
manner	way
necessitate	require
obtain	get
occasion, vb.	cause
peruse	read
place, vb.	put
portion	part
possess	own, have
present, vb.	give
preserve	keep
prior	earlier
prior to	before
proceed	go (ahead)
purchase	buy

Formal Word	*Ordinary Word*
receive	get
relate	tell
remain	stay
remainder	rest
remove	take away, haul off
request, vb.	ask
retain	keep
secure	get
subsequently	later, afterwards
subsequent to	after
sufficient	enough
summon	send for, call
terminate	end
utilize	use

former; latter. These should apply only to a series of two. The *former* is the first of two, the *latter* the second of two. In contexts with more than two elements, *first* should be used rather than *former*, *last* rather than *latter*.

Former and *latter* can bewilder the reader when coupled with numbers—e.g.: "The *former* are liberals first and Catholics second, the *latter* Catholics first, liberals second" (*Commonweal*). (A possible revision, based on the fuller text: *Catholic liberals are liberals first and Catholics second; liberal Catholics are Catholics first and liberals second.*)

May one have a *latter* without an explicit *former*? Yes, as long as there are two identifiable elements.

formidable is preferably pronounced /**for**-mə-də-bəl/, not /for-**mid**-ə-bəl/.

formula. Pl. *formulas* or *formulae*. The native plural, ending in *-s*, is preferred in all but scientific writing. See PLURALS (B).

forsake > forsook > forsaken. *Forsake* is sometimes corrupted into *foresake*—e.g.: "It *foresakes* [read *forsakes*] the rounded look of the previous Camry for a crisper, squarer silhouette" (*USA Today*). See FOR- & IRREGULAR VERBS.

for sure is colloquial for *certain* or *certainly*.

forte (= a person's strong point) has long been thought to be preferably pronounced with one syllable, like *fort*. That's because the word is originally French, in which the word is so pronounced. But most speakers of AmE use the two-syllable version (/**for**-tay/), probably under the influence of the Italian *forte*, a two-syllable word referring to a musical notation to play loudly. Though it might have been nice to keep the two words separate in pronunciation, that hasn't happened—and the two-syllable version can no longer be condemned.

fortitude refers to inner strength, willpower, and courage. Yet writers often seem to use it in reference to physical strength, stamina, or endurance—e.g.: "Talk-show host David Brudnoy showed off his physical *fortitude* [read *prowess*], bearhugging a reporter and lifting her off the floor" (*Boston Globe*).

fortuitous, strictly speaking, means "occurring by chance," not "fortunate." The traditional sense remains fairly strong—e.g.: "Unless the victim dies, the law cannot assume that the transgressor really meant to kill—even though whether the victim lives or dies might be entirely *fortuitous*" (*L.A. Times*).

Meanwhile, of course, the word is commonly misused for *fortunate*, in itself a very unfortunate thing—e.g.: "My choice of Leeds University was quite *fortuitous* [read *lucky* or *fortunate*]. A few weeks before the university session was scheduled to begin, I was given a scholarship to study in England" (*Wash. Post*).

In the phrases *fortuitous accident* and *fortuitous coincidence*, the word *fortuitous* bears the right sense but is redundant: every accident or coincidence is fortuitous. Writers using those phrases, though, almost invariably mean "fortunate" or "lucky"—e.g.: "Without that *fortuitous accident* [read *lucky accident*] of layout, even Conran's space might have stayed empty" (*N.Y. Times*).

forum. The preferred plural is *forums*, not *fora*. E.g.: "Even so, the debate over bigness—and how big is too big for corporate entities—continues in many different *forums*" (*L.A. Times*). But some writers, especially in law, persist in using the pedantic *fora*. See PLURALS (B).

forwent. See **forego.**

founder. See **flounder.**

foyer. The better pronunciation for this word is /**foy**-ər/, not the affected /**foy**-ay/ or /fwah-**yay**/.

fracas (= a noisy fight; brawl) is pronounced /**fray**-kəs/. Pl. *fracases*.

fractious. See **factional.**

FRAGMENTS, SENTENCE. See INCOMPLETE SENTENCES.

fragrant. For a humorous MALAPROPISM, see **flagrant.**

Frankenstein. In Mary W. Shelley's novel *Frankenstein* (1818), Dr. Victor Frankenstein creates a gruesome creature that eventually kills the doctor's brother and sister-in-law, and tries but fails to kill the doctor before ending his own life. Strictly speaking, then, a *Frankenstein* (usually capitalized) is a creator of a monster or other destructive agency, while a *Frankenstein's monster* is either a monster that turns on its creator or a destructive agency that cannot be controlled.

But popular usage has created a monster of its own: *Frankenstein* has come to refer to the creature itself. Today this ubiquitous usage must be accepted as standard—e.g.: "A visit to 'Bordello of Blood' is like a date with *Frankenstein* on Prozac: It's a bloated, lumbering, bloody bore" (*Dallas Morning News*).

free; for free. Because *free* by itself can function as an adverb in the sense "at no cost," some critics reject the phrase *for free*. Yet while it's true that *for free* is a casualism, the expression is far too common to be called an error. Sometimes the syntax all but demands it—e.g.: "[S]oft-dollar arrangements . . . include various services like research and information that big institutional clients receive *for free* from brokers" (*Wall St. J.*). That same writer, however, omitted the *for* when it wasn't needed: "That research is sent *free* to the client" (same).

freedom. See **liberty.**

freedom of; freedom from. Both are correct, the first being preferred by most writers on style. Note the shift in forms: *freedom of speech* but *freedom from oppression*, *pestilence*, *coercion*, etc.

free gift. This REDUNDANCY—the result of advertisers' attempted assurances that you'll really get something for nothing—isn't used by careful writers. But that's not to say it's not used—e.g.: "Volunteers at the 20th annual Tammi Tuck Wrap-a-thon distributed *free gifts* [read *gifts*] to the children in West Palm Beach" (*Palm Beach Post*).

free rein is the correct spelling of this phrase—not *free reign*. The allusion is to horses, not to kings or queens. But some writers have apparently forgotten the allusion—e.g.: "Holmgren was quoted in a New Orleans paper as saying his players have a fairly *free reign* [read *free rein*] to enjoy New Orleans during their stay there. However, he did warn them about talking to 'weird women' " (*Charleston Gaz.*). See **rein.**

FRENCH WORDS. See GALLICISMS.

frequently. This adverb can be ambiguous when used with a plural subject and verb. Do individuals do something frequently, or is the characteristic true of a group that may do something only once? Note the MISCUE here: "A study last year by Jack Hadley of the Georgetown University School of Medicine showed that uninsured patients arrived at the hospital sicker than those with health insurance, and died in the hospital more *frequently*" (*Newsweek*). If the phrase *more frequently* is placed after the conjunction *and*, the miscue disappears.

fridge, a shortened form of *refrigerator*, is so spelled—not *frig*.

friend. This word has settled into some exceptional idioms: *a friend of mine*; *he is friends with me*; *she made friends with me*; *he has been a friend to me*. Handle them with care.

For more on *a friend of mine*, see POSSESSIVES (D).

friendlily. See ADVERBS (B).

frijol /free-**hohl**/ (= a bean used in Mexican cuisine) forms the plural *frijoles* /free-**hoh**-leez/, which typically refers to refried beans. Because the plural is much more common than the singular, it's hardly surprising that the BACK-FORMATION *frijole* has emerged as a singular form. Avoid it.

-FUL. See PLURALS (F).

full complement. For the mistaken phrase *full compliment*, see **compliment.**

fulsome (= abundant to excess; offensive to normal tastes or sensibilities) is loosely used when "very full" is the intended sense. It has become a SKUNKED TERM because this loose sense is so common, especially in the expression *fulsome praise*. Usually the true sense of that expression is something like "lavish praise"—e.g.: "Just before Mobutu was run out of his lair in Kinshasa, National Public Radio played some old audiotapes of the *fulsome* [read *lavish*] praise heaped on this corrupt blackguard by Presidents Reagan and Bush" (*Boston Globe*).

fun, traditionally a noun, has come into vogue as an adjective—but only as a casualism. Perhaps the origin of this extension lies in the frequency of *fun* as a predicate nominative, as in *This is fun*. In that sentence, *fun* can be taken as being either a noun or an adjective. For speakers who consider it the latter, it's no significant change to say, instead, *This is a fun thing to do*. Still, the usage seems casual at best—e.g.: "To liven things up the last few weeks of the season, some resorts create *fun* events to entice customers" (*Sacramento Bee*).

R.W. Burchfield notes that "in serious writing, it (so far) lacks a comparative and a superlative" (*MEU3*). That may be true of serious writing, but not of spoken AmE (especially among those born after 1960 or so)—e.g.: " 'It's always *funner*,' says 13-year-old Jeff Oehrlein, 'to be where the parents aren't' " (*Wash. Post*)./" 'We came down here to watch the people. That's the *funnest* part,' said Jeff Daniel, 28, of Ventura" (*L.A. Times*). But to traditionalists, these forms remain blemishes in writing and speech alike.

fungus. Pl. *fungi*: /**fən**-jɪ/, not /**fəng**-gɪ/. See PLURALS (B).

further. See **farther.**

furtherest is a dialectal term not to be found in good writing—except in dialogue involving nonstandard speech. But the word mars a good many pieces—e.g.: "*Furtherest* [read *Furthest*] along is an investigation of the disclosure in life insurance policies" (*Wash. Post*).

furthermore, adv. & conj. This word is quite proper, of course, but its heaviness can weigh down a passage. A quicker word—such as *and*, *also*, *besides*, or even *moreover*—usually serves better.

further to your letter. This phrase, like *enclosed please find*, epitomizes business JARGON. If you want to write effective letters, don't use it.

fuse, n.; **fuze.** A *fuse* is a wick or other combustible cord for an old-fashioned explosive. A *fuze* is for more high-tech explosives: it's a mechanical or electronic device used for detonations.

In a different sense, *fuse* refers to a component that protects an electrical circuit by preventing it from melting. Thus, the two CLICHÉS derive from the different senses of the word: *blow a fuse* from the electrical-component sense, and *have a short fuse* from the wick sense.

FUSED PARTICIPLES. A. The General Rule. H.W. Fowler gave the name "fused participle" to a participle that is (1) used as a noun (i.e., a gerund), and (2) preceded by a noun or pronoun not in the possessive case—thus "Me going home made her sad" rather than the preferred "My going home made her sad." The fused participle is said to lack a proper grammatical relationship to the preceding noun or pronoun. Yet no one today doubts that Fowler overstated his case in calling fused participles "grammatically indefensible" and in never admitting an exception. The grammarians Otto Jespersen and George Curme have cited any number of historical examples and have illustrated the absolute necessity of the fused participle in some sentences (barring a complete rewrite)—e.g.: "The chance of that ever happening is slight."

But Fowler had a stylistic if not a grammatical point. Especially in formal prose, the possessive ought to be used whenever it is not unidiomatic or unnatural. In the following sentences, then, possessives would have been better used than the nouns and pronouns in the objective case: "The pattern of our life, which now involves *me spending* [read *my spending*] some days each week totally alone so as to write, proves to be creative and necessary for all of us" (*Times* [London])./ "Now when 11-year-old Shelby Young rides the bus to Loudon Grade School, he doesn't worry about the older *kids soaking* [read *kids' soaking*?] him with water guns" (*Concord Monitor*). (In that sentence, the difference in meaning is slight: as currently worded *the older kids soaking him* seems elliptical for *the older kids who are soaking him*; in fact, the writer probably meant to say *their soaking him*—hence *the older kids' soaking him*. The question is what he's not worrying about: the *kids* or the *soaking*.)

B. Exceptions. There are many exceptions to this rule of style. For example, there's typically no choice of construction when you're using nonpersonal nouns <he was responsible for the luggage having been lost>, nonpersonal pronouns <she couldn't accept nothing being done about the problem>, and groups of pronouns <he regretted some of them being left out in the rain>.

fuze. See **fuse.**

-FY. Most verbs ending in *-fy*—from the French *-fier* or Latin *-ficare* "to do or make"—are preceded by an *-i-* (e.g., *classify*, *mollify*, *mortify*, *pacify*). But a few of them aren't: *liquefy*, *putrefy*, *rarefy*, *stupefy*. The reason for the difference is merely that the corresponding infinitives in French and Latin are spelled with an *-e-* (*liquefier*, etc.), and the words were borrowed directly into English from those infinitives. In any event, it's a common error to misspell these words *-ify*. The same mistaken switch of *-e-* to *-i-* occurs in the corresponding nouns, which should be *liquefaction*, *putrefaction*, *rarefaction*, and *stupefaction*.

G

gaffe; gaff, n. *Gaffe* = (1) a blunder in etiquette; faux pas; or (2) a blatant error. *Gaff* (a rarer word) = (1) a large iron hook used for fishing; (2) a metal spur; (3) a trick or swindle; (4) harsh treatment, abuse; or (5) (BrE) a cheap theater.

Gaffe is sometimes misspelled *gaff*—e.g.: " 'His biggest risk,' Mr. Schoen said, 'is that something will happen and he will make another *gaff* [read *gaffe*] as he did in 1989' " (*N.Y. Times*).

gait (= a manner of walking) is sometimes confused with *gate*—e.g.: "Eddie squinted at the ball through thick black-framed glasses, his spindly legs and stooped shoulders giving him an awkward *gate* [read *gait*]" (*Hartford Courant*).

gallant. In all senses as an adjective, this word is best pronounced /**gal**-ənt/. (In the sense "polite," it may also be pronounced /gə-**lant**/.) As a noun, however, the word is pronounced either /gə-**lahnt**/ or /gə-**lant**/.

GALLICISMS appear frequently in modern prose—e.g., *coup de grace*, *tour de force*, *succès d'estime*, *cul-de-sac*, *blasé*, *tête-a-tête*, and *joie de vivre*. None of these is unduly recherché, to use yet another. But foreignisms of any kind become affectations when used in place of perfectly good English terms—e.g., *peu à peu* for *little by little*, or *sans* for *without*.

One stylist of high repute cautions sternly against all but thoroughly anglicized Gallicisms: "Of *Gallicisms* . . . it is perhaps not necessary to say much: they are universally recognized as a sign of bad taste, especially if they presuppose the knowledge of a foreign language. A few foreign words, such as *cliché*, have no English equivalent and are in current use; and there may be others [that] are desirable. But except in technical works it will generally be found possible to avoid them" (Herbert Read, *English Prose Style*, 1952).

On whether to italicize words borrowed from French and other languages, see ITALICS (B).

gambit (= ploy) for *gamut* (= an entire range or extent) is a MALAPROPISM: "Participants run the *gambit* [read *gamut*] of age and experience from 14-year-old riders to men in their early 20s with very little exposure to the bulls" (*Albany Times Union*).

gantlet; gauntlet. Although the latter is more common in most senses, the former is still preferred in one of them. One runs the *gantlet* (= a kind of ordeal or punishment) but throws down the *gauntlet* (= a glove). The trend, however, is to use *gauntlet* for all senses. Like many trends, this one is worth resisting: keep *gantlet* for the ordeal. E.g.: "They tortured him last year, dragged him through a senseless frat-boy *gauntlet* [read *gantlet*] that accomplished nothing" (*Chicago Sun-Times*). And many writers do resist it—e.g.: "The streetside culinary *gantlet* of hot grease and grills—stands selling everything from tacos to burgers to funnel cakes, pierogis and pizza—was shuttered, awaiting the evening rush" (*Cleveland Plain Dealer*).

Likewise, the word *gauntlet* is correctly used in the phrase *throwing down the gauntlet* (= issuing a challenge)—e.g.: "Anyone who passes her has thrown down the *gauntlet*" (*N.Y. Times*).

gaol. See **jail.**

gas. See **fluid.**

gases, not *gasses*, is the plural form of the noun *gas*. Still, for the verb *gas*, *gassed* is the accepted past tense and *gasses* is the third-person singular form. Cf. **bus.** See SPELLING (B).

gauntlet. See **gantlet.**

gay. In 1980, a well-known language critic commented: "[The] special-interest use of *gay* undermines the correct use of a legitimate and needed English word. It now becomes ambiguous to call a cheerful person or thing gay; to wish someone a gay journey or holiday, for example, may have totally uncalled-for over- and undertones and, in conservative circles, may even be considered insulting. The insulting aspect we can eventually get rid of; the ambiguous, never. What do we do about it? If we energetically reject *gay* as a legitimate synonym for *homosexual*, it may not be too late to bury this linguistic abomination" (John Simon, *Paradigms Lost*, 1980).

Hardly anyone today would dispute, though, that it's too late to contain the word. *Gay* is now all but universal in referring to homosexuals, both male and female. Its stronger associations, however, are with men, so that we have the phrase *gay and lesbian affairs*, as if lesbians weren't gay. The homosexual sense of *gay* first appeared in the mid-20th century; before that the word did, however, bear the derogatory senses "leading an immoral life" and "(of a woman) engaging in prostitution" (*SOED*).

But is Simon's point about ambiguity a valid one? Consider the following passage, from a book published in 1993. Was Hoccleve homosexual?

> **Hoccleve, Thomas** (c.1369–c.1450) poet, began to work as a clerk/copyist in the Privy Seal in about 1378, and had his salary raised to £10 a year in 1399, and to £13 6s.8d in 1408. This, with his private means of £4 a year, should have been adequate, but his pay was often late and he lived a gay bachelor life—dressing fashionably, travelling to the office by boat, eating and dining in taverns, and entertaining pretty girls. All this we know from "La Mâle Règle," a poem which includes a plea to the Treasurer, asking for his back pay. A few years later, his long-awaited benefice having failed to materialize, he married, for love.
>
> Antony Kamm, *Collins Biographical Dictionary of English Literature* 216 (1993).

Readers are likely to believe, at first, that he was homosexual—because of the word *gay*. By the end of the passage, most readers will be convinced that Hoccleve was heterosexual and that the author has simply used *gay* in an old-fashioned way. A few might finish the passage thinking that Hoccleve was bisexual. But almost any observant reader will have spent some time considering Hoccleve's sexuality—to the detriment of the information that's actually being conveyed. The writer would have been well advised to avoid the traditional sense of *gay*; it's now all but obsolete.

The new sense of *gay* is standard. Trying to reclaim the old sense is an exercise in futility. Meanwhile, there's much to be said for gays' having a more or less neutral term to describe themselves—something besides the familiar old DYSPHEMISMS.

gender has long been used as a grammatical distinction of a word according to the sex assigned (usually arbitrarily) to a given noun. It has newly been established in the language of the law in phrases such as *gender-based discrimination*, a use disapproved as jargonistic by some authorities. What this adds to *sex discrimination*—besides eight letters and one hyphen—one can only guess.

But in recent years, *sex* has narrowed its meaning to designate a set of physical characteristics, while *gender* increasingly denotes the social and psychological distinctions between man and woman (at least in academic circles). For example, most academics today would use *gender* in place of *sex* in the following sentence: "Given strong patriarchal traditions here, it is hardly surprising that the criticism is often put in ways that emphasize the two leaders' *sex*, even if Bangladesh has had plenty of reason in 22 years of nationhood scarred by military coups and assassinations to conclude that men in power are no less likely than women to be governed by the whims of personality and ambition" (*N.Y. Times*). As worded, the sentence might even contain a MISCUE for some readers; that is, one might expect the sentence to be completed differently—e.g.: "Given strong patriarchal traditions here, it is hardly surprising that the criticism is often put in ways that emphasize the two leaders' *sex*, which by all accounts is becoming more frequent."

generally has three basic meanings: (1) "disregarding insignificant exceptions" <the level of advocacy in this court is generally very high>; (2) "in many ways" <he was the most generally qualified applicant>; (3) "usually" <he generally leaves the office at five o'clock>. Sense 3 is the least good in formal writing, although at times it merges with sense 1.

genial. See **congenial.**

genie; jinni; djinni. Although these words overlap, *genie* more commonly denotes the magic spirit that, when summoned, carries out its master's wishes (the best-known one living inside Aladdin's lamp). A *jinni*, on the other hand, is a spirit or demon that, according to Muslim mythology, appears on Earth in human or animal form and exercises supernatural powers. *Djinni* is a variant spelling of *jinni*.

Both words have multiple plural forms. *Genie* forms *genies* or, less good, *genii*. (See PLURALS (B).) *Jinni* forms *jinn* (which itself sometimes wrongly appears as the singular) or *jinns* (corresponding to the incorrect singular *jinn*).

GENITIVES. See POSSESSIVES.

gentleman. A. General Use. *Gentleman* should not be used indiscriminately as a genteelism for *man*, the generic term. *Gentleman* should be reserved for reference to a cultured, refined man. It is a sign of the times that "[n]o word could be, it seems, more thoroughly out of style than *gentleman*" (*Sunday Times* [London]).

In BrE, the word formerly referred to a man of independent means and not working gainfully.

B. And *gentleperson*. This word is occasionally used as a neutral term in salutations, especially in the plural, but it has never lost its look of jocularity. *The Second Barnhart Dictionary of New English* (1980) says of *gentleperson*, "often used humorously or ironically." E.g.: "*Gentlepeople* don't read other *gentlepeople's* e-mail" (*Chicago Trib.*).

genus. The only plural form included in many dictionaries is *genera*, but both the *OED* and *RH2* include the variant *genuses*. That variant has become fairly common, and it is undeniably more comprehensible to more people—e.g.: "Both *genuses* have a blue daisylike flower" (*S.F. Chron.*). Still, somewhat surprisingly, *genera* predominates in modern usage—e.g.: "Although up to 90 species of plants are called rattan, most [that] are used in furniture are from two *genera*, Calamus and Daemonorops, climbing palms growing high in the primary forests of Southeast Asia" (*Chapel Hill Herald*). See PLURALS (B). Cf. **species.**

get. A. Generally. *Get* is good English. Yet many writers want to avoid it because they consider it too informal; they prefer *obtain* or *procure*, two FORMAL WORDS. The same tendency is at work here that leads some writers to shun *before* in favor of *prior to*, *later* in favor of *subsequent to*, and the like. But confident, relaxed writers use the word *get* quite naturally—e.g.: "Duke was obviously referring to some of the conference championship teams or playoff winners that either *got* lucky or hot during the playoffs or played an unimpressive schedule to win a conference title and gain an automatic berth" (*N.Y. Times*). Although some pedants have contended that *get* must always mean "to obtain," any good dictionary will confirm that it has more than a dozen meanings, including "to become." So the example quoted above is quite proper. And it's entirely acceptable to use such phrases as *get sick*, *get well*, *get rich*, and *get angry*.

B. Inflection: get > got > gotten,

got. The past participle *gotten* predominates in AmE, *got* in BrE. See IRREGULAR VERBS.

C. *Have got* for *have* or *must*. The phrase *have got*—often contracted (as in *I've got*)—has long been criticized as unnecessary for *have*. In fact, though, the phrasing with *got* adds emphasis and is perfectly idiomatic—e.g.: "For this offense to work, *he's got* to be able to do more than dump the ball off desperately to his receivers" (*Wash. Post*).

The main error to watch out for is omitting *have* in either its full or its contracted form. That is, such expressions as *I gotta leave now* and *I got a $10 bill in my billfold* aren't in good use. But *I've got to leave now* and *I've got a $10 bill in my billfold* are good English. Cf. **better** (A).

get rid of. See PHRASAL VERBS.

gibe; jibe; gybe; jive. *Gibe* is both noun and verb. As a noun, it means "a caustic remark or taunt"—e.g.: "Irving Lewis . . . personified the faceless civil servants who, for all the *gibes* about pointy-headed bureaucrats, make government work" (*N.Y. Times*). *Jibe* is generally considered a verb only, meaning "to accord with, to be consistent with"—e.g.: "The sight just doesn't *jibe* with the image of her character" (*Texas Monthly*). *Gybe*, a sailing term meaning primarily "to shift a sail from one side of a vessel to the other while sailing before the wind," is so spelled in BrE but is usually spelled *jibe* in AmE. *Jive*, like *gibe*, is both noun and verb. As a noun, it refers either to swing music or to the argot of hipsters. As a verb, it means "to dance to swing music" or "to tease"—e.g.: "Snipes and Harrelson previously *jived* and juked and ragged their way through 'White Men Can't Jump,' so they're old hands at this" (*Buffalo News*).

Unfortunately, some writers misuse *jive* for *jibe*—e.g.: "The new songs were clamorous and spacey, with distorted hooks and extended feedback that *jived* [read *jibed*] well with the futuristic stage lighting" (*Allentown Morning Call*)./ "Former deputy prosecutor Lawrence Taylor . . . believes the district attorney's media-driven loser image doesn't *jive* [read *jibe*] with reality" (*L.A. Times*).

gift, it may be surprising to learn, has acted as a verb since the 16th century. And now it's much on the rise—e.g.: "Her sales price must be measured against your cost, plus any gift tax attributable to the difference between the value of the property when *gifted* and your cost" (*St. Louis Post-Dispatch*). Though this usage is old, it is not now standard. English has the uncanny ability, however, to transform nouns into verbs and to revive moribund usages. Twenty years ago *contact* was objected to as a verb, though it had been used that way since the early 19th century; few writers now feel uncomfortable using the word as a verb. See NOUNS AS VERBS.

Gift may end up in the same class. A perceived difference, however, is that we already have a perfectly good verb (*give*) and even a secondary verb for formal contexts (*donate*). The objection to *contact* was only that it made people uncomfortable, but there was no existing equivalent—*get in touch with* being much more cumbersome. So cautious writers may prefer to keep *gift* as a noun only. One is accustomed to thinking of *gifted children*, but not of *gifted stock*.

gipsy. See **gypsy.**

girl. This word is widely (and understandably) regarded as an affront when used in reference to an adult, just as *boy* would be. But for a female minor, *girl* is the appropriate word.

given name. See **surname.**

gladiolus—/gla-dee-**oh**-ləs/ or (pretentiously) /glə-**dɪ**-ə-ləs/—is the singular form. The plural form is *gladioluses* or *gladioli*, pronounced /gla-dee-**oh**-lee/ or /-lɪ/. See PLURALS (B).

But because *gladiolus* is sometimes

wrongly taken to be a plural, especially in speech, the mistaken form *gladiola* has emerged. It is an arrant mistake that should be stamped out. E.g.: "Minutes later they crowd into Celsa Garcia's house, delivering their figures of Joseph and Mary to a makeshift corner altar that Ms. Garcia, 65, has draped with garlands of *gladiolas* [read *gladioluses*] and pine" (*N.Y. Times*).

go, meaning "say," is seemingly part of every American teenager's vocabulary. It occurs most often in the past tense, while recounting a conversation: "Then he *went*, like, 'No way!' " This is low-level slang. Cf. BE-VERBS (B) & **like** (C).

goes without saying, it. This phrase isn't generally suitable for formal contexts, although it may be appropriate in speech or in informal prose. Often, an editor is justified in thinking that if it goes without saying, then it need not be said.

good(-)faith. See **bona fide** (A) & ***bona fides*** (A).

got, p.pl.; **gotten.** See **get** (B).

governmental; government, adj. When we have an adjective (*governmental*) to do the job, we need not resort to a noun (*government*) to do the work of the adjective. Though the trend today is to write *government agency*, the stylist writes *governmental agency*. These are the niceties of writing that make the reader's task a little easier, and that distinguish between polished and ordinary prose.

graduate, vb. The traditional idiom (dating from the 16th century) was that the school *graduated* the student or the student *was graduated* from the school. By extension (during the 19th century), a student was said to *graduate* from the school. Those two uses of the verb are standard.

But in the mid-20th century, usage began to shift again: students were said to *graduate* college (omitting the *from* after *graduate*). This wording is not good usage, but it's increasingly common—e.g.: "Today three quarters of boys and half of girls have had sex by the time they *graduate* [read *graduate from*] high school" (*Newsweek*)./ " 'I have a reading disorder,' Leschuk says, yet he struggles to think of any friends who *graduated* [read *graduated from*] college who are doing as well" (*USA Today*).

graffiti. *W10* notes that this plural, originally Italian, "is sometimes used with a singular verb as a mass noun <the *graffiti* is being covered with fresh paint . . . >." But the word has not gone as far down this road as, say, *data*. (See **data.**) The word still sometimes appears as a plural—e.g.: "During the past year *graffiti* have begun to appear in cities" (*Time*). See PLURALS (I). Likewise, the traditional singular, *graffito*, still sometimes appears when the sense is undeniably singular and the mass noun would be inappropriate—e.g.: "[T]he young Indian submerged in the menacing urban emptiness of a London ghetto where the least offensive *graffito* says 'Go Home to Pakistan' " (*Wash. Post*). See COUNT NOUNS AND MASS NOUNS.

grammatical error. Because *grammatical* may mean either (1) "relating to grammar" <grammatical subject> or (2) "consistent with grammar" <a grammatical sentence>, there is nothing wrong with the age-old phrase *grammatical error* (sense 1). It's as acceptable as the phrases *criminal lawyer* and *logical fallacy*.

granddad; grandpa. These colloquial terms for *grandfather* are so spelled. *Grandad* and *granpa* are variant forms to be avoided. But *grandpa* is sometimes shortened to *gramp*, *grampa*, or *gramps*, all three of which are recognized as good colloquial AmE.

grandparenting. See **parenting.**

grateful; gratified. The distinction is well established. *Grateful* = appreciative, thankful <I'm grateful for your help>. *Gratified* = pleased, satisfied <we're gratified that you'll attend our party>.

gratuitous; fortuitous. These two words are occasionally confounded. *Gratuitous* = (1) done or performed without obligation to do so <gratuitous promises>; or (2) done unnecessarily <gratuitous criticisms>. *Fortuitous* = occurring by chance <fortuitous circumstances>. See **fortuitous.**

GRAVE ACCENT. See DIACRITICAL MARKS.

gray; grey. The former spelling is more common in AmE, the latter in BrE; both are old, and neither is incorrect. Still, *greyhound* is an invariable spelling.

Great Britain consists of England, Scotland, and Wales—all three on the island known to the Romans as *Britannia*. It differs from *United Kingdom*, which also includes Northern Ireland.

grey. See **gray.**

grievous is frequently misspelled and mispronounced *grievious*, just as *mischievous* is frequently misspelled and mispronounced *mischievious*. These are grievous and mischievous malformations. Cf. **mischievous.**

grisly; grizzly. *Grisly* = ghastly, horrible <grisly murders>. *Grizzly* = (1) grayish; or (2) of or relating to the large brown bear that inhabits Western North America. Each word is sometimes misused for the other. Most commonly, *grizzly* displaces *grisly* from its rightful position—e.g.: "[T]hat night the television news is full of the *grizzly* [read *grisly*] horror of it all" (*Wash. Post*). But the opposite error also occurs—e.g.: "Dolphins, storks, cranes, pelicans, *grisly* [read *grizzly*] bears, an 8-foot map of Texas: Joe Kyte has stuffed them all" (*Pitt. Post-Gaz.*).

grow, v.t. Although this verb is typically intransitive <he grew two inches taller over the summer>, its transitive use has long been standard in phrases such as *grow crops* and *grow a beard.*

Recently, however, *grow* has blossomed as a transitive verb in nonfarming and nongrooming contexts. It is trendy in business JARGON: *growing the industry*, *growing your business*, *growing your investment*, and so on. But because many readers will stumble over these odd locutions, the trend should be avoided—e.g.: "To this common mix Quantum has added a clever way to keep the teams' collective vision focused on how to *grow* [read *expand* or *develop*] the business rather than just on how to cooperate inside" (*Fortune*).

guerrilla (Sp. "raiding party") = a member of a small band of military fighters who, mostly through surprise raids, try to harass and undermine occupying forces. The word is preferably so spelled—not *guerilla*.

The MALAPROPISM *gorilla forces* occasionally surfaces.

gybe. See **gibe.**

gypsy is the standard spelling. *Gipsy* is a variant form.

H

ha—the interjection that expresses surprise, triumph, discovery, anger, and various other states of mind—is so spelled. *Hah* is a variant form.

For laughter, *ha-ha* is the usual spelling.

habituation. See **addicted.**

had better. See **better (A).**

hair's breadth; hair's-breadth; hairbreadth; hairsbreadth. Although most American dictionaries list *hairbreadth* first as both noun and adjective, that is one of the less common forms. The standard terms today are *hair's breadth* as a noun <victory by a hair's breadth> and *hair's-breadth* as an adjective <a hair's-breadth victory>. E.g.: "In 1972, we came within a *hair's breadth* of being arrested by Franco's Spanish police" (*Boston Globe*). The other forms are NEEDLESS VARIANTS.

The phrase is sometimes wrongly written *hare's breath* or *hair's breath*—e.g.: "CBS won by a *hare's breath* [read *hair's breadth*], followed by ABC and NBC, in a close race" (*Orange County Register*)./ "The Harvest Moon Inn, a *hair's breath* [read *hair's breadth*] away from achieving four-star status in the mere months of its existence, is clearly on the rise" (*Asbury Park Press*).

hale, vb., = to compel to go. This is the correct verb in the idiom *hale into court*. Unfortunately, though, the verb is often mistakenly written *hail*—e.g.: "Then he was *hailed* [read *haled*] into court on assault and battery charges" (*Riverside Press-Enterprise*).

hale and hearty is the SET PHRASE meaning "strong and healthy." But writers often get one or the other of the words wrong, and occasionally both—e.g.:

- "In another incident, the *hail and hardy* [read *hale and hearty*] boys of Ovett got good and drunk and decided to have some fun with the little ladies" (*Houston Chron.*).
- "Sir Donald is *hail* [read *hale*] *and hearty* and able to appreciate it" (*Daily Telegraph*).
- "But the big loggerheads, a threatened species, are *hale and hardy* [read *hale and hearty*] now after months of recuperation at the museum" (*Virginian-Pilot*).

half. A. ***Half (of).*** The preposition *of* is often unnecessary. Omit it when you can—e.g.: "Everyone else can still write off only *half* the cost of that cinnamon roll" (*Time*)./ "Nearly *half of* [read *half*] the people in Cuba receive economic help from family and friends in the United States" (*Fresno Bee*). Of course, when a pronoun follows, the *of* is typically needed <half of them are>. See (B).

B. ***Half of them (is) (are).*** Although we say *half of it is*, we should say *half of them are*. For the principle underlying the latter phrase, see SYNESIS.

C. ***A half dozen*** **and** ***half a dozen.*** For this noun phrase, either *a half dozen* or *half a dozen* is good form. Avoid *a half a dozen*. When the phrase is used as an adjective, it becomes a PHRASAL ADJECTIVE that should be hyphenated <a half-dozen twirlers with the band>.

D. ***Two halves.*** This phrase is often redundant—e.g.: "Peel your own or buy peeled fresh squash cut into *two halves* [read *halves*]" (*Providence J.-Bull.*).

On the plural *halves*, see PLURALS (G).

half-yearly. See **biannual.**

hallucination; delusion. A *hallucination* results from disturbed perceptions, as when a person "hears voices" or sees ghosts. A *delusion* results from disturbed thinking, as when a person incorrectly imagines that he or she is being persecuted. Cf. **illusion.**

hamstring, vb. *Hamstrung* is the settled past-tense and past-participial form. Although this form has no etymological basis—that is, the verb comes from the noun *hamstring* and not from any form of the verb *string* (we don't "string the ham")—the past tense *hamstringed* hardly exists today and strikes most readers as pedantic. E.g.: "Anderson was in fine physical form, still striking all the characteristic moves of a *hamstringed* [read *hamstrung*], drunken marionette" (*Seattle Times*).

handful. A. Plural. The word is *handfuls*, not *handsful*. See PLURALS (F).

B. *Handful is* or *handful are*. When followed by a plural noun, *handful* typically takes a plural verb—e.g.: "Today there *is* [read *are*] only a handful of residents in what is left of the white section of town" (*N.Y. Times*). See SYNESIS.

handicraft (= [1] an art or avocation requiring manual skill; or [2] an article made by manual skill) is the standard noun. *Handcraft*, n., is a NEEDLESS VARIANT.

But the verb *handcraft* (= to fashion by hand) and the adjective *handcrafted* are perfectly good. In fact, sometimes *handicraft* is wrongly asked to do their work—e.g.: "Dress up a wooden container with a selection of *handicrafted* [read *handcrafted*] tiles" (*S.F. Chron.*).

handkerchief /**hang**-kər-chif/. Pl. *handkerchiefs*—not *handkerchieves*. See PLURALS (G).

hand-wringing. See **wring (B).**

hangar; hanger. The shelter for airplanes is spelled *hangar*. All other senses belong to the spelling *hanger*. But that spelling sometimes invades the domain of *hangar*—e.g.: "[They] convert[ed] scores of old warehouses into offices and production sites, and airplane *hangers* [read *hangars*] into sound stages" (*L.A. Times*).

hanged; hung. Coats and pictures are *hung*, and sometimes so are juries. But criminals found guilty of capital offenses are *hanged*—at least in some jurisdictions. E.g.: "The six officers were executed by a firing squad and the two civilians were *hanged*, the radio said" (*Chicago Trib.*).

But just because it's a person doesn't mean that *hanged*—which implies execution and near-certain death as a result of the suspension—is always the right word. If a person is suspended for amusement or through malice, and death isn't intended or likely, then *hung* is the proper word—e.g.: "He charges that authorities did little or nothing after he complained at various times of being attacked by dogs, shot at, beaten with a rake and tortured while being *hanged* [read *hung*] upside down" (*Denver Post*). In Italy in 1944, Benito Mussolini and his mistress were executed and then their bodies *hung* upside down, but press reports often say incorrectly that they were *hanged*—e.g.: "Hitler decided to do so after hearing that Partisans had captured and shot Italian dictator Benito Mussolini, and *hanged him* [read *hung his body*] upside down in Milan plaza" (*Cleveland Plain Dealer*). See IRREGULAR VERBS.

hanger. See **hangar.**

happily means "fortunately," not "in a happy manner," when used as here: "*Happily*, some things never change" (*Santa Fe New Mexican*). See SENTENCE ADVERBS. Cf. **hopefully.**

harass may be pronounced either /**har**-is/ or /hə-**ras**/. The former is often considered preferable, but the latter prevails in AmE. The word is often misspelled *harrass*. See SPELLING (A).

harassment. During the Senate's confirmation hearings on the appointment of Justice Clarence Thomas in October 1991, senators were divided over whether to say /**har**-is-mənt/ or /hə-**ras**-mənt/ (and over other issues as well). Because the proceedings were closely watched throughout the country, the correct pronunciation became a popular subject of discussion. Although in BrE /**har**-is-mənt/ predominates—and many Americans (therefore?) consider it preferable—in AmE /hə-**ras**-mənt/ is standard.

hardly. In dialect, this word appears in at least three erroneous forms: *can't hardly* (for *can hardly*), *not hardly* (for *hardly*), and *without hardly* (for *almost without*). See **can't hardly & not hardly.**

hardy; hearty. *Hardy* = bold, vigorous, robust. *Hearty* = (1) warm and enthusiastic <a hearty greeting>; (2) strong and healthy <a hearty rancher>; (3) (of food) nourishing, satisfying <a hearty meal>; or (4) (of an eater) needing or demanding plenty of food <a hearty appetite>. Although sense 2 of *hearty* overlaps somewhat with *hardy* (and is therefore avoided by some careful writers), the other senses don't. Still, some writers confuse the two words—e.g.:

- Sense 1: "A *hardy* [read *hearty*] welcome home to Cleo Parker Robinson and the 18 members of her dance troupe" (*Rocky Mountain News*).
- Sense 3: "Milwaukee Bucks center Alton Lister . . . settled in on the more secluded side of the counter for a *hardy* [read *hearty*] meal after a practice with the team" (*Milwaukee J. Sentinel*).
- Sense 4: "It is an immensely popular spot that has been serving huge portions of gutsy food to enthusiastic *hardy* [read *hearty*, and delete *enthusiastic*] eaters for nearly three years" (*N.Y. Times*).

Sometimes, too, *hearty* is misused for *hardy*. We speak of *hardy* (not *hearty*) plants—e.g.: "At first, Thronson's customers were mostly public agencies seeking cheap, *hearty* [read *hardy*] plants to adorn highways and public buildings" (*Portland Oregonian*).

harebrained is the correct form; *hairbrained* is the common blunder. The misspelling falls just short of being what it attempts to denote—e.g.: "But what makes the episode such a delight is that it takes us inside the goofy mind of Helms and his *hairbrained* [read *harebrained*] sidekick" (*Baltimore Sun*)./ "By contrast Richard Rauh is consistently funny and convincing as the *hairbrained* [read *harebrained*] vice president who can't find his way to the Senate but ends up with the beauty queen by default" (*Pitt. Post-Gaz.*).

healthful; healthy. Strictly speaking, *healthy* refers to a person (or personified thing) in good health, *healthful* in reference to whatever promotes good health. E.g.: "[L]ow-fat dairy products . . . will keep us feeling *healthy* and good about ourselves, she says. A vegetarian, Barnes takes *healthful* dishes to parties" (*Dayton Daily News*). In fact, though, many writers use *healthy* when they mean *healthful*, and *healthy* threatens to edge out its sibling. Such a development would be unhealthful, since it would lead to a less healthy state of the language.

hear. See **listen.**

heart-rending is sometimes nonsensically written *heart-rendering*—e.g.: "He returns to his regular style on a cover of Larry Graham's R&B classic, a *heart-rendering* [read *heart-rending*], emotional 'One in a Million You' " (*Albany Times Union*). Of course, the verb *rend* (= to split, tear) has nothing to do with the verb *render* (= to make, perform, provide). See MALAPROPISMS.

hearty. See **hardy.**

heaven's sake. So written—not (as often erroneously written) *heavens' sake*, *heavens sake*, *heaven's sakes*, or *heaven sakes*.

height has a distinct /t/ sound at the end. To pronounce or write this word as if it were *heighth* is less than fully literate—e.g.: "Second-seeded Syracuse had intermittent difficulties with No. 15 Coppin State's zone defenses, but Syracuse's *heighth* [read *height*] and strength won out" (*Richmond Times Dispatch*). The mistake may occur for any of several reasons: (1) other words conveying measurement end in *-th* (e.g., *depth*, *width*, *breadth*); (2) people might confuse its ending with that of *eighth;* or (3) *highth* is an archaic variant formerly used in southern England. See PRONUNCIATION (B).

heinous /**hay**-nəs/—rhyming with "pain us"—is one of our most commonly mispronounced words. It is also frequently misspelled *heinious*—e.g.: "[It was as if] Maris had committed some *heinious* [read *heinous*] crime in threatening Ruth's record" (*Providence J.-Bull.*).

helpmate; helpmeet. *Helpmeet*, now archaic, was the original form, yet folk etymology changed the spelling to *-mate*, which is now the prevalent form. (See ETYMOLOGY (D).) In fact, *helpmate* is now nearly nine times more common than *helpmeet*.

Here's the story behind the development of the words. *Helpmeet* is a compound "absurdly formed" (as the *OED* puts it) from the two words *help* and *meet* in Genesis: "an help meet for him" (Gen. 2:18, 20), in which *meet* is really an adjective meaning "suitable." Some writers still use *helpmeet*—e.g.: "Naturally, I am a loyal and patient *helpmeet* whose only reward is a smile on the lips of my beloved—a smile, and ceaseless extravagant praise" (*S.F. Chron.*). But *meet* was widely misunderstood as *mate*, and the form *helpmate* sprang up and has long been predominant—e.g.: "She leads the choir, works with its youth and is her husband's steadfast and (usually) cheerful *helpmate*" (*St. Petersburg Times*).

Helpmate means "a companion or helper," and it need not refer to a spouse—e.g.: "We need to talk about the frustrations you face when you rely on a computer—Mac or IBM-compatible—as electronic *helpmate*" (*Palm Beach Post*).

help to. In most contexts, the better usage is to omit *to* after *help*—e.g.: "The accord also *helps to* [read *helps*] avoid a destabilizing competition in northeast Asia among Communist-ruled North Korea and two of its immediate neighbors, Japan and China" (*Milwaukee Sentinel*).

hence. This adverb has several meanings, listed here in decreasing order of frequency: (1) "for this reason; therefore" <your premise is flawed; hence, your argument fails>; (2) "from this source" <she grew up in Colorado; hence her interest in mountain climbing>; (3) "from this time; from now" <the millennium is two years hence>; or (4) "from this place; away" <the park is three miles hence>.

From hence for *hence* (in senses 3 and 4) is an ARCHAISM.

he or she. A. Generally. The traditional view, now widely assailed as sexist, was that the masculine pronouns are generic, comprehending both male and female. One way to avoid the generic masculine *he, his,* and *him* is to use—not at every turn, but sparingly—*he or she*, *his or her*, and *him or her*. E.g.: "The notion that a business can teach a customer about *his or her* desires will reshape industries, he says" (*Fin. Times*).

Another way to avoid the problem—not possible in all contexts—is to pluralize the antecedent of the pronoun. E.g.: "If *children* think *they* look different—because *they* feel a lot bigger or a lot smaller or a lot thinner than *their* peers—it calls extra attention to *them* and can make *them* uncomfortable" (*Boston Herald*). The disadvantage of such a wording is that it often too strongly suggests a singleness of mind in the group, as opposed to the uniqueness of an individual mind. This despite, in the example given, an implication of unique differences.

He or she is by no means a newfangled concession to feminism. In 1837, the English Wills Act stated: "And be it further enacted, That every Will made by a Man or Woman shall be revoked by *his or her* Marriage (except a Will made in exercise of Appointment . . .)." See SEXISM (B).

B. *He/she.* Sometimes this gets quite out of hand. But it's rare to see such an exquisite example as this: "If a child is not corrected when he/she first misspells a word, by the time he/she is in eighth grade, the errors are so ingrained they are never even noticed. . . . I think it is a disservice to the child to let him/her go along for seven years and then tell him/her that the spelling is all wrong" (*Ariz. Republic / Phoenix Gaz.*). What about letting him/her go seven years using *he / she* and *him / her*, when reasonable readers will think that he/she is off his/her rocker? See VIRGULE.

herb, n.; **herbal,** adj. Although *herb* is pronounced /ərb/, *herbal* has traditionally been pronounced /**hər**-bəl/. Today, however, /**ər**-bəl/ predominates in AmE. It therefore seems more natural to most American readers to sip *an herbal tea*, not *a herbal tea*. But *herbicide*, with an aspirated *h-*, should be preceded by *a*, not *an*. See **a (A).** Cf. **homage & humble.**

heretofore. See **up to now.**

hiccup; hiccough. The first is the standard spelling; the second is a variant form arrived at through folk etymology. See ETYMOLOGY (D).

Hiccup, vb., makes *hiccuped* and *hiccuping* in AmE, *hiccupped* and *hiccupping* in BrE. See SPELLING (B).

highfalutin (= pretentious, pompous) is preferably so spelled, as opposed to *highfaluting*, *highfalutin'*, or *hifalutin.* But the variants persist—e.g.: "Chief among these are the geo people—those apostles of geopolitics, geostrategies and all the *hifalutin'* [read *highfalutin*] rest—who argue against the 'sentimentality' of human rights and democratic concerns" (*Newsweek*). The *W10* spelling is *highfalutin*, without the apostrophe and with *high* spelled out. The *OED*, recording the word as an Americanism dating from the mid-19th century, has two spellings: *highfalutin* (first) and *highfalutin'*. The *Funk & Wagnalls New Standard Dictionary* (1942) records *hifalutin* (without the apostrophe) as a variant spelling; the main entry is under *highfalutin.* (Other variants listed there are *highfaluten* and *highfaluting.*) The best course is to do two things: spell the word *highfalutin*, and avoid being what it denotes.

highlight > highlighted > highlighted. *Highlit* is a variant past-tense and past-participial form that occasionally surfaces—e.g.: "The story is read aloud at a speed suggesting a preliterate user, [and] *highlit* [read *highlighted*] words are defined at a level appropriate for a smart 5th grader" (*Wash. Post*).

highly regarded. See **regard (B).**

hijack. Vehicles and airplanes are *hijacked*, not people. E.g.: " 'It's horrifying, because it's like a kidnapping,' said Greg Britt, a 34-year-old language instructor from Atlanta who was *hijacked* [read *abducted* or *held up*] in a cab at knife point last year, then ordered to make 12 separate withdrawals from automatic-teller machines—six before midnight and six after the new day began, when he was able to withdraw more" (*Boston Globe*).

The word is often misspelled *highjack*—e.g.: "Buildings are bombed and planes are *highjacked* [read *hijacked*]" (*Richmond Times Dispatch*).

hippopotamus. The plural is preferably *hippopotamuses*, not *hippopotami.*

The preferred form appears almost four times more frequently than the other. See PLURALS (B).

historical. A. And *historic*. *Historical*, meaning "of or relating to or occurring in history," is called upon for use far more frequently. *Historic* means "historically significant" <the Alamo is a historic building>. An event that makes history is *historic*; momentous happenings or developments are *historic*—e.g.: "The Supreme Court's *historic* decision about whether mentally competent, dying patients and their doctors have the right to hasten death won't be known for months" (*USA Today*).

A documented fact, event, or development—perhaps having no great importance—is *historical*. E.g.: "Despite the *historical* data, some people just don't feel comfortable knowing their loan's rate can drift up 5 or 6 points" (*Chicago Sun-Times*).

Examples of *historic* used incorrectly for *historical* could easily run for several pages—e.g.: "The odds are now on a further easing of monetary policy and there is a good *historic* [read *historical*] correlation between falling interest rates and a rising stock market" (*Fin. Times*).

The far less common mistake is misusing *historical* for *historic*—e.g.: "Gary Pinkel didn't know what to expect after Toledo and Nevada found themselves going into a *historical* [read *historic*] overtime in the Las Vegas Bowl" (*Austin American-Statesman*). See -IC.

B. *A historic(al)*; *an historic(al)*. On the question whether to write *a* or *an historic(al)*, see **a** (A).

hitherto. See **up to now.**

HIV virus. For this redundant acronym, see ABBREVIATIONS (B).

Hobson's choice. A. Generally. This ever-growing CLICHÉ has loosened its etymological tether. Tradition has it that Thomas Hobson (1549–1631), a hostler in Cambridge, England, always gave his customers only one choice among his horses: whichever one was closest to the door. Hence, in literary usage, a *Hobson's choice* came to denote no choice at all—either taking what is offered or taking nothing.

Though purists resist the change, the prevailing sense in AmE is not that of having no choice, but of having two bad choices—e.g.: "[T]he city then foists a *Hobson's choice* upon its electorate: Either vote to tax the city's property owners with a sizable bond issue, or just endure the increasingly unsafe streets and bridges" (*Seattle Times*). In a sense, this usage isn't much of a SLIPSHOD EXTENSION. After all, the choice of either taking what is offered or taking nothing must often be two poor options.

B. Article with. Traditionally—and still in BrE—the phrase takes no article; that is, you are faced not with *a Hobson's choice* but with *Hobson's choice*. In AmE, though, the phrase usually takes either *a* or *the* (as in the preceding example).

C. *Hobbesian choice*. Amazingly, some writers have confused the obscure Thomas Hobson with his famous contemporary, the philosopher Thomas Hobbes (1588–1679). The resulting MALAPROPISM is beautifully grotesque: "The trail points to the Beaver—who really doesn't give a damn—and will lead to a *Hobbesian choice* [read *Hobson's choice*] for his son: the truth vs. loyalty to the Old Man" (*L.A. Times*)./"[Y]our children and grandchildren will be faced with a *Hobbesian choice* [read *Hobson's choice*]: Either they support vastly higher taxes on their own incomes or sharply cut back Social Security and Medicare to their parents and grandparents" (*Esquire*). See DOUBLE BOBBLES.

hoi polloi (= the common people, the masses). Because *hoi* in Greek means "the (plural)," *the hoi polloi* is technically redundant. But the three-word phrase predominates and ought to be accepted.

What shouldn't be accepted, though, is the growing misuse of *hoi polloi* to refer to the elite. This might occur through a false association with *hoity-toity* (= arrogant, haughty) or *high and mighty*—e.g.: "You may shell out $75 or $80 per person, sans tax and tip, for the Tribute experience, but, trust me: This is money very well spent. Which is why Tribute has been drawing Detroit power brokers and the *upper-end hoi polloi* [read, perhaps, *upper crust*] since it opened in April" (*Detroit News*).

holistic (= [1] of or relating to holism, i.e., the theory [esp. as applied in medicine] that organisms have an existence other than as the mere sum of their parts; or [2] relating to or concerned with complete systems rather than with their component parts) is so spelled. But the word is fairly often misspelled *wholistic*—e.g.: "So Duke started the long journey toward recovery, sampling traditional veterinarian medicine, canine acupuncture, obedience techniques, *wholistic* [read *holistic*] medicine, and animal behavior modification" (*Denver Post*).

holocaust (Gk. "burnt whole") is one of our most hyperbolical words, beloved of jargonmongers and second-rate journalists. The historical sense from World War II, of course, is beyond question. Figurative applications of the term, however, are often questionable. Here it is used to no avail in reference to a scandal: "He would soon be engulfed in a *holocaust* of painful controversy that would maim several lives, wound hundreds of other people, and jostle the foundations of the fashion industry." Inherent in the sense of the word, whether literal or figurative, is the idea of a complete burning; thus, it may be used appropriately of fires, but not, for example, of floods.

Also, of course, it brings to most modern minds the Nazi extermination of European Jews during World War II. When referring to that ghastly series of atrocities, the word is capitalized. And because of its association with those acts of genocide, the word is generally seen as inappropriate when used in reference to deaths that are (1) not caused by malice and (2) not on a massive scale. E.g.: "History has a way of repeating itself, doesn't it? I consider what happened in Chicago this summer—the poor dying in their own apartment buildings [from the heat wave]—America's own *Holocaust* . . . . Who is responsible for this inhumane negligence?" (*Roanoke Times & World News*). (That terrible heat wave in Chicago caused nearly 200 deaths, but it shouldn't have been called a *holocaust*—especially not with a capital *H*.) See ETYMOLOGY (C).

homage is best pronounced /**hom**-ij/. It is a silly (but quite common) pretension to omit the /h/ sound. Cf. **herb & humble.**

home. See **house.**

home in, not *hone in*, is the correct phrase. In the 19th century, the metaphor referred to what homing pigeons do; by the early 20th century, it referred also to what aircraft and missiles do.

And by the late 20th century, some writers had begun mistaking the phrase by using the wrong verb, *hone* (= to sharpen) instead of *home*—e.g.: "When Pomeroy joined the Berklee faculty, the school was only 10 years old and just beginning to *hone* [read *home*] in on jazz education" (*Boston Herald*).

homely; homey. These two words have undergone DIFFERENTIATION. *Homey* means "characteristic of a home; homelike." *Homely* originally shared this sense, but it gradually was extended to mean "simple, unpretentious." From there, the word was extended further to the sense that is prevalent in AmE today: "unattractive in appearance; plain." R.W. Burchfield points out that if *homely* refers to a British woman, it means that she is "adept at housekeeping, warm and welcome" (*MEU3*). A *homely* American woman, however, is simply unattractive.

homogeneous; homogenous. *Homogeneous* (five syllables) is the usual and the etymologically preferable form—not *homogenous*. *Homogeneal*, *homogenetic*, and *homogenetical* are rare forms to be avoided; they have failed to become standard and should be laid to rest.

hone in. See **home in.**

honorarium. Pl. *honoraria* or *honorariums*. Though the latter has much to commend itself as a homegrown plural—and is *The New York Times*' preferred plural—*honoraria* generally prevails in AmE and BrE alike. See PLURALS (B).

hoof. Pl. *hooves*—preferably not *hoofs*. E.g.: "That's what makes the rodeo such a rip-snortin', wild fandango of bucking, swirling cayuses and bulls, flying *hooves*, sweat, sawdust and daredevil cowboys" (*Denver Post*). (See PLURALS (G).) In modern print sources, *hooves* is five times more common.

But the adjective *hoofed* is so spelled—not *hooved*. E.g.: "He's seen Powell load animals into a trailer—a place where most four-legged *hooved* [read *hoofed*] animals don't want to go" (*Memphis Commercial Appeal*).

hopefully. Four points about this word. First, it was widely condemned from the 1960s to the 1980s. Briefly, the objections are that (1) *hopefully* properly means "in a hopeful manner" and shouldn't be used in the radically different sense "I hope" or "it is to be hoped"; (2) if the extended sense is accepted, the original sense will be forever lost; and (3) in constructions such as "Hopefully, it won't rain this afternoon," the writer illogically ascribes an emotion (*hopefulness*) to a nonperson. In a way, *hopefully* isn't analogous to *curiously* (= it is a curious fact that), *fortunately* (= it is a fortunate thing that), and *sadly* (= it is a sad fact that). How so? Unlike all those other SENTENCE ADVERBS, *hopefully* can't be resolved into any longer expression involving the word *hopeful*—but only *hope* (e.g., *it is to be hoped that* or *I hope that*).

Second, whatever the merits of those arguments, the battle is now over. *Hopefully* is now a part of AmE, and it has all but lost its traditional meaning—e.g.: "That way, if one of them gets stuck in traffic on the way to the ceremony, the other will—*hopefully*—still make it there in time" (*Fortune*). Sometimes, the word is genuinely ambiguous (if the original meaning is considered still alive)—e.g.: "Dave Krieg will take the snaps and, *hopefully*, hand off to RB Garrison Hearst" (*USA Today*). (Is Krieg hoping for the best when Hearst runs? Or is the writer hoping that Krieg won't pass the football or hand off to another running back?) Indeed, the original meaning *is* alive, even if moribund—e.g.: "Officials recently have pointed *hopefully* to signs of increased usage of the garage" (*Boston Globe*).

Third, some stalwarts continue to condemn the word, so that anyone using it in the new sense is likely to have a credibility problem with some readers—e.g.:

- "Where we do not move forward, we regress. To be sure, it begins with slight lapses. Errors of usage—confusing 'disinterest' with 'uninterest,' using 'hopefully' for 'it is to be hoped.' And then, with astonishing swiftness, the rot sets in" (*N.Y. Times*).
- "In the 1969 Usage Panel survey [*hopefully*] was acceptable to 44 percent of the Panel; in the most recent survey it was acceptable to only 27 percent" (*AHD*).
- "Professor Michael Dummett, an Oxford logician, condemns the new usage of *hopefully* because only a person can be hopeful, and in many such cases there is nobody around in the sentence to be hopeful" (*Daily Telegraph*).

Fourth, though the controversy swirling around this word has subsided, it is now a SKUNKED TERM. Avoid it in all senses if you're concerned with your credibility: if you use it in the traditional way, many readers will think it odd; if you use it in the newish way, a few readers will tacitly tut-tut you.

hors d'oeuvre. Although this term serves as both the singular and the plural in French, the anglicized plural *hors d'oeuvres* has become standard in English. See PLURALS (B) & SPELLING (A).

house; home. In the best usage, the structure is always called a *house*. Thus, it is not good form to speak of a recently built *home* that hasn't yet been sold. Nor should one point to the building and call it one's *home*: it's a *house* in the best English. The word *home* connotes familial ties.

The plural *houses* should be pronounced /**howz**-əz/, not /**hows**-əz/.

however. A. Beginning Sentences with. It seems everyone has heard that sentences should not begin with this word—not, that is, when a contrast is intended. But doing so isn't a grammatical error; it's merely a stylistic lapse, the word *But* ordinarily being much preferable. (See **but (A)**.) The reason is that *However*—three syllables followed by a comma—is a ponderous way of introducing a contrast, and it leads to unemphatic sentences. E.g.: "*However,* Gross forced third baseman Alan Andrews to pop up" (*Pitt. Post-Gaz.*). (Better: *But Gross forced third baseman Alan Andrews . . . .*)

But when used in the sense "in whatever way" or "to whatever extent," *however* (not followed by a comma) is unimpeachable at the beginning of a sentence. E.g.: "*However* tiresome the politics of this skirmish may seem, Greene has a point" (*Ariz. Republic/Phoenix Gaz.*).

B. Emphasizing Certain Words. Assuming that *however* isn't put at the front of a sentence, the word has the effect of emphasizing whatever precedes it. If you say "Jane, however, wasn't able to make the trip," you're presumably contrasting Jane with others who were able to go. But if the story is about Jane alone, and the fact that she had been hoping to make a trip, the sentence should be "Jane wasn't able, however, to make the trip." Some otherwise good writers don't seem to understand this straightforward point of rhetoric.

C. Undue Delay in the Sentence. Because of the point established in (B), it's quite unwise to put the *however* very far into a long sentence. The cure is an initial *But*—e.g.: "We use data only for individuals from the former West Germany in this study, *however*, and restrict our attention to data reported for the years prior to 1989, the year of reunification" (*J. Hum. Resources*). (Read: *But we use data only for individuals from the former West Germany in this study. And we restrict our attention to the years before 1989, the year of reunification.*)

D. Playing a Role in Run-On Sentences. Like a few other adverbs—notably *therefore* and *otherwise*—*however* often plays a role in RUN-ON SENTENCES. These sentences don't appear nearly as often in print as they do in informal writing, student papers, and the like. They read something like this: "I wanted to go on the trip, however, there wasn't a slot available." One cure, of course, is a semicolon after *trip*. But the better cure is usually to give the sentence an initial *Although*-clause: "Although I wanted to go on the trip, there wasn't a slot available."

human, n. Purists long objected to *human* as a shortened form of *human being*, but today it's so pervasive—even in formal writing—that it should be accepted as standard.

humankind; mankind. *Humankind*, a 17th-century creation, is unexceptionable, while *mankind* is, to many people, a sexist word. The prudent writer will therefore resort to *humankind*—e.g.: "They are so convinced of its authenticity and importance to *humankind* that they have created the Turin Shroud Center, a research facility that mixes hard science and deep faith" (*Denver Post*). See SEXISM (C).

humble is preferably pronounced with the *h-* sounded: /**həm**-bəl/. But the pronunciation without an aspirated *h-* has somehow become common in AmE, especially in the South.

In Humble, Texas (near Houston), the residents all say /**əm**-bəl/. That pronunciation has led local writers to use *an* before the proper name—e.g.: "West Brook got on the board early in the second quarter following *an Humble* fumble" (*Houston Chron.*). Most out-of-town readers would probably find that phrase odd-looking. But locals know better—and proudly so. See **a (A).** Cf. **herb & homage.**

hundred /**hən**-drəd/ is sometimes mispronounced /**hən**-drit/ or /**hə**-nərd/. See PRONUNCIATION (B).

hung. See **hanged.**

hutzpa(h). See **chutzpah.**

huzzah, an exclamation of joy or approval for formal occasions, is the standard spelling. *Huzza* is a variant form. Of course, *hurrah* and *hurray* are more common—and much less formal.

HYBRIDS, or words composed of morphemes from different languages (such as *telephone* [Gk. *tele-* + L. *phone*]), have become quite common over the past 50 years. One occasionally finds them criticized in older literature—e.g.:

- "*Ize* and *ist* 'are Greek terminations, and cannot properly be added to Anglo-Saxon words. *Ist* is the substantive form, *ize* the verbal.' Jeopard*ize* is one of the monsters made by adding *ize* to an English verb. *Jeopard* means to put in peril—and jeopard*ize* could mean no more .... So, also, is the Anglo-Saxon *er* (sign of the doer of a thing) 'incorrectly affixed to such words as *photograph* and *telegraph*'; the proper termination is *ist*: *photographist, telegraphist*, the same as *paragraph—paragraphist*. *Geographer* and *biographer* are exceptions firmly fixed in the language" (Ralcy Husted Bell, *The Worth of Words*, 1902).
- "*A-* (not) is Greek; *moral* is Latin. It is at least desirable that in making new words the two languages should not be mixed" (H.W. Fowler & F.G. Fowler, *The King's English*, 1906).
- "Neologisms . . . should be formed with some regard to etymological decency; the marriage of a so very English word as *swim* with a so very Greek vocable *stad* strikes one as an unseemly misalliance" (Eric Partridge, *U&A*).

Today, though, only a few Classics professors object. As an American lexicographer once observed, "Not many people care whether a word has Greek and Latin elements mixed in it" (M.M. Mathews, *American Words*, 1959). Perhaps this is because of our increasing ignorance of Classical tongues. Whatever the cause, though, modern neologists have little regard for the morphological integrity of the words they coin.

Virtually all the hybrids condemned by H.W. Fowler in *MEU1* (e.g., *amoral, bureaucracy, cablegram, climactic, coastal, coloration, gullible, pacifist, racial, speedometer*) are now passed over without mention even by those who consider themselves purists. Other hybrids that Fowler didn't mention also fall into this class:

antedate
antibody
aqualung
automobile
biocide
claustrophobia
ecocide
epidural
likable
lumpectomy
megaton
meritocracy
merriment
monorail
naturopathy
postwar
retrofit
riddance
semi-yearly
telegenic
television
transship

We also have our own fringe hybrids: *botheration*, *raticide*, *scatteration*, and *monokini*.

One rarely hears complaints about hybrids, though Mario Pei once called the legal term *venireman* a product of "the worst kind of hybridization (. . . half Latin, half Anglo-Saxon)" (*Words in Sheep's Clothing*, 1969). The nonsexist *veniremember*, of course, solves that problem.

Other hybrids are widely accepted. *Breathalyzer* (formerly *drunkometer*) has become standard, although in 1965 Ernest Gowers wrote that the term was "stillborn, it may be hoped" (*MEU2* at 253). *Creedal* is a near-commonplace hybrid. And Fowler may not be resting in peace.

HYPALLAGE /hI-**pal**-ə-jee/, known also as the transferred epithet, is a figure of speech in which the proper subject is displaced by what would logically be the object (if it were named directly). Usually hypallage is a mere idiomatic curiosity. It has a distinguished lineage—a famous example being Shakespeare's line from *Julius Caesar*: "This was the most unkindest cut of all" (3.2.183). It was not the *cut* that was unkind, but rather the *cutter*. Hence the object has become the subject.

In any number of everyday phrases, an adjective logically modifies not the noun actually supplied, but an implied one—e.g.:

angry fight
cruel comments
cynical view
disgruntled complaints
drunken parties
elementary classroom
English-speaking countries
feminine napkin
handicapped parking
hasty retreat
humble opinion
impeachable offense
nondrowsy cold medicine
overhead projector
permanent marker
provincial attitude
unfair criticisms
well-educated home

Generally, this figure of speech is harmless, even convenient. Pedants who complain about almost any phrase like the ones listed ("But the marker itself isn't permanent, is it?") are simply parading their own pedantry. Perhaps the phrase that most commonly gives rise to spurious objections is *The book says* . . .—which is perfectly good English.

HYPERCORRECTION. Sometimes people strive to abide by the strictest etiquette, but in the process behave inappropriately. The very motivations that result in this irony can play havoc with the language: a person will strive for a correct linguistic form but instead fall into error. Linguists call this phenomenon "hypercorrection"—a common shortcoming.

This foible can have several causes. Often, it results from an attempt to avoid what the writer wrongly supposes to be a grammatical error. (See SUPERSTITIONS.) At other times, it results from an incomplete grasp of a foreign grammar, coupled with an attempt to conform to that grammar. Yet again, it sometimes results from a misplaced sense of logic overriding a well-established idiom. A few of the most common manifestations are enumerated below.

A. False Latin Plurals. One with a smattering of Latin learns that, in that language, most nouns ending in *-us* have a plural ending in *-i*: *genius* forms *genii*, *nimbus* forms *nimbi*, *syllabus* forms *syllabi*, *terminus* forms *termini*, and so on. The trouble is that not all of them do end in *-i*, so traps abound for those trying to show off their sketchy knowledge of Latin:

Hypercorrect Plural	*Latin Plural*	*English Plural*
apparati	apparatus	apparatuses
fori	fora	forums
ignorami	[A vb. in L.]	ignoramuses

Hypercorrect Plural	*Latin Plural*	*English Plural*
isthmi	[Gk. sing. n.: *isthmos*]	isthmuses
mandami	[A vb. in L.]	mandamuses
mittimi	[A vb. in L.]	mittimuses
nexi	nexus	nexuses
octopi	[Gk. pl. *octopodes*]	octopuses
prospecti	prospectus	prospectuses
stati	status	statuses

B. *Between you and I.* Some people learn a thing or two about pronoun cases, but little more. They learn, for example, that it is incorrect to say "It is me" or "Me and Jane are going to school now." (See **it is I.**) But this knowledge puts them on tenterhooks: through the logical fallacy known as "hasty generalization," they come to fear that something is amiss with the word *me*—that perhaps it's safer to stick to *I*. They therefore start using *I* even when the objective case is called for: "She had the biggest surprise for Blair and *I* [read *me*]."/ "Please won't you keep this between you and *I* [read *me*]." These are gross linguistic gaffes, but it is perennially surprising how many otherwise educated speakers commit them. See **between (C)** & PRONOUNS (B).

Many writers and speakers try to avoid the problem by resorting to *myself*, but that is hardly an improvement. See **myself.**

C. Number Problems. Sometimes, in the quest for correctness, writers let their sense of grammar override long-established idioms. They may write, for example, "A number of people was there," when the correct form is "A number of people were there." Or they will write, "A handful of problems arises from that approach," instead of "A handful of problems arise from that approach." For more on these correct but "antigrammatical" constructions, see SYNESIS & **number of.**

D. Redundantly Formed Adverbs. The forms *doubtless*, *much*, and *thus* are adverbs, yet some writers overcompensate by adding *-ly*, thereby forming barbarisms: *doubtlessly*, *muchly*, and *thusly*. See ADVERBS (D), **doubtlessly & muchly.**

E. *As* for *like*. When writers fear using *like* as a conjunction, they sometimes fail to use it when it would function appropriately as a preposition or adverb. Thus, "She sings like a bird" becomes "She sings as a bird." But the latter sentence sounds as if it is explaining the capacity in which she sings. The hypercorrection, then, results in a MISCUE. See **like (A).**

F. *Whom* for *who*. Perhaps writers should get points for trying, but those who don't know how to use *whom* should abstain in questionable contexts. That is, *against whom*, *for whom*, and the like may generally be instances in which the writer knows to choose *whom*. But things can get moderately tricky—e.g.: "In 'An Independent Woman,' Barbara is confronted by an African-American burglar, *whom* [read *who*] she realizes is well-educated but desperate" (*Fresno Bee*). Although *whom* in that sentence may seem to be the object of *realizes*, in fact it is the subject of the verb *is*. See **who** & PRONOUNS (B).

G. Unsplit Infinitives Causing Miscues. Writers who have given in to the most widespread of SUPERSTITIONS—or who believe that most of the readers have done so—avoid all split infinitives. They should at least avoid introducing unclear modifiers into their prose. But many writers do introduce them, and the result is often a MISCUE or ambiguity—e.g.: "Each is *trying subtly to exert* his or her influence over the other" (Mark H. McCormack, *What They Don't Teach You at Harvard Business School*, 1984). In that sentence, does *subtly* modify the participle *trying* or the infinitive *to exert*? Because we cannot tell, the sentence needs to be revised in any of the following ways: (1) *Each is subtly trying to exert his or her influence over the other*, (2) *Each is trying to exert his or her influence subtly over the other*, (3) *Each is trying to subtly exert his* *or her influence over the other*, or (4) *Each is trying to exert his or her subtle influence over the other*. See SPLIT INFINITIVES.

H. Unsplit Verb Phrases. A surprising number of writers believe that it's a mistake to put an adverb in the midst of a verb phrase. The surprise is for them: every language authority who addresses the question holds just the opposite view—that the adverb generally *belongs* in the midst of a verb phrase. (See ADVERBS (A).) The canard to the contrary frequently causes awkwardness and artificiality—e.g.: "I *soon will be calling* you." (Read: *I will soon be calling you.*) See SUPERSTITIONS (C).

I. Prepositions Moved from the Ends of Sentences. "That is the type of arrant pedantry up with which I shall not put," said Winston Churchill, mocking the priggishness that causes some writers and speakers to avoid ending with a preposition. See PREPOSITIONS (B) & SUPERSTITIONS (A).

J. Borrowed Articles for Borrowed Nouns. When a naturalized or quasi-naturalized foreignism appears, the surrounding words—with a few exceptions, such as *hoi polloi*—should be English. Thus, one refers to *finding the mot juste*, not *finding le mot juste* (a common error among the would-be literati). But see **hoi polloi.**

K. Overrefined Pronunciation. Some foreignisms acquire anglicized pronunciations. For example, in AmE *lingerie* is pronounced in a way that the French would consider utterly barbarous: /lon-jə-**ray**/, as opposed to /la[n]-**zhree**/. (See **lingerie.**) But for a native speaker of AmE to use the latter pronunciation sounds foolish. Another French word that gives some AmE speakers trouble is *concierge*: it should be pronounced /kon-see-**erzh**/, not /kon-see-**er**/. See **concierge.**

Similarly, American and British printers refer to the more traditional typefaces—the ones with small projections coming off the straight lines—as *sans serif* /sanz-**ser**-if/, not /sahnz-sə-**reef**/. The latter pronunciation may show a supposed familiarity with the French language (though *serif* is Dutch), but it belies an unfamiliarity both with publishing and with the English language.

Even native-English words can cause problems. The word *often*, for example, preferably has a silent *-t-*, yet some speakers (unnaturally) pronounce it because of the spelling. The next logical step would be to pronounce *administration* /ad-min-i-**stray**-tee-on/, and all other words with the *-tion* suffix similarly. See PRONUNCIATION (A).

HYPHEN [-]. Generally, AmE is much less hospitable to hyphens than BrE. Words with prefixes are generally made solid: *displeasure* (not *dis-pleasure*), *preshrunk* (not *pre-shrunk*), *postdebate* (not *post-debate*), *preordain* (not *pre-ordain*). This no-hyphen style seems aesthetically superior, but reasonable people will differ on such a question. They can agree, however, that the hyphen must appear when an ambiguity or MISCUE is possible without it—e.g., *pre-judicial* (career), *re-sign* (the letter). See CO- & RE- PAIRS.

But in one context, AmE is quite hospitable to the hyphen. That's in the realm of PHRASAL ADJECTIVES. Here's the rule: if two or more consecutive words make sense only when understood together as an adjective modifying a noun that follows, those words (excluding the noun) should be hyphenated. Thus, you hyphenate *special-interest money*, but only because *money* is part of the phrase; if you were referring to this or that *special interest*, a hyphen would be wrong. Thus:

credit card	*but*	credit-card application
electoral college		electoral-college procedures
forest products		forest-products stocks
high frequency		high-frequency sounds
minimum height		minimum-height requirement

small business	*but*	small-business perspectives
used record		used-record store

Wilson Follett had it right when he said, in reference to this phrasal-adjective hyphen: "Nothing gives away the incompetent amateur more quickly than the typescript that neglects this mark of punctuation or that employs it where it is not wanted" (*MAU*).

hypnotism; hypnosis. These words aren't quite interchangeable. One might use either term to name the art of mesmerism, but one would never say, "He is under *hypnotism.*" *Hypnotism* refers only to the practice or art; *hypnosis* refers either to the practice or to the state of consciousness itself.

hypnotize is pronounced /**hip**-nə-tɪz/. The erroneous /**hip**-mə-tɪz/, with an /m/ sound, is all too common. See PRONUNCIATION (B).

I

I; me. See FIRST PERSON, PRONOUNS (A), (B) & **it is I.**

-IBLE. See **-ABLE (A).**

-IC; -ICAL. There are enough adjective pairs ending in these suffixes to fill up an entire page. Suffice it to say that you should keep a couple of good dictionaries nearby to help you decide which adjective to use. But keep in mind the two "desirable tendencies" cited by H.W. Fowler (*MEU1*): favoring DIFFERENTIATION where it exists (as with *economic* vs. *economical* and *historic* vs. *historical*) and rejecting NEEDLESS VARIANTS that are truly needless (such as *biologic* or *ecologic*). See **economic (A)** & **historical (A).**

ID; I.D. The first is preferable for this shortened form of *identification*. In the second, the periods should indicate that the initials *I* and *D* each stand for something. But they don't: everybody knows that *I.D.* is simply shorthand. Given the illogic of the periods—and the trend in AmE away from periods in abbreviations—the form *ID* is better. See ABBREVIATIONS (A).

identical takes either *with* or *to*. Historically, *with* has been considered better because one has *identity with* something or someone, not *to* it. *Identical to* was not widely used until the mid-20th century. The *OED*'s illustrative examples contain only the phrase *identical with*. But today, especially in AmE, *to* predominates.

The phrase *same identical*—more often heard than seen—is redundant. E.g.: "From dawn to darkness they [cult members] lived *the same, identical* [read *identical*], controlled lives" (*Seattle Times*).

identify with. This phrase has become a cant phrase, associated especially with slang of the 1960s and 1970s <I can really identify with her>. Here it's inappropriately used in reference to early-19th-century historical figures: "In the end, the difference was that Jefferson *identified with* Virginia while Marshall *identified with* the United States" (*Charleston Gaz.*). Neither Jefferson nor Marshall would have identified with writing like that.

ideology. So spelled. But many writers misunderstand its ETYMOLOGY, believing the word is somehow derived from our modern word *idea*, and thus misspell it *idealogy*. In fact, like several other words beginning with *ideo-* (e.g., *ideograph*), *ideology* passed into English through French (*idéologie*) and has been spelled *ideo-* in English since the 18th century. Although the bungled spelling has become common enough that it's listed in some dictionaries, that isn't a persuasive defense of its use. Cf. **minuscule.**

id est. See **i.e.**

idiosyncrasy. So spelled, though often erroneously rendered *-cracy* (as if the word denoted a form of government)—e.g.: "Their *idiosyncracies* [read *idiosyncrasies*] are patrician" (*N.Y. Times*).

i.e., the abbreviation for *id est* (L. "that is"), introduces explanatory phrases or clauses. Although the abbreviation is appropriate in some scholarly contexts, the phrase *that is* is more comprehensible to the average reader.

Formerly it was said that in speaking or reading, the abbreviation should be rendered *id est*. But this is never heard today, whereas the abbreviated letters *i.e.* are occasionally heard. See **e.g.**

Generally, a comma follows *i.e.* in AmE (though not in BrE). E.g.: "[T]he implicit assumption is that the fountains were designed for some wading—

i.e., 'interactive' participation" (*Wash. Post*)./ "There was absolutely no need for any U.S. network to 'cover' (*i.e.*, 'interpret') the funeral" (*Indianapolis Star*).

if. A. And *whether*. It's good practice to distinguish between these words. Use *if* for a conditional idea, *whether* for an alternative or possibility. Thus, *Let me know if you'll be coming* means that I want to hear from you only if you're coming. But *Let me know whether you'll be coming* means that I want to hear from you about your plans one way or the other.

B. *If, and only if*. This adds nothing but unnecessary emphasis to *only if*. E.g.: "Such a 'homocentrist' position takes the human species to define the boundaries of the moral community: you are morally considerable *if, and only if,* [read *only if*] you are a member of the human species" (*New Republic*). The variation *if, but only if,* which sometimes occurs in legal writing, is unnecessary and even nonsensical for *only if*.

C. For *though, even if,* or *and*. Some writers use *if* in an oddly precious way—to mean "though," "though perhaps," "even if," or even "and." Though several dictionaries record this use, it's not recommended because it typically carries a tone of affectedness—e.g.: "Their presentation is passionate; their prose hectic, *if* [read *and*] occasionally hectoring; their Darwin ambitious, angry and agitated" (*Sunday Times* [London]).

if and when is a legalistic phrase of questionable validity. H.W. Fowler enumerated a number of suspicions that keen readers are likely to have about users of this phrase: "There is the suspicion that he is a mere parrot, who cannot say part of what he has often heard without saying the rest also; there is the suspicion that he likes verbiage for its own sake; there is the suspicion that he is a timid swordsman who thinks he will be safer with a second sword in his left hand; there is the suspicion that he has merely been too lazy to make up his mind between *if* and *when*" (*MEU1* at 254). In short, don't use the phrase because it can almost invariably be improved on—e.g.: "Dodger Executive Vice President Fred Claire has signed a new three-year contract amid rumors that former manager Tom Lasorda would be interested in assuming Claire's post *if and when* [read *if*] the club is sold to Rupert Murdoch" (*L.A. Times*).

if it be. See SUBJUNCTIVES.

ignoramus. Until 1934 in England, if a grand jury considered the evidence of an alleged crime insufficient, it would endorse the bill *ignoramus*, meaning literally "we do not know" or "we know nothing of this." By the early 17th century, though, the word *ignoramus* had come to mean, by extension, "an ignorant person." In 1615, George Ruggle wrote a play called *Ignoramus*, about a lawyer who knew nothing about the law; this fictional lawyer soon gave his name to all manner of know-nothings, whether lawyers or nonlawyers.

The modern nonlegal meaning appears most frequently—e.g.: "There's no surprise—or challenge—in watching a sycophantic, misogynistic *ignoramus* like Burdette win out over the self-effacing, truth-loving Hutchinson" (*Chicago Trib.*).

The plural is *ignoramuses*. The form *ignorami* is a pseudo-learned blunder, since *ignoramus* is a verb and not one of the Latin nouns ending in *-us*. See PLURALS (B) & HYPERCORRECTION (A).

ignorant; stupid. Fastidious users of language distinguish between these terms. *Stupid* refers to innate ability, whereas *ignorant* refers merely to the state of one's knowledge on a particular subject. Geniuses are *ignorant* of many facts, but that doesn't make them *stupid*. But *stupid* people are *ignorant* of even the most basic facts.

-ILE; -INE. Most words with these endings are best pronounced with the *-i-*

short rather than long. Thus: *agile* /**aj**-əl/, not /**aj**-ɪl/; *genuine* /**jen**-yoo-in/, not /**jen**-yoo-ɪn/. But as with any rule of pronunciation, there are many exceptions, among them *infantile* /**in**-fən-tɪl/, *magazine* /mag-ə-**zeen**/, and *turpentine* /**tər**-pən-tɪn/.

ilk. Originally, this Scottish term meant "the same"; hence *of that ilk* meant "of that same [place, territory, or name]" <McGuffey of that ilk>. By extension during the 19th century—from a misunderstanding of the Scottish use—*ilk* came to mean "type" or "sort" <Joseph McCarthy and his ilk>. Because there is little call outside Scotland for the original sense, the extended use must now be accepted as standard—e.g.: "Rooney embodies the old-guard 'family' owner whose *ilk* is dwindling in the league" (*Atlanta J. & Const.*). Still, one occasionally encounters puzzling uses that seem worthy of disapproval—e.g.: "It is also maddening to know there exists the human *ilk* that would, for whatever twisted motive, drag our young over the line" (*San Diego Union-Trib.*). The sentence would surely be improved by changing *the human ilk that* to *people who*.

ill. The comparative form of this adjective is *worse*, the superlative *worst*. The adverb is *ill*, *illy* being an illiterate form that is acceptable neither in formal writing nor in nondialectal informal writing. *Ill* itself acts as an adverb—e.g.: "There he had knocked a hole in the roof and poured in gasoline, a primitive technique *that illy fit* [read *ill-fitting* or *that ill fitted*] the Waldbaum evidence" (*N.Y. Newsday*). For other adverbs with a superfluous *-ly*, see ADVERBS (D).

illegal; illicit; unlawful. These terms are fundamentally synonymous, although *illicit* carries moral overtones <illicit love affairs> in addition to the basic sense of all three: "not in accordance with or sanctioned by law."

Illegal is not synonymous with *criminal*, though some writers mistakenly assume that it is. Anything against the law—even the civil law—is, technically speaking, "illegal."

For two MALAPROPISMS involving *illicit*, see **illicit.**

illegible; unreadable. *Illegible* = not plain or clear enough to be read (used of bad handwriting or defaced printing). *Unreadable* = too dull or obfuscatory to be read (used of poor writing).

illicit. This adjective, meaning "illegal," appears in two MALAPROPISMS. First, it is sometimes used for *elicit* (= to bring out)—e.g.: "The NFL tempered Cincinnati's first free agent signing Wednesday when it raised the league's salary cap $500,000, making it $2.5 million higher than in 1994 and *illiciting* [read *eliciting*] more fears from Bengals General Manager Mike Brown for the future" (*Cincinnati Enquirer*).

Second, and perhaps more surprisingly, the word is sometimes misused for *solicit*—e.g.: "Pele was banned from the World Cup draw last December after accusing Texiera of *illiciting* [read *soliciting*] bribes for Brazilian television rights" (*Chicago Sun-Times*).

For more on the word, see **illegal.**

Illinois is pronounced /il-ə-**noy**/—not /il-ə-**noyz**/. See PRONUNCIATION (B).

ILLOGIC. A. Generally. The writer on language who would dare drag logic into the discussion must do so warily. For centuries, grammarians labored under the mistaken belief that grammar is nothing but applied logic and therefore tried to rid languages of everything illogical.

But to paraphrase Justice Oliver Wendell Holmes, the life of the language has not been logic: it has been experience. No serious student believes anymore that grammatical distinctions necessarily reflect logical ones. Our language is full of idioms that defy logic, many of them literary and many colloquial. We should not, for example, fret over the synonymy of *fat chance* and *slim chance*. Applying "linguistic logic" to established ways of saying things is a misconceived effort.

We see this misconception today when armchair grammarians insist that *grammatical error* is an Irish bull; that *I don't think so* is wrong in place of *I think not*; that *the reason why* is wrong (no more so, certainly, than *place where* or *time when*); that *a number of people* must take a singular, not a plural, verb (see SYNESIS); or that, in *Don't spend any more time than you can help*, the final words should be *can't help*. When logic is used for such purposes, it is worse than idle: it is harmful.

That does not mean, of course, that logic is of no concern to the writer. For rhetorical purposes, logic is essential. Some readers will seek out holes in the logic; but almost all readers will be distracted if they notice this type of problem. In evaluating our own writing, therefore, we should strictly follow idiom and usage, but otherwise apply logic.

The exercise will tighten your prose. Since idiom does not yet prefer *could care less*, much less require it, write *couldn't care less*. Logically speaking, if you say you *could care less*, then you're admitting that you care to some extent. (See **couldn't care less.**) Logic will help you avoid saying *I was scared literally to death*, because you'll recognize the literal meaning of *literally*—and you're still alive to report how scared you were. Likewise, logic would have you banish thoughtless words such as *preplanned*.

Logic promotes clear thinking. To avoid the ills catalogued below, consider closely how your words and sentences relate to one another.

B. Illogical Comparison. This lapse occurs commonly in locutions like *as large if not larger than*, which, when telescoped, becomes *as large than*; properly, one writes *as large as if not larger than*. (See CANNIBALISM.) Similar problems occur with classes. For example, when members of classes are being compared, a word such as *other* must be used to restrict the class: "Representative democracy is better than any [other] political system in the world."

Another problem of comparison occurs when the writer forgets the point of reference in the comparison: "Like many others in Los Angeles, the quake helped Mr. Becker decide to leave" (*N.Y. Times*). (This is a fine dangling modifier: the quake joined many others in L.A. in persuading Mr. Becker to leave.)/ "But the bone marrow transplant Mr. Getty is to receive is different from the earlier *cases* [read *ones* or *transplants*] because the marrow is being processed so that it consists of only two types of cells" (*N.Y. Times*). (You don't compare a *transplant* to a *case*, which in medicine comprises the whole situation—the patient, the doctors, the injection, and everything else relating to the patient's problem.) For related issues, see **better than any (other)** & **vice versa.**

C. Danglers and Misplaced Modifiers. Every dangler or misplaced modifier, in some degree, perverts logic, sometimes humorously—e.g.: "I saw the Statue of Liberty flying into Newark." To avoid these disruptions of thought, remember that a participle should relate to a noun that is truly capable of performing the participle's action. Another example: "The 1993 law, which was invalidated before it went into effect, required pregnant teenagers or their doctors to notify a parent or guardian at least 48 hours before undergoing abortions" (*Amarillo Daily News*). Who is getting abortions? This sentence literally suggests that doctors are getting abortions, but that they must notify their parents first.

For a fuller discussion of these matters, see DANGLERS & MISCUES (B).

illusion; delusion. These words are used differently despite their similar meanings. An *illusion* exists in one's fancy or imagination. A *delusion* is an idea or thing that deceives or misleads a person (hence a *deluded* person). *Delusions* are dangerously wrong perceptions; *illusions* are also wrong perceptions, but the term is less pejorative. Cf. **hallucination.**

illy. See **ill.**

IM-. See **EN-.**

immanent. See **imminent.**

immigrate; emigrate. *Immigrate* = to migrate into or enter (a country). *Emigrate* = to migrate away from or exit (a country). Perhaps it is indicative of the relative worth of the two forms of government that before the Soviet Union collapsed in the late 20th century, the United States was plagued by illegal *immigration* and the Soviet Union by attempts at illegal *emigration*.

Emigrate is to *immigrate* as *go* is to *come*, or as *take* is to *bring*. And just as those other two pairs are sometimes misused, *emigrate* and *immigrate* sometimes get reversed—e.g.: "The store is owned by Maria Guadalupe Flores, a native of Mexico who *emigrated* [read *immigrated*] into the U.S. at age 17" (*St. Paul Pioneer Press*).

imminent; eminent; immanent. *Imminent* = certain and very near; impending <imminent danger>. *Eminent* = distinguished; of excellent repute <Moore is an eminent cardiac surgeon>. (See **eminently.**) *Immanent* (primarily a theological term) = inherent; pervading the material world <the immanent goodness of the divine will>.

These words are misused in more ways than one might suppose. *Imminent*, of course, ousts *eminent* from its rightful place (perhaps the most common misusage)—e.g.: "While making employees 'raise their hands to go to the bathroom,' may have a 19th century ring to it, such rules may be *imminently* [read *eminently*] sensible on assembly lines" (*Rocky Mountain News*). But *eminent*, likewise, sometimes wrongly displaces *imminent*—e.g.: "[T]here are exemptions from the warrant requirement if . . . an investigator determines there is *eminent* [read *imminent*] danger" (*Fla. Today*). Finally, *immanent* sometimes appears where *imminent* belongs—e.g.: "Had it been an A priority—signifying present or *immanent* [read *imminent*] danger to life—any police car in the city would have been ordered to the scene, he said" (*L.A. Times*).

immoral; unmoral; amoral. These three words have distinct meanings. *Immoral*, the opposite of *moral*, means "evil, depraved." The word is highly judgmental. *Unmoral* means merely "without moral sense, not moral," and is used, for example, of animals and inanimate objects. *Amoral*, perhaps the most commonly misused of these terms, means "not moral, outside the sphere of morality; being neither moral nor immoral." It is loosely applied to people in the sense "not having morals or scruples."

immunity; impunity. An *immunity* is any type of exemption from a liability, service, or duty—or (of course) a bodily resistance to an illness. *Impunity* is exemption from punishment.

I'm not sure that; I'm not sure whether. The first phrase means "I doubt" <I'm not sure that we can make it in time>; the second means "I wonder; I don't know" <I'm not sure whether Shakespeare died in the 16th or the 17th century>. (He died in the 17th—in 1616.) Cf. **doubt (A).**

impact, v.i. & v.t. *Impact* has traditionally been only a noun. In recent years, however, it has undergone a semantic shift that has allowed it to act as a verb. Thus uses such as the following have become widespread (and also widely condemned by stylists):

- "The researchers concluded that this low level of intensity may have *impacted* [read *affected*] the results" (*Tampa Trib.*).
- "Selig told Bush his ties to the Rangers could create an appearance of conflict of interest if he had to make decisions that

impacted [read *affected*] the franchise" (*Pitt. Post-Gaz.*).
- "[B]reast-feeding can be *impacted* [read *affected*] by visitation and custody decisions" (*Ft. Lauderdale Sun-Sentinel*).

These uses of the word would be applauded if *impact* were performing any function not as ably performed by *affect* or *influence*. If *affect* as a verb is not sufficiently straightforward in context, then the careful writer might use *have an impact on*, which, though longer, is probably better than the jarring impact of *impacted*. Reserve *impact* for noun uses and *impacted* for wisdom teeth. See NOUNS AS VERBS & VOGUE WORDS.

Interestingly, *impact* as a verb might have arisen partly in response to widespread diffidence about the spelling of *affect*. See **affect.**

impartable; impartible. These are two different words. *Impartable* = capable of being imparted. *Impartible* = indivisible. In the first, the prefix *im-* is intensive; in the second, it's negative. See -ABLE (A).

impel. See **compel.**

impinge; infringe. *Impinge* is used intransitively only; it is followed by *on* or *upon* <they impinged on the voter's rights>. *Infringe*, by contrast, may be either transitive or intransitive <to infringe someone's rights> <to infringe on someone's rights>.

Though *impinge* and *infringe* are often used as if they were interchangeable, we might keep in mind the following connotations from the literal senses: to *impinge* is to strike or dash *upon* something else; to *infringe* is to break in and thereby damage, violate, or weaken.

impious is pronounced /**im**-pee-əs/, not /im-**pɪ**-əs/.

implicit, meaning "implied" and functioning as a correlative of *explicit*, has come to be misused in the sense "complete, unmitigated" <I have implicit trust in her> <I trust her implicitly>. The *OED* labels this usage both erroneous and obsolete. With its resurgence in recent years, one can still call it erroneous but no longer obsolete—e.g.: "Such *implicit* [read *complete* or simply delete *implicit*] trust heralds a new dawn in married life—until we get the next sex poll, and spouses revert to normal" (*Ariz. Republic*).

implied; express. These adjectives are correlative <there are no express or implied warranties>. *Expressed* is sometimes incorrectly contrasted with *implied*.

impractical; impracticable. Although the words overlap, there is a subtle difference. *Impractical* = not capable of being put to good use <this advice was immediately seen as impractical>. *Impracticable* = not feasible; not capable of being accomplished <their plans for expansion were rendered impracticable once the company moved its headquarters>.

imply. See **infer.**

imprudent; impudent. *Imprudent* = rash; indiscreet. *Impudent* = insolently disrespectful; shamelessly presumptuous.

impugn (= to challenge, call into question) is sometimes misused for *impute* (= to ascribe or attribute)—e.g.: "Overall, Kupetz rejected the notion that a court should simply ignore the actual intention of the parties and *impugn* [read *impute*] constructive intent in every instance" (*J. Commercial Lending*).

impunity. See **immunity.**

impute. See **impugn.**

IN-. See EN- & NEGATIVES (A).

in; into. These prepositions usually aren't interchangeable, and care must be taken in choosing between them: *in* denotes position or location, and *into* denotes movement. Thus, a person who swims *in* the ocean is already there, while a person who swims *into* the ocean is moving from, say, the mouth of a river. There are some exceptions, however, especially with popular idioms <Go jump in a lake>.

in actual fact. See **actual fact.**

in behalf of; on behalf of. See **behalf.**

Inc. Unless otherwise required by syntax, a comma need not follow this abbreviation—e.g.: "Pantheon, Inc. was founded in 1998." Nor does a comma have to precede it, although typically one does. On that point, it's best to follow the individual company's preference. Cf. **Jr.**

incapable; unable. The words are basically synonymous, with perhaps a slight difference in connotation. *Incapable* suggests a permanent lack of ability <an incapable worker>, while *unable* often suggests a temporary lack of ability <I'm unable to accept your offer right now>. But these are hardly absolutes: if you're *unable* to lift 500 pounds, there's no implication that you'll soon be able to.

in case; in cases in which. See **case.**

incentivize; incent, vb. These NEOLOGISMS—dating from the mid-1970s—have become VOGUE WORDS, especially in American business JARGON. E.g.:

- "Together, the programs represent the most aggressive *incentivizing* to date by Honda" (*Atlanta J. & Const.*). (A possible revision: *Together, the programs provide the best incentives that Honda has ever offered.*)
- "And you know, we shouldn't *incent* [read *provide incentives for*] all the wrong behaviors. Right now, what we're doing is *incenting* [read *encouraging*] young girls to leave home, to not marry the person they're . . . having a child with because they won't get the welfare check if they're married" (*Boston Globe*).
- "Today it is management—usually *incentivized by stock options and the like* [read *having stock options and other incentives*]—that seeks to be recognized by institutional shareholders" (*L.A. Bus. J.*).

Incentivize, an -IZE barbarism, is more than twice as common as *incent*, a BACK-FORMATION. There is no good incentive to use either one.

inchoate, pronounced /in-**koh**-it/ in AmE and /**in**-koh-ət/ in BrE, means "just begun, not yet fully developed." The prefix is an intensive *in-*, not a negative or privative *in-*. Thus the BACK-FORMATION *choate* (= complete)—premised, as it is, on the notion that *inchoate* is a negative—makes little sense. But it's now established in law <choate lien>.

incidentally. This SENTENCE ADVERB commonly introduces casual asides and minor digressions—e.g.: "The dictionary says a schmuck is a person who is 'clumsy or stupid; an oaf.' (*Incidentally*, there are four people named Oaf with phone listings.)" (*Houston Chron.*)./ "*Incidentally*, the best-tailored trousers have a cuff, from 1 1/4 to 1 1/2 inches wide" (*Chicago Sun-Times*). H.W. Fowler's observation, though too harsh, still holds a kernel of truth: "those who find it most useful are not the best writers" (*MEU1*).

inclement (= unmerciful, stormy) is increasingly replaced by the MALAPROPISM and NONWORD *inclimate*. Because *inclement weather* is such a common phrase—either a SET PHRASE or a CLICHÉ, depending on whom one asks—many have come to hear the phrase as a redundant comment on the *climate* as well as the *weather*. Hence the erroneous *inclimate weather*—e.g.: "Because of the soggy turf and *inclimate* [read *inclement*] weather Thursday, the Bears practiced at South Park instead of behind their traditional Halas Hall facility" (*Chicago Trib.*). Of course, the preferred pronunciation (/in-**klem**-ənt/)—as opposed to the secondary one (/**in**-klə-mənt/)—would help everyone spell the word correctly. But that preferred pronunciation is becoming more endangered year by year.

incognito (= [1] in disguise; or [2] under an assumed name) is sometimes misused for *incommunicado* (= unable, unwilling, or forbidden to communicate with others)—e.g.: "COCEI members who were held *incognito* [read *incommunicado*] later reported being severely beaten by state police until they signed confessions" (*San Diego Union-Trib.*). Although the traditional pronunciation was /in-**kog**-ni-toh/, the standard today is /in-kog-**nee**-toh/.

incomparable; uncomparable. *Incomparable* = so good or so heightened as to be beyond comparison <her incomparable artistry>. *Uncomparable* = not subject to comparison <apples and oranges are uncomparable>. The words are pronounced /in-**kom**-pər-ə-bəl/ and /ən-**kom**-pər-ə-bəl/.

INCOMPLETE SENTENCES. A. Fragments. Grammarians typically define *fragment* as a part of a sentence punctuated as if it were complete. Usually denoting an error—as opposed to literary license—the term *fragment* (or *frag.*) appears frequently in the marginal jottings of high-school and college English teachers. That is to say, some high-school and college students don't know how to write complete sentences. Thus, elementary grammars warn against constructions such as the following one, in which a main clause and a subordinate clause are each written as a complete sentence:

> We usually go to the fair in the evening. Because everything is more glamorous under the lights.
>
> Ex. fr. Philip Gucker, *Essential English Grammar* 133 (1966).

The fragment might be corrected in any of several ways:

> We usually go to the fair in the evening because everything is more glamorous under the lights.

> We usually go to the fair in the evening; everything is more glamorous under the lights.

> We usually go to the fair in the evening. Everything is more glamorous under the lights.

This type of elementary problem rarely occurs in the writing of those who know enough about writing to be able to construct complete sentences. (The more frequent problem is RUN-ON SENTENCES, which occur when writers punctuate two sentences as if they were one.) Therefore, basic advice on avoiding fragments—"don't write a phrase or dependent clause as if it were a complete sentence"—is of limited utility to most writers. Further, for reasons discussed in (B), that advice might be misleading.

B. Incomplete Sentences in Informal Writing. Grammarians' definitions of the word *sentence* range widely. Here's a sampling:

- "A sentence is a group of words containing a subject and a predicate and expressing a complete thought" (C. Rexford Davis, *Toward Correct English*, 1936).
- "A complete sentence says something about something" (Robert M. Gorrell & Charlton Laird, *Modern English Handbook*, 1956).
- "Sentence [means] a group of words consisting of a finite verb and its subject as well as any complement that may be present and any modifiers that belong to the verb, to the subject, to the complement, or to the entire statement, the whole group of words constituting a grammatically complete statement, i.e., a statement that is clearly not part of a larger structure" (Ralph M. Albaugh, *English: A Dictionary of Grammar and Structure*, 1964).
- "A sentence is a combination of words

so connected as to express a complete thought: Man is mortal. Is man mortal? How mortal man is!" (James G. Fernald, *English Grammar Simplified*, 1979).

Given that the word *complete* appears in each of those definitions, one might surmise—as many writers believe—that it is impossible to write an *incomplete* sentence and still be within the bounds of good usage.

Yet the more sophisticated grammarians have long qualified the notion of "completeness." The great linguist Otto Jespersen defined *sentence* as "a (relatively) complete and independent unit of communication . . . —the completeness and independence being shown by its standing alone or its capability of standing alone, *i.e.* of being uttered by itself" (*Essentials of English Grammar*, 1933). Similarly but more specifically, C.T. Onions defined *sentence* as a group of words—or sometimes a single word—that makes a statement <I'm a tennis enthusiast>, a command <Open the window>, an expression of a wish <Let's go>, a question <How are you?>, or an exclamation <What a deal!> (*Modern English Syntax*, 1971). More recently still, a grammatical dictionary states that a sentence "usually" has a subject and a predicate (Sylvia Chalker & Edmund Weiner, *The Oxford Dictionary of English Grammar*, 1994).

It appears possible, then, to have an "incomplete" sentence—i.e., one in which the subject or the verb is at best implicit. Jespersen called one type "amorphous sentences," noting both that they are "more suitable for the emotional side of human nature" and that it would be impossible to say precisely what is "left out" (*Essentials of English Grammar*). Examples are *Yes!/ Goodbye!/ Thanks!/ Nonsense!/ Of course!/ Why all this fuss?/ Hence his financial difficulties!* (*id.*).

At least ten types of verbless sentences occur in modern prose. As the examples below illustrate, the important quality in each type is that the sentence be short enough that the reader will recognize it as purposely incomplete:

- Transitional: "One other thing. If they're not needed for a month or two, they never complain" (James W. McElhaney, "How I Write," in *Scribes J. Legal Writing*, 1994).
- Afterthought: "It is tempting to set Cardozo and Corbin over against them as the engineers of its destruction. Tempting and by no means untrue" (Grant Gilmore, *The Death of Contract*, 1974).
- Emphatic: "No sooner had the group adjusted to that setback than they suffered another: The hike between rivers turned out to be ten miles, not ten kilometers. Uphill. On an overgrown trail of ice-slick mud" (*American Way*).
- Negating: "All a dying man could utter would be a prejudgement. Which is absurd" (Christopher Ricks, *T.S. Eliot and Prejudice*, 1988)./ "Several past efforts at translating Kelsen have been sad, broken-backed affairs. Not Hartney's" (*TLS*).
- Explanatory: "For the compromise theory the question of justice is a question of balance, and the balance is both impersonal and intuitive. Impersonal because individuals become the instruments of achieving aggregate quantities—of equality as much as of utility. Intuitive because the correct balance must be a matter of inarticulate 'feel' " (Ronald Dworkin, *A Matter of Principle*, 1985).
- Elaborating: "Or he may confess and avoid: for instance, by admitting that the sheriff had a *capias* to arrest the servant but asserting that he had used excessive violence. And so on, until an affirmative is negatived" (J.H. Baker, *An Introduction to English Legal History*, 1990).
- Qualifying or recanting: "The Age of Aquarius has finally dawned in Presidential politics. Sort of" (*N.Y. Times*).
- Imitating the mind's processing of information: "What kind of boy was this? I had to know. I looked up. I looked directly at him. A skinny fellow with glasses. Small-boned and loose-limbed, and not so tall as I'd first thought. Wear-

ing a loose-fitting jacket and baseball cap. Not, in my estimation, 'cute' " (*Roanoke Times & World News*).
- Urgent: "Never mind the discounts and the espresso; patronize your independent bookseller. Soon. And often" (*Forbes*).
- Lively, staccato effect: "Men rather than women, black men if possible. Older people rather than younger. Discerning rather than deferential. Shepherds rather than sheep, football buffs rather than football widows, fans of 'L.A. Law' rather than 'NYPD Blue.' And though there are no longer any blank slates when it comes to O.J. Simpson . . . it's better that they get their news from 'MacNeil/Lehrer' or Newsweek than 'Geraldo!' or The Star. [¶] Among lawyers and jury consultants that is the consensus prescription for Mr. Simpson's ideal juror" (*N.Y. Times*).

Whatever the purpose, though, the incomplete or verbless sentence carries some degree of risk. You risk not being expert enough to carry it off adroitly. You risk your readers' being suspicious about whether you have carried it off. You should therefore be wary: "Most writers . . . use the incomplete sentence sparingly, except in reports of conversation. It is a special device, to be used for special effects. In the hands of anyone but an expert, it is usually unsuccessful because the basic patterns have not been established, and missing ideas cannot be supplied" (Robert M. Gorrell & Charlton Laird, *Modern English Handbook*, 1956).

Generally, incomplete or verbless sentences of the acceptable type are not classified as "fragments," but technically they are precisely that. Thus, it is possible, in good usage, to write fragments. Possible but difficult.

in connection with is always a vague, loose connective, often used in reporting wrongdoing. Occasionally—very occasionally—it is the only connective that will do. Use it as a last resort—e.g.: "The F.B.I. was searching for Mr. Bailey *in connection with* the stabbing of his friend, Demming F. Rocker 3d" (*N.Y. Times*). Here, Bailey might have been wanted for help in solving the crime; no official accusations had been lodged.

But when criminal charges have been officially made, *in connection with* is almost always too fuzzy—e.g.: "Bonds, 26, whose last address was 4 Linden St., Winthrop, is wanted on multiple warrants *in connection with* [read *for*] an April armed robbery at a Dorchester pizza restaurant" (*Boston Herald*).

incredible; incredulous. *Incredible* (= unbelievable) has become a VOGUE WORD to describe something that astounds, especially in a pleasing way—e.g.: "Moore combined this with meditations on the *incredible* [read *rare*? *priceless*?] paintings she found in a warehouse several months after Sargent's death in 1978" (*Chicago Sun-Times*).

Incredulous = unbelieving, skeptical. E.g.: "It took Shoup about 10 minutes to convince George that he wasn't joking. Then he had to convince [George's] wife, who was equally *incredulous*" (*Dayton Daily News*). But *incredulous* is sometimes misused for *incredible* or *unbelievable*—e.g.: "[T]he delays that were tolerated by the Canadian justice system are absolutely *incredulous* [read *incredible*]" (*Montreal Gaz.*).

INDEFINITE PRONOUNS. See PRONOUNS (C).

indexes; indices. For ordinary purposes, *indexes* is the preferable plural—e.g.: "A list of contributors and several *indexes* are included" (*N.Y. Times*). (See PLURALS (B).) *Indices*, though less pretentious than *fora* or *dogmata*, is pretentious nevertheless. Some writers prefer it in technical contexts, as in mathematics and the sciences.

Though not the best plural for *index*, *indices* is permissible in the sense "indicators"—e.g.: "Various *indices*, from satellite photos of crops in the Third World, to emergency room reports of overdoses in America's inner cities, make possible rough estimates of the quantities of drugs being produced and reaching America's streets" (*Chattanooga Times*). Cf. **appendixes.**

indicate shouldn't appear where *say*, *state*, *show*, or *suggest* will suffice—e.g.: "[M]emos between White House staffers *indicated* [read *said* or *suggested*] that McAuliffe had checked to make sure the call had been made" (*S.F. Chron.*).

indices. See **indexes.**

indicia, the plural of the obsolete word *indicium* (= an indication, sign, token), is treated as a singular noun forming the plurals *indicia* and *indicias*, the former being preferred: "The 1980s takeover cases identified several *indicia* of due care in a board's deliberation" (*Corporate Board*).

INDIRECT QUESTIONS. See QUESTIONS, DIRECT AND INDIRECT.

individual was formerly thought to be a newfangled barbarism as a noun substituting for *man*, *woman*, or *person*. Certainly, those more specific terms are generally to be preferred over *individual*, but this word should no longer be stigmatized. Still, *individual* is best confined to contexts in which the writer intends to distinguish the single person from the group or crowd.

indorse. See **endorse.**

induction. See **deduction.**

-INE. See -ILE.

INELEGANT VARIATION. H.W. Fowler devised the name "elegant variation" for the ludicrous practice of never using the same word twice in the same sentence. When Fowler named this vice of language in the 1920s, *elegant* was almost a pejorative word, commonly associated with precious overrefinement. Today, however, the word has positive connotations. E.g.: "The book is exceedingly well edited, and several essays are *elegantly* written."

Lest the reader think that the subject of this article is a virtue rather than a vice in writing, it has been renamed unambiguously: *in*elegant variation. The rule of thumb with regard to undue repetition is that one should not repeat a word in the same sentence if it can be felicitously avoided; this is hardly an absolute proscription, however.

Perhaps the most famous example is *elongated yellow fruit* as the second reference for *banana*. Thus Charles W. Morton named "the elongated-yellow-fruit school of writing," citing these examples:

billiard balls	=	the numbered spheroids
Bluebeard	=	the azure-whiskered wife-slayer
Easter-egg hunt	=	hen-fruit safari
milk	=	lacteal fluid
oysters	=	succulent bivalves
peanut	=	the succulent goober
truck	=	rubber-tired mastodon of the highway

("The Elongated Yellow Fruit," in *A Slight Sense of Outrage*, 1955). As Morton explains, this sin "lies somewhere between the cliché and the 'fine writing' so dreaded by teachers of English Composition. . . . It does bespeak an author who wishes to seem witty, knowledgeable, and versatile . . . . It can also bespeak an author who is merely pompous" (*id.*).

There is even a book full of these things, in which a minister is "an old pulpit pounder," a prizefighter is "a braggart of the squared circle," and a vegetarian is "a confirmed spinach-addict" (see J.I. Rodale, *The Sophisticated Synonym Book*, 1938).

The basic type of variation found objectionable by Fowler is the simple change from the straightforward term to some slightly more fanciful or formal synonym, as here:

- "This is Allen's first *directing* bid since 1989's 'Crimes and Misdemeanors'—he won the *helming trophy* [read *directing trophy* or *trophy for directing*] for 1977's 'Annie Hall'—and his 11th writing nomination" (*Daily Variety*).

- "Pakistan's top court has ruled that male doctors may no longer perform *autopsies* on female corpses, saying *postmortems* [read *autopsies*] by the opposite sex show disrespect for the dead" (*Fresno Bee*).
- "[The price controls] imposed by this budget will cause more distortions, more animosity among patients, hospitals and *doctors* and more thoughts among *physicians* [read *doctors*] of quitting and joining labor unions" (*Asian Wall St. J.*).

Equally common in modern prose is the switch from one form of a word to another—e.g.:

- "But it's not just those with a *sanguinary* view. Those with a *sanguine*—make that *super-sanguine*—view are eyeing California, too" (*San Diego Union-Trib.*).
- "During the hoopla about Vice President Dan Quayle's remark about Murphy Brown, his critics reminded him that she is a *fictional* character. Well, Murphy might be *fictitious*, but so am I, according to the same critics" (*St. Louis Post-Dispatch*). See **fictitious.**
- "Now just 27, he's a thoughtful and gifted writer, but he's in something of a *collegiate* rut. Or maybe the patience of those of us not in a *collegial* rut has just worn thin" (*Variety*).
- "For delayed coking, this means having to cope with greater quantities of vacuum *residuum* with a higher carbon *residue*" (*Hydrocarbon Processing*).

Certain pairs may lend themselves to this snare: *arbiter* and *arbitrator*, *adjudicative* and *adjudicatory*, *investigative* and *investigatory*, *exigency* and *exigence*. In fact, it sometimes seems that amateurish writers believe that NEEDLESS VARIANTS were made for this specific stylistic purpose.

Sometimes the variation leads to real confusion. For example, in the following headline, the reader must wonder at first whether *victim* and *loved one* refer to the same person: "Victim's Family Can Witness Death of Loved One's Killer" (*Austin American-Statesman*). The solution there would be to delete *Victim's*.

"[T]he point to be observed," wrote H.W. Fowler, "is that, even if the words meant exactly the same, it would be better to keep the first selected on duty than to change guard" (*MEU1* at 132).

in excess of is verbose for *more than*, *exceeding*, or some other word—e.g.: "Within hours a storm with maximum wind velocities *in excess of* [read *exceeding*] a hundred miles an hour swept across southern England and Wales" (*Atlantic Monthly*).

infectious. See **contagious.**

infer, properly used, means "to deduce; to reason from premises to a conclusion"—e.g.: "We get no sense of the man himself from this book except what we can *infer* from the biographical facts that Mr. Magida presents" (*N.Y. Times*).

But writers frequently misuse it when *imply* (= to hint at; suggest) would be the correct word—e.g.: "So they obliged him, publishing his life story in its March 24th issue, without *inferring* [read *implying*] that he was going to die" (*N.Y. Times*)./ "One [response] was a bright and chatty letter that clearly *inferred* [read *implied*] that Grandma had put her message across" (*Sarasota Herald-Trib.*).

infest (= to inhabit either parasitically or in menacingly large numbers) is sometimes, in a gross MALAPROPISM, confused with *invest*—e.g.: "Cited: Harvest from about 1,470 Boise National Forest acres in Logging Creek and French Creek drainages will thin stands of *insect-invested* [read *insect-infested*] trees" (*USA Today*).

infinitely (= endlessly, limitlessly) for *eminently* (= to a high degree) is either gross OVERSTATEMENT or a MALAPROPISM. It's a surprising error even in our hyperbole-ridden culture—e.g.: "The voice is quite pleasant, really. Low, well-modulated and *infinitely* [read *eminently*] reasonable, it is the voice of a good person" (*San Diego Union-Trib.*).

inflammable. See **flammable.**

inflict; afflict. These terms are occasionally confused. *Afflict* takes *with*; *inflict* takes *on*. Living things, especially humans, are *afflicted with* diseases; inanimate objects, especially scourges or punishments, are *inflicted on* people. But misusing *inflict* for *afflict* is increasingly common—e.g.: "While other urban superintendents were trying to hide the depths of the problems *inflicting* [read *afflicting*] their school systems, Alice Pinderhughes, who passed away last Thursday at age 74, was at least honest" (*Baltimore Sun*). See OBJECT-SHUFFLING.

influence. The first syllable receives the primary accent (/**in**-floo-ənts/), not the second (/in-**floo**-ənts/). That's so whether the part of speech is noun or verb. See PRONUNCIATION (B).

informant; informer. Both terms are used in reference to those who confidentially supply police with information about crimes. *Informant* is twice as common in American legal contexts, *informer* slightly more common in British ones. The Evanses wrote that *informant* is neutral, whereas *informer*, which acquired strong connotations of detestation in the 17th and 18th centuries, remains a connotatively charged term (*DCAU*). Although that statement doesn't hold true for legal writing, it does in most other contexts. See INELEGANT VARIATION.

infringe. See **impinge.**

ingenious; ingenuous. These words, virtual antonyms, are frequently confused. *Ingenious* means "clever, skillful, inventive." *Ingenuous* means "artless, simple, innocent."

ingenuity once corresponded to *ingenuous*, and *ingeniosity* (last used in 1608) to *ingenious*. Through a curious historical reversal of the role of *ingenuity*, it came to mean "ingeniousness." *Ingenuousness* was the only term left to do the work of the noun corresponding to the adjective *ingenuous*. Thus, although *ingenuity* appears to be the correlative of *ingenuous*, it no longer is.

ingenuous. See **ingenious.**

inimical (= hostile, injurious, adverse) is almost a CLICHÉ in place of *adverse* <a position inimical to the best interests of the university>. *Inimicable* for *inimical* is a fairly common error. The *OED* records *inimicable* as a "rare" adjective, but it should be even rarer than it is—e.g.: "World attention is as *inimicable* [read *inimical*] to tyranny as sunlight is to fungus" (*Atlanta J. & Const.*).

INITIALESE. See ABBREVIATIONS (C).

INITIALISMS. See ABBREVIATIONS (A).

initiate—a FORMAL WORD for *begin*, *open*, or *introduce*—is appropriate when referring to taking the first step in an important matter. Although you may *begin* an interview, *begin* a conversation, or *begin* a lecture, you *initiate* a series of high-level negotiations. But it is ludicrous to say that you *initiate* a telephone call.

in lieu of. A. Generally. A borrowing from French, the phrase *in lieu of* (lit., "in place of") is now English, and *instead of* will not always suffice in its stead—e.g.: "The two were arraigned before a town of Montezuma justice and sent to the Cayuga County Jail *in lieu of* $100,000 bond or $50,000 cash bail" (*Syracuse Herald-J.*).

B. For *in view of*. The day after President Clinton announced his health-care plan in the fall of 1993, a radio host, broadcasting from the White House lawn, said to his listeners: "This morning we're going to discuss what state health care means *in lieu of* the President's new federal plan." This mistake—which is spreading—results from a confusion of *in view of* and *in light of*, either of which would have sufficed in that sentence. As it is, *in lieu of* is a MALAPROPISM when used for either of the other phrases.

innocent. See **not guilty** (A).

in order to; in order for; in order that. The phrase *in order to* is often wordy for the simple infinitive—e.g.: "*In order to* [read *To*] control class sizes, the district will also place seven portable classrooms at the four schools" (*Idaho Statesman*). The primary exception occurs when another infinitive is nearby in the sentence—e.g.: "The controversy illustrates how the forces of political correctness pressure government *to grow* in size and arbitrariness *in order to pursue* a peculiar compassion mission" (*Baltimore Sun*).

In order for, which is followed by a clause, is often wordy for *for*—e.g.: "*In order for* [read *For*] the RCE scheme to be reliable, both detectors must get exactly the same amount of illumination" (*Electronic Eng'g Times*).

Finally, *in order that*, which needs no reduction, begins a noun phrase expressing purpose. It is usually followed by *may* or *might*—e.g.: "*In order that* the child reader *may* emulate the generous whale, the first three books in the series . . . all come with a peel-off sticker on the back cover" (*N.Y. Times*)./ "[T]hey are glad that the big guy closed down the shop for three days this week *in order that* the lads *might* grab some holiday cheer" (*Boston Herald*).

input, n. & v.t. This jargonmonger's word—dating from the 18th century as a noun and from the mid-1940s as a verb—is one that careful writers tend to avoid. E.g.: "They want to help devise the budget and have more *input* [read *say*] in whether deans and vice presidents receive tenure" (*Rock Hill Herald*)./ "After last week's loss to the Flyers, though, Campbell has wondered aloud if, even with the great effort *and input* [delete *and input*] of his stars, the Rangers have enough talent to enjoy more than spasmodic success" (*Village Voice*).

The usual past-tense form is *inputted*—e.g.: "Some people had middle initials *inputted* and others didn't, and some names were misspelled" (*New Republic*). As in that example, *input* is fairly common in COMPUTERESE.

inquiry. A. Pronunciation. *Inquiry* may be pronounced either /in-**kwɪr**-ee/ or /**in**-kwə-ree/.

B. And *enquiry*. In AmE, *inquiry* is the standard spelling in all senses. In BrE, *enquiry* is equivalent to *question*, whereas *inquiry* means "an official investigation." See EN-.

C. And *query*. While *query* refers to a single question, *inquiry* may refer also to a series of questions or a sustained investigation. Occasionally writers misuse *query* for *inquiry*—e.g.: " 'You've really got a couple of things that are problematic, notwithstanding the idea that a married woman could be counted as unmarried because she kept her maiden name,' said Richard Steffen, a Speier staffer who launched *a query* [read *an inquiry*] into the state's record-keeping system" (*S.F. Chron.*).

in receipt of. This phrase, to be avoided as OFFICIALESE and COMMERCIALESE, is invariably inferior to *have received* or *has received*. Instead of *We are in receipt of your letter*, say *We have received your letter*.

in regard to. See **regard** (A).

insidious; invidious. A distinction exists between these words. *Insidious* = (of persons and things) lying in wait or seeking to entrap or ensnare; operating subtly or secretly so as not to excite suspicion—e.g.: "Many Indians still fear that economic liberalization will bring with it cultural imperialism of a particularly *insidious* kind—that

'Baywatch' and burgers will supplant Bharatanatyam dances and bhelpuri" (*Wash. Post*).

Invidious = offensive; repulsive. This term often refers to discrimination, as it has for more than two centuries—e.g.: "The example familiar to us is segregation. In 1896, the justices said there was nothing *invidious* about separating black people unless they chose to see it that way. That pretense . . . could hardly be maintained in 1954" (*New Orleans Times-Picayune*).

instantly; instantaneously. *Instantly* = at once, directly and immediately. *Instantaneously* = (of two events that occur) so nearly simultaneously that any difference is imperceptible.

insurance. A. Pronunciation. This word is pronounced with the primary accent on the second syllable: /in-**shuur**-ənts/—not /**in**-shər-ənts/. See PRONUNCIATION (B).

B. Two Species. Insurance is of two kinds. One is insurance against accidents: buildings burning, ships sinking, cars colliding, being injured, and the like. The other—in BrE frequently called *assurance*—is provision for designated persons on the occurrence of death (*life insurance* [AmE] or *life assurance* [BrE]).

insure. See **assure.**

intelligent; intellectual, adj. One who is *intelligent* has an innate ability to learn quickly and to solve problems easily <an intelligent young child>. One who is *intellectual* enjoys using his or her intelligence for scholarly or philosophical pursuits <a quiet, intellectual woman who spends most of her time in bookstores>.

intense; intensive. The conventional advice is to shun *intensive* wherever *intense* will fit the context. That advice is sound. *Intensive* is really a philosophical and scientific term best left to philosophers and scientists. Other writers can work well enough with *intense*—e.g.: "Anti-tobacco lawyers complain that the *intensive* [read *intense*] scrutiny serves another purpose too—intimidating some clients into giving up their claims to keep embarrassing personal information from becoming public" (*Houston Chron.*). But *intensive* is now customary in PHRASAL ADJECTIVES such as *capital-intensive*, *labor-intensive*, *time-intensive*, and the like.

intensive purposes, for all. For this error, see **for all intents and purposes.**

INTER-; INTRA-. These prefixes have quite different meanings. *Inter-* means "between, among." *Intra-* means "within, in." Thus *interstate* means "between states" and *intrastate* means "within a state." American bureaucrats and businesspeople have recently created any number of NEOLOGISMS with these prefixes, primarily with *inter-*: *interagency*, *interbranch*, *intercorporate*, *intermunicipal*, and the like.

interface, v.i., is jargonmongers' talk. E.g.: "This man possesses the ability to *interface* and relate with people from all social and economic levels." *Interface* should be left to COMPUTERESE.

in terms of is often indefensibly verbose. Whenever you can replace it with a simple preposition, do so—e.g.: "Each of the paintings 'rates' a different area of Wisconsin, *in terms of* [read *for*] the quality of its towns" (*Milwaukee J. Sentinel*).

But in the sense "expressed by means of," the phrase is quite defensible—e.g.: "At the same time, he describes Sibelius's symphonies *in terms of* visual, personal drama, evoking not only smashings and submersions, but also dreamlike journeys through forests and snow" (*N.Y. Times*).

interpretative; interpretive. Generally, one forms the adjective on the model of the noun form of a word. Hence *prevention* yields *preventive*, not *preventative*; *determination* yields *determinative*, not *determinive*; *administration* yields *administrative*, not *administerive*. And with *interpretation*, the traditionally correct adjective is *interpretative* (= having the character or function of interpreting; explanatory). E.g.: "[C]rews continue to work on restrooms, a parking lot and *interpretative* displays near the McMillin Bridge off Washington 162, he said" (*Tacoma News Trib.*).

But *interpretive* has gained ground in the last 50 years—so much so that it's about five times more common than *interpretative*. E.g.: "Morrison, also a founding member of Bolsa Chica Conservancy, said her first goal will be to train more volunteer hosts for the conservancy's *interpretive* center" (*L.A. Times*). Fight the good fight, if you like, and stick to *interpretative*. But *interpretive* seems sure to drive it out in coming years.

in the circumstances. See **circumstances (A).**

in the course of is often wordy for *during* or *while*—e.g.: "Billingsley got to know the widow Doss pretty well *in the course of* [read *during*] the investigation" (*Jupiter Courier* [Fla.]).

in the final analysis; in the last analysis. Both CLICHÉS are likely to detract from your prose. You might better simply state the proposition without this tepid lead-in.

intimately. For a misuse of *intricately* for this word, see **intricately.**

into. See **in.**

INTRA-. See INTER-.

intramural = conducted within the limits of an organization or body, esp. of an educational institution. The term is misused when the sense extends beyond one college or university—that is, it is impossible to have a competition remain intramural if there are competitors from elsewhere: "They are also trying to determine if there has been any recent contact between Harvard and Dartmouth, like *intramural* sports" (*N.Y. Times*). (The sentence might be improved by writing, after the comma, *such as sporting events between intramural champions*).

intricately (= complexly; in a complicated way) is sometimes misused for *intimately* (= in a close, personal way)—e.g.: "Carolyn J. Schutz, 61, the secretary of Elmhurst's Epiphany Evangelical Lutheran Church who was *intricately* [read *intimately*] involved in relief work for the area's poor, died Sunday in Elmhurst Memorial Hospital" (*Chicago Trib.*).

INVERSION. Awkward are most, though not all, grammatical inversions. They seem to be on the rise in journalism—e.g.: "*Said* the silver-haired Rotblat, a professor emeritus of physics at the University of London: 'I hope the recognition will help other scientists to recognize their social responsibility' " (*L.A. Times*).

The inversions especially to be avoided are those whose existence is attributable to amateurish literary striving. The problem with these is that, "like the atmospheric inversion that is blamed for smog, the inversion of sentences creates a kind of linguistic smog that puts the reader to work sorting out the disarranged elements, causes his eyes to smart, and perhaps makes him wish he were reading something else. . . . Straining for variety in sentence structure is usually the cause. Tired of starting with the subject and adding the predicate, some writers make a mighty effort and jump out of the frying pan into the smog" (Roy H. Copperud, *American Usage and Style*, 1980).

The following sentence is typical: "*Unaffected would be* the marriage benefit of the current law, which gives a married couple a lower effective tax rate than an unmarried couple if one spouse has much less income than the other" (*L.A. Times*). (A possible revision: *The marriage benefit of the current law would be unaffected. It gives a married couple . . . .*)

Often those who invert are no better at grammar than they are at style. Thus they have problems with singulars and plurals, being unable to distinguish the inverted predicate from the subject—e.g.: "Our oldest son is now driving, and with privilege *comes* [read *come*] new challenges and more gray hair for me" (*Orlando Sentinel*)./ "With increased life expectancy *comes* [read *come*] increased expectations" (*Las Vegas Rev.-J.*).

invest. For the blunder of using *invest* for *infest*, see **infest.**

invidious. See **insidious.**

in view of. See **in lieu of (B).**

in virtue of. See **virtue of.**

invite. Use it in the traditional way—as a verb. Avoid it as a noun displacing *invitation*—e.g.: "Reno's office reports that while she got several *invites* [read *invitations*], Mark Johnson of Media General News Service asked first" (*Am. Journalism Rev.*)./ "In the meantime, he isn't counting on many *invites* [read *invitations*] to cocktail parties" (*Fortune*).

invoke. See **evoke.**

irregardless, a semiliterate PORTMANTEAU WORD from *irrespective* and *regardless*, should have been stamped out long ago. But it's common enough in speech that it has found its way into all manner of print sources—e.g.: "*Irregardless* [read *Regardless*] of the Big Ten outcome, Knight said he is gratified with IU's improvement over last season" (*Louisville Courier-J.*). Although this widely scorned NONWORD seems unlikely to spread much more than it already has, careful users of language must continually swat it when they encounter it.

IRREGULAR VERBS. A. The Forms. There are two types of verbs—regular (or "weak") and irregular (or "strong"). Irregular verbs form the past tense or past participle in unpredictable ways, usually by changing the vowel of the present-tense form, without the addition of an ending (e.g., *begin*, *began*; *rise*, *rose*; *wring*, *wrung*). Regular verbs, by contrast, form the past tense by adding *-ed*, *-d*, or *-t* to the present tense.

Irregular verbs are sometimes called "strong" verbs because they seem to form the past tense from their own resources, without calling an ending to their assistance. The regular verbs are sometimes called "weak" verbs because they cannot form the past tense without the aid of the ending (most often *-ed*).

All told, English now has fewer than 200 strong (or irregular) verbs. The trend is against the irregular forms: "For many centuries there has been a steady loss in favor of the weak class" (George O. Curme, *English Grammar*, 1947). Here are some of the most common irregular forms:

Present Tense	*Past Tense*	*Past Participle*
arise	arose	arisen
be	was	been
bear	bore	borne
beat	beat	beaten
become	became	become
beget	begot	begotten
begin	began	begun
behold	beheld	beheld
bend	bent	bent
beseech	besought	besought
bet	bet	bet
bid	bade	bidden
bind	bound	bound
bite	bit	bitten
bleed	bled	bled
blow	blew	blown
break	broke	broken
breed	bred	bred
bring	brought	brought
build	built	built
burst	burst	burst
buy	bought	bought
cast	cast	cast
catch	caught	caught

Present Tense	*Past Tense*	*Past Participle*
cleave (= to split)	cleft	cleft
cling	clung	clung
come	came	come
cost	cost	cost
creep	crept	crept
cut	cut	cut
dig	dug	dug
do	did	done
draw	drew	drawn
drink	drank	drunk
drive	drove	driven
eat	ate	eaten
fall	fell	fallen
feed	fed	fed
feel	felt	felt
fight	fought	fought
find	found	found
flee	fled	fled
fling	flung	flung
fly	flew	flown
forbear	forbore	forborne
forbid	forbade	forbidden
forecast	forecast	forecast
forget	forgot	forgotten
forgive	forgave	forgiven
freeze	froze	frozen
get	got	gotten
give	gave	given
go	went	gone
grind	ground	ground
grow	grew	grown
hang (a picture)	hung	hung
hide	hid	hidden
hit	hit	hit
hold	held	held
hurt	hurt	hurt
keep	kept	kept
kneel	knelt	knelt
knit	knit	knit
know	knew	known
lay (= to place)	laid	laid
lead	led	led
leave	left	left
lend	lent	lent
let	let	let
lie (= to rest)	lay	lain
light	lit	lit
lose	lost	lost
make	made	made
meet	met	met
mistake	mistook	mistaken
pay	paid	paid
put	put	put

Present Tense	*Past Tense*	*Past Participle*
quit	quit	quit
read	read	read
rend	rent	rent
rid	rid	rid
ride	rode	ridden
ring	rang	rung
rise	rose	risen
run	ran	run
say	said	said
see	saw	seen
seek	sought	sought
sell	sold	sold
send	sent	sent
set	set	set
sew	sewed	sewn
shake	shook	shaken
shed	shed	shed
shine	shone	shone
shoot	shot	shot
show	showed	shown
shrink	shrank	shrunk
sing	sang	sung
sink	sank	sunk
sit	sat	sat
slay	slew	slain
sleep	slept	slept
slide	slid	slid
sling	slung	slung
slink	slunk	slunk
slit	slit	slit
sow	sowed	sown
speak	spoke	spoken
speed	sped	sped
spend	spent	spent
spit	spat	spat
split	split	split
spread	spread	spread
spring	sprang	sprung
stand	stood	stood
steal	stole	stolen
stick	stuck	stuck
sting	stung	stung
stink	stank	stunk
strew	strewed	strewn
stride	strode	stridden
strike	struck	struck
string	strung	strung
strive	strove	striven
swear	swore	sworn
sweat	sweat	sweat
sweep	swept	swept
swim	swam	swum
swing	swung	swung
take	took	taken

Present Tense	Past Tense	Past Participle
teach	taught	taught
tear	tore	torn
tell	told	told
think	thought	thought
throw	threw	thrown
thrust	thrust	thrust
tread	trod	trodden
wear	wore	worn
weave	wove	woven
weep	wept	wept
win	won	won
wind	wound	wound
wring	wrung	wrung
write	wrote	written

B. Past-Participial Adjectives No Longer Used as Verb Forms. Many past participles no longer exist as verbs in good usage, but continue as adjectives. For examples discussed in entries throughout this book, see **cleave** (*cloven*), **laden, proved** (*proven*), **saw** (*sawn*), **shave** (*shaven*), **stricken** & **swell** (*swollen*).

C. AmE vs. BrE. Sometimes, the choice between two past-tense or (more commonly) past-participial forms depends on which major strain of English one is working in. AmE prefers *gotten*, BrE *got*. Two similar pairs are *hewed* (AmE) and *hewn* (BrE), *waked* (AmE) and *woken* (BrE).

D. Dialectal Forms. One characteristic of dialect is the use of past participles in place of past-tense verbs—e.g., *it begun a moment ago*, *he swum*, *the shirt shrunk*, *the grass sprung up*, *she sung loudly*, etc. For examples discussed in various entries, see **drink** (*I drunk it all*), **sink** (*he sunk*) & **swim** (*she swum*).

Another dialectal trait is the use of past-tense verbs for past participles—e.g., *she had began piano lessons*, *he's been bit by a snake*, etc. See **begin (B)** (*had began*), **bite** (*had bit*), **drink** (*had drank*) & **shake** (*was shook*).

Still another characteristic of dialect is the use of regular past forms for irregular verbs—e.g., *the shirt shrinked*, *the bee stinged me*, *he sweared he'd never let it happen*, *he swinged at the ball*, etc. For examples discussed in various entries, see **bet** (*betted*), **cast** (*casted*), **knit** (*knitted*), **shrink** (*shrinked*) & **strew** (*strewed*).

Finally, dialects have many irregular past forms differing from those of standard English. See **bring (A)** (*brung*), **buy (A)** (*boughten*), **climb (A)** (*clomb* and *clumb*), **drag** (*drug*), **drown (A)** (*drownded*), **overflow** (*overflown*), **ride** (*rid*), **sling** (*slang*), **snuck** & **swell** (*swoll*, *swole*). Occasionally, some of these become standard; for example, see **fit.**

For the related issue of phrases like *might should have*, see DOUBLE MODALS.

E. Choice Between *-ed* and *-'d*. See -ED.

irrelevant is sometimes, through METATHESIS, made *irrevelant*. And this spurious form appears in otherwise literate publications—e.g.: "Indeed, his experience in the city just goes to show that while some may consider the Paris fashion scene *irrevelant* [read *irrelevant*], the city can still build careers" (*Boston Globe*).

irrevocable; unrevokable. The first—the preferred form—is pronounced /i-**rev**-ə-kə-bəl/, not /ir-ə-**voh**-kə-bəl/. (See PRONUNCIATION (B).) *Unrevokable* is a NEEDLESS VARIANT.

On *irrevocable* as an uncomparable adjective, see ADJECTIVES (B).

irritate. See **aggravate.**

-ISE. See -IZE.

issue of whether; issue whether. See **whether (C).**

it. This EXPLETIVE and pronoun often appears too many times in one sentence. Careful writers restrict it (*it*, that is) to one meaning in a given sentence—no more. The most common sloppiness is to use the expletive *it* and the personal pronoun *it* in the same sentence—e.g.: "For anyone who really watches the program, *it* is obvious that *it* is not a 'political attack' on Catholicism" (*Salt Lake Trib.*). (A possible revision: *Anyone who watches the program will see that it is not a "political attack" on Catholicism.*)

Also, avoid the double expletive—two filler words in a single phrase. One filler *it* will do—e.g.: "*It* is evident that *it* will become necessary to hike taxes from year to year as federal and state dollars dwindle" (*Miami Times*). (A possible revision: *The city will surely have to hike taxes each year as federal and state dollars dwindle.*)/ "Now, coach Dave Wannstedt says, *it* is apparent that *it* will take more time for Hughes to acclimate himself to the backfield" (*Chicago Trib.*). (A possible revision: *Now, coach Dave Wannstedt says, Hughes will need more time to acclimate himself to the backfield.*)

When used after a passive-voice verb, *it* often gives the misimpression that it's a pronoun with an antecedent. E.g.: "The burial was to take place at Highgate, and *it* was intended to take the body by train from Winooski to Cambridge Junction over the defendant's road and thence over the connecting road to Highgate." (The full passive is *it was intended (by someone) to take the body*; yet, on first reading, *it* appears to refer to *burial.*)/ "Despite her prediction that the economic recovery will be slow, *it* is expected that the company will flourish during the next few quarters." (*It* seems at first to refer to *economic recovery* when in fact it is merely an expletive.) See MISCUES.

In short, delete *it* when you can; and if you need it, keep it to one meaning within a sentence.

ITALICS. A. Generally. H.W. Fowler cautioned that many people, though competent in their own special subjects, don't have enough writing experience to realize that they shouldn't try to achieve emphasis by italicizing every tenth sentence (*MEU1*). With experience comes the competence to frame sentences so that emphatic words fall in emphatic places. (See SENTENCE ENDS.) Also, the writer learns the techniques of subtle repetition—the type that reinforces an idea without cloying.

Ralph Waldo Emerson overstated the case: " 'Tis a good rule of rhetoric [that] Schlegel gives—'In good prose, every word is underscored,' which, I suppose, means, Never italicize" ("Lectures and Biographical Sketches," in 10 *Complete Works of Emerson*, 1904). By the same reasoning, of course, one might say we should abolish question marks, exclamation points, and even commas. The point is to italicize only when one *must*.

B. Foreign Phrases. If an imported term hasn't been fully naturalized, it should appear in italics—e.g.: *au mieux* (Fr. "on the best terms"); *cogito, ergo sum* (L. "I think, therefore I am"); *dolce far niente* (Ital. "sweet idleness"); *Weltschmerz* (Ger. "depression or pessimism caused by comparing the world's actual circumstances with ideal ones"). But because English is such a diverse language—having drawn from the resources of dozens of other languages—it is quite hospitable to foreign-looking words. That is, they become easily naturalized. And when that happens, the terms are written in ordinary roman type. The words are italicized here only because they're being referred to as words—e.g.: *caveat emptor* (L.), *décolletage* (Fr.), *gestalt* (Ger.), *glasnost* (Russ.). A good dictionary usually provides guidance on which words should be italicized.

For more on foreignisms, see GALLICISMS & LATINISMS.

itemization is often unnecessary for *list*.

it is I; it is me. Generally, of course, the nominative pronoun (here *I*) is the complement of a linking verb <this is she> <it was he>. But *it is me* and *it's me* are fully acceptable, especially in informal contexts: "both forms, 'It is I' and 'It is me,' are correct—one by virtue of grammatical rule, the other by virtue of common educated usage" (Norman Lewis, *Better English*, 1961). And, of course, those with even a smattering of French know that *It's me* answers nicely to *C'est moi*. Good writers have long found the English equivalent serviceable—e.g.:

- "It is not *me* you are in love with" (Richard Steele, *The Spectator*, 1712).
- "But Silver . . . called out to know if that were *me*" (Robert Louis Stevenson, *Treasure Island*, 1883).
- "[N]ot more than four people know that *it is me*" (Raymond Paton, *Autobiography of a Blackguard*, 1924).
- "It's only *me*" (Ian Anderson, "Aqualung" [song lyric], 1971).

E.B. White told an amusing story about the fear that so many writers have of making a mistake: "One time a newspaper sent us to a morgue to get a story on a woman whose body was being held for identification. A man believed to be her husband was brought in. Somebody pulled the sheet back; the man took one agonizing look, and cried, 'My God, it's her!' When we reported this grim incident, the editor diligently changed it to 'My God, it's she!' " (E.B. White, "English Usage," in *The Second Tree from the Corner*, 1954).

Similar problems arise in the third person, as in *it is him*. When the contraction appears, *Newsweek* makes the phrase *it's him*—e.g.: "Rostenkowski simply signed an expense-account voucher for stamps that Smith converted into cash. The first time he says he witnessed the alleged scheme, in 1989, 'I was no doubt taken aback when I saw his [Rostenkowski's] name on the [$2,000] voucher. I couldn't believe it was him.' [¶] Most Democrats on Capitol Hill still can't believe *it's him*" (*Newsweek*). See PRONOUNS (B).

its; it's. The possessive form of *it* is *its*; the contraction for *it is* is *it's*. But the two words are often confounded—e.g.: "For all *it's* [read *its*] faults, . . . this is a pretty interesting film" (*Cincinnati Post*)./"The best moment . . . brings out some energy and droll humor, but *its* [read *it's*] not enough to keep this unfocused piece from meandering off to nowhere" (*Minneapolis Star Trib.*). (See SPELLING (A).) Also, the possessive *its* should never be used—as it sometimes is—as a personal pronoun in place of *his*, *her*, or *his or her*.

it's me. See **it is I.**

I wonder. See QUESTIONS, DIRECT AND INDIRECT.

-IZE; -ISE. Adding the suffix *-ize* (or *-ise* in BrE) to an adjective or noun is one of the most frequently used ways of forming new verbs. Many verbs so formed are unobjectionable—e.g.: *appetize*, *authorize*, *baptize*, *capsize*, *familiarize*, *recognize*, *sterilize*, and *symbolize*. The religious leader Norman Vincent Peale popularized (ahem) the suffix in the mid-20th century: " '*Picturize*, *prayerize*, and *actualize*' was Peale's key formula" (*Christianity Today*).

But NEOLOGISMS ending in *-ize* are generally to be discouraged, for they are invariably ungainly and often superfluous. Thus we have no use for *accessorize*, *artificialize*, *audiblize*, *cubiclize*, *fenderize* (= to fix a dented fender), *funeralize*, *ghettoize*, *Mirandize*, *nakedize*, and so on. Careful writers are wary of new words formed with this suffix.

J

jail; gaol. The first is the AmE spelling; the second, the BrE variant. Both words, of course, are pronounced /jayl/.

jam (= [1] a fruit jelly; or [2] a congested or otherwise difficult situation) is sometimes misused for *jamb* (= the vertical sidepost of a doorway, window frame, or other framed opening)—e.g.: "The wide woodwork around the *door jams* [read *doorjambs*] highlights the Victorian wallpaper" (*Pitt. Post-Gaz.*).

jarful. Pl. *jarfuls*, not *jarsful*. See PLURALS (F).

JARGON refers to the special, usually technical idiom of any social, occupational, or professional group. It arises from the urge to save time and space—and occasionally to conceal meaning from the uninitiated. The subject has magnified importance today because we live "[i]n an age when vague rhetoric and incomprehensible jargon predominate" (*Times* [London]).

Jargon covers a broad span of vocabulary. For the commonplace medical phrase *heart bypass surgery*, a range of jargon is available. There's the technically precise (and more verbose) *coronary artery bypass graft*. From that phrase comes the acronym *CABG*, referred to in medical slang as *cabbage* <we're going to have to give him a cabbage>. Some heart surgeons, who would have nothing to do with such slang, prefer the pompously arcane *myocardial revascularization*. But whatever the name, it's all bypass surgery.

Doctors also have several ways of saying that a patient is on a respirator (or ventilator). Some, of course, say that a patient is *on the respirator* or *on the ventilator*. Others, being fond of slang, say that the patient is *on the blower*. But then there are the stuffed-shirt doctors who say precisely the same thing in the most pretentious possible way: the patient is *being given positive-pressure ventilatory support*.

Similar levels of jargon exist in other fields. Consider AIRLINESE. In the late 1990s, a captain announced, in midflight: "We're about to *traverse an area of instability*, so I've *illuminated* the fasten-seatbelts sign." When a flight attendant was asked how she would say the same thing, she said: "We're going to *encounter some light chop*, so I've *turned on* the fasten-seatbelts sign." Another said, "We're about to *go through some choppy air*, so please fasten your seatbelts." Those quotations progress from the most to the least jargonistic—or, to put it judgmentally from the passenger's perspective, from the least to the most admirable.

True, jargon is sometimes useful shorthand for presenting ideas that would ordinarily need explaining in other, more roundabout ways for those outside the specialty. Jargon thus has a strong in-group property, which is acceptable when one specialist talks with another.

But jargon is unacceptable when its purpose is to demonstrate how much more the speaker or writer knows as a specialist than ordinary listeners or readers do. The intended audience, then, is the primary consideration in deciding which words will be intelligible.

In his book *On the Art of Writing* (2d ed. 1943), Sir Arthur Quiller-Couch set out the two primary vices of jargon: "The first is that it uses circumlocution rather than short straight speech. It says: '*In the case of* John Jenkins deceased, the coffin' when it means 'John Jenkins's coffin'; and its yea is not yea, neither is its nay nay; but its answer is *in the affirmative* or *in the negative*, as the foolish and superfluous *case* may be. The second vice is that it habitually chooses vague wooly abstract nouns rather than concrete ones" (*id.* at 105). "To write jargon is to be perpetually shuffling around in a fog and cotton-wool of abstract terms" (*id.* at 117). See ABSTRACTITIS, DOUBLESPEAK & ABBREVIATIONS (C).

jealousy; envy. The careful writer distinguishes between these terms. *Jealousy* is properly restricted to contexts involving affairs of the heart; *envy* is used more broadly of resentful contemplation of a more fortunate person.

jemmy. See **jimmy.**

jewelry; jewellery. The first is the AmE spelling; the second is BrE.

jibe. See **gibe.**

jimmy; jemmy. A burglar's crowbar is spelled *jimmy* in AmE, *jemmy* in BrE.

jinni. See **genie.**

jiujutsu. See **jujitsu.**

jive. See **gibe.**

jobsite. One word.

joint cooperation is a REDUNDANCY.

join together is a REDUNDANCY that should be allowed to survive only in the marriage service, and there only because it is a bona fide remnant of Elizabethan English.

Jones's. See POSSESSIVES (A).

Joneses. See PLURALS (E).

joust. The traditional view is that this word should be pronounced either /jəst/ or /joost/. But almost all Americans say /jowst/; this pronunciation must be considered not just acceptable, but—because of its overwhelming prevalence, coupled with no good reason for opposing it—preferable. Let the orthoepic jousting cease.

Jr. is increasingly used restrictively, with no comma before it: "Louis V. Gerstner Jr., the new chairman of I.B.M., began his campaign yesterday to revive the world's largest computer maker by announcing an $8.9 billion program to cut the company's costs sharply" (*N.Y. Times*). Journalistic stylebooks—such as the AP's and the UPI's—prefer this approach, probably because newspapers generally disfavor optional commas.

And comma-less *Jr.* has logic on its side. But in the mid-1990s, when a group of eminent lawyers and judges with names bearing the abbreviation were polled, they unanimously stated a preference for the comma. That's the traditional approach.

Both forms are correct. The comma-less form has logic, and probably the future, on its side. The with-comma form has recent (not ancient) tradition on its side. Posterity will be eager to discover, no doubt, how this earth-shattering dilemma unfolds in the decades ahead. One consideration that militates in favor of the comma-less form is that, in a sentence, one comma begets another: "John Jones, Jr. was elected" seems to be telling Jones that Jr. was elected. With a comma before *Jr.*, another is needed after: "John Jones, Jr., was elected."

judging. For *judging* as an acceptable dangling modifier, see DANGLERS (E).

judgment. This is the preferred form in AmE and in British legal texts, even as far back as the 19th century. *Judgement* is prevalent in British nonlegal texts.

judicial; judicious. *Judicial* = (1) of, relating to, or by the court <judicial officers>; (2) in court <judicial admissions>; (3) legal <the Attorney General took no judicial action>; or (4) of or relating to a judgment <judicial in-

terest at the rate of four percent annually>. Sense 4, which is confined to legal contexts, is suspect because it hasn't yet gained admission to most dictionaries.

Judicious is a much simpler word, meaning "well considered, discreet, wisely circumspect." E.g.: "[T]he duo put on a lively show that was highlighted by the *judicious* use of video and an inflatable cow skull" (*Houston Post*).

jujitsu; jujutsu; jiujutsu. Although the Japanese term is *ju-jutsu*, the phonetic spelling *jujitsu* has become the established form in both AmE and BrE. The others are variant forms in English.

juncture. The phrase *at this juncture* should be used in reference to a crisis or a critically important time—e.g.: "*At this* critical *juncture* in history, the people of China need and deserve our support and friendship" (*Chicago Trib.*). Such phrases as *critical juncture* and *pivotal juncture* are not truly redundant, since *juncture* alone typically wouldn't suffice in place of those phrases.

But the phrase *at this juncture* isn't equivalent merely to "at this time" or "now." When used with these meanings, it's a pomposity—e.g.: "While the city has not initiated the program with much grace or deftness, that is no reason to make things even messier at this late *juncture* [read *date*]" (*Austin American-Statesman*).

Junior. On whether to include a comma with the abbreviation *Jr.*, see **Jr.**

junkie (= a drug addict) is the standard spelling. *Junky* is a variant form.

junta; junto. Of Spanish origin, *junta* (= a political or military group in power, esp. after a coup d'état) is pronounced either /**hoon**-tə/ or /**jən**-tə/. It is much more common in AmE than its altered form, *junto* /**jən**-toh/, which has undergone slight DIFFERENTIATION to mean "a self-appointed committee having political aims."

jurist. In BrE, this word is reserved for those having made outstanding contributions to legal thought and legal literature. In AmE, it is loosely applied to every judge of whatever level, and sometimes even to nonscholarly practitioners who are well respected.

jury. In AmE, this is a COLLECTIVE NOUN, and it therefore takes a singular verb <the jury has spoken>. To emphasize the individual members of the jury, we have the word *jurors* <the jurors have spoken>. In BrE, however, it is common to see a plural verb with *jury* <the jury have spoken>.

just, like *only*, must be carefully placed—e.g.: " 'America needs a decade of renewal and reform,' he [Richard D. Lamm, a presidential candidate] said. 'It *just doesn't* [read *doesn't just*] need a new President—it needs a whole decade of reform and renewal' " (*N.Y. Times*). See **only.**

just deserts (= the treatment one truly deserves) is occasionally misrendered *just desserts*. Sometimes, of course, it's a playful pun, as when a bakery is called *Just Desserts*. But sometimes it's sloppiness or pure ignorance—e.g.: "The deliciously wicked Francis Urquhart gets his *just desserts* [read *just deserts*] in this third installment of the story [the film *The Final Cut*]" (*Memphis Commercial Appeal*). In that example, the adverb *deliciously* creates a nonsensical echo in the wrong word *desserts*.

just exactly. Although this REDUNDANCY is common in speech, it shouldn't appear in careful writing (apart from dialogue)—e.g.: "*Just exactly* [read *Just*] how good are the big, fast and skillful Flyers?" (*Boston Herald*).

For a similar phrase involving *exact*, see **exact same.**

juvenilely. See ADVERBS (B).

juxtaposition is a noun, not a verb. Although one may *position* a thing, one may not *juxtaposition* two things. *Juxtapose* is the correct verb form—e.g.: "The intended irony of Luther's skewed morality *juxtapositioned* [read *juxtaposed*] against the President's lack of morality is not particularly subtle or original" (*Bloomington Pantagraph*). See NOUNS AS VERBS.

K

karat. See **carat.**

kerchief. Pl. *kerchiefs*—not *kerchieves.* See PLURALS (G).

ketchup; catchup; catsup. The first spelling greatly predominates in modern usage. It has the advantages of phonetically approximating and of most closely resembling the word's probable source, the Malay word *kĕchap*, meaning "fish sauce."

khaki (= a brownish-yellow fabric of twilled cotton or wool) is frequently misspelled *kahki.*

kidnap(p)ing. The spelling with *-pp-* is, by convention, preferred. But the inferior spelling *kidnaping* occasionally appears.

kill . . . dead is a REDUNDANCY popularly promoted (alas) in television commercials touting insecticides that, it is said, will "kill bugs dead."

kimono (= a long, loose Japanese robe) is frequently misspelled *kimona.*

kind of. A. Meaning "somewhat." *Kind of* is a poor substitute for *somewhat, rather, somehow,* and other adverbs. It properly functions as a noun, however, signifying category or class in phrases such as *this kind of paper.* Cf. **sort of.** See **these kind of.**

B. *What kind of (a).* With this phrasing, not only is the *a* unnecessary—it is typical of illiterate speech. Thus, *It depends on what kind of vacation you want,* not *It depends on what kind of a vacation you want.*

kitty-cornered. See **cater-cornered.**

knapsack (= a lightweight frameless backpack) is frequently misspelled *napsack.*

knave (= a rogue) is sometimes confused with *nave* (= the main body of a church)—e.g.: "She told me to enter the *knave* [read *nave*] of the church, then step into a small room where there was a wooden partition in the wall" (*S.F. Chron.*).

kneel > knelt > knelt. In modern print sources, the past-tense and past-participial *knelt* is at least five times more common than its variant *kneeled.* See IRREGULAR VERBS.

knickknack is so spelled, with a *-kk-* in the middle. *Nicknack* is a variant form.

knife. Pl. *knives.* See PLURALS (G).

knit > knit > knit. The past-tense and past-participial *knitted* is a variant form. Cf. **fit.** See IRREGULAR VERBS.

knowledgeable. So spelled—not *knowledgable.*

known /nohn/ is often mispronounced /**noh**-ən/, as if it had two syllables.

kudos (/**kyoo**-dohs/, /**kyoo**-dahs/, or /**koo**-dohz/)—from the Greek word *kydos* "glory"—is a singular noun meaning "praise, glory." It is sometimes erroneously thought to be a plural—e.g.: "Dresser . . . has received *several kudos* [read *much kudos* or *several rave reviews*] for 'Better Days' since it premiered in 1986" (*L.A. Times*).

As a result of that mistake, *kudo* (a false singular) and *kudoes* (a mistaken plural) have come to plague many texts—e.g.: "Whether you nail me when you think I'm wrong or toss me *a kudo* [read *kudos*] when you agree, I rely on you for ideas and criticism" (*St. Louis Post-Dispatch*)./ "This is a great-looking show, too: *Kudoes* [read *Kudos*] to the customer (Ambra Wakefield) and choreographer (Lee Martino)" (*Orange County Register*).

kummerbund. See **cummerbund.**

kumquat (= a small citrus fruit resembling a tiny orange) is the standard spelling. *Cumquat* is a variant form.

L

label, vb., makes *labeled* and *labeling* in AmE, *labelled* and *labelling* in BrE. See SPELLING (B).

labor, v.t. See **belabor.**

laden. A. As a Past Participle Equivalent to *loaded*. *Laden* survives today as a participial adjective <a laden barge> and not as a past participle. To use *laden* as a part of the verb phrase is to be guilty of ARCHAISM, although it is still used in shipping contexts <the ship was laden by union workers>. But sometimes, in literary contexts, *laden* is simply the better word <with rue my heart is laden>.

B. For *ridden*. *Ridden* is the more general term, meaning "infested with," "full of," or "dominated, harassed, or obsessed by." *Laden* has not shed its strong connotation of "loaded down." Hence a place might be *laden* with things if they had been stacked there; or, more plausibly, a truck or barge might be *laden* with goods. But figuratively, *laden* fails as an effective adjective if the original suggestion of loading is ignored. E.g.: "This winter she's going to teach herself how to use the GIS computerized mapping system so she can map out *mosquito-laden* [read *mosquito-ridden*] areas and make it easier on the workers" (*Virginian-Pilot*).

ladies' man; lady's man. The phrase is commonly written both ways, but *ladies' man* is more in keeping with the sense of *many* women. Some dictionaries seem to misdefine the phrase: "a man very fond of the company of women and very attentive to them" (*WNWCD*); "a man who shows a marked fondness for the company of women or is esp. attentive to women" (*W10*). The main element is missing there, because such a man could still be so oafish as to seem repulsive to women. That is, a *ladies' man* must be not only fond of women but also extremely popular with them. See **lady.**

lady. This word has become increasingly problematic. Though hardly anyone would object to it in the phrase *ladies and gentlemen*, most other uses of the term might invite disapproval—depending on the readers' or listeners' views about SEXISM. It isn't a SKUNKED TERM, but it's gradually becoming something like one.

laid; lain. See **lay.**

LAMBDACISM. See PRONUNCIATION (C).

lament, v.t., should not be made intransitive by the addition of a preposition—e.g.: "They should be used to it by now, having *lamented over* [delete *over*] one-point defeats to both Kansas City and San Francisco" (*Nashville Banner*).

lamentable is pronounced either /**lam**-ən-tə-bəl/ or /lə-**men**-tə-bəl/. Traditionally, the first of these pronunciations has been considered the better one.

large, unlike *great*, is not a word that can be idiomatically coupled with other words denoting measure, such as *breadth, depth, distance, height, length, weight*, or *width*. But writers often misuse *large* when *great* would be the right word—e.g.: "About 46 percent of the state's bridges are not wide or high enough, have lanes that are too narrow or can't handle *large* [read *great*] weights or high speeds" (*St. Louis Post-Dispatch*).

large-size, adj. This PHRASAL ADJECTIVE is usually redundant. Although *large-size apparel* is defensible, *large-size business* is not.

largess (= generous giving; munificence) is the standard spelling. *Largesse*, the French form, is an archaic variant. Still, the usual pronunciation is the Frenchified /lahr-**zhes**/.

last rites (= a sacrament in which a priest blesses and prays for a person who has fallen critically ill or been grievously injured) is occasionally misrendered *last rights*—e.g.: "Less than a year later, he would give her son, Albie, his *last rights* [read *last rites*] as he lay dying in a hallway" (*Boston Herald*).

Another term for *last rites* is *extreme unction*. But strictly speaking, the sacrament became obsolete with reforms that the Roman Catholic Church made in 1972.

late, the is elliptical for *lately* (i.e., recently) *deceased*. How long this can be used of a dead person depends on how recently that person died, but anything more than five years or so is going to strike most readers as odd (e.g., *the late John F. Kennedy*). Of course, there's no absolute statute of limitations; the question is whether a fair number of reasonable readers would know or need to be reminded that the person has recently died. But the expression serves as more than just a reminder. It also offers a note of respect—and perhaps even a touch of sorrow. Thus, in the fall of 1997 people said *the late Princess Diana* not because anybody needed to be reminded that she had died in August of that year—everyone knew it—but because people mourned her death.

later. A. Without Temporal Context. *Later* should not be used unless a proper time frame has been established. E.g.: "As Salman Rushdie, *later the target of an Islamic fatwa calling for his death* [read *who was to become the target of an Islamic fatwa calling for his death*], stated in 1985, ..."

B. *Later on.* The distinction between *later* and *later on* rests on two points: euphony and formality. Occasionally, *later on* simply sounds better in a sentence. It is always less formal—e.g.: "What you spend today sets the course for how much you'll 'need' *later on*" (*Money*). Cf. **early on.**

LATINISMS. In the English language, Latin words and phrases typically fall into any of six categories: (1) the ones that are now so common that they're barely recognizable as Latin (*bonus*, *quorum*, *vice versa*); (2) the ones that are reduced to abbreviations in scholarly contexts (*e.g.*, *i.e.*, *ibid.*, *id.*); (3) the ones used in JARGON of doctors, lawyers, and scientists (*metatarsus*, *habeas corpus*, *chlorella*); (4) the mottoes and maxims used especially in ceremonial contexts (*E pluribus unum*, *Sic transit gloria mundi*); (5) the ones that literate people know and occasionally find useful (*ipse dixit*, *non sequitur*, *rebus*, *mutatis mutandis*); and (6) the truly rare ones that characterize SESQUIPEDALITY (*ceteris paribus*, *hic et ubique*, *ignoratio elenchi*). Increasingly, the view among stylists today is that unless you know that your audience is fairly erudite, categories 3 through 6 are dangerous territory.

On whether to italicize words borrowed from Latin and other languages, see ITALICS (B). On pluralizing Latin terms, see PLURALS (B) & HYPERCORRECTION (A).

latter. See **former.**

laudable; laudatory. *Laudable* = deserving praise. *Laudatory* = expressing praise. The distinction is the same as that between *praiseworthy* (= laudable) and the active *praiseful* (= laudatory). But the misuse of *laudatory* for *laudable* is lamentably common—e.g.: "Indeed, like Nixon before him, a jaundiced view of Clinton and his motives causes many to oppose or at least look askance at even his most *laudatory* [read *laudable*] goals" (*Hartford Courant*).

lawful. See **legal.**

lay; lie. A. The Distinction. Very simply, *lie* (= to recline, be situated) is intransitive—it can't take a direct object

<he lies on his bed>. But *lay* (= to put down, arrange) is always transitive—it needs a direct object <please lay the book on my desk>. The verbs are inflected as follows:

Verb	Present Tense	Past Tense	Past Participle	Present Participle
lay, v.t.	lay	laid	laid	laying
lie, v.i.	lie	lay	lain	lying

Because *lie* is intransitive, it has only an active voice <lie down for a while>. And because *lay* is transitive, it may be either active <he laid the blanket over her> or passive <the blanket was laid over her>. See PASSIVE VOICE.

To use *lay* without a direct object, in the sense of *lie*, is nonstandard <I want to lay down> <he was laying in the sun>. But this error is very common in speech. In fact, some commentators believe that people make this mistake more often than any other in the English language.

The most unusual of these inflected forms, of course, is *lain*, but most writers have little difficulty getting it right—e.g.: "Katrina Kuratli said she and her husband, Dan, had just *lain* down in their bedroom when the bomb went off around 10:45 p.m." (*L.A. Times*). See IRREGULAR VERBS.

B. *Lay* for *lie*. This is one of the most widely known of all usage errors—e.g.:

- "Mr. Armstrong [debating against Alan Dershowitz] was not to be outdone . . . . But Mr. Dershowitz did not *lay* [read *lie*] down" (*N.Y. Times*).
- "This Christmas give a gift that's been *laying* [read *lying*] around for twelve years" (*Atlantic Monthly*).
- "But Walters did not ask any questions, investigators said. He ordered the two to get out of the car and *lay* [read *lie*] on the ground, according to Strouse's girlfriend" (*S.F. Chron.*).

Similarly, although a sickness can *lay you low*, if you're in that position you're *lying low*—e.g.: "Back when James A. Baker 3d was *lying low* over at the White House, the first invisible chief of staff, cynics in the West Wing said he was trying to avoid being tied too closely to a Presidential campaign that seemed headed for the political dump" (*N.Y. Times*). But American journalists get it wrong as often as they get it right—e.g.: "Another reason I *laid low* [read *lay low*] was to be in a position to help a friend back out of what he now must know to be a dead end" (*N.Y. Times*).

Another common mistake is *laying in wait* for *lying in wait*—e.g.: "Police say several armed assailants may have been *laying* [read *lying*] in wait at East 39th Street and Park Avenue" (*Indianapolis Star*).

C. *Laid* for Past-Tense *lay*. The *lay*-for-*lie* error also occurs with the past-tense forms—e.g.: "He *laid* [read *lay*] down flat on the ground and looked around for an object or landmark he might have missed from a higher angle" (*Amarillo Daily News*).

D. *Laid* for *lain*. Not surprisingly, the same mistake occurs with the past participles as well—e.g.: "[T]he players—performers—will take on a problem that has *laid* [read *lain*] dormant since Peter Ueberroth caved in to the umps" (*Boston Globe*).

E. *Lain* for the Past-Participial *laid*. This is a ghastly example of HYPERCORRECTION, that is, choosing the more far-fetched (and, as it happens, wrong) term in a contorted attempt to be correct—e.g.: "Earlier in the day, several people had *'lain hands'* [read *'laid hands'*] on Zachary and prayed for him. This is common at the crusades, as many people seem to think that God has anointed them" (*Orlando Sentinel Trib.*).

layman; layperson; lay person. *Layman* is the most common among these terms and is commonly regarded as unexceptionable—in reference to members of both sexes, of course. E.g.: "James Wilkinson, the 55-year-old *layman* who carried the cross at the head of Princess Diana's funeral procession, said he had never experienced anything like Saturday's ceremony" (*L.A. Times*). Still, modern writers increasingly avoid *layman* on grounds of SEXISM.

Layperson is an Americanism that originated in the early 1970s. Though much less common than *layman*, it does frequently appear, especially in the one-word form—e.g.: "Since [1979], the school's principals have been *laypersons*, and most of the sisters have given up teaching duties" (*Baton Rouge Advocate*).

For the reasons for avoiding *layperson*, like all other words ending with the suffix *-person*, see SEXISM (C).

lay off. See **fire.**

lay of the land; lie of the land. The first is the usual AmE form, the second the BrE, for this phrase meaning (1) lit., "the arrangement of an area's terrain; topography"; or (2) fig., "the facts of a given situation; the current state of affairs."

layperson; lay person. See **layman.**

lead > led > led. The form *lead* is sometimes wrongly used for *led*, perhaps on the mistaken analogy of *read* / *read*, and perhaps also because of confusion with the metal—e.g.: "Dr. Stewart, a co-author of the study, established her reputation in the field of radiation and health with her findings, published in 1956, that prenatal X-rays had *lead* [read *led*] to an increase in cancer deaths among children in Britain" (*N.Y. Times*). See IRREGULAR VERBS.

lean > leaned > leaned. The form *leant* /lent/ as a past tense and past participle is becoming obsolete.

leapt; leaped. Both are acceptable past-tense and past-participial forms for the verb *leap*. Because *leapt* is pronounced /lept/, the mistaken form *lept* is frequently encountered—e.g.: "John J. Sirica *lept* [read *leapt*] to his feet, shouting, 'It ain't fair. It ain't fair!' " (*N.Y. Times*). In fact, though, *leapt* is steadily being displaced by *leaped*: in frequency of use, the two forms are neck-and-neck in modern print sources.

learned; learnt. In AmE, the past tense is *learned*; in BrE, it's often *learnt*. To use *learnt* in AmE is an affectation.

As an adjective, *learned* has two syllables /**lər**-nəd/, and as a past-tense verb, one /lərnd/. The adjective means "possessing or showing broad or systematic knowledge; erudite."

leave alone; let alone. Traditionally, there has been a distinction: *leave me alone* means "leave me by myself (in solitude)"; *let me alone* means "stop bothering me." But only extreme purists will fault someone who uses *leave alone* in the nonliteral sense. Today that phrase is far more common than *let alone*. E.g.: "Good Samaritan VanVelkinburg told them to *leave* him *alone* and go away" (*Denver Post*).

Let alone is also used colloquially to mean "not to mention" or "much less" <he no longer drinks beer or wine, let alone bourbon or tequila>.

led. See **lead.**

legal; lawful; licit. *Legal* is the broadest term, meaning either (1) "of or pertaining to law, falling within the province of law," or (2) "established, permitted, or not forbidden by law." These two senses are used with about equal frequency.

Lawful and *licit* share sense 2 of *legal*: "according or not contrary to law, permitted by law." *Lawful* is quite common <driving in a lawful manner>. The least frequent of these terms is *licit* <licit acts> <the licit use of force>, which usually occurs in direct contrast to *illicit*.

Lawful should not be used in sense 1 of *legal*, as it sometimes is—e.g.: "The judgment must be affirmed if there is sufficient evidence to support it on any *lawful* [read *legal*] theory, and every fact issue sufficiently raised by the evidence must be resolved in support of the judgment." See **illegal.**

LEGALESE. Despite popular prejudices, not all uses of legal language are bad. But unnecessarily complex legal JARGON—or "legalese"—is widely viewed by legal scholars as the source of many problems: (1) it alienates people from their legal system; (2) it besots its users—namely, lawyers—who think they're being more precise than they really are; and (3) it doesn't communicate efficiently, even to other lawyers, despite occasional claims to the contrary. For comprehensive treatments, see David Mellinkoff, *The Language of the Law* (1963); and Bryan A. Garner, *A Dictionary of Modern Legal Usage* (2d ed. 1995). For a plain-language law dictionary, see *Black's Law Dictionary* (pocket ed. 1996).

legation. See **embassy.**

legitimate, v.t.; **legitimize; legitimatize.** The first is preferred in all senses and is by far the most common of the three forms. E.g.: "These putative acts of the Israelis, the *Globe* wrote, 'made all their compatriots into targets for revenge'—neatly *legitimating* Shiite terror" (*New Republic*). *Legitimize* and *legitimatize* are both NEEDLESS VARIANTS. Though formed incorrectly, the former is much more common than the latter. See -IZE.

lend. See **loan.**

lengthy. Throughout the 19th century, many BrE speakers considered this word an ugly Americanism. But it is now standard throughout the English-speaking world. The only restriction is that it should refer to books, talks, or arguments, with the implication of tedium. It shouldn't refer to physical distances, as here: "Women longshoremen sometimes have to drive *lengthy* [read *long*] distances to find one [a toilet] or to locate someone with a key" (*Virginian-Pilot & Ledger Star*).

lens. So spelled—not *lense*. But the misspelling occurs fairly often, as something like a BACK-FORMATION from the plural—e.g.: "Raunchy Lisa 'Left Eye' Lopez—who got her nickname after wearing a condom over one *lense* [read *lens*] of her glasses—makes no apologies for her behaviour" (*Daily Record*).

lept. See **leapt.**

less. A. And *fewer*. Strictly, *less* applies to singular nouns <less tonic water, please> or units of measure <less than six ounces of epoxy>. *Fewer* applies to plural nouns <fewer guests arrived than expected> or numbers of things <fewer than six limes are left>. See COUNT NOUNS AND MASS NOUNS.

The exception in using *fewer* occurs when count nouns are so great as to render the idea of individual increments meaningless. So *less* is used correctly with time and money—e.g.: "On that mantra, Larry Clark has built a $45 million-a-year company in *less* than five years" (*Ariz. Bus. Gaz.*). But if the units of time are countable as a whole, and not by fractions, then *fewer* is called for <fewer days abroad> <fewer weeks spent apart>.

Hence we say *less documentation* but *fewer documents*; *less argumentation* but *fewer arguments*; *less whispering* but *fewer remarks*; *less ambiguity* but *fewer ambiguities*; *less of a burden* but *fewer burdens*; *less material* but *fewer items*; *less fattening* but *fewer calories*.

But *less* for *fewer* is an all-too-frequent error: "She says it, but fact is, she's a linguist—a student of words. We need more of them, not *less* [read *fewer*]; more words, more students" (*Newsweek*).

B. And *lesser*. *Lesser*, like *less*, refers to quantity, but is confined to use as an adjective before a noun and following an article <the lesser crime>, thus performing a function no longer idiomatically possible with *less*. Dating from the 13th century, this formal usage allows *lesser* to act as an antonym of *greater*.

let alone. See **leave alone.**

liable (= subject to or exposed to) should not be used merely for *likely*. *Li-*

able best refers to something the occurrence of which risks being permanent or recurrent. E.g.: "What you don't know is *liable* to hurt you—and your building" (*Buildings*).

Liable has three syllables (/**lɪ**-ə-bəl/), not two, and is thus pronounced differently from *libel*.

liaison is pronounced either /lee-**ay**-zahn/ or /**lee**-ə-zən/, the first being more common in both AmE and BrE; /**lay**-ə-zahn/ is a mispronunciation. (See PRONUNCIATION (B).) The nontechnical senses of the word are (1) n., "an illicit love affair"; (2) n., "communication established for the promotion of mutual understanding; one who establishes such communication"; and (3) adj., "acting as an intermediary" <liaison officer>.

The word is commonly misspelled *laison* and (especially) *liason*.

libel. See **defamation.**

liberty; freedom. These synonyms have connotative distinctions. *Freedom* is the broader, all-encompassing term that carries strong positive connotations. *Liberty*, slightly less emotive, generally suggests the past removal of restraints on specific freedoms.

libido. Although dictionaries once recorded /li-**bɪ**-doh/ as the preferred pronunciation, /li-**bee**-doh/ is now the established preference in AmE.

library is pronounced /**lɪ**-brer-ee/—not /**lɪ**-ber-ee/. See PRONUNCIATION (B).

licit. See **legal.**

licorice (/**lik**-ə-rish/ or /**lik**-ə-ris/) is the standard spelling. *Liquorice* is a variant form. This word shouldn't be confused with its uncommon homophone, *lickerish* (= lascivious, lecherous).

lie forms *lay* in the past tense and *lain* as past participle, except when *lie* means "to utter a falsity" <the witness lied>. See **lay.**

lie of the land. See **lay of the land.**

life-and-death; life-or-death. Although the sense is "relating to a matter of life *or* death," idiom has sanctioned *and* in this phrase, not *or* <various life-and-death decisions>.

lifelong; livelong. *Lifelong* = lasting for all or most of one's life <Seymour's lifelong dream was to conduct the New York Philharmonic>. *Livelong* = (of a time period) whole, entire <"the eyes of Texas are upon you, all the livelong day">.

lighted; lit. Both are standard past-tense and past-participial forms. The usual forms are *lighted* as an adjective <a lighted torch> and as a past participle <is the fire lighted yet?>. *Lit* is unimpeachable as a past tense <she lit the fire>. See IRREGULAR VERBS.

light-year. Despite its appearance, this term is a measure of distance, not time. A *light-year* is the distance that light travels in one year in a vacuum (about 5.88 trillion miles). Although some figurative uses accurately reflect distances <the next town seemed light-years away>, the popular mind makes the term refer to time—e.g.: "And needless to say, the special effects are *light years ahead* of what Disney had in the '60s" (*Santa Rosa Press Democrat*). It's bad science and poor usage.

like; as. A. *Like* as a Conjunction. In standard usage, *like* is a preposition that governs nouns and noun phrases, not a conjunction that governs verbs or clauses. Its function is adjectival, not adverbial. Hence one does not write, properly, "He argued this case *like* he argued the previous one," but, "He argued this case *as* he argued the previous one." If we change *argue* to *argument*, *like* is correct: "His argument in this case was *like* his argument in the previous one." Frequently, then, *like* needs to be replaced by the proper conjunction *as* (or *as if*)—e.g.: "It looks *like* [read *as if*] the sales clerks are ahead of the hitters so far" (*St. Louis Post-*

Dispatch)./ "Star-crossed lovers, they are—*like* [read *as*] in the play—sprung from two households, both alike in dignity" (*Boston Globe*).

This relatively simple precept is generally observed in writing, but has been increasingly flouted in American speech. Examples of *like* used conjunctively can be found throughout the Middle English period; but the usage has been considered nonstandard since at least the 17th century.

B. *As* for *like*. This is a form of HYPERCORRECTION—trying so hard to avoid error that you end up falling into an opposite error. Ernest Gowers saw the problem: "A fashion seems to be growing, even among some good writers, to prefer *as* to *l.* not only, rightly, as a conjunction, but also, ill-advisedly, as a prepositional adjective" (*MEU2*). E.g.: "*As* [read *Like*] most people, I have been fortunate to have many mentors in life" (*CBA Record*). Cf. **in common with.**

C. As a Vogue Word and Verbal Tic. California is often credited with popularizing *like* as a space-filler: "California's biggest contribution to the American language is the use of the most versatile word ever—you guessed it, 'like.' Like, a word preceding every, like, noun and, like, verb, is almost the only description needed in a word where adjectives are, like, becoming a dying breed" (*Wash. Times*).

Since the 1980s, *be like* is also a juvenile colloquialism equivalent to *said* in relating a conversation—e.g.: "And I was like, 'Yes, I do.' But he was like, 'No you don't.' And so I was like, 'If you're just going to contradict me, then . . . .' " In teenagers, this usage is all but ubiquitous. In adults, it shows arrested development.

-LILY. See ADVERBS (B).

lingerie. Although the French pronunciation is /la[n]-**zhree**/, the established AmE pronunciation is /lon-jə-**ray**/. No advertiser would consider affecting a French pronunciation because it would seem ludicrous to an American audience.

liquid. See **fluid.**

listen; hear. To *listen* is to try to hear. To *hear* is simply to perceive with the ear, whether with effort or not.

lit. See **lighted.**

literally = (1) with truth to the letter; or (2) exactly; according to the strict sense of the word or words. *Literally* in the sense "truly, completely" is a SLIPSHOD EXTENSION. E.g.: "Behavioralists and postbehavioralists alike, *literally* or figuratively, learn what they know of science from the natural sciences, from the outside." (Read: *Behavioralists and post-behavioralists alike learn what they know of science from the natural sciences, from the outside.*)

When used for *figuratively*, where *figuratively* would not ordinarily be used, *literally* is distorted beyond recognition: "When I got to practice, I was stunned by the overwhelming fear the press had of Lombardi . . . *literally* petrified. He held everyone at bay and did very few interviews" (*San Diego Union-Trib.*).

literature is pronounced /**lit**-ər-ə-chuur/—not /**lit**-ər-ə-tyoor/. See PRONUNCIATION (B).

littler; littlest. These forms—the comparative and superlative for *little*—are perfectly good, although some writers have gotten the odd idea that they're not.

livelong. See **lifelong.**

load, n.; **lode.** Although they have similar etymologies, their meanings have fully diverged. *Load* (in its basic senses) means "a quantity that can be carried at one time" or, by extension, "a burden" <a load of work> <a load off my mind>. *Lode* carries the narrow meaning "a deposit of ore," as well as the figurative sense "a rich source or supply." The correct phrase, then, is *mother lode* (= an abundant supply), not *mother load*.

loan; lend. In formal usage, *lend* is the verb and *loan* the noun. The verb *loan* is considered permissible, however, when used to denote the lending of money (as distinguished from the lending of things).

loathe; loath; loth. *Loathe* is the verb meaning "to abhor, detest." *Loath* (with its needless variant *loth*) is an adjective meaning "reluctant." The verb spelling is often wrongly used for the adjective—e.g.: "Even young fans, usually *loathe* [read *loath*] to adopt the musical tastes of their parents, are bewildered" (*USA Today*).

lobby. The legislative senses derive ultimately from the architectural sense of the word. In 19th-century AmE, *lobby* came to denote (through the linguistic process known as metonymy) the persons who habitually haunt the lobby of a legislative chamber to carry on business with legislators and especially to influence their votes.

As a verb, *lobby* has come to mean: (1) to frequent legislative chambers for the purpose of influencing the members' official business <the group lobbied against the proposed reforms>; or (2) to promote or oppose (a measure) by soliciting legislative votes <the organization lobbied a measure through the House>.

The agent noun is *lobbyist*, meaning "one who lobbies." The term originated during the American Civil War.

lode. See **load.**

lodestar (= a guiding light or principle) is so spelled—not *loadstar*.

LOGIC. See ILLOGIC.

logical fallacy. See **grammatical error.**

look over. See **overlook.**

lose; loose, v.t.; **loosen.** *Lose*, v.t., = to suffer the deprivation of; to part with. *Loose* is both an adjective meaning "unfastened" and a verb meaning "to release; unfasten." *Loosen* bears a similar meaning, but while *loose* generally refers to a complete release <loosing criminals on the community>, *loosen* generally refers to a partial release <loosening one's belt>. Additionally, *loosen* is figurative more often than *loose* is.

Loose is sometimes misused for *lose*—e.g.: "Some aides close to James A. Baker 3d, Mr. Bush's top political adviser, say Mr. Baker is increasingly leaning to the view that the President stands to *loose* [read *lose*] more than he could gain from debating" (*N.Y. Times*).

loth. See **loathe.**

lour; lower, vb. *Lower*—as a virtual synonym of *glower* (= to scowl), and pronounced with the same vowel sounds /**low**-ər/—is so spelled in most AmE dictionaries. *Lour*, the standard BrE spelling, is listed as a variant form. That's unfortunate, because the spelling *lower* is an instant and inevitable MISCUE. We'd be well advised to use *lour* instead, as the British do—e.g.: "His first lead was in Terence Fisher's 'The Curse of the Werewolf' (1961), where his *louring* looks were seen to advantage" (*Observer*).

lovelily. See ADVERBS (B).

low; lowly. Each can function as both adjective and adverb: *a low profile*; *the car rides low*; *a lowly peasant*; *bow lowly before the king*. Because of the potential ambiguity, ensure that either word's meaning is clear from the context.

lower, vb. See **lour.**

low-key, adj., is the standard spelling. *Low-keyed* is a variant form.

lowly. See **low.**

lustful; lusty. *Lustful* is the narrower word, meaning "driven or excited by sexual lust" <long, lustful looks>. E.g.: "People of any sexual orientation can be violent or *lustful*" (*USA Today*).

Lusty is broader and typically lacks the other word's sexual connotations; it means either "vigorous, robust, hearty" <a lusty appetite> or "spirited, enthusiastic" <a lusty performance of *The Tempest*>. E.g.: "The UT-Chattanooga pep band has a nice routine where it plays a *lusty* version of the classic Chattanooga Choo-Choo" (*Tennessean*).

Sometimes writers misuse *lusty* for *lustful*—e.g.: "The affair included 400 e-mail communications, cyber sex and, finally, long and *lusty* [read *lustful*] phone calls" (*Sun-Sentinel*).

luxurious; luxuriant. *Luxurious* = characteristic of luxury <luxurious hotel>. *Luxuriant* = growing abundantly; lush <luxuriant foliage>. Each word is sometimes confused with the other—e.g.: "The Hostess House has the feeling of a large, *luxuriant* [read *luxurious*] home with plush velvet furnishings, an oak dance floor, a large fireplace and enclosed decks and patios" (*Columbian*)./ "Every general he describes had at least a moustache, if not mutton chops and a *luxurious* [read *luxuriant*] growth of beard" (*Rock Hill Herald*).

M

machination. The first syllable is preferably pronounced /mak/, not /mash/.

MACRON. See DIACRITICAL MARKS.

mad. Although this word has various nuances, the two primary senses are (1) "demented, insane," and (2) "angry." Unfortunately, sense 2—though predating Shakespeare and actually used by him—became stigmatized during the early 20th century as somehow substandard. The stigma should never have attached. The word is less formal than *angry*, *ireful*, *wrathful*, or *wroth*, but it's perfectly acceptable and has been for centuries.

majority. A. For *most*. When *most* will suffice, use it in place of *majority*—e.g.: "*The majority* [read *Most*] of the budget increase is due to the long-awaited expansion or replacement for city hall" (*Tampa Trib.*). *Majority* is most helpful in discussing votes—e.g.: "And let's not forget that a *majority* of Michigan voters approved term limits" (*Detroit News*).

B. Number. *Majority* is sometimes a COLLECTIVE NOUN that takes a singular verb, but sometimes (through SYNESIS) it's a plural demanding a plural verb—e.g.: "It is unwise, however, to become complacent, especially when the *majority seems* to have done just that" (*Tulsa Trib. & Tulsa World*).

Especially in the phrase *a majority of (people or things)*—with the *of-* phrase spelled out—the word *majority* is generally treated as a plural in both AmE and BrE. E.g.: "Since the *majority* of shops that will open tomorrow *were* also open last Sunday, most shoppers will be hard put to notice the difference that the law has made" (*Independent*). Still, the sentence could be advantageously recast: *Since most shops that will open tomorrow were . . . .*

make do (= to manage with what happens to be available, however inadequate it may be) is distressingly often written *make due*, a blunder—e.g.: "[T]housands of Wall Streeters will have to *make due* [read *make do*] with modest increases" (*Boston Globe*). For more on this type of verb, see PHRASAL VERBS.

MALAPROPISMS are words that, because they are used incorrectly, produce a humorous effect. The term derives from the character Mrs. Malaprop in Richard Brinsley Sheridan's play *The Rivals* (1775). Mrs. Malaprop loves big words, but she uses them ignorantly to create hilarious solecisms and occasionally embarrassing double entendres. One of Mrs. Malaprop's famous similes is *as headstrong as an allegory on the banks of the Nile*. Elsewhere, she refers to the *geometry* of *contagious countries*.

What most sources do not point out is that Sheridan borrowed the device from Shakespeare, who used it quite often for comic effect, always in the mouths of lower-class characters who are unsuccessfully aping the usage of their social and intellectual betters and saying something quite different (sometimes scandalously different) from what they meant to say. For example, Elbow, the incompetent constable in *Measure for Measure*, says of a bawdy house that it is "a respected [read *suspected*] house" (2.1.162). Several equally hilarious misusages—in this scene and others—have the judge standing bemused as both the accused and the accuser get their meanings tangled up.

A well-known example of a Shakespearean malapropism that skirts sacrilege is Bottom the Weaver's garbled version of 1 Corinthians 2:9, delivered near the end of *A Midsummer Night's Dream*: "The eye of man hath not heard, the ear of man hath not seen, man's hand is not able to taste, his tongue to conceive, nor his heart to report, what my dream was" (4.1.211–14).

Modern examples aren't hard to come by. One lawyer apparently mistook *meretricious* (= superficially attractive but false, like a prostitute) for *meritorious*, with embarrassing consequences: he asked a judge to rule favorably on his client's "meretricious claim." Similarly, Senator Sam Ervin recalled a lawyer who, in arguing that his client had been provoked by name-calling (*epithets*), said: "I hope that in passing sentence on my client upon his conviction for assault and battery, your honor will bear in mind that he was provoked to do so by the *epitaphs* hurled at him by the witness" (Paul R. Clancy, *Just a Country Lawyer*, 1974).

Other illustrations are *nefarious* (= evil) for *multifarious* (= greatly varied) <ties, shirts, shoes, belts, socks, and all the other nefarious parts of one's wardrobe>; *voracity* (= greediness with food) for *veracity* (= truthfulness) <How dare you attack my voracity!>; and *serial* for *surreal* <it was truly a serial experience>.

For other examples, see **behest, climactic, confess (B), effrontery (A), equivalent (B), for all intents and purposes, gambit, guerrilla, heartrending, Hobson's choice (C), illicit, inclement, infest, infinitely, in lieu of (B), odious, perpetuate, uncategorically & unmercilessly.**

male, adj.; **masculine; manly; manlike; mannish.** All these terms mean "of or relating to men," but their uses can be finely distinguished. *Male* is the most neutral <male-pattern baldness>. *Masculine* shares this neutral sense <masculine traits>, but often suggests the positive qualities traditionally associated with men <his masculine confidence was no charade>. *Manly* carries the positive connotations of *masculine* <manly strength and vigor>. *Manlike* most often refers to nonhumans <a tribe of manlike apes>. *Mannish* typically has negative connotations, especially in reference to a woman <she had a mannish appearance>.

Although these terms bear interesting historical distinctions, in modern usage some of them—particularly *manly* and *mannish*—are considered politically incorrect: *manly* because it suggests that women don't possess the admirable qualities denoted, and *mannish* because it typically applies to women in a derogatory sense. Cf. **female.** See SEXISM (C).

malodorous. See **odorous.**

-MAN. See SEXISM (C).

man and wife. Since the 1960s, this phrase has been steadily decreasing in frequency. The reason, presumably, is that it does not accord the woman an equal status—i.e., she is referred to only by her marital status. A more balanced phrasing is *husband and wife*. See SEXISM (E).

mankind. See **humankind.**

manly; manlike; mannish. See **male.**

manner, in a ——. This phrase typifies the style of a writer whose prose reads slowly. *In a professional manner* should be *professionally*; *in a rigid manner* should be *rigidly*; *in a childish manner* should be *childishly*. Good editors do not leave such phrases untouched.

Still, some phrases cannot be made into *-ly* adverbs: *in a Rambo-like manner*; *in a determined manner* (few editors would choose *determinedly*—see -EDLY); *in a catch-as-catch-can manner*. In many such phrases, though, the word *way* would be an improvement over *manner*. See ADVERBS. Cf. **manner in which & nature.**

manner in which is often unnecessarily verbose for *how* or *way*—e.g.: "Those larger issues—the foreign money contributions, the conduit money, the virtual merging of Clinton campaign and Democratic Party coffers and the generally reckless *manner in which* [read *way*] the Democrats raised funds for the 1996 presidential campaign—continue to demand vigorous investigation and prosecution" (*Wash. Post*).

manpower. See SEXISM (C).

mantle; mantel. *Mantle* means, among other things, "a loose robe," and is frequently used in figurative senses <mantle of leadership> <mantle of greatness>. E.g.: "The tributes flowing in suggest a *mantle* of modern sainthood falling upon her" (*San Diego Union-Trib.*). *Mantel* is a very different word, meaning "a structure of wood or marble above or around a fireplace; a shelf." E.g.: "Display some of your prized possessions on a shelf or on top of a *mantel* or windowsill" (*San Diego Union-Trib.*).

Each word is sometimes confused with the other—e.g.: "With key veterans like Byron Scott and Kenny Gattison gone from the inaugural season team, the *mantel* [read *mantle*] of leadership fell to Anthony and Edwards" (*Vancouver Sun*)./ "Now it's five autumns later, and there is no Heisman on his *mantle* [read *mantel*], no No. 1 ranking on his resume and no more time to waste" (*Cleveland Plain Dealer*).

many; much. *Many* is used with count nouns (i.e., those that comprise a number of discrete or separable entities). *Much* is used with mass nouns (i.e., those that refer to amounts as distinguished from numbers). Hence, *many persons* but *much salt.* Here *much* is used incorrectly: "We do not have *much* [read *many*] facts here." (Cf. *less* for *fewer*, noting that *less* is the correlative of *much*, whereas *fewer* is the correlative of *many.*) See COUNT NOUNS AND MASS NOUNS.

marked is pronounced /markt/, as one syllable. The pronunciation /**mar**-kəd/, in two syllables, is a vestige of the correct adverbial pronunciation /**mar**-kəd-lee/.

masculine. See **male.**

MASCULINE AND FEMININE PRONOUNS. See SEXISM (B).

MASS NOUNS. See COUNT NOUNS AND MASS NOUNS.

masterful; masterly. Traditionally, *masterful* has described a powerful, even bullying, superior; *masterly* has described the skill of a master of a profession or trade. A master craftsman is *masterly*; a boorish tyrant is *masterful.* Which is the correct term in the following sentence? "Though Britain's Derek Jacobi looks about as much like Adolph Hitler as Archie Bunker, he evokes the Fuhrer with *masterful* verve." (The actor is *masterly*; Hitler was *masterful.*)

Perhaps one reason the two words are so frequently confounded is that when an adverb for *masterly* is needed, *masterfully* seems more natural than *masterlily.* (See ADVERBS (B).) Indeed, "He writes *masterfully*" strikes one as much less stilted than "He writes *masterlily.*" This problem with the adverbial form threatens to destroy a useful distinction between the two adjectival forms. So if an adverb is needed, try *in a masterly way.*

MATCHING PARTS. See PARALLELISM.

maximum, n. & adj.; **maximal,** adj. More and more frequently, *maximum* (like *minimum*) acts as its own adjective. E.g.: "[T]he officials can levy the *maximum* amount under the cap and refund taxes if budget projections remain intact" (*Chicago Trib.*). *Maximal* usually means "the greatest possible" rather than merely "of, relating to, or constituting a maximum." E.g.: "Hill says upgrades in both insulation and ventilation must be made for *maximal* effectiveness" (*Asheville Citizen-Times*).

The plural of the noun *maximum* is

either *maximums* or *maxima*, preferably the former—e.g.: "It set 15-month *maximums* on various kinds of debt" (*S.F. Examiner*). See **minimum** & PLURALS (B).

may; might. These words occupy different places on a continuum of possibility. *May* expresses likelihood <we may go to the party>, while *might* expresses a stronger sense of doubt <we might be able to go if our appointment is canceled> or a contrary-to-fact hypothetical <we might have been able to go if George hadn't gotten held up>.

Some sentences present close calls—e.g.: "If one of his coaches did something wrong, he says, he *may* [or *might*] be able to forgive" (*Chron. of Higher Education*). If that statement comes on the heels of alleged wrongdoing by a coach, then *may* is the better word. But if it's a purely hypothetical question, *might* would be preferable.

Difficulties are especially common in negative forms, in which *may not* can be misread as meaning "do not have permission" <you may not come with me>. If the writer is using a negative in supposing or hypothesizing or talking about future possibilities, the phrase should probably be *might not*—e.g.: "This myth assumes that the softness of the breasts in the very early postpartum period will last for three days; it *may* [read *might*] not" (*Mothering*).

Misusing *might* for *may* runs contrary to the tendency to suppress SUBJUNCTIVES in modern English. But it does occur—e.g.: "Power surge *might* [read *may*] have triggered outages for up to 2 million people" (*Austin American-Statesman*). (*Might* suggests that the outages didn't occur; they did.)

For the distinction between *may* and *can*, see **can (A)**.

me; I. See FIRST PERSON & PRONOUNS (A), (B).

meat out. See **mete out.**

media; medium. Strictly speaking, the first is the plural of the second <the media were overreacting>. But *media*—as a shortened form of *communications media*—is increasingly used as a mass noun <the media was overreacting>; that usage still makes some squeamish, but it must be accepted as standard. See COUNT NOUNS AND MASS NOUNS.

But it's still possible to draw the line at *medias*, which has recently raised its ugly head—e.g.: "The staff will use several *medias* [read *media*] and visuals to help get their points across" (*Virginian-Pilot & Ledger Star*).

Mediums is the correct plural when the sense of *medium* is "a clairvoyant or spiritualist"—e.g.: "Contact is initiated by the deceased, and no psychics, *mediums* or devices are involved" (*St. Petersburg Times*). Otherwise, the form should be avoided—e.g.: "Reporters for printed *mediums* [read *media*] also focus criticism on television for using all-purpose experts to express an opinion on a wide variety of subjects" (*N.Y. Times*).

memento. So spelled—not *momento*. Pl. *mementos*. See PLURALS (C).

memorandums; memoranda. *Memorandum* is always the singular noun. Either *memorandums* or *memoranda* is correct as a plural. Shakespeare used *memorandums* (*Henry IV, Part 1* 3.3.158), and that form now predominates. One nice thing about *memorandums* is that it will help curb the tendency to misuse *memoranda* as a singular, as in the erroneous form *this memoranda is late*.

mental attitude is a common REDUNDANCY. The phrase might have made good sense when it was common to think of a person's *physical attitude* (i.e., posture and carriage), but those days are no more. E.g.: "Positive *mental attitude* [read *attitude*] will be the topic addressed by former University of Tennessee basketball coach Ray Mears" (*Knoxville News-Sentinel*).

mercy killing. See **euthanasia (A).**

METAPHORS. A *metaphor* is a figure of speech in which one thing is called by the name of something else, or is said to be that other thing. Unlike *similes*, which use *like* or *as*, metaphorical comparisons are implicit—not explicit. Skillful use of metaphor is one of the highest attainments of writing; graceless and even aesthetically offensive use of metaphors is one of the commonest scourges of writing.

Although a graphic phrase often lends both force and compactness to writing, it must seem contextually agreeable. That is, speaking technically, the *vehicle* of the metaphor (i.e., the literal sense of the metaphorical language) must accord with the *tenor* of the metaphor (i.e., the ultimate, metaphorical sense), which is to say the means must fit the end. To illustrate the distinction between the vehicle and the tenor of a metaphor, in the statement *that essay is a patchwork quilt without discernible design*, the makeup of the essay is the tenor, and the quilt is the vehicle. It is the comparison of the tenor with the vehicle that makes or breaks a metaphor.

A writer would be ill advised, for example, to use rustic metaphors in a discussion of the problems of air pollution, which is essentially a problem of the bigger cities and outlying areas. Doing that mismatches the vehicle with the tenor.

Yet the greater problem occurs when one metaphor crowds another. The purpose of an image is to fix the idea in the reader's or hearer's mind. If disparate images appear in abundance, the audience is left confused or sometimes laughing, at the writer's expense. This problem is more forgivable in oratory than in writing, for with the latter the perpetrator can be charged with malice aforethought. Oratorical falls from grace are legion. Some time ago someone collected the oratorical gems of Michigan legislators: "This bill goes to the very heart of the moral fiber of the human anatomy."/ "From now on, I am watching everything you do with a fine-toothed comb." The following classic example comes from a speech by Boyle Roche in the Irish Parliament, delivered in about 1790: "Mr. Speaker, I smell a rat. I see him floating in the air. But mark me, sir, I will nip him in the bud." Perhaps the supreme example of the comic misuse of metaphor occurred in the speech of a scientist who referred to "a virgin field pregnant with possibilities."

Dormant metaphors sometimes come alive in contexts in which the user had no intention of reviving them. In the following examples, *progeny*, *outpouring*, and *behind their backs* are dormant metaphors that, in most contexts, don't suggest their literal meanings. But when they're used with certain concrete terms, the results can be jarring—e.g.:

- "[T]his Note examines the doctrine set forth in *Roe v. Wade* and its *progeny*" (*Brooklyn L. Rev.*). (*Roe v. Wade*, of course, legalized abortion.)
- "The slayings also have generated an *outpouring of hand wringing* from Canada's commentators" (*Wash. Post*). (Hand-wringing can't be poured.)
- "But managers at Hyland Hills have found that, for whatever reasons, more and more young skiers are *smoking behind their backs*. And they are worried that others are setting a bad example" (*N.Y. Times*). (It's a fire hazard to smoke behind your back.)

Yet another pitfall for the unwary is the CLICHÉ-metaphor that the writer renders incorrectly, as by writing *taxed to the breaking point* instead of *stretched to the breaking point*. See SET PHRASES.

METATHESIS. This term refers to the transposition of letters or sounds in a word or phrase. Historical examples abound (e.g., the modern words *bird* and *third* from Old English *bridd* and *thridda*). But modern examples—such as *ax* for *ask*, *irrevelant* for *irrelevant*, and the like—are to be avoided in standard English. For entries discussing various modern examples, see **anem-**

one, calvary, chaise longue, irrelevant, nuclear & relevant.

mete out, v.t. (*mete* from an Old English word for "measure"), is the correct phrase, not *meet out* or *meat out*—e.g.: "Washington's penalty . . . marks the first time the maximum fine of $10,000 has been *meeted out* [read *meted out*] since O'Brien asked the NBA board of governors to expand his disciplinary powers" (*Wash. Post*)./ "He said, 'It's not a matter of enforcement, but a problem of *meating out* [read *meting out*] justice' in dealing with juveniles" (*Wheeling, W. Va., Intelligencer*).

methodology, strictly speaking, means "the science or study of method." But it is now widely misused as a fancy equivalent of *method* or *methods*—e.g.: "Defenders of *scientific methodology* [read either *scientific methods* or *the scientific method*] were urged to counterattack against faith healing, astrology, religious fundamentalism and paranormal charlatanism" (*N.Y. Times*).

might. See **may** & SUBJUNCTIVES.

might can; might could; might ought. See DOUBLE MODALS.

militate. See **mitigate.**

millennium [L. *mille* "thousand" + *annus* "year"] forms two plurals: *millennia* and *millenniums*. The predominant plural is *millennia* in AmE and *millenniums* in BrE, but either is acceptable on both sides of the Atlantic. (See PLURALS (B).) And the trend in major AmE publications is to use *-iums*.

The word is often deprived of one *-n-* and misspelled *millenium*. In fact, this misspelling has even found its way into a proper name: the hotel across from the World Trade Center in New York City is called *The Millenium*. Perhaps that should be called not a proper name but an improper name. See SPELLING (A).

minimize; minimalize. The latter is a mistaken form—e.g.: "Paperwork has been *minimalized* [read *minimized*]" (*Fedgazette*)./ "TV director Brian Large *minimalizes* [read *minimizes*] the damage by relying on closeups" (*Denver Post*).

minimum, n. The plural form recorded in dictionaries is *minima*, but few aside from scientists use it. The form *minimums*, though not recorded in many dictionaries, ought to be accepted as standard. It's already quite common—e.g.: "New Jersey's requirements were already higher than the new *minimums*" (*N.Y. Times*). Cf. **maximum.** See PLURALS (B).

miniscule. See **minuscule.**

minuscule. So spelled, not *miniscule*.

minutia (= a trivial detail; a trifling matter) is the singular of the plural *minutiae*. Though much less common than the plural, *minutia* is hardly unknown. Unfortunately, it is almost always misused for the plural—e.g.: "Even as a relatively quiet investor, Seheult can quote such *minutia* [read *minutiae*] as traffic counts on the nearby freeway" (*Bus. Press/Cal.*). The phrases should be *lost in the minutiae*, *statistical minutiae*, and *day-to-day minutiae*—never *minutia*.

misappropriate. See **embezzle.**

misbelief. See **disbelief.**

mischievous /**mis**-chə-vəs/ is so spelled. *Mischievious* is a common misspelling and mispronunciation /mis-**chee**-vee-əs/—e.g.: "Epps performs with a *mischievious* [read *mischievous*] air" (*Virginian-Pilot*). Cf. **grievous.** See PRONUNCIATION (B).

MISCUES. A miscue is an inadvertent misdirection that causes the reader to proceed momentarily with an incorrect assumption about how—in mechanics or in sense—a sentence or passage will end. The misdirection is not serious enough to cause a true ambiguity because, on reflection, the reader can figure out the meaning. Thus:

> The court decided the question did not need to be addressed.

The mere omission of *that* after the verb *decided* induces the reader to believe that *the question* is the direct object—that is, to believe (if only for an immeasurably short moment) that the court decided the question. In fact, of course, the court decided not to decide the question.

Miscues are of innumerable varieties; the only consistent cure is for the editor or self-editor to develop a keen empathy for the reader. Part of what the editor or self-editor must do, then, is to approach the text as a stranger might. Further, though, a good edit must involve the kind of skeptical reading in which one imagines how one reader in ten might misread the sentence.

Following are discussions of six of the most common causes of miscues.

A. Unintended Word Association. Sometimes, two words in a passage seem to go together—because they frequently *do* go together—but in the particular instance aren't intended to. This commonly occurs in two ways.

First, a word appearing late in a passage sometimes seems to echo an earlier word to which it really has no relation. For example, in the final clause of the following sentence, *barred* suggests some relation to *disbarred* in the opening sentence: "[I]n 1948 he was found guilty of unprofessional conduct and *disbarred* for three years by a federal judge. The decision was appealed and reversed three years later. In 1958 Fisher, a thin-faced, thinning-haired socialite, was censured by the Illinois Supreme Court for actions against clients—but the Chicago Bar Association had asked that he be *barred* from practice for five years" (Murray T. Bloom, *The Trouble with Lawyers*, 1970).

Second, readers can be misled into WORD-SWAPPING. For example, the phrase *visual imagery* suggests picturesqueness (as opposed to picaresqueness) in the following sentence: "Given the rich *visual imagery* of Cervantes's picaresque romance, this is certainly a production that can appeal to both deaf and hearing audiences" (*Evening Standard*). Similarly, the phrase *army regimen* suggests *regiment* (= a military unit): "She shows Rabin, full of grandfatherly pride at the family's third generation of warriors for Israel, his prime ministerial curiosity about how the *army regimen* had changed since his day" (*Chicago Sun-Times*).

In the following examples, some interesting things occur on first reading. Flattery induces a woman to have sex, somebody engages in murderous attacks, and fans are kept from going:

- "Flattery induced a woman to submit to intercourse by pretending to perform a surgical operation. He was convicted of rape" (Glanville Williams, *Textbook of Criminal Law*, 1978). (A man named Flattery committed a crime, but his name suggests the wile he might have used in committing it. The miscue might be removed by referring to *Mr. Flattery* instead of *Flattery*.)
- "Small-minded, episodic *murder attacks* the basis of our taken-for-granted values so fundamentally that it generates anxiety" (*Sunday Times* [London]). (It looks on first reading as if the noun phrase *murder attacks* is the subject, but *murder* is the subject and *attacks* is the verb.)
- "Texas and Dallas officials said they would be disappointed to lose the game and said they were taking steps in an attempt to *keep* fans *from* both schools *going* to Dallas" (*Dallas Morning News*). (*Keep* means "retain" in that sentence, but the proximity of *from* makes it read as if it meant "prevent.")

B. Misplaced Modifiers. When modifying words are separated from the words they modify, readers have a hard time processing the information. Indeed, they are likely to attach the modifying language first to a nearby word or phrase—e.g.:

- "The 39-year-old San Francisco artist has beaten the odds against him by living—no, thriving—with the virus that causes AIDS for 14 years" (*Time*). (Does the virus cause AIDS for 14 years?)
- "Both died in an apartment Dr. Kevorkian was leasing after inhaling carbon monoxide" (*N.Y. Times*). (This word order has Dr. Kevorkian inhaling carbon monoxide and then leasing an apartment.)
- "Professor David Buss, above, conducts *a class on the psychology of mating on the UT campus* [read *a class at UT on the psychology of mating*]" (*Austin American-Statesman*).

C. Remote Antecedents. When a word refers to an antecedent, the true antecedent should generally be the closest possible one—e.g.: "There are various reasons that juries hang, some better than others" (Robin Lakoff, *Talking Power: The Politics of Language in Our Lives*, 1990). (The writer means *some reasons*, not *some juries*, but some readers won't see this immediately.)/ "They [judicial appointments] are often given to those with political connections, which may handicap women" (*Globe & Mail*). (Political connections may handicap women? No: The fact that judicial appointments are often given to those with political connections may handicap women. The *which* has a vague referent in the quoted sentence.)

D. Failure to Hyphenate Phrasal Adjectives. Forgetting to put hyphens in PHRASAL ADJECTIVES frequently leads to miscues. For example, does the phrase *popular music critic* refer to a critic in popular music or to a sociable music critic? If it's a critic of popular music, the phrase should be *popular-music critic*. See HYPHEN.

E. Misleading Phraseology. Some writers omit a needed object, leaving readers to deduce an incorrect one. For example, according to the following sentence, with whom did Nicole Simpson talk? "Nicole Simpson talked about her troubles with O.J. only 'when she was having a really bad day' " (*Wash. Post*). The writer means to say, "Nicole Simpson talked *to friends* about her troubles with O.J.," but as written the sentence looks as if it might be, "Nicole Simpson talked *with O.J.* about her troubles . . . ." The original might have been improved merely by inserting *to friends* after *talked*.

Sometimes, the first word in an adverbial phrase (*up the coast of New England*) sometimes seems to be part of a verb (*blew up*): "The storm also blew up the coast of New England" (*Austin American-Statesman*).

F. Ill-Advisedly Deleted *that*. The widespread but largely unfounded prejudice against *that* leads many writers to omit it when it is necessary—e.g.: "Commissioner Karen Sonleitner pointed out any policy changes approved after Sept. 1 could be subject to the state's Property Rights Act" (*Austin American-Statesman*). (Insert *that* after *pointed out*.)/ "Skinner said he believes many prisoners contract AIDS behind bars" (*Chicago Sun-Times*). (Insert *that* after *believes*.) See **that (B).**

misinformation. See **disinformation.**

MISPLACED MODIFIERS. See DANGLERS, ILLOGIC (C) & MISCUES (B).

mistrustful. See **distrustful.**

mitigate; militate. *Mitigate* = to make less severe or intense <the new drug mitigates the patient's discomfort>. *Militate* = to exert a strong influence <Harry's conflicting schedule militates against an October 17 meeting>.

Mitigate against is incorrect for *militate against*. Edmund Wilson called it "William Faulkner's favorite error" (*The Bit Between My Teeth*, 1965). Faulkner's failings aside, the error is surprisingly common—e.g.: "She is the full-time student service coordinator, and one of her jobs is to interpret violence and *mitigate* [read *militate*] against children's natural tendency to perceive it as normal" (*Boston Globe*)./

"In general, the speed of mass communication *mitigates* [read *militates*] against exploring an issue carefully as people's attention span decreases in correlation with shorter, rapid-fire presentation" (*L.A. Times*).

momentarily. Strictly speaking, this word means "for a moment," not "in a moment." But the latter sense is widespread, and the word has therefore become ambiguous—e.g.: "I'll be able to talk with you *momentarily*."

momento. See **memento.**

moneys; monies. The first is the more logical and the preferred form, but *monies* is a frequent variant. See PLURALS (D).

But why do we need a plural at all? Why doesn't the COLLECTIVE NOUN *money* suffice? The answer lies in idiom. While *money* generally functions in collective senses <we made a lot of money on that deal>, *moneys* is frequently used, especially in financial and legal contexts, to denote "discrete sums of money" or "funds" <many federal and state moneys were budgeted for the disaster relief>.

more; most. See COMPARATIVES AND SUPERLATIVES & **all (C).**

more honored in the breach. See **breach, more honored in the.**

more important(ly). As an introductory phrase, *more important* has historically been considered an elliptical form of "What is more important . . . ," and hence the *-ly* form is sometimes thought to be the less desirable. Yet three points militate against this position. First, if we may begin a sentence "*Importantly*, the production appeared first off Broadway . . . ," we ought to be able to begin it, "*More importantly*, ..." See SENTENCE ADVERBS.

Second, the ellipsis does not work with analogous phrases, such as *more notable* and *more interesting*. Both of those phrases require an *-ly* adverb—e.g.: "*More notably*, the Dust Brothers are responsible for the production of Beck's Grammy-winning album, 'Odelay' " (*Grand Rapids Press*).

And third, if the position is changed from the beginning of the sentence in any significant way, the usual ellipsis becomes unidiomatic and *-ly* is quite acceptable—e.g.: "Shrage believes that the strategy should not be to reverse the intermarriage rate, as some activists argue, but to make sure that intermarried couples embrace Judaism and, *more importantly*, commit to raising their children as Jews" (*St. Louis Post-Dispatch*).

more unique. See ADJECTIVES (B) & **unique.**

most —in the sense "quite, very, almost"—has traditionally been considered poor usage. At best, it's a casualism—e.g.: "[T]he shredded lamb, encased in a flaky crust, was seasoned deliciously and was *most* [read *quite*] enjoyable" (*Chicago Sun-Times*). See **very (A).**

most important(ly). See **more important(ly).**

mouses. This plural—as opposed to *mice*—is correct when the reference is to timid people or computer gadgets. This conforms to our use of *lice* for more than one insect and *louses* for more than one cad. See PLURALS (H).

much. See **many.**

muchly is now considered substandard—a NONWORD—though several centuries ago it was not so stigmatized. *Much* is the preferred form in all adverbial contexts. But *muchly* occasionally finds its way into print—e.g.: "Stern steers his well-cast ensemble through its entertaining, *muchly* [read *quite* or *highly*] predictable course" (*Buffalo News*). For other adverbs with a superfluous *-ly*, see ADVERBS (D).

MUTE E. In English, a verb's unsounded final *-e* is ordinarily dropped before the *-ing* and *-ed* inflections: *create, creating, created; rate, rating, rated; share, sharing, shared.* Exceptions to this rule are verbs ending in *-ee*, *-ye*, and *-oe*; these do not drop the *-e* before *-ing*, but they do drop it before *-ed*: *agree, agreeing, agreed; dye, dyeing, dyed; hoe, hoeing, hoed.*

The suffix *-able* often causes doubt when it is appended to a base ending in a mute *-e*. Generally, the *-e* is dropped when *-able* is added, but a number of exceptions exist in BrE (e.g., *hateable, hireable, liveable, nameable, rateable, ropeable, saleable, sizeable, unshakeable*). See -ABLE (A).

The almost universal exception to the AmE rule of dropping the *-e* before a vowel is that it should be kept if it's needed to indicate the soft sound of a preceding *-g-* or *-c-*, or to distinguish a word from another with a like spelling, as in *change, changeable; hinge, hingeing; trace, traceable.* But even this exception to the rule is not uniform: *lunge* yields *lunging*. Because the given form of a word when inflected is easily forgotten and often the subject of disagreement even among lexicographers, the best course is to keep an up-to-date and reliable dictionary at hand.

One other difference between AmE and BrE is noteworthy: in AmE, the mute *-e* is dropped after *-dg-* in words such as *acknowledgment, fledgling,* and *judgment*, whereas the *-e* is typically retained in BrE (*acknowledgement, fledgeling,* and *judgement*). But British legal writers usually prefer the spelling *judgment*. See **judgment.**

mutual; common. It's possible to refer to a couple's *mutual* devotion, but not their *mutual* devotion to their children. The reason is that whatever is *mutual* is reciprocal—it's directed by each toward the other. E.g.: "So consider the matter a quid pro quo, a *mutual* exchange of affection between Zereoue and Mountaineer fandom" (*N.Y. Newsday*).

But when the sense is "shared by two or more," then the word is *common*—not *mutual. Friend in common* is preferable to *mutual friend*, although the latter has stuck because of Dickens's novel (the title to which, everyone forgets, comes from a sentence mouthed by an illiterate character). Careful writers continue to use *friend in common*.

myriad. The more concise phrasing involves using this word as an adjective <myriad drugs>, not as a noun <a myriad of drugs>. Here the better use is illustrated: "Back when we still thought America was a melting pot instead of a collection of hyphens, the crux of combining *myriad* nationalities into one was in that oath" (*Baltimore Sun*).

myself is best used either reflexively <I have decided to exclude myself from consideration> or intensively <I myself have seen instances of that type>. But *myself* shouldn't appear as a substitute for *I* or *me*. Using it that way is thought somehow to be modest, as if the reference were less direct. Yet it's no less direct, and the user may unconsciously cause the reader or listener to assume an intended jocularity, or that the user is somewhat doltish. E.g.: "The exclusion of women and women's concerns is self-defeating. For instance, *myself and other women in Hollywood* [read *many women in Hollywood, including me,*] would deliver millions of dollars of profit to the film industry if we could make films and television shows about the lives of real women" (*L.A. Times*)./ "My wife and *myself* [read *I*] were in a religious cult for over 15 years before the leader fell over dead" (*Bloomington Pantagraph*). See FIRST PERSON.

N

naive; naïve; naif; naïf. The standard adjective is *naive* (without a diaeresis), the standard noun *naif* (again, no diaeresis). The others are variant forms. *Naive* (= amusingly ingenuous) is sometimes misused for the noun *naif* (= a naive person)—e.g.: "But you are not a political *naive* [read *naif*]" (*N.Y. Times*). Maybe the author thought that, because he was addressing a woman, he should feminize the form. But in English, *naif* is not considered sex-specific.

The adjective is pronounced /nah-**eev**/, the noun /nah-**eef**/.

naiveté; naivete; naïveté; naivety. The first of these—a half-GALLICISM that keeps the accent but loses the diaeresis—is the standard form in AmE. Avoid the variants. The word is pronounced /nah-eev-**tay**/ or /nah-ee-və-**tay**/.

Naivety, which is chiefly BrE, is pronounced /nah-**eev**-tee/ or /nah-**ee**-və-tee/.

native-born citizen. This phrase, though it has been fairly common since the 19th century, reeks of REDUNDANCY—e.g.: "Some immigrants come to America as boat people, dirt poor and speaking no English, and within a decade are part of the professional class—suggesting that any poor *native-born* [read *native*] citizen has only his own sloth to blame" (*San Diego Union-Trib.*).

The modern temptation to brace the adjective *native* may come from two sources. First, in American law, the noun *native* has come to mean either (1) "a person born in the country"; or (2) "a person born outside the country of parents who are (at the time of the birth) citizens of that country and who are not permanently residing elsewhere." Sense 2 represents a slide in meaning, but the writer quoted above could not possibly have wanted to protect against that extended meaning. Second, the phrase *Native American*, meaning *American Indian*, has recently popularized a secondary meaning of *native*, one having to do with heritage and not with birthplace: "one of the original or usual inhabitants of a country, as distinguished from strangers or foreigners; now *esp.* one belonging to a non-European race in a country in which Europeans hold political power" (*OED*).

nature, of a ——. Good editors routinely revise this stilted phrase, which takes four words to do the work of one. If, for example, you can say someone is *of a generous nature*, you can invariably say the person is simply *generous*. Cf. **manner.**

nauseous (= inducing nausea) for *nauseated* (= experiencing nausea) has become so common that to call it an "error" is to exaggerate. Even so, careful writers follow the traditional distinction in formal writing: what is *nauseous* makes one feel *nauseated*. As of the early 1990s, the U.S. Supreme Court, in its seven uses of either word, had maintained a perfect record.

But other writers have spread the peccadillo—e.g.: "[H]e takes $30,000 worth of AIDS-related drugs a year, which leave him horribly *nauseous* [read *nauseated*]" (*N.Y. Daily News*).

Nauseous is pronounced /**naw**-shəs/.

necessary. See **possible (B).**

NEEDLESS VARIANTS, two or more forms of the same word without nuance or DIFFERENTIATION—and seemingly without even hope for either—teem in the English language. They're especially common in the outer reaches of the language—in technical vocabulary. Unfortunately, the unnecessary coexistence of variant forms (e.g., adjectives ending in *-tive* and *-tory*) leads not to precision in technical writing but to uncertainties about authorial intention. The trusting reader silently thinks, "The writer used *investigative* on the last page but now has pressed into service *investigatory*—is a distinction intended?"

"[I]t is a source not of strength," wrote H.W. Fowler, "but of weakness, that there should be two names for the same thing [by-forms differing merely in suffix or in some such minor point], because the reasonable assumption is that two words mean two things, and confusion results when they do not" (*MEU1* at 373). The confusion is perhaps greatest when the writer who is fond of INELEGANT VARIATION discovers the boundless mutations of form that exist in unabridged dictionaries: *submission* will appear in one sentence, *submittal* in the next; *quantify* on one page, *quantitate* on the next; and so on.

"On the other hand," we are advised to take note, "it may be much too hastily assumed that two words do mean the same thing; they may, for instance, denote the same object without meaning the same thing if they imply that the aspect from which it is regarded is different, or are appropriate in different mouths, or differ in rhythmic value or in some other matter that may escape a cursory examination" (*MEU1* at 373). Hence the nonlawyer should not jump to assume that *necessaries* is uncalled for in place of *necessities*; that *acquittance* has no place alongside *acquittal*; that *recusancy* is yet another needless variant of *recusal*; that *burglarize* is as good for a British audience as it is for an American one; and so forth.

Any number of entries throughout this work attempt to ferret out and discriminate between cognate words with established or emerging distinctions and those that seem, at present, to have neither. To the extent possible, words and phrases rightly classifiable as needless variants ought to be dropped from the language.

NEGATIVES. A. Negative Prefixes. The primary negative prefixes in English are *in-* (assimilated in many words to *il-*, *im-*, *ir-*), *un-*, *non-*, and *anti-*. For purposes of simple negation, *in-* is the most particularized of these prefixes, since it generally goes only with certain Latin derivatives (e.g., *inaccessible, inarticulate, intolerant*). *Un-* usually precedes most other adjectives, including Latin derivatives ending in *-ed* (e.g., *undiluted*, *unexhausted*, *unsaturated*). *Non-* is the broadest of the prefixes, since it may precede virtually any word. It often contrasts with *in-* or *un-* in expressing a nongradable contrast, rather than the opposite end of a scale—e.g.: *nonscientific* (= concerned with a field other than science) as opposed to *unscientific* (= not in accordance with scientific principles). *Anti-*, of course, has the special sense "against."

As a general rule, try to find the most suitable particularized prefix—and if none is really suitable, try *non-*.

But consistency is often difficult to find with particular roots. For example, *unsaturated fats* has the corresponding noun *nonsaturation*, not *unsaturation*. Likewise, we have *indubitable* but *undoubted*, *irresolute* but *unresolved*, *irrespective* but *unrespected*. From a typographical standpoint, negative prefixes cause trouble with PHRASAL ADJECTIVES, as in *uncross-examined witness*. Wordings that are less compressed are usually preferable; hence, *a witness who wasn't cross-examined*.

On whether to hyphenate prefixes such as *non-*, see HYPHEN.

B. *Not un-*; *not in-*. Double negatives such as *not untimely* are often used quite needlessly in place of a more straightforward wording such as *timely*. When the negatives serve no such identifiable purpose, they ought to be avoided. To say, for example, that the point is *not uninteresting* or that somebody's writing is *not unintelligible* is probably to engage in a time-wasting rhetorical flourish.

C. Periphrastic Negatives. Generally *we disagree* is preferable to *we do not agree*—except that the latter may be slightly more emphatic. Directness is better than indirectness; hence, *violate* rather than *fail to comply with*; *violate* rather than *do not adhere to*; and the like.

D. *Not . . . all.* On the problems caused by this phrasing, see **all (B).**

neither. A. Number. As a pronoun, *neither* is construed as a singular. That is, it should take a singular verb, and any object of that verb should also be singular. Thus, *neither of the offers was a good one* is grammatically better than *neither of the offers were good ones*.

But often it's not that simple. In the first example below, the plural *themselves* is necessary to avoid an awkward or sexist construction. In the second example, however, there is no danger of SEXISM because the company isn't mixed—and therefore the singular would be the better choice. E.g.: "*Neither* of my parents worked for *themselves*, and that was a strike against me" (*St. Petersburg Times*)./ "*Neither* of these two men placed *themselves* [read *himself*] into the police and fire retirement system" (*Virginian-Pilot*).

B. Beginning Sentences with. It is permissible to begin a sentence with *neither*—just as it is with *nor*—when embarking on yet another negative subject. E.g.: "*Neither* are they outraged at themselves for playing racial politics by insidiously implying, or outright accusing, every black Clinton Cabinet member of being either a crook or incompetent, or both" (*Nashville Banner*). See **nor (A).**

C. Pronunciation. In AmE generally, **/nee-th̲ər/** is the preferred pronunciation; **/nɪ-th̲ər/** is a mildly pretentious variant in most parts of the country. But in BrE, **/nɪ-th̲ər/** is usual.

neither . . . nor. A. Singular or Plural Verb. This construction takes a singular verb when the alternatives are singular or when the second alternative is singular—e.g.: "*Neither* Haley *nor* Rowell *were* [read *was*] charged with setting the Macedonia fire" (*St. Louis Post-Dispatch*). Cf. **either (C).**

Moreover, the verb should precisely match the form mandated by the second of the alternatives. E.g.: "*Neither* Barton *nor* I *am* saying that equities aren't a great long-term place to be" (*Fortune*). Of course, there are several possible variations, among them these:

> Neither you nor I *am* right.
> Neither she nor I *am* right.
> Neither you nor he *is* right.
> Neither I nor she *is* right.
> Neither he nor you *are* right.
> Neither I nor you *are* right.

But ignorance of this principle commonly leads to errors—e.g.: "Neither you nor I *is* [read *am*] likely to change the world" (Jefferson D. Bates, *Writing with Precision*, 1988).

Of course, when both alternatives are plural, the verb is plural—e.g.: "*Neither those goals* nor *the overall themes* of the conference *fit* the extremist image conjured up by some critics of the gathering, like Senators Bob Dole and Phil Gramm" (*N.Y. Times*).

B. Number of Elements. These CORRELATIVE CONJUNCTIONS should generally frame only two elements, not more. Though it's possible to find modern and historical examples of *neither . . . nor* with more than two elements, these are unfastidious constructions. When three or more are involved, it's better not to say *They considered neither x, y, nor z.* Instead, say *They didn't consider x, y, or z.* Or it's permissible to use a second *nor* emphatically in framing three elements: *They considered neither x, nor y, nor z.* Cf. **either (A).**

C. Parallelism. Not only should there be just two elements, but also the elements should match each other syntactically. (See PARALLELISM.) E.g.:

- "At the same time, many of Aristide's followers express concern that some ex-members of the army and its paramilitary allies who carried out a campaign of terror here have *neither been dis-*

armed nor brought [read *been neither disarmed nor brought*] to justice" (*Wash. Post*).
- "But Indonesia's ongoing record of improving the quality of life for all East Timorese should *neither be overlooked nor undone* [read *be neither overlooked nor undone*] by those who seek to exploit historical divisions among the East Timorese people for political gain" (*Wash. Times*).
- "Secret Service spokesman Jim Makin said Merletti intended *neither* to offend *nor infringe* [read *nor to infringe*] on agents' free-speech rights" (*Chicago Sun-Times*).

D. *Neither . . . or.* This phrasing is a gross lapse—e.g.: "West . . . reiterated that *neither* he *or* [read *nor*] his staff considered the past generosity of the families seeking plots" (*S.F. Chron.*).

NEOLOGISMS, or invented words, are to be used carefully and self-consciously. Usually they demand an explanation or justification, since the English language is already well stocked. New words must fill demonstrable voids to survive, and each year a few good ones get added to the language. Some become VOGUE WORDS; others are slow to achieve acceptance; still others, denoting scientific innovations, might never become widely known. Fortunately, lexicographers monitor new entrants into the language and periodically publish compilations such as these: Sara Tulloch, *The Oxford Dictionary of New Words* (1991); John Algeo, *Fifty Years Among the New Words* (1991); and Anne H. Soukhanov, *Word Watch* (1995).

nephew; niece. Legally speaking, are the children of a spouse's siblings one's *nephews* and *nieces*? No: it's only by courtesy that they're so called.

New Orleans is acceptably pronounced either /noo-**or**-lee-ənz/ or /noo-**or**-lənz/. Avoid /noo-or-**leenz**/.

news is now regarded as a singular noun, not a plural—e.g.: "By now, such good *news has* become commonplace" (*Milwaukee J. & Sentinel*).

nice = (1) subtle, precise <a nice question> <a nice distinction>; or (2) good, attractive, agreeable, pleasant <they're nice people> <it's a nice vacation package>. Although purists formerly objected to sense 2, it's now universally accepted among reputable critics. Still, the word is so vague in that sense—as a generalized expression of approval—that stylists typically work to find a more concrete term to express their meaning.

nicknack. See **knickknack.**

niece. See **nephew.**

nimrod. According to all the standard dictionaries—such as *W10* and the *SOED*—this word means "a skillful hunter." The term derives from the name of a king of Shinar (Nimrod), who is described in Genesis as a mighty hunter. Although the word is often used in this traditional sense, the late-20th-century slang meaning is "a simpleton; dunderhead; blockhead"—e.g.: "Hey all you mack daddies (cool guys) out there: if you don't want to sound like a *nimrod* (geek) on your next trip to kili cali (Southern California), don't get all petro (worried)" (*Wash. Post*)./ "Thus we wind up with the tableau of several hundred more or less disgruntled *nimrods* trudging along like cattle through a process that is at best inefficient, at worst absurd" (*Denver Post*). Though this sense isn't recorded in the standard dictionaries—not even the most up-to-date ones—it certainly exists and is well known among the younger generations. For now, it remains slang. But it surely threatens to kill off the hunter sense.

no. Pl. *noes*, preferably not *nos*. See PLURALS (C). Cf. **yes.**

nobody. See **no one** & PRONOUNS (C).

noisome is often misconstrued as meaning "noisy; loud; clamorous." In fact, it means "noxious; malodorous." (Cf. **fulsome.**) The word is related etymologically to *annoy*.

NOMINALIZATIONS. See BURIED VERBS.

NOMINATIVE AND OBJECTIVE CASES. See PRONOUNS (A), (B).

NON-. See NEGATIVES (A).

nonbelief. See **disbelief.**

none = (1) not one; or (2) not any. Hence it may correctly take either a singular or a plural verb. E.g.: "There are many lessons that society can learn from Mother Teresa's life . . . . But *none is* as powerful as the lessons that Mother Teresa said she learned from the poor" (*Orlando Sentinel*)./ "Sexton stressed—several times—that all the meats are farm-raised and USDA-approved and *none are* endangered" (*Sacramento Bee*). Generally speaking, *none is* is the more emphatic way of expressing an idea. But it's also the less common way, and it therefore sounds somewhat stilted. Cf. **no one.**

NONRESTRICTIVE RELATIVE PRONOUNS. See **that** (A).

NONWORDS. H.W. Fowler's formidable American precursor, Richard Grant White, wrote incisively about words that aren't really words:

> [A]s there are books that are not books, so there are words that are not words. Most of them are usurpers, interlopers, or vulgar pretenders; some are deformed creatures, with only half a life in them; but some of them are legitimate enough in their pretensions, although oppressive, intolerable, useless. Words that are not words sometimes die spontaneously; but many linger, living a precarious life on the outskirts of society, uncertain of their position, and cause great discomfort to all right thinking, straightforward people.
>
> *Words and Their Uses* 184 (rev. ed. 1899).

His polemical tone and hyperbole were characteristic: they were purposeful.

Among the words that he labeled nonwords are three that might still be considered so: *enthused, experimentalize, preventative*. But with most of the others he mentioned, he proved anything but prophetic—they're now standard: *accountable, answerable, controversialist, conversationalist, donate, exponential, jeopardize, practitioner, presidential, reliable, tangential*. The lesson is that in any age, stigmatizing words is a tough business—no matter how good the arguments against them might be.

This book contains entries on dozens of terms that might be considered nonwords by White's standards. Among the more prominent ones are these (each of which is treated separately in this book):

analyzation (see **analysis**)
doubtlessly
fastly
forebearance (see **forbearance**)
illy (see **ill**)
inclimate (see **inclement**)
irregardless
muchly
uncategorically
unmercilessly
unrelentlessly

The term *nonword* itself might seem to be a nonword because it doesn't appear in most dictionaries. But be assured that it's a word: it appears in *RH2* and the *OED*.

no object. This phrase, literally speaking, should mean "not a goal; not something considered worth achieving." In fact, though, writers use it to mean "no obstacle" or "no objection"—e.g.: "If you would love a fast, handsome car, and if money is *no object* [read *no obstacle*], take a close look at the 911" (*Fresno Bee*). The nonsense of the phrase is apparent especially in the following example, in which *object* bears a double sense, through ZEUGMA: "So now it's on to Florida and the Marlins, where money is *no object* but winning is"

(*Lakeland Ledger*). In that sentence, seemingly, money is no object (= no obstacle) but winning is an object (= a goal); thus, *object* means different things with the different subjects.

no one; nobody. Generally, *no one* is somewhat more formal and literary than *nobody*. In AmE, both are treated as singular nouns and therefore as singular antecedents <no one in his right mind would care>. But today, as indefinite pronouns, they're often treated as plural to avoid SEXISM—e.g.: "Yes, Germany was ringed by enemies, but this was just the right time for a bold move, the fuhrer figured. *No one* in *their* right mind would expect it" (*N.Y. Newsday*). See CONCORD & PRONOUNS (C). Cf. **none.**

noplace is a barbarism for *nowhere*—e.g.: "As the Joads' plight continues to worsen there's no work, no food, *noplace* [read *nowhere*] decent to live" (*Knoxville News-Sentinel*). Cf. **anyplace & someplace.**

nor. A. Beginning a Sentence. *Nor*, like *neither*, may begin a sentence—e.g.: "[T]he uttering of a word is not a consequence of the uttering of a noise, whether physical or otherwise. *Nor* is the uttering of words with a certain meaning a consequence of uttering the words" (J.L. Austin, *How to Do Things with Words*, 1965). In that construction, of course, the word *nor* needn't follow a *neither*. See **neither (B).**

B. For *or*. When the negative of a clause has appeared at the outset of an enumeration, and a disjunctive conjunction is needed, *or* is generally better than *nor*. The initial negative carries through to all the enumerated elements—e.g.: "There have been *no* bombings *nor* [read *or*] armed attacks by one side against the other" (*L.A. Times*). Sometimes, the best solution is to replace *nor* with *and no*—e.g.: "Florida, with its large elderly population, has *no* income *nor* [read *and no*] estate tax" (*Portland Oregonian*). See **not (B).**

normality; normalcy. The first has long been considered superior to the second. Born in the mid-19th century and later popularized by President Warren G. Harding, *normalcy* has never been accepted as standard by the best writing authorities. It still occurs less frequently than *normality*, and it ought to be treated as a NEEDLESS VARIANT. Careful editors continue to prefer *normality*—e.g.: "Set to emerge officially from the University of Chicago next week, the landmark study, called the 'National Health and Social Life Survey,' shatters many preconceptions in its attempts to define *normality*" (*Chicago Trib.*).

north; northward(s); northerly. See DIRECTIONAL WORDS.

nosy (= unduly inquisitive; prying) is the standard spelling. *Nosey* is a variant form.

not. A. Placement of. When used in a construction with *all* or *every*, *not* is usually best placed just before that word. E.g.: "But *every* team *does not* expect more. Kansas does" (*Houston Chron.*). (A possible revision: *But not every team expects more. Kansas does.*)/ "While *every* letter *cannot* be answered, your stories may be used in future columns" (*Raleigh News & Observer*). (A possible revision: *While not every letter can be answered . . . .*) See **all (B).**

B. *Not . . . nor*. This construction should usually (when short clauses are involved) be *not . . . or*. E.g.: "As parents, we need to encourage our children to focus on our inner character, *not* on our superficial traits *nor* [read *or*] on marketing-driven peer expectations" (*Lancaster New Era*).

C. In Typos. *Not* is a ready source of trouble. Sometimes it becomes *now*, and sometimes it drops completely from the sentence. This tendency helps explain why some newspapers use CONTRACTIONS such as *shouldn't* and *wouldn't*: the negative is unlikely to get dropped. See **not guilty (A).**

D. *Not only . . . but also.* See **not only . . . but also.**

not all. See **all** (B).

notary public. Pl. *notaries public*—not *notary publics*. E.g.: "County Clerk Mary Jo Brogoto said *notary publics* [read *notaries public*] should call the office at 881-1626 before picking up their commissions in Independence" (*Kansas City Star*). See PLURALS (F).

not . . . because. See **because** (B).

not guilty. A. And *innocent.* The two aren't quite synonymous. To be *innocent* is to be blameless. To be *not guilty* is to have been exonerated by a jury of a crime charged—regardless of actual blame.

Many writers blur the distinction—e.g.: "A San Francisco jury found him *innocent* [read *not guilty*] of the charge in 1988" (*L.A. Times*). Yet journalists may have a defensible reason for avoiding the term *not guilty*: they're concerned about typographical errors with *not*, which can easily become *now*. Fair enough. But writers who do have enough time for careful proofreading shouldn't sacrifice accuracy in this way.

B. *Not guilty beyond a reasonable doubt.* This phrasing is ambiguous. The standard by which a jury decides criminal charges is this: a defendant is guilty only if the evidence shows, beyond a reasonable doubt, that he or she committed the crime. Otherwise, the defendant is not guilty. Thus, we say that a defendant was not found *guilty beyond a reasonable doubt*.

But it doesn't follow that we should also say that a defendant was found *not guilty beyond a reasonable doubt*. Is that *not guilty (beyond a reasonable doubt)* or *not guilty-beyond-a-reasonable-doubt*? The latter idea makes more sense—e.g.: "The question is whether a judge can reach a contrary conclusion on the second charge—deciding that though a defendant was *not guilty beyond a reasonable doubt*, he nonetheless probably committed the crime" (*Chicago Trib.*).

Yet many readers will misconstrue the phrase. Thus, regardless of the writer's intention, some will think of *not guilty beyond a reasonable doubt* as a strong vindication—rather than as the slight vindication it is (we, the jury, had the slightest bit of reasonable doubt, so we had to find the defendant not guilty). The writer might have gotten it right in the following sentence, but nonlawyers are likely to be misled: "When you know all the facts [of the O.J. Simpson case], you'll see that the prosecutors failed to meet their burden of proof, and how, contrary to the court of public opinion, the jury arrived at their verdict of 'not guilty beyond a reasonable doubt' " (*Tulsa World*).

If somebody is found not guilty, say *not guilty*. Omit the standard (*beyond a reasonable doubt*) to prevent a MISCUE.

not hardly. This robust barbarism is fine if your purpose is to show dialect, but it doesn't otherwise belong in the serious writer's vocabulary—e.g.: "Is there a more logical place for Moorpark than the Marmonte League? *Not hardly*. [Read *Hardly.*] But logic often has nothing to do with it" (*L.A. Times*).

not in-. See NEGATIVES (B).

not only . . . but also. These CORRELATIVE CONJUNCTIONS must frame syntactically identical sentence parts—e.g.:

- "Many board games, electronic toys and computer programs *are not only enjoyable but also provide* [read *not only are enjoyable but also provide*] educational benefits" (*Montreal Gaz.*). (In that revision, the conjunctions frame two verb phrases. Another possible revision: *Many board games, electronic toys, and computer games are not only enjoyable but also educational.* The conjunctions frame two adjectives.)
- "It *not only* will save construction costs, *but also* the cost of land acquisition and demolition" (*Cincinnati Enquirer*). (A

possible revision: *It will save not only construction costs, but also the cost of land acquisition and demolition.* The conjunctions frame two noun phrases.)

- "These foundation-like funds are useful *not only* for small donors *but also* for big donors who don't want to hassle with the red tape" (*Forbes*). (The conjunctions frame two *for*-phrases.)

See PARALLELISM.

One common issue in *not-only* constructions is whether it's permissible to omit the *also* after *but*. Actually, this simply makes the prose less formal—e.g.: "[Perret] seeks to secure Grant's reputation *not only* as a successful general *but* as a military genius" (*N.Y. Times*).

notorious may mean either "famous" or "infamous," though it usually carries connotations of the latter, i.e., "unfavorably known." *Notoriety* is generally more neutral, although it is becoming tinged with the connotations of its adjectival form.

not un-. See NEGATIVES (B).

NOUN PLAGUE is Wilson Follett's term for the piling up of nouns to modify other nouns (*MAU* at 229). When a sentence has more than two nouns in a row, it generally becomes much less readable. The following sentence is badly constructed because of the noun-upon-noun syndrome, which (sadly) is more common now than in Follett's day: "Consumers complained to their congressman about *the National Highway Traffic Safety Administration's automobile seat belt 'interlock' rule.*" One can hardly make it to the SENTENCE END to discover that we're talking about a rule. (Actually, many writers today would leave off the possessive after *Administration.*) In the interest of plague control, the following rewrite is advisable: *the "interlock" rule applied to automobile seat belts by the National Highway Traffic Safety Administration.*

Readability typically plummets when three words that are structurally nouns follow in succession, although exceptions such as *fidelity life insurance* certainly exist. But the plague is virtually never endurable when four nouns appear consecutively, as when writers refer to a *participation program principal category* or the *retiree benefit explanation procedure.* Occasionally one encounters even longer strings: in 1997, a major national bank circulated a form entitled *Government Securities Dealership Customer Account Information Form*—which might be something of a record.

Finally, it is worth sounding a caution against loading a single statement with too many abstract nouns ending in *-tion*. The effect isn't pleasing:

- "Police must [study] . . . how to defuse volatile *situations* and how to instruct victims on *prosecution* and *protection options* the law provides" (*Cleveland Plain Dealer*).
- "This work led to a *consideration* of additional important attributes of *information* and *communication* media within *organizations*" (*MIS Q.*).
- "All of the 'classic' *assumptions* that are at the basis of the terms 'culture' and 'intercultural differences' find *expression* in this *intervention*. That is why the *situation* at the Center is not a *question* of organizational change" (*J. Applied Behavioral Science*).

For more on words ending in *-tion*, see BURIED VERBS. See also SOUND OF PROSE.

NOUNS AS ADJECTIVES. English has long been noted for its ability to allow words to change parts of speech. The transmutation of nouns into adjectives is one of the most frequently seen shifts of this kind. Usually the change is unobjectionable, as in the first word in each of the following phrases: *body weight*, *insurance policy*, *telephone wires*, *home repairs*, *family problems*.

Occasionally, however, semantic shifts of this kind give rise to ambiguities or play tricks on the reader. For example, it would be unwise for one writing about a statute concerning invalids to call it an *invalid statute.* To make a somewhat different point, the reader's expectations are subverted when a noun is used adjectivally in place of the more usual adjective. E.g.: "Police would have access to the fingerprints for *investigation* [read *investigative*] purposes only after obtaining a court order" (*Morning News Trib.*).

Often, of course, the sense conveyed is different when one uses the noun adjectivally as opposed to the adjective form. For example, a *pornography commission* seems to mean something different from *pornographic commission* (which is somehow difficult to visualize). But at other times, the two ways of phrasing the idea are synonymous, as in *prostate cancer* vs. *prostatic cancer* or *pronoun problem* vs. *pronominal problem*. The main difference is that, in such pairs, the more usual phrasing uses the noun (*prostate cancer*, *pronoun problem*). Only specialists use adjectives such as *prostatic* and *pronominal*. Or, for that matter, *adjectival* (over *adjective*, adj.).

Finally, relations often become vague when nouns that would normally follow prepositions are adjectives placed before nouns, and the relation-bearing prepositions are omitted. Thus, *victim awareness* is a vague phrase; does it mean *on the part of*, *by*, *of*? E.g.: "*Victim awareness* gained momentum in the early 1980s, with the passage of the Victim and Witness Protection Act." We can deduce that the intended sense is *awareness (on the part of the public) of victims and their rights*, but perhaps we should not ask our readers to have to make such deductions. The same sort of uncertainty infects *victim restitution* (= full restitution to the victim of a crime).

NOUNS AS VERBS. A type of semantic shift less common than the noun-to-adjective shift is the noun-to-verb shift. Perhaps because this shift is less common, it is more noticeable whenever it occurs. The result is often slangy—e.g.:

- " 'The Firm' . . . for a time even out-*box-officed* 'Jurassic Park' " (*Cleveland Plain Dealer*).
- "[H]e'd be as busy *ambassadoring* in Rome as he's been *mayoring* in Boston" (*Boston Globe*).
- "Samples were *air-expressed* to Atlanta for testing" (*Ft. Lauderdale Sun-Sentinel*).

Although some writers enjoy referring to *fast-tracking* budgets, *tasking* committees, and *mainstreaming* children, be wary of these innovations. They reek of JARGON.

Increasingly, too, people are turning noun phrases into awkward PHRASAL VERBS even when much simpler verbs are available. This phenomenon typically involves an evolution from the simple verb to the noun phrase and then to the phrasal verb. For example, hotel staffers frequently deal with customers who, when checking in, request a different room from their preassigned one—that is, they *change rooms*. The staffers then refer to this as a *room change*, and that phrase becomes so customary among those staffers that they begin using it as a verb. So in some hotels—especially in New York—it's not uncommon to hear someone at the front desk say, "Did you *room-change*?" Of course, the more natural question would be, "Did you change rooms?"

For other examples of noun-to-verb shifts, see **author, gift, impact, juxtaposition, office, premier** (where *premiere* is discussed) & **reference.**

On the related phenomenon of using adjectives as verbs, see ADJECTIVES (D).

now. On the typographical error of *now* for *not*, see **not (C) & not guilty (A).**

nowhere; nowheres. The first is standard. The second is a dialectal word. Cf. **anywhere.**

nuclear is pronounced /**noo**-klee-ər/—not /**noo**-kyə-lər/. Though presidents and other educated persons have had difficulty pronouncing the word correctly, if you can do it you should. See PRONUNCIATION (B). Cf. METATHESIS.

number. See **amount.**

number of, a. Some pedants think that correctness dictates *a number of people is*. One critic, for example, refers to "the growing habit of using plural verbs with singular nouns," adding: " 'A number of voters were unhappy' illustrates the offense" (*Nashville Banner*).

But *a number of* is generally—and quite correctly—paired with a plural noun and a plural verb, as in *there are a number of reasons*—e.g.: "A growing *number* of U.S. service companies *are* pursuing an international 'good management' seal of approval called ISO 9000" (*BusinessWeek*)./ "Although most Jefferson scholars have considered the rumor unlikely, a gradually increasing *number*—including late historians Page Smith and Fawn Brodie—*have* given credence to the Hemings story" (*U.S. News & World Report*). This construction is correct because of the linguistic principle known as SYNESIS.

NUMERALS. A. General Guidance in Using. The best practice is to spell out all numbers ten and below and to use numerals for numbers 11 and above. This "rule" has five exceptions:

1. If numbers recur throughout the text or are being used for calculations—that is, if the context is quasi-mathematical—then numerals are usual.
2. Approximations are usually spelled out (*about two hundred years ago*).
3. In units of measure, words substitute for rows of zeros where possible (*$10 million, $3 billion*), and numerals are used with words of measure (*9 inches, 4 millimeters*).
4. Percentages may be spelled out (*eight percent*) or written as numbers (*8 percent* or *8%*).
5. Numbers that begin sentences must always be spelled out. (See (B).)

B. Not Beginning Sentences with. It is stylistically poor to begin a sentence—or a paragraph—with a numeral <1997 saw the publication of no fewer than 3,700 mystery novels>. Some journals, such as *The New Yorker*, would make that sentence begin, *Nineteen ninety-seven saw* . . . . But most writers and editors would probably simply begin the sentence some other way, as by writing, *In 1997, no fewer than 3,700 mystery novels were published*.

C. Round Numbers. Except when writing checks or other negotiable instruments, omit double zeros after a decimal: *$400* is better form than *$400.00*.

D. Decades. As late as the 1970s, editors regularly changed *1970s* to *1970's*. Today, however, the tendency is to omit the apostrophe. See DATES (D) & APOSTROPHE.

E. Describing Votes. The preferred method for reporting votes is to use numerals separated by an en-dash <a 5–4 decision> <voted 164–58 against the proposal>. This method, which gives the reader more speed than spelling out the numbers, is standard today.

F. Cardinal and Ordinal. A *cardinal number* expresses amount (e.g., *one, two, three*). An *ordinal number* expresses place in a series (e.g., *first, second, third*). Occasionally, cardinal numbers are mistakenly used for ordinal numbers—e.g.: " 'It wasn't really a ballet class. It was more of a modern dance class, sort of an introduction to ballet,' Roy explained with the weariness of someone reciting a response for the *umpteenth million* [read *umpteen-millionth*] time" (*Austin American-Statesman*).

O

O; Oh. Although the distinction isn't always observed, there is one: *O* denotes either a wish or a classically stylized address <Praise the Lord, O Jerusalem—Psalm 147>, while *Oh* expresses a range of emotions from sorrow to pain to shock to longing <Oh! You frightened me!>. *O* is always capitalized; *oh* may be lowercase if it occurs in midsentence <I was just thinking that, oh, I miss my home>.

OBJECT-SHUFFLING. This term describes what unwary writers often do with verbs that require an indirect as well as a direct object. E.g.: "He continued the medicine a few days longer, and then *substituted the penicillin with tetracycline* [read *substituted tetracycline for the penicillin* or *replaced the penicillin with tetracycline*]." This use of *substitute* for *replace*, resulting from a confusion over the type of object that each verb may take, is labeled "incorrect" in the *OED*.

Unfortunately, there is no simple rule for determining which verbs are reversible and which are not. One must rely on a sensitivity to idiom and a knowledge of what type of subject acts upon what type of object with certain verbs. It is perfectly legitimate, for example, either to *inspire* a person *with* courage or to *inspire* courage *in* a person; but the switch does not work with similar words such as *instill* and *inculcate*. Good teachers *instill* or *inculcate values into* students, but cannot properly be said to *instill* or *inculcate students with* values. For an additional example, see **inflict.**

oblivious. Although this word takes the preposition *of* in its strictest sense ("forgetful"), the more popular meaning today is "unmindful; unaware; unobservant." And in this sense it may take either *to* or *of*—*to* being the more common choice. But fastidious speakers and writers continue to prefer *of*—e.g.: "He confesses that he was *oblivious to* [read *oblivious of*] his son, and the evidence he supplies is persuasive" (*Newsweek*).

OBSCURITY, generally speaking, is a serious offense. Simple subjects are often made needlessly difficult, and difficult subjects are often made much more difficult than they need to be.

Obscurity has myriad causes, most of them rooted in imprecise thought or lack of consideration for the reader. The following examples are winners of a "Bad Writing Contest" held in New Zealand in 1997. All three are from English professors—the first two American and the third British:

- "The visual is *essentially* pornographic, which is to say that it has its end in rapt mindless fascination; thinking about its attributes becomes an adjunct to that, if it is unwilling to betray its object; while the most austere films necessarily draw their energy from the attempt to repress their own excess (rather than from the more thankless effort to discipline the viewer)" (Fredric Jameson, *Signatures of the Visible*, 1992).
- "If such a sublime cyborg would insinuate the future as post-Fordist subject, his palpably masochistic locations as ecstatic agent of the sublime superstate need to be decoded as the 'now all-but-unreadable DNA' of the fast deindustrializing Detroit, just as his Robocop-like strategy of carceral negotiation and street control remains the tirelessly American one of inflicting regeneration through violence upon the racially heteroglassic wilds and others of the inner city" (Rob Wilson's essay in an anthology entitled *The Administration of Aesthetics*, 1994).
- "The lure of imaginary totality is momentarily frozen before the dialectic of desire hastens on within symbolic

chains" (Frederick Botting, *Making Monstrous: Frankenstein, Criticism, Theory*, 1991).

One might try to defend this obtuseness on grounds that the subjects are metaphysical, but the defense will be to little avail.

The root of the problem is largely psychological: "Most obscurity, I suspect, comes not so much from incompetence as from ambition—the ambition to be admired for depth of sense, or pomp of sound, or wealth of ornament" (F.L. Lucas, *Style*, 1962). More bluntly still: "The truth is that many writers today of mediocre talent, or no talent at all, cultivate a studied obscurity that only too often deceives the critics, who tend to be afraid that behind the smoke-screen of words they are missing the effectual fire, and so for safety's sake give honour where no honour is due" (G.H. Vallins, *The Best English*, 1960).

For more on different types and causes of obscurity, see ABBREVIATIONS (C), ABSTRACTITIS, AIRLINESE, COMMERCIALESE, COMPUTERESE, JARGON, LEGALESE & OFFICIALESE. For the antidote, see PLAIN LANGUAGE.

observance; observation. The DIFFERENTIATION between these two words is complete. *Observance* = heeding; obeying; the act of following a custom or rule. *Observation* = scrutiny; study; a judgment or inference from what one has seen.

obviously, like other dogmatic words (*clearly, undoubtedly, undeniably*), is one that writers tend to rely on when they're dealing with difficult, doubtful propositions. Be wary of it. See **clearly.**

octopus. Because this word is actually of Greek origin—not Latin—the classical plural is *octopodes* /ok-**top**-ə-deez/, not *octopi*. But the standard plural in AmE and BrE alike is *octopuses*. Still, some writers mistakenly use the supposed Latin plural—e.g.: "[T]he nearby mangrove swamps have become nurseries and breeding grounds for a whole new ecosystem, including sponges, *octopi* [read *octopuses*], shrimp, oysters, sharks, fiddler crabs, and man" (*Christian Science Monitor*). See PLURALS (B) & HYPERCORRECTION (A).

odious (= hateful, repulsive) derives from *odium* (= hatred; the reproach that attaches to an act that people despise). Although the word has nothing to do with *odor*, some writers blunder in thinking that it does—e.g.: "Often, the chemist rented a hotel room for the final mixing, while continuing to make the more *odious-smelling* [read *malodorous*] ingredients in the woods" (*Wash. Post*).

odorous; odoriferous; malodorous. *Odorous* = smelly <an odorous room>. *Malodorous* carries even stronger negative connotations <a malodorous bathroom>. *Odoriferous*, a frequently misused term, has historically had positive connotations in the sense "fragrant" <odoriferous rose gardens>. It shouldn't be used in reference to foul odors. *Odiferous*, an erroneous shortening of *odoriferous*, is often misused for *odorous* or *malodorous*—e.g.: "I was in the Texas Panhandle, typically maligned for its harsh weather, *odiferous* [read *malodorous*] feedlots, and dull, wind-whipped landscape—flat as a tortilla and practically treeless" (*Texas Monthly*). See DOUBLE BOBBLES.

-OES. See PLURALS (C).

of. A. Signaling Verbosity. However innocuous it may appear, the word *of* is, in anything other than small doses, among the surest indications of flabby writing. Some fear that *of* and its resulting flabbiness are spreading: "Clearly, *of* is now something more than a mere preposition. It's a virus" (*N.Y. Times*). The only suitable vaccination is to cultivate a hardy skepticism about its utility in any given context. If it proves itself, fine. Often, though, it will merely breed verbosity—e.g.:

- "In spite *of* the fact that a great percentage *of* the media coverage *of* Muslims mainly targets the negative actions *of* some splinter groups and several individuals, there are still a shrinking number *of* people who are still under the false impression that Al-Islam is a 'bloody and dangerous religion,' as the Bishop puts it" (*Cleveland Call & Post*). (A possible revision: *Because the media continually put Muslims in a negative light, some continue to believe that Al-Islam is a "bloody and dangerous religion," as the Bishop puts it.* [Five *of*s to none; 56 words to 28; and heightened logic in the revision.])
- "By the mid-1980s, many *of* these politicians were seen as a big part *of* the problem not only in terms *of* poor economic performance but also in terms *of* political authoritarianism" (*J. Asian & Afr. Studs.*). (A possible revision: *By the mid-1980s, many of these politicians were seen as having contributed to the problem both through poor economic performance and through political authoritarianism.* [Four *of*s to one; 32 words to 25.])
- "In light *of* the high number *of* requests from retail investors, the Treasury can expect to top the million mark in terms *of* numbers *of* small shareholders participating in the privatization" (*Wall Street J. Eur.*). (A possible revision: *Given the high demand from retail investors, the Treasury can expect that more than a million small shareholders will participate in the privatization.* [Four *of*s to none; 31 words to 23.])

As the examples illustrate, reducing the *of*s can, even at the sentence level, greatly improve the briskness and readability of the prose. See PREPOSITIONS (A).

B. Intrusive *of*. The word *of* often intrudes where it doesn't idiomatically belong, as in *not that big of a deal*, *not too smart of a student*, *somewhat of an abstract idea*, etc. Cf. **too (C)**.

For the opposite tendency—omitting a necessary *of*—see **couple (of) dozen.**

C. Superfluous in Dates. *December of 1987* should be *December 1987.* See DATES (B).

D. For *have*. Because the spoken *have* (especially in a contraction) is often identical in sound with *of* <I should've done it>, semiliterate writers have taken to writing *should of*, *could of*, and *would of*. But the word is *have*, or a contraction ending in *'ve*, and it should be written so.

E. *Of a . . . nature*. See **nature.**

offense; offence. The first is the AmE spelling; the second is BrE. In AmE and BrE alike, the word is preferably accented on the second syllable: /ə-**fen[t]s**/. Unfortunately, because sports talk puts the accent on the first syllable (/**of**-en[t]s/), many American speakers have adopted this pronunciation even in the word's legal sense. The sound of it puts the literate person's teeth on edge. Cf. **defense.**

In BrE, and to a lesser extent in AmE, lawyers commonly distinguish *crimes* (at common law) from *offenses* (created by statute). It is common in both speech communities to use *offense* for the less serious infractions and *crime* for the more serious ones. Lawyers would not speak of the "offense" of murder. Nor would they refer to the "crime" of parking a car in the wrong place.

office, vb., has become a commonplace expression among American businesspeople, but not among fastidious users of language. Although *office* is recorded as a verb from the 16th century, the new vogue began in the Southwest during the 1980s within the oil-and-gas industry. Gradually it has spread to other fields and has started to overrun the country. No one seems to *have an office* anymore; instead, everyone *offices.* E.g.: "[T]he Uptown area is most attractive to prospective tenants wanting the lure of downtown without the high costs associated with *officing* there" (*Dallas Bus. J.*). This is a classic example of the problem discussed under NOUNS AS VERBS.

OFFICIALESE = the language of officialdom, characterized by bureaucratic turgidity and insubstantial fustian; inflated language that could be readily translated into simpler terms. E.g.: "Let us now proceed to perambulate down the corridor to procure our midday foodstuffs." As translated: "Let's go down the hall for lunch."

Officialese is governed by four essential rules. First, use as many words as possible. Second, if a longer word (e.g., *utilize*) and a shorter word (e.g., *use*) are both available, choose the longer. Third, use circumlocutions whenever possible. Fourth, use cumbersome connectives when possible (e.g., *as to, with regard to, in connection with, in the event of*, etc.).

Among the linguistically unsophisticated, puffed-up language seems more impressive. Thus, police officers never *get out of their cars*; instead, they *exit their vehicles*. They never *smell* anything; rather, they *detect it by olfaction*. They *proceed* to a *residence* and *observe* the suspect *partaking of food*. Rather than *sending* papers to each other, officials *transmit* them (by hand-delivery, not by fax). And among lawyers, rather than *suing*, one *institutes legal proceedings against* or *brings an action against*. For sound guidance on how to avoid officialese, see Ernest Gowers, *The Complete Plain Words* (2d ed. 1973); J.R. Masterson & W.B. Phillips, *Federal Prose: How to Write in and/or for Washington* (1948). Cf. PLAIN LANGUAGE.

officious. In Samuel Johnson's day, *officious* had positive connotations ("eager to please"). Today, however, it means "meddlesome; interfering with what is not one's concern." E.g.: "Over the years, the most *officious* and obnoxious customs officials I encountered were those in India" (*Atlanta J. & Const.*). But in the context of diplomacy, the word has a strangely different sense: "having an extraneous relation to official matters or duties; having the character of a friendly communication, or informal action, on the part of a government or its official representatives" (*OED*) <an officious communication>.

But some mistakenly think it means "official-looking"—e.g.: "He still lived in the same old dormitory, but in a bigger and more *officious* room."

offing, in the. This is the correct, idiomatic phrase—not *on the offing*.

off of is much inferior to *off* without the preposition—e.g.: "It wasn't as though Porch was looking for a tall bridge to jump *off of* [read *off*] after last week's loss" (*Virginian-Pilot & Ledger Star*).

often. A. Pronunciation. The educated pronunciation is /**of**-ən/, but the less adept say /**of**-tən/. (See PRONUNCIATION (B).) Similar words with a silent *-t-* are *soften, fasten, listen*, and *whistle*.

B. And *oftentimes*; *oft*; *ofttimes*. These literary ARCHAISMS are NEEDLESS VARIANTS of *often*. Substituting *often* is almost always (not merely often) good—e.g.: "Smoke and smells from nearby concession stands *ofttimes* [read *often*] wafted over the courts" (*Wall St. J.*). About the only time *oft* is justified is when it's part of a PHRASAL ADJECTIVE <an oft-quoted passage>.

of which. See **whose.**

Oh. See **O.**

OK; O.K.; okay. Each of these is OK—but nowadays the first is the most OK of all.

olden. Apart from the SET PHRASE *olden times* and the CLICHÉ *olden days*, this adjective doesn't generally appear in good writing (except in that of Shakespeare and his contemporaries). Today, the word describes itself: it's a creaky ARCHAISM.

older; oldest. See **elder.**

on; upon. These synonyms are used in virtually the same ways. The distinctions are primarily in tone and connotation. *On*, the more usual word, is generally preferable: it's better to write *put the groceries on the counter* than *put the groceries upon the counter*. But *upon* is the better word for introducing a condition or event—e.g.: *Upon receiving the survey, fill it out completely*. See **upon.**

on behalf of. See **behalf.**

once. By convention, *once* isn't hyphenated either adverbially <a once powerful monarch> or adjectivally <the once and future king>. Cf. **then (A).**

one and one (is) (are). See SUBJECT–VERB AGREEMENT (G).

one and the same is occasionally misrendered *one in the same*.

one another. See **each other (B).**

one of the [+ pl. n.] who (*or* that). This construction requires a plural verb, not a singular one. After the *who* or *that*, the verb should be plural because *who* is the subject, and it takes its number from the plural noun to which *who* or *that* refers—e.g.: "It is one of the few writing texts that *is* [read *are*] worth reading." The reason for this construction becomes apparent when we reword the sentence: "Of the writing texts that *are* worth reading, it is one." But many writers wrongly think that *one* is the (singular) subject—e.g.: "Manos said Ohio is one of only 15 states that *lacks* [read *lack*] some form of merit selection for judges" (*Beacon J.*).

only is perhaps the most frequently misplaced of all English words. Its best placement is precisely before the words intended to be limited. The more words separating *only* from its correct position, the more awkward the sentence; and such a separation can lead to ambiguities. (Cf. **just & solely.**) E.g.:

- "[T]he prosecution was hindered from seeking a conviction on attempted manslaughter charges because Seles elected not to testify at the hearing and *only provided her medical records shortly before* [read *provided her medical records only shortly before*] the trial was to begin" (*USA Today*).
- "So far, the county proposes that PDA [planned-development agriculture] *only be allowed for about* [read *be allowed for only about*] 15 areas in the eastern county" (*Sarasota Herald-Trib.*).
- "In the U.S., boys *only seem to go for girl heroes when* [read *seem to go for girl heroes only when*] they are teamed up with male partners as in the Power Rangers" (*Variety*).

H.W. Fowler is surprisingly permissive on this point: "[T]here is an orthodox position for the adverb, easily determined in case of need; to choose another position that may spoil or obscure the meaning is bad; but a change of position that has no such effect except technically is both justified by historical & colloquial usage & often demanded by rhetorical needs" (*MEU1*). The problem with Fowler's view is that what for one person is merely "technically" obscure may for another person be a full-fledged ambiguity.

On *only* as an uncomparable adjective, see ADJECTIVES (B).

only if. See **if (B).**

opossum; possum. *Opossum* is standard. But *possum* appears predominantly (and correctly) in the phrase *play possum* (= to play dead or pretend to be asleep)—and only in that phrase.

The misspellings *opposum* and *oppossum* have arisen doubtless from the influence of *opposite*—e.g.: "The ratlike *opposum* [read *opossum*] is prevalent in the area" (*Boston Globe*).

oppress; repress. *Oppress*, which has connotations that are more negative, means "to subject (a person or a people) to inhumane or other unfair treatment; to persecute." *Repress* means either (1) "to keep under control" or (2) "to reduce (persons) to a subordinate position."

optimum. *Optimum* is the noun, but *optimal* is—optimally speaking—the better adjective. Hence, the phrase should be *optimal advantage*, not *optimum advantage*.

-OR; -ER. See -ER (A).

-OR; -OUR. Although all agent nouns except *saviour* (BrE) take *-or* in both AmE and BrE (e.g., *actor, investor*), the general distinction is that AmE nouns end in *-or*, BrE nouns in *-our*. That distinction occurs primarily in abstract nouns. Hence the British write *behaviour, colour, flavour*, and *humour*, whereas Americans write *behavior, color, flavor*, and *humor*. The following words, however, end in *-or* on both sides of the Atlantic: *error, horror, languor, liquor, pallor, squalor, stupor, terror, torpor*, and *tremor*. *Glamour* is the primary exception to the *-or* rule in AmE.

In BrE, nouns ending in *-our* change to *-or* before the suffixes *-ation, -iferous, -ific, -ize*, and *-ous* (e.g., *coloration, honorific*). But *-our* keeps the *-u-* before *-able, -er, -ful, -ism, -ist, -ite*, and *-less* (e.g., *honourable, labourer, colourful*).

oral. See **verbal.**

ordinal numbers. See **cardinal numbers** & NUMERALS (F).

Oregon /**or**-i-gən/ is frequently mispronounced /**or**-ə-gon/ or /**or**-ee-gon/.

orient; orientate. The latter is a NEEDLESS VARIANT of *orient*, which means "to get one's bearings or sense of direction." Sadly, the longer variant (a BACK-FORMATION from *orientation*) seems especially common in BrE: "Not everyone, even in *market-orientated* [read *market-oriented*] America, is wholly happy with what is happening" (*Sunday Times* [London]). Cf. **disorient.**

-OS. See PLURALS (C).

otherwise. A. And *other*. Pedants insist that *other* is the adjective, *otherwise* the adverb—and that it's wrong to use *otherwise* as an alternative to an adjective <no real impact, substantial or otherwise>. Wilson Follett believed that "[t]o pronounce this *otherwise* inadmissible would be to fly in the face of a strongly established usage. But usage, which can allow it on sufferance, cannot prevent it from being rejected by more exact writers" (*MAU*). In fact, though, this usage is so strongly established that—to most educated speakers—*other* would sound incorrect. E.g.: "Cowboys simply aren't cowboys—urban or *otherwise*—without a pair of boots between them and the ground" (*Dallas Morning News*).

Of course, *otherwise* often functions adverbially as well—e.g.: "Paul Sanchez . . . said his business has been booming, financially and *otherwise*" (*Albuquerque Trib.*).

B. As a Conjunction. This slipshod usage, which leads to RUN-ON SENTENCES, occurs primarily in BrE. *Otherwise* shouldn't connect two clauses in a compound sentence—e.g.: "The alliance needs to receive clearance from London, Washington and Brussels by November *otherwise* BA and American may not be able to launch joint services in time for next summer's timetable" (*Independent*). (Put a period or semicolon after *November* and a comma after *otherwise*.)

-OUR. See -OR.

ours. See POSSESSIVES (C).

out loud. See **aloud.**

outside of is inferior to *outside*—e.g.: "Italian goods have done well *outside of* [read *outside*] the Continent because the lira has fallen 15% vs. the U.S. dollar in the past year" (*BusinessWeek*). Cf. **off of.**

When *outside of* appears in the sense *apart from* or *aside from*, either of those phrases would be more serviceable—e.g.: "*Outside of* [read *Apart from* or *Aside from*] economies of scale in purchasing and merged back-room operations, Pillowtex reaps Fieldcrest's well-known brands in sheets, comforters, [and] towels" (*N.Y. Times*).

over. A. For *more than*. This is acceptable as a casualism—e.g.: "Reagan won the election by *over* a million votes" (*History Today*)./ "He breaks off . . . from reporting the injustices inflicted on Beethoven's Fifth Symphony (well *over* a hundred pages) to voice vigorous approval of Carlos Kleiber" (*N.Y. Times*). Cf. **above (A).**

B. *Over-* as a Combining Form. See **overly.**

overall is a VOGUE WORD, often a lame SENTENCE ADVERB. Many sentences would read better without it—e.g.: "*Overall, national brands* [read *National brands*] and designer-label jeans, which held 70% of the market in 1993, have seen their share slip to 65%" (*BusinessWeek*)./ "*Overall, Wada* [read *Wada*] says Toyota has doubled its engineering output over the past four years" (*Fortune*).

overdo; overdue. The first is the verb (= to do too much), the second the adjective (= past due, late). But the two are sometimes confounded—e.g.: "With 140 children, the program is an idea that was long *overdo* [read *overdue*]" (*Boston Globe*)./ " 'If you have blue eyes, bring them out. But when you do, don't *overdue* [read *overdo*] it with too much makeup or jewelry' " (*L.A. Times*).

overflow > overflowed > overflowed. Some writers mistakenly use *overflown* as the past participle of *overflow*—e.g.: "Though waste was found in a lagoon at the farm, some waste had *overflown* [read *overflowed*] at a lift station designed to pump it from four hog houses to the lagoon" (*Wilmington Morning Star*).

overlay; overlie. To *overlay* is to spread (something) on top of; to overspread <she intended to overlay the culture plates with bacteria>. To *overlie* is either to lie above <this dramatic change in funding overlies the whole debate about rural property and inequality> or to smother by lying on <when it stopped rolling, the meteorite would overlie some rare Japanese plants for more than a week>.

As with *lay* and *lie*, the most common error is to use *overlay* when the proper word is *overlie*. One signal of the misuse is putting the present participle *overlaying* at the beginning of the sentence—e.g.: "*Overlaying* [read *Overlying*] these hypernaturalistic scenes are evocations of the slain woman's spirit intoning nonsense rhymes in a high girlish voice" (*N.Y. Times*). See **lay.**

overlook; oversee; look over. The first is sometimes misused for the second. To *overlook* is to neglect or disregard. To *oversee* is to supervise or superintend. *Look over* is also differentiated from *overlook*; it means "to examine."

overly. Although it's old, dating from about the 12th century, *overly* is almost always unnecessary because *over-* may be prefixed at will: *overbroad*, *overrefined*, *overoptimistic*, *overripe*, etc. When it's not unnecessary, it's merely ugly. Some authorities consider *overly* semiliterate, although the editors of the Merriam-Webster dictionaries have used it in a number of definitions. Certainly this adverb should be avoided whenever possible, though admittedly *over-* as a prefix sometimes just doesn't sound right (*overburdensome*). Yet it usually serves well—e.g.: "To supporters, Duke's initiative was a worthy, if *overly ambitious* [read *overambitious*], effort" (*N.Y. Times*). When *over-* is awkward or ugly-sounding, another word is invariably at the ready—e.g.: "Hence the UN inspectors were not *overly* [read *especially*] skeptical when they started their work of scrutinizing Iraq's arsenal of weapons of mass destruction" (*Boston Globe*).

oversee. See **overlook.**

Overstatement. In polemical prose, such words as *clearly*, *patently*, *obviously*, and *indisputably* generally weaken rather than strengthen the statements they preface. They have been debased by overuse. Some critics have noted that a writer who begins a sentence with one of these words is likely to be leading up to something questionable. See **clearly.**

Unconscious overstatement is also a problem. It is never good to overstate one's case, even in minor, unconscious ways, for the writing will thereby lose credibility. Unless the purpose is to be humorous or satirical, good writers avoid exaggeration.

owing, adj.; **owed.** Although *owing* in the sense of *owed* is an old and established usage <$45 was owing on the bill>, the more logical course is simply to write *owed* where one means *owed*. The active participle may sometimes cause ambiguities or mislead the reader if only for a second—e.g.: "Taxpayers who owe taxes for 1996 still have to pay the balance *owing* [read *owed*] by April 30" (*Vancouver Sun*). See PASSIVE VOICE.

owing to (= because of) is an acceptable dangling modifier now primarily confined to BrE—e.g.: "Prolonged rain in the West Country has caused today's meeting at Newton Abbot to be abandoned *owing to* waterlogging" (*Independent*). Yet it does occur in AmE—e.g.: "There's a great deal of humor in the story, *owing to* the ironic distance that this method of telling lends to the tale" (*Indianapolis Star*). Cf. **due to.** See DANGLERS (E).

Oxymorons. This term, originally a Greek word meaning "keenly foolish" or "sharply dull," denotes an immediate contradiction in terminology. Thus:

amateur expert
exact estimate
found missing
intense apathy
mandatory choice
nonworking mother
organized mess
standard deviation
sure bet

Among language aficionados, collecting and inventing cynical oxymorons is a parlor game; they enjoy phrases that seem to imply contradictions, such as *military intelligence*, *legal brief*, and *greater Cleveland*.

Writers sometimes use oxymorons to good effect—e.g.: "And there was, moreover, an irresponsibly giddy antigovernment fervor among the more *sophomoric House freshmen*" (*Newsweek*). The main thing to avoid is the seemingly unconscious incongruity such as *increasingly less* or *advancing backwards*.

P

pair is the singular noun <one pair of shoes is missing>, *pairs* the plural <three pairs of shoes are in stock>. But many writers and speakers misuse *pair* as if it were plural—e.g.: "The ASU outburst matched a 9-year-old record set ironically enough by Miami when Greg Ellena and Rusty DeBold hit two apiece in a five-homer game against Stanford in 1985. In addition to Cruz's and Williamson's *pair* [read *pairs*], Todd Cady hit a solo shot—his 11th—for the team's first run" (*Austin American-Statesman*).

pajamas; pyjamas. The former is the AmE spelling, the latter BrE. The word is best pronounced /pə-**jah**-məz/, not /pə-**ja**-məz/.

pale, beyond the. This phrase, which means "bizarre, outside the bounds of civilized behavior," derives from the legal sense of *pale* from English history ("a district or territory within specific bounds, or subject to a particular jurisdiction"). In medieval Ireland, the district around Dublin, settled by the English and considered a law-abiding area, was known as the *Pale* or *within the Pale*. The land beyond that area was characterized as wild "bandit country." Today, whatever is *beyond the pale* is a forbidden area or subject.

Modern writers often mangle the phrase by writing *pail* instead of *pale*—e.g.: "To have a panel of citizens and the Commonwealth's Attorney . . . call for the board members' resignations with such harsh and demeaning language, however, is beyond the *pail* [read *pale*]" (*Virginian-Pilot & Ledger-Star*).

pamphlet. This word is pronounced with the *-ph-* as if it were an *-f-*: /**pam**-flət/. Many people incorrectly say /**pam**-plət/. See PRONUNCIATION (B), (D).

paparazzi (= photographers who follow celebrities, often aggressively, in hopes of snapping candid photos) is a plural; *paparazzo* is the singular. Originally Italian—invented for Federico Fellini's film *La Dolce Vita* (1960)—the term first surfaced in English in the mid-1960s. Unfortunately, because the singular form is so rare, some writers have begun using the misbegotten double plural *paparazzis*—e.g.: "The *paparazzis* [read *paparazzi*] even left the Clintons to find her [Princess Diana] on the Vineyard" (*Boston Herald*). On 31 August 1997, the day when Princess Diana died after a car crash while being chased by paparazzi, many television commentators used the incorrect form—no doubt spreading the mistake among the millions of listeners.

papier-mâché. So spelled—not *paper-mâché*. E.g.: "This morning, when the gates open at 8 a.m., the lifesized *paper-mache* [read *papier-mâché*] band will start to play with the flick of a switch in the Circus Museum" (*Albany Times Union*). Although American dictionaries spell the phrase with the DIACRITICAL MARKS, it's often spelled without the circumflex over the *-a-*.

Even so, the word is best pronounced /pay-pər-mə-**shay**/—not /pah-pyay-mə-**shay**/.

PARALLELISM—the matching of sentence parts for logical balance—helps satisfy every reader's innate craving for order and rhythm. By phrasing parallel ideas in parallel grammatical constructions, you show the reader how one idea relates to another. You supply correspondences. Stylists have long emphasized the importance of matching phrase to like phrase:

- "One of the first requisites for the writing of good clean sentences is to have acquired the art of enumeration, that is, of stringing together three or four words or phrases of identical grammatical value without going wrong" (H.W. Fowler, *MEU1*).

- "No long complex sentence will hold up without parallel construction. Paralleling can be very simple. Any word will seek its own kind, noun to noun, adjective to adjective, infinitive to infinitive" (Sheridan Baker, *The Practical Stylist*, 1998).
- "How do you make ideas parallel? In a series, all the items should be alike, whether all nouns, all gerunds, all infinitives, all phrases or all clauses. If a series of verbs is used, they should all be in the same tense, voice and mood. Subjects of parallel clauses should be in the same person and number. When two phrasal prepositions or conjunctions are used together, both need to be present in their entirety" (Brian S. Brooks & James L. Pinson, *Working with Words*, 1993).

With CORRELATIVE CONJUNCTIONS and with lists (even short ones), noun should be matched with noun, adjective with adjective, adverb with adverb, etc. Avoid a mixture—e.g.:

- "The poem is derivative, ceremonial, and *an elegy* [read *elegiacal*]" (D.S. Brewer, *Chaucer*, 1960). (Another possible revision: *The poem is derivative and ceremonial; it is an elegy.*)
- "John Baker is conservative and *a traditionalist*" (Murray Teigh Bloom, *The Trouble with Lawyers*, 1970). (A possible revision: *John Baker is conservative and traditional.* Or: *John Baker is a conservative and a traditionalist.*)
- "Webb, who batted .104 last season, had two doubles, three walks *and scored three times* [read *and three runs*]" (*Austin American-Statesman*).

parameters. Technical contexts aside, this jargonistic VOGUE WORD is not used by those with a heightened sensitivity to language. To begin with, only a specialist in mathematics or computing knows precisely what it means: it is a mush word. Second, when it does have a discernible meaning, it is usurping the place of a far simpler and more straightforward term. Although it abounds in AmE, it doesn't occur in the best writing—e.g.:

- "Similarly, his [Frank Zappa's] music broke down barriers even as it expanded *parameters*" (*Austin American-Statesman*). (How could it not expand "parameters" if it is breaking down barriers? A possible revision: delete *even as it expanded parameters.*)
- "In March, school board members set *parameters* [read *guidelines*] for the search, saying they would consider only those with superintendent experience and a doctorate" (*Charleston Post & Courier*).
- "At 14 months, babies already know a lot about the *parameters* [read *limits*] of their safe little world" (*N.Y. Times*).

Sometimes *perimeter*, the meaning of which has influenced the senses of *parameter*, is used ostensibly so that the writer can sidestep any criticisms for the use of *parameter*. Although this usage makes literal sense, a clearer expression is available—e.g.: "Some of the nation's foremost experts in medicine, law and politics will discuss the 25th Amendment to the U.S. Constitution, which *sets perimeters for* [read *establishes procedures in the event of*] presidential disability and [determines] when the president must transfer power to the vice president" (*Greensboro News & Record*). And in any event, *perimeter* is best left to physical senses <the fort's perimeter>.

paramount means "superior to all others" or "most important"—not merely "important." E.g.: "It is *extremely paramount* [read *extremely important* or *paramount*] that effective deployment of sworn deputies must begin with the distribution of these workers on a proportionate-need basis" (*St. Petersburg Times*). See **tantamount** & ADJECTIVES (B). Cf. **penultimate.**

pardon me. See **excuse me.**

Parentheses [( )]. These marks enclose words, phrases, and even whole sentences (but usually not more than a whole paragraph). If what is enclosed is a full sentence, the closing parenthesis follows the end punctuation; if not, the end punctuation is placed outside, as in the previous sentence here. More specifically, parentheses are used in four ways. First, they indicate interpolations and remarks by the writer of the text <Mrs. X (as I shall call her) now spoke>. Second, they specify, in one's own running text, an authority, definition, explanation, reference, or translation <according to Fowler (*MEU1*), it is correct to . . . >. Third, in reporting a speech, they sometimes indicate interruptions by the audience <"Finally—(laughter)—no, I'm really coming to an end now—(laughter)—let me say . . .">. Fourth, parentheses separate reference letters or figures that do not need a full stop, e.g., (1)(a).

The first of those uses comes into play most frequently. The main test for whether a parenthetical construction works is whether the rest of the sentence makes sense without it. That's because words contained within parentheses do not affect the syntax of the rest of the sentence. E.g.: "We must determine whether each (or both) children are entitled to tickets." The writer of that sentence could have avoided this error (*each children are*) by reading the sentence without the parenthetical phrase.

Virtually any punctuation mark is subject to an annoying overuse, but this is especially true of parentheses, which to be effective must be used sparingly. When they appear at all frequently, they tire the reader's eye, add to the burden of decoding, and deaden the reader's interest. Sentences can sag with all the qualifying parentheticals.

parenthesis /pə-**ren**-thə-sis/, the singular noun, forms the plural *parentheses* /pə-**ren**-thə-seez/. But because the plural is more common than the singular, some speakers use the mistaken BACK-FORMATION *parenthese* (wrongly pronounced /pə-**ren**-thə-see/). The error rarely occurs in writing.

parenting, a VOGUE WORD meaning "the raising of a child by its parents," is a fairly recent coinage: *W10* dates it from 1958. It began as JARGON used by psychologists, sociologists, and self-help practitioners, but spread into the general language during the 1980s. Its relative *grandparenting* is much rarer.

parimutuel, n., = a form of gambling in which those who have bet on winning numbers share in the total stakes, after deduction of a management fee. The word is sometimes misspelled *paramutual*, *paramutuel*, or *parimutual*.

part. See **portion.**

partake is construed with either *in* or *of* in the sense "to take part or share in some action or condition; to participate." *In* is the more common preposition in this sense—e.g.: "From 5 to 5:30 p.m., members will meet and *partake in* a wine and cheese reception" (*Tampa Trib.*).

Of is common when the sense is "to receive, get, or have a share or portion *of*"—e.g.: "So should one *partake of* Chinese cuisine, British history and Clint Eastwood?" (*Courier-J.*).

partially; partly. Whenever either word can suffice in a given context, *partly* is the better choice. *Partially* occasionally causes ambiguity because of its other sense "in a manner exhibiting favoritism."

party is a legalism that is unjustified when it merely replaces *person*. If used as an elliptical form of *party to the contract* or *party to the lawsuit*, *party* is quite acceptable as a term of art. E.g.: "Either *party* may enforce the terms of this contract, and in the event that either *party* must use attorneys to effect such enforcements, then such expenses and other fees may be charged against the other *party*." Fred Rodell's quip is worth remembering: "Only The Law insists on making a 'party' out of a single person" (*Woe Unto You, Lawyers!*, 1939).

The word has become something of a popularized technicality on restaurant waiting lists <the Butterworth party> —a usage so convenient and so commonplace now that any objection is bootless.

passable; passible. *Passable* = (1) capable of being passed, open; or (2) acceptable. *Passible* (a rare term) = feeling; susceptible to pain or suffering. The primary error is to misuse *passible* for *passable*, especially in sense 2—e.g.: "They get *passible* [read *passable*] fake identification like driver's licenses in the border states and then look for work" (*Harrisburg Patriot & Evening News*).

pass away. This phrase—sometimes shortened to *pass* <she passed last week>—is the most common EUPHEMISM for *die*.

passed is sometimes misused for *past*—e.g.: "He said that in addition to the organizers' decision to exclude the openly homosexual group from the parade, 'there have been other efforts as well to eliminate some of the other excesses associated with the parade, the drinking and rowdy behavior present in years *passed* [read *past*]' " (*N.Y. Times*).

passerby. Pl. *passersby*. See PLURALS (F).

passible. See **passable.**

PASSIVE VOICE. A. Generally. Many writers talk about passive voice without knowing exactly what it is. In fact, many think that any BE-VERB signals passive voice, as in:

> The quotation is applicable to this point.

But that sentence is actually in active voice—even though it's badly in need of editing. Most professional editors would change *is applicable* to *applies*, but they wouldn't call it "passive" because it's not. It's just a flabby *be*-verb.

The point about passive voice is that the subject of the clause doesn't perform the action of the verb. Instead, you back into the sentence:

> Passive: The deadline was missed by the applicant.

> Active: The applicant missed the deadline.

And, of course, in the passive form, it's possible to omit the actor altogether—a prime source of unclarity. Sometimes it amounts to responsibility-dodging:

> Passive: The deadline was missed.

As anyone who follows political discourse knows, the passive voice is a staple of politicians.

The unfailing test for passive voice is this: you must have a *be*-verb plus a past participle (usually a verb ending in *-ed*). Thus, constructions such as these are passive:

is	discussed
are	believed
was	sent
were	delivered
been	served
being	flattered
be	handled
am	given

Sometimes, though, the *be*-verb won't appear. It's simply an implied word in the context. For example:

> Recently I heard it suggested by a friend that too many books appear with endnotes.

Grammatically speaking, that sentence contains the implied verb *being* after the word *it*, so it's in the passive voice. To make it active, you'd write:

> Recently I heard a friend suggest that too many books appear with endnotes.

What's the real problem with using passive voice? There are three. First, passive voice usually adds a couple of unnecessary words. Second, whenever it doesn't add those unnecessary words, it fails to say squarely who has done what. That is, a *by*-phrase is necessary to show the actor (*The book was written* vs. *The book was written by Asimov*). Third, the passive subverts the normal word order for an English sentence, making it harder for readers to process the information.

The opposite of each of those liabilities appears as a gain in the active voice: it saves words, says directly who has done what, and meets the reader's expectation of an actor–verb–object order.

Sometimes, of course, you'll be justified in using the passive voice. There's no absolute prohibition against it—and anyone who tries carrying out such a prohibition would spoil a piece of writing. Among the times when you'll want the passive in a given sentence are these:

- When the actor is unimportant.
- When the actor is unknown.
- When you need to put the punch word at the end of the sentence.
- When you want to hide the actor's identity.
- When the focus of the passage is on the thing being acted upon.
- When the passive simply sounds better.

Still, professional editors find that these six situations don't account for more than about 15% to 20% of the contexts in which the passive appears.

That means you ought to have a presumption against the passive, unless it falls into one of the categories just listed.

B. The Double Passive. The problem here is using one passive immediately after another. E.g.: "This document refers to the portion of the votes *entitled to be cast* by virtue of membership in the union." (Votes are not *entitled to be cast*; rather, persons are *entitled to cast* votes.)/ "Had the new vaccine *been intended to have been injected* into the patient, he would have been warned to avoid drinking alcohol." (A possible revision: *If the new vaccine had been intended for injection into the patient . . . .*)

The problem is common with the verb *seek* (and sometimes *attempt*), especially in legal contexts—e.g.: "[T]here is no evidence that any improper influence *was sought to be exercised* by me or anybody else over any official decision" (President Bill Clinton as quoted in the *N.Y. Times*). (A possible revision: *There is no evidence that I or anybody else tried to influence any official decision.*) Fowler wrote that "monstrosities of this kind . . . are as repulsive to the grammarian as to the stylist" (*MEU1* at 121).

A few double passives are defensible—e.g.: "Offerings made in compliance with Regulation D *are not required to be registered* with the SEC under the Securities Act." As Ernest Gowers noted, "In legal or quasi-legal language this construction may sometimes be useful and unexceptionable: *Diplomatic privilege applies only to such things as are done or omitted to be done in the course of a person's official duties. / Motion made: that the words proposed to be left out stand part of the Question*" (*MEU2* at 139). But these are of a different kind from *are sought to be included* and *are attempted to be refuted*, which can be easily remedied by recasting. The principle is that if the first passive-voice construction can be made active—leaving the passive infinitive intact—the sentence is correctly formed. Here, for example, a recasting of the first passive verb form into the active voice clarifies the sense:

> Passive/Passive: The prisoners were ordered to be shot.
> Active/Passive: He ordered the prisoners to be shot.

But in the following example, a recasting of the first passive verb into the active voice does not make sense:

> Passive/Passive: The contention has been attempted to be made.
> Active/Passive: He attempted the contention to be made.

The last-quoted sentence is un-English. Sense can be restored to it by casting both parts in the active voice:

> Active/Active: He attempted to make the contention.

A final caution, from William Zinsser: "The difference between an active-verb style and a passive-verb style—in clarity and vigor—is the difference between life and death for a writer" (*On Writing Well*, 1994).

past. This word occurs in many redundant phrases, such as *past history*, *past track record*, and *past experience*. All of these are REDUNDANCIES because the noun denotes something that by its very nature is rooted in the past.

pastime is sometimes misspelled *past-time*. The misspelling derives from a misunderstanding of the word's origin: *pastime* derives from *pass* (v.t.) + *time*, not *past* + *time*.

patent, n., v.t. & adj. In the adjectival sense of "obvious, apparent," the preferred pronunciation is /**payt**-ənt/. In all other senses and uses, the pronunciation is /**pat**-ənt/.

pathos. See **bathos.**

pay. A. Inflected Forms: *pay* > *paid* > *paid*. *Payed* is a startlingly frequent error for *paid*—e.g.: "He got charged with harassment after a supermarket fistfight, a violation, and *payed* [read *paid*] a $250 fine" (*N.Y. Newsday*).

B. And *pay up*. The PHRASAL VERB *pay up* means "to discharge (a debt) completely." *Pay* may refer to partial or total payments. Thus, because of this slight DIFFERENTIATION, *up* is not a needless particle. See PHRASAL VERBS.

peaceable; peaceful. Generally, *peaceful* refers to a state of affairs; *peaceable* refers to the disposition of a person or a nation. The two words overlap some, but a strict DIFFERENTIATION is worth encouraging.

pejorative is so spelled, though often mistakenly spelled *perjorative*—e.g.: "By 'radical' I mean not the commonly used political *perjorative* [read *pejorative*] but the original definition" (*N.Y. Times*). Though once pronounced /**pee**-jər-ə-tiv/, the preferred pronunciation today is /pə-**jor**-ə-tiv/.

penultimate (= next-to-last) is sometimes misused for *ultimate*: "The classic surfer movie, 'The Endless Summer,' caught a new wave this week in Superior Court here. . . . In the complaint, *Hynson v. Brown*, 694180, Hynson claims that August was set up with a new car, a tavern and, eventually, a surfboard business by Brown, with proceeds from the *penultimate* surfer movie" (*L.A. Daily J.*). Could any movie be dubbed the next-to-last surfing movie of all time? Cf. **paramount & tantamount.**

people; persons. The traditional distinction—now a pedantic one—is that *people* is general, *persons* specific. Thus, one would refer to *300 people who had assembled* but to *the twelve persons on the jury*. *Persons* has been considered better for small, specific numbers. But *twelve persons on the jury* seems stuffy to many readers, and most native speakers of AmE would say *twelve people on the jury*. In contexts like that one, *people* has long been used and is surely the more natural phrasing.

PER- as a prefix typically means "through," as in *perspire* (= to emit sweat through the pores) and *pervade* (= to spread throughout). But in certain ARCHAISMS—such as *perchance*, *perfervid*, and *perforce*—it's an intensive.

per. See **a (B) & as per.**

percent; per-cent; per cent; per cent.; per centum. This sequence illustrates in reverse the evolution of this word, originally a phrase. Today it is best spelled as a single word. The plural of *percent* is *percent*; adding an *-s*, though not uncommon, is substandard.

In most writing, *75%* is easier to read than *75 percent* or (worse yet) *seventy-five percent*.

percentage. Even though this word is technically a singular, it's usually construed with a plural verb when followed by *of* plus a plural noun (or when the *of*-phrase is implied)—e.g.: "Women often have little say about finances at home or at work, while a greater *percentage* than ever before *are* the sole breadwinners" (*Christian Science Monitor*).

But when the sentence is inverted, and the verb precedes the noun, a singular verb is required. That is, even though you say *a higher percentage of them are*, you also say *there is a higher percentage of them*. E.g.: "No statistics exist to prove or disprove the widespread perception that there *are* [read *is*] a higher percentage of lesbians than gay men in the military" (*Newsweek*).

PERIOD [.]. This punctuation mark is used for two purposes. First, it ends all sentences that are not questions or exclamations. The next word normally begins with a capital letter. Second, it has traditionally indicated abbreviations, but this use is on the decline. See ABBREVIATIONS (A).

If a point marking an abbreviation comes at the end of a sentence, it also serves as the closing full stop. E.g.: "She also kept dogs, cats, birds, etc." But where a closing parenthesis or bracket intervenes, a period is required: "She also kept pets (dogs, cats, birds, etc.)." When a sentence concludes with a quotation that ends with a period, question mark, or exclamation mark, no further period is needed. E.g.: "He cried, 'Be off!' [no period] But the child would not move."

periodic; periodical. These two have undergone DIFFERENTIATION. *Periodic*, the more general word, means "occurring at regular intervals" <periodic reviews of employee performance>. (The word also has specialized meanings in mathematical and scientific contexts.) *Periodical* is now usually restricted to mean "published at regular intervals" <periodical newsletters>. And, of course, *periodical* is used as a noun meaning "a publication issued at regular intervals" <the doctor's office subscribed to a dozen or more periodicals>.

period of, for a. This phrase is usually verbose—e.g.: "If your grandchildren or great-grandchildren lived with you *for a period of a year or more* [read *for a year or more*], section (d) of this bill would ensure that they would always be able to visit with the grandparent that kept them" (*Ark. Democrat-Gaz.*).

period of time is usually unnecessary in place of either *period* or *time*.

permission; acquiescence. *Permission* connotes an authorization to do something, whereas *acquiescence* connotes the passive failure to object to someone's doing something.

permit. See **allow.**

pernickety. See **persnickety.**

perpetuate (= to make last indefinitely; prolong) and *perpetrate* (= to commit or carry out) are surprisingly often confounded. Although *WDEU* says that "actual examples of mistaken use are in extremely short supply," the following list could easily be multiplied:

- "In 1988, Federal District Judge James L. Kinf dismissed the suit as baseless, accused Mr. Shean of knowingly *perpetuating* [read *perpetrating*] a fraud and fined the Christie Institute" (*N.Y. Times*).
- "[T]hey assemble to pray for an end to the violence *perpetuated* [read *perpetrated*] on an innocent member of the human race" (*Sacramento Bee*).
- "Of course, a good detective may have a clear idea of who has *perpetuated* [read *perpetrated*] the crime" (*BusinessWorld*).

See MALAPROPISMS.

perquisite; prerequisite. *Perquisite* (often shortened to *perk*) = a privilege or benefit given in addition to one's salary or regular wages <executive perquisites such as club memberships>. *Prerequisite* = a previous condition or requirement <applicants must satisfy all five prerequisites before being interviewed>. Although *WDEU* says there is "almost no evidence of the words' being interchanged," the confusion certainly does occur—e.g.: "Have executive salaries, bonuses and other corporate *prerequisites* [read *perquisites*] been cut, or will the proposed rate increase maintain them?" (*Wash. Post*).

persecute. See **prosecute.**

persevere is pronounced /pər-sə-**veer**/. Because the word is frequently a victim of the intrusive *-r-* (/pər-sər-**veer**/), it is often misspelled *perservere*. The corresponding noun, *perseverance*, has been similarly victimized. See PRONUNCIATION (B), (C) & SPELLING (A).

persnickety; pernickety. Although the latter is the older form, *persnickety* is now about five times more common than *pernickety* in AmE.

-PERSON. See SEXISM (C).

persons. See **people.**

persuade; convince. In the best usage, one *persuades* another *to do* something but *convinces* another *of* something. Avoid *convince to*—the phrasing *she convinced him to resign* is traditionally viewed as less good than *she persuaded him to resign*.

Either *convince* or *persuade* may be used with a *that*-clause. Although *persuade that* occurs mostly in legal contexts, it does appear elsewhere—e.g.: "But at the same time he's *persuaded that* he has to take advantage of the message of tolerance that is part of Muhammad's legacy" (*San Diego Union-Trib.*)./ "The merger has received preliminary approval from the UC Board of Regents, which was *persuaded that* the agreement would avert financial problems at UCSF" (*S.F. Examiner*).

peruse (= to read with great care) is pompous and stilted in business correspondence. That is, the word shouldn't be used merely as a fancy substitute for *read*. It is pronounced /pə-**rooz**/; the corresponding noun is *perusal* /pə-**rooz**-əl/.

Some writers misuse the word as if it meant "to read quickly" or "scan"—e.g.: "Combs takes off his round sunglasses, quickly *peruses* [read *glances through*] the stack of documents, asks a few questions and then signs several, but requests changes in others" (*L.A. Times*).

-PH-. See PRONUNCIATION (D).

phase. See **faze.**

Ph.D. (L. *Philosophiae Doctor* "Doctor of Philosophy") requires the lowercase *-h-* and both periods.

phenomenon. Pl. *phenomena*. (See PLURALS (B).) Several errors occur. First, and perhaps most commonly, the plural form is increasingly misused as a singular—e.g.: "No social *phenomena* [read *phenomenon*] highlights the change better than the explosive growth of religious cults" (*Chicago Trib.*). Second, more strangely, the term *phenomenon* is sometimes mistakenly used as a plural—e.g.: "[T]hese irregularities could explain several *phenomenon* [read *phenomena*] in the earth including the well-known jerkiness in the planet's rotational rate" (*N.Y. Times*). Third, even though *phenomena* is the accepted plural, some people erroneously write *phenomenons*—e.g.: "The seven-day week, alone among the components of the calendar, has always been thought to be a product of divine instruction or social convention, not set by natural *phenomenons* [read *phenomena*] as the day, month and year are" (*Kansas City Star*). Finally, the word is surprisingly often misspelled *phenomenum*—e.g.: "But to those trying to get a grip on the Hingis *phenomenum* [read *phenomenon*], it didn't matter" (*Ft. Lauderdale Sun-Sentinel*).

PHRASAL ADJECTIVES. A. General Rule. When a phrase functions as an adjective—an increasingly frequent phenomenon in late-20th-century English—the phrase should ordinarily be hyphenated. Most professional writers know this; most nonprofessionals don't.

The primary reason for the hyphens is that they prevent MISCUES and make reading easier and faster. Following are some examples culled from *The Wall Street Journal* and *The New York Times*:

advance-free loan
bikini-clad blondes
birds-and-bees metaphor
blue-jeans-and-T-shirt crowd
credit-card applications
draft-choice compensation
flat-panel computer screens
general-election attack
get-out-the-vote activities
modern-dance festival
much-talked-about strategies
open-air market
stronger-than-expected second-quarter profit
take-it-or-leave-it shot
weaker-than-usual results
year-to-year rise

In any single issue of either paper, you will find many more phrasal adjectives than these.

Upon encountering a phrasal adjective, the reader isn't misled into thinking momentarily that the modifying phrase is really a noun itself. It matters a great deal, for example, where you put hyphens in *last known criminal activity report*.

Some guides might suggest that you should make a case-by-case decision, based on whether a misreading is likely. You're better off with a flat rule (with a few exceptions noted below) because almost all sentences with unhyphenated phrasal adjectives will be misread by *someone*. (See HYPHEN.) The following examples demonstrate the hesitation caused by a missing hyphen: "One last pop on this whole question of incivility of discourse, the *much argued over* [read *much-argued-over*] issue of whose speech has been more inflammatory and socially destructive than whose" (*Newsweek*).

Readability is especially enhanced when the hyphens are properly used in two phrasal adjectives that modify a single noun—e.g.:

county-approved billboard-siting restriction
long-latency occupational-disease cases
13-year-old court-ordered busing plan
24-hour-a-day doctor-supervised care

Some writers—those who haven't cultivated an empathy for their readers—would omit all those hyphens.

B. Exception for *-ly* Adverbs. When a phrasal adjective begins with an adverb ending in *-ly*, the convention is to drop the hyphen—e.g.: "With the *hotly-contested* [read *hotly contested*] Second Congressional District primary six days away, supporters of Sen. Bob Smith gathered last night just as curious about a race two years away and a candidate who hasn't said yet whether he's running" (*Concord Monitor*). But if the *-ly* adverb is part of a longer phrase, then the hyphen is mandatory (*the not-so-hotly-contested race*).

C. Suspension Hyphens. When two phrasal adjectives have a common element at the end, and this ending portion (usually the last word) appears only with the second phrase, insert a suspension hyphen after the unattached words to show their relationship with the common element. The hyphens become especially important when phrases are compounded in this way—e.g.: "Detroit is . . . positioning the new class of compacts as the centerpiece of an old-fashioned, '50s- and '60s-style all-out autumn advertising blitz" (*Time*). Here the hyphens are omitted, to the reader's puzzlement: "They lived in the small city of Apopka, Florida, located *in the fern and foliage growing region* [read *in the fern- and foliage-growing region*] north of Orlando."

D. Duration or Amount. When phrasal adjectives denote durations or amounts, plurals should be dropped—e.g.: "The report doesn't disclose whether Annie Bell was born after a normal *nine months pregnancy* [read *nine-month pregnancy*]." Likewise, one should write *14-hour-a-day schedule, three-week hiatus, 2,000-bottle wine cellar,* and *25,000-volume library*. The exception is with fractions, in which the plural is retained <a two-thirds vote>.

PHRASAL VERBS are verbs that comprise more than one word, often a verb and a preposition (acting as an adverbial particle). Thus politicians *put up with* the press, and vice versa; striking workers *hold out* for more benefits; arguing family members *work out* their problems; campers must *make do* with the supplies they have; legacies are *handed down* from one generation to the next; gardeners work to *get rid of* weeds; overworked employees, like candles left too long, *burn out;* boxers are *knocked out*—and unwed mothers *knocked up*.

Rhetoricians have taken two positions on these verbs. On the one hand, some recommend using them whenever they're natural-sounding because they lend a relaxed, confident tone—hence *get rid of* instead of the Latin-derived *eliminate, phase out* instead of *gradually discontinue*. On the other hand, because phrasal verbs often add to the number of words (though not syllables) in a phrase, some rhetoricians prefer avoiding them—hence *handle* instead of *deal with, resolve* instead of *work out*. In the end, this tension isn't resolvable (or can't be worked out) as a matter of general principle: one's judgment will depend on the context.

Three caveats are in order with phrasal verbs.

First, when using one, be certain to include the entire phrase and not just the primary verb. Don't say that two things *cancel each other* if what they're really doing is *canceling out each other* (or *canceling each other out*). And don't say that you're *drawing the resources* if you're *drawing on the resources*.

Second, don't use a phrasal verb if the adverbial particle is simply baggage that doesn't add to meaning. Thus, don't say *meet up with* if *meet* suffices. Don't say *divide up* if *divide* suffices. The same is true of others such as *calculate out* (*calculate*); *continue on* (*continue*); *liven up* (*liven*); and *separate out* (*separate*). E.g.: "Competition in high schools . . . has not *slackened off* [read *slackened*]" (Roger Buckley, *Japan Today*, 1990). It is true, though, that DIFFERENTIATION has occurred with several phrases, such as *die off* (*die*), *face up to* (*face*), and *lose out* (*lose*). With these phrases, the particles add a nuance to the verb.

Third, although the corresponding nouns are often solid (*breakdown, lockout, phaseout, shutout, workout*), the verb forms should remain two words. Some writers, especially in BrE, tend to use hyphens that don't belong in the verbs—e.g.: "But Mr. Bush's speech suggests that the administration has overcome its initial doubts and is determined to *lock-in* [read *lock in*] still further nuclear weapons reductions" (*Fin. Times*).

physician-assisted suicide. See **euthanasia (B).**

pianist is pronounced either /pee-**an**-ist/ or /**pee**-ə-nist/. The first is the unpretentious AmE pronunciation; the second is an older BrE one.

pique, vb., = (1) to irritate; or (2) to excite or arouse. The most common phrase in sense 2 is *pique one's interest*—e.g.: "He views the Internet primarily as a way to *pique* the interest of potential customers and to familiarize them with his gallery" (*Houston Chron.*). But some writers erroneously make the phrase *peak one's interest*—

e.g.: "What really *peaked* [read *piqued*] Jones's interest was McVeigh's attempted phone call to Strassmeir" (*Village Voice*).

pitiable; pitiful; piteous; pitiless. *Pitiable* = calling for or arousing pity <their pitiable living conditions were shown internationally>. *Pitiful*, strictly, means "feeling pity," but in modern speech and writing it is almost always used in the sense "contemptible" <a pitiful attempt>. The word *piteous* is archaic and poetic—not a word for ordinary uses. *Pitiless* = showing no pity <pitiless determination to increase profits>.

plagiarize is often misspelled *plagarize* or *plagerize*. E.g.: "The article accused the author of leaning heavily—far too heavily—on editorial assistance, even *plagarizing* [read *plagiarizing*] the idea for his acclaimed novel, 'Being There' " (*Seattle Times*).

PLAIN LANGUAGE. Albert Einstein once said that his goal in stating an idea was to make it as simple as possible but no simpler. He also said: "Most of the fundamental ideas of science are essentially simple, and may, as a rule, be expressed in a language comprehensible to everyone" (*The Evolution of Physics*, 1938). If that's true of science, surely it's true of most subjects.

But there is little reason for hope when so many writers seem to believe that to appear competent or smart, they must state their ideas in the most complex manner possible. Of course, this problem plagues many fields of intellectual endeavor, as the philosopher Bertrand Russell noted:

> I am allowed to use plain English because everybody knows that I could use mathematical logic if I chose. Take the statement: "Some people marry their deceased wives' sisters." I can express this in language [that] only becomes intelligible after years of study, and this gives me freedom. I suggest to young professors that their first work should be written in a jargon only to be understood by the erudite few. With that behind them, they can ever after say what they have to say in a language "understanded of the people." In these days, when our very lives are at the mercy of the professors, I cannot but think that they would deserve our gratitude if they adopted my advice.
>
> Bertrand Russell, "How I Write," in *The Basic Writings of Bertrand Russell* 63, 65 (Robert E. Egner & Lester E. Denonn eds., 1961).

But the professors have not heeded Russell's advice. Since he wrote that essay in the mid-1950s, things have gotten much worse in fields such as biology, economics, law, linguistics, literary criticism, political science, psychology, and sociology.

Consider the following passage from a tax statute, a 260-word tangle that is as difficult to fathom as any mathematical theorem:

> 57AF(11) Where, but for this sub-section, this section would, by virtue of the preceding provisions of this section, have in relation to a relevant year of income as if, for the reference in sub-section (3) to $18,000, there were substituted a reference to another amount, being an amount that consists of a number of whole dollars and a number of cents (in this sub-section referred to as the "relevant number of cents")—
>
> (a) in the case where the relevant number of cents is less than 50—the other amount shall be reduced by the relevant number of cents;
>
> (b) in any other case—the other amount shall be increased by the amount by which the relevant number of cents is less than $1.
>
> (12) Where, but for sub-section (5), this section would, by virtue of the preceding provisions of this section, have effect in relation to a relevant year of income as if, for the reference in sub-section (3) to $18,000, there were substituted a reference to another amount, being an amount that consists of a number of whole dollars and a number of cents (in this sub-section referred to as the "relevant number of cents") then, for the purposes of the application of paragraph 4(b)—
>
> (a) in a case where the relevant number of cents is less than 50—the other amount

> shall be reduced by the relevant number of cents; or
>
> (b) in any other case—the other amount shall be increased by the amount by which the relevant number of cents is less than $1.
>
> Income Tax Assessment Act [Australia] § 57AF(11), (12) (as quoted in David St. L. Kelly, "Plain English in Legislation," in *Essays on Legislative Drafting* 57, 58 [David St. L. Kelly ed., 1988]).

That is the type of prose that prompts an oft-repeated criticism: "So unintelligible is the phraseology of some statutes that suggestions have been made that draftsmen, like the Delphic Oracle, sometimes aim deliberately at obscurity" (Carleton K. Allen, *Law in the Making*, 1964).

With some hard work, the all-but-inscrutable passage above can be transformed into a straightforward version of only 65 words:

> If either of the following amounts is not in round dollars, the amount must be rounded off to the nearest dollar (or rounded up to the next whole dollar if the amount is 50 cents or more):
>
> (a) the amount of the motor-vehicle-depreciation limit; or
>
> (b) the amount that would have been the motor-vehicle-depreciation limit if the amount had equaled or exceeded $18,000.
>
> Revision based on that of Gavin Peck (quoted in Kelly at 59).

Few would doubt that the original statute is unplain and that the revision is comparatively plain. True, to comprehend the revision the reader must know what a "motor-vehicle-depreciation limit" is, but some things can be stated only so simply.

But shouldn't learned professionals be allowed complex verbiage? That is, shouldn't they express themselves in more sophisticated ways than nonprofessionals do?

These questions need serious answers because they present the most serious impediment to the plain-language movement. There are essentially four answers.

First, those who write in a difficult, laborious style risk being unclear not only to other readers but also to themselves. When you write obscurely, you're less likely to be thinking clearly. And you're less likely to appreciate the problems that are buried under such convoluted prose.

Second, obscure writing wastes readers' time—a great deal of it, when the sum is totaled. An Australian study conducted in the 1980s found that lawyers and judges take twice as long deciphering legalistically worded statutes as they do plain-language revisions. See Law Reform Commission of Victoria, *Plain English & the Law* 61–62 (1987).

Third, simplifying is a higher intellectual attainment than complexifying. Writing simply and directly is hard work, and professionals ought to set this challenge for themselves. In fact, the hallmark of all the greatest stylists is precisely that they have taken difficult ideas and expressed them as simply as possible. No nonprofessional could do it, and most specialists can't do it. Only extraordinary minds are capable of the task. Still, every writer—brilliant or not—can aim at the mark.

Fourth, the very idea of professionalism demands that writers not conspire against nonspecialists by adopting a style that makes their writing seem like a suffocating fog. We should continually ask ourselves how the culture stacks up when we consider the durable truth expressed by Richard Grant White: "As a general rule, the higher the culture, the simpler the style and the plainer the speech" (*Words and Their Uses*, 1870).

playwrighting; playwriting. The second, a corrupt form of the first, is lamentably common—e.g.: "He leaps from the university classroom into *playwriting* [read *playwrighting*] and acting, much as Alan Helms leapt into bed, with little evident thought" (*Nation*). See SPELLING (A).

pleaded; pled. Traditionally speaking, *pleaded* is the best past-tense and past-participial form. Commentators on usage have long said so. And in any event, *pleaded* is the predominant form in both AmE and BrE—e.g.: "Only Nadia knew of his plans, and she *pleaded* with him not to leave her" (*Dallas Morning News*).

please find enclosed. See **enclosed please find.**

please RSVP. See **RSVP.**

pled. See **pleaded.**

plenitude. So spelled. The word is derived from the Latin *plenus* "full"—the source also of *plenary*. Unfortunately, through confusion with the word *plenty*, the misspelling *plentitude* has become common—e.g.: "Moore coaxes out colors and pictorial incidents from his canvases, creating a *plentitude* [read *plenitude*] of sensation" (*Boston Herald*).

Of course, the phrase *a plenitude of* can very often be shortened to a simple *much* or *many*.

plentiful; plenteous. No distinction in meaning being possible, writers should prefer the prevalent modern form, *plentiful. Plenteous* is archaic and poetic.

plow, n. & vb., is the standard spelling in AmE. *Plough* is the BrE form.

plumb, adj., means "perfectly straight, vertical," and by extension—as a colloquialism—"entirely, wholly" <I'm plumb tired>. But some writers confuse the spelling by associating it somehow with fruit—e.g.: "Shelley, a 13-week-old springer spaniel, looks *plum-tired* [read *plumb tired*] during an obedience class at Temple Terrace Recreation Center on Tuesday night" (*St. Petersburg Times*).

PLURAL POSSESSIVES. See POSSESSIVES (B).

PLURALS. A. Generally. Most nouns form their plurals simply by adding *-s*—thus *books, songs, xylophones*. But if a word ends with the sound of *-s-*, *-sh-*, *-ch-*, or *-z-*, the plural is formed by adding *-es*—thus *buses, thrushes, churches,* and *buzzes*. Occasionally, a single final consonant is doubled—thus *fez* makes *fezzes*.

Several exceptions exist in words derived from Old English: *child–children, ox–oxen, man–men, woman–women, mouse–mice, louse–lice, foot–feet, goose–geese, tooth–teeth*.

B. Borrowed Words. References to this subentry appear throughout this book. That's not to say that each such term is elaborated on here but only that the principles governing the words are explained here.

Words imported into the English language from other languages—especially Greek, Latin, French, and Italian—present some of the most troublesome aspects of English plurals. Many imported words become thoroughly naturalized; if so, they take an English plural. But if a word of Latin or Greek origin is relatively rare in English—or if the foreign plural became established in English long ago—then it typically makes its foreign plural.

One reliable guide is this: if in doubt, use the native-English plural ending in *-s*. That way, you'll avoid the mistakes involved in HYPERCORRECTION, which is rampant with foreign plurals (as when people say or write *ignorami* instead of *ignoramuses*, thereby betraying something quite ironic). H.W. Fowler called the benighted stab at correctness "out of the frying-pan into the fire" (*MEU1*). Many writers who try to be sophisticated in their use of language make mistakes such as *ignorami* and *octopi*—unaware that neither is a Latin noun that, when inflected as a plural, becomes *-i*. The proper plural of the Greek word *octopus* is *octopodes*; the proper English plural is *octopuses*.

Thus, as a general matter, if it's a close call, use the native plural. In music, it's better to say *allegros* than *allegri*; *concertos* than *concerti*; *contraltos* than *contralti*; *solos* than *soli*; *sopranos* than *soprani*; and *virtuosos* than *virtuosi*. In publishing, it's better to say *appendixes* than *appendices*; *compendiums* than *compendia*; *Festchrifts* than *Festchriften* (from German); and *thesauruses* than *thesauri*. It's pedantic and prissy to say that politicians enter *auditoria*, ascend the *rostra*, and speak in favor of *referenda*.

But exceptions certainly exist. Literate people say *crises*, not *crisises*; *criteria*, not *criterions*; *hypotheses*, not *hypothesises*; and *phenomena*, not *phenomenons*. Medical and biological researchers say *bacilli*, not *bacilluses*; *fungi*, not *funguses*; *ova*, not *ovums*; *stimuli*, not *stimuluses*; and *thalami*, not *thalamuses*. Few other people ever use those words.

Some are very close calls. *Cactuses* predominates in common usage, but *cacti* is the more frequent form in botanical contexts. *Formulas* is generally better than *formulae* (and *spectrums* than *spectra*), but not in scientific contexts. There is significant movement toward *honorariums*, but *honoraria* still predominates; the same is true of *penumbras* and *penumbrae*. *Millenniums* and *millennia* are neck-and-neck, the former predominating in BrE and the latter in AmE.

And some variant forms have started undergoing DIFFERENTIATION. *Phalanxes* is the plural referring to groups of people; *phalanges* is the term for bones in the fingers and toes. *Protozoans* is the term for a few microorganisms that go by that name, but *protozoa* is typically used for large numbers. *Staff* generally makes *staffs*, but the musical staff is pluralized *staves*. *Stigmas* is better than *stigmata* except in religious contexts <the stigmata of Christ>.

French words also present problems. *Bête noire* makes *bêtes noires*; *chargé d'affaires* makes *chargés d'affaires*; *fait accompli* makes *faits accomplis*; *force majeure* makes *forces majeures*; *nouveau riche* makes *nouveaux riches*. But the trend is to anglicize French plurals. Thus, *bon mots* is now much more common than *bons mots*. Likewise, the phrases in the left column outnumber those in the right:

bon vivants	bons vivants
chaise longues	chaises longues
cul-de-sacs	culs-de-sac
filet mignons	filets mignons

C. Nouns Ending in *-o*. No consistent rules are possible for plurals of words ending in *-o*. But some weak guidelines might be ventured. First, words used as often in the plural as in the singular usually have *-oes* (*embargoes*, *heroes*, *noes*, *potatoes*, *vetoes*). A majority of American dictionaries agree on the following plurals ending in *-oes*:

buffalo	buffaloes
cargo	cargoes
desperado	desperadoes
domino	dominoes
echo	echoes
fiasco	fiascoes
grotto	grottoes
mango	mangoes
manifesto	manifestoes
mosquito	mosquitoes
motto	mottoes
peccadillo	peccadilloes
stucco	stuccoes
tomato	tomatoes
tornado	tornadoes
torpedo	torpedoes
volcano	volcanoes

Some are close calls. For example, American dictionaries tend to list *peccadilloes* before *peccadillos*, but is that term any more naturalized than *banjo* (which forms *banjos*)?

Second, alien-looking words (e.g., *imbroglio*), proper names (e.g., *the Florios*—that is, the Florio family), words that are seldom used as plurals (e.g., *bravados*), words in which *-o* is preceded by a vowel (e.g., *portfolios*), and shortened words (e.g., *photo*) typically don't take the *-e-*. Among the many words that don't have an *-e-* are these: *albinos*, *avocados*, *cameos*, *curios*, *gazebos*, *innuendos*, *mementos*, *piccolos*, and *tuxedos*.

Good dictionaries contain the preferred spellings. If it's possible to cite a trend, the plurals with *-e-* seem very slightly on the decline. But it's a slow, weak trend.

D. Nouns Ending in *-y*. If a word ending in *-y* is preceded by a vowel, the plural is formed by adding an *-s*—e.g.:

alloy, alloys
asprey, aspreys
chimney, chimneys
donkey, donkeys
journey, journeys
money, moneys
monkey, monkeys

But if a word ending in *-y* isn't preceded by a vowel, the plural is formed by omitting the *-y* and substituting *-ies*—e.g.:

bankruptcy, bankruptcies
gully, gullies
mercy, mercies
opportunity, opportunities
pony, ponies
story, stories
sty, sties
supply, supplies

There are two exceptions in the second category. First are proper names: *Busby* becomes *Busbys*, *Kingsly* becomes *Kingslys*, and so on. (See (E).) Second are words ending in *-quy*: *colloquy* becomes *colloquies*, and *obloquy* becomes *obloquies*.

E. Proper Names. Although few books on grammar mention the point, proper names often cause problems as plurals. The rule is simple: most take a simple *-s*, while those ending in *-s*, *-x*, or *-z*, or in a sibilant *-ch* or *-sh*, take *-es*. Thus:

Singular Form	*Plural Form*
Adam	Adams
Adams	Adamses
Bush	Bushes
Church	Churches
Cox	Coxes
Flowers	Flowerses
Jones	Joneses
Levy	Levys
Lipschutz	Lipschutzes
Mary	Marys
Rabiej	Rabiejs
Shapiro	Shapiros
Sinz	Sinzes
Thomas	Thomases

Plurals such as these are often erroneously formed by calling, say, Mr. and Mrs. Sinz either *the Sinz* or *the Sinz'*. The latter form, with the apostrophe, merely results from confusion with possessives—and it isn't even a good possessive: the correct possessive is *Sinz's* in the singular and *Sinzes'* in the plural. See (A) & POSSESSIVES (B).

F. Compound Nouns. Certain compound nouns and hyphenated terms make their plurals by adding *-s* to the main word—e.g.:

aides-de-camp
battles royal
brothers-in-law
commanders-in-chief
consuls general
courts-martial
editors-in-chief
fathers-in-law
heirs presumptive
knights-errant
maids of honor
men-of-war
mothers-in-law
notaries public
poets laureate
postmasters general
rights-of-way
sergeants-at-arms
sisters-in-law

The American and British practices differ on the method of pluralizing *attorney general*. In AmE, it's *attorneys general*; in BrE, it's *attorney-generals*.

Words in which the noun is now disguised add *-s* at the end of the word, as with all compounds ending in *-ful*:

armfuls
bagfuls
barrelfuls
basketfuls
bottlefuls
bucketfuls
cupfuls
forkfuls
glassfuls
handfuls
jarfuls
lapfuls
lungfuls

mouthfuls
pailfuls
platefuls
pocketfuls
potfuls
roomfuls
scoopfuls
shovelfuls
spoonfuls
tablefuls
tablespoonfuls
teaspoonfuls
tubfuls

A few phrases fall into this category, such as *cul-de-sacs* (see (B)) and *Johnny-come-latelies*.

But when the addition is merely a preposition—and the noun isn't disguised—the *-s-* is added internally, as in *passersby*, *hangers-on*, *listeners-in*, *lookers-on* (more typically *onlookers*), and *lyings-in*.

G. Nouns Ending in *-f*. Some words change in the plural from a final *-f* to *-ves*, but others simply become *-fs*. Following are the main ones that change:

beef, beeves (fattened cattle)
calf, calves
elf, elves
half, halves
hoof, hooves
knife, knives
leaf, leaves
life, lives
loaf, loaves
scarf, scarves
self, selves
sheaf, sheaves
shelf, shelves
thief, thieves
wharf, wharves
wife, wives
wolf, wolves

And these are the ones that preferably don't change:

beef, beefs (types of meat)
dwarf, dwarfs
handkerchief, handkerchiefs
kerchief, kerchiefs
oaf, oafs
proof, proofs
roof, roofs
staff, staffs (but *staves* in music)

Note, however, that the plural of *still life* is *still lifes*.

H. Differentiated Forms. Despite the exceptional forms mentioned in (A)—the ones deriving from Old English (e.g., *foot–feet*)—in two of those cases there are exceptions to the exceptions. When *mouse* refers to the computer gadget that the user points and clicks with, the plural is *mouses*. And when *louse* refers to a scoundrel or cad, the plural is *louses*. See **mouses.**

I. Mass (Noncount) Nouns. A recent trend in the language is to make plurals for mass nouns—i.e., general and abstract nouns that cannot be broken down into discrete units and that therefore should not have plural forms. One example of this phenomenon is the psychologists' and sociologists' term *behaviors*, as if the ways in which people behave are readily categorizable and therefore countable. Granted, one can have good or bad behavior, but not, traditionally speaking, *a* good behavior or *a* bad behavior.

Increasingly, though, speakers of English think of *technologies* and *methodologies* as being discrete things. And to weather forecasters, it makes perfect sense to speak of *humidities* and *accumulations*. In part, this trend seems to show two things: first, an affection for abstract terms; and second, a resulting tendency to reify those abstract terms. See COUNT NOUNS AND MASS NOUNS.

J. Plural Possessives. See POSSESSIVES (B).

plus, n., forms the plural *pluses*—preferably not *plusses*.

p.m. See **a.m.**

POINTING WORDS (technically known as "deictic terms")—words like *this*, *that*, *these*, *those*, and *it*—point directly at an antecedent. A pointing word should always have an identifiable referent. But this doesn't mean that *this* or *these* must always have a noun immediately following it. Most grammarians take a more relaxed position: "The antecedent of *this* and *that* may be any single noun .... *This* and *that* may also refer to a phrase, clause, or sentence, or even to an implied thought. Reference of this kind must, however, be immediately clear and apparent; otherwise the thought will be obscure" (James G. Fernald, *English Grammar Simplified*, 1979). Fernald is not alone: "*This*, like *that*, is regularly used to refer to the idea of a preceding clause or sentence: 'He had always had his own way at home, and this made him a poor roommate.'/'The company train their salesmen in their own school. This [More formally: This practice] assures them a group of men with the same sales methods'" (Porter G. Perrin, *Writer's Guide and Index to English*, 1950) (bracketed language in original). Perrin's notation in his second example accurately describes the difference between *this* and *this practice*: it is a question of formality, not of correctness.

Actually, the grammarians' rule against vague reference is just that—a rule that forbids ambiguities of the kind illustrated here: "The most important activity is the editing of a college newspaper. *This* has grown with the college" (ex. drawn fr. Summers & Patrick, *College Composition*, 1946). What has grown with the college? Editing? The newspaper? The importance of editing the college newspaper? You simply cannot tell what the writer intended—if indeed the writer knew.

All one needs, then, is a sensitivity to antecedents, whether explicit or implicit. Good writers routinely use pointing words to refer to something that, although clear, is less specific than a particular noun—e.g.:

- "As a language [English] is highly unified; more so than many tongues spoken by a far smaller number of people. *This* raises the question of the probable future of English" (Albert H. Marckwardt, *American English*, 1958).
- "Kanemaru and Takeshita have come so close to differing publicly in recent months that some analysts believe an open split may be only a question of time. *This*, however, overlooks the historical relationship between the two men" (*Far Eastern Econ. Rev.*).
- "The Puritan hatred of Laud was well nigh insane. A leading MP speaks of the 'wicked tenets' of his Arminianism. *This* because the poor Archbishop believed in free will" (*Fin. Times*).

The test for knowing when the word *this* is acceptable in such a context is this: ask yourself, This what? If an answer comes immediately to mind, the word *this* is probably fine. If none comes immediately to mind, you probably need to add a noun. But a word of warning: inserting an abstract noun or noun phrase such as *fact*, *idea*, *practice*, or *state of affairs* often mars the style.

For a related problem with the relative pronoun *which*, also a pointing word, see REMOTE RELATIVES.

point of view. See **viewpoint.**

point out; point to; point up. *Point out* = to call attention to <she pointed out the four withering geraniums> <she pointed out the health benefits of eating lots of vegetables>. *Point to* = to direct attention to (as an answer or solution) <they could point to no good reason for closing the facility>. *Point up* = to illustrate <this case points up a key pitfall of the prosecutors' seeking capital punishment>.

police, though a COLLECTIVE NOUN, is generally construed as a plural both in AmE and in BrE <the police aren't here yet>. The word is pronounced /pə-**lees**/—not /**poh**-lees/. See PRONUNCIATION (B).

politically; politicly. *Politically* = in a political way; in a way that involves politics. *Politicly* = in a politic (i.e., judicious or prudent) way. The latter, of course, is much less common—e.g.: "'Is that a duck or a cormorant?' Bruce Babbitt asked, resting his paddle on his chino-covered leg, looking at a distant water bird. 'We have both,' raft guide Katy Strand told him *politicly*" (*Richmond Times-Dispatch*).

politick, v.i.; **politicize.** *Politick*, a BACK-FORMATION from *politics*, at one time was not recognized as an acceptable word. Today it is more common in AmE than in BrE; it means "to engage in partisan political activities." *Politicize* has the similar sense "to act the politician," but also the broader sense "to render political" <politicizing judicial elections>.

politics may be either singular or plural. Today it is more commonly singular than plural <politics is a dirty business>, although formerly the opposite was true. Cf. **economics.**

pompon; pompom. The decorative tuft of strands used by cheerleaders is correctly called a *pompon*—e.g.: "There were gymnastics teams doing backflips down Elk Grove Boulevard, marching bands, officers on horseback, *pompon* squads, Boy Scout troops, and the usual assortment of politicians" (*Chicago Trib.*). But because so many people mishear the word, and because of the tendency toward reduplicative sounds, *pompon* has become altered to *pompom*—e.g.: "Home of the state champion *pompom* [read *pompon*] squad and a General Motors Buick plant, it turned out to be a potential lodging industry jewel" (*Chicago Trib.*). Today, the correct *pompon* outranks *pompom* by a margin of more than four to one.

pore (= to read intently) is sometimes misused for *pour* (= to make [a liquid] flow downward). This blunder occurs in writing not pored over carefully enough by a good proofreader—e.g.: "Ms. Besso . . . now spends her evenings *pouring* [read *poring*] over brochures from Boston, Boulder, Colo., and Nashville" (*N.Y. Times*). This mistake probably appears primarily because the verb *pore* appears less often in print than in speech.

portion; part. There are connotative differences. *Portion* = share (as of an estate or of food). It is an entity cut (or as if cut) away from the whole <his portion of the profits> <her portion of the grain>. *Part*, in contrast, merely connotes a constituent piece of the whole <part of a house, a country, etc.>.

PORTMANTEAU WORDS. Lewis Carroll improvised this term to denote words formed by combining the sounds and meanings of two different words. (Linguists use the term *blend*.) Thus *insinuendo* combines *insinuation* with *innuendo*; *quasar* is from *quasi* and *stellar*; *aerobicise* derives from *aerobic exercise*. Other recent innovations are *avigation*, from *aviation* and *navigation*; *pictionary* for *picture-filled dictionary*; and *videbut* for *video debut*.

Most portmanteau words are nonce words that do not gain currency; others, like *brunch* (*breakfast* + *lunch*), become standard. Among portmanteau coinages are these:

Amerasian (*American* + *Asian*)
breathalyzer (*breath* + *analyzer*)
brotel (*brothel* + *hotel*)
chortle (*chuckle* + *snort*)
defamacast (*defamatory* + *broadcast*)
Franglais (*Francais* + *Anglais*)
futilitarian (*futile* + *utilitarian*)
galimony (*gal* + *alimony*)
galumph (*gallop* + *triumph*)
jazzercise (*jazz* + *exercise*)
motel (*motor* + *hotel*)
Oxbridge (*Oxford* + *Cambridge*)
palimony (*pal* + *alimony*)
quelch (*quell* + *squelch*)
simulcast (*simultaneous* + *broadcast*)
slurk (*slink* + *lurk*)
smog (*smoke* + *fog*)
Spanglish (*Spanish* + *English*)
sportscast (*sports* + *broadcast*)
stagflation (*stagnation* + *inflation*)
televangelist (*television* + *evangelist*)

Some portmanteau words lend an air of jocularity—e.g.: "The skinny [on Federal Express]? When you *absotively posilutely* have to get it there" (*Buffalo News*).

POSSESSIVES. A. Singular Possessives. To form a singular possessive, add *-'s* to most singular nouns—even those ending in *-s* and *-x* (hence *witness's*, *Vitex's*, *Jones's*, *Nichols's*). E.g.: "Noting *Congress's* move to regulate maternity hospitalization, managed-care advocates predict that politicians would legislate health care" (*U.S. News & World Rep.*). Although the *AP Stylebook* (6th ed. 1996) calls for nothing more than an apostrophe if the word already ends in *-s* (p. 163), most authorities who aren't journalists demand the final *-s* as well (i.e., *Bill Forbis's farm*, not *Bill Forbis' farm*). See William Strunk, Jr. & E.B. White, *The Elements of Style* 1 (3d ed. 1979).

There are three exceptions to this rule. The first is the standard one: Biblical and Classical names ending in *-s* take only an apostrophe, hence *Jesus' suffering*, *Moses' discovery*, *Aristophanes' plays*, *Grotius' writings*. (No extra syllable is added in sounding the possessive form.) The second exception is for words formed from a plural. Thus *General Motors* should make *General Motors'*, not *General Motors's*—e.g.: "A merger by General Motors will excite great interest in an enforcement agency simply because of *General Motors's* [read *General Motors'*] size" (E.W. Kintner, *An Antitrust Primer*, 1973). The third exception (a minor point) is discussed at (J).

B. Plural Possessives. For most plural possessives, use the ordinary plural form and add an apostrophe to the final *-s*: *Smiths'*, *Joneses'*, *bosses'*, *octopuses'*. The one exception is for plurals not ending in *-s*, for which *-'s* is added as in the singular possessive: *brethren's*, *children's*, *men's*, *women's*.

Writers sometimes confound the singular and plural possessives, most commonly by misusing the singular for the plural—e.g.: "I don't much admire the *Wales's* [read *Waleses'*] taste in expensive schools" (*Guardian*). (The reference was to the Prince and Princess of Wales.)/ "According to the lawsuit, on the day before he died, a classmate walked into the *boy's bathroom* [read *boys' bathroom* (because it's a school bathroom)] and interrupted Shawn before he could hang himself with a shirt" (*Austin American-Statesman*).

C. Absolute Possessives. The words *hers*, *ours*, *theirs*, and *yours* are sometimes termed "absolute" or "independent" possessives because they occur when no noun follows. No apostrophe appears in these words, which are often in the predicate <the house was ours> <the fault was theirs>. Sometimes, though, they can occur as subjects <hers was a gift that anyone would envy>. See UNDERSTOOD WORDS.

Occasionally, an absolute possessive occurs when it shouldn't—usually in combination with ordinary possessives. E.g.: "If a new relationship breaks up, your teen may feel very protective of you and feel stress about both *yours* [read *your*] and his or her vulnerability" (*Seattle Times*).

D. Double Possessives. Some people erroneously stigmatize *a friend of mine* or *an acquaintance of John's*, in which both an *of* and a possessive form appear: "[T]he double possessive is redundant, and it should be avoided in careful speech and formal writing. In short, don't be too 'possessive,' i.e., redundant, when indicating possession or ownership in your writing or speech. Form the possessive case by adding an *'s* or by using the preposition *of*. Just don't get carried away and do both at the same time" (Michael G. Walsh, "Grammatical Lawyer," in *Practical Lawyer*, Jan. 1996).

But this age-old idiom has appeared consistently since the days of Middle English. And it is widely approved:

- "The double genitive [i.e., double possessive] is required whenever a word indicating ownership is placed after *of*. For example, *he found a bone of the dog's* and *he found a bone of the dog* mean different things; and *he found a toy of the child* is meaningless" (Evans & Evans, *DCAU*).
- "By an old and well-established English idiom, sometimes called the double genitive, possession may be shown by two

methods at the same time, by an *of*-phrase and by a possessive form of the substantive. 'You are no friend of mine.' [Possession is shown by the prepositional *of*-phrase and by the possessive form *mine*.]" (R.W. Pence & D.W. Emery, *A Grammar of Present-Day English*, 1963).

- "Using both the *s*- and *of*-genitives together is an English idiom of long and respectable standing. It is especially common in locutions beginning with *that* or *this* and usually has an informal flavor: 'that boy of Henry's'; 'friends of my father's'; 'hobbies of Jack's.' It is useful in avoiding [an] ambiguity . . . : 'Jane's picture' is resolved either as 'the picture of Jane' or 'the picture of Jane's' " (Porter G. Perrin, *Writer's Guide and Index to English*, 1965).

The double possessive appears in good writing and typically causes no trouble. Occasionally, however, it can be improved on—e.g.: "Many *colleagues of Dr. Siegel's* [read *of Dr. Siegel's colleagues*] have said they were shocked by the allegations about a man whom they have long considered to be a reserved, somewhat academic person" (*N.Y. Times*).

E. Joint Possessives: *John and Mary's house*. For joint possession, an apostrophe goes with the last element in a series. If you put an apostrophe with each element in the series, you signal individual possession. E.g.:

John and Mary's house. (Joint)
John's and Mary's houses. (Individual)
America and England's interests. (Joint)
America's and England's interests. (Individual)

In the last two examples, *interests* is plural (regardless of the possessives) merely as a matter of idiom: we typically refer to *America's interests*, not *America's interest*.

F. Names as Adjectives. When a proper name is used as an adjective, it isn't a possessive and thus doesn't take an apostrophe. Hence "the Cubs [not *Cubs'*] game is at 1:00 today." The following example incorrectly uses an apostrophe because the name *Fields* (referring to a single person) is being used adjectivally: "One source who attended the fundraiser said it generated at least $50,000 for the *Fields'* [read *Fields*] campaign" (*New Orleans Gambit*).

G. Possessives of Names Made with Possessives. It is common for businesses to be named with a proper single name in possessive form, such as *McDonald's*. Although possessive in form, these are functionally nouns, as in *McDonald's brings you a new kind of meal*. How, then, does one make a possessive of the noun *McDonald's*? Literally, it would be *McDonald's'*, as in *Try McDonald's' new dinner combos!* But good phrasing requires *the new dinner combos at McDonald's*.

H. Inanimate Things. Possessives of nouns denoting inanimate objects are generally unobjectionable. Indeed, they allow writers to avoid awkward uses of *of*—e.g.: *the book's title, the article's main point, the system's hub, the envelope's contents, the car's price tag*. See **of (A)**.

The old line was that it's better to use an "*of* phrase rather than the *'s* to indicate possession when the possessor is an inanimate object. Write *foot of the bed*, not *the bed's foot*" (Robert C. Whitford & James R. Foster, *Concise Dictionary of American Grammar and Usage*, 1955). *Foot of the bed*, of course, is a SET PHRASE, so the example is not a fair one. As a general principle, though, whenever it's not a violation of idiom, the possessive in *'s* is preferable <the hotel's front entrance> <the earth's surface>.

But such possessives can be overdone. For example, avoid using the possessive form of a year—e.g.: "Mr. Rogers, 41, took the show by storm in 1993, winning 28 blue ribbons and the Show Sweepstakes with a total of 1,120 points (which really upped the ante: *1992's winner* [read *the 1992 winner*] scored only 387 points)" (*N.Y. Times*).

I. Phrasal Possessives. Avoid phrasal possessives when possible, so that you don't end up with sentences like this: "That strange man who lives down the block's daughter was arrested last week." (Read: *The daughter of that strange man who lives down the block was arrested last week.*) The form with *of*, though slightly longer, is correct. Sometimes, too, the sentence can be fixed in some way other than by inserting an *of*—e.g.: "These statements do let women in on *the man in question's view* of our half of humanity." (Read: *These statements do let women in on how the man in question views our half of humanity.*)

As always, there are exceptions—two of them. With a phrase such as *mother-in-law*, the possessive is acceptable and widely used <my mother-in-law's sister>. The other established phrasal possessives are variations on *anybody else's*: "Once alerted, the janitor could find *no one else's* umbrella." See **else's.**

J. Attributive Nouns Ending in *-ed*. Words ending in *-ed* become awkward as possessives. This happens primarily in law. With such phrases as *the insured's death* or *the deceased's residence*, it's better to use an *of*-phrase—hence *the death of the insured* and *the residence of the deceased*. (Or you might try *the decedent's residence*.)

K. Possessives Followed by Relative Pronouns. The relative pronoun *who* stands for a noun; it shouldn't follow a possessive because the possessive (being an adjective, not a noun) can't properly be its antecedent. In the sentence that follows, *Esterhazy's* is a possessive adjective modifying the UNDERSTOOD WORD *voice*, but the writer meant *who* to refer to *Esterhazy*: "Or there may have been inimical voices raised among the committee, such as Palffy's or Nikolaus Esterhazy's, *who* just then had had an unpleasant brush with the composer" (George R. Marek, *Beethoven*, 1969). (Read: *Or there may have been raised among the committee inimical voices, such as those of Palffy or Nikolaus Esterhazy. The latter had just had an unpleasant brush with the composer.*) The poor grammar in the original sentence raises another question: to whom does the *who* refer—Esterhazy alone, or both Esterhazy and Palffy? The revision assumes that the reference is to Esterhazy alone. Otherwise, the wording would be *both of whom*.

L. Units of Time or Value. The idiomatic possessive should be used with periods of time and statements of worth—hence *30 days' notice*, *three days' time*, *20 dollars' worth*, and *several years' experience*. E.g.: "Under Japanese law, 10 judges of the 15-member Supreme Court, the nation's top court, must be legal experts with at least *10 years experience* [read *10 years' experience*]" (*Ariz. Daily Star*). In that sentence, of course, it would also be possible to write *with at least 10 years of experience*.

M. Titles of Books, Films, and the Like. Do you say *Garner's "A Dictionary of Modern American Usage"* or *Garner's "Dictionary of Modern American Usage"*? That is, if you're introducing a title with a possessive, do you include an initial article (*A* or *The*) in the title? Including the article gets the full title of the book, but omitting it seems less stilted. Eric Partridge liked the former phrasing (*U&A*); others prefer the latter (e.g., *Words into Type*, 1974). In fact, though, either style is likely to bother some readers.

Kingsley Amis has found a sensible approach: "Speakers of English understandably feel that a noun, or modifier-plus-noun, will take a maximum of one article or possessive or other handle and shy away from saying anything like 'Graham Greene's *The Confidential Agent*' or 'Anthony Burgess's *A Clockwork Orange*' or 'A.N. Other's *He Fell Among Thieves*.' . . . To behave properly you have to write, for instance, 'Graham Greene's thriller, *The Confidential Agent*' and 'Anthony Burgess's fantasy of the future, *A Clockwork Orange*' and 'Kafka's novel [or whatever it is] *The Castle*' " (*The King's English*, 1997).

N. *Goodness' sake* and *conscience' sake*. The traditional view is that in the phrases *for goodness' sake* and *for* *conscience' sake*, no final *-s* is added to the possessive. In practice, writers follow this exception with *goodness* but not with *conscience* (the prevalent form in AmE being *conscience's sake*). The reason is probably that *for goodness' sake* is so common. In fact, 50% of the time in modern prose, writers omit the possessive altogether, making it *for goodness sake*.

The best course is probably to stick with the traditional forms so that they're parallel: *goodness' sake* and *conscience' sake*.

possible. A. And *practicable.* *Practicable* (= feasible; possible in practice) is only a little narrower than *possible* (= capable of happening or being done). The more problematic words are *practical* and *practicable*. See **practical.**

B. For *necessary.* This error occasionally appears in the odd, unidiomatic phrase *more difficult than possible*—e.g.: "The movie goes overboard trying to make the parents' day more difficult than *possible* [read *necessary*]" (*Columbus Dispatch*). The writer seems to have been thinking of *as difficult as possible*. See SWAPPING HORSES.

possum. See **opossum.**

postscript. See **P.S.**

potentiality is jargonistic when used (as it usually is) merely for the noun *potential*. E.g.: "They must seek to find meaning for their life, and to give something unique from their *potentiality* [read *potential*] for experience" (*Asheville Citizen-Times*).

The one justifiable sense of *potentiality* is "the state or quality of possessing latent power or capacity capable of coming into being or action" (*SOED*)—e.g.: "In every child who is born, under no matter what circumstances . . . the *potentiality* of the human race is born again" (*Ariz. Republic*).

pour. For the misuse of this verb for *pore*, see **pore.**

practical; practicable. Though similar, these words should be distinguished. *Practical* = manifested in practice; capable of being put to good use <a practical guide to horse-breeding>. Its opposite is *theoretical. Practicable* = capable of being accomplished; feasible; possible <videoconferencing soon became practicable over standard telephone lines>.

Occasionally *practicable* is misused for *practical*—e.g.: "The articles in The Syracuse Newspapers and comments by the Syracuse SkyChiefs Board of Directors were very interesting and extremely *practicable* [read *practical*]" (*Syracuse Post-Standard*). See **possible (A).**

In both words, the first syllable is stressed: /**prak**-ti-kəl/ and /**prak**-ti-kə-bəl/.

precede; proceed. These words are sometimes confused even by otherwise literate persons. Both may mean "to go ahead," but in different senses. *Precede* = to go ahead of; to come before <the Japanese husband preceded his wife by ten steps>. *Proceed* = to go ahead; to continue <they proceeded into the hall>.

Preceed, a misspelling, confuses the two words. It occurs in print surprisingly often—e.g.: "He asked the audience to vote for politicians who solve problems, instead of focusing on the storms that *preceed* [read *precede*] the solutions" (*Cincinnati Enquirer*).

So does the misuse of *proceed* for *precede*—e.g.: "Representative Charles B. Rangel of New York, the senior Democrat on the Ways and Means Committee, and one of the leading liberals in Congress, *proceeded* [read *preceded*] Mr. Archer to the microphone" (*N.Y. Times*).

precipitate, adj.; **precipitous.** These words are quite different, though often confused. *Precipitate* = sudden; hasty; rash; showing violent or uncontrollable speed. The word is applied to actions, movements, or demands. *Precipitous* = like a precipice; steep. It is applied to physical things—rarely to actions, except when the metaphor of steepness is apt. *Precipitous* is frequently misused for *precipitate*—e.g.: "We are not asking for a *precipitous* [read *precipitate*] decision on the directorship" (*Chicago Trib.*).

precipitation; precipitancy; precipitance. *Precipitation* = (1) something that condenses from a vapor and falls (as rain or snow) <a forecast of freezing precipitation overnight>; or (2) the bringing about of something suddenly or unexpectedly <precipitation of a riot>. *Precipitancy* = sudden or rash haste <we shouldn't act with precipitancy>. Although *precipitation* has sometimes overlapped with *precipitancy*, this overlap is undesirable. Finally, *precipitance* is a NEEDLESS VARIANT of *precipitancy*.

precipitous. See **precipitate.**

predate = (1) to have existed before (something else); or (2) to devour as prey; prey upon. Sense 2, not recorded in most dictionaries, is a newfangled BACK-FORMATION from *predation*. And it doesn't fill a void: *prey* is an age-old verb that does the job. E.g.: "The colorful fish are easily seen and *predated* [read *preyed*] upon, and once a dominant male disappears, a remarkable event occurs" (*Louisville Courier-J.*).

For sense 1, see **antedate.**

predominate, adj., is a NEEDLESS VARIANT for *predominant*. In good usage, *predominate* is the verb, *predominant* the adjective. Because readers may be confused by *predominate* as an adjective, *predominant* should be reserved for this job—e.g.: "[J]azz must still undergo [de-ghettoizing] to dispel the *predominate* [read *predominant*] images of it as banal happy-time entertainment and primitive, spontaneous emotionalism" (*N.Y. Times*). Cf. **preponderant.**

preferable, inherently a comparative adjective, shouldn't be preceded by *more*—e.g.: "All hands involved have decided that inconveniencing Suns fans is *eminently more preferable than* [read *much preferable to*] risking the chance that just one person in the known universe misses a chance to see Michael Jordan" (*Baltimore Sun*). See COMPARATIVES AND SUPERLATIVES & ADJECTIVES (B).

Also, the word takes *to*, not *than*—e.g.: "A high down payment also helps an applicant's cause, as does the type of loan sought—a 15-year fixed being *more preferable than* [read *preferable to*] a 30-year fixed, for example" (*Chicago Sun-Times*).

Preferable is accented on the first syllable, not the second: /**pre**-fər-ə-bəl/, not /pri-**fər**-ə-bəl/. See PRONUNCIATION (B).

PREFIXES, NEGATIVE. See NEGATIVES (A).

preliminary to for *before* is a silly pomposity—e.g.: "*Preliminary to* [read *Before* or *Just before*] announcing his departure, he had some kind words for his colleagues." Cf. **prior.**

premier, adj.; **premiere,** n. Aside from the part-of-speech distinction, three observations are in order. First, *premier*, the adjective meaning "first in importance or rank," is often pretentious in place of *first* or *foremost*. Second, *premiere*, the noun meaning "a first performance," is not in good use as a verb. (See NOUNS AS VERBS.) Third, the accent is no longer used in the noun—hence *premiere*, not *première*.

preowned is now a common EUPHEMISM for *used*. Used-car dealers are especially fond of this DOUBLESPEAK—e.g.: "Why settle for an Accord or Taurus when you can have a *preowned* Cadillac for about the same price?"

preplan is illogical for *plan* because planning must necessarily occur beforehand—e.g.: "[I]n return you get an interactive touch screen display that will beep a warning if you take a wrong turn and stray from its *preplanned* [read *planned*] route" (*Santa Fe New Mexican*).

preponderant; preponderate, adj. The latter is a NEEDLESS VARIANT that often occurs in the adverb *preponderately*—e.g.: "[T]he statistical patter . . . has thus far indicated that AIDS and its transmission are *preponderately* [read *preponderantly*] linked to homosexual practices" (*Daily Mail*).

Preponderate should be used only as a verb—e.g.: "[I]ts market share has declined each year as cars equipped for unleaded gasoline have *preponderated*, and lead gas is projected essentially to disappear by about 1990" (*Chicago Trib.*). Cf. **predominate.**

PREPOSITIONS. A. The Preposition Quotient. In lean writing, it's a good idea to minimize prepositional phrases. In flabby prose, a ratio of one preposition for every four words is common; in better, leaner writing, the quotient is more like one preposition for every ten or fifteen words.

Five editorial methods can tighten sentences marred with too many prepositions. First, the prepositional phrase can be deleted as surplusage; for example, it's often possible in a given context to change a phrase such as *senior vice president of the corporation* to *senior vice president*—if the corporate context is already clear. Second, uncovering BURIED VERBS often eliminates as many as two prepositions; thus, *is in violation of* becomes *violates*. Third, it's sometimes possible to replace a prepositional phrase with an adverb; so *she criticized the manuscript with intelligence* becomes *she criticized the manuscript intelligently*. Fourth, many prepositional phrases resolve themselves into POSSESSIVES; thus, *for the convenience of the reader* becomes *for the reader's convenience*. And finally, a change from PASSIVE VOICE to active often entails removing a preposition; so *the ball was hit by Jane* becomes *Jane hit the ball*. See **of** (A).

B. Ending Sentences with Prepositions. The spurious rule about not ending sentences with prepositions is a remnant of Latin grammar, in which a preposition was the one word that a writer could not end a sentence with. But Latin grammar should never straitjacket English grammar. If the SUPERSTITION is a "rule" at all, it is a rule of rhetoric and not of grammar, the idea being to end sentences with strong words that drive a point home. (See SENTENCE ENDS.) That principle is sound, of course, but not to the extent of meriting lockstep adherence.

The idea that a preposition is ungrammatical at the end of a sentence is often attributed to 18th-century grammarians. But that idea is greatly overstated. Robert Lowth, the most prominent 18th-century grammarian, wrote that the final preposition "is an idiom, which our language is strongly inclined to: it prevails in common conversation, and suits very well with the familiar style in writing" (*A Short Introduction to English Grammar*, 1782). The furthest Lowth went was to urge that "the placing of the preposition before the relative is more graceful, as well as more perspicuous; and agrees much better with the solemn and elevated style" (*id.*). That in itself is an archaic view that makes modern writing stuffy; indeed, Lowth elsewhere made the same plea for *hath*: "*Hath* properly belongs to the serious and solemn style; *has* to the familiar" (*id.*). But in any event, Lowth's statement about prepositions was hardly intended as a "rule."

Winston Churchill's witticism about the absurdity of this bugaboo should have laid it to rest. When someone once upbraided him for ending a sentence with a preposition, he rejoined, "That is the type of arrant pedantry up with which I shall not put." Avoiding a preposition at the end of the sentence sometimes leads to just such a preposterous monstrosity.

Perfectly natural-sounding sentences end with prepositions, particularly when a verb with a preposition-particle appears at the end (as in *follow up* or *ask for*). E.g.: "The act had no causal connection with the injury complained *of*." When one decides against such formal (sometimes downright stilted) constructions as *of which*, *on which*, and *for which*—and instead chooses the relative *that*—the preposition is necessarily sent to the end of the sentence: "This is a point on which I must insist" becomes far more natural as "This is a point that I must insist on." And consider the following examples:

Correct and Natural	*Correct and Stuffy*
people worth talking to	people to whom it is worth talking
What are you thinking about?	About what are you thinking?
the man you were listening to	the man to whom you were listening
a person I have great respect for	a person for whom I have great respect

In 1947, a scholar summed up the point: "Those who insist that final prepositions are inelegant are taking from the English language one of its greatest assets—its flexibility—an advantage realized and practiced by all our greatest writers except a few who, like Dryden and Gibbon, tried to fashion the English language after the Latin" (Margaret M. Bryant, *College English*, 1947).

Good writers don't hesitate to end their sentences with prepositions if doing so results in phrasing that seems natural:

- "The peculiarities of legal English are often used as a stick to beat the official *with*" (Ernest Gowers, *Plain Words: Their ABC*, 1954).
- "[I]n the structure of the 'coherent sentence,' such particles are necessary, and, strip the sentence as bare as you will, they cannot be entirely dispensed *with*" (G.H. Vallins, *The Best English*, 1960).
- "It was the boys in the back room, after all, whom Marlene Dietrich felt comfortable drinking *with*" (*N.Y. Times*).

See **which & that.**

C. Redundant Prepositions. Writers often repeat prepositions unnecessarily when there are intervening phrases or clauses. E.g.: "Sue is survived by her beloved husband, Roy C. Walker, *with whom* she shared her life *with* for 63 years" (*Austin American-Statesman*). (Delete the second *with*.) Paul McCartney, in his hit song "Live and Let Die," made a similar error: "But if this ever-changing world *in which* we live *in* makes you give in and cry, just live and let die." McCartney might have improved the lyrics by writing *in which we're livin'*.

prerequisite. See **perquisite.**

prescribe. See **proscribe.**

presently contains an ambiguity. In the days of Shakespeare, it meant "immediately." Soon its meaning evolved into "after a short time" (perhaps because people exaggerated about their promptitude). This sense is still current. Then, chiefly in AmE, it took on the additional sense "at present; currently." This use is poor, however, because it both causes the ambiguity and displaces a simpler word (*now* or, if more syllables are necessary, *currently*)—e.g.: "Carol *presently* [read *now*] has a one-elephant show (I am not making this up) going at the Clarion Hotel in downtown San Diego" (*Columbus Dispatch*). Cf. **momentarily.** See also **at this time.**

present time, at the. This phrase is wordy for *now*.

present writer. Unless self-mockery is intended, this phrase is today generally considered inferior to *I* or *me*. See FIRST PERSON.

Presidents' Day; Presidents Day. The spelling with the apostrophe is better and more common. *Presidents' Day* is not a federal legal holiday; *Washington's Birthday* is the name officially adopted by the Federal Government for the third Monday in February. But several states call it *Presidents' Day*—perhaps so that Abraham Lincoln's birthday (Feb. 12), which is not a legal holiday, can be celebrated jointly. Cf. **Veterans Day.**

presiding juror. See **foreman (B).**

pretend as though for *pretend that* (by analogy to *act as though*) is unidiomatic.

pretty, adv., is still considered informal or colloquial <a pretty good drawing>. It sometimes conveys a shade of doubt—*pretty clear* being less certain in some readers' minds than *clear.* See WEASEL WORDS.

prevalent is accented on the first, not the second, syllable: /**prev**-ə-lənt/.

preventive; preventative. The strictly correct form is *preventive* (as both noun and adjective), though the corrupt form with the extra internal syllable is unfortunately common—e.g.: "The scientific discoveries . . . have led biotech researchers to develop two classes of vaccines: *preventative* [read *preventive*], such as traditional inoculations against polio, influenza, or rubella; and therapeutic, where the immune system is primed to fend off the recurrence of certain diseases such as skin cancer" (*Boston Globe*). In modern print sources, *preventive* is about five times more common than *preventative.*

previous to for *before* is highfalutin—e.g.: "*Previous to* [read *Before*] this award, the Police Department had received at least $11 million under the 1994 crime bill alone" (*Sacramento Bee*). See **prior.**

prideful. See **proud.**

principal; principle. A. The Senses. Generally, it's enough to remember that *principal* (= chief, primary, most important) is usually an adjective and that *principle* (= a truth, rule, doctrine, or course of action) is virtually always a noun. Although *principle* is not a verb, we have *principled* as an adjective.

But *principal* is sometimes a noun—an elliptical form of *principal official* <Morgan is principal of the elementary school> or *principal investment* <principal and interest>.

B. *Principal* for *principle.* This is a fairly common blunder—e.g.: "The Ways and Means bill approved today, after more than a month of deliberation and voting, preserves two of the central *principals* [read *principles*] put forth by the President: universal coverage and the requirement that employers assume 80 percent of its cost for their workers" (*N.Y. Times*).

C. *Principle* for *principal.* This mistake is perhaps even more common—e.g.: "Bowers was a *principle* [read *principal*] figure in one of college basketball's nastiest scandals in recent years after she made allegations of NCAA violations by the Baylor men's team in memos to university officials" (*Austin American-Statesman*).

D. *Principal* as an Uncomparable Adjective. See ADJECTIVES (B).

prior; previous. The adjectives *prior* and *previous* for *earlier* are each within the stylist's license; *prior to* and *previous to* in place of *before* are not.

In fact, *prior to*—one of the most easily detectable symptoms of COMMERCIALESE and LEGALESE—is terribly overworked. As Theodore Bernstein once pointed out, one should feel free to use *prior to* instead of *before* only if one is accustomed to using *posterior to* for *after.* See *The Careful Writer* 347 (1979). Cf. **previous to & subsequent to.**

prioritize; priorize. Writers with sound stylistic priorities avoid these words. *Prioritize,* dating from the mid-1960s, typifies bureaucratic bafflegab—e.g.: "The rate at which an objective is achieved should reflect the degree to which that component of the plan has been *prioritized.*" (Read: *Do the most important things first.*) Instead of *prioritize,* conservative writers tend to use *set priorities* or *establish priorities*. In time, of course, *prioritize* might lose its bureaucratic odor. But that time has not yet arrived.

Much less common than *prioritize* is the illogically formed *priorize*, a fairly obscure Canadianism—e.g.: "Of course, the finance minister will, for the benefit of his colleagues, '*priorize*' [read *establish priorities for*] the promises made by the new regime" (*Toronto Star*). See -IZE.

privilege is often misspelled *priviledge*—e.g.: "A season badge, which includes grounds and clubhouse *priviledges* [read *privileges*] throughout the tournament, is $80" (*Chicago Sun-Times*).

proactive = (of a person, policy, etc.) creating or controlling a situation by taking the initiative or anticipating events; ready to take initiative, tending to make things happen (*SOED*). Though, as a VOGUE WORD, *proactive* is widely viewed with suspicion, it's occasionally useful as an antonym of *reactive*. It seems to fill a gap in the language—one not adequately filled by *assertive* or any other common word.

probably /**pro**-bə-blee/ is frequently mispronounced /**pro**-blee/ and even /**pro**-lee/. See PRONUNCIATION (B).

proceed. See **precede.**

prodigality; profligacy. The former means "lavishness, extravagance." The latter means primarily "salaciousness, licentiousness," but it also shares the sense of the former.

prodigious (= [1] abnormal; or [2] amazing, marvelous) for *prestigious* (= having prestige) is a MALAPROPISM—e.g.: "The rich and famous of decades gone by came here to float in serenity. In 1984, the *prodigious* [read *prestigious*] hotel was accorded National Historic Landmark status" (*Wash. Times*).

profess innocence. See **confess (B).**

profligacy. See **prodigality.**

prognosis. See **diagnosis.**

PRONOUNS. A. The Basics. The English pronouns are as follows:

Singular Pronouns

	Nominative	*Objective*
First Person	I	me
Second Person	you	you
Third Person	he, she	him, her

Plural Pronouns

	Nominative	*Objective*
First Person	we	us
Second Person	you	you
Third Person	they	them

There are four essential rules of pronouns. First, if the pronoun is the subject of a clause, it must always be in the nominative case <she is friendly>. Second, if the pronoun is the object of a verb, it must be in the objective case <the atmosphere made her feel friendly>. Third, if a pronoun is the object of a preposition, it must always be in the objective case <it was the fault of them, not their children>. If a prepositional phrase contains two or more objects, all the objects are in the objective case <please tell only me and him>. *Like*, a preposition, is followed by the objective case <you're starting to sound like me> <they looked like us>. Fourth, if the pronoun is the subject of an infinitive, it must be in the objective case <she wanted him to sing another song>.

B. Confusion of Nominative and Objective Cases. One might think that a work of this kind, catering as it does to serious writers, could pass over the differences between subjects and objects in pronouns. But debilitated grammar seems ubiquitous—e.g.:

- "My mother was busy raising my brother and *I* [read *me*]."/ "Give Al Gore and *I* [read *me*] a chance to bring America back." Bill Clinton, accepting the Democratic nomination for President of the United States, 16 July 1992.
- "As for *we* [read *us*] poor slobs who were out of the loop—any loop—we did what Dallasites had always done: We took it on faith that the city was virtually recession-proof" (*D Mag.*).
- "What the public knows about Mr. Kelly's life at home since his surrender in Switzerland is more or less what he, his parents and Mr. Puccio have chosen to disclose: scenes of Mr. Kelly passing the time with vigorous exercise and of *he* [read *him*] and his parents declaring his innocence, as seen on a recent broadcast of ABC's 'Turning Point' " (*N.Y. Times*).
- "[T]okens predicting the future were buried in each dish . . . a coin for one who would become wealthy and a ring for *he or she* [read *him or her*] who would marry" (*Irish America*).

For *between you and I*, see **between (C)** & HYPERCORRECTION (B). For *it's me*, see **it is I.** For pronouns after *than*, see **than (B).**

Occasionally, writers avoid the strictly correct form merely to avoid seeming pedantic. One trying for a natural tone might understandably shrink from *I* in this example: "There are now so many casinos in the Upper Midwest that somebody has actually written a guidebook for gamblers who want to know what the places are like. [¶] And that somebody is *me*" (*St. Paul Pioneer Press*). The word *I*, technically, should serve as the predicate nominative after the linking verb *is*. That is, the pronoun in the predicate denotes the same person as the subject (*somebody*), so the predicate takes the nominative form because of that interchangeability. But *me* is much more common today in a sentence like that one.

Ernest Gowers gave sound advice here: "[T]he prepositional use of *than* is now so common colloquially (*He is older than me; they travelled much faster than us*) that the bare subjective pronoun in such a position strikes the readers as pedantic, and it is better either to give it a more natural appearance by supplying it with a verb or to dodge the difficulty by not using an inflective pronoun at all" (*MEU2*). Following are three good examples involving comparatives in which, strictly speaking, a pronoun in the nominative case should follow the word *than*: "What makes the story even juicier is that Pamela, 74, has allegedly been feuding for years with her two former stepdaughters, both of them slightly older than *her*—and one of whom may face financial difficulties" (*Newsweek*)./ " 'It's clear that actually a lot of people they protect are in more danger than *me*—if you're a member of the royal family or, more recently, if you were the secretary of state for Northern Ireland' " (*Newsweek*, quoting Salman Rushdie).

C. Indefinite Pronouns: Number. Traditionally, indefinite pronouns (*anyone, anybody, everyone, everybody, no one, nobody, someone,* and *somebody*) have been considered invariably singular. Indeed, as the subject of a verb, each of those terms must be singular—e.g.:

- "There's just one problem: Hardly *anybody* is riding" (*Syracuse Post-Standard*).
- "*Everyone* was gleeful, full of the spirit of Hanukkah" (*Denver Post*).
- "He releases bad news when *nobody* is looking" (*Omaha World-Herald*).

For an example of *anyone . . . are*, see **anyone (D).**

But often, as in the following sentences, the sense undoubtedly carries the idea of plurality: "Since *everyone* there was Japanese, and none of *them* had ever traveled abroad, *they* needed a translator."/ "*Everybody* was crouched behind furniture to surprise me, and *they* tried to. But I already knew *they* were there." Try changing *them* to *him* and *they* to *he*, and you end up with deranged writing.

Other sentences present closer calls, but the trend is unmistakable—e.g.: "Being so down-to-earth she accepts *everybody* for who *they* are, and so is unlikely to treat them any differently from the way she deals with anybody else" (*Sunday Times*).

Although *everyone* and *everybody* carry the strongest suggestions of plurality, the other indefinite pronouns are almost as natural with *they* and *them*. That's because *they* has increasingly moved toward singular senses. (See SEXISM (B).) Disturbing though these developments may be to purists, they're irreversible. And nothing that a grammarian says will change them.

D. Overeager Pronouns. See ANTICIPATORY REFERENCE.

E. Restrictive and Nonrestrictive Relative Pronouns. See **that** (A).

PRONUNCIATION. A. General Principles. The best course is to follow the pronunciation current among educated speakers in one's region. A few words have universally accepted pronunciations and rejected mispronunciations; where prescriptions on pronunciation appear in this book, the preferred pronunciation is generally preferred across geographic boundaries.

H.W. Fowler still speaks to us with clarion wisdom: "The ambition to do better than our neighbours is in many departments of life a virtue; in pronunciation it is a vice; there the only right ambition is to do as our neighbours" (*MEU1* at 466).

But when it comes to words that are seldom pronounced by English-speaking people—as with any learned word—the advice to conform with our neighbors' pronunciation becomes problematic. For here we find diversity, not uniformity—the result of the infrequent occasions when the words are pronounced. And when there are diverse opinions among reasonable and educated people, there must be considerable leeway.

B. Commonly Mispronounced Words. Many troublesome words are listed throughout this book, with the correct pronunciation noted. Here are 50 of the most frequently mispronounced words in AmE:

	Correct	*Incorrect*
affluent	**af**-loo-ənt	ə-**floo**-ənt
album	**al**-bəm	**al**-bləm
almond	**ah**-mənd	**al**-mənd
applicable	**ap**-li-kə-bəl	ə-**pli**-kə-bəl
asked	askt	ast, aksd
asterisk	**as**-tə-risk	**as**-tə-rik
athlete	**ath**-leet	**ath**-ə-leet
cement	sə-**ment**	**see**-mint
comparable	**kom**-pə-rə-bəl	kəm-**par**-ə-bəl
comptroller	kən-**troh**-lər	**komp**-troh-lər
concierge	kon-see-**erzh**	kon-see-**er**
coupon	**koo**-pon	**kyoo**-pon
descent	di-**sent**	**dee**-sent
Detroit	di-**troyt**	**dee**-troyt
ebullient	i-**buul**-yənt	**eb**-yə-lənt
ecstatic	ek-**sta**-dik	e-**sta**-dik
escape	es-**kayp**	ek-**skayp**
et cetera	et-**set**-ə-rə	ek-**set**-ə-rə
extraordinary	ek-**stror**-di-ner-ee	ek-strə-**or**-di-ner-ee
fifth	fifth	fith
flaccid	**flak**-sid	**fla**-səd
grocery	**groh**-s[ə]-ree	**groh**-shree
height	hɪt	hɪtth
hundred	**hən**-drəd	**hə**-nərd, **hən**-drit
hypnotize	**hip**-nə-tɪz	**hip**-mə-tɪz
Illinois	il-ə-**noy**	il-ə-**noyz**
influence	**in**-floo-ənts	in-**floo**-ənts
insurance	in-**shuur**-ənts	**in**-shər-ənts
interesting	**in**-trə-sting	**in**-ə-res-ting
intravenous	in-trə-**vee**-nəs	in-trə-**vee**-nee-əs
irrevocable	i-**rev**-ə-kə-bəl	ir-ə-**voh**-kə-bəl
liaison	lee-**ay**-zahn	**lay**-ə-zahn
library	**lɪ**-brer-ee	**lɪ**-ber-ee
literature	**lit**-ər-ə-chuur	**lit**-ər-ə-tyoor
mirror	**mir**-ər	**mir**-ə
mischievous	**mis**-chə-vəs	mis-**chee**-vee-əs
nuclear	**noo**-klee-ər	**noo**-kyə-lər
often	**of**-ən	**of**-tən
pamphlet	**pam**-flət	**pam**-plət
persevere	pər-sə-**veer**	pər-sər-**veer**
police	pə-**lees**	**poh**-lees
preferable	**pre**-fər-ə-bəl	pri-**fər**-ə-bəl
probably	**pro**-bə-blee	**pro**-blee, **pro**-lee
realtor	**reel**-tər	**reel**-ə-tər

	Correct	*Incorrect*
schism	**si**-zəm	**ski**-zəm, **shi**-zəm
secretary	**se**-krə-ter-ee	**se**-kə-ter-ee
sherbet	**shər**-bət	**shər**-bərt
substantive	**səb**-stən-tiv	**səb**-stə-nə-tiv, səb-**stan**-tiv
wash	wahsh	wahrsh
zoology	zoh-**ol**-ə-jee	zoo-**ol**-ə-jee

Some CONTRACTIONS are also commonly mispronounced. For example, *couldn't*, *didn't*, and *wouldn't* are sometimes mouthed as if the *-d-* were emphasized in the second syllable: /**kuu**-dənt/, rather than the correct /**kuud**-ənt/, etc.

C. Lambdacism and Rhotacism. These are two of the most common defects in pronunciation: *lambdacism* denotes the imperfect sounding of *-l-* (as by making it sound like an *-r-* or *-y-*), and *rhotacism* denotes the imperfect sounding of *-r-* (as by making it a *-w-* or *-l-*). In some children, these mispronunciations occur at an early stage of development and are soon outgrown; for them, *Mary had a little lamb* can sound like *Mawy had a yitto yam*. Sometimes, though, these defects are never outgrown; they become minor speech impediments. Sometimes, too, pronunciations exhibiting rhotacism characterize regional speech, as in President John F. Kennedy's pronunciation of *idea* /I-**deer**/ and *Cuba* /**kyoo**-bər/. In the words listed in (B), one sees the intrusive *-r-* (*persevere*) and the omitted *-r-* (*mirror*), both of which are types of rhotacism; and the intrusive *-l-* (*album*), which is a type of lambdacism.

D. The Mispronounced *-ph-*. In several words—notably, *diphtheria*, *diphthong*, *naphtha*, *ophthalmology*, and *pamphlet*—people tend to change the /f/ sound of the *-ph-* to a /p/ sound. Avoid these mispronunciations.

E. Bibliography. For books on pronunciation, see the Select Bibliography at the end of this book.

prophesy; prophecy. *Prophesy* /**pro**-fə-sI/ is the verb meaning "to predict or foretell"; *prophecy* /**pro**-fə-see/ is the noun meaning "a prediction or foretelling." *Prophesy* is sometimes incorrectly made *prophesize*—e.g.: "As Jesus rode through Jerusalem, many of the Jews waved palm branches and hailed him as the king of Israel because of clues . . . that had been *prophesized* [read *prophesied*] in Scripture" (*Ariz. Republic*).

proscribe; prescribe. *Proscribe* = to prohibit. *Prescribe* = to impose authoritatively. But some writers apparently think that *proscribe* is simply a fancier form of *prescribe*—e.g.: "Before commencing formal discovery, plaintiff's counsel may wish to focus a great deal of effort on discovery of facts *outside of* [read *outside*] the litigation vehicles *proscribed* [read *prescribed*] by statute" (*L.A. Daily J.*).

prosecute; persecute. *Prosecute* = to begin a case at law for punishment of a crime or of a legal violation. *Persecute* = to oppress, coerce, treat unfairly, often out of religious hatred. Occasionally the two are confounded—e.g.: "Asked why they figure Philips has not actively *persecuted* [read *prosecuted*] violators, sources cite 'pure negligence' and a 'lack of organization' on the part of the company" (*Billboard*).

prostrate; prostate. These are very different words, but they are sometimes confused. In its verb sense, to *prostrate* oneself is to kneel down in humility or adoration. As an adjective, *prostrate* means either "lying facedown" or "emotionally overcome." The noun *prostate*, by contrast, refers to the gland found in male mammals, surrounding the urethra at the base of the bladder.

The most common mistake is to write *prostrate gland* instead of *prostate gland*—e.g.: "For operations on major blood vessels and the *prostrate* [read *prostate*] gland, the death rate was 200" (*Newsweek*).

protagonist. Literally, *protagonist* = the chief character in a drama. By extension, it means "a champion of a cause." It should not be used loosely in reference to any character in a drama or any supporter of a cause—only to the chief one. But the SLIPSHOD EXTENSION is commonplace—e.g.: "Its half-dozen intertwined *protagonists* [read *characters*], all played by fine, serious actors, are sensitive, right-thinking human beings who worry about the world" (*L.A. Times*).

Protagonist is all too frequently confused with *antagonist*—e.g.: "Keanu Reeves and Dennis Hopper star as the dueling *protagonists* [read *antagonists*]" (*Christian Science Monitor*).

Perhaps the most objectionable watering-down of the meaning of *protagonist* occurs when it is used as an equivalent of *proponent*—e.g.: "Rep. Henry Gonzalez, the Texas Democrat who chairs the housing subcommittee, is the *protagonist* [read *proponent*] of this legislation that also would increase the number of adjustable rate mortgages the FHA may insure" (*San Diego Union-Trib.*).

proud; prideful. The connotative distinction to bear in mind is that *prideful* suggests excessive pride, haughtiness, and disdain. *Prideful* is also moralistic in tone.

proved; proven. *Proved* is the universally preferred past participle of *prove*. But *proven* often ill-advisedly appears—e.g.: "Yet it was another 'Game of the Century,' matching teams that had *proven* [read *proved*] thus far to be unbeatable" (*Boston Globe*).

In AmE, the past participle *proved* is much more common than *proven*, which, like *stricken*, properly exists only as an adjective—e.g.: "But that strategy of occupation and settlement is a *proven* failure—if the object is peace" (*Palm Beach Post*).

P.S.; postscript. The former (usually in capitals and with periods) is, of course, an abbreviation for the latter. In ordinary writing, you're better off spelling out the word—that is, "The postscript added nothing substantial to the letter" is clearer and smoother than "The P.S. added nothing substantial to the letter."

In letter-writing, a second postscript is abbreviated *P.P.S.*

psych, vb.; **psyche,** n. & vb. *Psych* /sɪk/ = (1) to analyze psychologically <don't try to psych my behavior>; (2) to figure out and anticipate correctly <I psyched out my professors and made all A's>; (3) to use intimidating ploys against <but all his gamesmanship didn't psych her out>; or (4) to get mentally prepared for an event <she psyched herself up before the competition>. As a verb, *psyche* is a variant spelling.

Psyche /**sɪ**-kee/ is best confined to its noun sense: "the human mind or soul."

psychology; psychiatry. *Psychology* is the science of the mind and behavior; *psychiatry* is the branch of medicine dealing with mental or behavioral disorders. A *psychiatrist* holds an M.D., whereas a *psychologist* does not.

PUNCTUATION is the cuing system by which writers signal their readers to slow down, pause, speed up, supply tonal inflections, and otherwise move more smoothly through sentences. Punctuation is like rhetoric: it's a way of giving emphasis and achieving clarity. Meanwhile, punctuation problems are often a prime indicator of poor writing: "[M]ost errors of punctuation arise from ill-designed, badly shaped sentences, and from the attempt to make them work by means of violent tricks with commas and colons" (Hugh Sykes Davies, *Grammar Without Tears*, 1951).

The basic marks—and their uses—are well known. Yet each one sometimes presents difficulties. Even the best writers should pay close attention to these matters because the more sophisticated the writing is, the subtler and more varied the punctuation becomes. And punctuating well is essential to writing solid sentences.

For help with various marks, see APOSTROPHE, BULLET DOT, COLON, COMMA, DASHES, ELLIPSIS DOTS, EXCLA-

MATION POINT, HYPHEN, PARENTHESES, PERIOD, QUESTION MARK, QUOTATION MARKS & VIRGULE.

purchase. See **buy (B).**

purposely; purposefully. *Purposely* = on purpose; intentionally. *Purposefully* = with a specific purpose in mind; with the idea of accomplishing a certain result. Some writers fall into INELEGANT VARIATION with these words—e.g.: "For someone to be guilty of witness tampering, they must have acted *purposely*. Accidentally interfering with a witness, for example, does not qualify. Because the indictments did not specify Montgomery acted *purposefully* [read *purposely*], Mohl 'quashed,' or voided, the indictments" (*Manchester Union Leader*).

pyjamas. See **pajamas.**

Q

QUADRI-; QUADRU-; QUADRA-. In Latinate words denoting four of something, *quadri-* is the usual form, as in *quadripartite* (= having four parts), *quadrillion* (= 10^{15} [consisting of four groups of three zeros after 1,000]), and *quadrivium* (= the four divisions of study in the medieval curriculum, consisting of arithmetic, geometry, astronomy, and music).

Quadru- is the usual form for words in which the second element begins with a *-p-*, as in *quadruped* (= a four-legged animal), *quadruple* (= to multiply by four), and *quadruplet* (= one of four children born at one birth). The two words in which *quadru-* precedes a word without a *-p-* are rare: *quadrumanous* (= four-handed) and *quadrumvirate* (= a group of four men united in some way).

Although Eric Partridge said that *quadra-* is "always wrong" (*U&A*), it appears unexceptionably in many terms deriving from Late Latin, such as *quadragesimal* (= of or relating to Lent) and *quadrangle* (= a four-sided figure). And 20th-century word coiners have devised words such as *quadraphonic* (= of or relating to a sound system with four loudspeakers) and *quadrathlon* (= an athletic contest involving four events).

But in one word especially—*quadriplegia*—the medial *-i-* is sometimes wrongly made *-a-*. About 10% of the time, the misspelling *quadraplegia* appears—e.g.: "[T]he sudden bending of the neck . . . can lead to spinal cord injury and permanent paralysis of both arms and legs (known as *quadraplegia* [read *quadriplegia*])" (*Chicago Trib.*).

quality. When used as an adjective meaning "of high quality," this is a VOGUE WORD and a casualism <a quality bottling company>. Use *good* or *fine* or some other adjective of better standing.

quandary = a mental state of perplexity or confusion <now that he's been told the truth, he's in a quandary about his next step>. The word best describes a state of mind and should not be detached from mental processes. That is, it shouldn't be used as a synonym of *problem*, *challenge*, *issue*, or *dilemma*—e.g.: "One of the most difficult *quandaries* [read *issues*] about assisted suicide stems from the uncertainty of medicine" (*Tampa Trib.*).

Because the *-ary* is unstressed, the misspelling *quandry* sometimes appears—e.g.: "The arrival of the REITs is putting the titans in a *quandry* [read *quandary*]" (*Boston Globe*).

quantify; quantitate. The latter is a NEEDLESS VARIANT newly popular with social scientists, whose word choice should never be treated as a strong recommendation.

quantum leap; quantum jump. These terms, once technical but now part of the popular idiom, date from the early 20th century. They denote "a sudden, extensive change (usu. an improvement) in the rate of progress." Although purists insist that, in physics, the change is merely abrupt but not necessarily large or dramatic, anyone using the term in that way is sure to be misunderstood in most contexts—even technical ones. The popular sense, involving a massive change, seems genuinely useful. Its only disadvantage is that it's now a VOGUE WORD and a CLICHÉ.

The phrase *quantum leap* is 20 times more common today than *quantum jump*.

quasi—pronounced /**kwah**-zee/ or /**kway**-zɪ/—means "as if; seeming or seemingly; in the nature of; nearly." In legal writing, *quasi* may stand alone as a word, but as a prefix it's generally hyphenated. The term has been prefixed to any number of adjectives and nouns, e.g., *quasi-compulsory*, *quasi-domicile*, *quasi-judicial*, and *quasi-monopoly*.

quelch is a malformed PORTMANTEAU WORD from *quell* and *squelch*, perhaps through a false association with *quench*. Although few dictionaries record it, it's hardly uncommon—e.g.: "He aggravated scholars even further by *quelching* [read *squelching*] hopes that he might release reams of hitherto unread Joyceana sealed in a suitcase in the Irish national library" (*Boston Globe*). (On the use of *aggravate* for *irritate* in that sentence, see **aggravate.**) What's the principle for deciding between *squelch* and *quell*? *Squelch* is better for the idea of stifling talk, emotions, thoughts, and the like. *Quell* is better for the idea of stifling a violent uprising or competitive bid.

query. See **inquiry (c).**

question as to whether. See **question whether.**

QUESTION MARK [?]. A question mark follows every question that expects an answer. Typically, the next word begins with a capital letter. "He asked me, 'Why are you here?' A foolish question." But it's also possible to have a midsentence question mark—e.g.: "Why should what is supposed to be a sacrament be performed with everyone looking on?—with that most desolating of all assemblages, a family reunion" (Edmund Wilson, "Things I Consider Overrated" (1920), in *From the Uncollected Edmund Wilson*, 1995). Most authorities recommend not placing a comma after the question mark in such a sentence; yet, though it seems a little old-fashioned, Wilson's em-dash after the question mark is quite acceptable.

A question mark is not used after indirect questions <He asked me why I was there>. See QUESTIONS, DIRECT AND INDIRECT.

A question mark may be placed in brackets after a word, phrase, or date whose accuracy is doubted <Sangad Anurugsa[?]>.

questionnaire —so spelled—is occasionally misspelled *questionaire*.

question of whether. See **question whether.**

QUESTIONS, DIRECT AND INDIRECT. A direct question—one explicitly posed—ends with a question mark. E.g.:

- "How can demand be controlled and stimulated?" (Helen E. Haines, *Living with Books*, 1950).
- "There are [other cultures that] seem to have largely succeeded in taming or repressing [envy]. What causes such differences? Is it perhaps the varying frequency of certain types of personality and character?" (Helmut Schoeck, *Envy: A Theory of Social Behavior*, 1970).
- "Does he or she have pockets deep enough to finance future rounds?" (*Nation's Bus.*).

But an indirect question—one posed at a distance from the actual asking—ends with a period. E.g.:

- "In Clarksdale, Miss., a motel desk clerk diplomatically inquired what we were doing in that city, having noted we were from Florida" (*St. Petersburg Times*).
- "Reamer himself, when asked what value he added, once replied, 'absolutely none' " (*Fortune*).
- "I wondered what he was thinking" (*Mothering*).

Writers sometimes err by putting a question mark after an indirect question, especially one beginning with *I wonder*—e.g.: "*I wonder* whether the NAACP would have considered it proper if the Ku Klux Klan had similarly paid off the plaintiffs in Brown v. The Board of Education?" (*Fresno Bee*). In that example, the question mark should be a period.

question whether; question as to whether; question of whether. The first is preferred. The other two are common prolixities. See **whether (B).**

queue, vb., makes *queued* and *queuing* (not *queueing*). For the sense of the noun as well as the verb, see **cue.**

queue up. See **cue (B).**

quick. Although *quick*, as an adverb, dates back to Middle English, *quickly* has long been considered preferable in serious writing. To say *she learns quick* is so casual as to be slangy. But some exceptions occur in SET PHRASES such as *Come quick!* (sometimes also *Come quickly!*) and *get-rich-quick schemes.* Some instances are close calls—e.g.: "Police said they believe that the explosives were stolen and dumped in the A.B. Jewell water reservoir by someone who wanted to get rid of them *quick*" (*Dallas Morning News*). Cf. **slow.**

quiet, n.; **quietness; quietude.** *Quiet* = silence; stillness; peace <the quiet of Wolfson College when the students had departed>. *Quietness* = the condition of being silent or still <they had mistakenly attributed her quietness to shyness>. *Quietude* = a state or period of repose <after a three-month quietude, he resumed work once again>.

quiet, v.t.; **quieten.** The preferred verb form is *quiet*. Chiefly a Britishism, *quieten* was considered a superfluous word by H.W. Fowler (*MEU1*). Avoid it.

quit = (1) to stop; or (2) to leave. For sense 1, the past tense is *quit* <he finally quit snoring>. For sense 2, which is more common in BrE than in AmE, the past tense is *quitted* <he quitted the suburbs and moved downtown>.

quorum. Pl. *quorums*. See PLURALS (B).

QUOTATION MARKS [" "]. Reserve quotation marks for five situations: (1) when you're quoting someone; (2) when you're referring to a word as a word <the word "that">; (3) when you mean so-called-but-not-really <if he's a "champion," he certainly doesn't act like one>; (4) when you're creating a new word for something—and then only on its first appearance <I'd call him a "mirb," by which I mean . . . >; and (5) when you're marking titles of magazine articles, book chapters, poems not published separately, and songs <having been put on the spot, she sang "Auld Lang Syne" as best she could>.

In marking quotations, writers and editors of AmE and BrE have developed different conventions for quotation marks (or "inverted commas," as the British call them). In AmE, double quotation marks are used for a first quotation; single marks for a quotation within a quotation; double again for a further quotation inside that; etc. In BrE, the practice is exactly the reverse at each step.

With a closing quotation mark, practices vary. In AmE, it is usual to place a period or comma within the closing quotation mark, whether or not the punctuation so placed is actually a part of the quoted matter. In BrE, by contrast, the closing quotation mark comes before any punctuation marks, unless these marks form a part of the quotation itself (or what is quoted is *less* than a full sentence in its own right). Thus:

AmE:	(1)	"Joan pointedly said, 'We won't sing "God Save the Queen." ' "
	(2)	"She looked back on her school years as being 'unmitigated misery.' "
BrE:	(1)	'Joan pointedly said, "We won't sing 'God Save the Queen'." '
	(2)	'She looked back on her school years as being "unmitigated misery".'

In both sets of examples, the outermost quotation marks indicate that a printed source is being quoted directly.

When question marks and exclamation marks are involved, AmE and BrE practice is the same. They're either inside or outside the end quotation mark depending on whether they're part of what's being quoted—e.g.: (AmE) "Did Nelson really say 'Kiss me, Hardy'?"/

(BrE) 'Did Nelson really say "Kiss me, Hardy"?' But when the question or exclamation mark is an integral part of what is being quoted, it is swept inside all quotation marks (i.e., inverted commas): (AmE) "Banging her fist on the table, she exclaimed, 'And that's *that*!' "/ (BrE) 'Banging her fist on the table, she exclaimed, "And that's *that*!" ' (Note that when the end of an interrogatory or an exclamatory sentence coincides with the end of another sentence that embraces it, the stronger mark of punctuation is sufficient to end *both* sentences. A period need not also be included.)

Colons and semicolons are placed outside quotation marks—e.g.: "John didn't shout 'Fire!'; he did, however, say that he smelled smoke."

As to quotations that are interrupted to indicate a speaker, AmE and BrE again show different preferences. In AmE, the first comma is placed within the quotation mark <"Sally," he said, "is looking radiant today">; in BrE, the first comma (usually) remains outside the inverted comma, just as though the attribution could be lifted neatly out of the speaker's actual words <'Sally', he said, 'is looking radiant today'>.

Finally, be cautious about using gratuitous quotation marks. Don't use them for PHRASAL ADJECTIVES, don't use them to be cute, and don't use them to suggest that the marked word or phrase is somehow informal or slangy. If you mean what you say, say it without hesitation. If you don't, then use other words. The following examples could be improved by removing the quotation marks and tweaking the sentences: "[F]eatures are the characteristics of a product or service that are 'built-in' when you buy it—in other words, 'the things it already comes with' " (Erica Levy Klein, *Write Great Ads*, 1990)./ "The individual, however, who truly 'made it happen' is our senior vice president, Jim Savage. . . . Since he and I are virtually always on the 'same page' in our philosophy and thoughts, I had a double advantage of having a dedicated, experienced, bright collaborator who made a magnificent contribution" (Zig Ziglar, *Ziglar on Selling*, 1991).

QUOTATIONS. A. Use of Quoted Material. The deft and incidental use of quotations is a rare art. Poor writers are apt to overuse block quotations (see (B)). Those who do this abrogate their duty, namely, to *write*. Readers tend to skip over single-spaced mountains of prose, knowing how unlikely it is that so much of a previous writer's material pertains directly to the matter at hand.

Especially to be avoided is quoting another writer at the end of a paragraph or section, a habit infused with laziness. Skillful quoters subordinate the quoted material to their own prose and use only the most clearly applicable parts of the previous writing. And even then, they weave it into their own narrative or analysis, not allowing the quoted to overpower the quoter.

B. Handling Block Quotations. The best way to handle them, of course, is not to handle them at all: quote smaller chunks. Assuming, though, that this goal is unattainable—as many writers seem to think it is—then the biggest challenge is handling a quotation so that it will actually get read. The secret is in the lead-in.

Before discussing how a good lead-in reads, let us look at how many of them read. They're dead:

- According to one authority: . . . .
- The author went on to state: . . . .
- The article concludes as follows: . . . .
- As stated by one critic: . . . .

Anyone who wants to become a stylist must vow to try *never* to introduce a quotation in this way. Readers are sure to skip the quotation.

With a long quotation, the better practice is to evoke the upshot of the quotation in the lead-in. Thus, the lead-in becomes an assertion, and the quotation becomes the support. Feeling as if the writer has asserted something concrete, the reader will often, out of curiosity, want to verify that assertion.

Consider, for example, how nicely three literary critics introduce quotations. First is Randall Jarrell, in his *Third Book of Criticism* (1965):

- "[H]is poetic rhetoric is embarrassingly threadbare and commonplace, as when he writes about his own lost belief: . . . ."
- "What he says about his childhood is true of his maturity: . . . ."
- "His obsessions, at their worst, are a moral and intellectual disaster and make us ashamed for him: . . . ."

Second is William Empson, in *Argufying: Essays on Literature and Culture* (1987):

- "The first reply of Lamb (3 October) begins with the words, 'Your letter was an inestimable treasure to me,' but the next one grieves that Coleridge is not settling down to a serious course of life, and the third (24 October) questions the doctrines that Coleridge has preached: . . . ."
- "Mr. Piper sometimes admits that a use of words by a Romantic is bad, but even so he considers it bad in a different way from what we think: . . . ."
- "[H]e quotes from 'A General Introduction for My Work' (1937) about the undirected hatred that sprouts in the modern world: . . . ."

Third is Hermione Lee, in her essay entitled "*Power*: Women and the Word," in *The State of the Language* (Christopher Ricks & Leonard Michaels eds., 1990):

- "Adrienne Rich, in an essay called 'Power and Danger,' gives a feminist history of the word as used against women: . . . ."
- "Any rewriting of women's history, as in this neutrally uninformative passage, has to center on the word: . . . ."
- "Toril Moi (arguing with Irigaray over the word *power*) writes these heartening words: . . . ."

How does such a lead-in work in the fuller context? Here's an example from the masterly Christopher Ricks:

> William Blake knew, whether or not torment may hereafter prove eternal, that eternity may itself be a torment to contemplate:
>
> Time is the mercy of Eternity; without Time's swiftness
> Which is the swiftest of all things: all were eternal torment.
>
> Christopher Ricks, *Beckett's Dying Words* 24 (1993).

When the writer gives the upshot in the introductory words, readers aren't left hunting for the quotation's central idea.

This method has the benefit not only of ensuring that the quotation is read, but also of enhancing the writer's credibility. For if the lead-in is pointed as well as accurate, the reader will agree that the quotation supports the writer's assertion.

C. Punctuating the Lead-In. Writers usually have four choices: a colon, a comma, a period (i.e., no lead-in, really—only an independent sentence before the quotation), or no punctuation. A long quotation ordinarily requires a colon—e.g.:

> My concern today is with what might be called the Higher Bibliography (*bibliology* would be a better word), and in particular with the superior historical certainty increasingly claimed for such investigations. Here, as a sample, is a characteristic pronouncement:
>
> When bibliography and textual criticism join [*sc.* in the editing of a definitive text], it is impossible to imagine one without the other. Bibliography may be said to attack textual problems from the mechanical point of view, using evidence which must deliberately avoid being colored by literary considerations. Nonbibliographical textual criticism works with meanings and literary values. If these last are divorced from all connection with the evidence of the mechanical process that imprinted meaningful symbols on a sheet of paper, no check-rein of fact or probability can restrain the farthest reaches of idle speculation. [Fredson Bowers, *On Editing Shakespeare and the Elizabethan Dramatists* 34–35 (1955).]

> On the contrary, I shall argue, the only check-rein on idle critical speculation is critical speculation that is *not* idle.
>
> F.W. Bateson, "The New Bibliography and the 'New Criticism,' " in *Essays in Critical Dissent* 1–2 (1972).

Some writers, though, let the lead-in and the quotation stand as separate sentences; that is, Bateson might have used a period instead of the colon when leading into the Bowers quotation. But the colon helps tie the quotation to the text and is therefore generally superior. A period would leave the quotation in a sort of syntactic limbo.

A comma typically introduces a short quotation that isn't set off from the rest of the text—e.g.:

> True, I can't quite match [Barzun's] example of the novelist who submitted a manuscript in which one of his characters spoke about seeing a play starring the Lunts; it came back to him from his publisher with the marginal suggestion, "Wouldn't the Hunts be better?"
>
> John Gross, "Editing and Its Discontents," in *The State of the Language* 282, 285 (Christopher Ricks & Leonard Michaels eds., 1990).

A colon would be permissible in place of that comma, but it would introduce the quotation more formally and give a stronger pause. With the comma, the reader glides more easily into the silly suggestion that Gross quotes.

When is it best to use no punctuation at all? Only when the introductory language moves seamlessly into the quoted material. E.g.:

> Thus, Wilson is able to say of the Dickens family penury and of Charles's childhood humiliations that they are biographical data
>
> worth knowing and bearing in mind, because they help us to understand what Dickens was trying to say. He was less given to false moral attitudes or to fear of respectable opinion than most of the great Victorians; but . . . the meaning of Dickens's work has been obscured by that element of the conventional which Dickens himself never quite outgrew.
>
> Janet Groth, *Edmund Wilson: A Critic for Our Time* 25 (1989).

The mere fact that what is being introduced is a block quotation does not mean that some additional punctuation is necessary.

D. American and British Systems. In AmE, quotations that are short enough to be run into the text (usually fewer than 50 words) are set off by pairs of *double* quotation marks ("..."). In BrE, quoted text that is not long enough to be a block quotation is set off by *single* quotation marks ('. . .'). See QUOTATION MARKS.

quote (properly a verb) for *quotation* is a casualism—e.g.: "Most of his really good *quotes*, which have an off-the-cuff originality when heard at a campaign rally, are rehashes from the book" (*N.Y. Newsday*). The problem with *quotation* is that, to the writer who hopes to deliver goods quickly, the three syllables sound and read as if they are slowing the sentence down. The single syllable of *quote*, meanwhile, sounds apt to such a writer. And it sounds more and more natural all the time, as it seems to predominate in spoken English. So although it remains informal for now, it's likely to gain ground in formal prose.

R

raccoon; racoon. The animal is North American, and the AmE spelling is *raccoon*. The BrE spelling—a variant form in AmE—is *racoon*. Presumably Americans have many more occasions to spell the word than Britons do.

rack. See **wrack.**

racket; racquet. For the implement used in net games, *racket* is standard. The variant form *racquet* appears in some proper names (e.g., the Palm Springs Racquet Club) seemingly because the "fancy" spelling looks more high-toned. Perhaps that also explains why, in the sport of squash, *racquet* has somehow become the predominant spelling. The same is true of *racquetball*, the related sport using short-handled rackets.

radiocast. See **broadcast.**

radius. The Latin plural *radii*, traditionally the preferred form, outnumbers *radiuses* by a 9-to-1 margin in modern print sources. E.g.: "[D]uring a turn, the two skis cut different *radii*—the outside ski carving a wider turn than the inside ski" (*Seattle Post-Intelligencer*).

railroad; railway. As nouns these words are virtually equivalent. *W2* makes the following distinction: "*Railroad* . . . is usually limited to roads [with lines or rails fixed to ties] for heavy steam transportation and also to steam roads partially or wholly electrified or roads for heavy traffic designed originally for electric traction. The lighter electric street-car lines and the like are usually termed *railways*." In BrE, however, streetcar lines are commonly called *trainlines* and the vehicles *traincars* or *trammy cars*.

Railroad is used universally as a verb <passenger railroading>, figuratively as well as literally—e.g.: "But we're Brooklynites, so watch out; we will not be *railroaded*" (*N.Y. Times*). This sense is now used in BrE as well as AmE.

raise. A. And *rear*. The old rule, still sometimes observed, is that crops and livestock are *raised* and children are *reared*. But today the phrase *born and raised* is about eight times more common than *born and reared*. E.g.: "Reynolds, born and *raised* in Texas and still carrying a trace of an accent, believes he'll come under fire" (*Chicago Sun-Times*). Indeed, *born and reared* is likely to sound affected in AmE.

B. And *rise*. The straightforward distinction is that *raise* (raise > raised > raised) is transitive, while *rise* (rise > rose > risen) is intransitive. Here the rule is followed: "For 40 years the farmer has *risen* at 4:00 in the morning to tend to his crops and *raise* his chickens." But the following example incorrectly uses *raise* as an intransitive verb: "Then it [an alligator] *raised up* [read *rose*] on all four legs and charged" (*St. Petersburg Times*).

rampant means "widespread, unrestrained" <a rampant epidemic>. Thus, bad things become *rampant in* places; places don't become *rampant with* bad things. Yet some writers get this backwards—e.g.: "Officials and residents in the area want to revive and showcase the glory that was Bronzeville before it becomes *rampant* [read *rife*] with large *tracks* [read *tracts*] of vacant land and dilapidated buildings" (*Dubuque Telegraph Herald*). (For the second error in that sentence, see **track.**)

ransack (= to search thoroughly, esp. for loot; pillage) is occasionally misspelled *ramsack*—e.g.: "After Kentland was *ramsacked* [read *ransacked*] by

Union troops during the Civil War, Kent rebuilt Kentland" (*Roanoke Times & World News*).

rap (= a negative allegation or reputation) typically appears in the phrase *bad rap* or *bum rap*. It's occasionally confused with the word *wrap* (= a material for covering something)—e.g.: "Even though Edgar Allan Poe gets a bum *wrap* [read *rap*] for 'just dying here,' his genealogy is deeply rooted in this city's history" (*Baltimore Sun*).

rappel (= to engage in the mountain-climber's maneuver of descending a precipice with a double rope) is sometimes confounded with the similar-sounding *repel*—e.g.: "[T]he soldiers-in-training climbed up and *repelled* [read *rappelled*] down mountains" (*Orange County Register*). Because the verb is accented on the second syllable (/ra-**pel**/), its inflected forms have a double *-l-*: *rappelled, rappelling*. See SPELLING (B).

rare; scarce. In the best usage, *rare* refers to a consistent infrequency, usually of things of superior quality <diamonds having more than three carats remain quite rare>. *Scarce* refers to anything that is not plentiful, even ordinary things that are temporarily hard to find <job opportunities are scarce this year>. Writers sometimes misuse *rare* for *scarce*—e.g.: "Flowers are frequent, usually in the warmer months, but fruit is *rare* [read *scarce*] in the Tampa Bay area" (*St. Petersburg Times*).

rarebit. See **Welsh rabbit.**

rarefaction /rar-ə-**fak**-shən/ = (1) the act or process of making less dense; the state of being less dense; or (2) the act or process of purifying; the state of being purified. The forms *rarefication* and *rarification* are erroneous.

rarefy (= [1] to make or become less dense or solid; or [2] to purify) is often misspelled *rarify*—e.g.: "Too often, when we wonder why government and its institutions cost so much, we gaze down for solutions, look to the bottom of the pond where real life goes on instead of peering into that murky but *rarified* [read *rarefied*] algae bloom" (*Boston Globe*). See -FY.

rarely ever, though old, is literally nonsensical—as many idioms are, of course. But this one is easily corrected to *rarely* or *rarely if ever*, usually the former—e.g.: "Zimmerman had *rarely ever* [read *rarely*] spoken of his own traumatic history with domestic violence" (*Hartford Courant*). Cf. **seldom ever.**

The phrasing *rarely or ever* has no justification at all—e.g.: "Three out of four of us questioned earlier this year said we *'rarely or ever'* [read *'rarely if ever'*] trust government" (*Peoria J. Star*).

rase. See **raze.**

rather. A. *Rather than.* This phrase can function either as a conjunction or as a preposition. As a conjunction (the more common use), *rather than* demands that the constructions on each side of it be parallel: "If we can, we will solve this problem diplomatically *rather than* forcibly." But as a preposition, *rather than* can connect nonparallel constructions: "*Rather than* staying home on a Saturday night, we went out to six different bars."

When *rather than* separates two verbs, it's often less awkward to convert the verbs into gerunds: "I've always liked *going* out rather than *staying* in." But sometimes *rather than* appears between simple verbs—e.g.: "[W]ith due respect to Shakespeare and others, we want our girls to *communicate* freely with the live world around them *rather than plunge* into musty old books" (Vladimir Nabokov, *Lolita*, 1955). Many modern writers would make that *rather than plunging*.

B. *Rather . . . instead of.* This phrasing, an example of SWAPPING HORSES, sometimes displaces what should be a straightforward *rather . . . than*—e.g.: "The tragedy of Ms. Charen's column is that it reveals a writer who would *rather* be glib and sarcastic *instead of* [read *than*] measured and sincere" (*Syracuse Herald-J.*).

rather unique. See ADJECTIVES (B).

rational. See **reasonable.**

raze (= to tear down) is the standard spelling. *Rase*, a variant, is chiefly BrE.

RE- PAIRS. Many English words beginning with the prefix *re-* take on different meanings depending on whether the prefix is hyphenated or closed up. Some of these words, whose two different senses with and without the hyphen should be self-explanatory, are:

re(-)bound
re(-)call
re(-)claim
re(-)collect
re(-)count
re(-)cover
re(-)create
re(-)dress
re(-)form
re(-)fund
re(-)lay
re(-)lease
re(-)mark
re(-)move
re(-)place
re(-)present
re(-)prove
re(-)search
re(-)sent
re(-)serve
re(-)sign
re(-)sound
re(-)store
re(-)treat

-RE; -ER. See -ER (B).

real is dialectal when used for *very*—e.g.: "Competition in recent years hasn't been *real* [read *very*] friendly" (*Wall St. J.*).

realtor; real-estate agent; estate agent. *Realtor* (= a real-estate agent or broker) has two syllables, not three: /**reel**-tər/, not /**reel**-ə-tər/. (See PRONUNCIATION (B).) This Americanism is ill-formed, since the *-or* suffix in Latin is appended only to verb elements, and *realt-* is not a verb element. But the term is too well established in AmE to quibble with its makeup. Its shortness commends it.

Some authorities suggest that it should be capitalized and used only in its proprietary trademark sense, that is, "a member of the National Association of Realtors"; that organization invented and registered the trademark in 1916. Few people seem to know about the trademark, and consequently in AmE the term is used indiscriminately of real-estate agents generally. In BrE, *real-estate agents* are known as *estate agents*; *realtor* is virtually unknown, and *real estate* is only a little better known.

rear. See **raise** (A).

rearward(s). See DIRECTIONAL WORDS (A).

reasonable; rational. Generally, *reasonable* means "according to reason; sensible"; *rational* means "having reason." Yet *reasonable* is often used in reference to persons in the sense "having the faculty of reason" <reasonable person>. When applied to things, the two words are perhaps more clearly differentiated: "In application to things *reasonable* and *rational* both signify according to *reason*; but the former is used in reference to the business of life, as a *reasonable* proposal, wish, etc.; *rational* to abstract matters, as *rational* motives, grounds, questions, etc." (George Crabb, *Crabb's English Synonymes*, 1917).

reason is because. This construction is loose, because *reason* implies *because* and vice versa. After *reason is*, you'll need a noun phrase, a predicate adjective, or a clause introduced by *that*. The best cure for *reason is because* is to replace *because* with *that*—e.g.: "Marcello (Jean Reno) has one frantic mission in life: to keep anyone from dying in the small Italian village where he lives. The *reason is because* [read *reason is that*] there are only three plots left in the local cemetery and his terminally ill wife, Roseanna (Mercedes Ruehl), wishes only that she be buried next to their daughter" (*Newark Star-Ledger*).

Variations such as *reason is due to* are no better—e.g.: "It's a challenge for any athlete to come back after four years of inactivity. The challenge is even greater when *the reason is due to injury* [read *the layoff is due to injury* or *injury is the cause*]" (*Tulsa Trib. & Tulsa World*).

reason why; reason that. Both forms are correct. It's an unfortunate SUPERSTITION that *reason why* is an objectionable REDUNDANCY. True, it is mildly redundant (as are *time when* and *place where*), but it has long been idiomatic, and good writers routinely use it—e.g.: "Prime-time programming may drain your brain, but there's no *reason why* your TV set should" (*Time*).

Moreover, *reason that* is often a poor substitute—as in any of the examples just quoted—just as *time that* and *place that* are poor substitutes when adverbials of time and place are called for. Cf. the indefensible REDUNDANCY **reason is because.**

rebound; re-bound. See RE- PAIRS.

rebut; refute. *Rebut* means "to attempt to refute." *Refute* means "to defeat (countervailing arguments)." Thus one who *rebuts* certainly hopes to *refute*; it is immodest to assume, however, that one has *refuted* another's arguments. *Rebut* is sometimes wrongly written *rebutt*.

recall; re-call. See RE- PAIRS.

receipt of, in. See **in receipt of.**

reckless (= heedless; rash; willfully careless), in a gross misspelling, sometimes appears as *wreckless*—which seems to denote precisely the opposite of what it's supposed to mean. As literacy in the higher sense has become ever shakier, this error has become disturbingly common—e.g.: "It begins with the cast making mindless revelry; the quality of movement is disturbingly loose and *wreckless* [read *reckless*]" (*Philadelphia Inquirer*)./ "Racette was charged with *wreckless* [read *reckless*] operation of a motor vehicle, speeding and failure to keep right, police said" (*Boston Globe*).

For more on *reckless*, see **wanton.**

reclaim; re-claim. See RE- PAIRS.

recognize /**re**-kəg-nɪz/ is often mispronounced /**re**-kə-nɪz/, without the *-g-* sounded.

recount; re-count. See RE- PAIRS.

recur; reoccur. The first means "to happen repeatedly, often at predictable intervals." The second means merely "to happen again."

REDUNDANCY. Washington Irving wrote that "redundancy of language is never found with deep reflection. Verbiage may indicate observation, but not thinking. He who thinks much says but little in proportion to his thoughts." Those words are worth reflecting on.

This linguistic pitfall is best exemplified, rather than discoursed on:

- "A woman with a permanent disability who claims she received a low *test* score for the law school entrance *exam test* because the testgivers wouldn't accommodate her has sued them for emotional distress" (*L.A. Daily J.*). (*Test* appears twice, once in the phrase *exam test*.)
- "Bush also went high profile, *choosing* as one of his *picks* baseball legend Nolan Ryan for a six-year term" (*Austin American-Statesman*). (*Choosing as one of his picks* is tautological. If it read, less colloquially, *choosing as one of his*

choices it would have been more obvious both to the writer and to the editors that the phrasing was redundant.)

- "Ms. Kwok believed *the cause of the heavy rainfall was due to two major factors* [read *the cause of the heavy rainfall was twofold* or *the heavy rainfall was due to two major factors*]" (*South China Morning Post*).
- "Unaware of the spider's *poisonous venom* [read *venom* or *poisonous bite*], Martinez grabbed a piece of *tissue paper* [read *tissue*] to get rid of it the way she normally gets rid of critters" (*Denver Post*).
- "That each creature from microbe to man is unique in all the world is amazing when you consider that every life form is assembled from *the same identical* [read *the same* or *identical*] building blocks" (*N.Y. Times*). See **identical.**

Samuel Johnson once advised writers to "avoid ponderous ponderosity." His repetition of word roots, of course, was purposeful. But many writers engage in such repetitions with no sense of irony, as in the phrases *build a building*, *refer to a reference*, *point out points*, *an individualistic individual*. In the sentence that follows, the repetition seems to be a thoughtless error: "Other issues include preserving a minimum set of *state-required requirements* [read *state-imposed requirements* or *state requirements*] like class size and teacher benefits in home-rule districts" (*Dallas Morning News*).

Though many of such mistakes look like unique ones—the result of semiconscious writing—some are so commonplace that they've been all but enshrined in the language. Adept editors must be alert to phrases like these:

absolute necessity
basic fundamentals
collaborate together
connect together
few in number
free gift
future forecast
future plans
general consensus of opinion
many . . . abound
merge together
mingle together
mix together
mutual advantage of both
pair of twins
pause for a moment
plead a plea
reason is because
reelected for another term
regress back
still continues to
surrounded on all sides
throughout the entire
visible to the eye

reek; wreak. These homophones are occasionally confused. *Reek*, vb., = to give off an odor or vapor <the house reeked of gas>. *Reek*, n., = an odorous vapor <the reek of garlic spoiled our conversation>. *Wreak* = to inflict, bring about <to wreak havoc>.

Reek havoc is a frequent blunder—e.g.: "Past hurricanes have *reeked* [read *wreaked*] havoc on this small fishing community of east Apalachicola" (*Christian Science Monitor*).

Also, *wreak* for *reek* is a surprisingly common slip-up—e.g.: "Though such a statement *wreaks* [read *reeks*] of hyperbole, Alexakis truly seemed more comfortable with the intimate give-and-take at this sold-out Middle East date on his solo tour" (*Boston Herald*). See **wreak.**

reference, as a verb meaning "to provide with references," is defensible. E.g.: "The cross-*referenced* chapter contains two subsections." The term has become a VOGUE WORD, however, as a synonym for *refer to*—e.g.: " 'And I would simply *reference* [read *refer to*] those of you who are out there working' " (*N.Y. Times* [quoting Bobby Ray Inman]). See NOUNS AS VERBS & COMPUTERESE.

referendum. Pl. *referendums* or *referenda*. In modern print sources, *referendums* is four times more common—and as the native plural, it ought to be preferred. See PLURALS (B).

reform; re-form. See RE- PAIRS.

refrain; restrain. Both mean generally "to put restraints upon," but *refrain* always concerns oneself in the sense "to abstain" <he refrained from exchanging scurrilities with his accuser>, whereas *restrain* concerns either someone else <the police illegally restrained the complainant from going into the stadium> or oneself (reflexively) <I couldn't restrain myself>.

Refrain is sometimes misused for *restrain*, as a reflexive verb—e.g.: "I had to *refrain myself* [read *restrain myself* or *refrain*] from snapping that I wasn't quite ready to date" (*Albuquerque J.*).

refund; re-fund. See RE- PAIRS.

refute. See **rebut.**

regard. A. As a Noun in *with regard to* and *in regard to*. The singular noun is correct. The plural form (as in *with regards to* and *in regards to*) is, to put it charitably, poor usage—e.g.: "In the case of Angel, it is [set] to a simple piano accompaniment, *and with regards to* [read *but with regard to* or, better, *but with*] Mimi and Roger, there is a musical gap when the line is spoken" (*L.A. Times*).

The acceptable forms are best used as introductory phrases. But even these may be advantageously replaced by a single word such as *concerning*, *regarding*, or *considering*, or even *in*, *about*, or *for*.

The plural *regards* is acceptable only in the phrase *as regards*. But some writers mistakenly use *with regards to*—e.g.: "He became furious at the mere mention of George F. Will, the columnist who accused him recently of 'judicial exhibitionism' *with regards to* [read *with regard to*] his trade-agreement ruling" (*N.Y. Times*).

B. As a Verb in *highly regarded* and *widely regarded*. The verb *regard* commonly appears in these two combinations. The one phrase, *highly regarded*, is a vague expression of praise; the other, *widely regarded as*, usually leads to words of praise—though it would certainly be possible to say that someone is *widely regarded as beneath contempt*. It's a mistake, however, to truncate the latter phrase—to say *widely regarded* in place of *highly regarded*: "Crotty has published four novels since leaving the newspaper, and he's *widely regarded* [read *highly regarded*] by both fiction writers and journalists."

regardless (= without regard to) should not be used for *despite* (= in spite of). E.g.: "Take heart. *Regardless* [read *Despite*] what happened Saturday, the Broncos will be performing in the Super Bowl Sunday" (*Rocky Mountain News*). Though longer, *regardless of* would also be acceptable in that sentence. See **irregardless.**

regardless whether is unidiomatic for *regardless of whether*—e.g.: "When he wanted to send troops to help end the civil war a year ago, President Clinton told a skeptical public and Congress that they would be withdrawn in December 1996 *regardless whether* [read *regardless of whether*] peace had been achieved" (*Fla. Times-Union*). See **whether (C).**

regards. See **regard (A) & as regards.**

regiment (= a military unit made up of several battalions) is coming to be misused for *regimen* (= a systematic plan designed to improve health, skills, etc.)—e.g.: "Wealthy people plagued with weak nerves and 'autointoxication' flocked to the San, as it was known, from all over the world to undergo a strict *regiment* [read *regimen*] of sinusoidal baths, Vibrotherapy, laughing exercises and five enemas a day" (*Miami Herald*).

regret. See **resent (B).**

regretful; regrettable. Errors made are *regrettable;* the persons who have made them should be *regretful*. The most common error is to misuse *regretful* for *regrettable*, especially in the adverbial forms—e.g.: "*Regretfully* [read *Regrettably*], the articles reflect a failure of contemporary liberalism and progressive politics" (*Chicago Sun-Times*).

rein; reign. Like many homophones, these words are frequently mistaken for each other in print—but perhaps no other pair is confused in so many different ways. Besides the blunders below, see **free rein.**

Rein in, not *reign in*, is the correct phrase for "to check, restrain." The metaphorical image is of the rider pulling on the reins of the horse to slow down (i.e., "hold your horses")—e.g.: "Though the White House has tried to *reign him in* [read *rein him in*], Roger Clinton (Secret Service code name: 'Headache') has ambitions to become more than the President's dysfunctional younger brother" (*Parade*).

The error also occurs with the noun forms: one holds the *reins*, not the *reigns*. E.g.: "Ron Low has a hold of the Oilers' *reigns* [read *reins*] for now, but should he not work out, look for former Canucks and Flyers coach Bob McCammon to take over as coach next season" (*Tampa Trib.*).

As further evidence of Murphy's Law at work, the opposite error (*rein* for *reign*) occurs as well—e.g.: "His *rein* [read *reign*] as Fort Meade's tobacco-chewing, play-calling leader ended abruptly in September 1993" (*Tampa Trib.*).

relate to is a voguish expression characteristic of popular American cant in the 1970s and 1980s <Southern writers can relate to what it's like growing up in Atlanta>. It is unlikely to lose that stigma.

relay; re-lay. See RE- PAIRS.

release; re-lease. See RE- PAIRS.

relegate; delegate. To *relegate* is to consign to an inferior position <because first-class was full, he was relegated to coach>. To *delegate* is to commit (powers or duties) to an agent or representative <Shirley delegated the task to her associate>, or to appoint (a person) as one's agent <I'll delegate you as my stand-in for tomorrow's meeting>.

relevant. The misspelling *revelant* is a classic example of METATHESIS, or the transposition of sounds in a word. The error is more frequent in speech than in writing, but it does appear surprisingly often in print—e.g.: "With drastic service cuts just around the corner for many New Yorkers, Schnieder's film and the subsequent discussion are as *revelant* [read *relevant*] as they were when Abe Beame was mayor" (*N.Y. Newsday*). President Harry S. Truman is said to have blundered often in this way.

remorselessly. A. And *unremorsefully.* These two terms are essentially equivalent. *Remorselessly* is far more common and somewhat more pejorative.

B. Mistakenly Made *remorsely.* Although *remorsely* isn't recorded in the *OED* or other dictionaries, some writers have taken to using it—apparently as a contracted form of *remorselessly*. E.g.: "Ever since then, the belt stars have been slowly but *remorsely* [read *remorselessly*] rising in the sky" (*Daily Mail*). The error is more common in BrE than in AmE.

REMOTE RELATIVES. "[E]very relative word which is used shall instantly present its antecedent to the mind of the reader, without the least obscurity" (Hugh Blair, *Lectures on Rhetoric*, Grenville Kleiser ed., 1911). Surprisingly few modern grammarians discuss what has become an increasingly common problem: the separation of the relative pronoun (*that, which, who*) from its antecedent. For example, in the sentence "The files sitting in the office that I was talking about yesterday are in disarray," the word *that*—technically—

modifies *office*, not *files*. But many writers today would intend to have it modify *files*. They would loosely employ a "remote relative."

The best practice is simply to ensure that the relative pronoun immediately follows the noun it modifies. As the following examples illustrate, lapses involving *which* are extremely common: "This will take the game back to its roots in the 1920s, when we had the Decatur Staleys, owned by Staley's starch company, *which* later became the Chicago Bears" (*Time*). (*Which* modifies *Decatur Staleys*—6 words and 2 nouns before. The Chicago Bears started out as Staley's starch company? Fascinating. Actually, the problem is the parenthetical phrase *owned by Staley's starch company*. A possible revision: *This will take the game back to its roots in the 1920s, when we had the Decatur Staleys, owned by Staley's starch company. That team later became the Chicago Bears*.)

The relative pronoun *that* is almost as troublesome, and when used remotely is even more likely to cause confusion—e.g.: "There is a word unrecognizable even to some crossword puzzle addicts *that* is useful in describing my strategy of survival between May and October. I estivate" (*N.Y. Newsday*). (*That* modifies *word*—8 words and 2 nouns before. A possible revision: *A word unrecognizable even to some crossword-puzzle addicts describes my strategy of survival between May and October. I estivate.*)

Even *who* is used remotely, and just as confusingly (especially if more than one person has been mentioned nearby)—e.g.: "She is the mother of four children *who* at age 15 aborted what would have been her first child, and evidently she seeks to redress that wrong" (*Fresno Bee*). (Who aborted whom? It reads as if the woman's four children aborted what would have been her first child. *Who* is intended to modify *mother*—4 words and 2 nouns before.)

At times, the remote relative may even appear in a phrase such as *in which*—e.g.: "The unexpected announcement renewed speculation about the 74-year-old Pope's broader state of health, particularly because he planned an important speech at the United Nations on the family *in which* he was expected to discuss the Vatican's views of the recent population conference in Cairo" (*N.Y. Times*). (*In which* modifies *speech*—8 words and 3 nouns before. A possible revision: *The unexpected announcement renewed speculation about the 74-year-old Pope's broader state of health, particularly because he planned an important speech at the United Nations on the family. In that speech, he was expected to discuss the Vatican's views of the recent population conference in Cairo.*)

As in the example just quoted, remote relatives often seem to result from the writer's ill-advised combining of two sentences into one. Among the advantages of avoiding remote relatives—such as preventing MISCUES and even ambiguities—is an improved average SENTENCE LENGTH.

For more on relative pronouns, see **that (A).**

remove; re-move. See RE- PAIRS.

remuneration. So spelled. *Renumeration* is an all-too-common misspelling and mispronunciation—e.g.: "Joseph Cammarata . . . said he . . . would recommend rejecting any settlement that did not include financial *renumeration* [read *remuneration*] for Jones" (*Christian Science Monitor*). Cf. METATHESIS.

renounce. See **denounce.**

renowned (= famous) is so spelled. *Reknowned* is wrong but fairly common for *renowned*. E.g.: "Byatt is *reknowned* [read *renowned*] for her intelligence" (*N.Y. Times*).

The noun form is *renown*; there is no verb (despite the past-participial adjective *renowned*). The adjective is sometimes wrongly written *reknown*—e.g.: "Michaels became *reknown* [read *renowned*] for 'The War Song' " (*San Diego Union-Trib.*).

The word is pronounced /ri-**nownd**/.

reoccur. See **recur.**

repay back. This phrase is redundant. Use *repay* or *pay back*—e.g.: "Students who obtain Stafford loans borrow at a reduced interest rate and wait until after graduation to *repay them back* [read *repay them* or *pay them back*]" (*Pitt. Post-Gaz.*).

repeat again; repeat back. Both are REDUNDANCIES.

repellent; repulsive. Both mean, literally, "causing to turn away." *Repulsive* is stronger; it applies to whatever disgusts or offends in the extreme <Fred's constant posing before mirrors and self-adulatory talk are only two examples of his repulsive narcissism>. *Repellent* is often more dispassionately descriptive <a sunblock that is repellent to insects>. Avoid *repellant*, a variant spelling of *repellent*.

replace; re-place. See RE- PAIRS.

repress. See **oppress.**

reputation. See **character.**

research; re-search. See RE- PAIRS.

resent. A. For *begrudge*. Unlike *begrudge*, *resent* shouldn't be used with a direct and an indirect object—e.g.: "It is easy for women to *resent men their easy access* to sexual arousal since our own is often wrapped in thick layers of guilt and insecurity" (*N.Y. Times*). The idiom should be *to begrudge men their easy access* because the verb *resent* always takes a simple direct object.

B. For *regret*. If it's within your control and you've done it, you *regret* it; if it's foisted on you, you *resent* it. E.g.: " 'I think that every person I know who likes me, who talked with Gail Sheehy, frankly *resents* [read *regrets*] having done so, because she so systematically manipulated and was so totally dishonest in the article' " (*Wash. Times* [quoting Speaker of the House Newt Gingrich]).

C. And *re-sent*. See RE- PAIRS.

reserve; re-serve. See RE- PAIRS.

resident. See **citizen** (A).

resign; re-sign. See RE- PAIRS.

resound; re-sound. See RE- PAIRS.

respecting. For *respecting* as an acceptable dangling modifier, see DANGLERS (E).

restaurateur. So spelled. *Restauranteur*, with an intrusive *-n-*, is a common error—e.g.: "Corporate spending is way down, *restauranteurs* [read *restaurateurs*] and caterers say" (*St. Petersburg Times*). The mispronunciation—resulting, of course, from the spelling of *restaurant*—may also be influenced by *raconteur*. See SPELLING (A).

restive = (1) intractable, stubborn, unmanageable; or (2) restless, nervous, unsettled. Although sense 1 is older, sense 2 has become more common. Some critics lament this development, but it seems irreversible—e.g.: "[M]any of the movers and shakers who control so much of New York's economic and financial life are already quite *restive* about the possible huge tax burden on those who live or work in New York" (*N.Y. Times*).

The more serious problem is that *restive* is sometimes misused for *restful*—e.g.: "*Restive* [read *Restful*] moment. Lori takes a time out from sports to relax in her living room" (*Fresno Bee*).

restore; re-store. See RE- PAIRS.

restrain. See **refrain.**

résumé. So spelled—with both accents. Some writers mistakenly omit the first one.

retch, v.i. This verb, meaning "to vomit or try to vomit," is amazingly often misspelled *wretch*—e.g.: "A few weeks ago I found myself stretching out on the couch and *wretching* into a bowl, nursing a headache the size of Montana" (*Ark. Democrat-Gaz.*). *Wretch*, of course, is a noun meaning either "a miserable person" or "a contemptible lowlife."

reticent (= reserved; unwilling to speak freely; taciturn) is frequently misunderstood as being synonymous with *reluctant*—e.g.: "Although the Marlins also have been *reticent* [read *reluctant*] to run (two steals in as many attempts), leadoff batter Devon White was hit by a pitch Sunday, promptly stole second and scored the first Florida run on Bobby Bonila's single" (*N.Y. Newsday*).

retreat; re-treat. See RE- PAIRS.

reurge; re-urge. In AmE, the word is solid: *reurge*.

reuse; re-use. In AmE, the word is solid: *reuse*.

revelant. For this erroneous form, see **relevant.**

revenge. See **avenge.**

revocable; revokable. The first is preferred; the word is pronounced /**re**-və-kə-bəl/. *Revokable* (as well as *revokeable*) is a NEEDLESS VARIANT. See **irrevocable.**

RHOTACISM. See PRONUNCIATION (C).

rid > rid > rid. *Ridded* is a variant form to be avoided—e.g.: "The fish-eating public had a heyday the last time Williams and Badger were *ridded* [read *rid*] of non-game fish" (*Spokane Spokesman Rev.*). See IRREGULAR VERBS.

ridden. See **laden (B).**

ride > rode > ridden. In dialect, *rid* is sometimes used as a past participle. See IRREGULAR VERBS.

rise. See **raise (B).**

rock 'n' roll; rock-'n'-roll; rock'n'roll; rock and roll; rock-and-roll; rock & roll. Each of these is listed in at least one major American dictionary. *Rock 'n' roll* is probably the most common; appropriately, it has a relaxed and colloquial look. *Rock and roll* and *rock-and-roll* are somewhat more formal than the others and therefore not very fitting with the music itself. The others are variant forms—except that *rock-'n'-roll*, with the hyphens, is certainly preferable when the term is used as a PHRASAL ADJECTIVE <the rock-'n'-roll culture of the 1960s>.

Fortunately, the editorial puzzle presented by these variations has largely been solved: almost everyone today refers to *rock music* or simply *rock*. Increasingly, *rock 'n' roll* carries overtones of early rock—the 1950s-style music such as "Rock Around the Clock," by Bill Haley and the Comets.

role; roll. These are sometimes confused. *Roll* has many senses, including breadstuff, but the only sense that causes problems is "a list or register" <the teacher took roll>. *Role*, by contrast, means "a function or part, as in a drama." E.g.: "She has no children with names such as Johnny, John, Peter, Paul, Mary or Martha. Instead, a sampling of names on one of her *roles* [read *rolls*] includes Tiana, Victoria, Carmen, Melissa, Christopher, Phillip, Tyler and Allegra" (*Amarillo Globe News*).

roof, n. Pl. *roofs*, not *rooves*. But the mistaken plural occurs with some frequency—e.g.: "The birds scoured yards for food, roosted in eaves and pooped liberally on tile *rooves* [read *roofs*]" (*Riverside Press-Enterprise*). Cf. **hoof.** See PLURALS (G).

roofed, not *rooved*, is the correct form—e.g.: "These new state farms and cooperatives—clusters of *tin-rooved* [read *tin-roofed*] huts nestling in valleys—have been attacked repeatedly by the rebels" (*Christian Science Monitor*). Cf. **hoof.**

row to hoe is an agricultural or gardening metaphor meaning "a challenging and perhaps arduous project" <it's going to be a tough row to hoe>. Sometimes it's ludicrously written *road to hoe*, especially in sportswriting—e.g.: "Red-hot North Carolina has a tough *road* [read *row*] to hoe" (*Newark Star-Ledger*).

RSVP; rsvp; R.S.V.P.; r.s.v.p. The first is the usual abbreviation of the French phrase *répondez s'il vous plaît* (= respond if you please)—the phrase for requesting responses to invitations. Because the phrase contains the polite idea of "please," it's a REDUNDANCY to say *please* RSVP.

Increasingly, AmE is making the acronym a verb meaning either "to respond" <have you RSVP'd yet?> or "to make reservations" <admission is free, but be sure to RSVP at least two days beforehand>. That's probably why *please* RSVP is becoming so common—e.g.: "If you have received an invitation, *please* RSVP [read *please respond*] . . . so the newspaper will be prepared to honor your organization" (*Ft. Worth Star-Telegram*). See ABBREVIATIONS (B).

RUN-ON SENTENCES do not stop where they should. The problem usually occurs when the writer is uncertain how to handle punctuation or how to handle such adverbs as *however* and *otherwise*, which are often mistakenly treated as conjunctions.

Some grammarians distinguish between a "run-on sentence" (or "fused sentence") and a "comma splice" (or "run-together sentence"). In a run-on sentence, two independent clauses—not joined by a conjunction such as *and*, *but*, *for*, *or*, or *nor*—are incorrectly written with no punctuation between them. Thus a run-on sentence might read: "I need to go to the store the baby needs some diapers." Correctly, it might read: "I need to go to the store; the baby needs some diapers."

With a comma splice, two independent clauses have merely a comma between them, again without a conjunction—e.g.: "I need to go to the store, the baby needs some diapers."

The presence or absence of a comma—and therefore the distinction between a run-on sentence and a comma splice—isn't usually noteworthy. So most writers class the two problems together as run-on sentences.

But the distinction can be helpful in differentiating between the wholly unacceptable (true run-on sentences) and the usually-but-not-always unacceptable (comma splices). That is, most usage authorities accept comma splices when (1) the clauses are short and closely related, (2) there is no danger of a MISCUE, and (3) the context is informal. Thus: "Jane likes him, I don't." But even when all three criteria are met, some readers are likely to object. And in any event a dash seems preferable to a comma in a sentence like that one.

Unjustified comma splices are rare in print, but they do sometimes occur—e.g.: "The remnants of Hurricane Opal will move north through the Tennessee Valley as a tropical storm this morning. Winds near the center of the storm will diminish rapidly, *however*, wind gusts over 60 miles an hour will persist around the storm center" (*N.Y. Times*). In that sentence, the mispunctuation makes for an ambiguous modifier because *however* could go with either the clause before or the clause after. The context suggests that the reading should be with a semicolon after *rapidly*. The best edit would be to replace *however* with *but*—and to delete the comma after it.

run the gantlet. See **gantlet.**

S

's. See POSSESSIVES.

sacrilegious (= violative of something sacred; profane) is so spelled. *Sacreligious* is a common misspelling.

salmon is pronounced /**sa**-mən/, not /**sal**-mən/. But *salmonella* is pronounced with the *-l-*: /sal-mə-**nel**-ə/.

same difference. This phrase is an illogical AmE casualism that is to be avoided not only in writing but in speech as well. "It's all the *same*," "It's the *same* thing," etc. are better.

sanction = (1) to approve; or (2) to penalize. The word is generally understood as bearing sense 1; thus lawyers, who use it primarily in sense 2, are likely to be misunderstood.

As a noun, *sanction* is burdened by the same ambiguity, meaning either (1) "approval" <governmental sanction to sell the goods>, or (2) "penalty" <the statute provides sanctions for violations of the act>. In phrases such as *give sanction to*, the word means "approval"—while *issue sanctions against* shows disapproval.

sank. See **sink.**

save, in the sense "except," is an ARCHAISM best avoided. But as the following examples illustrate, it still occasionally appears—e.g.: "Everyone, *save* [read *except*] for a handful of brief, part-time employees, came back" (*Buffalo News*).

saw > sawed > sawed. The past participle *sawn* is archaic except in attributive uses—e.g.: "A *sawn*-off sweatshirt worn by the beach blonde [Pamela Anderson Lee] is on the auction block for an estimated $1,500 to $2,000" (*Toronto Star*). Even so, *sawed-off shotgun* outranks *sawn-off shotgun* by an 18-to-1 margin.

As a verb form, *sawed* is preferable—e.g.: "The complex could use many of the logs previously chipped for pulp or *sawn* [read *sawed*] into log-grade lumber, company officials said" (*Portland Oregonian*).

say; state, vb. Whenever possible, use *say* rather than *state*. The latter typically sounds stilted. But there is a substantive as well as a tonal difference: *say* means "to tell; to relate," while *state* means "to set out (formally); to make a specific declaration."

scarce. See **rare.**

scarf. Although *scarfs* is listed in most dictionaries as the standard plural, *scarves* is nearly 15 times more common in modern print sources. So *scarves* should be accepted as the preferred form. See PLURALS (G).

Scotch, adj.; **Scottish; Scots,** adj. F.T. Wood, an Englishman, writes: "The Scots (or Scotch?) themselves are less particular than the English in the matter of these three words [*Scotch, Scottish,* and *Scots*]" (*Current English Usage*, 1962). He recommends *Scots* for the noun denoting the people; and *Scottish* when referring to characteristics of the country.

James Boswell, a Scottish lawyer, used *Scotch law* throughout his *Life of Johnson*, and occasionally *Scottish law* as well. Even modern British writers do not use the terms consistently. But one might defensibly say that the preferred forms are *Scots law*, but *Scottish procedure, Scottish arbitration, Scottish legal forms. Scotch*, recorded in the *OED* as a "contracted variant of *Scottish*," is best avoided by those in doubt.

It is sometimes said that *Scotch* should be used of material objects, as

Scotch tartans, *Scotch whisky*, and *Scotch thistle*.

sculpt; sculpture, v.t.; **sculp.** Although the preferred verb has long been thought to be *sculpture* <to sculpture a bust>, *sculpt* (a BACK-FORMATION from *sculptor*) is now the predominant form and should be accepted as standard. *Sculp* is a NEEDLESS VARIANT.

For the agent noun, *sculptor* is preferred over *sculpturer*.

Scylla and Charybdis, between. As described by Homer, *Scylla* /**sil**-ə/ was a sea monster who had six heads (each with a triple row of teeth) and twelve feet. Though primarily a fish-eater, she was capable of snatching and devouring (in one swoop) six sailors if their ship ventured too near her cave in the Strait of Messina. (In the accounts of later writers, she is rationalized into a rocky promontory.) Toward the opposite shore, not far from Scylla's lair, was *Charybdis* /kə-**rib**-dis/, a whirlpool strong enough thrice daily to suck into its vortex whole ships if they came too close.

Thus, to say *between Scylla and Charybdis* is a close literary equivalent of *between a rock and a hard place*. The main difference between the phrases is that there is no comfort between a rock and a hard place; there is a safe, though precarious, way to proceed between Scylla and Charybdis. Both phrases are CLICHÉS.

seasonable; seasonal. *Seasonable* = (1) happening during the right season; opportune <for us, an August trip to Aspen is quite seasonable: we don't ski>; or (2) (of weather) suitable to the time of year <seasonable April showers>. *Seasonal* = (1) of or relating to the seasons of the year, or any one of them <El Niño has caused seasonal changes in weather>; or (2) dependent on the seasons, as certain trades <seasonal shipping patterns>.

seem. On the sequence of tenses in phrases such as *seemed to enjoy* (as opposed to *seemed to have enjoyed*), see TENSES (A).

seldom ever. In this phrase—which seems to be a collapsed form of *seldom if ever*—the word *ever* is superfluous. E.g.: "And as everyone knows, Fleck, who *seldom ever* [read *seldom*] missed a meeting, will attend those sessions as long as he is able" (*Allentown Morning Call*). Cf. **rarely ever.**

self-addressed stamped envelope. Though sometimes condemned, this phrase is now firmly entrenched in AmE (especially in the abbreviated form *SASE*). *Self-addressed* isn't merely "addressed by oneself," but commonly means "addressed for return to the sender." The prefix *self-* prevents vagueness: an envelope that's merely *addressed* could be addressed to anybody.

self-admitted; self-confessed. These are common redundancies—e.g.: "Rep. Gerry E. Studds, 53, and Rep. Barney Frank, 50, . . . are *self-admitted* [read *admitted*] homosexuals, but that is not automatically grounds for Congressional expulsion" (*Parade*)./ "A court that frees a *self-confessed* [read *confessed*] murderer on a technicality would seem to bear responsibility for any harm that criminal may do in the future" (Mario Pei, *Words in Sheep's Clothing*, 1969).

self-complacent is redundant. *Complacent* is sufficient—e.g.: "You will remind the *self-complacent* [read *complacent*] to stop and think of their fellow men" (*Boston Herald*).

self-confessed. See **self-admitted.**

SEMI-. See BI-.

semiannual (AmE); **half-yearly** (BrE). See **biannual.** On the hybrid form *semi-yearly*, see HYBRIDS.

SEMICOLON [;]. This punctuation mark—a kind of "supercomma"—separates sentence parts that need a more distinct break than a comma can signal, but that are too closely connected to be made into separate sentences. Typically these will be clauses of similar importance and grammatical construction.

Four uses are common.

First, it is sometimes used to unite two sentences that are more closely connected than most others; typically, as in this very sentence, there is no conjunction between clauses. E.g.: "The speaker knows that he has allowed his imagination some leeway; thus, even after he has frightened himself with his questions, he can turn and challenge the very premise of his meditation" (Richard Ohmann, *English in America*, 1976). Often, this semicolon signals an antithesis—e.g.:

- "He did not lead; he followed" (John Wain, "Byron: The Search for Identity," 1963).
- "The evil lover is not prudent; he is simply wicked" (W. Ross Winterowd, *Rhetoric: A Synthesis*, 1968).
- "Malamud promises an oeuvre; Bellow, at fifty-one, has already achieved one" (Anthony Burgess, "The Jew as American," 1968).

Second, the semicolon sometimes separates coordinate clauses in long, complex sentences. This use was much more common in the 19th century than it is today—e.g.:

- "But Elizabeth was not formed for ill-humour; and though every prospect of her own was destroyed for the evening, it could not dwell long on her spirits; and having told all her griefs to Charlotte Lucas, whom she had not seen for a week, she was soon able to make a voluntary transition to the oddities of her cousin, and to point him out to her in particular notice" (Jane Austen, *Pride and Prejudice*, 1813).
- "The system which had addressed him in exactly the same manner as it had addressed hundreds of other boys, all varying in character and capacity, had enabled him to dash through his tasks, always with fair credit, and often with distinction; but in a fitful, dazzling way that had confirmed his reliance on those very qualities in himself, which it had been most desirable to direct and train" (Charles Dickens, *Bleak House*, 1853).
- "If the memory which we have uncovered does not answer our expectations, it may be that we ought to pursue the same path a little further; perhaps behind the first traumatic scene there may be concealed the memory of a second, which satisfies our requirements better and whose reproduction has a greater therapeutic effect; so that the scene that was first discovered only has the significance of a connecting link in the chain of association" (Sigmund Freud, "The Aetiology of Hysteria" (1896), in *The Freud Reader*, 1989).

Third, the semicolon separates items in a series when any element in the series contains an internal comma—e.g.:

- "Greek developments include *pimplemi* and *pletho*, 'to fill,' *pleres*, *pleos*, 'full'; *poly-*, 'much,' with comparative *pleios* and superlative *pleistos*; *polemos*, 'war'; and *polis*, 'city' " (Mario Pei, *The Families of Words*, 1962).
- "I wish to acknowledge the valuable help of a number of superior editors in the composition of this book: Neal Kozodoy of *Commentary*; Erich Eichman and Hilton Kramer of *The New Criterion*; John Gross, formerly of the *Times Literary Supplement*; and Carol Houck Smith, of W.W. Norton" (Joseph Epstein, *Plausible Prejudices: Essays on American Writing*, 1985).
- "Between 1815 and 1850 Americans constructed elaborate networks of roads, canals, and early railroad lines; opened up wide areas of newly acquired land for settlement and trade; and began to industrialize manufacturing" (Sean Wilentz, "Society, Politics, and the Market Revolution," in *The New American History*, 1997).

Fourth, the semicolon sometimes appears simply to give a weightier pause than a comma would. This use is discretionary. A comma would do, but the writer wants a stronger stop—e.g.: "There is never anything sexy about Lautrec's art; but there also is never anything deliberately, sarcastically anti-feminist in it" (Aldous Huxley, "Doodles in the Dictionary" (1956), in *Aldous Huxley: Selected Essays*, 1961).

The most common misuse of the semicolon is to place it where a colon belongs. Thus, it's not so uncommon to see, in a business letter, a semicolon after the salutation: "Dear Sarah; . . . ." But the semicolon stops the forward movement of a statement, whereas a colon marks a forward movement. In any given published example, the error might simply be a typographical error. But it happens too commonly to be routinely a typo—e.g.: "In addition to those whose names appear as contributors, I am especially grateful to the following for their valuable assistance in the preparation of the Second Edition; Luciano Berio, Juilliard School of Music; David Burrows, New York University; . . ." (Willi Apel, *Harvard Dictionary of Music*, 1972). In that sentence, of course, the first semicolon should be a colon; the others are correct.

sensuous; sensual. Although these words derive from the same root (*sens-*, meaning "appeal to the senses"), they have undergone DIFFERENTIATION. *Sensuous* = of or relating to the five senses; arousing any of the five senses. The word properly has no risqué connotations, though it is gravely distorted by hack novelists. Here it is correctly used: "Words thus strung together fall on the ear like music. The appeal is *sensuous* rather than intellectual" (W. Somerset Maugham, "Lucidity, Simplicity, Euphony," in *The Summing Up*, 1938).

Sensual = relating to gratification of the senses, esp. sexual; salacious; voluptuous <sensual desires>. This is the word intended by the hack novelists who erroneously believe that *sensuous* carries sexy overtones. *Sensual* is correctly used here: "Lartigue shows a land where a benevolent sun shines on women and water, cars, painted fingernails, tennis champs, swimmers—a *sensual* topography of blonde and brunette" (*N.Y. Times*). And it's badly misused here: "There is something special about naked babies, a purely *sensual* [read *aesthetic*?] sight devoid of sexuality" (*San Diego Union-Trib.*).

SENTENCE ADVERBS qualify an entire statement rather than a single word in the sentence. A sentence adverb does not resolve itself into the form *in a —— manner*, as most adverbs do. Thus, in *Happily, the bill did not go beyond the committee*, the introductory adverb *happily* conveys the writer's opinion on the message being imparted. The following words are among the most frequent sentence adverbs ending in *-ly*:

accordingly
admittedly
arguably
concededly
consequently
curiously
fortunately
importantly
interestingly
ironically
legally
logically
mercifully
oddly
paradoxically
regrettably
sadly
strangely
theoretically

Improvising sentence adverbs from traditional adverbs like *hopefully* (= in a hopeful manner) and *thankfully* (= in a thankful manner) is objectionable to many stylists but seems to be on the rise. Avoid newfangled sentence adverbs of this kind. And in formal prose, even those like *hopefully* and *thankfully* shouldn't appear. Though increasingly common, they have a tarnished history. See **hopefully & thankfully.**

Because sentence adverbs reveal the writer's own thoughts and biases, writers often overuse them in argumentation—but danger lurks in words such as *clearly*, *obviously*, *undoubtedly*, and *indisputably*. See **clearly** & OVERSTATEMENT.

SENTENCE ENDS. Rhetoricians have long emphasized that the punch word in a sentence should come at the end:

- "[T]he most emphatic place in a clause or sentence is the end. This is the climax; and, during the momentary pause that follows, that last word continues, as it were, to reverberate in the reader's mind. It has, in fact, the last word. One should therefore think twice about what one puts at a sentence-end" (F.L. Lucas, *Style*, 1955).
- "[A] word or phrase gains importance by being placed at the beginning or the end of a sentence. The end is the more important position of the two, for the sentence that trails off in a string of modifiers runs downhill in interest. By saving an important part of the predicate till the end, you emphasize the main idea" (Alan H. Vrooman, *Good Writing: An Informal Manual of Style*, 1967).
- "Because the end of a sentence is the last thing a reader sees, it is a position of emphasis. Don't use it to express minor thoughts or casual information. Don't write 'Both candidates will appear here in July, if we can believe the reports.' (This is correct only if you want to stress the doubtfulness of the reports.) Don't write 'Pray for the repose of the soul of John Bowler, who died last week in Cleveland.' (Your reader will start wondering what he was doing in Cleveland.)" (Daniel McDonald, *The Language of Argument*, 1986).

Yet the point eludes writers who end sentences with a flat phrase such as *in many cases*; with a date that isn't critical; or with the very noun phrase that appeared at the beginning.

One way to test how effective your sentences are is to read them aloud, exaggerating the last word in each sentence. If the reading sounds awkward or foolish, the sentence should probably be recast.

SENTENCE FRAGMENTS. See INCOMPLETE SENTENCES.

SENTENCE LENGTH. What is the correlation between sentence length and readability? No one knows precisely. Rhetoricians and readability specialists have long suggested aiming for sentences of varying lengths, but with an average of about 20 to 25 words. And empirical evidence seems to bear out this rough guideline. In 1985, three authors calculated figures for several publications, using extensive samples:

Publication	Average Sentence Length
Pittsburgh Press	20
Reader's Digest	20.4
Popular Mechanics	21.8
Science Digest	22
Field & Stream	22.8
Newsweek	24
Time	24.4
Scientific American	24.9
New York Times	26.6
Wall Street Journal	27

Source: Gary A. Olson et al., *Style and Readability in Business Writing* 102 (1985).

They arrived at a provocative conclusion: "Varying your sentence length is much more important than varying your sentence pattern if you want to produce clear, interesting, readable prose" (*id.*).

If you're aiming for an average sentence length of 20 to 25 words, some sentences probably ought to be 30 or 40 words, and others ought to be 3 or 4. Variety is important, but you must concern yourself with the overall average.

Standards have changed, of course, with time. In the 18th and 19th centuries, the long sentence was much more commonplace than it is today. For many modern readers, long sentences read too slowly. They are plodding. They waste time. While long sentences slow the reading and create a solemn, portentous impression, short sentences speed the reading and the thought. For the modern writer, it's "a counsel of perfection never to write a sentence without asking, 'Might it not be better shorter?' " (F.L. Lucas, *Style*, 1962).

SERIAL COMMA. See COMMA.

series. Though serving as a plural when the need arises, *series* is ordinarily a singular <the series is quite popular>. But it is also a noun of multitude, so that the phrase *a series of things* takes a plural verb—e.g.: "There *have* been a *series* of such incidents as refugees from both sides have begun reconstructing houses" (*Ariz. Republic & Phoenix Gaz.*). See SYNESIS.

The form *serieses* is an archaic plural that still occasionally appears—e.g.: "The Braves have posted an unfathomable 6–0 mark at Busch this year, winning three-game *serieses* [read *series*] in April and July" (*Peoria J. Star*).

SESQUIPEDALITY is the use of big words, literally those that are "a foot and a half" long. Although the English language has an unmatched wealth of words available for its users, most of its resources go untapped. The *OED* contains more than 500,000 words, yet even highly educated people have only about 10% of that number in their working vocabulary.

This discrepancy gives rise to a tension between two ideals. On the one hand, vocabulary-builders have long maintained that a rich personal wordstock is your key to success. On the other hand, writing guides are full of advice to shun big words.

So which of these two views is correct? It's entirely possible to resolve the seeming paradox and to hold that they're both essentially right. Build your vocabulary to make yourself a better reader; choose simple words whenever possible to make yourself a better writer.

The last part of that antithesis is hard for some wordsmiths to accept. And it needs tempering, because hard words have a legitimate literary tradition. English has inherited two strains of literary expression, both deriving ultimately from ancient Greek rhetoric. On the one hand is the plain style now in vogue, characterized by unadorned vocabulary, directness, unelaborate syntax, and earthiness. (This style is known to scholars as Atticism.) On the other hand we have the grand style, which exemplifies floridity, allusiveness, formal and sometimes abstruse diction, and rhetorical ornament. Proponents of this verbally richer style (called Asiaticism) proudly claim that the nuances available in the "oriental profusion" of English synonyms make the language an ideal putty for the skilled writer to mold and shape precisely. The Asiaticist sees the opulence of our language as providing apt terms for virtually every conceivable context.

Still, using the abundant resources of English is widely, if not wisely, discouraged. This attitude is as old as Modern English. During the 16th century, when our language had just begun to take its modern form, learned Englishmen who enriched their lexically impoverished tongue with Latin and Greek loanwords were vilified as "smelling of inkhorn" or as "inkhornists." Thus one of the more notable borrowing neologists of the Renaissance, Sir Thomas Elyot, author of *The Governour*, wrote in 1531: "Divers men, rather scornying my benefite ['beneficence,' i.e., adding to the English wordstock] than receyving it thankfully, doo shew them selves offended (as they say) with my straunge termes." The "straunge termes" this redoubtable inkhornist gave us include *accommodate, education, frugality, irritate, metamorphosis, persist,* and *ruminate*. He sought not to parade his formidable erudition, but rather "to augment our Englyshe tongue, wherby men shulde as well expresse more abundantly the thynge that they conceyved in theirs hartis (wherefore language was ordeyned) havinge wordes apte for the purpose." In retrospect, of course, the efforts of Elyot and others like him were not in vain because they enriched the language.

The dilemma, though, remains: to what extent is it advisable to use big words? The Fowler brothers generally thought it inadvisable: "Prefer the familiar word to the far-fetched" (*The King's English*, 1906). But "prefer" begs an important question: how strong is this preference to be? Sheridan Baker elaborates the idea more fully, and quite sensibly:

> "What we need is a mixed diction," said Aristotle, and his point remains true 24 centuries and several languages later. The aim of style, he says, is to be clear but distinguished. For clarity, we need common, current words; but, used alone, these are commonplace, and as ephemeral as everyday talk. For distinction, we need words not heard every minute, unusual words, large words, foreign words, metaphors; but, used alone, these become bogs, vapors, or at worst, gibberish. What we need is a diction that weds the popular with the dignified, the clear current with the sedgy margins of language and thought.
>
> Sheridan Baker, *The Practical Stylist* 133 (8th ed. 1998).

Intermingling Saxon words with Latin ones gives language variety, texture, euphony, and vitality. The best writers match substance with form. They use language precisely, evocatively, even daringly. So we shouldn't assume that Hemingwayan spartanism is the only desirable mode, unless we're ready to indict T.S. Eliot, H.L. Mencken, Vladimir Nabokov, Edmund Wilson, John Updike, and many another masterly writer.

Having established a reputable pedigree for the judicious employment of unfamiliar words, we can approach a standard for discriminating between useful and relatively useless abstrusities. Consider words as analogues to mathematical fractions, both being symbols for material or conceptual referents: would a self-respecting mathematician say 12/48 instead of 1/4 just to sound more erudite? Certainly not. Likewise a writer or speaker generally should not say *obtund* when the verbs *dull* and *blunt* come more readily to mind. Nor would one say *saponaceous* for *soapy*, *dyslogistic* for *uncomplimentary*, or *macrobian* (or *longevous*) for *long-lived*.

Of course, it's impossible to set down absolute rules about words that are and are not useful. Still, it's almost always degenerate to avoid the obvious by clothing it in befogged terminology, as one might by writing *arenaceous* or *sabulous* for *sandy*, *immund* for *dirty*, *nates* for *buttocks*, or *venenate* for the verb *poison*. In the words of Coleridge, "Whatever is translatable in other and simpler words of the same language, without loss of sense or dignity, is bad."

But what about the mathematician who arrives at 15/16? Is it really best to round off the fraction to 1? Maybe in some contexts, but not in all—certainly not in the professional context. (One is reminded of the school district in the Deep South that once decided that 3.14159 was too much for children to learn and therefore stipulated that the value of pi was 3. Or worse, of the Midwestern state legislature that, in 1896, set pi equal to 4.) Likewise with the writer who, when describing an asthenic person, should not balk at using *asthenic* rather than the vaguer *weak*, because the former evokes the distinct image of muscular atrophy, which the latter lacks. And why engage in circumlocutions when a single word neatly suffices?

One could make similar arguments for thousands of other English words. *Coterie* and *galere* have almost identical meanings—something like "a group of persons united for a common interest or purpose"—but no everyday word exists for this notion. The same is true of *cathexis, eirenicon, gravamen, obelize, oriflamme, protreptic*, or any of numberless other examples. Samuel Johnson came closest to rationalizing his sesquipedalian penchant when he wrote: "It is natural to depart from familiarity of language upon occasions not familiar. Whatever elevates the sentiments will consequently raise the expression; whatever fills us with hope or terror, will produce some perturbation of images and some figurative distortions of phrase."

Certainly you might have occasion to use abstruse vocabulary for reasons other than stylistic dignity or the lack of a simpler term. Three stand out. First, it's often desirable to avoid the apt but voguish word. To select one of several examples, in the days when *aggravate* was first coming to be widely used for "irritate, annoy," the fastidious speaker or writer could either combat the word's debasement and use it correctly or seek refuge in *exacerbate*. As a result, *exacerbate* is no longer an unusual word. (And of course, *make worse* is always an available standby.)

Second, big words can often have a very humorous effect, though the fun is limited to those who can understand them. Such jocular phrases as *campanologist's tintinnabulation* (= bell-ringer's knell), *alliaceous halitosis* (= garlic breath), *pernoctative nepotation* (= riotous carousing through the night), and *bromidrotic fug* (= sweaty stench) can be delightfully amusing.

A third reason for waxing lexiphanic is to soften one's scurrility—to abstract it so that one's audience does not immediately visualize an unpleasant image. For example, R. Emmett Tyrell, the political analyst, once used *fecal-buccal* to describe certain politicians. He couldn't—and wouldn't—have said that if he'd been forced to simplify.

In the end, there seem to be three legitimate stances for the writer. The first is that if you truly want to communicate with a wide readership, you have to build your core of small words. The second is that if one of your purposes is to educate, use challenging words while allowing the context to reveal their meanings, as in the following examples:

- *umbrelliferous*: "His arms were like pipes, and had a way of branching from his shoulders at sharp angles so that the umbrella-bearing, or *umbrelliferous*, limb, for example, shot up on a steeply ascending vertical before articulating crisply at the elbow into a true vertical" (Patrick McGrath, *Blood and Water and Other Tales*, 1988).
- *enucleate* [A psychiatrist talking to a woman in love with a madman]: "Appearances to the contrary, Edgar Stark is a deeply disturbed individual." "I know this, Jack." "I wonder if you do. Do you know what he did to that woman after he killed her?" She said nothing. "He decapitated her. Then he *enucleated* her. He cut her head off, and then he took her eyes out" (*id.*).
- *synaesthesia*: "The *synaesthesia* (mixing of senses) of 'visible sob' might seem too rich to apply to a golf ball, if it didn't occupy the climactic position in the description" (David Lodge, *The Art of Fiction*, 1992).

The third stance is that if you know you're writing for a specific audience with a prodigious vocabulary—whether one particular reader or the intelligentsia generally—then use hard words that are truly unsimplifiable. But question your motives: are you doing it to express yourself well, or are you just showing off?

SET PHRASES. Bits of language sometimes become fossilized, and when they do it's foolish to try to vary them. Thus *carved in stone* should never become *carved in shale*, or whatever variation one might lamely invent. Nor, to cite another example, should one change *comparing apples and oranges* to *comparing apples and pomegranates*. Wilson Follett called set phrases "inviolable" (if not quite inviolate): "[T]he attempt to liven up old clichés by inserting modifiers into the set phrase is a mistake: the distended phrase is neither original, nor unobtrusive, nor brief, and sometimes it has ceased to be immediately clear, as in *They have been reticent to a tactical fault*" (*MAU*).

In addition to the fault of inserting modifiers into set phrases, two other faults commonly occur.

First, it is wrong to force a set phrase into ungrammatical contexts—e.g.: "This was reported to *we the people*." Although the well-known phrase *we the people* derives from the Declaration of Independence, it was necessarily in the nominative case in Jefferson's sentence. In this one, the syntax calls for the objective *us*.

Second, it's poor style to aim at novelty by reversing the usual order of a phrase, as by writing *well-being and health* instead of *health and well-being*, or *hearty and hale* instead of *hale and hearty*. Cf. INELEGANT VARIATION.

sex. See **gender.**

SEXISM. A. Generally. If you start with the pragmatic premise that you want to avoid misleading or distracting your readers, then you'll almost certainly conclude that it's best to avoid sexist language. Regardless of your political persuasion, that conclusion seems inevitable—if you're a pragmatist.

But does avoiding sexism mean resorting to awkward devices like *he/she*? Surely not, because that too would distract many readers. What you should strive for instead—if you want readers to focus on your ideas and not on the political subtext—is a style that doesn't even hint at the issue. So unless you're involved in a debate about sexism, you'll probably want a style, on the one hand, that no reasonable person could call sexist, and on the other hand, that never suggests you're contorting your language to be nonsexist.

B. The Pronoun Problem. English has a number of common-sex general words, such as *person*, *anyone*, *everyone*, and *no one*, but it has no common-sex singular personal pronouns. Instead, we have *he*, *she*, and *it*. The traditional approach has been to use the masculine pronouns *he* and *him* to cover all persons, male and female alike. That this practice has come under increasing attack has caused the single most difficult problem in the realm of sexist language. Other snarls are far more readily solvable.

The inadequacy of the English language in this respect becomes apparent in many sentences in which the generic masculine pronoun sits uneasily. Lawyers seem to force it into the oddest contexts—e.g.: "If a testator fails to provide by will for *his* surviving spouse [a *she*?] who married the testator after the execution of the will, the omitted spouse shall receive the same share of the estate *he* [i.e., the spouse] would have received if the decedent left no will" (Unif. Probate Code, 1989).

"There are," as H.W. Fowler noted (with contributions from Ernest Gowers),

> three makeshifts: first, *as anybody can see for himself or herself*; second, *as anybody can see for themselves*; and third, *as anybody can see for himself*. No one who can help it chooses the first; it is correct, and is sometimes necessary, but it is so clumsy as to be ridiculous except when explicitness is urgent, and it usually sounds like a bit of pedantic humour. The second is the popular solution; it sets the literary man's [!] teeth on edge, and he exerts himself to give the same meaning in some entirely different way if he is not prepared to risk the third, which is here recommended. It involves the convention (statutory in the interpretation of documents) that where the matter of sex is not conspicuous or important the masculine form shall be allowed to represent a person instead of a man, or say a man (*homo*) instead of a man (*vir*).
>
> *MEU2*.

At least two other makeshifts are now available. The first is commonly used by American academics: *as anybody can see for herself*. Such phrases are often alternated with those containing masculine pronouns, or, in some writing, appear uniformly. Whether this phraseology will someday stop sounding strange to most readers only time will tell. This is one possibility, however, of: (1) maintaining a grammatical construction; and (2) avoiding the awkwardness of alternatives such as *himself or herself*.

But the method carries two risks. First, unintended connotations may invade the writing. In the 1980s, a novel was published in two versions, one using generic masculine pronouns and the other using generic feminine pronouns; the effects on readers of the two versions were reported to have been startlingly different in ways far too complex for discussion here. Second, this makeshift is likely to do a disservice to women in the long run, for it would probably be adopted only by a small minority of writers: the rest would continue with the generic masculine pronoun.

A second new makeshift has entered Canadian legislation: *as anybody can see for themself*; *if a judge decides to recuse themself*. (Donald L. Revell et al., " 'Themself' and Nonsexist Style in Canadian Legislative Drafting," 10 *English Today* 10 (1994).) The word *themself* fills the need for a gender-neutral reflexive pronoun, but many readers and writers—especially Americans—bristle at the sight or the sound of it. Thus, for the legal writer, this makeshift carries a considerable risk of distracting readers.

Typographical gimmickry may once have served a political purpose, but it should be avoided as an answer to the problem. Tricks such as *s/he*, *he/she*, and *she/he*—and even the gloriously misbegotten double entendre, *s/he/it*—are trendy, ugly, distracting, and often unpronounceable. If we must have alternatives, *he or she* is the furthest we should go. See **he or she.**

For the persuasive writer—for whom credibility is all—the writer's point of view matters less than the reader's. Thus, if one is writing for an unknown or a broad readership, the only course that does not risk damaging one's credibility is to write around the problem. For this purpose, every writer ought to have available a repertoire of methods to avoid the generic masculine pronoun. No single method is sufficient. Thus, in a given context, one might consider doing any of the following:

- Delete the pronoun reference altogether. E.g.: "Every manager should read memoranda as soon as they are delivered *to him* [delete *to him*] by a mail clerk."
- Change the pronoun to an article, such as *a* or *the*. E.g.: "An author may adopt any of the following dictionaries in preparing *his* [read *a*] manuscript."
- Pluralize, so that *he* becomes *they*. E.g.: "A student should avoid engaging in any activities that might bring discredit to *his* school." (Read: *Students should avoid engaging in any activities that might bring discredit to their school.*)
- Use the relative pronoun *who*, especially when the generic *he* follows an *if*. E.g.: "If a student cannot use standard English, *he* cannot be expected to master the nuances of the literature assigned in this course." (Read: *A student who cannot use standard English cannot be expected to master the nuances of the literature assigned in this course.*)
- Repeat the noun instead of using a pronoun, especially when the two are separated by several words. E.g.: "When considering a manuscript for publication, the editor should evaluate the suitability of both the subject matter and the writing style. In particular, *he* [read *the editor*] . . . ."

Though the masculine singular personal pronoun may survive awhile longer as a generic term, it will probably be displaced ultimately by *they*, which is coming to be used alternatively as singular or plural. (See CONCORD (B).) This usage is becoming commonplace—e.g.:

- "*Anyone* who has subscribed to the Literary Review for more than one year may join, as long as *they* are proposed by a writer known to the committee" (*Sunday Times* [London]).
- "It is assumed that, if *someone* is put under enough pressure, *they* will tell the truth, or the truth will emerge despite the teller" (Robin T. Lakoff, *Talking Power: The Politics of Language in Our Lives*, 1990).
- "*Anyone* planning a dissertation on Hollywood's fling with yuppie demonology

> will want to include 'The Temp' in *their* calculations" (*N.Y. Times*).

Speakers of AmE resist this development more than speakers of BrE, in which the indeterminate *they* is already more or less standard. That it sets many literate Americans' teeth on edge is an unfortunate setback to what promises to be the ultimate solution to the problem.

C. Words with *man-* and *-man*. "For the lawyer more than for most men, it is true that he who knows but cannot express what he knows might as well be ignorant." That sentence opens Chapter 1 of Henry Weihofen's *Legal Writing Style* (2d ed. 1980)—a sentence that, ironically, is flanked by warnings against sexist language (pp. vii, 19–20). If Weihofen were writing today, no doubt he would express himself in neutral language.

Throughout the English-speaking world, writers' awareness of sexism rose most markedly during the 1980s. In September 1984, the Commonwealth Attorney-General's Department in Canberra, Australia, issued a press release entitled "Moves to Modify Language Sex Bias in Legislation." The release stated that "[t]he Government accepts that drafting in 'masculine' language may contribute to some extent to the perpetuation of a society in which men and women see women as lesser beings." The press release recommended, "[w]here possible and appropriate, avoidance of the use of words ending in *man*, such as *chairman, serviceman, seaman,* and so on."

In a similar vein, American businesspeople and journalists have begun to write in more neutral language, sometimes obtrusively neutral—e.g.: "When the blow-dried *anchorperson* [read *newscaster*?] on the 11 o'clock news tells you the market rose or fell 100 points, you have learned absolutely nothing" (*Forbes*)./ "The ice cream mixture is placed in the frozen canister and turned automatically, thus eliminating the use of salt, ice and *personpower* [read *labor* or *toil*]" (*Fresno Bee*).

As a nonsexist suffix, *-person* leaves much to be desired. For every *chairperson, anchorperson, draftsperson, ombudsperson,* and *tribesperson,* there is a superior substitute: *chair, anchor, drafter, ombuds,* and *tribe member.* Words ending in *-person* are at once wooden and pompous.

Some of the extremes to which the trend has been taken seem absurd, such as *herstory* (to avoid *his*), *womyn* (to avoid *men*), and the like. For the more ardent reformers, the line-drawing often doesn't seem to be tempered with good sense. For example, in 1992, *Time* magazine reported:

> NASA will no longer refer to "manned" flights but will describe the missions as "habitated" and "uninhabitated," or "crewed" and "uncrewed." Says a NASA spokesman: "We have been ordered to delete any reference by sex, on the grounds that 'manned' flight is crude and 'crewed' is p.c." Even so, some sociologists are still not satisfied. They prefer "space flight by human beings." Female astronauts find these linguistic aerobics foolish. Says one: "Common sense is the victim of all this rhetoric."
>
> "Lost in Space: Common Sense," *Time*, 1992.

For other entries dealing with this and related issues, see **chair, foreman, humankind & male.**

D. Differentiated Feminine Forms. Several word endings mark feminine forms (as in *authoress, comedienne, confidante, majorette,* and *tutrix*). As a whole, these are very much on the wane.

For example, words ending in *-ess,* such as *poetess* and *authoress,* are mostly archaic in AmE. (BrE is more hospitable to them; it's not unusual to see references to *manageresses* in British newspapers.) At some point they acquired a derogatory tinge, and they've never been the same. The quite understandable tendency has been to avoid sex-specific terms if the person's sex is beside the point. And it usually is beside the point when identifying a *poet*, an *author*, or a *waiter*. Not everyone agrees that this is true of *actors*: although some women insist that they are *actors*, the Academy of Motion Picture Arts and Sciences retains the "Best Actor" and "Best Actress" categories. Still, the support for *actress* (but not for "Best Supporting Actress") seems to be eroding.

It is jarring to hear phrases such as *female booksalesman* or the Air Force's *female airman*. But it isn't at all jarring—except to insufferable pedants—to read or hear about a woman's being an *author* or *waiter*.

As for words ending in *-trix*, the law seems to be one of two last bastions for such terms—e.g.: *executrix, prosecutrix, testatrix*. But even in law these terms are moribund. Increasingly, lawyers refer to women as *executors, prosecutors,* and *testators*. The other bastion? Sadomasochism—with *dominatrix*.

For other words with differentiated suffixes, see the entries at **blond, brunet(te), fiancé & waiter.**

E. Equivalences. Among the subtler problems of nonsexist usage is to refer to men and women in equivalent terms: not *man and wife*, but *husband and wife*; not *chairmen* and *chairs* (the latter being female), but *chairs* (for all); not *men* and *girls* (a word that diminishes the status of an adult female), but *men* and *women*.

Even *Mr.*, on the one hand, as contrasted with *Miss* or *Mrs.*, on the other, causes problems on this score. Differentiating between one woman and another on the basis of her marital status is invidious, really, if we do not make the same distinction for men. The idea that it matters as an item of personal information whether a woman is married—but that it doesn't matter whether a man is married—is surely an outmoded one. Though many people once considered *Ms.* an abomination, it is today accepted as the standard way of addressing a married or unmarried woman. Unless the writer knows that a woman prefers to use *Mrs.* or *Miss*, the surest course today is to use *Ms.*

F. Statute of Limitations. Those committed to nonsexist usage ought to adopt a statute of limitations that goes something like this: in quoted matter dating from before 1980, passages containing bland sexism—such as the use of the generic *he* or of *chairman*—can be quoted in good conscience because in those days the notions of gender-inclusiveness were entirely different from today's notions. Although it is quite fair to discuss cultural changes over time, it is unfair to criticize our predecessors for not conforming to present-day standards. How could they have done so? Therefore, using "[*sic*]" at every turn to point out old sexist phrases is at best an otiose exercise, at worst a historically irresponsible example of mean-spiritedness.

shake > shook > shaken. Occasionally *shook* appears erroneously as the past-participial form—e.g.: "Exercise rider Kelly Rycroft was *shook* [read *shaken*] up Wednesday morning when a horse he was pulling up was struck from behind by a bolting horse" (*Vancouver Sun*). See IRREGULAR VERBS.

shall; will. Grammarians formerly relied on the following paradigm, which now has little utility:

Simple Futurity

First person	I shall	we shall
Second person	you will	you will
Third person	he will	they will

Determination, Promise, or Command

First person	I will	we will
Second person	you shall	you shall
Third person	she shall	they shall

But with only minor exceptions, *will* has become the universal word to express futurity, regardless of whether the subject is in the first, second, or third person. *Shall* is now mostly restricted to two situations: (1) interrogative sentences requesting permission or agreement <shall we all go outside?> <shall I open the present

now?>; and (2) legal documents, in which *shall* purportedly imposes a duty <the tenant shall obtain the landlord's permission before making any changes to the premises>. In both of those situations, *shall* seems likely to persist, but in law it is declining because of increased recognition of its hopeless ambiguity as actually misused by lawyers. See Garner, *A Dictionary of Modern Legal Usage* 939–41 (2d ed. 1995).

Professor Gustave Arlt of the University of California summed it up well, writing in the late 1940s: "The artificial distinction between *shall* and *will* to designate futurity is a superstition that has neither a basis in historical grammar nor the sound sanction of universal usage. It is a nineteenth-century affectation [that] certain grammarians have tried hard to establish and perpetuate. . . . [T]hey have not succeeded" (quoted in Norman Lewis, *Better English*, 1961).

And if the distinction isn't real, there's simply no reason to hold on to *shall*. The word is peripheral in AmE.

shave > shaved > shaved. *Shaven* exists only as a past-participial adjective <clean-shaven face>. Cf. **proved.**

s/he. See SEXISM (B).

sheaf. Pl. *sheaves*. See PLURALS (G).

sheath, n.; **sheathe,** vb. It's an error to use *sheathe* as a noun or *sheath* as a verb—e.g.: "Madame de Sevigne's friend, the Sun King, tamed his subjects by urging them to *sheath* [read *sheathe*] their swords and help with his nightshirt or hold his candle as he got undressed" (*Fin. Times*)./ "The device features a mechanism that secures the needle, point and all, inside a plastic *sheathe* [read *sheath*] at the same time that the user withdraws it from the skin" (*Lancaster New Era*). Just remember the difference between *breath* (n.) and *breathe* (vb.).

Sheath forms the plural *sheaths*, not *sheathes*—e.g.: "Don Davis makes each of the hand-tooled leather *sheathes* [read *sheaths*] that come with his knives" (*Denver Post*).

shed > shed > shed. Avoid *shedded*—e.g.: "Prosecutors plainly want to suggest that the missing bags contained both the knife they believe Mr. Simpson used to murder Nicole Brown Simpson and Ronald L. Goldman, and blood-soaked clothes he quickly *shedded* [read *shed*] before boarding his flight to Chicago" (*N.Y. Times*). See IRREGULAR VERBS.

sherbet /**shər**-bət/ is commonly mispronounced with an intrusive *-r-*: /**shər**-bərt/. Because of this mispronunciation, the word is sometimes wrongly spelled *sherbert*. See PRONUNCIATION (B).

shone; shined. The former is the past tense of the intransitive *shine* <the sun shone>, the latter the past tense of the transitive *shine* <he shined his shoes>. But writers occasionally use *shined* where *shone* is the word they want—e.g.: "And neither *shined* [read *shone*] like the oft-dormant Texas running game that has produced only two 1,000-yard rushers since Earl Campbell and none since Eric Metcalf in 1987" (*Austin American-Statesman*). See IRREGULAR VERBS.

Shone is sometimes confused with *shown*—e.g.: "The sun *shown* [read *shone*] brightly and it seemed like happily ever after when Tessler and Miller exchanged vows" (*Pitt. Post-Gaz.*).

shoo-in (= a candidate or competitor who is sure to win), a colloquialism deriving from the idea of "shooing" something (as a pet), is so spelled. Yet *shoe-in* is a frequent error—e.g.: "Gray . . . is considered a *shoe-in* [read *shoo-in*] for re-election" (*Baltimore Sun*).

shook. See **shake.**

shoot, n.; **chute.** The latter means (1) "an inclined channel or passage"; (2) "a waterfall or water slide"; or (3) "a parachute." *Shoot* is the standard spelling for all other senses. *Chute* is sometimes misspelled *shute*—e.g.: "The river sucked me right down the *shute* [read *chute*] of a Class Two rapid" (*Ft. Lauderdale Sun-Sentinel*).

should; would. *Should* appears with the first, second, and third persons to express a sense of duty <I really should go with you>; a condition <if Bess should call, tell her I'll be back at 4 o'clock>; or an expectation <they should be here in five minutes>. *Would* appears with all three persons to express habitual practice <every day the golfers would start lining up at 6:30 a.m.>; a hypothetical <she would do it if she could>; or a preference <I would like to see you>. See **would.**

shouldn't ought. See DOUBLE MODALS.

should of. See **of** (D).

show > showed > shown. *Showed* is less good than *shown* as the past participle. And in the PASSIVE VOICE, *shown* is mandatory <he was shown to have lied>. See IRREGULAR VERBS.

shrink > shrank > shrunk. Some writers mistakenly use *shrinked* as a past tense and past participle—e.g.: "Texas country-folk chanteuse Katy Moffatt's latest album needs to be *shrinked* [read *shrunk*] before it's played" (*Boston Herald*).

Others wrongly use *shrunk* as a past tense rather than as a past participle, as in the movie title *Honey, I Shrunk the Kids!* (1989). Examples are hardly scarce—e.g.: "Then I sent it to the cleaners, and it *shrunk* [read *shrank*] back to its normal size" (*People*). See IRREGULAR VERBS.

shy preferably makes *shier* and *shiest* in AmE. *Shyer* and *shyest* are primarily BrE forms. *Shyly* is so spelled—not *shily*.

sic. **A. Generally.** *Sic* (= thus, so), invariably bracketed and usually set in italics, is used to indicate that a preceding word or phrase in a quoted passage is reproduced as it appeared in the original document. *Sic* at its best is intended to aid readers, who might be confused about whether the quoter or the quoted writer is responsible for the spelling or grammatical anomaly. This interpolation has been much on the rise: in published writings, its use has skyrocketed since the mid-20th century.

B. Benighted Uses. Some writers use *sic* meanly—with a false sense of superiority. Its use may frequently reveal more about the quoter than about the writer being quoted. For example, a recent book review of an English book contained a *sic* in its first sentence after the verb *analyse*, which was so spelled on the book's dust jacket. In AmE, of course, the preferred spelling is *analyze*; in BrE, however, the spelling *analyse* is not uncommon and certainly does not deserve a *sic*. In fact, all the quoter (or overzealous editor) demonstrated was an ignorance of British usage.

sick, adj.; **sickly,** adj. & adv. While *sick* means "ill," *sickly* (adj.) means "habitually ill" <a sickly young man> or "associated with sickness" <a sickly complexion>. Because *sickly* is an adverb as well as an adjective, the term *sicklily* is a NEEDLESS VARIANT. See ADVERBS (B).

sight. See **site.**

sight unseen. From a strictly logical point of view, the phrase makes little sense. In practice, however, it has an accepted and useful meaning: "(of an item) bought without an inspection before the purchase." See ILLOGIC (A).

Sometimes the phrase is erroneously written *site unseen*—e.g.: "Experts say the Web could be even more dangerous than the telephone because the medium will soon showcase virtual walkthroughs of property and homes for sale, in which purchases could be hustled *site unseen* [read *sight unseen*]" (*San Diego Union-Trib.*). See **site.**

significance; signification. These should be distinguished. *Significance* = (1) a subtly or indirectly conveyed meaning; suggestiveness; the quality of implying; or (2) the quality of being important or significant. *Signification* = (1) the act of signifying, as by symbols; or (2) the purport or sense intended to be conveyed by a word or other symbol.

simplistic, a pejorative adjective meaning "oversimple, facile," became a VOGUE WORD during the 1980s and 1990s: "With adults, a word catches on and it becomes a hobbyhorse that we ride to death. Remember when early critics of President Reagan's economic plans called them 'simplistic.' It was a word seldom used until then, but once let loose in the '80s, it was on every tongue. When someone didn't like something but couldn't articulate why, he'd call it 'simplistic' " (*Atlanta J. & Const.*).

Some misuse the word as a synonym for *simple*—that is, not as a pejorative at all. E.g.: "Replay is not the answer. That sounds like a nice, *simplistic* [read *simple*] fix but what the NFL really needs is to improve its officiating and have better coordination among the officials" (*S.F. Chron.*).

Too simplistic is a venial REDUNDANCY—e.g.: "Tom Dimmit, principal of Golden High School in the Jefferson County school district, says even that [proposal] is *too simplistic* [read *simplistic*]" (*Rocky Mountain News*).

since. See **as** (A).

singlehanded, adv.; **singlehandedly.** The preferred adverb is *singlehanded*, but only when the word follows the verb <she did it singlehanded>. When the adverb precedes the verb, *singlehandedly* is called for <she singlehandedly brought the corporation back from the brink of bankruptcy>.

sink > sank > sunk. Sometimes the past participle wrongly ousts the past-tense form—e.g.: "Unwilling to release a weighty satchel of carefully collected magazine samples, he *sunk* [read *sank*] unceremoniously into an apartment swimming pool" (*Dallas Morning News*). See IRREGULAR VERBS.

site; sight. This is yet another example of homophonic confusion. A *site* is a place or location; a *sight* is (among other things) something seen or worth seeing. The following example is an unusually close call: "The intern liked to ask the 42-year-old lawyer, who was working for the firm as an independent contractor, for advice ranging from how to maintain integrity as a lawyer to what *sights* [read *sites*?] he should visit in California" (*N.Y. Times*). Why a close call? Because a *site* is a place, but one talks about *seeing the sights*.

The phrase *set one's sights* is a SET PHRASE meaning "to aim at" or "to have as one's ambition." Writers sometimes mangle the phrase, most commonly by writing *sites* for *sights*—e.g.: "Immediately after accepting the fourth-place medal at the Division II state meet, Vest set his *sites* [read *sights*] on winning the title next year while setting a state record" (*Cincinnati Enquirer*). Cf. **sight unseen.**

skid > skidded > skidded. *Skid* is incorrect in the past tense—e.g.: "Deputies said Brooks' southbound car *skid* [read *skidded*] out of control on a curve" (*Indianapolis News*).

skim milk; skimmed milk. Though the latter was the original form, *skim milk* is now standard, outstripping the other in frequency of use by an 8-to-1 margin.

SKUNKED TERMS. When a word undergoes a marked change from one use to another—a phase that might take ten years or a hundred—it's likely to be the subject of dispute. Some people (Group 1) insist on the traditional use; others (Group 2) embrace the new use, even if it originated purely as the result of WORD-SWAPPING or SLIPSHOD EXTENSION. Group 1 comprises various members of the literati, ranging from language aficionados to hard-core purists; Group 2 comprises linguistic liberals and those who don't concern themselves much with language. As time goes by, Group 1 dwindles; meanwhile, Group 2 swells (even without an increase among the linguistic liberals).

A word is most hotly disputed in the middle part of this process: any use of it is likely to distract some readers. The new use seems illiterate to Group 1; the old use seems odd to Group 2. The word has become "skunked."

Hopefully is a good case in point. Until the early 1960s, the word appeared only infrequently—almost always with the meaning "in a hopeful manner" <she watched hopefully as her son, having teed off, walked down the first fairway>. Then a new use came into vogue, in the sense "one hopes; I hope; it is to be hoped" <hopefully, they'll get it done on time>. The Group 1 objectors were vocal (for reasons explained under **hopefully**), and for a time the word acquired a bad odor. But with time the odor has faded, so that only a few diehards continue to condemn the word and its users.

To the writer or speaker for whom credibility is important, it's a good idea to avoid distracting *any* readers or listeners—whether they're in Group 1 or Group 2. Thus, in this view, *hopefully* is now unusable: some members of Group 1 continue to stigmatize the newer meaning, and any member of Group 2 would find the old meaning peculiar.

Among the skunked terms discussed at their own entries are **data, decimate, effete, fulsome & transpire.**

slander. See **defamation.**

sleight of hand. This term—meaning "a hand-trick or other display of dexterity"—is the native English equivalent of *legerdemain*. *Sleight* derives from the Middle English word *sleahthe* (= wisdom, cleverness). Although in the early 14th century it was recorded as *slight*, the word we now know by that spelling is a quite different Anglo-Saxon word. It's a fairly common mistake, though, to write *slight* for *sleight*—e.g.: "But in the Senate nothing ever seems to be that simple or easy—not when you have wizards of parliamentary *slight* [read *sleight*] of hand at work" (*Boston Herald*).

slew, n. (= a large number), which most commonly appears in the phrase *whole slew*, is sometimes miswritten *slough* (= a stagnant bog—pronounced /sloo/)—e.g.: "Watch for a whole *slough* [read *slew*] of indictments to be issued today stemming from a major cargo theft ring involving baggage handlers at O'Hare Airport" (*Chicago Sun-Times*). Sometimes, too, it's wrongly made *slue* (= an act of rotating or veering)—e.g.: " 'GoldenEye' . . . has one insane villain, two beautiful women (one good, one bad) and a *slue* [read *slew*] of high-tech gadgets" (*San Antonio Express-News*). For still further confusion between these words, see **slough (A).**

sling > slung > slung. As a past-tense form, *slang* is dialectal. See IRREGULAR VERBS.

slink > slunk > slunk. *Slank* is incorrect in the past tense. See IRREGULAR VERBS.

SLIPSHOD EXTENSION. Several entries in this dictionary refer to this one. "Slipshod extension" denotes the mistaken stretching of a word beyond its accepted meanings, the mistake lying in a misunderstanding of the true sense. It occurs most often, explained H.W. Fowler, "when some accident gives currency among the uneducated to words of learned origin, and the more if they are isolated or have few relatives in the vernacular" (*MEU1* at 540). Today, one might rightly accuse not only the uneducated, but the educated as well, of the linguistic distortion of *lit-*

erally and *protagonist*, to name but two of many possible examples. See **literally & protagonist.** For other examples, see **alibi, dilemma, factor, hopefully, verbal & viable.**

slough. A. Pronunciation. Depending on the meaning, this word can rhyme with *through*, *bough*, or *rough*.

As a noun, *slough* /sloo/ = (1) a muddy bog; or (2) a place ridden with immorality. (*Slew* and *slue*, which are frequent misspellings of this word, are actually different words. See **slew.**)

The pronunciation /slow/ is a chiefly BrE variant in the noun senses.

As a verb, *slough* is pronounced /sləf/ (see (B)).

B. Misspelled *sluff* as a Verb. *Slough off* (= [1] to shed an outer skin; or [2] to cast off, discard) is sometimes incorrectly written *sluff off* (a phonetic spelling)—e.g.: "As he delves deeper into a lousy world in which people steal children for money, he expands, *sluffs* [read *sloughs*] off his lethargy and assumes the role of avenger" (*Grand Rapids Press*).

As a slang term, *sluff* means "to be lazy; shirk responsibilities" <Johnny, have you been sluffing again?>. In this sense the phonetic spelling is passable. The usual PHRASAL VERB is *sluff off* <Jaynie, have you been sluffing off again?>.

slow has long been treated as an immediate adverb, i.e., one not requiring the *-ly* suffix. It is ill-informed pedantry to insist that *slow* can be only an adjective. Though *slowly* is the more common adverb, and is certainly correct, *slow* is often just as good in the adverbial sense. Euphony should govern the choice. For example, Coleridge wrote, in "The Complaint of a Forsaken Indian Woman": "I'll follow you across the snow,/ You travel heavily and *slow*." The usage is common today—e.g.: "While his proposal doubtless goes too *slow* for some legislative leaders, he is wise to steer a moderate tax-cutting course" (*Charleston Post & Courier*). In deciding whether to use *slow* or *slowly* as the adverb, let rhythm and euphony be your guides. You'll undoubtedly prefer *slowly* in most situations, but occasionally *slow* will sound better. As the mystery writer Rex Stout once quipped, "Not only do I use and approve of the idiom 'Go slow,' but if I find myself with people who do not, I leave quick" (as quoted in Norman Lewis, *Better English*, 1961). Cf. **quick.**

sluff off. See **slough (B).**

slung. See **sling.**

slunk. See **slink.**

smell > smelled > smelled. *Smelt* is now exclusively BrE.

smite > smote > smitten. See IRREGULAR VERBS.

snuck is a nonstandard past tense and past participle of *sneak* common in American dialectal and informal speech and writing. The standard past form is *sneaked*. Surprisingly, though, *snuck* appears half as often in American writing as *sneaked*—e.g.: "The next day, Gowdy and I *snuck* [read *sneaked*] off camera to a mesquite thicket where birds were flying thick and fast" (*Ariz. Republic*). Cf. **drag.**

so. A. Beginning Sentences with. Like *And* and *But*, *So* is a good word for beginning a sentence. Each of these three is the informal equivalent of the heavier and longer conjunctive adverb (*Additionally*, *However*, and *Consequently* or *Therefore*). Rhetoric, not grammar, is what counts here. The shorter word affords a brisker pace—e.g.: "Under a state law enacted last year, prisoners must serve at least 85 percent of their sentences, but the state Supreme Court has ruled that the change cannot be applied retroactively. *So* Mark Brown is out walking around" (*Lancaster New Era*).

B. For *very*. The casualism of substituting *so* for *very* should be avoided in formal writing. E.g.: "He cannot reason *so well* [read *very well*]."

C. The Construction *so . . . as*. See **as . . . (A).**

sole (= the one and only; single) shouldn't be used with a plural noun, as it sometimes is. *Only* is the better choice—e.g.: "Pakistan's soldiers seem to be the *sole* [read *only*] people in the country with a sense of duty and national responsibility" (*Toronto Sun*).

solely. Like *only*, this word is sometimes misplaced syntactically—e.g.: "Orick said that although the educational programs are sponsored by Purdue University, they are not *solely related* [read *related solely*] to preservation of agricultural farmlands" (*Indianapolis News*). See **only.**

Also, the word is fairly frequently misspelled *soley*—e.g.: "Since playing basketball as a freshman, Prentiss has concentrated *soley* [read *solely*] on softball" (*San Antonio Express-News*).

solicit. A. For *elicit*. To *solicit* a response is to request it. To *elicit* a response is to get it. But some writers confuse the two, usually by misusing *solicit* for *elicit*—e.g.: " 'The way the question was worded didn't *solicit* [read *elicit*] the type of response I think we were looking for,' Ekberg said" (*Seattle Times*). The following example contains a slight ambiguity—is the core group to ask 4,000 people or to get 4,000 to cooperate? "Sentient representatives expect the core group to *solicit* [read *elicit?*] responses from about 4,000 people" (*Orange County Register*).

B. And *solicitate*. *Solicitate*, a NEEDLESS VARIANT of *solicit*, is an erroneous BACK-FORMATION from *solicitation*. It serves no purpose—e.g.: "Among those Watson has *solicitated* [read *solicited*] advice from was Roy Williams" (*USA Today*)./"Packwood *solicitated* [read *solicited*] jobs for his estranged wife" (*Charleston Daily Mail*).

somebody; someone. The words are equally good; euphony should govern the choice. *Someone* is often better by that standard. Each is a singular noun that, for purposes of CONCORD, is the antecedent of a singular pronoun. *Some one* as two words is an obsolete spelling.

On treating these terms as singular or plural, see PRONOUNS (C).

someplace for *somewhere* is out of place in formal prose. But it's acceptable in speech. Cf. **anyplace & noplace.**

somewhat. The phrasing *somewhat of a* has traditionally been considered poor because it treats *somewhat*—principally an adverb—as a pronoun. Instead of *somewhat of a lackluster performance*, write either *a somewhat lackluster performance* or *something of a lackluster performance*. E.g.: "Neuheisel . . . is *somewhat* [read *something*] of a natural when he's chatting up one of his guys, even with towels flying" (*Sports Illustrated*). See **of (B).**

sort of, adv., a casualism that hedges what would otherwise be a direct statement, should be avoided in polished writing. The following sentence would be improved by dropping it: "It used to be easy to think of McElwee as a *sort of* [delete *sort of*] literary novelist, but one with no chance of getting a movie option" (*Village Voice*). Cf. **kind of (A).**

sound bite. So spelled—not *sound byte*. E.g.: "Although this was a fairly logical prediction to make, knowing the teams, their styles, and their media sound *bytes* [read *bites*] throughout the week, Kawakami hit the nail on the head" (*L.A. Times*). The metaphor is of a bite-sized quotation, especially on video. *Byte*, on the other hand, denotes a string of eight binary digits (*bits*) processed as a unit by a computer.

SOUND OF PROSE. Every writer is occasionally guilty of having a tin ear. But the effective writer is self-trained not to write in a way that distracts with undue alliteration, unconscious puns, accidental rhyming, or unseemly images. These clunkers are sure to irritate some readers. And although clunkers are never entirely escapable, writers can learn to minimize them—most helpfully by acquiring the habit of reading their prose aloud.

A. Undue Alliteration or Rhyme. I.A. Richards, in a classic book, wrote: "But in most *prose*, and more than we ordinarily *suppose*, the opening words have to wait for *those* that follow to settle what they shall mean" (*The Philosophy of Rhetoric*, 1936). This type of wordplay—assuming it is wordplay—should be undertaken cautiously because it declares that the writer is being wry or coy.

Intentional but ineffective alliteration is one thing. Thoughtless alliteration is quite another—e.g.:

- "The Jaguars also signed wide receiver Jimmy Smith to a new contract, and came *to* terms *to two* other draft picks" (*Austin American-Statesman*). (There are too many *tos* and *twos* here; one comes to terms *with* someone, not *to* someone.)
- "That makes some *sense, since* [read *sense because*] a child who has mouth-runs is going to have a hard time winning friends" (*Albany Times Union*).
- "Critics of this new approach say it squelches distinctive programming by pushing stations to adopt more successful, *uniform formats* [read *consistent formats*]" (*N.Y. Times*).

Other phrases susceptible to this problem include *instead of a steady*, *tempted to attempt*, *net debt schedule*, and *need not know*. See ALLITERATION.

B. Awkward Repetition. Too much repeating of sounds can enfeeble your style, especially if two different forms of the same root appear close together—e.g.:

- "The major role of *legislative* liaisons is to answer *legislators'* [read *lawmakers'*] questions about the impact of proposed *legislation* [read *bills*] on various agencies" (*Chicago Sun-Times*).
- "If you're getting the *impression* [read *idea*] we weren't *impressed* with our $20,000 test truck, you're right" (*N.Y. Newsday*).
- "[I]t set aside $3.25 million . . . to cover expected losses from *liquidating liquid* crystal display screens and other assets left over from the Epson deal" (*St. Petersburg Times*). (Change *liquidating* to *selling*.)

soundtrack is so written (or sometimes *sound track*)—not *sound tract*. The *track* in the phrase denotes the segment in a motion picture or videotape where sound, as opposed to visual camera work, is reproduced. But some writers err by writing *tract*—e.g.: "Some of the sound *tracts* [read *tracks*] may have to be 'bleeped' " (*Houston Chron.*). For other misuses, see **track.**

sour grapes is one of the most commonly misused idiomatic METAPHORS. It is not a mere synonym of *envy* or *jealousy*. Rather, as in Aesop's fable about the fox who wanted the grapes he could not reach, *sour grapes* denotes the human tendency to disparage as undesirable what one really wants but can't get (or hasn't gotten). For example, a high-school boy who asks a girl for a date and is turned down might then insult her in all sorts of puerile ways. That's a case of sour grapes.

But the traditional and correct use of the phrase seems to be on the wane. Some uses are downright incoherent—e.g.: "Great Britain's reaction [in the Falklands War] was more a case of *sour grapes* and wounded pride than any genuine desire to right a terrible wrong" (*Time*). (The British reaction couldn't have been "sour grapes" because [1] Great Britain did not disparage the Falklands as undesirable—it wanted to keep them as a territory; and [2] Britain was successful in the effort.) The more typical misuse looks like this: "Is someone trying to jinx *Good Will Hunting*'s chances for a screenwriting Oscar? Perhaps a competitor's *sour grapes* [read *envy*] over the film's success?" (*Daily Variety*).

sow, vb. **A. Inflection: *sow* > *sowed* > *sown*.** In the past participle, *sowed* is a variant form. In modern sources, *sown* predominates by a 6-to-1 margin. See IRREGULAR VERBS.

B. *Sowing wild oats*. To *sow* is to scatter seed. By extension, to *sow one's wild oats* is to engage in youthful promiscuity or other excess. Some writers, though, mistake *sow* (/soh/) with its homophone *sew* (= to stitch with needle and thread)—e.g.: "Primarily, Ios attracts a young Scandinavian crowd that spends the summer *sewing* [read *sowing*] its oats on the nude beaches and in the wild discos" (*L.A. Times*). Sometimes the metaphor appears to be misunderstood. A father, for example, cannot sow the son's oats: "Snelling's *oats were sewn* [*sic*] early in big-time college basketball by his father, Ray Snelling, who played at Southwest Missouri State University in the late 1960s" (*St. Louis Post-Dispatch*). It's hard to suggest a solution for that sentence, which reflects woolly thinking. But perhaps a better phrasing would be *roots were planted*.

Also, this is traditionally a male-only metaphor, since only males have the seed to sow. Only if you take the phrase as a dead metaphor does it work in reference to females. But many readers will find the following sentence hopelessly incongruous: "But how does a '90s girl *sow her wild oats*?" (*N.Y. Newsday*).

spay (= to neuter by removing the ovaries from [a female animal]) is used so often in the past-tense and past-participial form (*spayed*) that it's sometimes confused with *spade*—e.g.: "'Task force will probe way to curb county's animal population. Suggestions: mandatory *spade and neuter* [read *spaying-and-neutering*] laws" (*USA Today*).

speaking. This word is among the few "acceptable danglers" or "disguised conjunctions" when used as a SENTENCE ADVERB—e.g.: "*Speaking* realistically, Ritchey still only hopes to 'capture' a small margin of the commuting population" (*Raleigh News & Observer*). (This might be a paraphrase of Ritchey, but the sentence doesn't have him speaking at all; the comment is the author's.)/ "Practically *speaking*, the proponents of government-funded health insurance for kids ignore the likeliest result of their plan" (*Colo. Springs Gaz. Telegraph*). (Again, the reader knows that the proponents aren't doing the speaking; the writer is.) See DANGLERS (E) & SENTENCE ADVERBS.

special. See **especial.**

species is both singular and plural. As a singular noun, it means "a group of similar plants or animals that can breed among themselves but not outside the group." From that sense the word's meaning has naturally been extended to "class" or "type" <a problem of this species is best left to the family to work out>. As a plural, *species* means "all the groups of similar plants or animals that can breed [etc.]." In the title of Charles Darwin's great work, *The Origin of Species* (1859)—among the most important books ever published—*species* is plural. Unfortunately, many publications insert an extra *the* before *Species*, as if Darwin had considered only the human species. Cf. **series.**

Some writers erroneously make *specie* a singular of *species*—e.g.: "The shrub, also known as southern spicebush, was listed in 1986 as an endangered *specie* [read *species*] by the U.S. Fish and Wildlife Service" (*Memphis Commercial Appeal*). (*Specie*, in its correct form, means "coined money." It has no plural, unless one means to refer to different types of coined money.)

And sometimes people mistake *species* for *sex*—e.g.: "And she was on the whole glad she didn't have to play the scene in which her co-star, Patsy Kensit, is attacked by moths, which required her to have 'rubber rings impregnated with female sex pheromones' sewn into her dress to attract the sex-starved *male species* [read *males*]" (*Independent*). Cf. **genus.**

speed > sped > sped. The best past-tense and past-participial form is *sped*, not *speeded*—except in the PHRASAL VERB *speed up* (= to accelerate) <she speeded up to 80 m.p.h.>.

SPELLING. **A. Common Misspellings.** Computerized spelling checkers have begun to eliminate many misspellings. But they don't catch all misspellings if the word is actually a different word, as when *not* is mistyped *now*. And to the extent that the word lists in the spelling checkers aren't sound, certain misspellings may become more widespread. For example, one spelling checker stops at *restaurateur*, recommending that it be replaced with the incorrect form *restauranteur*. All in all, though, spelling checkers are quite helpful.

Here are 25 of the most commonly misspelled words in the English language. Naturally, they're spelled correctly here:

accommodate
committee
consensus
definitely
embarrass
expedite
grammar
harass
hors d'oeuvre
innovate
inoculate
lieu
millennium
minuscule
misspelling
noticeable
occurrence
pavilion
persevere
playwright
receive
restaurateur
separate
supersede
ukulele

Three CONTRACTIONS are also constantly being misspelled: *it's*, *they're*, and *you're*. See **its, their & your.**

Among the less usual words that are difficult to spell are *iridescent*, *kimono*, *naphtha*, and *syzygy*.

B. Doubling of Final Consonants in Inflected Forms. Apart from words ending in *-l* and exceptions noted below, all English-speaking countries follow the same rules on doubling. When a suffix beginning with a vowel is added, the final consonant of the word is repeated only if (1) the vowel sound preceding the consonant is represented by a single letter (hence *bed, bedding* but *head, heading*); or (2) the final syllable bears the main stress (hence *oc-'cur, oc-'curred* but *'of-fer, 'of-fered*). Among the more commonly misspelled words are these: *biased*, *focused*, *benefited*, *transferred*.

There are exceptions. Unaccented syllables in inflected words are often spelled differently in AmE and in BrE. Americans generally do not double a final *-l* before the inflectional suffix, whereas the British generally do. Thus:

AmE	**BrE**
canceled, canceling	cancelled, cancelling
dueled, dueling	duelled, duelling
funneled, funneling	funnelled, funnelling
initialed, initialing	initialled, initialling
labeled, labeling	labelled, labelling
marshaled, marshaling	marshalled, marshalling
parceled, parceling	parcelled, parcelling
signaled, signaling	signalled, signalling
totaled, totaling	totalled, totalling
traveled, traveling	travelled, travelling
unraveled, unraveling	unravelled, unravelling

The British–American split is seen also in words like *jewel(l)er*, *pupil(l)age*, *tranquil(l)er*, and *travel(l)er*, the British preferring *-ll-* over the *-l-* used by Americans. But there are exceptions:

British writers use the forms *paralleled, paralleling*—just as Americans do—presumably to avoid the ungainly appearance of four *-l*-s in quick succession.

BrE doubles the final consonant after a fully pronounced vowel in words such as *kidnapped, -ing* and *worshipped, -ing*. (One exception is *galloped, galloping*.) In AmE, *kidnapping* is preferred over *kidnaping* (see **kidnap(p)ing**) as an exceptional form (as with *formatted, formatting*), though *worshiped, -ing* follows the general rule of no doubling after unaccented syllables. *Programmed* and *programming* are the preferred spellings on both sides of the Atlantic, the single *-m-* spellings being secondary variants in AmE.

There are a few other exceptions in AmE. *Bayonet* (with the accent on the final syllable) would seemingly make *bayonetted*, but the dictionaries all list *bayoneted* first. Likewise with *chagrined*, *combated*, and *coroneted*—all with an accent on the final syllable. But these forms are few. And with the verb *combat*, the possibility of a MISCUE seems great enough that *combatted* and *combatting* ought to be preferred—despite what the dictionaries say.

Writers and editors should make themselves aware of these minor transatlantic differences in spelling and avoid inserting a bracketed *sic* when quoting a foreign text. See ***sic*** **(B)**.

C. Words with *-ie-* or *-ei-*. The old rule—*i* before *e*, except after *c*, or when sounded as *a*, as in *neighbor* and *weigh*—generally holds. Two notable exceptions are *counterfeit* and *seize*.

D. Compounds. The normal process in modern English is for separate words used habitually to become hyphenated, then fused into a single word (e.g., *to day* became *to-day* in the 19th century and then *today* in the 20th). Because the process is constantly at work, it's difficult to be definite about the status of some terms. For example, *database* went rapidly from *data base* through *data-base* to *database*; and many writers simply skipped the intermediate step. The same tendency is now seen as people begin to write *word-processing* as a solid word.

spirt. See **spurt.**

spit (= to expectorate) is inflected in three possible ways:

spit > spat > spat
spit > spat > spit
spit > spit > spit

Good authority can be found for the first two; the third finds less enthusiastic support. The recommendation here is to follow the first, as good writers generally do—e.g.: "On Tuesday night, he shook hands with John Hirschbeck, the umpire in whose face he *had spat* seven months earlier" (*Boston Globe*). See IRREGULAR VERBS.

Avoid *spit* as the past-tense or past-participial form. It sounds dialectal—e.g.: "Outspoken basketball star Charles Barkley, who once *spit* [read *spat*] at hecklers at a game in New Jersey and has fought critics outside the arena, has appeared frequently in ads for Nike shoes and McDonald's burgers" (*Miami Herald*).

Spit (= to use a spit or skewer) makes *spitted* as the past tense and past participle—e.g.: "We saw *spitted* small birds being barbecued at the Oktoberfest" (*Christian Science Monitor*).

SPLIT INFINITIVES. A. Generally. H.W. Fowler divided the English-speaking world into five classes: (1) those who neither know nor care what a split infinitive is; (2) those who do not know, but care very much; (3) those who know and condemn; (4) those who know and approve; and (5) those who know and distinguish (*MEU1*). It is this last class to which, if we have a good ear, we should aspire.

An infinitive, of course, is the tenseless form of a verb preceded by *to*, such as *to dismiss* or *to modify*. Splitting the infinitive is placing one or more words between *to* and the verb, such as *to summarily dismiss* or *to unwisely modify*. For the infinitive to be truly split, the intervening word or words must follow *to* directly <to satisfactorily have finished>. E.g.: "Supporters of defense projects and opponents of how the president used his new line-item veto power joined forces yesterday *to decisively reject* President Clinton's line-item veto of military construction programs" (*San Diego Union-Trib.*). If the adverb follows any other part of the infinitive, there's no split <to have satisfactorily finished>.

Although few armchair grammarians seem to know it, some split infinitives are regarded as perfectly proper:

- "The evidence in favor of the judiciously split infinitive is sufficiently clear to make it obvious that teachers who condemn it arbitrarily are wasting their time and that of their pupils" (Sterling A. Leonard, *Current English Usage*, 1932).
- "[T]he split infinitive is in full accord with the spirit of modern English and is now widely used by our best writers" (George O. Curme, *English Grammar*, 1947).
- "[The English language gives us] the inestimable advantage of being able to put adverbs where they will be most effective, coloring the verbs to which they apply and becoming practically part of them. . . . If you think a verb cannot be split in two, just call the adverb a part of the verb and the difficulty will be solved" (Joseph Lee, "A Defense of the Split Infinitive," in *Mass. L.Q.*, 1952).
- "To deliberately split an infinitive, puristic teaching to the contrary notwithstanding, is correct and acceptable English" (Norman Lewis, *Better English*, 1961).

See SUPERSTITIONS (B).

B. Splits to Be Avoided. If a split is easily fixed by putting the adverb at the end of the phrase and the meaning remains the same, then avoiding the split is the best course:

Split: "It is not necessary *to here enlarge* upon those points."

Unsplit: "It is not necessary *to enlarge* upon those points *here*."

This is an excellent example of the capricious split infinitive, which only jars the reader. Similar examples turn up frequently—e.g.: "[M]aybe the intense distrust many voters feel toward their government institutions have led them *to almost automatically vote* [read *to vote almost automatically*] against anything the Legislature supports" (*Ariz. Republic / Phoenix Gaz.*). (Notice also the subject–verb disagreement: *distrust* is the subject, and the verb should be *has.*)/ "Last year three-time Doral champion Raymond Floyd revamped the course, adding, among other things, 18 bunkers *to, he says, 'put* [read *in order, he says, to 'put*] the teeth back in the monster' " (*Sports Illustrated*).

Wide splits are generally to be avoided—e.g.: "We encourage both spouses to utilize the best efforts *to understandingly, sympathetically, and professionally try* to work out a compromise." (A possible revision: *We encourage both spouses to try to work out a compromise understandingly, sympathetically, and professionally.*) But sometimes—for effect—they may be justified: "[I]f there is no other way to make our point, we ought to boldly go ahead and split. We should also be willing to sometimes so completely, in order to gain a particular effect, split the infinitive as to practically but quite consciously run the risk of leaving the *to* as far behind as the last runner in the London Marathon. Grammar is made for man, not man for grammar" (*Times* [London]).

C. Justified Splits. A number of infinitives are best split. Perhaps the most famous is from the 1960s television series *Star Trek*, in which the opening voice-over included this phrase: *to boldly go where no man* (or, in the revival of the 1980s and 1990s, *where no one*) *has gone before*. The phrase sounds inevitable partly because it is so familiar, but also because the adverb most naturally bears the emphasis, not the verb *go*.

And that example is not a rarity. Consider: *She expects to more than double her profits next year*. We cannot merely move the adverbial phrase in that sentence—to "fix" the split, we would have to eliminate the infinitive, as by writing *She expects that her profits will more than double next year*, thereby giving the sentence a different nuance. (The woman seems less responsible for the increase.)

Again, though, knowing when to split an infinitive requires a good ear and a keen eye. Otherwise, the ability to distinguish—the ability Fowler mentioned—is not attainable. *To flatly state*, for example, suggests something different from *to state flatly*. In the sentences that follow, unsplitting the infinitive would either create an awkwardness or change the sense:

- "White House officials said they hope Wellstone and Moseley-Braun can be persuaded *to quietly drop* their objections and allow the bill to pass when the Senate returns from its vacation" (*Minneapolis Star Trib.*).
- "With no ready templates available—the only other 'nearby' track, in Vancouver, was judged too dark, static and simplistic—the two had *to pretty well make up* Speed Zone Go Kart Raceway from scratch" (*Edmonton J.*).
- "Issues that most feminists support, such as abortion rights and equal treatment for gays and lesbians, seem *to directly contradict* Christian teachings" (*Raleigh News & Observer*).

Distinguishing these examples from those under (B) may not be easy for all readers. Those who find it difficult might advantageously avoid all splits.

D. Awkwardness Caused by Avoiding Splits. Occasionally, sticking to the old "rule" about split infinitives leads to gross phrasing. The following sentences illustrate clumsy attempts to avoid splitting the infinitive. In the first example, the adverb may be placed more naturally than it is without splitting the infinitive; in the second and third examples, a split is called for:

- "Linda Dishman . . . said Monday that Mahony was *attempting unfairly to deflect* attention away from what she said was illegal demolition of a city-protected landmark" (*L.A. Times*). (What was unfair: the attempting or the deflecting? Read either *was unfairly attempting to deflect* or *was attempting to unfairly deflect*.)
- "Democrats fought for an increase in the minimum wage and *hope quickly to pass* [read *hope to quickly pass*] an expansion of the family leave act" (*Pitt. Post-Gaz.*).
- "[T]he ordinance is not *expected immediately to solve* [read *expected to immediately solve*] problems with the throbbing, low-frequency bass notes from a local club in the Cromwell Square Shopping Center" (*Hartford Courant*).

E. Ambiguities. When the first of several infinitives is split and the initial *to* is the only one, an ambiguity results—e.g.: "The legislation would make it a federal crime *to physically block* access to clinics, damage their property or injure or intimidate patients and staff" (*Dallas Morning News*). There's a problem in interpretation: does *physically* modify the verbs *damage*, *injure*, and *intimidate*, as well as *block*? One hopes that the problem is merely with the journalist's paraphrase and not with the legislation itself.

splutter; sputter. These words are largely synonymous. But *splutter* is the newer word: it probably formed as a blend of *splash* and *sputter*. See PORTMANTEAU WORDS.

spurt; spirt. Most AmE dictionaries list *spirt* merely as a variant of *spurt*. H.W. Fowler suggested a valuable DIFFERENTIATION: use *spirt* in the sense "gush, jet, flow" <a spirt of blood> <oil spirts up from the ground>, and reserve *spurt* for "sprint, burst, hustle" <work done in spurts> <Bailey spurted past>. So far, however, this distinction hasn't taken hold.

SQUARE BRACKETS. See BRACKETS.

squelch. See **quelch.**

stadium. Although several dictionaries seem to prefer *stadia* as the plural, *stadiums* is the more natural and the more usual form. *Stadiums* is also 30 times more common—e.g.: "[D]ozens of *stadiums* have sprouted up all over the country in recent years" (*Baltimore Sun*). See PLURALS (B).

staff. In most senses, the plural is *staffs*. But in music (as well as some archaic senses), the preferred plural is *staves*—though *staffs* occasionally appears even in musical contexts. See PLURALS (G).

standpoint. See **viewpoint.**

state, vb. See **say.**

start. See **begin (A).**

stationary; stationery. The first is the adjective (= remaining in one place, immobile), the second the noun (= writing paper or envelopes).

On *stationary* as an uncomparable adjective, see ADJECTIVES (B).

status (/**sta**-dəs/ or /**stay**-dəs/) forms the plural *statuses* (or, in Latin, *status*), not *stati*. See HYPERCORRECTION & PLURALS (B).

staunch; stanch. *Staunch* is preferable as the adjective ("trustworthy, loyal"), *stanch* as the verb ("to restrain the flow of [usu. blood]"). But in practice the adjective is sometimes undesirably used for a verb—e.g.: "Until now, his most notable move was *staunching* [read *stanching*] the flow of red ink by closing New York Newsday in 1995" (*Boston Globe*).

staves. See **staff.**

steal. See **embezzle.**

stick with; stick to. Both phrases are acceptable in figurative senses <stick with it!> <stick to it!>. *Stick with* predominates in AmE, *stick to* in BrE.

stigma. Pl. *stigmas* or *stigmata*. The English plural (*-mas*) is preferable in most contexts. But *stigmata* carries the specialized sense "bodily marks resembling the crucifixion wounds of Jesus Christ." See PLURALS (B).

stimulus. Pl. *stimuli*. This word has not traditionally made a native-English plural, but a few writers have nevertheless experimented with *stimuluses*—e.g.: "The octopus is meant not to symbolize industry or productivity, but as an example of the kind of visual *stimuluses* [read *stimuli*] that America is producing" (*St. Louis Post-Dispatch*). See PLURALS (B).

story; storey. For the floor or level of a building, *story* is AmE and *storey* BrE. The plural forms are *stories* and *storeys*. See PLURALS (D).

straighten; straiten. These two verbs have different meanings. *Straighten* = to make or become straight. *Straiten* = (1) to make narrow, confine; or (2) to put into distress, esp. financial hardship. Because *straiten* is the rarer word, it is sometimes wrongly displaced by *straighten*—e.g.: "[W]hile most farmers were in *straightened* [read *straitened*] circumstances and too old-fashioned to want machinery, he believed Gridley Gerhardt to be forward-looking and prosperous" (*Christian Science Monitor*).

straitjacket; straightjacket. The latter form is a common error for *straitjacket*—e.g.: "Teachers of the subject assigned editorials by rhetorical types until it was realized that such *straightjacketing* [read *straitjacketing*] of students was destructive of talent, not a developer of it" (Curtis D. MacDougall, *Principles of Editorial Writing*, 1973).

strait-laced (= rigidly narrow in moral matters; prudish) referred originally, in the 16th century, to a tightly laced corset—*strait* meaning "narrow" or "closely fitting." Over time, writers have forgotten the etymology (or they never learned it in the first place) and have confused *strait* with *straight*.

Hence the erroneous form *straight-laced*—e.g.: "Perhaps this city is just too *straight-laced* [read *strait-laced*] to learn how bikes and cars can coexist" (*Wash. Post*).

stratagem. So spelled—though the mistaken *strategem*, on the analogy of *strategy*, appears about 20% as often as the correct spelling. Though the words *stratagem* and *strategy* are etymologically related, they came into English by different routes, and their spellings diverged merely as a matter of long-standing convention. What happened is that the Latin *strategema* became *stratagema* in Romance languages such as French. (The *Century Dictionary* calls the Romance spelling "erroneous.") *Stratagem* came into English in the 15th century, through French. But it wasn't until the early 19th century that English and American writers borrowed *strategy* (originally a Greek term) from Latin. Hence our incongruous spellings today.

stratum. Pl. *strata*. (See PLURALS (B).) *Strata* should not be used as a singular, but it sometimes is—e.g.: "By contrast with the atmosphere of, say, Sinclair Lewis's 'Main Street,' in which an afternoon call or the purchase of a shirtwaist might occasion endless talk among every *strata* [read *stratum*] of a community, minding our own business has become a cardinal virtue" (*N.Y. Times*).

strew. A. As a Verb: *strew* > *strewed* > *strewn*. A variant past-participial form is *strewed*, but *strewn* is standard—e.g.: "Autumn leaves may be *strewn* across the surface in lieu of a centerpiece" (*Memphis Commercial Appeal*). See IRREGULAR VERBS.

B. As a Noun. This is an uncommon usage; *W3* defines it as "a number of things scattered about; a disorderly mess." Because it is so rare, a good replacement might be the better-known, similar-sounding *slew*—e.g.: "Ordinary people could be heard earnestly offering a *strew* [read *slew*] of views that, at their most human turning, veered toward the confessional" (*N.Y. Times*).

stricken. A. Generally. Though *stricken* often appears as a past participle, grammatical authorities have long considered it inferior to *struck*. It's an ARCHAISM except when used as an adjective <a stricken community>. The past-participial use is ill-advised—e.g.: "A noncompete agreement that bans a person from ever setting up a competing company in the same geographical location will be *stricken* [read *struck*] down by the courts as too restrictive" (*Wis. State J.*).

B. *"Strickened."* The participial usage has given rise to the mistaken use of *stricken* for *strike* as a present-tense verb—e.g.: "He was *strickened* [read *stricken*] Friday night while doing what he loved—watching the Attleboro High football team play" (*Providence J.-Bull.*). See IRREGULAR VERBS.

stride > strode > stridden. The past participle *stridden*, as well as its variant form *strode*, rarely appears. See IRREGULAR VERBS.

strive > strove > striven. The past tense seems to cause the most trouble—e.g.: "Negotiators *strived* [read *strove*] to get South African power-sharing talks back on track" (*Wall St. J.*). See IRREGULAR VERBS.

stupid. See **ignorant.**

St. Valentine's Day. See **Valentine's Day.**

subject. See **citizen** (B).

SUBJECT-VERB AGREEMENT. A. General Rule. The simple rule is to use a plural verb with a plural subject, a singular verb with a singular subject. But there are complications. If a sentence has two or more singular subjects connected by *and*, use a plural verb. Yet if the subjects refer to the same person or thing, use a singular verb <the apple of his eye and the source of his inspi-

ration is Heather>. And if the sentence has two singular subjects connected by *or*, *either . . . or*, or *neither . . . nor*, use a singular verb. See **either (C) & neither . . . nor (A).**

B. False Attraction to Noun Intervening Between Subject and Verb. This subheading denotes a mistake in number usually resulting when a plural noun intervenes between a singular subject and the verb. The writer's eye is thrown off course by the plural noun that appears nearest the verb—e.g.:

- "The stalled barges and the towboats that push them along are costing the industry as much as $500,000 a day, but the ripple effect of these disruptions *are* [read *is*] incalculable" (*N.Y. Times*).
- "Evaluation of rookies and free agents *are* [read *is*] the fundamental reason for playing these games" (*Dallas Morning News*).
- "Its history of domination by neighboring countries *sharpen* [read *sharpens*] a stubborn independence" (*N.Y. Times*).

This error sometimes occurs when two nouns, seeming to create a plural, intervene between the subject and the verb—e.g.: "Barefaced *defiance* of morals and law *were* [read *was*, because the subject is *defiance*] illegal" (Lawrence M. Friedman, *Crime and Punishment in American History*, 1993). See SYNESIS.

The reverse error, plural to singular, also occurs—e.g.: "While the types of illness covered *varies* [read *vary*] from one insurer to another, most pay out for heart disease, certain types of cancer and strokes" (*Int'l Herald Trib.*).

C. False Attraction to Predicate Noun. Occasionally a writer incorrectly looks to the predicate rather than to the subject for the noun that will govern the verb. The "correct" way of phrasing the sentence is often awkward, so the writer is well advised to find another way of stating the idea—e.g.: "You can use live or artificial bait to catch these fish. My favorite *are* topwater plugs, plastic jigs and live green backs or shrimp" (*St. Petersburg Times*). (Read: *My favorites are* or *My favorite bait is . . . .*)

D. Compound Subjects Joined Conjunctively. If two subjects joined by *and* are different and separable, they take a plural verb—e.g.: "At the same time, the democratic process and the personal participation of the citizen in his government *is* [read *are*] not all we want" (Charles P. Curtis, Jr., *Lions Under the Throne*, 1947). (*The democratic process* and *personal participation* are different things.)

But sometimes the two subjects joined by *and* express a single idea, and hence should take a singular verb <their confusion and uncertainty is understandable>. This is the case with *spaghetti and meatballs*, which denotes a single dish and therefore takes a singular verb <spaghetti and meatballs is great comfort food>.

E. Misleading Connectives. The phrases *accompanied by*, *added to*, *along with*, *as well as*, *coupled with*, and *together with* do not affect the grammatical number of the nouns preceding or following them. When such a phrase joins two singular nouns, the singular verb is called for—e.g.: "The late Walter Haight of sainted memory, *along with myself* [read *along with me*], *were* [read *was*] phoning a play-by-play of the scene back to the *Post*'s sports department" (*Wash. Post*). (On the reason for changing *myself* to *me* in that sentence, see **myself.**)

F. Plural Units Denoting Amounts. In AmE, a plural noun denoting a small unit by which a larger amount is measured generally takes a singular verb—e.g.: "Five hours *are* [read *is*] enough time."/ "Fifteen minutes *pass* [read *passes*] more quickly than you might think." See COLLECTIVE NOUNS & SYNESIS.

G. *One and one (is) (are).* Both forms are correct. It's possible to treat *one and one* as a single mathematical idea, so that the appropriate verb is *is*. Or it's possible to treat the two *ones* separately—hence *are*.

The same is true of multiplication: both *four times four is sixteen* and *four times four are sixteen* are correct. But the singular is much more common and more natural in modern usage.

H. *Thing after thing (is) (are).* This construction takes a singular verb—e.g.: "Assault after assault on the M'Naghten Rules *were* [read *was*] beaten off until 1957" (H.L.A. Hart, "Changing Conceptions of Responsibility," in *Punishment and Responsibility*, 1968).

I. Subject Area Implied. Some writers fall into the habit of implicitly prefacing plural nouns with UNDERSTOOD WORDS such as *the idea of*, *the field of*, or even *the fact of*. To be sure, some of these wordings are perfectly idiomatic—"Torts is my favorite area of the law."

But the habit should not extend beyond the reach of idiomatic comfort. Consider the following title, over an article by Ray and Tom Magliozzi: "Duplicate Cars Means Customer Pays More for Name" (*Amarillo Daily News*). In that title, there is an implied subject—something like *the fact of having . . . means*. But the phrasing looks sloppy.

J. *One in five*; *one of every five*. This construction takes a singular: *one in three is not admitted*, *one of every five achieves a perfect score*, etc.

K. Decades. Decades customarily take plural verbs: *the 1930s were a tough time in America*. The following sentence is unidiomatic: "The 1950s *is* [read *are*] remembered more for *its* [read *their*] sociology than for *its* [read *their*] politics" (*Time*).

L. An Unusual Plural. By convention—and through the principle of SYNESIS—a singular abstract noun may take a plural verb if it's modified by two or more adjectives referring to different varieties of things denoted by that noun. E.g.: "*Eastern* and *Western art differ* in many fundamental ways."/ "*Classical* and *modern philosophy are* not radically different fields of study." One way of analyzing those sentences is to say that the first adjective has an implied noun after it. See UNDERSTOOD WORDS.

M. *A number of people (is) (are).* See SYNESIS & **number of.**

N. *One of those who (is) (are).* See **one of the [+ pl. n.] who (*or* that).**

O. *Each* as Subject. See **each (A).**

P. *What* as Subject. See **what.**

Q. Inversion. See INVERSION & **there is.**

R. Alternatives. See **either (C)** & **neither . . . nor (A).**

SUBJECT-VERB SEPARATION. The core words in a sentence are the subject and the verb. They are related both in sense and in grammar. And related words should go together. If you separate them too much, the sentence goes asunder—e.g.: "Jurors' *need* to hear that testimony again just minutes before reaching a verdict *puzzled* experts" (*USA Today*). (A possible revision: *When jurors said they needed to hear that testimony again, and just minutes later reached a verdict, the experts were puzzled.* Or: *The experts were puzzled when jurors said they needed to hear that testimony again, and just minutes later reached a verdict.*)/ "*Plans* unveiled Wednesday for a pair of looping reliever roads connecting vast tracts of land south of Forest Drive *have* been roundly panned by many residents" (*Annapolis Capital*). (A possible revision: *Many residents have criticized plans unveiled Wednesday for a pair of looping reliever roads connecting vast tracts of land south of Forest Drive.*)

SUBJUNCTIVES. In modern English, the subjunctive mood of the verb appears primarily in six contexts: (1) conditions contrary to fact <if I were king> (where the indicative would be *am*); (2) suppositions <if I were to go, I wouldn't be able to finish this project> (where the indicative would be *was*); (3) wishes <I wish that I were able to play piano> (where the indicative would be *was*); (4) demands <I insisted that he go> (where the indicative would be *goes*); (5) suggestions <I suggest that she think about it a little longer> (where the indicative would be *thinks*); and (6) statements of necessity <it's

necessary that they be there> (where the indicative would be *are*).

Although subjunctives are less common in English than they once were, they survive in those six contexts. While suppositions and wishes are the most common examples in conversation, the others are most common in writing. And they're worth keeping.

subscribe. For the misuse of *ascribe* for *subscribe*, see **ascribe.**

subsequently. A. For *later*. Using the four-syllable word in place of the two-syllable word is rarely, if ever, a good stylistic choice.

B. And *consequently*. Though both words contain the sense "following" or "occurring later," *consequently* has an added causal nuance: "occurring because of."

subsequent to is a pomposity for *after* or *later*, just as *prior to* is for *before*. E.g.: "Such an atmosphere was created *subsequent to* [read *after*] the June 1989 Tiananmen Square massacre" (*Ariz. Republic*).

substantive. A. Pronunciation. *Substantive*—a commonly mispronounced word—has three, not four, syllables: /**səb**-stən-tiv/. The common error in AmE is to insert what is technically known as an epenthetical *-e-* after the second syllable: /**səb**-stə-nə-tiv/. Still another blunder is to accent the second syllable: /səb-**stan**-tiv/. See PRONUNCIATION (B).

B. For *substantial*. *Substantial* is the more general word, meaning "of considerable size, quantity, or importance; real; ample." *Substantive* is more specialized, appearing most often in old-fashioned grammars (in which *substantive* means "noun") and in law (in which it serves as the adjective corresponding to *substance* and as the antonym of *procedural* <substantive rights>). Some writers misuse *substantive* for *substantial*—e.g.: "Facing a $290 million deficit this year, L.A. is hard pressed to meet the cops' demands for a *substantive* [read *substantial*] raise" (*Newsweek*).

succinct. The first *-c-* has a /k/ sound: /sək-**sinkt**/. Cf. **accessory (B) & flaccid.**

sufficient. See **adequate (A) & enough,** adj.

sufficiently. See **enough,** adv.

sumptuous; sumptuary. These words have almost opposite senses. *Sumptuous* = excessively luxurious; made or produced at great cost <a sumptuous feast>. *Sumptuary* = relating to or designed to regulate expenditures <sumptuary regulations>.

Sumptuous is sometimes misspelled *sumptious*, perhaps under the influence of *scrumptious*—e.g.: "If you have a leftover fish, you can convert it into a *sumptious* [read *sumptuous* or, depending on meaning, *scrumptious*] soup in a matter of minutes" (*St. Louis Post-Dispatch*).

sum total of. This phrase is technically a REDUNDANCY—"sum" meaning "total"—but it's a venial one not likely to disappear from the modern lexicon. And the phrase can be especially useful for emphatic purposes in such lines as *the sum total of our knowledge*—although sticklers would probably prefer *totality* there.

sunk. See **sink.**

SUPERLATIVES. See COMPARATIVES AND SUPERLATIVES.

supersede. A. Spelling. This word—from the Latin root *-sed-* "to sit," not *-ced-* "to move"—is properly spelled with an internal *-s-*, not a *-c-*. But so many other English words end in *-cede* or *-ceed* that many writers unconsciously distort the spelling of *supersede*. Spelling it correctly is one of the hallmarks of a punctilious writer. The misspelling occurs in some surprising places—e.g.: "For now, their legal battle in California mostly centers on jurisdiction, whether the state's gun laws *supercede* [read *supersede*] those enacted locally" (*Boston Globe*). See SPELLING (A).

B. Misused for *surpass* or *beat*. Sportswriters have begun using this word as a synonym of *beat*: thus, one team is said to "supersede" another when it wins a game. E.g.: Tim Cowlishaw, "Cowboys *Superseded* [read *Beaten*] by Redskins: Dallas Defense Overpowered in 35–16 Loss" (*Dallas Morning News*). And other writers have misused the word for *surpass*—e.g.: "Arguably, Russia *supersedes* [read *surpasses*] even England in the publication of Shakespeare's works and the staging of his plays" (*Wall St. J.*).

SUPERSTITIONS. In 1926, H.W. Fowler used the term "superstitions" to describe, in the field of writing, "unintelligent applications of an unintelligent dogma" (*MEU1*). Experts in usage have long railed against them as arrant nonsense, yet they retain a firm grip—if not a stranglehold—on the average person's mind when it comes to putting words on paper. Indeed, these superstitions are bred in the classrooms in which children and adolescents learn to write.

Most of these superstitions are treated elsewhere in this book, in the entry to which the reader is referred at the end of each subentry. For additional perspectives on these points, below are collected some brief statements by respected authorities on style, grammar, and usage.

A. Never End a Sentence with a Preposition. "The origin of the misguided rule is not hard to ascertain. To begin with, there is the meaning of the word 'preposition' itself: stand before. The meaning derives from Latin, and in the Latin language prepositions do usually stand before the words they govern. But Latin is not English. In English prepositions have been used as terminal words in a sentence since the days of Chaucer, and in that position they are completely idiomatic" (Theodore M. Bernstein, *Miss Thistlebottom's Hobgoblins: The Careful Writer's Guide to the Taboos, Bugbears, and Outmoded Rules of English Usage*, 1971). See PREPOSITIONS (B).

B. Never Split an Infinitive. "The practice of inserting an adverb between the infinitive sign [*to*] and the infinitive has steadily increased during the last hundred years, and goes on increasing still. Even a slight examination of the best and the worst contemporary production, both in England and America, will make clear that the universal adoption of this usage is as certain as anything in the future well can be" (Thomas R. Lounsbury, *The Standard of Usage in English*, 1908)./ "The notion that it is a grammatical mistake to place a word between *to* and the simple form of a verb, as in *to quietly walk away*, is responsible for a great deal of bad writing by people who are trying to write well. Actually the rule against 'splitting an infinitive' contradicts the principles of English grammar and the practice of our best writers" (Evans & Evans, *DCAU*)./ "There is no point in rearranging a sentence just to avoid splitting an infinitive unless it is an awkward one" (Porter G. Perrin, *Writer's Guide and Index to English*, 1965). See SPLIT INFINITIVES (A).

C. Never Split a Verb Phrase. "In a compound verb (*have seen*) with an adverb, that adverb comes between the auxiliary and the participle ('I have *never* seen her'); or, if there are two or more auxiliaries, immediately after the first auxiliary ('I have *always* been intending to go to Paris'); that order is changed only to obtain emphasis, as in 'I never have seen her' (with stress on 'have') . . . . There is, however, a tendency to move an adverb from its rightful and natural position for inadequate reasons, as in 'Oxford must *heartily* be congratulated' " (Eric Partridge, *U&A*)./ "Because of their misconception as to what a split infinitive really is, some have reached the erroneous conclusion that an adverbial modifier must never be placed between parts of a compound verb phrase, with the result that they write in such an eccentric style as 'I greatly have been disappointed' instead of writing naturally 'I have been greatly disappointed'" (R.W. Pence & D.W. Emery, *A Grammar of Present-Day English*, 1963). See ADVERBS (A).

D. Never Begin a Sentence with *And* or *But*. "Next to the groundless notion that it is incorrect to end an English sentence with a preposition, perhaps the most wide-spread of many false beliefs about the use of our language is the equally groundless notion that it is incorrect to begin one with 'but' or 'and.' As in the case of the superstition about the prepositional ending, no textbook supports it, but apparently about half of our teachers of English go out of their way to handicap their pupils by inculcating it. One cannot help wondering whether those who teach such a monstrous doctrine ever read any English themselves" (Charles Allen Lloyd, *We Who Speak English*, 1938). See **and (A)** & **but (A).**

E. Never Write a One-Sentence Paragraph. "A paragraph may contain but one sentence . . . [or] two sentences; but usually it contains more than two" (Adams S. Hill, *The Foundations of Rhetoric*, 1896)./ "[T]o interpose a one-sentence paragraph at intervals—at longish intervals—is prudent. Such a device helps the eye and enables the reader (especially if 'the going is heavy') to regain his breath between one impressive or weighty or abstruse paragraph and the next" (Eric Partridge, *U&A*)./ "Basically, there are three situations . . . that can occasion a one-sentence paragraph: (a) when you wish to emphasize a crucial point that might otherwise be buried; (b) when you wish to dramatize a transition from one stage in your argument to the next; and (c) when instinct tells you that your reader is tiring and would appreciate a mental rest-station" (John R. Trimble, *Writing with Style*, 1975).

F. Never Begin a Sentence with *Because*. So novel and absurd is this superstition that seemingly no authority on writing has countered it in print. It appears to result from concern about fragments—e.g.: "Then the group broke for lunch. Because we were hungry." Of course, the second "sentence" is merely a fragment, not a complete sentence. (See INCOMPLETE SENTENCES (A).) But problems of that kind simply cannot give rise to a general prohibition against starting a sentence with *because*. Good writers do so frequently—e.g.: "*Because* of the war the situation in hospitals is, of course, serious" (E.B. White, "A Weekend with the Angels," in *The Second Tree from the Corner*, 1954)./ "*Because* the relationship between remarks is often vague in this passage, we could not rewrite it with certainty without knowing the facts" (Donald Hall, *Writing Well*, 1973).

G. Never Use *since* to Mean *because*. "There is a groundless notion current in both the lower schools and in the world of affairs that *since* has an exclusive reference to time and therefore cannot be used as a causal conjunction. . . . No warrant exists for avoiding this usage, which goes back, beyond Chaucer, to Anglo-Saxon" (Wilson Follett, *MAU*)./ "It is a delusion that *since* may be used only as an adverb in a temporal sense ('We have been here since ten o'clock'). It is also a causal conjunction meaning *for* or *because*: 'Since it is raining, we had better take an umbrella'" (Roy H. Copperud, *American Usage and Style: The Consensus*, 1980). See **as (A).**

H. Never Use *between* with More Than Two Objects. "When Miss Thistlebottom taught you in grammar school that *between* applies only to two things and *among* to more than two, she was for the most part correct. *Between* essentially does apply to only two, but sometimes the 'two' relationship is present when more than two elements are involved. For example, it would be proper to say that 'The President was trying to start negotiations between Israel, Egypt, Syria and Jordan' if what was contemplated was not a round-table conference but separate talks involving Israel and each of the other three nations" (Theodore M. Bernstein, *Dos, Don'ts & Maybes of English Usage*, 1977). See **between (A).**

I. Never Use the First-Person Pronouns *I* and *me*. "[I]f you want to write like a professional just about the first thing you have to do is get used to the first person singular. Just plunge in and write 'I' whenever 'I' seems to be the word that is called for. Never mind the superstitious notion that it's immodest to do so. It just isn't so" (Rudolf Flesch, *A New Way to Better English*, 1958). See FIRST PERSON.

J. Never Use Contractions. "Your style will obviously be warmer and truer to your personality if you use contractions like 'I'll' and 'won't' when they fit comfortably into what you're writing. 'I'll be glad to see them if they don't get mad' is less stiff than 'I will be glad to see them if they do not get mad.' There's no rule against such informality—trust your ear and your instincts" (William Zinsser, *On Writing Well*, 1985). See CONTRACTIONS (A).

K. Never Use *you* in Referring to Your Reader. "Keep a running conversation with your reader. Use the second-person pronoun whenever you can. Translate everything into *you* language. *This applies to citizens over 65 = if you're over 65, this applies to you. It must be remembered that = you must remember. Many people don't realize = perhaps you don't realize.* Always write directly to *you*, the person you're trying to reach with your written message. Don't write in mental isolation; reach out to your reader" (Rudolf Flesch, *How to Be Brief: An Index to Simple Writing*, 1962)./ "Not only does the use of *you* eliminate the passive and make sentences more readable, it directs the writing where it should be directed: to the reader. The 'you attitude' is reader-oriented rather than writer-oriented" (Gary A. Olson et al., *Style and Readability in Business Writing*, 1985).

supplement, n.; **complement,** n. A *supplement* is simply something added <a dietary supplement>. A *complement* is a wholly adequate supplement; it's something added to complete or perfect a whole <that scarf is a perfect complement to your outfit>.

For the misuse of *compliment* for *complement*, see **compliment.**

surname; Christian name; forename; given name. The *surname* (or *last name*) is common to all the members of a family. In many cases it was derived from physical characteristics, occupations, or locations and later transmitted to descendants (e.g., Smith); in other cases it indicated paternity (e.g., Davidson). Such names came to be called *surnames* from the sire or father. The modern custom is that a woman who marries may, but need not, add her husband's surname to her own (e.g., Hillary Rodham Clinton).

The *Christian name* (or *first name*) is older; it was the baptismal name and in medieval England was the only name. Surnames were given later to differentiate (e.g., Robert the Younger).

The first name of a non-Christian is better called a *forename* or *given name*—or simply *first name*. E.g.: " 'Woranoj' is the *first name* [or *forename* or *given name*] and 'Anurugsa' the *last name* [or *surname*] of my friend in Bangkok."

surrounding circumstances. See **circumstances (B).**

swam. See **swim.**

SWAPPING HORSES while crossing the stream is H.W. Fowler's term for vacillating between two constructions (*MEU1* at 589). Thus, someone writes that *the rate of divorce is almost as high in Continental Europe, other things being equal, than it is in the United States*. The first *as* needs a second one in answer, but instead is ill greeted by *than*. See **as . . . as (D).**

Examples don't exactly abound in modern prose, but they're not rare either—e.g.: "He has given the Tilden, Simonsen, Hugo Muller and Pedler *lectureships* [read *lectures*] of the Royal Society of Chemistry" (*Fin. Post*). (He has been given—or awarded—lectureships and has given lectures, but he hasn't given lectureships.)/ "Beardstown coach Don Dillon would *rather* have Maltby handing off *instead of* [read *than*] catching passes" (*Bloomington Pantagraph*). (*Rather* is completed by *than*, not *instead of*; but *instead of* would suffice if *rather* were omitted.)

SWAPPING WORDS. See WORD-SWAPPING.

sweat > sweat > sweat. Although *sweated* is a variant past tense and past participle, *sweat* is the standard form—e.g.: "He was dressed in white cowboy hat and boots, and a pearl-gray western jacket that he *sweat* through" (*Boston Herald*). See IRREGULAR VERBS.

But in quasi-figurative phrases <we really sweated over that one!> <they sweated it out>, the past forms are *sweated*—e.g.: "Inside, you'll find . . . a celebration of the valedictorians, who have *sweated out* straight A's and are finishing high school at the top of their respective classes" (*Spokane Spokesman-Rev.*).

swell > swelled > swelled. The form *swollen*—quite correct as an adjective <swollen ankles>—is a variant past participle. The term *swoll* is a dialectal form sometimes encountered, usually in recorded speech—e.g.: "Up to the time I started to get all *swoll'* up like a pizened pup, it had been a fairly remarkable weekend" (*S.F. Chron.*). *Swole* is a variant spelling of this word, both in AmE dialect and in BrE—e.g.: "We heard an unprecedented number of Dan Ratherisms, including every single colorful Texas simile except, '*Swole* up like an old mule's prostate' " (*Advertising Age*). See IRREGULAR VERBS (D).

swim > swam > swum. The past tense and past participle are often confused—e.g.: "They *swum* [read *swam*] on" (*Santa Rosa Press Democrat*). See IRREGULAR VERBS (D).

syllabus. Pl. *syllabuses* or *syllabi*. American teachers are fond, perhaps overfond, of the Latin plural. Ernest Gowers wrote that "[t]he plural *-buses* is now more used than *-bi*" (*MEU2*). He was right: in AmE, *syllabuses* outstrips *-bi* by a 2-to-1 margin. (In legal writing, oddly, the ratio is 50 to 1 the other way: *syllabi* over *-buses*.) See PLURALS (B).

SYLLEPSIS. See ZEUGMA.

sympathy. See **empathy.**

sync, short for *synchronism* or *synchrony*, is preferred to *synch*. E.g.: "[T]hose 'uncorrelated' world markets are moving much more in *synch* [read *sync*] with each other than they once did" (*Nat'l Rev.*). *Sync* is nearly five times more common than *synch*.

SYNESIS. In some contexts, meaning—as opposed to the strict requirements of grammar or syntax—governs SUBJECT–VERB AGREEMENT. Henry Sweet, the 19th-century English grammarian, used the term "antigrammatical constructions" for these triumphs of logic over grammar. (Expressions in which grammar triumphs over logic are termed "antilogical.") Modern grammarians call the principle underlying these antigrammatical constructions "synesis" (/**sin**-ə-sis/).

The classic example of an antigrammatical construction is the phrase *a number of* (= several, many). It is routinely followed by a plural verb, even though technically the singular noun *number* is the subject <a number of people were there>. (See **number of.**) Another example occurs when a unit of measure has a collective sense. It can be plural in form but singular in sense—e.g.: "*Three-fourths is* a smaller quantity than we had expected."/ "*Two pounds* of shrimp *is* all I need."

If these constructions are grammatically safe, similar constructions involving COLLECTIVE NOUNS are somewhat more precarious. The rule consistently announced in 20th-century grammars is as follows: "Collective nouns take sometimes a singular and sometimes a plural verb. When the persons or things denoted are thought of as individuals, the plural should be used. When the collection is regarded as a unit, the singular should be used" (George L. Kittredge & Frank E. Farley, *An Advanced English Grammar*, 1913). Generally, then, with nouns of multitude, one can justifiably use a plural verb.

Among the common nouns of multitude are *bulk*, *bunch*, *flood*, *handful*, *host*, *majority*, *mass*, *minority*, *multitude*, *percentage*, *proportion*, and *variety*. Each of these is frequently followed by *of* [+ plural noun] [+ plural verb]—e.g.:

- "A great *variety* of clays *were* available to Mississippian potters in the Southeast" (*Am. Antiquity*).
- "Republicans in California see Boxer as a vulnerable target, and a *host* of them *are* actively considering the race" (*L.A. Times*).
- "Of these 3,000, however, just a small *proportion are* enrolled in courses such as Foundations of Health or Human Sexuality" (*USA Today*).
- "A *handful* of them *are* world-class operations" (*Colo. Springs Gaz. Telegraph*).
- "[T]he *majority* of them *were* brought over by the autocratic tyrant, led astray, divided, slandered and finally violently suppressed" (*Wall St. J.*).
- "Only a small *percentage are* chosen as All-America Selections" (*Austin American-Statesman*).

These nouns of multitude are not just acceptably treated as plural. Most of them are preferably so treated when they're followed by *of* and a plural noun. Perhaps the best-known example is *a lot*, which no one today thinks of as having a singular force <a lot of people were there>.

Occasionally an ambiguity arises—e.g.: "*There is* now *a variety of* antidepressant drugs that can help lift these people out of their black moods." If the sense of *a variety of* is "several," then *are* is the appropriate verb; if the sense of the phrase is "a type of," then *is* is the appropriate verb. Either way, though, a writer would be wise to reword a sentence like that one.

But the nouns *amount*, *class*, and *group* all typically call for singular verbs—e.g.: "[T]his *class* of organizations *was* far more prevalent in the developing countries" (*Society*)./ "[A] small *group* of conservative congressmen *are* [read *is*] thinking about drafting a bill requiring U.S. companies to translate the names of their businesses locating here into Spanish" (*San Antonio Express-News*).

There may be little or no logical consistency in the two sets of examples just given—justifiable plurals and less justifiable ones—but the problem lies just outside the realm of logic, in the genius of the language. It is no use trying to explain why we say, on the one hand, *that pair of shoes is getting old*, but on the other hand, *the pair were perfectly happy after their honeymoon*.

For more on grammatical agreement generally, see CONCORD & COLLECTIVE NOUNS.

systematic; systemic. *Systematic* = (1) carried out according to an organized plan; or (2) habitual, deliberate. *Systemic* = affecting an entire system; systemwide. Typically, *systemic* should be replaced by *systematic* unless the reference is to systems of the body <autoimmune and other systemic disorders> or metaphors based on bodily systems <our political order has been debilitated by a series of systemic problems>.

T

table, v.t., has nearly opposite senses in AmE and BrE. By *tabling* an item, Americans mean postponing discussion for a later time, while Britons mean putting forward for immediate discussion. Thus Americans might misunderstand the following sentence: "MPs from both sides of the Commons will tomorrow *table* parliamentary questions demanding to know what official action has been taken to uncover the facts" (*Sunday Times* [London]).

take. See **bring (B).**

taken aback. This phrase (meaning "shocked or stunned, usu. by something someone has done") is sometimes wrongly written—or wrongly said—*taken back*. E.g.: " 'Nothing to do with me?' She was completely *taken back* [read *taken aback*]. 'I can't just stand by and see Sarah being cheated on' " (*Good Housekeeping*).

talisman. Pl. *talismans*. Sometimes the erroneous *talismen* appears for the singular or plural, especially the latter—e.g.: "The boy soldiers wear old shredded Zairian army uniforms or jeans and T-shirts, often with *talismen* [read *talismans*] or plastic rosary beads around their necks" (*Cleveland Plain Dealer*).

talk to; talk with. The first suggests a superior's advising or reprimanding. The second suggests a conversation between equals, with equal participation.

tantalize = to torment by sight or promise of a desired thing kept just out of reach. The verb *tantalize* is derived from the Greek myth about Tantalus, the son of Zeus and the nymph Pluto. After becoming the king of Lydia, he offended the gods by divulging the gods' secrets to mortals. Because the father of Tantalus was divine, Tantalus (though not a god) was himself immortal and thus could not be executed for his crime. Instead, as an eternal punishment, he was plunged into a river of Hades, up to his chin, while overhead boughs of edible fruit hung temptingly near. Whenever he dipped to drink, the water receded; whenever he stretched to eat, a wind blew the laden boughs out of reach.

Although it's sometimes hard to be sure from the context, *tantalize* often seems to be misused for *titillate* (= to excite sensually)—e.g.: "Kama Sutra tells the truth about eros: that no matter how *tantalizing* [read *titillating*?] sex can be, without love, it is unruly, destructive and lonesome-making" (*Ft. Lauderdale Sun-Sentinel*).

tantamount (= equivalent) is sometimes misused for *paramount* (= supreme, preeminent)—e.g.: "Clearly written contracts, carefully outlining duties and functions, are of *tantamount* [read *paramount*] importance" (*Harrisburg Patriot & Evening News*). See **paramount.** Cf. **penultimate.**

technical; technological. The distinction is sometimes a fine one. *Technical* = (1) of or relating to a particular science, art, or handicraft; or (2) of or relating to vocational training. *Technological* = (1) of or relating to the science of practical or industrial arts; or (2) of or relating to innovative gadgetry and computers. *Technological* connotes recent experimental methods and development, whereas *technical* has no such connotation.

teeming with (= to abound; be in plentiful supply) should be followed by a count noun <the pond is teeming with fish> <our suggestion box is teeming with slips>. But sometimes it's misused for *rich in*, when applied to abstract noncount nouns—e.g.: "Lancaster County is *teeming with* [read *rich in*] history" (*Lancaster New Era*).

Teeming is also sometimes misspelled *teaming*—e.g.: "Helen King of Riverside wasn't surprised when I recently reported that Mystic Lake is *teaming* [read *teeming*] with fish" (*Riverside Press-Enterprise*).

telecast. See **broadcast.**

teleconferencing. See **conferencing.**

telegraph, vb.; **telegram,** n. To *telegraph* is to send a *telegram*. Although *telegram* has also been recorded as a verb since the mid-19th century, it has only sporadically so appeared and has never become standard—e.g.: "When [Oscar Levant] was suspended for insulting a local sponsor, Frank Lloyd Wright, not noted for his TV viewing, *telegrammed* [read *telegraphed*] support for Oscar" (*L.A. Times*).

tell; say. Idiomatically speaking, you *say* that something is so, or you *tell* someone that something is so. *Tell*, in other words, needs a personal direct object. You don't *tell* that something is so—e.g.: "After reviewing emergency procedures, he *told* [read *said*] that he would let me fly it" (*Lancaster New Era*). Still, it's permissible to say *tell that to your father* and the like—e.g.: "OK, RWD is better for towing, but *tell that to the owner* of a 4-cylinder engine" (*Chicago Trib.*). In this usage, *tell that to* is a SET PHRASE.

temerity (= rash boldness) is sometimes confused with *timidity*. In the following example, the writer's meaning isn't at all clear—e.g.: "There's a wonderful moment when Hal actually has the *temerity* to place his hand on his father's shoulder, a *timid* gesture of affection that he immediately is made to regret" (*Wash. Post*).

temperature. A. Pronunciation. *Temperature* is pronounced /**tem**-pə-rə-chər/ or /**tem**-prə-chər/, not /**tem**-pə-rə-tyuur/, which is extremely pedantic, or /**tem**-pə-chər/, which is slovenly. A combination of the precious and the slovenly, /**tem**-pə-tyuur/ is humorously affected.

B. For *fever*. In colloquial English, *temperature* has been used in the sense "fever" since the late 19th century. But this usage is illogical because everything has a temperature, in the general sense of the word. The better choice is *fever*—e.g.: "One day recently, Christopher was running a *temperature* [read *fever*]" (*Providence J.-Bull.*). Of course, it's acceptable to say that someone is *running a temperature of 104*—because the word *temperature* makes perfect sense when it's coupled with a specific number.

tenant (= a renter) is now often misused for *tenet* (= a principle or doctrine), a gross solecism—e.g.: "The Clinton legislation, which embraces many of the *tenants* [read *tenets*] supported in education legislation passed in the Bush Administration, calls for the reconfiguration of American public schools" (*N.Y. Times*).

TENSES. A. Generally. The following table shows the basic tenses in English with the verb *be* conjugated. The labels *1st*, *2nd*, and *3rd* stand for first person, second person, and third person.

Indicative Mood

	Present Tense	
	Sing.	**Pl.**
1st	I am	We are
2nd	You are	You are
3rd	He is	They are
	Past Tense	
	Sing.	**Pl.**
1st	I was	We were
2nd	You were	You were
3rd	She was	They were
	Future Tense	
	Sing.	**Pl.**
1st	I will be	We will be
2nd	You will be	You will be
3rd	He will be	They will be

Present Perfect Tense

	Sing.	Pl.
1st	I have been	We have been
2nd	You have been	You have been
3rd	She has been	They have been

Past Perfect Tense

	Sing.	Pl.
1st	I had been	We had been
2nd	You had been	You had been
3rd	He had been	They had been

Future Perfect Tense

	Sing.	Pl.
1st	I will have been	We will have been
2nd	You will have been	You will have been
3rd	She will have been	They will have been

Subjunctive Mood

Present Tense

	Sing.	Pl.
1st	(If) I be	(If) we be
2nd	(If) you be	(If) you be
3rd	(If) he be	(If) they be

Past Tense

	Sing.	Pl.
1st	(If) I were	(If) we were
2nd	(If) you were	(If) you were
3rd	(If) she were	(If) they were

Present Perfect Tense

	Sing.	Pl.
1st	(If) I have been	(If) we have been
2nd	(If) you have been	(If) you have been
3rd	(If) he has been	(If) they have been

Past Perfect Tense

	Sing.	Pl.
1st	(If) I had been	(If) we had been
2nd	(If) you had been	(If) you had been
3rd	(If) she had been	(If) they had been

B. Sequence of. The term *sequence of tenses* refers to the relationship of tenses in subordinate clauses to those in principal clauses. Generally, the former follow from the latter.

In careful writing, the tenses agree both logically and grammatically. The basic rules of tense sequence are easily stated, although the many examples that follow belie their ostensible simplicity in practice.

(1) When the principal clause has a verb in the present (*he says*), present perfect (*he has said*), or future (*he will say*), the subordinate clause has a present-tense verb. Grammarians call this the primary sequence.
(2) When the principal clause is in past tense (*he said, he was saying*) or past perfect (*he had said*), the subordinate clause has a past-tense verb. Grammarians call this the secondary sequence.
(3) When a subordinate clause states an ongoing or general truth, it should be in the present tense regardless of the tense in the principal clause—thus *He said yesterday that he is Jewish*, not *He said yesterday that he was Jewish*. This might be called the "ongoing-truth exception."

The primary sequence is often mangled—e.g.: "Mrs. Yager faces a possible sentence of up to 60 years in prison, although neither side expects that the maximum sentence *would* [read *will*] be imposed if she *was* [read *is*] convicted" (*N.Y. Times*).

But the secondary sequence also causes problems—e.g.: "Mr. Noriega limited his own movements even further, avoiding windows and even the shaded palm court out of fear that snipers *will* [read *would*] gun him down" (*Wall St. J.*).

An exceedingly common problem occurs with (tenseless) infinitives, which, when put after past-tense verbs, are often wrongly made perfect infinitives—e.g.: "Guest . . . had had plenty of time *to have challenged* [read *to challenge*] on either side" (*Sporting Life*)./ "It would have been unfair to the coauthors, he said, *to have listed* [read *to list*] Dr. Lu among them" (*N.Y. Times*). Cf. **would have liked.**

Finally, some writers mistakenly ignore the ongoing-truth exception—e.g.: "It hadn't escaped my notice that many modern texts, like many older ones, *were* [read *are*] self-referential, or concerned with the pleasures of 'recognition' " (*London Rev. of Books*). If, as in that example, the point is continuously true—that is, it couldn't have changed since the time of the writing—then present tense is appropriate even for a verb that follows a past-tense verb.

On a related subject, see DOUBLE MODALS.

C. Threatened Obsolescence of Perfect Tenses. Perhaps the heading here is overdrawn, but a distressingly large number of educated speakers of English are at least mildly hostile to perfect tenses. There are three: the present perfect, the past perfect (or pluperfect), and the future perfect. And they're worth some attention.

First, the present perfect tense is formed with *have* [+ past participle], as in *I have done that.* Either of two qualities must be present for this tense to be appropriate: indefiniteness of past time or a continuation to the present. This tense sometimes represents an action as having been completed at some indefinite time in the past—e.g.:

> I *have played* more than 1,000 rounds of golf.
> They *have seen* Ely Cathedral before.

But sometimes, too, the present perfect indicates that an action continues to the present—e.g.:

> I *have played* cards nonstop since 3:00 yesterday.
> They *have toiled* at the project for three years now.

If either of those qualities is missing—imprecision about time or (if the time is precise) continuation to the present—then the present perfect isn't the right tense.

Apart from the urge to convert this tense to simple when the perfect is needed, the most common error is to use the perfect form when the time is definite but the action doesn't touch the present—e.g.: "I *have played* [read *played*] cards nonstop from 3:00 to 5:00 p.m. yesterday."/ "They *have toiled* [read *toiled*] at the project for three years until last month." If, as in those examples, the action is wholly in the past—and the time is relatively definite—the simple past is called for.

Second, the past perfect tense is formed with *had* [+ past participle], as in *I had done that.* This tense represents an action as completed at some definite time in the past—that is, before some other past time referred to. E.g.:

> I *had* already *taken* care of the problem when you called yesterday.
> By June 26 the money *had disappeared.*

Third, the future perfect tense is formed with *will* (or *shall*) [+ *have* + past participle], as in *I will have done that.* This tense represents an action that will be completed at some definite time in the future—e.g.:

> She *will have published* her second book by the time she's 30.
> They *will have gone* to sleep by midnight.

Of these three types, the present perfect causes the most confusion. Some writers mistakenly equate it with PASSIVE VOICE—to which it has no relation. Others simply want to cut *have*. They may call this economizing, but it's almost always a false economy. And if the *have*-cutters ever become numerous enough, they will have done (that's future perfect) the language serious harm.

terminate. See **fire.**

territory; dependency; commonwealth. The distinctions in AmE are as follows. *Territory* = a part of the United States not included within any state but organized with a separate legislature (*W10*). Guam and the U.S. Virgin Islands are *territories* of the United States; Alaska and Hawaii were formerly *territories. Dependency* = a land or territory geographically distinct from the country governing it, but belonging to it and governed by its laws. The Philippines was once a *dependency* of the United States. *Commonwealth* = a political unit having local autonomy but voluntarily united with the United States. A few states are called *commonwealths*, but mostly one thinks of Puerto Rico and the Northern Mariana Islands as *commonwealths*. Puerto Rico is sometimes referred to as a *dependency*, but its proper designation is *commonwealth*.

In BrE, *commonwealth* = a loose association of countries that recognize one sovereign <the British Commonwealth>.

than. A. For *then*. This error is so elementary that one might fairly wonder whether it is merely a lapse in proofreading. But it occurs with some frequency—e.g.: "Mr. Bennett did wake up several times, hoping to hear good news, if not about himself, *than* [read *then*] at least about the two stars of the film, Nigel Hawthorne, nominated for best actor, or Helen Mirren, nominated for best actress" (*N.Y. Times*). This error is extremely common, perhaps because the two words are almost homophones in some dialects of AmE. In any given instance, though, the error might be typographical. For the opposite error, see **then (B).**

B. Case of Pronoun After: *than me* or *than I*? Traditionally, grammarians have considered *than* a conjunction, not a preposition—hence *He is taller than I (am).* The rule is that the pronoun after *than* gets its case from its function in the completed second clause of the sentence—though, typically, the completing words of the second clause are merely implied. See UNDERSTOOD WORDS.

That view has had its detractors, including Eric Partridge, who preferred the objective case: *You are a much greater loser than me* (*U&A*). Even William Safire plumps for the objective case: "The hard-line Conjunctionites have been fighting this battle a long time. Give them credit: they had to go up against the poet Milton's treatment of *than* as a preposition—*than whom* in 'Paradise Lost'—and against Shakespeare's 'a man no mightier than thyself or me' in 'Julius Caesar' " ("Than Me?", *N.Y. Times*, Apr. 1995).

For formal contexts, the traditional usage is generally best; only in the most relaxed, colloquial contexts is the prepositional *than* acceptable. Here it seems ill advised: "What makes the story even juicier is that Pamela, 74, has allegedly been feuding for years with her two former stepdaughters, both of them slightly older than *her* [read *she*]—and one of whom may face financial difficulties" (*Newsweek*). See PRONOUNS (B).

thankfully = in a manner expressing thanks; gratefully <after being saved so unexpectedly, they thankfully said goodbye>. The word should not be misused in the sense "thank goodness; I am (or we are) thankful that." (Cf. **hopefully.**) Following is an example of the all-too-common fall from stylistic grace: "[R]est assured, there will be no singing, no dancing and, *thankfully* [read *thank goodness*], no hokey Disney presentation" (*Baltimore Sun*). See SENTENCE ADVERBS.

that. A. And *which*. You'll encounter two schools of thought on this point. First are those who don't care about any distinction between these words, who think that *which* is more formal than *that*, and who point to many historical examples of copious *which*es. They say that modern usage is a muddle. Second are those who insist that both words have useful functions that ought to be separated, and who observe the distinction rigorously in their own writing. They view departures from this distinction as "mistakes."

Before reading any further, you ought to know something more about these two groups: those in the first probably don't write very well; those in the second just might.

So assuming you want to learn the

stylistic distinction, what's the rule? The simplest statement of it is this: if you see a *which* without a comma before it, nine times out of ten it needs to be a *that*. The one other time, it needs a comma. Your choice, then, is between comma-*which* and *that*. Use *that* whenever you can.

Consider the following sentence: "All the cars that were purchased before 1995 need to have their airbags replaced." It illustrates a *restrictive* clause. Such a clause gives essential information about the preceding noun (here, *cars*) so as to distinguish it from similar items with which it might be confused (here, cars that were purchased from 1995 on). In effect, the clause restricts the field of reference to just this one particular case or class of cases—hence the term *restrictive*. Restrictive clauses take no commas (since commas would present the added information as an aside).

Now let's punctuate our sample sentence differently and change the relative pronoun from *that* to *which*: "All the cars, *which* were purchased before 1995, need to have their airbags replaced." This version illustrates a *nonrestrictive* clause. Such a clause typically gives supplemental, nondefining information. Here, we already know from the context which cars we're talking about. The sentence informs us that the cars need their airbags replaced—oh, and by the way, they were all bought before 1995. The incidental detail is introduced by *which* and set off by commas to signal its relative unimportance.

Restrictive clauses are essential to the grammatical and logical completeness of a sentence. Nonrestrictive clauses, by contrast, are so loosely connected with the essential meaning of the sentence that they might be omitted without changing the meaning.

Hence, three guidelines. First, if you cannot omit the clause without changing the basic meaning, the clause is restrictive; use *that* without a comma. Second, if you can omit the clause without changing the basic meaning, the clause is nonrestrictive; use a comma plus *which*. Third, if you ever find yourself using a *which* that doesn't follow a comma, it probably needs to be a *that*.

B. Wrongly Suppressed *that*. As a relative pronoun or relative adverb, *that* can be suppressed in any number of constructions (e.g., *The dog you gave me* rather than *The dog that you gave me*). But in formal writing *that* is often ill-advisedly omitted, creating a MISCUE, even if only momentarily—e.g.: "Son acknowledges being a member of a discriminated minority—his grandfather emigrated from the Korean Peninsula to work in the coal mines—may have helped him turn his eyes abroad early" (*L.A. Times*). (Insert *that* after *acknowledges*.)/ "They believed prisoners should be placed in isolation and educated" (*Worcester Telegram & Gaz.*). (Insert *that* after *believed*.)

The writers who ill-advisedly omit *that* seem deaf to their ambiguities and miscues. When one instance occurs in a piece of writing, more are sure to follow. The following examples come from the same article—which contains six more errors of the same variety: "But the state *charged the lease deal* [read *charged that the lease deal*], signed in 1991, sprang from a web of fraud and deceit" (*Sunday Star-Ledger*)./ "During more than a year of negotiations and bureaucratic processing, the Karcher group *claimed the property* [read *claimed that the property*] was worth $2 million when it really was only worth $850,000, the state said" (same).

C. Used Excessively. Those who rabidly delete *that* (see (B)) seem to be overreacting to those who use it excessively—e.g.: "In a 1990 book of his successes and misadventures, *News of My Death . . . Was Greatly Exaggerated* (a tiresomely self-centered, but nonetheless bright and lucid analysis of the '80s boom-to-bust cycle), Hall points out, among other things, *that* while the problem as of '86 and '87 was *that* no one had any money, the bigger problem *that* had fomented *that* circumstance was *that* everyone had had too much money" (*D Mag.*). (A possible revision:

In 1990 Hall wrote a book about his successes and misadventures: News of My Death . . . Was Greatly Exaggerated. *It's tiresomely self-centered, but it's still a bright and lucid analysis of the '80s boom-to-bust cycle. In his view, although the problem in '86 and '87 was that no one had any money, this resulted from an even bigger problem: in the early '80s, everyone had too much money.* [Five *thats* to one.])

D. As a Pointing Word. See POINTING WORDS.

theater; theatre. The first is the usual spelling in AmE, the second in BrE. See -ER (B). The word is pronounced /**thee**-ə-tər/, not /**thee**-ay-tər/ or /thee-**ay**-tər/.

the fact that. See **fact that.**

their; they're. A book like this one need not explain such elementary distinctions. So it will not. But: "Liberals are again trying to explain why they lost their fifth presidential election in 20 years. They've been talking about what *they're* [read *their*] party should be for" (*Wall St. J.*). For still another common mistake, see **there.** See also SPELLING (A).

theirs. See POSSESSIVES (C).

then. A. As an Adjective. *Then* should not be hyphenated when used in the sense "that existed or was so at that time" <the then mayor of San Diego>.

B. For *than*. This is a distressingly common error, especially in newsprint —e.g.: "[H]e enjoyed much more autonomy with 'Face/Off' *then* [read *than*] he did with his other movies" (*Salt Lake Trib.*). For the reverse error, see **than (A).**

there for *they're* or *their* is an embarrassing confusion of homophones. It's the type of solecism one expects from a grade-school student, not from a professional writer or editor. But it occurs as a common inadvertence in journalism—e.g.: "With money saved by not paying property tax, people could keep *there* [read *their*] homes in better condition, afford vacations and buy more" (*Indianapolis Star*).

there is; there are. A. As Signals of Clutter. These phrases, though sometimes useful, can also be the enemies of a lean writing style, as several commentators have observed. When are the phrases defensible? When the writer is addressing the existence of something. That is, if the only real recourse is to use the verb *exist*, then *there is* or *there are* is perfectly fine—e.g.: "*There is* no positive relationship between aid levels and economic growth" (*Fortune*).

Otherwise, though, the phrase should typically be cut—e.g.: "*There is* wide support among congressional Republicans for a flat tax" (*Dallas Morning News*). (A possible revision: *Congressional Republicans tend to support a flat tax.* Or: *Many congressional Republicans support a flat tax.*) The phrase *there is wide support* has become a CLICHÉ among political commentators. And it does exactly what *there is* tends to do: it robs the sentence of a good strong verb.

B. Number with. The number of the verb is controlled by whether the subject that follows the inverted verb is singular or plural. Mistakes are common—e.g.: "With an onslaught of fresh new talented female R&B groups, there *is* [read *are*] several ways you, the consumer, can decipher whether or not you should purchase their products" (*N.Y. Amsterdam News*). See EXPLETIVES & INVERSION.

these. See POINTING WORDS.

these kind of; these type of; these sort of. These are illogical forms that, in a bolder day, would have been termed illiteracies. Today they merely brand the speaker or writer as slovenly. They appear most commonly in reported speech, but sometimes not—e.g.: "But by making *these type of incidents* [read *this type of incident*] racial, he not only is doing his player a disservice, he is failing her as a father" (*L.A. Times*).

Of course, it's perfectly acceptable to write *these kinds* or *these types* or *these sorts*, as many writers conscientiously do—e.g.: "I told my sister that setting up her own Website would allow her to propagate *these kinds* of activities" (*Fortune*).

they. On the use of this word as a singular term, see CONCORD (B), PRONOUNS (C) & SEXISM (B).

they'd better; they better. See **better** (A).

they're. See **their.**

this. See POINTING WORDS.

tho. See **although.**

those. See POINTING WORDS.

those kind of; those type of; those sort of. See **these kind of.**

though. See **although.**

though . . . yet. See CORRELATIVE CONJUNCTIONS.

thrive > thrived > thrived. *Thrived*, not *throve*, is the better past tense—e.g.: "He released them and—with no natural predators—they *throve* [read *thrived*] in the abundant wetlands" (*Cleveland Plain Dealer*). Likewise, *thrived*, not *thriven*, is the better past participle.

thru, a variant spelling of *through*, should be shunned. Oddly, it appears in parts of the Internal Revenue Code.

tie makes, in the present participle, *tying*. *Tieing*, though common, is incorrect—e.g.: "As Dillehay said, *tieing* [read *tying*] overhand knots is 'the kind of thing nature cannot do' " (*Boston Globe*).

TILDE. See DIACRITICAL MARKS.

till; until. *Till* is, like *until*, a bona fide preposition and conjunction. Though less formal than *until*, *till* is neither colloquial nor substandard. It's especially common in BrE, but it still occurs in AmE. Yet the myth of the word's low standing persists; some writers and editors mistakenly think that *till* deserves a bracketed *sic*. If a form deserves a *sic*, it's the incorrect *'til*. Worse yet is *'till*, which is abominable—e.g.: "A month or two remain *'till* [read *till*] you grab your dancing shoes, plus a crew of pals or that special date" (*Denver Post*).

tiro. See **tyro.**

title, v.t. See **entitle.**

TITULAR TOMFOOLERY. Nowadays almost any APPOSITIVE can become a title. This trend is primarily an outgrowth of newspapers and magazines, which create descriptive titles for people, often with initial capitals. Thus, instead of *Timothy McVeigh, the convicted bomber*, writers want to say *convicted bomber Timothy McVeigh*, or, worse yet, *Convicted Bomber Timothy McVeigh* (as if the "title" deserved capitals).

Officer, granted, is a title to be prefixed to a person's name <Officer James Nelson>. *Garbage collector* is not. Yet journalistic writing teems with references to people such as *garbage collector Bill Jones*. This trend originated in an understandable desire for economy in both words and punctuation, since most appositives require articles (*a* or *the*) and commas. Yet the result is often a breeziness that hardly seems worth the effort of repositioning the words from their traditional placement—e.g.: "The district attorney also said he would request a new trial for one of the four policemen acquitted in the 1991 beating of *black motorist Rodney King* [read *Rodney King, a black motorist*]" (*Wall St. J.*)./ "*Frequent contributor Michael Kaplan* [read *Michael Kaplan, a frequent contributor,*] taps in to this energy in the interview gracing our cover, 'On the Record' . . . . *Frequent contributor Ken McAlpine* [read *Ken McAlpine, another frequent contributor,*] does some hip-hop and flip-flop of his own as he checks out the guys who wear the striped shirts and whistles for the National Football League" (*American Way*).

to all intents and purposes. See **for all intents and purposes.**

together appears in many a REDUNDANCY, such as *blend together, connect together, consolidate together, couple together, join together,* and *merge together.* These phrases should be avoided.

For the distinction between *altogether* and *all together,* see **altogether.**

together with. See SUBJECT–VERB AGREEMENT (E).

too. A. Beginning Sentences with. When it means "also," *too* should not begin a sentence, although there is a tendency in facile journalism to use the word this way. Instead of *Too, we shouldn't forget,* write *Also, we shouldn't forget* or, better, *And we shouldn't forget.* Words such as *moreover, further,* and *furthermore* also serve ably in this position.

B. For *very*. This informal use of *too* almost always occurs in negative constructions <it's not too common>. But there are exceptions <you're too kind>.

C. *Too* [+ adj.] *a* [+ n.]. This idiom being perfectly acceptable, there is no reason to insist on the artificiality of *a too* [+ adj. + n.]; that is, *too good a job* is better than *a too good job.* E.g.: "But Monica is *too nice a person* for that kind of behavior" (*Houston Chron.*). For the bad form *too good of a,* see **of (B).**

tortuous; torturous; tortious. *Tortuous* = full of twists and turns <a tortuous path through the woods>. *Torturous* = of, relating to, or characterized by torture <torturous abuse>. *Tortious* = (1) of or relating to a civil wrong (i.e., a tort) for which a person can sue <tortious liability>; or (2) constituting a tort <a tortious act>.

toward. A. And *towards*. In AmE, the preferred form is *toward; towards* is prevalent in BrE. See DIRECTIONAL WORDS (A).

B. Pronunciation. The word is preferably pronounced /tord/, not /twahrd/ or /tə-**wahrd**/.

C. Misused for *to*. *Toward* implies movement. It shouldn't be used when the sentence would be served by *to* or *against*—e.g.: "The parks and recreation department has no objections *toward* [read *to*] selling the West Suffield School" (*Hartford Courant*).

track is sometimes misused for *tract* (= a parcel of land) in the phrase *tract of land*—e.g.: "It's easy to be saddened by change, especially when that change means development gobbling up what longtime Floridians remember as vast *tracks* [read *tracts*] of vacant land, fields of flowers and quiet beaches" (*Tampa Trib.*). The opposite error also sometimes occurs—e.g.: "[T]he prompt will always display the path of the current directory to help you keep *tract* [read *track*] of where you are in the filing system" (*PC Mag.*).

transpire. The traditionally correct meaning of this word is "to pass through a surface; come to light; become known by degrees." But that sense is now beyond redemption, though writers should be aware of it. Today, of course, the popular use of *transpire* is as a FORMAL WORD equivalent to *happen, occur,* or *take place.* But when used in that way, *transpire* is a mere pomposity displacing an everyday word—e.g.: "Conversation remains at a hushed level, as if something of earth-shattering importance or heart-breaking intrigue is *transpiring* [read *occurring*] at all times" (*S.F. Examiner*).

Another loose usage occurs (not *transpires*) when *transpire* is used for *pass* or *elapse*—e.g.: "Three days *transpired* [read *passed*] between the call and discovery of the dead child" (*Albany Times Union*).

All in all, *transpire* fits the definition of a SKUNKED TERM: careful writers should avoid it altogether simply to avoid distracting any readers, whether traditionalists or revolutionaries.

tread > trod > trodden. *Trod* is a variant past participle. Although many American dictionaries (surprisingly) list *untrod* as the standard adjective in preference to *untrodden*, the latter form is four times more common. See IRREGULAR VERBS.

triumphant; triumphal. Persons are *triumphant* (= celebrating a triumph), but events and actions are *triumphal* (= of, relating to, or constituting a triumph).

trod; trodden. See **tread.**

trooper; trouper. *Trooper* = (1) a cavalry soldier or horse; (2) a police officer mounted on horseback; or (3) a state police officer. *Trouper* = (1) a member of an acting troupe; or (2) one who handles adversity well. The proper expression, then, is *real trouper* (sense 2), not *real trooper*. Yet while the correct form is more common, the incorrect form seems to be gaining ground—e.g.: "Recently, our beloved 16-year-old cat, Casey, was stricken with cancer. Nevertheless, she was a real *trooper* [read *trouper*] until the end" (*St. Louis Post-Dispatch*).

true facts. This is a common REDUNDANCY, especially in legal writing—e.g.: "Two Sandwich teachers accused of showing a sexually explicit foreign film to a class of seventh-graders say they have done nothing wrong and are being fired from their jobs without the *true facts* [read *facts*] of the incident being revealed" (*Boston Herald*). Writers debase the word when they qualify *facts* with an adjective like *true* or *incorrect*. We ought to be able to rely on the facts being facts, instead of having to wonder whether the writer failed to describe what kind of facts they are. Cf. **actual fact.**

try and is, in AmE, a casualism for *try to*—e.g.: "Mr. Kemp, who seemed intent on slowing his normally rapid speaking pace, accused the Administration of 'demagoguery' in using 'fear' to *try and* [read *try to*] panic older voters with charges that Republicans endanger the health of the Medicare program" (*N.Y. Times*). In BrE, however, *try and* is a standard idiom.

tsar. See **czar.**

twofold, threefold, fourfold, and the like should each be spelled as one word.

two halves. See **half (D).**

tying. So spelled—not *tieing*. See **tie.**

type of—like *kind of*, *sort of*, and *variety of*—is often used unnecessarily and inelegantly. But when the word *type* does appear, it must have its *of*—which is unfortunately dropped in the following examples. They are typical of the modern American colloquial trend: "The Cloister is exquisitely beautiful and fine for a different *type person* [read *type of person*]" (*Atlanta J. & Const.*).

For the phrase *these type of*, see **these kind of.**

tyro (= a beginner, novice) is the standard spelling in AmE. *Tiro* predominates in BrE. Pl. *tyros* (or, in BrE, *tiros*). See PLURALS (C).

U

ukulele. So spelled—not *ukelele.* See SPELLING (A).

ultimate destination. See **destination.**

ultimately = (1) in the end <she ultimately reached her destination>; or (2) basically; fundamentally <the two words are ultimately related>. Cf. **penultimate.**

ultimatum. Pl. *ultimatums.* E.g.: "The 49ers president delivered an ultimatum to a town that doesn't respond to *ultimata* [read *ultimatums*]" (*S.F. Examiner*).

umlaut. See DIACRITICAL MARKS.

unable. See **incapable.**

unanimous appears in various redundant phrases, such as *unanimously of one opinion, entirely unanimous,* and *completely unanimous.* See ADJECTIVES (B).

unaware; unawares. Properly, *unaware* is the adjective <I am unaware of that book> and *unawares* the adverb <the rainstorm caught us unawares>. Thus, *taken unaware* and *caught unaware* are mistakes for the SET PHRASES *taken unawares* and *caught unawares*—e.g.: "Reportedly, he has had the ailments for months but the Flyers were caught *unaware* [read *unawares*]" (*Boston Globe*).

unbeknown; unbeknownst. Some authorities suggest that both forms are humorous, colloquial, and dialectal. Others say that *unbeknown* is preferred over the dialectal *unbeknownst.* These inconsistent pronouncements—reflecting mostly BrE usage—serve as confusing guides.

In AmE, neither can really be called dialectal or colloquial, since the words are essentially literary. In current AmE usage, *unbeknownst* far outranges *unbeknown* in frequency, and it must therefore be considered at least acceptable. But *unbeknownst,* like other *-st* forms (e.g., *whilst, amidst*), seems to come less naturally to AmE. So there's much to be said for preferring *unbeknown*—e.g.: "*Unbeknown* to her, though, Christmas was the day a curse transformed him from a handsome but vain young prince into the ugly, angry Beast" (*L.A. Times*).

unbelief. See **disbelief.**

uncategorically is a silly but distressingly common MALAPROPISM for *categorically* (= unconditionally, without qualification). And it has gotten wide exposure. In 1991, Judge Clarence Thomas, testifying before the Senate Judiciary Committee, "uncategorically" denied that he had discussed pornographic materials with Ms. Anita Hill: " 'Senator, I would like to start by saying unequivocally, *uncategorically,* that I deny each and every single allegation against me today' " (*N.Y. Times*). Cf. **unmercilessly & unrelentlessly.**

uncharted (= unmapped), as in *uncharted territory,* is often wrongly written *unchartered*—e.g.: "He believes this latest frontier in communications is an *unchartered* [read *uncharted*] territory bound to attract Wild West–type outlaws" (*Minneapolis Star Trib.*). An airplane might be *unchartered* if it had no scheduled flights. But unknown territory is *uncharted,* not *unchartered.*

uncomparable. See **incomparable.**

UNCOMPARABLE ADJECTIVES. See ADJECTIVES (B).

unctuous. So spelled. *Unctious* is a fairly common misspelling—e.g.: "Most unbelievably *unctious* [read *unctuous*]: Ginger Spice of the Spice Girls, after winning Best Dance Video: 'Lady Diana had real girl-power'" (*Boston Globe*).

underestimate is often misused for *overestimate* when writers intend the phrase *impossible to overestimate*. The misuse renders the phrase illogical—e.g.: "While it's true baseball's draft generally can't be judged for about four years—a player's average development time—it's impossible to *underestimate* [read *overestimate*] its importance" (*Wash. Post*). This error is akin to using *could care less* for *couldn't care less*. See **couldn't care less** & ILLOGIC.

underhanded; underhand, adj. The shorter form is much older <underhand dealings>, but *underhanded* is now more than twice as common and must be accepted as standard—e.g.: "[P]artisans accused each other of unnecessary delay and *underhanded* negotiating tactics" (*Wis. State J.*). Increasingly, *underhand* is confined to literal senses <because he hurt his shoulder, the tennis champion is temporarily having to use an underhand serve>.

underlie. So spelled. *Underly* is an infrequent blunder—e.g.: "They [want to restore] principles that some, maybe even most, people believe to *underly* [read *underlie*] the cornerstone of our cultures: human relationships, love, marriage" (*Santa Fe New Mexican*). Writers fall into the error because they more commonly see the adjectival participle *underlying* than the uninflected verb.

Underlay is properly the past tense of *underlie*—e.g.: "Atkins gets the doggedness, the country-boy simplicity that *underlay* Dunne's unquestioning devotion to duty, as well as the fey quality of his madness" (*Plain Dealer*). But the word is sometimes used wrongly for *underlie*—e.g.: "As the ground thaws in the spring, the moisture is kept from draining downward by the *underlaying* [read *underlying*] ice" (*Providence J.-Bull.*).

UNDERSTOOD WORDS are common in English, and they usually aren't very troublesome if we can mentally supply them. Often they occur at the outset of sentences. *More important* is short for *what is more important*; *as pointed out earlier* is short for *as was pointed out earlier*.

In a compound sentence, parts of a verb phrase can carry over from the first verb phrase to the second, in which they are understood: "Gorbachev has demanded that Lithuania suspend the declaration of independence before the blockade can be lifted and *talks begun*." (That sentence is considerably more elegant than it would have been if the second verb phrase had appeared in full: *talks can be begun*.)

On verbs supposedly "understood" whose absence detracts from clarity, see BE-VERBS (A).

under the circumstances. See **circumstances (A).**

underway; under way. Some dictionaries record the term as two words when used adverbially, one word when used as an adjective preceding the noun <underway refueling>. In the phrases *get underway* (= to get into motion) and *be underway* (= to be in progress), the term is increasingly made one word, and it would be convenient to make that transformation, which is already underway, complete in all uses of the word.

unequivocal; unequivocable. The latter is erroneous, yet the error is surprisingly common. Most dictionaries list only the former, but some writers are undaunted—e.g.: "Coach Joan Stolarik can say *unequivocably* [read *unequivocally*] that her team will win when Wilson Hunt swims against Wilson Fike" (*News & Observer*).

uniform. See ADJECTIVES (B).

uninterest. See **disinterest.**

uninterested. See **disinterested.**

unique. Strictly speaking, *unique* means "being one of a kind," not "unusual." Hence the phrases *very unique*, *quite unique*, *how unique*, and the like are slovenly. The *OED* notes that this tendency to hyperbole—to use *unique* when all that is meant is "uncommon, unusual, remarkable"—began in the 19th century. However old it is, the tendency is worth resisting.

But who can demand responsible use of the language from an ad writer who is loose enough to say, in a national advertisement, that a certain luxury sedan is "so unique, it's capable of thought"? And what are we to make of the following examples?

- "This year the consensus among the development executives seems to be that there are some fantastically funny, very exciting, *very, very unique* talents here" (*Time*).
- "Residents of college basketball's *most unique* unincorporated village were in place yesterday afternoon, the day before their Blue Devils will face North Carolina" (*N.Y. Times*).
- "Turns out the University of Wisconsin football team is in the process of doing something *quite unique*" (*Wis. State J.*).

Arguably, our modern culture lacks and does not *want* absolutes, in intellectual life or in language. But stick with the uncomparable *unique*, and you may stand out as almost unique. See ADJECTIVES (B).

United Kingdom. See **Great Britain.**

unlawful. See **illegal.**

unleash. The word is premised on the idea that a threatening or vicious animal can be let off a leash. But a surprising number of writers have misunderstood and written the meaningless *unlease*—e.g.: "But Mr. Williams *unleases* [read *unleashes*] a fiery temper at managers who fail to make budget" (*N.Y. Times*).

unlike in. Though some critics have called the phrase a "gaucherie" and worse, *unlike in*—in which *unlike* takes on an adverbial sense—is now common in AmE and BrE alike. Of all the instances in which *unlike* appears, it is followed by *in* about 2% of the time—meaning, statistically, that it's quite frequent. E.g.: "But *unlike in* the primary, Cropp won't be running with the support of John Ray's well-financed mayoral campaign" (*Wash. Post*).

unmercilessly is a MALAPROPISM and NONWORD on the order of *uncategorically*. *Mercilessly*, of course, is the word—e.g.: "He worked with top-flight professionals and drilled them *unmercilessly* [read *mercilessly*]" (*Wash. Post*). Cf. **uncategorically & unrelentlessly.**

Though it adds another syllable, *unmercifully* also suffices—e.g.: "And still, Stevie Wonder seemed intent on taking his sweet, soulful time, teasing us *unmercifully*, making us sweat for his presence" (*Boston Globe*).

unmoral. See **immoral.**

unorganized. See **disorganized.**

unreadable. See **illegible.**

unrelentlessly is a solecism for either *unrelentingly* or *relentlessly*. Ironically, this NONWORD literally suggests just the opposite of the intended meaning—e.g.: "He has *unrelentlessly* [read *relentlessly* or, better, *faithfully*] served as a committee person involved in parks and recreation, fire prevention, police and emergency services, highway management, budget control and youth and school advisory committees" (*Syracuse Post-Standard*). Cf. **unmercilessly & uncategorically.**

unremorsefully. See **remorselessly** (A).

unrevokable. See **irrevocable.**

unsatisfied. See **dissatisfied.**

until. In the phrase *up until*, the *up* is superfluous, though it's common in speech. Use either *until* or *up to*—e.g.: "*Up until* [read *Until*] about 30 years ago, Sisters of Mercy were the teachers; today, lay teachers dominate" (*Hartford Courant*). See **till.**

unwed. See **wed.**

unwieldy, an adjective meaning "difficult to handle" <unwieldy packages>, often seems to be mistaken for an adverb ending in *-ly*—e.g.: "And it doesn't require an *unwieldly* [read *unwieldy*], lengthy tournament to improve the situation" (*Denver Post*).

upon is a FORMAL WORD, often unnecessary in place of *on*—e.g.: "Beneath his likeness sits a table *upon* [read *on*] which participants place the fabric after prostrating themselves three times" (*L.A. Times*). In short, *upon* is inferior when a shorter, simpler, and more direct word will suffice.

Yet *upon* is quite justifiable when the sense is *upon the occasion of*, or *when* (something) *occurs*—e.g.: "*Upon* disembarking from their chartered plane and boarding the team bus on the tarmac, they proceeded to have a fender bender—with a 727" (*Pitt. Post-Gaz.*).

up to now is a comfortably idiomatic equivalent of *heretofore* and *hitherto*—e.g.: "So why did Gaffney, *up to now* a staunch supporter of the deal and a close ally of the governor, create what is likely to be three months of political pandemonium?" (*N.Y. Newsday*).

upward(s). Although *upward* is generally the preferred adverb and adjective in AmE, the form ending in *-s* has become established in the SET PHRASE *upwards of* (= more than)—e.g.: "If she's right, the stock could rise *upwards of* 61% to $35 by the end of next year" (*Money*). See DIRECTIONAL WORDS (A).

urban; urbane. *Urban* = (1) of, relating to, or located in a city; or (2) characteristic of city life. *Urbane* = suave; sophisticated; debonair. Occasionally *urbane* is misused for *urban*—e.g.: "Looking at a computer as a miracle machine is akin to spouting the glories of dense *urbane* [read *urban*] living or fossil fuels" (*Countryside & Small Stock J.*).

use; utilize; utilization. *Use* is the all-purpose noun and verb, ordinarily to be preferred over *utilize* and *utilization*. *Utilize* is both more abstract and more favorable connotatively than *use*.

used to, not *use to*, is the phrase meaning "formerly"—e.g.: "We didn't *use to* [read *used to*] think of politics in quite these terms" (*Time*). *Didn't used to* (= formerly didn't) is the informal equivalent of the rarely encountered phrase *used not to*—e.g.: "Choosing the car of the year is getting to be a messy business. It *didn't used to* be that way" (*Albany Times Union*).

user-friendly. See COMPUTERESE.

utilize; utilization. See **use.**

V

v.; vs. Both are acceptable abbreviations of *versus*, but they differ in application: *vs.* is more common except in names of law cases, in which *v.* is the accepted abbreviation.

Valentine's Day; Valentine Day; Valentines Day. Although the formal name is *St. Valentine's Day*, this is rarely encountered. The standard term today is *Valentine's Day*. Avoid the two variant forms.

variety. When the phrase *a variety of* means "many," it takes a plural verb—e.g.: "Words, songs and rituals are a few of the many things that color our experience, and *a variety of* them *are* found in religious services" (*Nat'l Catholic Rptr.*). In fact, it's erroneous in that context to use a singular verb—e.g.: "There *is* [read *are*] *a variety of* dwelling types, including houses, row houses and apartments, so that younger and older people, singles and families, poor and the wealthy, may live there" (*Sun-Sentinel*). See SYNESIS.

vehement is pronounced /**vee**-ə-mənt/, not /və-**hee**-mənt/.

vehicle. The *-h-* is not pronounced. Hence: /**vee**-i-kəl/.

The word itself is often a prime example of OFFICIALESE, as when a police officer refers to *exiting the vehicle and engaging in foot pursuit* (= getting out of the car and running after a suspect). Some auto manufacturers have made their warranties easier to decipher by taking the simple step of substituting *car*, *truck*, *minivan*, or the like for the abstract *vehicle*. See ABSTRACTITIS & PLAIN LANGUAGE.

venal; venial. *Venal* = purchasable; highly mercenary; amenable to bribes; corruptible <the continent's most spectacularly venal dictator>. *Venial* = slight (used of sins); pardonable; excusable; trivial <absolution for venial sins>. Writers sometimes misuse *venal* for *venial*—e.g.: "For all the failings of nature, Murphy's play makes clear that the *venal* [read *venial*] sins of the leaders were as much to blame" (*Boston Herald*).

venue = (1) the proper or a possible place for the trial of a lawsuit; or (2) the place where an event is held <the venue will be Madison Square Garden>. In sense 2, it's a VOGUE WORD—e.g.: "After more than 300 years, the Covent Garden piazza is still London's most popular *venue* [read *place*] for street performers" (*Cleveland Plain Dealer*).

verbal = (1) of, relating to, or expressed in words, whether written or oral; or (2) of, relating to, or expressed through the spoken word; oral. Many regard sense 2 as a SLIPSHOD EXTENSION. In fact, given the primary sense, the movie producer Samuel Goldwyn wasn't really very ironic when he remarked, "A *verbal* contract isn't worth the paper it's written on." After all, a written contract *is* verbal. The phrase requires *oral*.

The error is especially acute when *verbal* is opposed to *written*—e.g.: "Take care with words, *verbal* [read *oral*] and written" (*Wash. Post*). Take care indeed!

VERBAL AWARENESS. To keep from making unconscious gaffes or MISCUES—as by referring to a *virgin field pregnant with possibilities*—writers must be aware of all the meanings of a word because its potential meanings can sabotage the intention. Careful users of language don't let a sign such as *Ears Pierced While You Wait* go unnoticed. Nor do they overlook the humor in the church bulletin that reads, *All women wishing to become Young Mothers should visit the pastor in his office.*

Likewise, writers ought not to refer to *Roe v. Wade and its progeny*—though several prominent writers have done just that. A heightening of verbal awareness would save writers from such oddities.

verbiage. This term has long had negative connotations, referring to language that is prolix or redundant. E.g.: "Fanatics sloughing through Stone's pseudo-Joycean jungle of *verbiage* might note . . . his overuse of sentence fragments and quick, cheap imagery" (*Village Voice*). Still, the *SOED* records a "rare" neutral sense: "diction, wording, verbal expression." Unfortunately, this unneeded sense has been revived in recent years, so that it's sometimes hard to say whether pejorative connotations should attach. E.g.: "In the past, Spencer's public commentary has fallen short of the righteous, high-minded *verbiage* displayed in Diana's eulogy" (*N.Y. Newsday*).

Strictly speaking, the phrase *excess verbiage* is a REDUNDANCY, given the predominant meaning of *verbiage*—e.g.: "None of the *excess verbiage* [read *verbiage*] would matter, of course, if 'Chasing Amy' had no aspirations beyond the windbag coarseness of a young director" (*Albany Times Union*).

Verbage for *verbiage* is a common error spawned perhaps by the analogy of *herbage*. E.g.: "But too often, investors need a magnifying glass and a law degree to get through the document's turgid, lengthy *verbage* [read *verbiage*]" (*USA Today*). This error might result partly from the common mispronunciation: /**vər**-bij/, rather than the correct /**vər**-bee-ij/.

VERBLESS SENTENCES. See INCOMPLETE SENTENCES.

VERBS. See TENSES.

versus. See **v.**

vertebra (= a single bone that, together with similar bones, forms the spinal column) has two plurals: *vertebrae* (/**vər**-tə-bree/ or /**vər**-tə-bray/) and *vertebras* (/**vər**-tə-brəz/). (See PLURALS (B).) The Latinate plural (*vertebrae*) is so common that some writers mistake it for a singular—e.g.: "There were fears that he could be crippled after the fall, but an operation successfully treated a fractured *vertebrae* [read *vertebra*]" (*Daily Telegraph*).

very. A. As a WEASEL WORD. This intensifier, which functions as both an adjective and an adverb, surfaces repeatedly in flabby writing. In almost every context in which it appears, its omission would result in at most a negligible loss. And in many contexts the idea would be more powerfully expressed without it—e.g.: "The *very* [delete *very*] outrageous statement by Earl Woods that his son would 'do more than anyone to change humanity' gives Woods a chance not only to survive his Miracle at the Masters, but to improve upon it" (*Tulsa Trib. & Tulsa World*). In that sentence—as in so many others—*very* actually weakens the adjective that follows. Cf. **clearly & obviously.**

B. *Very disappointed*, etc. *Very* modifies adjectives (*sorry*, *sick*, etc.) and not, properly, past participles (*disappointed*, *engrossed*, etc.). Wilson Follett wrote that "finer ears are offended by past participles modified by *very* without the intervention of the quantitative *much*, which respects the verbal sense of an action undergone. Such writers require *very much disappointed*, *very much pleased*, *very much engrossed*, *very well satisfied*, etc." (*MAU*). E.g.: "Now in their early 30s and *very changed* [read *very much changed*], they have a reunion" (*Houston Chron.*).

As Follett has noted, "Only a few adjectives from verbs—*tired*, *drunk*, and possibly *depressed*—have shed enough of their verbal quality to stand an immediately preceding *very*" (*MAU*). *Very interested* is another acceptable idiom, although *very much interested* seems preferable. When a past participle has become thoroughly established as an adjective (e.g., *drunk*), it takes *very* rather than *very much*.

But the best solution to this knotty problem is often simply to substitute *quite* for *very*. That is, it's quite acceptable to say *quite disappointed*, *quite engrossed*, and so on.

veteran. *Former veteran* is redundant —e.g.: "[S]ometime after World War II, the Postal Service began to develop an inbred, bloated paramilitary culture. The 'generals'—many of them *former veterans* [read *veterans*]—who ran the place administered rigid rules from the Domestic Mail Manual, a tome the size of the New York City telephone book" (*Wash. Post Mag.*).

Veterans Administration. *Veterans* takes no apostrophe.

Veterans Day; Veterans' Day. The spelling without the apostrophe is preferred—both in everyday usage and by the statute establishing the legal holiday. The former official name for the Nov. 11 federal holiday was *Armistice Day*. Cf. **Presidents' Day.**

via = (1) by way of (a place); passing through <they flew to Amarillo via Dallas>; or (2) by means of, through the agency of <we sent the letter via fax>. Sense 2, a casualism, is questionable whenever a simple preposition would suffice. Ernest Gowers called it a vulgarism in *MEU2*, and Wilson Follett (*MAU*) and Theodore Bernstein (*The Careful Writer*) concur. But like it or not—and there's no longer any reason not to—*via* is now standard in sense 2. It has come to supplant *through* whenever the latter word doesn't feel quite right—e.g.: "From its one store in Carytown, his company has sold furniture to customers throughout the country *via* its World Wide Web site" (*Richmond Times Dispatch*).

viable originally meant "capable of living; fit to live," a sense that still applies in many phrases, such as *a viable fetus*. By acceptable extension it has come to refer figuratively to any idea or thing that might flourish. But in this use it's a VOGUE WORD that can often be improved on—e.g.: "They now have a *viable* [read *plausible*] successor to the Speaker in New York Congressman Bill Paxon" (*New Republic*).

The word has lately been the victim of SLIPSHOD EXTENSION, when used in the sense "feasible, practicable" <a viable plan>. One writer has noted that "dictionaries now give [as definitions for *viable*] *real*, *workable*, *vivid*, *practicable*, *important*, newer definitions that seem only to confirm the critics' complaints that the word has had the edge hopelessly ground off it" (Roy Copperud, *American Usage and Style*, 1980).

Thus it is sometimes hard even to know what a writer means with *viable*—e.g.: "The white cotton shirt is still *viable* [read *acceptable* or, possibly, *a possibility*], but it could also be traded for a softer, sheer-mesh top" (*Dallas Morning News*). Cf. **feasible.**

vice; vise. In AmE, a *vice* is an immoral habit or practice, and a *vise* is a tool with closable jaws for clamping things. But in BrE, the tool is spelled like the sin: *vice*.

vice versa (= the other way around; just the opposite) should be the fulcrum for reciprocal referents <he liked her and vice versa>. But some writers misuse the term in trying to imply something different from (or sometimes even analogous to) what they've just said—e.g.: "They have eased restrictions to an odd-even rationing system under which residents at odd addresses can water on odd days of the month, and *vice versa*" (*Portland Oregonian*). (A possible revision: . . . *residents at odd addresses can water on odd days of the month, and those at even addresses on even days.*)/ "The higher the put trading, the more bullish the indication and *vice versa*" (*Barron's*). (A possible revision: *The higher the put trading, the more bullish the indication; the lower the put trading, the more bearish the indication.*)

victory. The phrase *win a victory* is a common but venial REDUNDANCY—e.g.: "The United Auto Workers has *won a victory in Northeast Ohio in its bid to unionize seat plants owned by Johnson Controls Inc.* [read *won in its bid to unionize seat plants in Northeast Ohio owned by Johnson Controls Inc.*]" (*Crain's Cleveland Bus.*).

victuals, pronounced /**vit**-əlz/, is spelled phonetically (*vittles*) only in colloquial usage.

videoconferencing. See **conferencing.**

viewpoint; point of view; standpoint. The first has been stigmatized by a few writers and grammarians who consider it inferior to *point of view*. Eric Partridge wrote that the term "has been deprecated by purists; not being a purist, I occasionally use it, although I perceive that it is unnecessary" (*U&A*). And John Simon says that "centuries of sound tradition have hallowed *point of view* as preferable to the Teutonism *viewpoint*" (*Paradigms Lost*, 1980).

Yet *viewpoint*, apart from being extremely common, conveniently says in one word what *point of view* says in three. The same holds true for *standpoint*. Today, no stigma should attach to either word.

violative. The phrase *to be violative of* is verbose for *to violate*. E.g.: "This proposal *is too flagrantly violative of the First Amendment* [read *violates the First Amendment too flagrantly*] to merit anything but condemnation" (*Virginian-Pilot*). See BE-VERBS (A).

The *OED* records *violative* from 1856 at the earliest, but the word appeared more than half a century before in a famous Supreme Court case, *Marbury v. Madison* (1803): "To withhold the commission, therefore, is an act deemed by the court not warranted by law, but *violative* of a vested legal right."

VIRGULE [/]. Known popularly as the "slash" and arcanely as the "solidus," the virgule is a punctuation mark that doesn't appear much in first-rate writing. Some writers use it to mean "per" <50 words/minute>. Others use it to mean "or" <and/or> or "and" <every employee/independent contractor must complete form XJ42A>. Still others use it to indicate a vague disjunction, in which it's not quite an *or* <the novel/novella distinction>. In this last use, the en-dash is usually a better choice. (See DASHES (B).) In all these uses, there's almost always a better choice than the virgule. Use it as a last resort.

But the virgule has several other, more legitimate uses as well: (1) to separate run-in lines of poetry <To be, or not to be: that is the question:/ Whether 'tis nobler in the mind to suffer/ The slings and arrows of outrageous fortune>; (2) to show pronunciations (as they're shown throughout this book) <*ribald* is pronounced /**ri**-bəld/>; (3) to separate the numerator and the denominator in a fraction <19/20>; and (4) in informal jottings, to separate the elements in a date <11/17/98>.

virtue of, by; in virtue of. *By virtue of*, not *in virtue of*, is now the idiomatic phrase. The latter is an ARCHAISM.

virtuoso. The plural is preferably *virtuosos*—not *virtuosi* (a pedantic form that is less than half as common). See PLURALS (B).

virus. Pl. *viruses*.

vis-à-vis (lit., "face to face") is a multihued preposition and adverb in place of which a more precise term is often better. The traditional sense is adverbial, "in a position facing each other." But the word is most often figurative. And as a preposition, *vis-à-vis* has been extended to the senses "opposite to; in relation to; as compared with." Although more straightforward phrases are often available, they're sometimes longer—e.g.: "That would have done far more to bolster California's economic competitiveness *vis-à-vis* other Western states where income levies are considerably larger" (*San Diego Union-Trib.*). (Possibly *in comparison with*?)/ "[S]mall, remote towns suffer from a number of deprivations—along with corresponding advantages—*vis-à-vis* big cities" (*New Republic*). (Possibly *in comparison with*?)

But shorter substitutes are often available—e.g.: "But I've often had this question *vis-à-vis* [read *about*] business lunches: Just how unusual and personalized can I be with them and not lose every client I've ever had?" (*N.Y. Times*).

vise. See **vice.**

visualize does not mean "to see," but "to see in the mind's eye." So it's silly to say, as some do, that they can't *visualize* very well because of the fog.

vocation. See **avocation.**

VOGUE WORDS are those faddish, trendy, ubiquitous words that have something new about them. They may be NEOLOGISMS or they may be old words in novel uses or senses. Often they quickly become CLICHÉS or standard idioms, and sometimes they pass into obscurity after a period of feverish popularity.

For whatever reason, vogue words have such a grip on the popular mind that they come to be used in contexts in which they serve little purpose. But as their popularity increases, their value diminishes. The following list is a representative collection:

bottom line
constructive
cost-effective
cutting edge, on the
definitely
dialogue, vb.
disconnect, n.
downside
downsize
empower; empowerment
environment
escalate (= to intensify)
eventuate
exposure (= liability)
framework
grow your business
guardedly optimistic
identify with <I can identify with you>
impact, vb.
interface
-IZE words
lifestyle
matrix
meaningful
need-to-know basis, on a
network, vb.
no-brainer
no-lose situation
no-win situation
-oriented (e.g., cat-oriented)
overly
parameters
politically correct (or P.C.)
proactive
relate, v.i. <I can relate to that>
resonate <Does that resonate with you?>
scenario
state-of-the-art
synergy
upside
user-friendly (see COMPUTERESE)
viable
wake-up call
win-win situation
worst-case scenario

When you put it all together, of course, it's ludicrous: "Language-wise, I am, like, majorly bummed by the way people abuse the mother tongue. This one's a no-brainer. Yo, I've got issues here, and this is my bottom line" (*Montgomery Advertiser*).

void, adj. See ADJECTIVES (B).

vs. See **v.**

W

waistcoat (= [in BrE] a vest) is best pronounced not as it's spelled, but instead /**wes-kət**/.

wait. See **await.**

waiter. If women can be actors and sculptors, then surely they can be *waiters*. Yet in looking for nonsexist alternatives to *waitress*, various groups have championed the silly terms *waitperson* and *waitron*. Let *waiter* do for either sex. See SEXISM (D).

waiver; waver. *Waiver* (= voluntary relinquishment of a right or advantage) is primarily a noun; *waver* (= to vacillate) is primarily a verb. It is a solecism to confuse the two—e.g.: "Mayor Koch . . . *waivered* [read *wavered*] between silence and support for months" (*N.Y. Times*)./ "Out of the school's 575 students, 38 have signed *wavers* [read *waivers*] to allow them not to wear the uniform" (*Orange County Register*).

wake; awake; awaken. The past-tense and past-participial forms of *wake* and its various siblings are perhaps the most vexing in the language. Following are the preferred declensions:

wake > woke > waked (or woken)
awake > awoke > awaked (or awoken)
awaken > awakened > awakened
wake up > woke up > waked up

See IRREGULAR VERBS. For the past participle, AmE prefers *waked*; BrE prefers *woken*.

wallet; billfold. The traditional distinction is that a *wallet* holds paper money unfolded and contains compartments for coins and the like, whereas a *billfold* (as the name suggests) holds it folded and does not contain extra compartments. But most people use the words interchangeably.

walrus. Pl. *walruses*.

wane; wax. *Wane* = to decrease in strength or importance. *Wax* (= [1] to increase in strength or importance; or [2] to become) is used primarily (in sense 2) in CLICHÉS such as *to wax poetic, eloquent*, etc., or (in sense 1) as a correlative of *wane* <her influence waxed and waned>.

wangle. See **wrangle.**

wanton; reckless. The word *wanton* usually denotes a greater degree of culpability than *reckless* does. A *reckless* person is generally fully aware of the risks and may even be trying and hoping to avoid harm. A *wanton* person may be risking no more harm than the *reckless* person, but he or she is not trying to avoid the harm and is indifferent about whether it results. In criminal law, *wanton* usually connotes malice, but *reckless* does not.

-WARD(S). See DIRECTIONAL WORDS (A).

wash /wahsh/ is frequently mispronounced with an intrusive *-r-*: /wahrsh/. See PRONUNCIATION (B), (C).

Washington's Birthday. See **Presidents' Day.**

waver. See **waiver.**

wax. See **wane.**

wean means either "to cause (a child or young animal) to become accustomed to food other than the mother's milk" or, by extension, "to withdraw (a person) gradually from a source of dependence." Thus, a person is typically *weaned off* something—e.g.: "Skeptics have claimed this decline in caseload would slow and then halt once the most employable welfare recipients were *weaned off* the rolls" (*Las Vegas Rev.-J.*).

But *weaned on*—used illogically in the sense "raised on, brought up with"—is a spreading contagion. E.g.: "For a culture *weaned on* [read *brought up on*] Hollywood's interpretation of romance, the very notion that any healthy, intelligent, attractive male might desire a woman over 35 is a radical concept" (*Vancouver Sun*).

we aren't. See **we're not.**

WEASEL WORDS. Theodore Roosevelt said, in a speech in St. Louis on May 31, 1916: "One of our defects as a nation is a tendency to use what have been called weasel words. When a weasel sucks eggs it sucks the meat out of the egg and leaves it an empty shell. If you use a weasel word after another there is nothing left of the other." Some writers have incorrectly assumed that the metaphor suggested itself because of the wriggling, evasive character of the weasel. In any event, sensitive writers are aware of how supposed intensives (e.g., *very*) actually have the effect of weakening a statement. Many other words merely have the effect of rendering uncertain or toothless the statements in which they appear. Among these are *significantly*, *substantially*, *reasonable*, *meaningful*, *compelling*, *undue*, *clearly*, *obviously*, *manifestly*, *if practicable*, *rather*, *somewhat*, *duly*, *virtually*, and *quite*. See **clearly** & **very.**

website. One word.

we'd = (1) we would; or (2) we had. Sense 2 has not held as much favor as sense 1, but it is common and typically doesn't cause any confusion because the past participle follows closely—e.g.: "*We'd* just arrived in Colorado . . . . *We'd* gone to sleep gliding through the farmlands of Missouri" (*Christian Science Monitor*).

wed > wedded > wedded. Although *wed* is no more than a variant past-tense form, it often displaces *wedded*—e.g.: "Last year, the singer [Dan Fogelberg] *wed* [read *wedded*] his longtime fiancée, Anastasia Savage, who shares his love of oil painting" (*Parade*). In the negative, the proper adjective is *unwed* <unwed mothers>.

we'd better; we better. See **better (A).**

Wednesday is pronounced /**wenz**-day/ or /**wenz**-dee/. But some precisians want to—and do—say /**wed**-nəz-day/, which is simply incorrect. As it happens, the first *-d-* has long been silent.

welcher. See **welsher.**

well, when forming an adjective with a past-participial verb, is hyphenated if placed before the noun (e.g., *a well-known person, a well-written book*), but it's typically not hyphenated if the phrase follows what it modifies (e.g., *a person who is well known, a book that is well written*).

welsher; welcher. The former is usual; the term means "one who shirks his or her responsibility," and most commonly refers to one who does not pay gambling debts.

Many natives of Wales consider the word insulting, though there is no etymological evidence supporting a connection with *Welsh* (= of, relating to, or hailing from Wales). Even so, the popular mind makes this connection, and the careful writer must be heedful.

Welsh rabbit; Welsh rarebit. For the term denoting a dish of melted cheese on toast or crackers, *Welsh rabbit* has long been considered standard. It seems, however, that some 18th-century literalist, noting the absence of bunny meat in the dish, corrupted the term through false etymology to *rarebit*. Today, both terms are still found, but unfortunately *Welsh rarebit* is about three times more common than *Welsh rabbit*. See ETYMOLOGY (D).

we're not; we aren't. Although both forms are extremely common, *we're not* is ten times more common than *we aren't*. And because the negative isn't contracted in *we're not*, the phrasing is more emphatic. E.g.: "*We're not* talking about a futuristic, Jetson-like electronic house where robots cook and clean. *We're not* even talking about so-called smart houses" (*San Diego Union-Trib.*).

west; westward(ly); westerly. See DIRECTIONAL WORDS.

wet > wetted > wetted. The past-tense and past-participial *wet* is inferior except in a few SET PHRASES <he wet his whistle with a couple of beers after mowing the yard> <Little Bobby has wet the bed again>. See **whet.**

wharf. The usual plural in AmE is *wharves*, but in BrE it's *wharfs*. See PLURALS (G).

what it is, is. Sentences with this ungainly construction are much on the rise—e.g.: "Clearly, this is no high-level policy debate. *What it is, is* payback time for middle-class voters" (*Chicago Trib.*). (A possible revision: *Clearly, this is no high-level policy debate. Instead, it's payback time for middle-class voters.*)

What happens is that the noun clause (*what it is*) needs a subject (the second *is*). But the better method in writing is to avoid the *what*-construction altogether and make the sentence more direct.

whereas has a cluster of literary senses, namely, "although; while on the one hand; on the contrary; but by contrast." These literary uses are a part of the general writer's idiom—e.g.: "Whereas both his parents have black hair, he has blond."

One usage critic has stated: "*Whereas* sounds stuffy. In spite of the objections of some grammarians, the common word is now *while*" (Rudolf Flesch, *The ABC of Style*, 1964). Yet *whereas* is better than *while* if the latter ambiguously suggests a time element, especially a clashing time element—e.g.: "*While* [read *Whereas*] I brought her to the office, George took her home." See **while.**

whet (= to sharpen or stimulate) commonly appears in the CLICHÉ *whet the appetite*. Unfortunately, though, *whet* is often confused with *wet*—e.g.: "More importantly, he *wet* [read *whetted*] the appetite of Atlanta and presumably much of the country for an Olympics that, at least in distances under a mile, could carry a red, white and blue tint" (*Ariz. Republic*). The error might occur in part because people tend to salivate when their appetites are stimulated; that is, the mouth becomes *wet*. But it's still the wrong word.

whether. A. *Whether or not.* Despite the SUPERSTITION to the contrary, the words *or not* are usually superfluous, since *whether* implies *or not*—e.g.: "In another essay, 'The Rules of the Game,' he discusses moral codes and *whether or not* [read *whether*] they work" (*Denver Post*).

But the *or not* is necessary when *whether or not* means "regardless of whether" <the meeting will go on whether or not it rains>. E.g.: "You can tap many of these resources *whether or not* you have an account with that fund company" (*Home PC*). If you add the word *regardless*, however, either it or *or not* is superfluous—e.g.: "[Who can use IRAs:] Couples with AGIs up to $150,000, singles to $95,000, *regardless of whether or not* [read *regardless of whether* or *whether or not*] they have retirement plans" (*Money*).

B. *As to whether.* The Fowler brothers describe this phrasing as "seldom necessary" in *The King's English* 344 (3d ed. 1931). That judgment still stands—e.g.: "Surprisingly, most folks have never taken the time to learn this skill . . . , [which] may *mean the difference as to whether* [read *determine whether*] someone with no pulse or respiration will live or die" (*Cincinnati Post*). See **question whether.**

C. *Of whether.* *Whether* usually directly follows the noun whose dilemma it denotes: *decision whether*, *issue whether*, *question whether*. (See **ques-**

tion whether.) But *regardless*, an adverb, makes *regardless of whether*. See **regardless whether.**

Although *issue whether* is typically better than *issue of whether*, the latter phrase has certain justifiable uses in which *of* is obligatory, usually when *issue* is modified by an adjective. E.g.: "Thompson [referred to] . . . the narrow legal *issue of whether* fund-raising calls made by either Clinton or Gore violated a federal law barring solicitation on federal property" (*Chicago Trib.*).

D. And *if*. See **if (A).**

which. A. Generally. This word, used immoderately, is possibly responsible for more bad sentences than any other in the language. Small wonder that James Thurber wrote: "What most people don't realize is that one 'which' leads to another. . . . Your inveterate whicher . . . is not welcome in the best company" ("Ladies' and Gentlemen's Guide to Modern English Usage," in *The Ways of Language*, 1967). E.B. White was like-minded: "The careful writer, watchful for small conveniences, goes *which*-hunting, removes the defining *whiches*, and by so doing improves his work" (William Strunk, Jr. & E.B. White, *The Elements of Style*, 1979).

For a full explanation of *which* vs. *that*, see **that (A).** Suffice it to say here that if you see a *which* with neither a preposition nor a comma, dash, or parenthesis before it, it should probably be a *that*.

B. Wrongly Applied to Persons. Unlike *that*—which can apply to either things or persons—*which* applies only to things. If persons are referred to, the nonrestrictive relative pronoun is *who*—e.g.: "Rights advocates and officials in Zaire protested the treatment of the illegal immigrants, some of *which* [read *whom*] were reportedly bound with tape" (*N.Y. Times*).

C. The Remote *which*. See REMOTE RELATIVES.

while for *although* or *whereas* is permissible and often all but necessary, despite what purists sometimes say about the word's inherent element of time. *While* is a more relaxed and conversational term than *although* or *whereas*, and it works nicely when introducing a contrast—e.g.: "Five of the nine Dallas school board members are white, *while* only 11 percent of Dallas' schoolchildren are white" (*Pitt. Post-Gaz.*). The *OED* traces this use back to Shakespeare in 1588 (*Love's Labour's Lost*).

Though the use is quite proper, writers must be on guard for the occasional ambiguity. For instance, does it denote time or contrast in the following sentence? "[The] former spokeswoman . . . claim[s] she was fired in April because she is white, *while* the hospital's management was seeking to build bridges to Tampa's black community" (*Tampa Bay Bus. J.*). The sense is surely a contrasting one, but the sentence undesirably causes the reader to hesitate.

Further, *while* shouldn't be used merely for *and*—e.g.: "Her father, J. Frank McKenna III, is a lawyer, *while* [read *and*] her mother, Colleen O'Shaughnessy McKenna, is the author of 17 children's books, many of which are set in Catholic schools" (*Pitt. Post-Gaz.*).

while away; wile away. The phrase *while away* (= to spend [time] idly) dates from the early 17th century and remains current—e.g.: "Guitarist Martin Barre doesn't *while away* his time listening to old Jethro Tull albums" (*Chicago Trib.*).

Wile away, a synonymous phrase dating from about 1800, began as a corrupt form but is included in modern dictionaries such as *W10* and *AHD* without any cautionary note. Most commonly, of course, *wile* is a noun meaning "a stratagem intended to deceive" or "trickery"; it may also function as a verb in the corresponding sense "to lure or entice." However old the mistaken form *wile away* is—and never mind that Charles Dickens used it—it is still inferior to *while away*. E.g.: "Before Kim Peek saw *Rain Man*, the 1988 award-winning movie loosely based on his life, he stayed home and *wiled* [read *whiled*] away the time working and reading books" (*Austin American-Statesman*).

who; whom. A. Generally. Edward Sapir, the philosopher of language, prophesied that "within a couple of hundred years from to-day not even the most learned jurist will be saying 'Whom did you see?' By that time the *whom* will be as delightfully archaic as the Elizabethan *his* for *its*. No logical or historical argument will avail to save this hapless *whom*" (*Language*, 1921). A safer bet might be that no one will be spelling *to-day* with a hyphen. In any event, writers in the late 20th and early 21st centuries ought to understand how the words *who* and *whom* are correctly used.

Who, the nominative pronoun, is used (1) as the subject of a verb <it was Kate who rescued the dog>; and (2) as the complement of a linking verb, i.e., as a predicate nominative <they know who you are>. *Whom*, the objective pronoun, is used (1) as the object of a verb <whom did you see?>; and (2) as the object of a preposition <the person to whom we're indebted>.

It's true that in certain contexts, *whom* is stilted. That has long been so: "Every sensible English speaker on both sides of the Atlantic says *Who were you talking to*? [—not *Whom*—] and the sooner we begin to write it the better" (J.Y.T. Greig, *Breaking Priscian's Head*, ca. 1930). But there are other constructions in which *whom* remains strong—and more so in AmE than in BrE. Although writers have announced the demise of *whom*, it persists in AmE—e.g.: "Even if things do come down to *whom* you know in this world, luck definitely figures in *whom* you meet" (*Fortune*).

The correct uses of *who* are sometimes tricky. But if the pronoun acts as the subject of a clause, it must be *who*, never *whom*—e.g.: "Alan Alda, *who* you quickly realize *is* sorely missed on TV, stars as Dan Cutler, a type-A personality advertising executive" (*Sun-Sentinel*). (*Who* is the subject of *is*.)

While the subject of a finite verb is nominative (*I know she is good*), the subject of an infinitive is in the objective case (*I know her to be good*). The same is true of *who* and *whom*. But that brings us to the next section.

B. The Objective *who*. Strictly, *whom* is always either an object or the subject of an infinitive. E.g.: "Do all you can to develop your intuition—this will help you to know when to act and when to wait, *whom* to be cautious about and *whom* to trust" (*Wash. Times* [horoscope]). If a horoscope writer can get it right, then you'd think that other journalists could as well. But often they don't—e.g.:

- "A polite, helpful 11-year-old *who* [read *whom*] everybody called Jake was fatally shot in his bedroom in this small rural town on Thursday, and a 13-year-old friend was charged hours later with killing him" (*N.Y. Times*).
- "And he [nominee Stephen G. Breyer] promised, following the admonition of the late Justice Arthur Goldberg, *who* [read *whom*] he served as a law clerk 30 years ago, to do his best to avoid footnotes" (*Wash. Post*).
- "Those friends include Myra Guarino, 62, of Valdosta, *who* [read *whom*] Mrs. Helms represents in a suit against the manufacturer of silicone breast implants" (*N.Y. Times*).

C. The Nominative *whom*. Among the toughest contexts in which to get the pronouns right are those involving linking verbs. We say, for example, *who it is* for the same reason we say *It is I*, but some very good writers have nodded. In any event, *whom* shouldn't be used as the subject of any finite verb—e.g.: "Police went to several addresses looking for a 17-year-old *whom* [read *who*] they thought was staying with his aunt" (*S.F. Chron.*). (*Who* is needed as the subject of *was*.) See HYPERCORRECTION (F).

William Safire takes an interesting approach for those who fear seeming pedantic (by using *whom*) or being incorrect (by using *who* for *whom*): "When *whom* is correct, recast the sentence" ("On Language," *N.Y. Times*, Oct. 1992). Thus *Whom do you trust?* becomes, in a political campaign, *Which candidate do you trust?* For those who hesitate over these questions of case, this approach might seem quite sensible. See PRONOUNS (B).

But one commentator, Steven Pinker, calls Safire's suggestion an "unacceptable pseudo-compromise" (*The Language Instinct*, 1994). And Pinker has a point: "Telling people to avoid a problematic construction sounds like common sense, but in the case of object questions with *who*, it demands an intolerable sacrifice. People ask questions about the objects of verbs and prepositions *a lot*" (*id.*). Moreover, a phrase such as *which person* is wordier and slightly narrower than *who* or *whom*. So realistically, we're stuck with the continuing struggle between *who* and *whom*.

D. Placement of the Relative Pronoun. See REMOTE RELATIVES.

who else's. See **else's** & POSSESSIVES (I).

whoever; whomever. Like *who* and *whom*, this pair is subject to more than occasional HYPERCORRECTION—e.g.: "Both teams want to run, so *whomever* [read *whoever*] controls the boards and doesn't throw the ball away too much will win" (*USA Today*). See PRONOUNS (B) & **who (C).**

whole, adj. See ADJECTIVES (B).

whom. See **who.**

whomever. See **whoever.**

whose. A. Meaning "of which." *Whose* may usefully refer to things <an idea whose time has come>. This use of *whose*, formerly decried by some 19th-century grammarians and their predecessors, is often an inescapable way of avoiding clumsiness—e.g.: "It was a door that opened into the twilight zone of credit repair, a shadowy world *whose* siren calls, dubious as they may sound, lure countless desperate souls" (*L.A. Times*).

The other possessive for *which*—namely, *of which*—is typically cumbersome. E.g.: "Western reluctance to intervene militarily in every foreign conflict is understandable. But it is disputable in the case of Bosnia, where fighting long ago turned from ethnic strife into a war of foreign aggression, *the continuation of which* [read *whose continuation*] would jeopardize European stability" (*Int'l Herald Trib.*).

B. Mistakenly Written *who's*. Whereas *whose* is the possessive form, *who's* is a contraction for *who is*. But writers often confuse the two—e.g.: "*Who's* [read *Whose*] fault is this? That depends on whom you ask" (*USA Today*).

whose else. See **else's** & POSSESSIVES (I).

widely regarded. See **regard (B).**

wile away. See **while away.**

will. See **shall.**

-WISE. Generally, avoid *-wise* phrases. They typically displace a more direct wording, and they're invariably graceless and inelegant—e.g.:

- "McCaskey (0–8) is the biggest school *population-wise*, but the smallest when it comes to youth soccer turnout" (*Lancaster New Era*). (A possible revision: *Although McCaskey (0–8) has the most students, it has the smallest turnout for youth soccer*.)
- "After a dull summer *book-wise* [read *in books* or *in the book trade*] . . . , the season of fairs, sales, readings and other book-related events gets off to a satisfying start this month" (*Wash. Post*).
- "*Content-wise*, the slacker story reveals what other less mass-minded magazines revealed long ago: Slackers are not really job-averse at all" (*Commercial Appeal*). (Surely the best approach

to revising that sentence is to delete *content-wise*.)

But some recent NEOLOGISMS seem to be earning their way. For example, *taxwise* is often better than *from the point of view of taxes* or some similar phrase—e.g.: "You can't fund an education IRA in any year you contribute to a prepaid tuition plan, now offered by 14 states. *Taxwise*, IRAs are better" (*Newsweek*).

with. This word is increasingly being used as a quasi-conjunction to introduce a tag-on idea at the end of a sentence. The sense is close to *and* <John went to Houston and Sarah went to Minneapolis, with me going to Chicago>. Avoid this sloppy construction—e.g.: "We separated, *with me carrying* [read *and I carried*] a couple thoughts back to the office" (*L.A. Times*).

with regard to. See **regard (A).**

with the exception of is verbose for *except*, *except for*, *aside from*, or *apart from*—e.g.: "European Union Members, *with the exception of* [read *except for*] Greece, recalled their envoys to Iran for consultations over the court verdict" (*L.A. Times*).

with the object of [+ vb. + -ing] is verbose for a simple infinitive, e.g., *with the object of preventing* in place of *to prevent*.

woke; woken. See **wake.**

wolf. Pl. *wolves*. See PLURALS (G).

wolverine; wolverene. The latter is a NEEDLESS VARIANT.

-WOMAN. See SEXISM (C).

womanly; womanlike; womanish. See **female.**

WORD-SWAPPING. It's something like a Murphy's Law of language: two words that can be confused will be confused. Sometimes, the more popular word will encroach on the less popular (as when *demean* takes over the sense *bemean* [= to make base or low; degrade]). But the opposite is the more common phenomenon: the less well-known word encroaches on the better-known one, as in these pairs:

effete	*gets used for*	effeminate
deprecate		depreciate
foreboding		forbidding
fortuitous		fortunate
incredulous		incredible
laudatory		laudable
proscription		prescription
reticent		reluctant

This book records hundreds of other examples.

How does this happen? Because people enjoy experimenting with words—not going so far as to engage in true SESQUIPEDALITY, but merely using slightly offbeat words that everyone has heard before—they'll replace an "expected" word with one that strikes them as more genteel. And they'll do this without ever bothering to look the word up in a dictionary.

In the old days, this psychological impulse probably didn't have a great effect on the language. But in an age of mass communications—when millions of people can be simultaneously exposed to a barbarous error in speech—the effect can be almost immediate. One speaker's carelessness with the language spreads as never before.

And because writing follows speech—as it must—these confusions, over time, get embedded in the language. The dictionaries record that *infer* sometimes means *imply*; that *precipitous* sometimes means *precipitate* (adj.); and that *regretfully* sometimes means *regrettably*. It's the lexicographer's duty to record what's happening in the language; if various words are in flux, then the dictionaries will reflect it.

That's where a good dictionary of usage comes in: it helps people understand which words are worth continuing the struggle to preserve in their traditional senses; which words are all but lost in the short term (SKUNKED

TERMS); and which words, though once confused, have simply undergone reversals in meaning and can't be objected to any longer. In any given day, various sets of words belong at different places on that continuum.

Rarely do the preservationists—the ones who want to keep traditional distinctions—prevail. Sometimes they do; more often they don't. But that doesn't mean the struggle is in vain. To the contrary: it means that these speakers and writers will be better equipped, among their contemporaries, to avoid thrashing about in the language. Among astute listeners and readers, they'll have a higher degree of credibility. There's much to be said for that.

worst. A. For *most*. *Worst* is a casualism when used as an equivalent of *most* <what they need worst is food>. It is related to *badly in need*. It occurs chiefly in reported speech—e.g.: "These reforms would help schools that need them *worst*—failing urban ones—where children have no alternatives" (*Cincinnati Enquirer*).

B. *Two worst*; *worst two*. The first is more logical, and is three times more common, than the second. *Worst two* is loose phrasing—e.g.: "Their *worst two* [read *two worst*] positions for offensive production have been catcher and third base" (*Chicago Trib.*).

would. Writers often use *would* to condition statements that really ought to be straightforward—e.g.: "I *would submit to you* [read *submit to you*] that very few presentations end with the audience saying, 'Well, that presenter really beat our brains out. He thrashed us good and proper' " (Ron Hoff, *"I Can See You Naked,"* 1992). (A better revision: *Very few presentations end with the audience . . . .*)/ "Mr. Kohl *would seem* [read *seems*] to have made another concession" (*N.Y. Times*). See **should** & SUBJUNCTIVES.

would have liked. This phrase should invariably be followed by a present-tense infinitive—hence *would have liked to go, would have liked to read,* not *would have liked to have gone, would have liked to have read*. The erroneous phrasings are very common—e.g.: "Clapp said he *would have liked to have seen* [read *would have liked to see*] more teams involved in postseason play" (*Ariz. Republic*). Nor is it correct to say *would like to have done,* because the sequence of events is then off. See TENSES (B).

would of. See **of** (D).

wrack; rack, vb. *Wrack* = to destroy utterly; to wreck. *Rack* = to torture or oppress. *Wrack* is also, and primarily, a noun meaning (1) "wreckage"; or (2) "utter destruction."

The idiom is *rack one's brains*. The root meaning of *rack* is to stretch, hence to torture by stretching. H.W. Fowler said that *rack* is a variant of *wrack* in *rack and ruin*, but *wrack* isn't a variant of *rack* as a transitive verb—e.g.: "After I had received Rose's letter begging my assistance and realized that I would soon need to borrow a large sum of money, I had *wracked* [read *racked*] my brains for some time to decide whom I should approach" (Susan Howatch, *Penmarric*, 1971).

Wrack commonly appears in the SET PHRASE *wrack and ruin*, for which *wreck and ruin* is an erroneous substitute—e.g.: "[T]his is all about . . . people whose morals will go to *wreck* [read *wrack*] and ruin now" (*N.Y. Times*).

wrangle; wangle. The two are occasionally confounded. *Wrangle* = to argue noisily or angrily. *Wangle* = (1) v.t., to accomplish or obtain in a clever way; (2) v.t., to manage (a thing) despite difficulties; or (3) v.i., to use indirect methods to accomplish some end. E.g.: "So, in 1990, he called the Detroit Lions and *wrangled* [read *wangled*] an invitation to camp" (*L.A. Times*).

wreak. The phrase *wreak havoc* (= to bring about difficulty, confusion, or chaos) is an established AmE idiom. (In BrE, the usual idiom is *play havoc*.) But *wreak havoc* has two variants to be avoided: *wreck havoc* and *work havoc*. E.g.: "An inner struggle was *working* [read *wreaking*] havoc on Tracey's normally cheerful demeanor" (*Atlantic Monthly*)./ "Lincoln Heights Police Chief Ernie McCowen said the four teens arrested in connection with the shooting have *wrecked* [read *wreaked*] havoc on the block for months" (*Cincinnati Enquirer*). *Wreak*, of course, is pronounced /reek/—not /rek/.

The past tense of *wreak* is *wreaked*, not *wrought*. For the confusion of *wreak* with *reek*, see **reek.**

wreath; wreathe. *Wreath* is the noun <a Christmas wreath>, *wreathe* the verb <they plan to wreathe the door in garlands>.

wreck and ruin. See **wrack.**

wreckless. See **reckless.**

wretch. For an interesting mistake involving this word, see **retch.**

wrier; wriest. See **wry.**

wring. A. Inflection: *wring* > *wrung* > *wrung*. The past-tense and past-participial forms of *wring* (= to squeeze or twist) are sometimes erroneously written *rung*—e.g.: "[O]n market days, it is possible to see a small boy grab a live chicken by the head and whip its body round and round in an arc until its neck is *rung* [read *wrung*]" (*Wash. Post*).

B. *Hand-wringing*. This phrase is sometimes mangled into *hand-ringing*—e.g.: "Mary Tyler Moore now gets by without the haunting, *hand-ringing* [read *hand-wringing*] insecurity that once dogged her everywhere she went" (*Toronto Sun*).

wrought. See **wreak.**

wrung. See **wring (A).**

wry makes the comparative *wrier* and the superlative *wriest* in AmE, *wryer* and *wryest* in BrE. But in both, the kindred adverb is *wryly*.

X

x-ed; x'd; xed. As the past tense for the verb meaning "to mark with an x, delete," the first is standard. The second and third are variant forms.

The present participle is preferably *x-ing*, not *x'ing*.

xerox is a registered trademark that is nevertheless used as a noun <he made a xerox of the document>, adjective <a xerox copy>, and verb <to xerox an article>. Sometimes the word is capitalized, but usually not—e.g.: "Several readers *xeroxed* my Sept. 14 column" (*Boston Globe*). Careful writers and speakers tend to use *photocopy* or some other similar word. *Zerox* is a common misspelling.

Xmas. This abbreviation for *Christmas* is popular in advertising. The X is not a Roman X but a Greek chi—the first letter in Christ's name (Gk. *Christos*). *Xmas* has no connection with Generation X, X-ray, or X as an algebraic variable.

X-ray; x-ray. Either form is correct, although the first is perhaps more common. Although *W10* suggests that the term is hyphenated as an adjective and verb (*X-ray*) but not as a noun (*X ray*), most other dictionaries hyphenate the term in all parts of speech. That makes good sense, and it's an easy rule to follow.

Y

y'all; ya'll. This Southernism is most logically *y'all*, not *ya'll*. Only the *you* of *you-all* is contracted. And in modern print sources, *y'all* is ten times more common. So *ya'll* deserves an edit—e.g.: " 'Geeeeeeez,' Puck yelled from above. '*Ya'll* [read *Y'all*] look like ants from up here' " (*Minneapolis Star Trib.*). See **you-all.**

yes. This word has two possible plurals: *yeses* and *yesses*. The better plural for the noun is *yeses* because, like *buses*, it follows the usual rule for nouns ending in *-s*. See PLURALS (A). Cf. **no.**

But the verb *yes* (recorded in *W3* but not *W10*) is inflected *yessed*, *yessing*. Therefore, the second-person singular verb is *yesses* <he's so uxorious that he yesses her constantly>.

yet. A. Beginning Sentences with. Like other coordinating conjunctions, *yet* is perfectly acceptable as a sentence starter. It's a rank SUPERSTITION to believe otherwise. E.g.: "Campaign professionals . . . are becoming the new breed of influence peddlers. *Yet* they don't need to register as lobbyists in Washington" (*Fortune*). Cf. **but (A).**

B. Idioms Involving *yet*. There are two common negative phrases revolving around this word: *no person has yet done something* and *the person has yet to do something*. Some writers have ill-advisedly conflated the two idioms to come up with their own brand of illogic—e.g.: "No artist has yet to capture the essence of the Thai sea" (*Island*). The writer has inadvertently suggested that every artist has already captured the essence of the Thai sea.

C. *As yet*. See **as yet.**

yoke; yolk. *Yoke* = (1) a twice-curved, usu. wooden beam with U-shaped brackets beneath to enclose the necks of two oxen or other draft animals <after a struggle, the oxen were fitted into the yoke>; or (2) a pair of animals suitable for yoking <a yoke of oxen>. *Yolk* = the yellow center of an egg <he liked omelettes made with egg whites—he didn't miss the yolks>. *Yoke* is sometimes a verb; *yolk* never is.

Sometimes the two are confused—e.g.: "A couple of Jacqueline Ott's sculptures are quite cunning: [for example,] two flat plywood umbrellas *yolked* [read *yoked*] together like Siamese twins" (*N.Y. Times*)./ "I was stunned by the mix of aquamarine, luscious tans, dusty reds, yellow of egg *yoke* [read *yolk*], the turquoise as mute as a lizard" (*Pitt. Post-Gaz.*).

you-all. Many educated speakers in the South and Southwest use *you-all* as the plural form of *you*. This is a convenient usage, since *you* alone can be either singular or plural—and therefore is sometimes ambiguous. (See PRONOUNS (A).) True, *you-all* is unlikely to spread beyond regional usage. But speakers who (like the author of this book) grew up with the phrase won't be easily dispossessed of it. It's handy. Cf. **y'all.**

you can't eat your cake and have it too; you can't have your cake and eat it too. The second phrasing, now the more common one, is sometimes stigmatized. Although the *eat–have* sequence is the traditional one, the *have–eat* sequence isn't necessarily illogical, as some critics assert. Assume that the phrase were *you can't spend your money and save it too*; why couldn't you just as easily say *you can't save your money and spend it too*? Essentially, that idea is perfectly analogous to the one involving cake.

you'd better; you better. See **better (A).**

your, the possessive form of the second person, is sometimes misused for *you're*, the contraction of *you are*. E.g.: "Just saying *your* [read *you're*] going to get fit this year doesn't mean you will unless you define what you mean by the term 'fit' and establish some step-by-step goals to help you accomplish your fitness resolution" (*Kansas City Star*). The opposite error also occurs, though less commonly—e.g.: " 'In boxing you don't have that kind of luxury or time. If you mess up in a fight or two, *you're* [read *your*] career could be over' " (*Lancaster New Era* [quoting an interviewee]). See SPELLING (A).

yours. See POSSESSIVES (C).

Z

zeitgeist. Though originally capitalized as a German noun, this word is now fully naturalized and should be lowercased in both AmE and BrE.

zero. When used as an adjective (as it rarely is), *zero* should modify a plural noun, not a singular one. The only number that takes a singular noun is *one*. E.g.: "In 1985, New York City had 71 days that were out of compliance with the EPA standard for carbon monoxide; that number declined to two days in 1991 and *zero day* [read *zero days* or *no days*] last year" (*Newsweek*).

The plural of the noun *zero* is *zeros*—not *zeroes*. See PLURALS (C).

ZEUGMA. This figure of speech, literally a "yoking together," involves a word's being a part of two constructions. Sometimes it results in a grammatical error, but sometimes it's simply a felicitous way of phrasing an idea. For example, sometimes a verb or preposition is applied to two other words in different senses, often literally in one sense and figuratively in the other, as in *she took her oath and her seat*. Often, the phrasing is both purposeful and humorous—e.g.:

- "Time flies like an arrow; fruit flies like a banana" (Groucho Marx).
- "I just *blew my nose, a fuse, and three circuit breakers*" (Jim Henson).
- "You held your breath and the door for me" (Alanis Morissette).
- "He turned my life and this old car around" (Sara Evans).

For another good example, see **no object.**

But sometimes zeugma is a kind of grammatical error, as when a single word refers to two or more words in the sentence when it properly applies to only one of them. One type, the nontransferable auxiliary, plagues writers who habitually try to express their ideas in the alternative—e.g.:

- "At the same time, the number of people magnets Disney *has or will put* on its property has multiplied" (*Orlando Bus. J.*). (*Put* is made both a past-tense and a present-tense verb; insert another *put* after *has*.)
- "Although outside professionals *have and will be called* in to work on the station, firefighters will do most of the work" (*Cincinnati Enquirer*). (Insert *been* after *have*; otherwise, *called* is nonsensically made both active and passive.)
- "U.S. policy toward Latin America *has and will continue to be held* hostage to the whims of the Senate Foreign Relations Committee and its chairman" (*Houston Chron.*). (*Has* doesn't match up with *be held*; insert *been* after *has*.)

Although commentators have historically tried to distinguish between *zeugma* and *syllepsis*, the distinctions have been confusing and contradictory. We're better off using *zeugma* in its broadest sense and not confusing matters by introducing *syllepsis*, a little-known term the meaning of which even the experts can't agree on.

zoology is pronounced /zoh-**ol**-ə-jee/—not /zoo-**ol**-ə-jee/. See PRONUNCIATION (B).

zwieback (= a sweetened bread that is baked and then sliced and toasted) is sometimes misspelled *zweiback*. The word is pronounced /**zwee**-bak/ or /**zwɪ**-bak/.

SELECT BIBLIOGRAPHY

English Dictionaries

The American Heritage Dictionary of the English Language. 3d ed. Boston & N.Y.: Houghton Mifflin, 1992.

The Concise Oxford Dictionary of Current English. 8th ed. Oxford: Clarendon Press, 1990.

Merriam-Webster's Collegiate Dictionary. 10th ed. Springfield, Mass.: Merriam-Webster, 1993.

The New Shorter Oxford English Dictionary. 2 vols. Oxford: Clarendon Press, 1993.

The Oxford English Dictionary. 2d ed. 20 vols. Oxford: Clarendon Press, 1989.

The Random House Dictionary of the English Language. 2d ed. N.Y.: Random House, 1987.

Webster's New World College Dictionary. 3d ed. N.Y.: Macmillan & Co., 1995.

Webster's Third New International Dictionary of the English Language. Springfield, Mass.: Merriam, 1961.

Usage

Bernstein, Theodore M. *The Careful Writer*. N.Y.: Atheneum, 1979.

Burchfield, Robert W. *The New Fowler's Modern English Usage*. Oxford: Oxford Univ. Press, 1996.

Evans, Bergen; and Cornelia Evans. *A Dictionary of Contemporary American Usage*. N.Y.: Random House, 1957.

Follett, Wilson. *Modern American Usage*. N.Y.: Hill & Wang, 1966. 2d ed. Erik Wensberg, ed. 1998.

Fowler, H.W. *A Dictionary of Modern English Usage*. Oxford: Clarendon Press, 1926. 2d ed. Ernest Gowers, ed. Oxford: Oxford Univ. Press, 1965.

Garner, Bryan. *A Dictionary of Modern American Usage*. N.Y.: Oxford Univ. Press, 1998.

Partridge, Eric. *Usage and Abusage*. 1942. 5th ed. Harmondsworth: Penguin Books, 1981.

Grammar

Curme, George O. *English Grammar*. N.Y.: Barnes & Noble Books, 1947.

Gordon, Karen Elizabeth. *The Deluxe Transitive Vampire: The Ultimate Handbook of Grammar for the Innocent, the Eager, and the Doomed*. N.Y.: Pantheon Books, 1993.

Jespersen, Otto. *Essentials of English Grammar*. N.Y.: Holt, 1933. Repr. University, Ala.: Univ. of Alabama Press, 1964.

Morsberger, Robert E. *Commonsense Grammar and Style*. 2d ed. N.Y.: Crowell, 1975.

Opdycke, John B. *Harper's English Grammar*. Rev. Stewart Benedict. N.Y.: Harper & Row, 1965.

Style

Baker, Sheridan. *The Practical Stylist*. 8th ed. N.Y.: Harper & Row, 1998.

Barzun, Jacques. *Simple and Direct*. Rev. ed. N.Y.: Harper & Row, 1985.

The Chicago Manual of Style. 14th ed. Chicago: Univ. of Chicago Press, 1993.

Strunk, William; and E.B. White. *The Elements of Style*. 3d ed. N.Y.: Macmillan & Co., 1979.

Trimble, John R. *Writing with Style: Conversations on the Art of Writing*. Englewood Cliffs, N.J.: Prentice-Hall, Inc., 1975.

Zinsser, William. *On Writing Well*. 6th ed. N.Y.: HarperPerennial, 1998.

Etymology

The Barnhart Dictionary of Etymology. Ed. Robert K. Barnhart. Bronx: H.W. Wilson, 1988.

The Merriam-Webster New Book of Word Histories. Springfield, Mass.: Merriam-Webster, 1991.

The Oxford Dictionary of English Etymology. Ed. C.T. Onions, with G.W.S. Friedrichsen and R.W. Burchfield. Oxford: Clarendon Press, 1966.

Partridge, Eric. *Origins: A Short Etymological Dictionary of Modern English*. 4th ed. London: Routledge & Kegan Paul, 1966.

Pronunciation

Bender, James F. *NBC Handbook of Pronunciation*. 3d ed. Rev. Thomas Lee Crowell, Jr. N.Y.: Crowell, 1964.

Elster, Charles Harrington. *The Big Book of Beastly Mispronunciations: The Ultimate Opinionated Guide for the Well-Spoken*. Boston & N.Y.: Houghton Mifflin Co., 1999.

Lewis, Norman. *Dictionary of Modern Pronunciation*. N.Y.: Harper & Row, 1963.

Punctuation

Carey, G.V. *Mind the Stop: A Brief Guide to Punctuation with a Note on Proof-Correction*. Harmondsworth, Middlesex: Penguin, 1971. Repr. 1977.

Gordon, Karen E. *The Well-Tempered Sentence: A Punctuation Handbook for the Innocent, the Eager, and the Doomed*. N.Y.: Ticknor & Fields, 1983.

Partridge, Eric. *You Have a Point There: A Guide to Punctuation and Its Allies*. London: Routledge & Kegan Paul, 1953. Repr. 1978.

Paxson, William C. *The Mentor Guide to Punctuation*. N.Y.: New Am. Lib., 1986.

The English Language

Baugh, Albert C.; and Thomas Cable. *A History of the English Language*. 3d ed. Englewood Cliffs, N.J.: Prentice-Hall, Inc., 1978.

Burchfield, Robert W. *The English Language*. Oxford: Oxford Univ. Press, 1985.

Burchfield, Robert W. *Unlocking the English Language*. N.Y.: Hill & Wang, 1991.

Crystal, David. *The Cambridge Encyclopedia of the English Language*. Cambridge: Univ. of Cambridge Press, 1995.

Flexner, Stuart Berg; and Anne H. Soukhanov. *Speaking Freely: A Guided Tour of American English*. N.Y.: Oxford Univ. Press, 1997.

Jespersen, Otto. *Growth and Structure of the English Language*. 9th ed. 1938. Repr. Chicago: Univ. of Chicago Press, 1982.

McArthur, Tom, ed. *The Oxford Companion to the English Language*. Oxford: Oxford Univ. Press, 1992.

Mencken, H.L. *The American Language* [one-volume abridged ed.]. Ed. Raven I. McDavid, Jr. N.Y.: Alfred A. Knopf, 1963.

CPSIA information can be obtained at www.ICGtesting.com
Printed in the USA
BVOW02s0252010414

349369BV00005B/11/P